INTERNATIONAL ORGANIZATION:
POLITICS & PROCESS

D1453194

International Organization: Politics & Process

Edited by

LELAND M. GOODRICH
&
DAVID A. KAY

THE UNIVERSITY OF WISCONSIN PRESS

Published 1973

The University of Wisconsin Press
Box 1379, Madison, Wisconsin 53701
The University of Wisconsin Press, Ltd.
70 Great Russell Street, London

Printings 1973, 1976

Printed in the United States of America

ISBN 0–299–06250–3 cloth, 0–299–06254–6 paper
LC 72–7986

The essays in this volume are collected from International Organization,
volumes 1–26

Contents

v

Introduction

The editors of this volume have thought that both students of inter-national organization and others who are broadly concerned with the cooperative approach to international problems, as exemplified on a global basis by the United Nations and its related agencies, would find some value in a selection of articles that have appeared in *International Organization* since its first publication in February 1947. To the query "Why this particular journal?" our response would be that it is the only scholarly journal exclusively devoted to the field during the last quarter of a century.

The reader is naturally interested to know the criteria that have guided us in making our selection, since the twenty-two articles in-cluded here represent only a small fraction of the total number of articles published. First of all, we should make it clear that individual excellence has not been the sole criterion by any means, although we have undoubtedly been influenced by that consideration. Nor has up-to-dateness been taken into account, since all the articles will be dated to some degree by the time this book reaches the reader, and especially since this collection is specifically intended to convey some sense of the development of institutions and of scholarly interests and approaches to them.

The pieces selected for inclusion were chosen primarily on the basis of their contribution to the understanding of a few general topics which constitute the framework of the book. Our title, *International Organi-zation: Politics and Process,* excludes many valuable articles dealing primarily with the structure and the legal basis of international organizations. Also, we have not thought it wise to include articles of a highly technical nature that would have interest only for a fairly limited readership. Possibly with less justification, we have not thought it desirable in general to include articles that form specialized parts of a comprehensive treatment of a larger topic; consequently, the importance to scholars of the annual special number of the journal is not at all adequately reflected here.

International Organization has completed its twenty-sixth year as a scholarly journal. The original Board of Editors was composed mainly of scholars who had seen service at San Francisco, either as staff members of the United States delegation or as members of the international secretariat that the Department of State had created to serve the Conference. The journal was initially sponsored and supported by the World Peace Foundation, whose original donor and trustees had recognized that the cause of peace could best be furthered through education. The then president of the Board of Trustees, Harvey H. Bundy, in his preface to the first number of the journal, described its purpose and the Foundation's action in supporting it as being "the dissemination of accurate information and informed comment on the manifold problems of international organization."

Like the institutions with which it has been concerned, *International Organization* has undergone great changes over the years, responding to the changing interests and demands of its readers and contributors, to the new approaches of scholars to the study of international relations, and above all, to the changes that have taken place in the state of international relations and the world environment in general. The journal first appeared at a time when the interest of serious students and the concerned public was very much centered on the United Nations and its related agencies. Though the League of Nations had failed, there was widespread conviction that a second try must be made. In colleges and universities as well as among the interested public, there was a desire for information and for guidance in understanding what the new organizations were, what they might be expected to accomplish, and what were the conditions of their success. There had been a substantial and varied literature on the League, but, because of their newness, there was little available on these agencies. *International Organization* therefore met a real need.

In the early years of the journal, the articles appearing in it were largely of a descriptive and explanatory nature. This was natural and justifiable, considering the scarcity of materials available to give the information needed at that time. Furthermore, in those early years, serious scholarship in the field was very much influenced by the legal and constitutional approach to organized international cooperation. After all, each international agency had its constitution, its legal basis, which had been the object of careful negotiation. Questions of the composition, powers, and operating procedures were thought to be of real significance in explaining the promise and effectiveness of an international organization. Furthermore, this interest in mechanism tended to be kept alive and strengthened by the "cold war" and the attention that it focused on voting procedure in United Nations organs, particularly the Security Council.

Notwithstanding the attention given to legal and constitutional aspects of the new international organizations, the early numbers of the journal also reflected the realization that these organizations, and particularly the United Nations, were called upon to function in a political environment, and that since they were voluntary associations of independent states, their effectiveness in achieving their declared purposes was dependent on the attitudes and policies of governments. In recognizing the need to place international organizations in a political context, the journal—its editors and contributors—reflected the views which had prevailed in the drafting of the Charter of the United Nations. Unlike the authors of the League Covenant, who had placed their chief reliance on legal obligations and constitutional arrangements in creating an international organization to prevent war, the authors of the Charter frankly recognized the weakness, and even the futility, of legal commitments and constitutional arrangements not supported by the common interests and the strength of the principal member states.

Recognition that international organization is a matter of politics as well as of law and constitutional structure naturally led to concern with some of the basic questions of politics as applied in an international context, questions related to the exercise of power and influence. While the Charter had recognized the special responsibilities of the major military powers in the maintenance of international peace and security and had accorded them privileged positions in the Security Council with respect to both membership and voting privileges, it had broken with all precedents in affirming the principles of equal voting power and decision by majority vote (simple or two-thirds) in the General Assembly. This purely procedural provision acquired great political importance during the period of the "cold war," since the General Assembly was seized upon by the Western members, under the leadership of the United States, as a means of circumventing the veto in the Security Council and mobilizing wide support.

The voting behavior of member states, their alignment on specific issues, and the influence of some members on others became matters of practical concern to national delegations and foreign offices, as well as being objects of theoretical concern to scholars, many of whom were already committed to the behavioral approach to the study of political phenomena. Margaret Ball's article, "Bloc Voting in the General Assembly," was a pioneer work in this area.[1] Subsequent articles in *International Organization,* articles in other periodicals, and monographs have explored this subject more fully with the use of more highly developed quantitative techniques. Scholars have recognized, however, that the explanation of voting behavior and the measuring of political influence cannot be undertaken exclusively in quantitative terms, since there are many factors that do not lend themselves to being stated thus. In "The Study of Political Influence in the General Assembly,"[2] Robert Keohane demonstrated the importance of a broader approach, through selective interviewing as well as the use of voting data and available documentation, for determining who influences whom, and how.

The Charter of the United Nations, while emphasizing the predominant role of global organizations, recognized that regional and more limited organizations had a place within the global system. Contrary to what was to be the course of organizational development, regional arrangements were given a place in the organization of international peace and security but not in the organization of economic and social cooperation. It soon became clear, however, that this was not to be true in practice. Responding to postwar developments which placed an emphasis on regional and limited-membership arrangements, numerous articles in the early years of *International Organization* were concerned with the description and analysis of this phenomenon, chiefly in the way of depicting the structure and functions of particular organizations and their relation to, and probable impact on, the global system.[3]

In the late fifties, interest in regionalism took a new turn, with the publication of *Political Community and the North Atlantic Area,* by Karl Deutsch and Associates.[4] This monograph showed the way to the use of the methods of historical sociology and suggested a theoretical framework for the study of the process of political integration, which, it was assumed, was the desired end-product of international organization. In his pioneering work, *The Unity of Europe,*[5] Ernst Haas used similar methods and theoretical concepts in a study of integration in Western Europe. His article, "International Integration: The European and the Universal Process,"[6] had a special significance, in that it resulted in a redirection of interest in, and the study of, regionalism by scholars. This was reflected not only by the nature of articles subsequently appearing in *International Organization,* but also in the literature on regionalism and integration published in the following years. For the most part, these studies have been concerned with further developing and refining the theoretical conclusions of Haas' earlier writings. A special number of *International Organization*[7] summarized the progress made in the development of regional integration theory during the period of a dozen years.

International organizations are not ends in themselves. Rather, they are means chosen by govenments for achieving common ends. Consequently, the questions must always be asked, with respect to any international organization and with respect to the method itself: How effective is it in achieving its purpose? What are the conditions of its success? What impact does it have upon its environment, more particularly on the attitudes and policies of its members?

In establishing the United Nations and its related agencies, the contracting parties committed themselves to a range of common purposes —the maintenance of international peace and security; cooperation in achieving conditions of economic and social progress and development; the political, economic, and social development of non-self-governing territories; and the furtherance of respect for human rights. Of these, maintenance of international peace and security was regarded as the primary commitment and responsibility of the new organization, since the achievement of this objective was considered to be the necessary condition of reaching the other goals.

It soon became clear after the United Nations began to function that it was not going to be able to achieve this purpose by the methods specified in the Charter. More particularly, failure of the permanent members to agree on the principles governing the agreements to be concluded under Article 43 meant that the Security Council would not have at its disposal the full range of enforcement measures enumerated in Articles 41 and 42. Furthermore, the deepening confrontation between East and West substantially reduced the likelihood that those means of peaceful settlement and persuasion available to the Council would in fact be used. The limited capacity of the Organization for achieving its primary purpose, accentuated by a state of international relations which restricted the use of even that limited capacity, was reflected in the articles appearing in *International Organization* during its first decade. In the existing state of political relations among the major powers, there was interest in alternative means of achieving security through self-defense arrangements under Article 51 (the North Atlantic Treaty) and the use of the General Assembly ("Uniting for Peace"); the particular situations in which peaceful methods (Chap. VI) and provisional measures (Art. 41) could be used with some degree of success; and the need for some reconsideration of collective security and enforcement in the light of international realities. The Korean experience was recognized as not being a precedent for future enforcement action, but rather as an accidental happening not likely to recur.[8] However, it illustrated a special political function that the United Nations was increasingly to perform in the years ahead, that of collective legitimization.[9]

After a decade of limited achievement and of disappointing results in the peace and security field, at least when measured against the hopes and expectations expressed in the Charter provisions, the United Nations in the middle fifties entered a period of revised hopes and substantial accomplishment. This change in United Nations fortunes was due in part to the lessening of East-West tension following the death of Stalin, but to a greater extent it was accounted for by the imaginative initiative and skillful diplomacy of the Secretary-General, Dag Hammarskjöld, who, by gaining the confidence of the major powers, was able to develop and make effective a peace-keeping role for the United Nations in situations where the United States and the Soviet Union had a common interest in limiting their involvement. Peace-keeping operations were, at the time of their major successes, viewed by many not only as opening up an important new area of constructive activity on the part of the United Nations in the maintenance of international peace and security, but also as indicative of an important institutional development taking the form of the assumption by, or the conferring upon, the Secretary-General of important responsibilities for initiating and directing these operations. Brian Urquhart, who played an important role as one of the Secretary-

General's principal collaborators in this work, gave authoritative expression to this point of view in his contribution to the special number *International Force—A Symposium,* edited by Lincoln P. Bloomfield.[10] It soon became apparent, however, that the problem of financing peacekeeping operations was of an even more critical nature than had been recognized at first. What was originally treated as simply a shortage of needed funds—a restriction that the Organization was not unaccustomed to—soon came to be recognized as basically a political crisis. The Soviet Union and other members were withholding funds in order to achieve basic institutional objectives—the restoration of the exclusive role of the Security Council, where the veto would prevail, and the denial to the Secretary-General of any independent role that he might claim. That the confrontation over the expenses of peace-keeping operations was and is of an essentially political nature, directed to the central issue of influence in the Organization, is the theme of Inis Claude's article on "The Political Framework of the United Nations' Financial Problems." [11]

The decade of the sixties was a critical period for the United Nations. While the Congo operation was a limited success, to the extent that it helped to preserve the unity of the Congo and to give the Congolese the opportunity to determine their own future without "cold war" involvement, failure of members to agree on the method of financing this and other similar operations in the future seriously reduced the prospect that this once promising form of United Nations activity would often be used. Displeased by the failure of other members to bear their share of the costs of peace-keeping and preoccupied with its own unfortunate involvement in Vietnam, the United States (which had in the past been the strongest great power proponent of United Nations action) seemed to be losing interest in the use of the United Nations for peace and security purposes. At the same time, as the consequence of the rapid progress of decolonization and the admission of many new Asian and African states to membership, resulting in the creation of a new majority, the priorities of the Organization, at least so far as the General Assembly was concerned, came to be altered. The new members were primarily concerned with the use of the Organization to bring about the complete liquidation of colonialism, the elimination of racial discrimination, and the economic and social development of the underdeveloped countries. They were interested in the use of the Organization for the maintenance of peace and security, to be sure, but chiefly to the extent that reduction and limitation of armaments might permit the use of greater resources for assistance in their own economic development, and that the enforcement provisions of the Charter might be used for eliminating colonialism and racial discrimination, on the assumption that these conditions constituted a threat to the peace.

For the work of the United Nations in assisting non-self-governing territories to achieve self-government or independence, the decade of the sixties was important not only because of the new emphasis given to it, but also because of the different approach that was adopted. Down to 1960, the activity of the Organization had been based on the principles that non-self-governing territories should eventually achieve self-government or independence, that the administering state should assist the territory to achieve that status, and that United Nations supervision should be exercised (in the case of trust territories) or limited persuasion used (in the case of other dependencies) to assure that assistance was effectively given, to guard against unnecessary delay in the granting of self-government, and to assist in determining the conditions under which the eventual goal would be realized. Furthermore, in discharging their responsibilities for the maintenance of international peace and security, the Security Council and the General Assembly indirectly contributed to this goal. While the United Nations played an important part in the substantial reduction of colonialism in this period, other forces were at work which independently, or in cooperation with or working through the United Nations, contributed mightily to the same result. Harold Jacobson, in his article "The United Nations and Colonialism: A Tentative Appraisal,"[12] gives one scholar's evaluation of the relative importance of the United Nations role and how its influence was exercised.

Down to 1960, the work of the United Nations had been largely based on Chapter XI of the Charter (Declaration Regarding Non-Self-Governing Territories) and Chapters XII and XIII providing for the international trusteeship system. Under both the Declaration and the trusteeship provisions, the approach was to be a gradualist one. The general idea was that self-government or independence would come when the people of a territory were ready for it. In the discussions on human rights in connection with the drafting of the Covenant there had been insistence on recognizing the right of self-determination, but this had not been given as much prominence, or made the basis for claims for immediate independence, as it was in the 1960 Declaration on

Granting Independence to Colonial Countries and Peoples. From 1960 on, under the relentless pressure of the new nations of Asia and Africa and their allies, United Nations activity was directed to achieving the complete eradication of colonialism, not by gradualist and orderly means, but rather by prompt termination of colonial relations without regard to degree of preparedness for independence. Not only were the members of the new majority in the General Assembly insistent on the elimination of racial discrimination, which was associated in their minds with colonialism, but to achieve these goals they were prepared to use all means of persuasion which the Charter provided, and even to tolerate the use of force. While their efforts met with considerable success, if measured by number of resolutions adopted, the practical results have been far less impressive, particularly in southern Africa. David Kay, in his "The Politics of Decolonization," [13] tells how the new states sought to achieve their ends in the parliamentary struggles of the General Assembly.

In the economic field, as in other areas, the words of the United Nations Charter are a relatively poor guide to what in fact has been the principal work of the Organization and its related agencies, and to the importance of their work in relation to what has been achieved by other means. Those who drafted the Charter were rightly concerned that stable and prosperous economic conditions be created and maintained in the postwar world, for they were convinced that the economic collapse of the thirties was largely responsible for the Second World War. Consequently, the Charter emphasizes, as specific purposes of the United Nations, higher standards of living, full employment, conditions of economic and social progress and development, and the solution of economic, social, health, and related problems. Provision is made for a number of specialized agencies, having wide international responsibilities in their areas of concern, to be brought into relation with the United Nations for achieving these purposes. For the most part the structure envisaged has been created. In fact, if anything, there has been an excessive proliferation of structure and a duplication of function. This organizational complex has been largely devoted, though by no means exclusively to one specific purpose, to the economic and social development of underdeveloped territories. Questions of trade policy, currency stability, foreign investments, and full employment policy which were thought to be so urgently in need of international cooperative action have for the most part been handled through other channels.

This emphasis on assistance in economic and social development has come about in part through recognition by the advanced countries of the interest they have in improving the economic and social conditions of the poverty-stricken areas of the world. The original program of technical assistance was United States inspired. Since the original programs were initiated, much of the pressure to improve, extend, and strengthen the assistance has come from the developing countries themselves. In fact, pressure has built up as the result of the expansion of membership, the appearance of the new majority in the Assembly, and the constant awareness of interested parties that, in spite of what is being done, the gap between rich and poor nations is getting wider instead of narrower.[14] A special number of *International Organization, The Global Partnership: International Agencies and Economic Development,* was devoted to surveying the progress being made in the organization of world society for economic cooperation and, more specifically, examining what is being done and with what success in organizing assistance offered by the developed nations to the underdeveloped and underprivileged. In the concluding chapter of that special number, Robert Asher gives "An Overview" of what had been achieved at that time.[15]

The capacity of international organization to adapt to new and unforeseen demands is nowhere better demonstrated than in the way in which the United Nations and its related agencies have responded to demands created by modern science and technology. It is to be noted that the Charter as written at San Francisco makes no specific reference to science and technology as such. Even the problems to which reference is made are largely envisaged in the context of prewar developments. The problem of regulation of armaments, for example, is conceived in such terms, with the consequence that no urgency is attached to achieving the necessary agreements. After all, the development of atomic power was still in the experimental stage, and the social consequences of the wider use of technologies already available were not fully appreciated. With the explosion of the first atomic device, the potentialities of the atomic weapon for mutual destruction came to be fully appreciated, and the approach to disarmament quickly shifted in United Nations practice from seeking first to create the necessary political conditions for arms control to an urgent attempt at the direct control of atomic weapons.

It was the failure of the direct approach to control of the use of atomic energy for purposes of destruction that led to attention's being given to the possible diversion of this new source of energy to peaceful uses. With President Eisenhower's proposal in his December 1953 address to the United Nations General Assembly that an international program for the peaceful use of atomic energy be inaugurated, the holding in 1955 of the first International Conference on the Peaceful Uses of Atomic Energy, and the establishment of the International Atomic Energy Agency as a going concern in 1957, the United Nations extended its interest in atomic energy from the essentially negative effort to limit its use in order to prevent universal destruction to the more positive approach of exploring ways and means of using it for the improvement of life on this planet.

While developments in atomic science and technology were the most spectacular manifestations of scientific and technological progress in the postwar years, those developments were only a part of major advances on a broad front which had profound implications for the well-being of the peoples of the world. It was recognized at an early point that this progress was uneven from state to state and that the degree of advance was closely related to the stage of economic development. Consequently, the sharing of scientific and technological knowledge and the development of facilities and personnel in underdeveloped areas became an important part of the total program in the early years of United Nations activity in development assistance. At a somewhat later time, in the sixties, there was a growing awareness that, along with the great contributions of modern science and technology to increased production, improved travel and communication, and greater material comfort there were certain emerging dangers that needed to be guarded against. They took various forms, including the exhaustion of essential resources, the degradation of the physical environment through pollution, and the growth of the world's population beyond the resources available to support it. It soon became apparent, however, that peoples and governments did not share these fears equally and had different priorities regarding immediate needs. Brazil, for example, as an important developing country, placed primary emphasis on development and suspected that those in developed countries who were advocates of population control and antipollution measures were trying to prevent the developing countries from reaching the same level of industrial development that they themselves had already attained. The 1972 Stockholm Conference was the first major effort on the part of the United Nations to cope with some of the many interrelated problems that modern science and technology have presented us with, and, it is hoped, may provide the means of dealing with. But science and technology only provide instruments that can be used for many and often conflicting ends; the effective use of them for environmental protection depends upon appropriate organization, policies, and administration, as the three articles by Daniel Cheever, Eugene Skolnikoff, and Kay and Skolnikoff seek to demonstrate.[16]

Scholars in the field of international organization have generally in the past defined their field in terms of relations between states, though there has been great flexibility in defining the nature of relations to be included. As against a tendency in the interwar period to define international organization in terms of the legal arrangements between states and the constitutional structures provided, the more recent practice, as we have observed, has been to recognize and to be concerned with the totality of the relations between states and the total environment within which the organization operates, and furthermore to recognize that that environment is not exclusively political in nature, but also economic, social, and technological. Recognition of this interdependence among various aspects of interstate relations naturally and logically leads to the further recognition of the interconnectedness of state relations and relations between what we have in the past considered to be nongovernmental or private groups and organizations, and to the realization of the importance of giving attention to these hitherto neglected relationships if we are to have a full understanding of international organization today. This new perspective has been given detailed elaboration and statement in the special number of *International Organization, Transnational Relations and World Politics,* edited by Robert O. Keohane and Joseph S. Nye, Jr.[17] Their summary and conclusions are included in this volume as the last chapter, suggesting some of the new questions that scholars need to consider in the coming years.

We come away from our review of what *International Organization* has published over the past twenty-six years convinced that transnational relations will provide one of the most important and challenging areas of policy and research in the years immediately ahead. It is our conviction that the current understanding of the evolving transnational political process and the role played by international organizations in that process is fundamentally incomplete; that most students are being presented in textbooks and class lectures with a view of the international political system that is no longer valid and that fails to convey the growth in number of transnational actors and the increased scope of international political issues involved; that we fail to fully understand the implications of the growing linkages between domestic and international policy and the increased interdependencies of our complex social systems; and that policy makers continue to receive advice and to act on the basis of this outmoded conception of the international political system.

Three of the most salient characteristics of the evolving transnational political system that, in our view, should receive increased attention from scholars and policy makers in the next decade are:

1. A sharply growing volume of transnational policy making involving subnational political units, national political units, nonstate actors, such as multinational corporations and transnational elite groups, and officials of regional and global international organizations.

2. An increased interdependence of complex social systems that is not yet adequately supported by transnational policy-making processes. In the areas of economics, science, and technology we are seeing the effects of this increased interdependence and are only beginning to struggle with the question of what the appropriate institutionalized multilateral channels for handling such interdependencies are.

3. The impotence of many existing international organizations. There is clearly a crisis in the failure of existing international organizations to perform their stated functions and to adapt to the challenges that now face the global system.

The articles contained in this volume bear evidence to the accelerating growth of intergovernmental organizations and international nongovernmental organizations and the even more rapid growth of tasks that such organizations have undertaken, although not always successfully, to perform. Both of these patterns are enriching and complicating the global political system and are crucially related to fundamental developments in transnational relations. The overwhelming evidence points to the conclusion that we are entering into a basically new arrangement of international political issues, policy, and actors. In our view it is this apparent relationship between the number and scope of activities of intergovernmental organizations and the nature and direction of long-range trends in international relations that will provide the strongest stimulus to a widening interest among both scholars and policy makers in the field represented by *International Organization.*

L. M. G.
D. A. K.

January 1973

NOTES

1. *International Organization* 5 (1951), 3–31; pp. 77–105 in this volume.

2. *International Organization* 21 (1967), 221–37; pp. 137–53 in this volume.

3. See Norman J. Padelford, "Regional Organization and the United Nations," *International Organization* 8 (1954), 203-16; pp. 383-96 in this volume.

4. Princeton: Princeton University Press, 1957.

5. Stanford: Stanford University Press, 1958.

6. *International Organization* 15 (1961), 366–92; pp. 397–423 in this volume.

7. *Regional Integration: Theory and Research,* edited by Leon N. Linberg and Stuart A. Scheingold, *International Organization,* vol. 24, no. 4 (Autumn, 1970).

8. See articles by William M. Jordan and Leland M. Goodrich, pp. 183–92 and 193–207.

9. See article by Inis L. Claude, Jr., pp. 209–21.

10. *International Organization,* vol. 17, no. 2 (Spring, 1963). See pp. 223–39 in this volume.

11. *International Organization* 17 (1963), 831–59; pp. 107–35 in this volume.

12. *International Organization* 16 (1962), 37–56; pp. 287–306 in this volume.

13. *International Organization* 21 (1967), 786–811; pp. 307–32 in this volume.

14. See Barbara Ward and others (eds.), *The Widening Gap* (New York: Columbia University Press, 1971).

15. *International Organization* 22 (1968), 432–58; pp. 241–58 in this volume.

16. The last of these is the concluding article of a special number, *International Institutions and the Environmental Crisis, International Organization* 26 (1972), 469-78; pp. 371-80 in this volume.

17. *International Organization,* vol. 25, no. 3 (Autumn, 1971).

PART I

INTERNATIONAL ORGANIZATION AND THE
INTERNATIONAL POLITICAL SYSTEM

FROM LEAGUE OF NATIONS TO UNITED NATIONS

by LELAND M. GOODRICH*

I.

On April 18, 1946, the League Assembly adjourned after taking the necessary steps to terminate the existence of the League of Nations and transfer its properties and assets to the United Nations. On August 1, this transfer took place at a simple ceremony in Geneva. Thus, an important and, at one time, promising experiment in international cooperation came formally to an end. Outside of Geneva, no important notice was taken of this fact. Within the counsels of the United Nations, there was an apparent readiness to write the old League off as a failure, and to regard the new organization as something unique, representing a fresh approach to the world problems of peace and security. Quite clearly there was a hesitancy in many quarters to call attention to the essential continuity of the old League and the new United Nations for fear of arousing latent hostilities or creating doubts which might seriously jeopardize the birth and early success of the new organization.

This silence regarding the League could well be understood at a time when the establishment of a general world organization to take the place of the discredited League was in doubt, when it was uncertain whether the United States Senate would agree to American participation, and when the future course of the Soviet Union was in the balance. Though careful consideration had been given within the Department of State to League experience in the formulation of American proposals, it was quite understandable that officers of the Department, in the addresses which they delivered and reports which they made on the Dumbarton Oaks Proposals, should have for the most part omitted all references to the League except where it seemed possible to point to the great improvements that had been incorporated in the new Proposals. Nor was it surprising, in view of the past relation of the United States to the League and the known antipathy of the Soviet Union to that organization, that Secretary of State Stettinius in his address to the United Nations Conference in San Francisco on April 26, 1945, failed once to refer to the League of Nations,

* LELAND M. GOODRICH, Professor of Political Science at Brown University and Professor of International Organization at the Fletcher School of Law and Diplomacy, was Secretary of the Committee on the Pacific Settlement of Disputes of Commission III at the United Nations Conference at San Francisco. He is co-editor of the *Documents on American Foreign Relations* series, co-author, with Edvard Hambro, of *Charter of the United Nations: Commentary and Documents,* and a former Director of the World Peace Foundation.

From Volume 1, No. 1 (1947), pp. 3–21.

or the part of an American President in the establishment of it.[1] In fact, from the addresses and debates at the San Francisco Conference, the personnel assembled for the Conference Secretariat, and the organization and procedure of the Conference, it would have been quite possible for an outside observer to draw the conclusion that this was a pioneer effort in world organization.[2] Since the United Nations came into being as a functioning organization there has been a similar disinclination on the part of those participating in its work to call attention to its true relation to the League of Nations.

While the circumstances which make it necessary for those officially connected with the United Nations to be so circumspect in their references to the League of Nations can be appreciated, the student of international organization is free, in fact is duty bound, to take a more independent and objective view of the relations of the two organizations. If his studies lead him to the conclusion that the United Nations is in large measure the result of a continuous evolutionary development extending well into the past, instead of being the product of new ideas conceived under pressure of the recent war, that should not be the occasion for despair, as we know from the past that those social institutions which have been most successful in achieving their purposes are those which are the product of gradual evolutionary development, those which in general conform to established habits of thought but which nevertheless have the inner capacity for adaptation to new conditions and new needs.

While progress largely depends upon the discovery and application of new ideas and techniques, it has always been considered the test of practical statesmanship to be able to build on the past, adapting what has been proven to be useful in past experience to the needs and requirements of the changing world. Thus the framers of the American Constitution, while they created much that was new, did not hesitate to draw heavily upon the institutions and principles which were a part of their common background of experience in America and in England. At the time of the establishment of the League of Nations, the view was commonly held, certainly with more justification than today in relation to the United Nations, that something really unique was being created. However, we have come to recognize that even the League system was primarily a systematization of pre-war ideas and practices, with some innovations added in the light of war experience. Sir Alfred Zimmern has expressed this fact very well in these words:

> . . . The League of Nations was never intended to be, nor is it, a revolutionary organization. On the contrary, it accepts the world

---

[1] United Nations Conference on International Organization, Document 15, P/3, April 27, 1945.

[2] For an authoritative description of the Conference, see Grayson Kirk and Lawrence H. Chamberlain, "The Organization of the San Francisco Conference," in *Political Science Quarterly*, LX (1945), p. 321.

of states as it finds it and merely seeks to provide a more satisfactory means for carrying on some of the business which these states transact between one another. It is not even revolutionary in the more limited sense of revolutionizing the methods for carrying on interstate business. It does not supersede the older methods. It merely supplements them.[3]

We have come to recognize the various strands of experience—the European Concert of Powers, the practice of arbitration in the settlement of disputes, international administrative cooperation, to mention only a few—which entered into the fabric of the League. Should we be surprised to find that what was true of the League of Nations is even more true of the United Nations?

Those who have thus far attempted a comparison of the United Nations with the League of Nations have, generally speaking, been concerned with pointing out the differences.[4] Furthermore, comparison has been made of the textual provisions of the Covenant and the provisions of the Charter, not taking into account actual practice under the Covenant. Such a basis of comparison naturally leads to an exaggerated idea of the extent of the gap which separates the two systems. If in similar fashion the Constitution of the United States as it existed on paper at the time it became effective in 1789 were compared with the Constitution as it is applied today, the conclusion undoubtedly would be that a revolution had occurred in the intervening period. Obviously, any useful comparison of the League and the United Nations must be based on the League system as it developed under the Covenant. If that is done, it becomes clear that the gap separating the League of Nations and the United Nations is not large, that many provisions of the United Nations system have been taken directly from the Covenant, though usually with changes of names and rearrangements of words, that other provisions are little more than codifications, so to speak, of League practice as it developed under the Covenant, and that still other provisions represent the logical development of ideas which were in process of evolution when the League was actively functioning. Of course there are many exceptions, some of them important. But the point upon which attention needs to be focused for the serious student of international affairs is that the United Nations does not represent a break with the past, but rather the continued application of old ideas and methods with some changes deemed necessary in the light of past experience. If people would only recognize this simple truth, they might be more intelligent in their evaluation of past efforts and more tolerant in their appraisal of present efforts.

---

[3] Alfred Zimmern, *The League of Nations and the Rule of Law*, London, 1936, p. 4.
[4] See, for example, Clyde Eagleton, "Covenant of the League of Nations and Charter of the United Nations: Points of Difference," in Department of State, *Bulletin*, XIII, p. 263.

II.

Space does not permit a detailed analysis with a view to establishing the exact extent to which the United Nations is a continuation of the League system. All that is attempted here is to consider the more important features of the United Nations system, particularly those with respect to which claims to uniqueness have been made, with a view to determining to what extent in general this continuity can be said to exist.

Relation to the Peace Settlement

One point that has been made in favor of the United Nations as a special claim to uniqueness is that its Charter is an independent instrument, unconnected with the treaties which are in process of being made for settling the political and economic issues of World War II.[5] In contrast, it is argued that the League, by virtue of the fact that its Covenant was made at the Paris Peace Conference, and incorporated in each of the peace treaties, was from the beginning so involved in the issues of the peace settlement that it was never able to overcome the initial handicap of being a League to enforce the peace treaties. It is true, of course, that under the Covenant and under other provisions of the peace treaties, the League had placed upon it certain responsibilities in connection with the carrying out of the peace settlement.[6] This connection was not, in the early years of the League, regarded as an unmixed evil. One distinguished observer, while recognizing that a principal function of the League was "to execute the peace treaties," concluded on the basis of the first years of experience that this connection on balance served a useful world purpose.[7] It might be suggested that the criticism that later came to be made of the League on the ground of its relation to the peace treaties was primarily an attack upon the treaties themselves and would have been directed against any international organization which proved incapable of revising them. Without further arguing this point, however, the question can be raised as to how different will be the relation of the United Nations to the peace settlement following World War II?

While the Charter is a separate instrument and was made at a conference called specially for the purpose, the United Nations will inevitably become intimately and directly associated with the peace treaties once they are made. For one thing the original Members of the United Nations were those states that were at war with one or more of the Axis powers at the time of the San Francisco Conference. Furthermore, the interpre-

[5] See, for example, Clyde Eagleton, "Covenant of the League of Nations and Charter of the United Nations: Points of Difference," in Department of State, *Bulletin*, XIII, p. 264.
[6] See, for example, the provision of the Treaty of Versailles relating to the administration of the Saar Basin and the protection of Danzig. *Treaty of Peace with Germany*, Part III, section IV, Annex, chapter II, and section XI.
[7] W. E. Rappard, *International Relations Viewed from Geneva*, New Haven, 1925, p. 14–16.

tation to date of the provisions of Article 4 of the Charter makes it clear that the conduct of a non-member state during the war is an important factor in determining whether that state shall be admitted to membership. While Article 107 dissociates the United Nations as a peace organization from action taken in relation to enemy states, once the peace treaties have been made they will become part of the existing economic and political order on the basis of which the United Nations will seek to maintain peace and security. It is difficult to see how an international organization for maintaining peace and security, such as the United Nations is, can do so on any other basis. Furthermore, in connection with the making of the peace treaties, we already see the United Nations being called upon to exercise important functions of administration or guarantee similar to those which the League was asked to perform. Thus the United Nations guarantee of the special regime for Trieste parallels very closely the League guarantee of Danzig in its basic conception, and the proposed role of the United Nations in connection with "territories detached from enemy states in connection with the Second World War"[8] is almost identical to that of the League in relation to "colonies and territories which as a consequence of the late war [World War I] have ceased to be under the sovereignty of the States which formerly governed them."[9]

In this same connection we should consider the respective powers and responsibilities of the two organizations in regard to the revision of the two peace settlements. One serious criticism made of the League of Nations was its ineffectiveness as an instrumentality for the revision of those provisions of the peace treaties which had come to be recognized as unfair and unjust. Under the Covenant of the League the Assembly was empowered to advise the revision of treaties which had become "inapplicable" and the consideration of international conditions whose continuation might affect the peace of the world.[10] This provision remained a dead letter from the beginning, due to the Assembly's lack of power of decision and means of enforcement.[11] How much more effective is the United Nations likely to be in this respect? According to Article 14 of the Charter the General Assembly may recommend measures for the peaceful adjustment of any situation, regardless of origin, which is likely to impair friendly relations among nations. While there is no specific mention made of the revision of treaties, the General Assembly is clearly authorized under this Article to discuss any situation having its origin in unsatisfactory treaty provisions and to make recommendations thereon.[12] There is, however,

---

[8] *Charter of the United Nations*, Article 77.
[9] *Covenant of the League of Nations*, Article 12, paragraph 1.
[10] *Ibid.*, Article 19.
[11] Frederick S. Dunn, *Peaceful Change*, New York, 1937, p. 106–11.
[12] See discussion in Leland M. Goodrich and Edvard Hambro, *Charter of the United Nations: Commentary and Documents*, Boston, 1946, p. 104–06.

no obligation on the part of Members to accept any recommendation that may be made. Thus the power conferred under this Article does not go substantially beyond that of the Assembly under Article 19 of the Covenant and there is the same chance, if not likelihood, that the United Nations will be ineffective as an instrument for treaty revision. Furthermore, while the Security Council is given broad powers to take necessary action to maintain peace and security, the powers which the Council has to bind Members are limited to those falling within the general category of enforcement action and do not extend to the power to impose upon parties to a dispute or states interested in a particular situation any particular terms of settlement or adjustment. That was made clear in the discussions at San Francisco.[13]

Basic Character of Two Organizations

The statement has been made that the United Nations is "potentially and actually much stronger" than the League of Nations.[14] That statement might lend itself to some misunderstanding, particularly in view of the fact that it is only one of many statements that have been made suggesting that the United Nations inherently is a more powerful organization and therefore more likely to achieve its purpose by virtue of the specific provisions of its Charter than was the League of Nations.

We can start, I think, with the fundamental proposition that the United Nations, as was the League of Nations, is primarily a cooperative enterprise and falls generally within the category of leagues and confederations instead of within that of federal unions. Except in one situation, neither the United Nations nor its principal political organs have the authority to take decisions binding on Members without their express consent. Without this power, it is impossible to regard the organs of the United Nations as constituting a government in the sense of the federal government of the United States. The essential character of the United Nations is specifically affirmed in the first of the principles laid down in Article 2 of the Charter where it is stated that "the organization is based on the principle of the sovereign equality of all its members." This principle was not expressly stated in the Covenant of the League of Nations, but was, nevertheless, implicit in its provisions.

Since both the United Nations and the League of Nations are based primarily upon the principle of voluntary cooperation, the point that needs special consideration is whether, more or less as an exception to the general principle, the Charter contains provisions which give to the organs of the United Nations greater authority than was vested in the corre-

---

[13] See Goodrich and Hambro, *op. cit.*, p. 152–53, 155–59.
[14] Louis Dolivet, *The United Nations: A* *Handbook on the New World Organization,* New York, 1946, p. 16.

sponding organs of the League. In this connection a great deal of emphasis has been placed upon the provisions of the Charter regulating voting in the General Assembly and the Security Council. It is, of course, true that under Article 18 of the Charter decisions of the General Assembly can be taken by a two-thirds majority of the members present and voting, instead of by unanimous vote of those present, as was the requirement for the League Assembly. It must be borne in mind, however, that on questions of policy the General Assembly can only recommend, and that consequently any decision taken is a decision to make a recommendation. Also, it is quite unfair to compare these provisions without taking into account the practice of the League Assembly under the Covenant. In several important respects the rule of the Covenant was interpreted so as to bring actual League practice fairly close to the provisions of the Charter.[15] For one thing, it was provided in the rules of the Assembly that a state which abstained from voting was not to be counted as present, with the result that abstention was a means by which certain of the consequences of the unanimity rule could be avoided. More important, however, was the rule which was established in the first session of the League Assembly, that a resolution expressing a wish, technically known as a "voeu," might be adopted by a majority vote. This had the effect of making possible a whole range of Assembly decisions by majority vote which did not differ in any important respect from decisions which may be taken by the General Assembly by majority or two-thirds votes.[16] Furthermore, it should be noted that the League Assembly early came to the conclusion that the decision to recommend an amendment to the Covenant under Article 26 might be taken by a majority vote,[17] with the result that the power of the Assembly to initiate amendments actually could be exercised more easily than under the Charter of the United Nations. Thus it would seem erroneous to view the provisions of the Charter with respect to the power of the General Assembly to make decisions as representing any fundamentally different approach from or any great advance over the comparable provisions of the Covenant of the League of Nations as interpreted in practice.

When we turn our attention to the Security Council we find admittedly that an important change has been made. Under the League Covenant the Council was governed by the unanimity rule except in procedural matters, and this proved a serious handicap, particularly when the Council was acting under Article 11 of the Covenant. It was possible for a member of the Council, accused of threatening or disturbing the peace, to prevent any effective action under this Article by the interposition

---

[15] See Margaret E. Burton, *The Assembly of the League of Nations*, Chicago, 1941, p. 175–205.

[16] See C. A. Riches, *Majority Rule in Inter-national Organization*, Baltimore, 1940, p. 24.

[17] League of Nations, *Records of the Second Assembly*, Plenary Meetings, p. 733–35. See also, Burton, *op. cit.*, p. 187.

of its veto, as happened in the case of Japanese aggression in Manchuria in 1931 and the threat of Italian aggression in Ethiopia in 1935. Under the Charter it is possible for a decision to be taken binding Members of the United Nations without their express consent. Furthermore, this decision may require specific acts upon the part of the Members of the United Nations and is not to be regarded as a simple recommendation as was the case with decisions taken by the League Council under Articles 10 and 16.

Nevertheless, there are important points to be kept in mind before we conclude that a revolutionary step has been taken. In the first place, a decision by the Security Council can only have the effect of a recommendation when the Security Council is engaged in the performance of its functions under Chapter VI, *i.e.* when it is seeking to achieve the pacific settlement or adjustment of a dispute or situation. Furthermore, while the decision of the Security Council with respect to enforcement action under Chapter VII is binding upon Members of the United Nations, including those not represented on the Security Council, such decisions cannot be taken without the concurrence of all the permanent members of the Security Council. Consequently, in a situation comparable to that of Japanese aggression against China in Manchuria in 1931 and the threat of Italian aggression against Ethiopia in 1935, where the League Council admittedly failed on account of the unanimity principle, the Security Council would be prevented from taking any decision. Under the Charter the Security Council has power, which the League Council did not have, to take action against the small powers, but the experience of the past would seem to show that it is not the smaller powers, acting alone, who are most likely to disturb the peace. When dealing with threats by smaller powers acting alone the League Council was reasonably effective; it failed only when small powers had the backing of great powers. In spite of important changes in the technical provisions of the Charter, one is forced to the conclusion that so far as the actual possession of power is concerned, the United Nations has not advanced much beyond the League of Nations and that in comparable situations much the same result is to be anticipated. In the last analysis under either system success or failure is dependent upon the ability of the more powerful members to cooperate effectively for common ends.

Finally, the provisions of the Charter with regard to amendments and withdrawal follow in all essential respects the provisions of the Covenant and the practices developed thereunder. Under both Charter and Covenant no amendment recommended by the Assembly can become effective until ratified by the great powers. The Covenant was a little more restrictive than the Charter in one respect, requiring ratification by all members of the League whose representatives composed the Council, plus a majority of all other members, thereby giving any Council member a "veto." On the other hand, the Charter, while limiting the "veto" to permanent members, requires approval by two-thirds of the Members of the United Nations. In practice, the charter provisions are not likely to have substantially different results.

Likewise, with respect to withdrawal, the League and the United Nations systems do not differ in any important respect. The Covenant of the League expressly permitted withdrawal under certain conditions which were not, however, enforced in practice.[18] The Charter says nothing about withdrawal but it is understood on the basis of a declaration adopted at San Francisco that the right of withdrawal can be exercised.[19] No doubt influenced by the League practice and conforming to it, it was decided that no legal conditions should be attached to the exercise of this right and that no attempt should be made to force a state to remain a Member, although it was made clear that a moral obligation to continue as a Member exists and that the right of withdrawal should only be exercised for very good reasons.

Basic Obligations of Members

Enumerated in Article 2 of the Charter are certain basic obligations of Members of the United Nations. These include the obligation to settle disputes by peaceful means in such a manner that international peace and security are not endangered, the obligation to refrain from the threat or the use of force against the territorial integrity or political independence of any state, and the obligation to give assistance to the United Nations in any action taken under the terms of the Charter. Similar commitments phrased in somewhat different language and with somewhat different meanings were to be found in various Articles of the Covenant.[20] From the point of view of form the Charter does represent a somewhat different approach in that these basic commitments are grouped together as Principles binding upon all Members. The phraseology of the Charter in certain respects undoubtedly represents improvement. For instance, the provision of Article 2, paragraph 4, by which Members are to refrain "from the threat or use of force against the territorial integrity or political independence of any state" represents an advance over the corresponding provisions of the Covenant which made it possible for members to take refuge in the technicality that an undeclared war in the material sense was no war and that therefore such use of armed force did not constitute a "resort to war." On the other hand, in one important respect, the basic

---

[18] Article 1, paragraph 2.

[19] For text, see UNCIO, *Verbatim Minutes of the Ninth Plenary Session*, June 25, 1945, Document 1210, P/20, p. 5–6; for text and comment, see Goodrich and Hambro, *op. cit.*, p. 86–89.

[20] Articles 10; 12, paragraph 1; 13, paragraphs 1 and 4; 15, paragraphs 1 and 6; 16, paragraphs 1 and 3; and 17.

obligations of the Members of the United Nations may prove to be less satisfactory since, in the matter of enforcement action, the obligation of the Members of the United Nations is to accept and carry out decisions of the Security Council and to give assistance to the United Nations in any action taken under the Charter, while under Article 16 of the Covenant, the obligation of members extended to the taking of specific measures against any state resorting to war in violation of its obligations under the Covenant. While this obligation was weakened by resolutions adopted by the Assembly in 1921, it nevertheless proved capable of providing the legal basis for important action against Italy in 1935.

III.

The element of continuity in the progression from League of Nations to United Nations is perhaps most obvious when we examine the structure of the two organizations. The General Assembly is the League Assembly, from the point of view of the basic principles of its composition, powers and procedures. We have already seen from an examination of voting procedures that the practical difference between the League provisions and their actual application and the Charter provisions has been greatly exaggerated. The powers of the General Assembly, as compared with those of the League Assembly, have been somewhat restricted, it is true. The General Assembly's powers of discussion under Article 10 of the Charter and succeeding articles are fully as broad and comprehensive as the League Assembly's powers under Article 3, paragraph 3 of the Covenant. Only in respect to the making of recommendations has the power of the General Assembly been limited, and this, it can be argued, is in line with the practice which developed under the Covenant according to which the Council, and not the Assembly, ordinarily dealt with disputes and situations which endangered peace and good understanding.[21] The significant difference is that under the Charter a party to a dispute cannot by its act alone transfer the dispute from the Council to the Assembly, as was possible under Article 15, paragraph 9, of the Covenant.

The Security Council, from the point of view of composition, is the old League Council. One important change, however, has been introduced into the Charter. The League Council had general responsibilities and functions, whereas the Security Council is a highly specialized organ. Instead of having one council with broad powers as did the League, the United Nations has three, among which the various functions and powers of the League Council are divided. To a certain extent this new set-up was anticipated in League practice. At the time when the League's prestige as a peace and security organization was low, the Assembly created a special committee known as the Bruce Committee to inquire

[21] See Burton, *op. cit.*, p. 284–374.

and report on the possibilities of giving the economic and social work of the League greater autonomy. This Committee recommended the establishment of a new organ to be known as the Central Committee for Economic and Social Questions to which would be entrusted the direction and supervision of the work of the League committees in this field.[22] This proposed Committee, while it never was set up, was in effect the forerunner of the present Economic and Social Council.

So far as the Trusteeship Council is concerned, there is a somewhat similar background of development. While the Council was responsible under the Covenant for the supervision of the administration of mandates, in actual practice the Council came to rely very heavily on the Mandates Commission which, under the Charter, has come to be elevated to the rank of a principal organ, responsible not to the Council but to the General Assembly. This very responsibility of the Trusteeship Council to the General Assembly was to some extent anticipated in the practice of the League. Over the protest of some members, the League Assembly early asserted and exercised the right to discuss and express its opinion on mandates questions. While the Council was technically responsible for the enforcement of the provisions of the Covenant, there can be little doubt but what the Assembly exercised a real influence both on Council action and upon the mandatory powers.[23]

The Secretariat of the United Nations is clearly a continuation of the League Secretariat, not only in name, but also largely in substance. While the Charter provisions would permit its organization on somewhat different lines, with separate staffs for the principal organs of the United Nations, it seems clear that the conception of a unified Secretariat has prevailed.[24] "The role of the Secretary-General as the administrator of the United Nations derives from that of his counterpart in the League of Nations," [25] but has clearly assumed greater importance and scope under the provisions of the Charter. Due to political circumstances and the personality of the first holder of the office, the Secretary-General of the League never came to exercise a strong guiding hand in the direction of the League's work. The Charter of the United Nations, however, both expressly and by implication, gives the Secretary-General greater power and seems to expect more constructive leadership from him. More particularly, the role which the Secretary-General will be called upon to play in connection with the coordination of the work of the specialized agencies will require the exercise of initiative and strong leadership.[26]

[22] League of Nations, Monthly Summary, August 1939, Special Supplement.
[23] See Quincy Wright, Mandates under the League of Nations, Chicago, 1930, p. 133–35.
[24] See Report of the Preparatory Commission of the United Nations, PC/20, 23 December 1945, p. 84–94; Walter H. C. Laves and Donald Stone, "The United Nations Secretariat," Foreign Policy Reports, October 15, 1946.
[25] Laves and Stone, op. cit., p. 183.
[26] Ibid., p. 186 et seq.

With respect to the Court, it is clearly recognized that, while it was decided to set up a new Court under a new name, it will be essentially the same as the Permanent Court of International Justice.[27] The fact that this Court is regarded as one of the principal organs of the United Nations does not in substance distinguish it from the Permanent Court. For purposes of expediency it seemed advisable to maintain the fiction that the Permanent Court of International Justice was independent of the League system, but a careful examination of the actual organization and work of the Court will leave no doubt that the Court functioned as fully within the framework of the League as will the International Court of Justice within the framework of the United Nations.

IV.

Like the League of Nations, the United Nations is a "general international organization" in the sense that its functions and actions cover the whole range of matters of international concern. Both the Preamble and the statement of Purposes contained in Article I of the Charter make this clear. In fact this generality of purpose and function is more explicitly stated in the Charter than it was in the Covenant, though in the practice of the League it came to be fully recognized. The Charter of the United Nations, in its general arrangement and substantive provisions, divides the major activities of the Organization into three categories: (1) the maintenance of international peace and security, by the pacific settlement of disputes and the taking of enforcement measures; (2) the promotion of international economic and social cooperation; and (3) the protection of the interests of the peoples of non-self-governing territories.

The Pacific Settlement of Disputes

The Charter system for the pacific settlement of disputes,[28] while differing from that of the League in many details of substance and phraseology, follows it in accepting two basic principles: (1) that parties to a dispute are in the first instance to seek a peaceful settlement by means of their own choice; and (2) that the political organs of the international organization are to intervene only when the dispute has become a threat to the peace, and then only in a mediatory or conciliatory capacity.

The obligation which Members of the United Nations accept under Article 2, paragraph 3 is to "settle their international disputes by peaceful means in such a manner that international peace and security, and justice, are not endangered." Under Article 34, paragraph 1, the parties to any

[27] UNCIO, Report of the Rapporteur of Committee IV/1, Document 913, IV/1/74 (1). See also Manley O. Hudson, "The Twenty-Fourth Year of the World Court," in *American Journal of International Law,* LX (1946), p. 1–52.

[28] For detailed analysis, see Leland M. Goodrich, "Pacific Settlement of Disputes," in *American Political Science Review,* XXXIX (1945), p. 956–970.

dispute "the continuance of which is likely to endanger the maintenance of international peace and security, shall, first of all seek a solution" by peaceful means of their own choice. Furthermore, by the terms of Article 36 of the Statute of the Court, Members may by declaration accept under certain conditions the compulsory jurisdiction of the Court. Declarations made by Members of the United Nations accepting the compulsory jurisdiction of the Permanent Court of International Justice and still in force are declared to be acceptances under this Article.

The legal obligations which Members of the United Nations have thus assumed are substantially the same as the obligations of League·members under the Covenant and supplementary agreements. The Covenant itself did not place upon members of the League the obligation to settle all their disputes by peaceful means. However, forty-six states accepted the compulsory jurisdiction of the Permanent Court by making declarations under Article 36 of the Statute.[29] By Article 2 of the General Pact for the Renunciation of War of 1928 (Kellogg-Briand Pact), the signatories agreed that "the settlement or solution of all disputes or conflicts of whatever nature or of whatever origin they may be . . . shall never be sought except by pacific means."

The powers of the United Nations organs for the pacific settlement of disputes are substantially the same as those of the principal organs of the League. Under the Charter, as under the Covenant, the functions of political organs in this connection are limited to discussion, inquiry, mediation and conciliation. It is clear from the words of the Charter and from the discussions at San Francisco, that the Security Council has no power of final decision in connection with its functions of pacific settlement.[30] The Charter does, however, seek to differentiate between the functions and powers of the General Assembly and the Security Council in a way that the Covenant did not do. More specifically it makes the Security Council primarily responsible for the maintenance of peace and security, does not permit a party to a dispute to have the matter transferred at its request to the General Assembly, and limits the power of the General Assembly in principle to that of discussion. This constitutes an important departure from the textual provisions of the League Covenant which gave the Council and Assembly the same general competence and expressly allowed a party, acting under Article 15, paragraph 9, to have a dispute transferred at its request to the Assembly. It is significant, however, that out of some 66 disputes that came before the League, only three were actually brought before the Assembly under this provision. It would thus appear, and this is the conclusion of a careful student of the Assem-

[29] See Manley O. Hudson, "The Twenty-Fourth Year of the World Court," *op. cit.*, p. 33.

[30] See UNCIO, Report of the Rapporteur of Committee III/2, Document 1027 III/2/31(1), p. 4.

bly,[31] that actual practice under the Covenant resulted in a differentiation of function. This the Charter seeks to make obligatory.

In certain other respects the Charter system departs from the League pattern, but the importance of these differences can be greatly exaggerated. The elimination of the requirement of unanimity in voting theoretically increases the power of the Security Council, as compared with the League Council, in dealing with disputes and situations, but considering that the Security Council can only recommend, and that in League practice, agreement of the great powers was likely to result in the necessary agreement among all members of the Council, the practical importance of this difference is not likely to be great. Furthermore, under the Charter provision is made for the consideration by the Security Council and General Assembly of situations as well as disputes, but this does not mean any increase in the powers of the United Nations organs, particularly the Security Council, as compared with those of the corresponding organs of the League. In fact, it can be argued that the provisions of the Charter suffer somewhat in flexibility and capacity for growth, as compared with the corresponding provisions of the Covenant, because of the greater detail and consequent rigidity of certain of its terms. A comparison of experience under the Charter to date in the peaceful settlement or adjustment of disputes and situations with that of the League gives little basis for a confident conclusion that the Charter system is inherently better than, or for that matter, significantly different from, that which operated under the terms of the Covenant.[32]

Enforcement Action

It is in respect to enforcement action that the provisions of the Charter seem to offer the most marked contrast to the provisions of the Covenant,[33] but here again when we compare the Charter provisions with the way in which the Covenant provisions were actually applied the differences do not appear so great. The League system, as originally conceived, was based on the principle that once a member had resorted to war in violation of its obligations under the Covenant, other members were immediately obligated to apply economic and financial sanctions of wide scope against the offending state. The Council was empowered to recommend

[31] See Margaret E. Burton, *The Assembly of the League of Nations*, p. 284 et seq.

[32] On the operation of the League system, see William E. Rappard, *The Quest for Peace*, Cambridge, 1940, p. 134–207; Burton, *op. cit.*, p. 284–374; and T. P. Conwell-Evans, *The League Council in Action*, London, 1929. On the work of the Security Council to date, see Clyde Eagleton, "The Jurisdiction of the Security Council over Disputes," in *American Journal of International Law*, XI (July, 1946), p. 513–33; and United Nations, *Report of the Security Council to the General Assembly*, A/93, October 3, 1946.

[33] For analysis of the United Nations system for the enforcement of peace and security, see Grayson Kirk, "The Enforcement of Security," in *Yale Law Journal*, LV (August 1946), p. 1081–1196.

military measures which members of the League were technically not required to carry out. As a matter of fact, in the one case where the provisions of Article 16 were given anything like a real test, the application of sanctions against Italy in 1936, acting under the influence of the resolutions adopted by the Assembly in 1921,[34] the members of the League established a mechanism for the coordination of their individual acts, and proceeded to apply selected economic and financial measures. No recommendation was made by the Council for the application of military measures.[35]

The Charter makes the Security Council responsible for deciding what enforcement measures are to be used to maintain the peace. Obligations arise for Members of the United Nations only when such decisions have been taken. This is a further development of the principle recognized in the 1921 Assembly resolutions and in the application of sanctions against Italy, that a central coordinating agency is needed to insure the taking of necessary measures with the maximum of effectiveness and the minimum of inconvenience and danger to the participating members. However, the provisions of the Charter go much further than did the Covenant in providing for obligatory military measures and advance commitments to place specific forces at the disposal of the Security Council. Even though certain members of the League, notably France, were insistent upon the need of specific military commitments, little was done in League practice to meet this need. The Geneva Protocol of 1924 was one notable attempt to meet this demand, by methods which in certain respects anticipated the Charter, but it never came into force. The framers of the Charter, no doubt recognizing this as a defect in the League system, sought to remedy the deficiency by providing in some detail for military agreements between members of the United Nations and the Security Council, and for a military staff committee to assist the Security Council in drawing up advanced plans and in applying military measures.

It can, however, be queried whether the Charter system will be more effective than the League system, in view of the requirement of unanimity of the permanent members of the Security Council. If we imagine its application in situations such as the Italian-Ethiopian and Sino-Japanese affairs, it is difficult to see how the United Nations would achieve any better results than did the League. Like the League, but for somewhat different technical reasons, the United Nations, in so far as its enforcement activities are concerned, is an organization for the enforcement of peace among the smaller states. If the permanent members of the Security Council are in agreement, it will be possible to take effective action under

---

[34] League of Nations, *Records of the Second Assembly*, Plenary Meetings, p. 803.
[35] For summary of this experience, see

International Sanctions (A Report by a Group of Members of the Royal Institute of International Affairs), London, 1938, p. 204–213.

the Charter. It is not likely that such agreement will be reached to take measures against one of these great powers or against a protégé of such a great power. Consequently the sphere of effective enforcement action by the United Nations is restricted in advance, even more perhaps than was that of the League. Within the area of possible operation, the actual effectiveness of the United Nations system will depend upon political conditions which, if they had existed, would have also assured the success of the League of Nations.[36]

Administration of Non-Self-Governing Territories

Here we encounter new names and phraseology in the United Nations Charter, but the substance is very much the substance of the League mandates system. There are, of course, important differences. For one thing, Chapter XI, "Declaration Regarding Non-Self-Governing Territories," is definitely an addition. The idea, however, is not new, as it has been accepted by various colonial administrations in recent years, and has found expression both in official statements and in authoritative writings on the subject.[37] However, it is new to have embodied in an international instrument a definite statement of principles binding upon all states engaged in the administration of non-self-governing territories and to place upon such states the additional obligation to make reports to an international authority.

So far as the trusteeship system, strictly speaking, is concerned, it follows in general the lines of the mandates system.[38] The three categories of A, B, and C mandates do not appear, but due to the freedom allowed in the drafting of trusteeship agreements, there can be the same, if not greater, variety of provisions. Like the League mandates system, the institution of the trusteeship system is not made obligatory for any particular territories; it is simply declared applicable to certain territories to the extent that they are placed under it by agreement. Following the practice under the mandates system, the trusteeship agreements, according to the Charter, are to be made by the states "directly concerned." They must in addition have the approval of the General Assembly or the Security Council, depending upon whether or not they apply to strategic areas, but neither organ has any authority to draft and put into effect a trusteeship agreement for any territory without the specific approval at least of the state in actual possession of it.

The machinery for supervision and the lines of responsibility have been changed in that for trusteeship areas other than strategic areas the ad-

---

[36] See Kirk, *op. cit.*, p. 1082.
[37] See, for example, Baron Lugard, *The Dual Mandate in British Tropical Africa*, 2nd ed., London, 1923.
[38] For detailed analysis of the United Nations trusteeship system, see Ralph J. Bunche, "Trusteeship and Non-Self-Governing Territories in the Charter of the United Nations," in *Organizing the United Nations*, Department of State Publication 2573.

ministrative authorities are responsible to the General Assembly and its agent, the Trusteeship Council. As has been pointed out above, however, this change as compared with the League mandates system, was to some extent anticipated in League practice by the right which the Assembly asserted and exercised to discuss and make recommendations with respect to the administration of mandated territories. There is, however, in the Charter one important power vested in the United Nations organs, though in somewhat qualified form, which the Council and Mandates Commission of the League did not have and the lack of which was regarded as a serious weakness of the League system. I refer to the provision for periodical visits to the trusteeship territories which should make it possible for the Organization to get information on the spot and thereby check upon and supplement the reports of the administrative authorities.

International Economic and Social Cooperation

Perhaps the most important advance of the Charter over the Covenant of the League is to be found in its provisions defining the objectives, policies, machinery and procedure of international economic and social cooperation. In this respect, the Charter offers a wide contrast to the Covenant, which had only three articles dealing specifically with the subject. In fact, the Preamble of the Covenant, containing the statement of purposes of the League, made no specific mention of cooperation in economic and social matters, though the very general phrase "in order to promote international order and cooperation" was relied upon to justify numerous activities for which no express authority was to be found.

It is, nevertheless, true that the League in practice was a quite different matter.[39] It has been generally observed that the most permanently worthwhile activities of the League of Nations were in the field of international economic and social cooperation. There was in the course of the League's existence a tremendous proliferation of organization and an impressive record of substantial achievement in making available necessary information, in promoting administrative and legislative action by member states, and in dealing directly with international economic and social evils by administrative action. We have seen how in 1939 the recognition of the scope and importance of this work led to the proposal that a Central Committee for Economic and Social Questions should be set up to coordinate League activities in this field.

Apart from the provision for a separate economic and social council there is one important organizational difference between the League and United Nations systems, a difference which may prove to be of great

[39] See, for example, Denys P. Myers, *Handbook of the League of Nations*, Boston, 1935, for evidence of the relative importance on a quantitative basis, at least, of the League's economic and social activities during the first fifteen years of the League's existence.

importance, depending upon how the provisions of the Charter are applied in practice. Whereas the League technical organizations dealing with health, economic and financial cooperation were developed within the framework of the League and operated under the general direction and control of the principal League organs, the approach of the United Nations has been a different one. This time we have proceeded on the assumption that special needs as they arise should be met by the creation of appropriate autonomous organizations and that subsequently, these organizations should be brought into relationship with each other and with the United Nations by agreements negotiated by the organs empowered to act in such matters. The result is that instead of having a number of technical organizations functioning within the general international organization and subject to the general direction and supervision of its principal organs, as under the League system, we now have a number of specialized inter-governmental agencies, each operating within a defined area and more or less independently of the others.

Such a system clearly has possibilities as to the range and type of action that may be taken which were denied to the League system operating more completely under the influence of political considerations. On the other hand, there are obviously certain advantages in having some effective coordination of the operation of these various agencies as there will be many points at which their interests and activities will overlap.[40] Under the Charter the proposal is to take care of these common concerns by the special agreements referred to above. It is too early to be certain as to what the practical consequences of this approach will prove to be.

V.

To the student of international organization, it should be a cause neither of surprise nor of concern to find that the United Nations is for all practical purposes a continuation of the League of Nations. Rather it would be disturbing if the architects of world organization had completely or largely thrown aside the designs and materials of the past. One cannot build soundly on the basis of pure theory. Man being what he is, and the dominant forces and attitudes of international relations being what they are, it is idle to expect, and foolhardy to construct the perfect system of world government in our day. Profiting from the lessons of past experience, we can at most hope to make some progress toward the attainment of a goal which may for a long time remain beyond our reach. The United Nations is not world government and it was not intended to be such. Rather it represents a much more conservative and cautious approach

[40] See Herman Finer, *The United Nations Economic and Social Council*, Boston, 1945, 121 p.; also *Report of the Preparatory Commission of the United Nations*, PC/20, December 23, 1945, p. 40–48.

to the problem of world order. As such, it inevitably falls into the stream of institutional development represented by the League of Nations and its predecessors. Different names may be used for similar things, and different combinations of words may be devised to express similar ideas. There may be changes of emphasis, and in fact important substantive changes, deemed desirable in the light of past experience or thought necessary in order to meet changed conditions. But there is no real break in the stream of organizational development.

The student of international organization must recognize the United Nations for what it quite properly is, a revised League, no doubt improved in some respects, possibly weaker in others, but nonetheless a League, a voluntary association of nations, carrying on largely in the League tradition and by the League methods. Important changes have occurred in the world distribution of power, in the world's economic and political structure, in the world's ideological atmosphere. These changes create new problems and modify the chances of success or failure in meeting them, but the mechanics remain much the same. Anyone desiring to understand the machinery, how it operates, the conditions of its success, must look to the experience of the past, and particularly to the rich and varied experience of that first attempt at a general international organization, the League of Nations.

INTERNATIONAL ORGANIZATION
AND WORLD POLITICS

CHARLES EASTON ROTHWELL

When the Soviet Union withdrew recently from the World Health Organization, a somewhat startled world learned that even the prevention of disease can be affected by world politics. The most cursory study of international organizations for other purposes discloses that none is immune to world social and political forces. On the contrary, they are in varying degree shaped and influenced by these forces, and in fact serve as vehicles for their expression.

The influence is not, however, wholly one-sided. The many international organizations created within the past seventy-five years have themselves become a force within the world community. They have modified the patterns of world politics significantly; and they have slowly begun to acquire the status of world institutions serving the needs of a commonwealth greater than the sum of the nations that compose it.

The United Nations proper and the numerous specialized agencies that round out the "United Nations system" are very young, institutionally speaking. The oldest of them was established within the memory of persons still living; several have been created within the past four years. Even the embryonic forms of international collaboration out of which they have evolved antedate them by less than a century.

It is the purpose of this study to explore the significance of these international organizations by viewing them in the milieu of world politics. In order to do so, it is necessary to describe the world forces that brought about their establishment, the influences that have shaped their development, and the effects which they have produced in the world community. Only with knowledge of these factors is it possible to form reasonable estimates of what may be expected of international organizations, now and in the future.

CHARLES EASTON ROTHWELL is Vice-Chairman of the Hoover Institute and Library on War, Revolution and Peace at Stanford University. He served with the Department of State from 1941 to 1946, was Executive Secretary of the United Nations Conference on International Organization in 1945, and later Secretary-General of the United States Mission to the United Nations. This article, in expanded form, will serve as the introductory chapter in a forthcoming book on *International Organization and World Politics*. The book will contain a series of case studies of organizations in various fields, one of which, "World Health and World Politics," by Charles E. Allen, will appear in a subsequent issue of *International Organization*.

From Volume 3, No. 4 (1949), pp. 605–19.

II

During the past century and a half, while international organizations have gradually been taking form, the world community has been shrinking physically but growing in terms of human interaction. Throughout this period, the nation state has been the prevailing unit of power and decision. Greater interaction among the peoples and political units composing the world community has on the one hand compelled nations to work together to satisfy their common needs. On the other hand, it has aggravated the forces that produce friction, within states and among them. More intimate contacts among nations and culture groups, coupled with other results of technological and institutional development, have tended to intensify old nationalisms, call forth new ones, provoke conflicts of interest, and create webs of tension. When the level of conflict and tension has exceeded the pressures for accommodation, hostile alignments have formed and wars have resulted. Although the wars have temporarily released tensions and raised the level of accommodation among nations, they have also served as powerful catalysts of change and sources of renewed tension and conflict.

Within the same period, the world community has undergone sweeping revolutionary changes. In part these have been radical advances in the technical bases of life typified by the so-called industrial and scientific revolutions. In part they have been fundamental changes in social structure, units of political power, and ideology, as illustrated by urbanization, imperialist expansion, and later totalitarian trends. Whatever their form, these vast and comparatively rapid transformations have been both creatures and creators of domestic upheaval and international conflict. Added together, the years of unrest, revolution, and war have exceeded those of orderly development during the past century and a half. Disturbance and flux have been more normal than abnormal in the nation-centered world of the nineteenth and twentieth centuries, and have been symptomatic of a global community in process of violent adjustment.

Counter forces making for world order have also been at work. Important among them has been the frightening costliness of cyclical tension and war, which has caused peoples and their governments to seek greater international tranquillity, especially in immediate post-war periods. More positive has been the increasing number of human needs that can be met in a world of greater interaction only through international cooperation. To these forces should be added the influence of a spreading network of international relationships, both private and public. These relationships, born of an emerging recognition of the international identity of special interest groups, have found expression in banking and commercial ties, in labor internationals, and in hundreds of private international organizations. They have, with notable exceptions, contributed to an orderly world because they thrive best in conditions of stability and peace.

The trends towards more rational behavior among nations have also been sustained by the prevailing intellectual and spiritual currents of the age. From the period of the Enlightenment well into the twentieth century, the prevalent stream of aspiration in western culture has been running toward an ordered world community. The emphasis has been upon progress, common humanity, universal law, political freedom, democracy, general well-being, and peace. These aspirations lent impetus to the movement for international order which culminated in the establishment of the League of Nations. Their resurgence during the second world war contributed to the founding of the United Nations. Superficially, at least, they have even gained wide acceptance within the young nations of non-western cultures that have emerged from crumbling colonial empires.

This system of ideals, which cradled the basic concepts of international organization, met no serious challenge until after 1920. Contrary ideals advanced by Treitschke, Gobineau, and others made little headway against the more liberal spirit of the age. To be sure, international practices were frequently out of line with prevailing aspirations, as the alliances preceding 1914 or the secret treaties of the first world war would suggest. This circumstance did not weaken the ideas favorable to a liberally organized world order, but in fact tended to strengthen them. Their popular acceptance was such that they were frequently venerated in high policy statements by the very governments that forgot them in practice. Until thirty years ago no great power of the late nineteenth and twentieth century presumed to deny the ideals of an orderly and peaceful world, even when behaving contrary to them. Statesmen, including Bismarck, even thought it necessary to defend and rationalize excursions into *realpolitik,* however cynically they may have regarded the ideals.

On the other hand, the nineteenth century synthesis of aspirations acquired positive creative influence when it found expression in the policy and action of states, particularly the great powers. This happened when such ideas coincided with the real national interests of these states as perceived by their governments. The fact of such coincidence in 1918 and again in 1945 was in large measure responsible for the founding of the League of Nations and the United Nations.

Nonetheless, the liberal heritage favorable to international organization has met revolutionary challenge within the last thirty years. It has been challenged from the right by fascism, which repudiated completely the ideal of a cooperative world order in favor of the hegemony of a martial nation and a master race. More recently, it has been challenged from the left by Soviet communism, which would substitute for the liberal (and "capitalist") world order a proletarian commonwealth of Stalinist orientation. The great impact which the fascist challenge had upon the world community resulted from the power which the fascist states wielded at their zenith, coupled with the appeal of a glamourized ideology to the discontented of this earth. Similarly, the challenge of Soviet communism derives potency from the vast power of the USSR and the attraction of the communist dream for dissatisfied peoples.

III

The state-centered world community has thus been characterized during the past century and a half by virulent nationalism, revolutionary change, and turbulent adjustment on the one hand, and by strong forces favorable to world order on the other. In that environment an increasing number of international agencies has been established to cope with an ever wider range of inter-state activities. This growth of organized international collaboration has been sufficiently vital to survive two world wars, the fascist challenge, and a world-wide depression. Although the wars have interrupted most international cooperation, one of their most striking consequences has been the new impetus and strength which they have imparted to the development of organized world order in the immediate post-war periods.

Each international organization came into being through a compact among national states. In no case did the establishment of a continuing international body represent a sharp break from the past. Whatever the purpose of the organization, it had almost without exception been preceded by *ad hoc* conferences, local or general, or by regional bodies exercising the same functions. In some instances, official international organizations such as the International Labor Organization and the United Maritime Consultative Council evolved from private international associations that pioneered the channels of cooperation. Not infrequently, as in the field of political adjustment and the maintenance of peace, the first continuing organization (the League of Nations) was built upon practices and conceptions deriving from several embryonic forms of cooperation. The historical process by which present organizations coalesced out of such antecedents is well illustrated in the century and a half of development that culminated in the founding of the World Health Organization in 1946, as related in an article on that subject scheduled to appear in a later issue of *International Organization.*[1]

1 "World Health and World Politics" by Charles E. Allen will appear in a forthcoming issue of *International Organization.*

Each organization became possible when a sufficient number of states recognized and were prepared to do something about a mutual need that could best be met through continuing channels of multilateral cooperation. The need itself, whether for international health measures, facilities for air travel or the preservation of peace, usually resulted from world changes wrought by technological development, and from the consequent increases of human interaction with their new demands, opportunities, and dangers.

Usually a need for international collaboration had existed for some time before governments got around to recognizing it. Most often the need had been discerned and proclaimed by individuals or by private associations, both national and international, long before it was acknowledged officially. In the field of labor standards, for instance, seven decades of agitation by individual reformers, trade unions, and welfare organizations was required to bring about the first official conference on this subject in 1890. Thirty more years had to elapse before the International Labor Organization could be founded upon a model afforded by the establishment of the private International Labor Association in 1900.

Moreover, the willingness of governments to do something about needs which they had recognized was usually subject to further delays. In the field of peace and security, for instance, the readiness to establish a general international security organization did not catch up with widely recognized necessity until after the cataclysm of the first world war. The need for an international body to facilitate trade, although acknowledged in the 1930's, was not transmuted into the establishment of the International Trade Organization until the second world war had aggravated general economic dislocation and produced a post-war groundswell of international cooperation.

Nations have likewise been disposed to experiment with international bodies earlier and more readily in those areas of relationship that impinge least upon vital or sanctified national interests. The first universal organizations created were those to foster postal communications, telecommunications, and similar services of obvious mutual advantage to many nations. Almost fifty years and a world war had to elapse after the founding of the Universal Postal Union before the states were prepared to join in a League of Nations to maintain peace and security.

In all fields, nations have shown a greater willingness to load organizations with functions and responsibilities than to endow them with authority. States have persisted in regarding the international organizations as their creatures, and have constructed them constitutionally as loose associations for specific purposes, with little or no power to bind the members. The quasi-legislative authority developed by the Universal Postal Union and the enforcement powers bestowed upon the Security

Council of the United Nations have been among the few exceptions to this norm, other than the administrative powers bestowed upon more restricted agencies such as the International Commission of the Danube.

Essentially, the states of the world, large and small, have looked upon international organizations as instrumentalities through which they could further some aspects of their respective national interests. In many cases these national interests have been narrowly conceived in terms of prestige, protection, or immediate advantage. On other occasions, such as the founding of the League of Nations and the United Nations, states have evinced more genuinely international and altruistic conceptions of national interest. Even in these instances, the identification of national aspirations with improved world order and well-being through collective effort has usually reflected a calculated decision that the state's interests would be better served in this manner.

Whatever the motives that may have prompted the creation of international bodies, states have tended to regard the advantages of membership in them as outweighing any surrender of the capacity for independent decision (sovereignty) that might be involved. The surrender has been tentative in all events, since member states have in almost every case reserved explicitly or implicitly the right to refuse compliance with what an organization decides, or to withdraw from it and regain freedom of decision.

IV

Once founded, international organizations have been subject to the same forces that conditioned their establishment, except as these have been modified by moral, psychological, and political influences created within the world community by the very existence of the organizations themselves. Fundamentally, individual member states have supported an organization to the extent that it served their national interests. This has varied with the interpretation of national interests at a given time, and with the size, power, and location of a state and its capacity to achieve its real interests more effectively through alternative channels.

In assessing the extent to which any given organization has served the national interest, governments have been subject to influence by a wide range of domestic and international factors. Not least among these factors in the non-totalitarian countries has been the activity of private organizations and special interests. Examples can be cited to show how these groups have caused governments to exploit or undermine international bodies; equally impressive instances can be shown of strong support for international organizations instigated by private associations.

Since the strength and effectiveness of an organization has depended upon the continuing support of a large majority of its numbers, including all the more powerful ones, the successful organization has been one whose performance has coincided broadly through time with the national interests of its member states. Phrased another way, the success of an international organization has depended upon the existence of a consensus among member states about the underlying idea or objective of the organization. Broad or universal consensus has meant a strong organization. A narrowing of the consensus, especially when coupled with militant opposition, has meant weakness and relative ineffectiveness. This result has been more pronounced, regardless of the nature or form of the organization, when the opposition has included one or more great powers, or coalitions of lesser states whose collective decision is critical in the world community.

The existence of a broad consensus of purpose has not necessarily meant that the member states have agreed upon all issues. It has meant rather a common willingness to use the instrumentalities of the organization for accomplishing mutual objectives or for accommodating differences of policy. Where there has been a healthy consensus to sustain the organization, there has usually been a high tolerance for disagreement on specific issues. Controversy has been containable within the framework of the organization and there has been no tendency to bolt it or to repudiate its decisions, a situation nicely illustrated by what has happened until recently within the succession of health organizations. This can be construed as meaning that the conflicts of national interest which produced disagreement were less important to the states concerned than other aspects of national interest which were served through continuing support of the organization. A series of successfully resolved issues has not only disclosed the existence of a broad consensus, but has tended to strengthen it. Conversely, hotly contested issues or those that could not be resolved, have usually indicated a straining or erosion of the consensus.

The extent to which a state may continue to support an organization and at the same time achieve the broadest range of its own national interests has depended primarily upon the size and power of the state. So important to an effective consensus is the continuing adherence of the great powers that they have, in practice, been permitted greater latitude for individualistic behavior than has been accorded to the smaller states. This has gone so far as to make it possible for a great power to remain within the organization even when it has sought to use the body for ulterior purposes or has failed to live up to its charter obligations.

These processes have been amply demonstrated in the histories of the League of Nations and the United Nations. In less spectacular form, they have also been evident in the records of other organizations.

V

The establishment of international organizations has obviously not by any magic put an end to the dynamic of world politics. Rather, these organizations, whatever their fields and functions, have provided new arenas in which the social and political forces of the world community contend for ascendency. The policies of the member states have been the primary vehicle for the expression of such forces, both within the organizations and in other channels of international intercourse. Needless to say, these political and social forces have exerted a powerful formative influence upon the organizations themselves, quite as much as upon the world community. This normal process has been dramatically evident in the trying years since 1945. An adequate understanding of it would help to clarify the true significance of the United Nations system and to explain some of the conflicts, failures, and frustrations that have perplexed or discouraged public observers.

The very existence of international organizations, however, has injected a new force into the world community and has altered the configurations of world politics. Regardless of the fact that the states which created international organizations have usually intended that they should remain simply instruments for inter-nation collaboration, they have inevitably become something more. They have acquired lives of their own and a distinctive international personality which has been manifested both symbolically and legally. Many organizations possess their own flags and symbols and have gradually established substantial privileges and immunities for their properties and personnel. To these achievements has recently been added express judicial recognition of the international personality of the United Nations. This was given by the International Court of Justice in an advisory opinion on April 11, 1949 which recognized the capacity of the United Nations to sue any nation for damages suffered by the organization or by its agents.[2] Beyond attaining such identity and capacity, international organizations have in some cases developed a certain immunity against those forces in world politics that might weaken or destroy them.

This development is attributable to several factors. In the first place, the functions which most of these young institutions perform have become virtually indispensable in our increasingly interactive world. The tasks of improving health, facilitating communications, promoting trade and financial stability, or maintaining peace have become so necessary, so extensive, and so complex that they can be dealt with only on a continuous and sys-

2 For text of the Court's opinion, see *International Organization*, III, p. 569–78.

tematic basis, with opportunity for long-range planning. This fact is eloquently attested in both the underlying concepts and the actual operations of the United Nations system.

Moreover, cumulative experience with international organizations has tended to create in the public mind attitudes favorable to their acceptance and their further development. The work of one organization such as the Universal Postal Union has made easier the establishment of others, in part by allaying national doubts and fears, in part by providing object lessons about mechanics and procedures. Organizational advances in less controversial fields have paved the way for the creation of international bodies to deal with the more politically-laden problems of peace and security. Experience with the League of Nations, despite its failures, has without question enhanced the expectation that governments will handle an even larger proportion of present-day problems through the United Nations system. To be sure, certain kinds of experience in international bodies, particularly those of primarily political purpose, has had a divisive rather than cohesive effect. Yet the prevailing trend appears to have been toward readier acceptance and support.

The purely personal element cannot be excluded from among the forces which have fostered the identity and influence of international bodies. All international organization has drawn strength from the creative leadership of outstanding personalities such as Wilson and Roosevelt, Robert Cecil, Jan Christian Smuts, and Cordell Hull. It has acquired stature from the roles played by such distinguished national statesmen as Briand, Paul-Henri Spaak, Mrs. Roosevelt, or Herbert Evatt. Equally important in building the identity of international bodies have been the solid administrative achievements of special agencies such as the Governing Commission of the Saar and spectacular accomplishments such as refugee resettlement under the League and the International Refugee Organization, or the Palestine armistices. These have, of course, acquired great dramatic impact when personalized in distinguished staff members such as Fritjof Nansen and Ralph Bunche.

Less conspicuous, perhaps, but more widespread has been the day-to-day impact of the labors of hundreds of international civil servants. Imbued, for the most part, with a truly international point of view, these members of organization staffs and secretariats have tended to give substance to the concept of international or world policy. Their work is a tangible symptom of the emergent world community. Through their efforts and through the influence of great personalities and dramatic achievements, international organizations — in particular the League of Nations and the United Nations — have become symbols to millions of people around the globe, encouraging them to give political expression within their own countries to aspirations which they associate with the international agencies. Even though these organizations have sometimes been used as symbols for purely nationalistic or ideological purposes, preponderant public reaction has been in the other direction.

International organizations have also acquired identity and strength from the legal and moral foundations upon which they rest. With some notable exceptions, these factors have exerted a cohesive influence upon the member states, despite their reservations about retaining freedom of action. The acceptance of membership in an organization is, after all, solemnized in a duly ratified treaty. The breaching of a treaty obligation, however frequently this may have occurred in the past seventy-five years, still carries the stigma of an affront to the world community and is not an act to be committed lightly. So likely is world opinion to disapprove behavior of this kind that states have usually sought to rationalize any breach by reinterpreting the original obligation. Such has been the course pursued by the Soviet Union, and by the United States as well, under the United Nations Charter.

This growth of international organizations in strength and prestige and the consequent support they have received from the nations of the world has been neither steady nor without interruption. It has been retarded during periods of increased tension, both economic and political; and it has been seriously disrupted when tensions have exploded into wars.

The present system of organizations, based fundamentally upon a liberal ideology, survived the challenge of fascism because the power of the fascist states was destroyed in war. What will be the outcome of the present Soviet and communist challenge remains to be seen. The present political and ideological bifurcation of the world is clearly reflected in the fact that the Soviet Union maintains membership in only two specialized agencies, the International Telecommunication Union and the Universal Postal Union, in addition to the United Nations proper (a pattern followed only in part by the Soviet satellites). Should the bifurcation continue and become more complete, the last formal ties might be severed by Soviet withdrawal from the remaining organizations. This would present a new situation in the world community. It would suspend any hopes for universal world order but probably would not eliminate any of the present organizations unless war should result. On the contrary, it might strengthen these organizations among the great majority of nations that constitute the non-Soviet world. There is significant evidence, however, that the Soviet Union will not burn its final bridges because of the material and political advantages it derives from the organizations of which it is a member.

VI

International organizations have exerted direct influence upon the forces of world politics by their very existence and by their activities. In general, this influence has been in the direction of orderly and rational world behavior, although on occasion it has contributed to disunity and disorder.

The organizations have been able to exert such influence because of the weight and prestige they have achieved; because they have become foci for the expression of world opinion; and because they have served as institutions through which contending political forces can be brought continuously face to face in a regularized manner. Beyond these factors, the force and influence of organizations has flowed from the concentration of economic and political power represented in their membership. These elements are usually blended in the effects produced by the activities of any given international organization, just as various elements are fused in the results produced by any domestic political body. It is difficult to segregate them and point to instances in which, for example, the intrinsic weight and prestige of an international body, apart from the power of its members or the other factors, has significantly modified world politics. The important fact is that the organization has altered the configurations of world forces.

The influence of international bodies has usually been greatest where their functions are generally recognized as having least political implication. This has been true, for instance, of the Universal Postal Union, which has gained such universal acceptance that it can require members to adhere to new postal conventions within a specified period or, in effect, lose the substantial benefit of free transit for mails throughout the entire territory of the Union. This sanction, the fruit of long development, has sufficed to keep even great powers in line.

In the area most laden with political content, that of maintaining peace and security, the influence of the League and the United Nations has been most effective when the case at issue has involved lesser states in situations removed from the spheres of great power contention. This could be said of the earlier successes of the League, such as the Aaland Island dispute and the Greco-Bulgarian incident. It is also in a measure true of the Kashmir and Indonesian cases within the United Nations, although neither of these has yet been resolved with the same degree of success that was true of the League episodes.

The influence of organizations which flows from their capacity to polarize world opinion has, on the other hand, been most marked in the political field. This undoubtedly has resulted from the fact that major political issues make the headlines and excite a greater public reaction than do the less dramatic questions of trade, labor, or economic development. The still unresolved problem of the control of atomic energy illustrates the kind of issue upon which the pressures of world opinion have had marked effect. They were at least partially responsible for producing in the recent Paris session of the General Assembly a large majority vote favorable to substantial international regulation. Even so, opinion pressures on this vital issue were insufficient to bring about Soviet capitulation. Far from quailing before public opinion on the atomic energy question, the Soviet Union sought on this issue, as on others, to make propaganda capital out of defying the majority view. It must be pointed out, however, that the Soviet Union has not been the only great power willing to disregard world opinion when it ran counter to the dictates of national interest. Both the United Kingdom and the United States found it possible to act contrary to widespread public sentiment elsewhere in the world at certain stages in the development in their respective stands on the Palestine issue. Even lesser powers have defied world reaction without drastic consequence, as has the Union of South Africa on the question of trusteeship for Southwest Africa. Each of these cases has reflected a circumstance in which that segment of a state's national interest which might have been served by currying favorable public reaction has been outweighed by other objects of national policy.

Although public reaction alone has had apparently limited influence upon national behavior, it has been more effective when combined with the composite political pressure that can be developed within international organizations. In the assemblies, councils, and commissions of the various organizations, the policies of any state are subject to immediate reaction, formal and informal, from the representatives of other nations. The influence which such collective reaction can produce upon the policies of even a great power was recently demonstrated when the United States apparently abandoned its indicated reversal of policy on Franco Spain in the face of widespread unfavorable reaction at Lake Success. In this instance, to be sure, American interests were better served by yielding to the views of certain European states. On the other hand, the Soviet Union has in most cases refused to be deflected from its predetermined policies by even numerous opposition; in fact, the USSR appears to believe that its national interests are advanced by the exploitation of such opposition.

The existence of international organizations has provided an opportunity for coalitions of smaller states to make felt their combined power and influence. These states, whose real national interests (conditioned by their lesser world responsibilities) tend to coincide with the "international conscience," have been able, in combination, to compel modifications in the positions of larger powers. This process was illustrated during the Paris session of the General Assembly by the small-power mediation on the Berlin issue. At the same time, the opportunity for small state influence is, like that of the great powers, susceptible of abuse. It can result in the kind of bloc-voting which defeated recent efforts of the General Assembly to find a solution for the problem of the Italian colonies.

International organizations modify the forces of world politics in yet another way — by serving their primary function as places of adjustment. They provide opportunities for graceful accommodation, both formally at the Council and on the Assembly floor, and informally behind the scenes. Conversations and negotiations on the spot are means for adjusting extreme positions to the collective norm. Unfortunately, this useful function has been impaired by the glare of publicity upon the formal debates which has tended to crystallize opposing policies and to reduce the possibilities for their reconciliation.

Even though formal accommodation may be impaired, greater understanding among governments frequently results from the bringing together of professional representatives with common interests in common problems. The process is most conspicuous at the technical level in general bodies like the United Nations and in organizations with specialized functions such as the Food and Agriculture Organization. At this level the government representatives are frequently technicians from the foreign offices and other administrative departments with a strong mutuality of professional interest that tends to balance or exceed their concern with the more political aspects of national interest. Despite the difficulties that sometimes result from the consideration of even technical questions without adequate reference to the political framework, the team efforts of technical experts have often had the effect of deepening intergovernmental understanding and have contributed to the success of many specialized international bodies. The diminished use by the United Nations in comparison with the League of Nations of experts who do not represent governments has deprived the present organization of one important channel for modifying purely national policies through impartial investigation and norm-setting. The effects of this change, itself a result of political pressures originating with the Soviet Union, is in part offset by the personal relationships and *esprit de corps* that often develop among representatives at the technical level.

VII

Despite the divisive forces of an essentially state-centered world that continue to assert themselves within international organizations, these bodies have been able to take collective action that expresses an international will greater than the composite will of the members. The organizations have served as media for formulating and symbolizing standards of world behavior; and they have facilitated the harmonizing of national interests in accordance with these standards. Or to put it another way, they have made possible a sublimation of conflicting national interests within collective decisions that offer superior advantages to the individual member states. By this process the organizations fulfill their function of segregating and registering the common international interests of all states.

Every organization, regardless of purpose, has achieved this quality of "internationalism" in some degree, varying usually with the political content of its activities. In terms of relative political content, and therefore relative capacity to perform "internationally," present-day organizations range all the way from the basically non-political Universal Postal Union to the United Nations Security Council, with no marked gap between some so-called "functional" organizations and those commonly designated as political. Even organizations at the non-political extreme, such as the UPU and the health organizations, have failed to perform in a wholly international manner. They have at times reflected strong national and ideological influences, usually when their activities have touched political and social issues incidental to their broadly accepted main purposes.

The capacity of all organizations to yield genuinely international results is highly responsive to the ebb and flow of general international tension. Major cleavages on the political front that paralyze great power agreement in the Security Council radiate to every area of international collaboration, with resulting friction, controversy and renewed assertion of national or ideological particularism. On the other hand, harmony at the political center facilitates work at the less political periphery.

International bodies at all points on the political scale have acquired through the years varying degrees of immunity to the influence of such tensions. This immunity, small indeed, but greater in the less political organizations, can be regarded as evidence of a net increment in genuine internationalism.

VIII

In the preceding sections, an effort has been made to set forth some general observations about the interrelation between international organizations and the forces of world politics. These remarks constitute merely a general framework of principle and hypothesis, and are intended as a guide for more intensive studies of particular organizations. One such study — an examination of organizations to deal with world health problems — has been made and will appear soon in *International Organization*. Others are in preparation.

In order to clarify the interaction between any given international organization and the influences of world politics, it should be essential to answer at least the following questions: 1) what needs and conditioning factors in the world community influenced the establishment and growth of international organization in the field under consideration and in what manner; 2) what expansion or contraction of functions has taken place and for what reasons; 3) to what extent and for what reasons has the authority of the organizations been increased or diminished; 4) in how far have the operations of this organization satisfied the needs for which it was created, found acceptance in the world community, and established new and controlling norms for the behavior of national states?

To answer the last question it is necessary to examine the performance of national states within the organization. Tests of the organization's usefulness, prestige and authority will be found in 1) increases or decreases of membership; 2) the willingness of member states to support the reasonable financial needs of the organization; 3) the attitudes and actions of member states on principal issues; and 4) their compliance or non-compliance with action agreed upon. Adequate explanations for these manifestations of national behavior must then be sought in the forces at work, both national and international.

Intensive case studies of this character should make it possible to understand better the role which international organization plays in the changing milieu of world politics. Based upon this understanding, more reliable estimates can be made of the extent to which international institutions have become rooted in the world community and exert a formative influence upon political and social forces. These estimates should provide one important indication of the degree to which the world community is developing toward a world society in which human interaction is guided by common values and regulated through universally accepted institutions.

Above all, such studies should shed light upon what might be called the "physiology" of world institutions. To achieve this purpose, they should so reveal the interaction between international organizations and world politics that those who seek to increase the strength and vitality of international institutions will be better aware of what to treat and how to go about it.

THE UNITED NATIONS IN THE ERA OF
TOTAL DIPLOMACY

William T. R. Fox

In George Orwell's *Animal Farm* all that finally remains of the animals' plans for a brave new world, a farm without Farmer Jones, a farm to be run by and for the animals themselves, is the slogan "Four feet good; two feet bad." As one reads the reports from Lake Success and Flushing Meadows one is tempted to say of the brave new world projected five years ago at San Francisco, the world of sovereign equality and great-power unanimity, that all that is left is the slogan "United Nations good; power politics bad." But here the analogy ends; for there is no agreement in the United Nations as to who is being good by supporting the spirit and the language of the Charter and who is being bad by playing power politics.

There is no agreement because in the struggle for the minds and hearts of people everywhere in the world during this era of "total diplomacy," an era in which will, intelligence, and resources are being mobilized to a degree which would be exceeded only in total war, the United Nations is a potent symbol.[1] The rulers of the opposing coalitions seek to capture it to promote their respective purposes, benign or evil as the case may be. This is perhaps just another example of behavior which is characteristic of the political process at all levels, domestic and international, the representation of the special or private interest as being identical with the general or public interest. Washington and Moscow have at least this characteristic in common, they seek to represent the special national interest as being in line with the general world interest. To the extent that the United Nations is believed to have a public, a special following of its own, we may expect Member states to woo that public and so bend the United Nations to their own purposes. They may in that effort often modify their behavior to make it socially more acceptable. Certainly the United States government has on countless occasions modified its position

William T. R. Fox is Professor at the School of International Affairs, Columbia University and is managing editor of "World Politics."

[1] "Total diplomacy" is an expression which Secretary Acheson first used in a speech, February 16, 1950. For the text, see *Strengthening the Forces of Freedom, Selected Speeches and Statements of Secretary of State Acheson*, Department of State Publication 3852, p. 15–19. It is noteworthy that in this discussion of total diplomacy there is not a single reference to the United Nations. By September 1950, Secretary Acheson was in his "Uniting for Peace" proposals urging that the United Nations play a critical role in mobilizing for "total diplomacy."

From Volume 5, No. 2 (1951), pp. 265–73.

in the councils of the United Nations to carry along with it the many other states whose support it must have if United States aims are to be presented to the world as in complete harmony with United Nations aims.[2]

The United Nations then is a potent symbol of man's aspirations for peace and security. As an instrument for the direct promotion of peace and security, is it anything more?[3] Its unsophisticated supporters certainly had far greater expectations in 1945; but some of these expectations were essentially unfulfillable. The United Nations would have worked perfectly only in a world so bent on peace that it would hardly have needed the United Nations.

It was born in a world that was being remade by forces far beyond the control of that fledgling world organization. The old Europe of several great powers was gone, and with it went the primitive collective security system which had prevented any one power from gaining world hegemony. The old colonial areas were spawning new sovereignties. Indeed, in a world in which the Philippines and Byelorussia were simultaneously receiving their first invitations to be separately represented in an interstate conference, it was hard any longer to say what sovereignty—and the sovereign equality so frequently referred to in the Charter—really meant; it was only clear that southern Asia would not henceforth be a European *Lebensraum*. In this new world it lay within the power of either one of two of the world powers to veto singlehandedly peace and security for the rest of the world. This veto was one of the elementary facts of political life and could not be eliminated by any combination of words in the charter of a world organization.

The Charter of San Francisco reflected this hard fact. The political veto of the Big Two found its reflection in the legal veto of the Big Five. With the multiplication of sovereignties in what we have learned to call the underdeveloped areas of the world and the failure of many European states to gain admission to the United Nations, the proportion of European representation has been sharply reduced.[4] The absence of Europe's full diplomatic representation has emphasized the commanding position of the Big Two; for it is from that continent with its tradition of skilled diplomacy and its still remaining great industrial power that a mediating

[2] In the United States effort to brand communist China as an aggressor, for example, the General Assembly resolution which finally accomplished that result reflected many concessions to those governments which had misgivings lest the United Nations seem to be used simply as the tail on an American kite.

[3] The proliferation of activities in the fields of health, welfare, statistics, etc., may have a long-range indirect consequence for the promotion of peace; but these activities are justified as good things in themselves, whether or not they contribute fundamentally to solving the problems of peace and war.

[4] Burma, Indonesia, Israel, Lebanon, Pakistan, the Republic of the Philippines, Syria and Yemen are sovereignties of recent origin who are Members of the United Nations. European states who were members of the League but who are not Members of the United Nations include Austria, Bulgaria, Eire, Finland, Germany, Hungary, Italy, Portugal and Spain.

influence might have been expected to emerge. The political veto of the colossus powers, whether surrounded by spontaneous collaborators or flanked by unwilling satellites was, if anything, strengthened by the Charter. The veto was inverted in matters of regional enforcement action. In this situation, according to Article 51 of the Charter, only unanimity among the Big Five can bring a Security Council decision to call off regional action initiated independently of the Council. The permanent members of the Security Council can thus veto not only enforcement action directed at themselves, but Council efforts to limit military action taken on their own initiative but in the name of regional enforcement action.

The bipolar distribution of power has, of course, influenced the operations of the United Nations even more than the language of its Charter.[5] China and France, for example, are not able to develop influence either in the Security Council or the General Assembly commensurate with their legal status as veto-possessing Members. The United States and the Soviet Union have, on the other hand, come to play dominant roles and might well have done so, veto or no veto.

Some other elementary facts of world politics have only become apparent in the postwar period. One of these is the Soviet leadership's belief that a gigantic anti-Soviet conspiracy of encirclement was in the making, a hypothesis which has doomed the Security Council to paralysis. This belief generated an unwillingness to cooperate which has created in the non-Soviet world a very deep distrust of all Soviet actions and a barrier to collaboration in every field. It has resulted in the very encirclement which the Soviet government feared. Of equal importance is the development of atomic weapons. This has enabled the western world to escape the full consequences of its precipitate and unreciprocated demilitarization and disarmament. It may also, paradoxically, by making general war less acceptable all around, have made feasible a more extensive resort to military action short of general war. The failure to negotiate a peace settlement has left the forces of the communist and the non-communist world confronting each other directly in Germany, Austria and Korea. Had a *de jure* settlement proved possible resorting their independence, each of these countries would have been valuable as buffers. It has thus come about that a charter designed to compel great-power collaboration has had to operate under a *de facto* peace settlement which makes this collaboration as difficult as possible.

The function of the United Nations under these changed conditions has

[5] Cf. Edward H. Buehrig, "The United States, the United Nations and Bi-Polar Politics," *International Organization*, IV, p. 573–584.

not been to coerce but to persuade, not to order but to recommend. As a forum for world opinion it has been used and abused. As an enforcement agency, its effectiveness has been measured by its capacity to evoke voluntary sacrifices by national governments. The precise military commitments envisioned by Articles 43 and 45 of the Charter would have made armed force available to the Security Council in advance of a diplomatic crisis. Presumably this force would have been available to support whatever decision the Security Council might have taken. In the Korean crisis, however, each government has determined for itself, after weighing the appropriateness of the Council action to meet the attack from north Korea, how much if any military support it would give to the Council's resolutions. Although General MacArthur is directing United Nations forces under a United Nations directive,[5a] he has international force at his disposal because the United Nations provided a rallying point for spontaneous collaboration against what was believed to be Soviet-inspired aggression. The Security Council resolutions of June 27 and July 7, 1950, made possible by the fortuitous absence from the Council table of the Soviet representative and the enforced absence of the representative of the Chinese People's Republic put the stamp of free world approval on the basic decision already taken by President Truman. By its resolution of July 7, 1950, "The Security Council . . . *recommends* that all members providing military forces . . . make such forces available to a unified command under the United States. . . . "[6] The forces which these United Nations resolutions made available for the Korean campaign were, in addition to the United States forces which President Truman's interpretation of American commitments under the United Nations Charter had already made available, the forces which the various Member states saw fit under pressure of domestic or free world opinion to provide. Whether such forces turned out to be large or small depended not upon United Nations resolutions but upon decisions of national governments; they were provided voluntarily on the basis of a recommendation of the Security Council, not as a result of compulsion or legal obligation. World opinion rather than world law is what has given the United Nations a prominent role in the Korean crisis.

Public opinion in that part of the world in which opinion remains relatively free, the base for that influence which the United Nations has, is powerful, but it is not all-powerful. Its limitations are suggested by an incident occurring at the Peace Conference of Paris in 1919. Australia's Prime Minister, Mr. Hughes, objected strenuously to Woodrow Wilson's

[5a] This article was written before General Ridgway's assumption of the United Nations command.

[6] Document S/1588, July 7, 1950.

effort to apply the principle of the mandate to the islands occupied by Australia in the course of the war. "Mr. Hughes, am I to understand," asked Wilson, "that if the whole civilized world asks Australia to agree to a mandate in respect of these islands, Australia is prepared to defy the appeal of the whole civilized world?" Hughes replied, "That's about the size of it, President Wilson."' The point to this story is not dulled by the fact that Australia did eventually accept some Pacific islands under mandate. It accepted them under mandate because Australia was not impervious to world opinion; but the mandate placed far less onerous burdens upon the mandatory than it would have had Hughes been more pliable.

It is rare indeed that such frankness is exhibited in negotiations and debates at Lake Success, but this anecdote suggests the basic strength and the basic weakness of the United Nations. Against a hard-headed and determined prime minister, Woodrow Wilson would have been helpless in his efforts to use the conscience of mankind as an instrument of international diplomacy. As it was, his success in frustrating Australian claims for annexation was limited. Australia received the islands as Class C mandates. For purposes of administration this was barely distinguishable from annexation. A contemporary leader of world opinion would have even less success today in using the United Nations to bring about a modification of Australia's "White Australia" policy or South Africa's policy in its former mandate from the League of Nations. For it is only to the extent that opinion *within* a country is open to influence from *without* that the United Nations can perform what we shall call its forum function. The United States, too, has pursued some policies which are beyond the reach of debate in any world organization, as the Commission on Human Rights may discover if a Covenant on Human Rights is ever debated on the floor of the United States Senate.[8]

With the totalitarian countries, however, the case is different and far more serious. For public opinion in those countries, if such a thing as public opinion can be said to exist, is so far as the United Nations is concerned beyond reach on *every* issue. The forum function of the United Nations can be performed only with respect to the public opinion of free peoples and in the free world it can be performed only to the extent that opinions are free to be reformed in the light of supranational discussion.

[7] P. Birdsall, *Versailles Twenty Years After*, Reynal and Hitchcock, 1941, p. 72; quoted in F. B. Chambers, C. P. Harris and C. C. Bayley, *This Age of Conflict*, rev. ed. Harcourt Brace, 1950, p. xvii.

[8] Senators from the South are not likely to look with favor on a Covenant of Human Rights which might provide a legal or a moral basis for condemning the practices of southern states in regard to the civil rights of negroes. Furthermore, any elaboration of economic and social rights is likely to disturb the more conservative members of the Senate.

The General Assembly has moved to the fore as the primacy of this forum function of the United Nations has come to be recognized. The Soviet representative's return to the Security Council in August 1950, gave new interest to the workings of that body, but Mr. Malik's spectacularly televised performance as Council President did not give it new importance. It is through the General Assembly that, on the basis of Secretary Acheson's proposals, new procedures are being developed for mobilizing against the disturbers of the peace.[9] In this era of total diplomacy the United Nations, even with its Security Council paralyzed, is regarded as an important resource in the effort to deter the aggressor and thus to avert total war. With improved methods for observation and investigation, with improved organization to keep the Assembly or one of its committees in a state of constant readiness to discuss and recommend, the aggressor power is left free to commit only those aggressions he is willing to commit even though he thereby alienates the United Nations' public.

The enforcement function has passed into other hands, as it inevitably had to pass if the victorious powers of World War II fell apart; and the wisdom of exempting regional enforcement action from the paralyzing requirement of great-power unanimity has been confirmed. Even apart from the unanimity requirements military action against a great-power aggressor is unlikely to wait upon the completion of procedures in which the aggressor prolongs the debate by parliamentary maneuver and deliberate confusion of issues. With the enforcement provisions of the Charter moribund the functions of the Security Council and the General Assembly have come to be very similar, and it would seem to be a matter of tactics rather than strategy whether at any given moment the General Assembly or the Security Council be chosen as the forum for spotlighting the aggressor or for educating public opinion against the contingency of aggression.

With respect to a third function, as an agency of conciliation, the record of the United Nations is much more impressive in adjusting differences within the non-Soviet world than across the main chasm of conflict. Indonesia and Palestine are cases in point. In adjusting differences between the Soviet and non-Soviet worlds, the United Nations record is barren. Total diplomacy is being carried on in an atmosphere which approaches, on both sides, total mistrust. There appears to be very little basis for conciliating particular issues. If, for example, the Russians believe that any atomic energy control scheme which the Americans are willing to support must conceal within itself some anti-Soviet trick and the Americans be-

---

[9] See the Draft Resolution on Uniting for Peace submitted by Canada, France, Philippines, Turkey, United Kingdom, United States and Uruguay to the fifth session of the General Assembly, October 7, 1950 (Document A/C.1/576); reprinted in *International Organization*, IV, p. 721.

lieve the same thing in reverse, the particular points of difference are not very important.

The use of the United Nations to rally world opinion against the disturbers of the peace may in fact have caused the United Nations to play a negative role as an agency of conciliation. Impassioned oratory, exchange of invectives and 47–5 votes may have rallied opinion, but they may also have hardened the positions of national governments. This will not always be regarded as an evil by those who are sure that their side is right. For them the problem is then not to conciliate or compromise with those who are believed to be wrong but to win wider approval for what is believed to be right.

The development of the forum function within the United Nations and of the enforcement function without may not have been a totally unforeseen contingency as John Foster Dulles' recent analysis of the official United States position at the San Francisco Conference suggests.[10] He had gone to the Conference feeling that the Dumbarton Oaks proposals put excessive dependence upon the postwar unity of the great powers, a unity which, as he said, "if it prevails, will itself assure peace." The task at San Francisco was, as he understood it, not so much to get small-power approval of what the Big Three had done at Dumbarton Oaks as that of "radically revising the Dumbarton Oaks Proposals so that the world organization could survive and accomplish something even if the Big Four should in the future fall out among themselves."[11] In this context, the crucial paragraphs of the Charter related not to vetoes over enforcement action or legally binding decisions, but to what were then widely believed to be fringe questions: the veto over discussion in the Security Council; other limitations on freedom of discussion in the General Assembly; and the liberation of regional agencies for enforcement action. With the position of the United States delegation prevailing on all three questions, the basis was laid for future by-passing of the Security Council's unanimity requirement.

Whether free world opinion and especially American opinion was not at this point cruelly misled so that the United Nations was oversold and the way paved for a cynical reaction against it is a question we need not at this point discuss. But if the United Nations' function was from the beginning the modest but important one which it has been performing and which Mr. Dulles says the United States delegation expected it to perform from the very first days at San Francisco, both public and private agencies for molding American opinion must bear some responsibility for the current resurgence of isolationism.

[10] *War or Peace*, Macmillan, 1950, Chapter 5.   [11] *Ibid.*, p. 36.

The United Nations has made a difference. It was not meant to be a world government, and the fact that it has not turned out to be a world government should not obscure its role. We cannot know in what ways the history of the postwar years would have been different if Winston Churchill had had his way and the conference on postwar international organization had been delayed until the time of a general peace conference. But some hypotheses as to what difference the United Nations has actually made may be set down which will help us bring into truer perspective the function of the United Nations in securing the values of a free society and securing them peacefully.

It may have saved Iran in 1946 by denying the Soviet Union the possibility of moving into that exposed country unobtrusively. It may have hastened the withdrawal of British and French troops from Syria and Lebanon by making it impossible for the troops to remain there unnoticed by world public opinion. It may have hastened the independence of Israel and thereby removed a powerful source of discord in the English-speaking world which might have rendered still more difficult the welding of a North American alliance system. It may have hastened the independence of Indonesia, facilitated thereby the liquidation of the western world's imperialist heritage and, conceivably, laid the basis for a future cooperation between the non-Soviet western world and the non-Soviet eastern world. It may have reduced the risk of war at the time of the Berlin crisis by providing "a third way as against the alternatives of humiliating surrender and violent defiance"[12] while the potentialities of the airlift were being discovered.

In this same crisis, after the airlift had been made to work, and it was the Soviet Union which seemingly had to choose between acquiescence and ultimatum, it provided the Soviet Union with a supplementary channel of diplomatic negotiation which brought Messrs. Jessup and Malik into contact (thus demonstrating that the United Nations does have some conciliatory function even through the Iron Curtain).

It may have facilitated responsible participation by the United States in world affairs. The constitutional vocabulary of the United Nations system is more familiar to Americans than the language of European diplomacy. It can be used to define American interests in the outside world in ways which American opinion can more readily grasp and to define them in ways which do not seem to threaten our free world collaborators. The Soviet bloc continues, of course, to describe American policy as imperialistic; but filtering United States policy through the United Nations has finally brought even Henry Wallace within the broad consensus which supports resistance to Soviet-inspired aggression.

[12] *Ibid.*, p. 59.

It may have further hastened the diplomatic isolation of the Soviet Union by putting that country in the position of having to use its veto repeatedly or having to modify its foreign policy. It may have made a bigger war sooner out of the Korean crisis; but in contributing to the broadening and deepening of this crisis it may have hastened the massive rearmament and effective collaboration of the non-Soviet world so as to increase the chance that the free world would survive that war free.

All these consequences were possible because the United Nations is an instrument for molding the attitudes of men whose minds are not completely enslaved by dictatorial government. Against this must be set the complete inability of the United Nations to circumvent what I earlier called the political veto of the Big Two. Either one of them can veto the peace and security of the rest of the world. Fortunately, neither can veto the rest of the world's response to that challenge. And in this era of total diplomacy that response will be articulated in great part through the United Nations.

International Organization and the International System

STANLEY HOFFMANN

Sᴘᴇᴄɪᴀʟɪsᴛs in the field of international organization have noted with some alarm a decline of interest among students and foundations in the study of the United Nations system. There has been a shift toward the study of regionalism and the theory of integration. The former shift reflects one reality of postwar world politics—the division of a huge and heterogeneous international system into subsystems in which patterns of cooperation and ways of controlling conflicts are either more intense or less elusive than in the global system. The interest in integration reflects both the persistence and the transformation of the kind of idealism that originally pervaded, guided, and at times distorted the study of international organization. We have come to understand that integration, in the sense of a process that devalues sovereignty, gradually brings about the demise of the nation-state, and leads to the emergence of new foci of loyalty and authority, is only one, and by no means the most important, of the many functions performed by global international organizations. This has led only in part to a more sober and searching assessment of these functions. It has resulted primarily in a displacement of interest toward those geographically more restricted institutions (like the European Communities) whose main task seems to be to promote integration.

Those who have remained concerned with the UN system have also gradually shifted their efforts. The heavy emphasis, advocated some years ago, on a comparative study of the institutions still expressed a willingness to detach or abstract international organization from the international system. But in recent years there has appeared a new approach—both more sweeping and more modest though not incompatible with comparative research.

It has become clear that international institutions, in their political processes

Sᴛᴀɴʟᴇʏ Hᴏꜰꜰᴍᴀɴɴ is a professor in the Government Department and a faculty associate at the Center for International Affairs, Harvard University, Cambridge, Massachusetts.
From Volume 24, No. 3 (1970), pp. 389–413.

and in their functions, reflect and to some extent magnify or modify the dominant features of the international system. Therefore, instead of concentrating on these institutions as if they were a closed universe, one ought to study them as patterns of cooperation and of muted conflict whose nature, evolution, effectiveness, and outcomes cannot be studied apart from the global system or from the relevant subsystem. In this respect the discussion of international organization by political scientists follows the same curve as the study of international law or of war.

Since international organizations provide procedures for cooperation or for the temperate pursuit of conflict, it is obvious that their effectiveness depends on the degree of moderation of the international system. A revolutionary system wracked by inexpiable power rivalries and ideological conflicts is one in which international organization is reduced to impotence as a force of its own and to the condition of a helpless stake in the competition of states. This was the fate of the League of Nations in its second decade. On the other hand, not every moderate international system need be one in which global international organization plays a major role. This is not due to any built-in conflict between the balance of power, the traditional moderating mechanism in international politics, and international organization: Such a conflict exists only with respect to one function of international organization, collective security. Rather it is due to two other facts. A moderate international system will be one in which global international organization plays a major role in the muting of conflict and the spread of cooperation only if, in the first place, there exists a broad procedural consensus among states which makes of multinational institutions the legitimate channels for the management of conflict and cooperation and if, in the second place, there exists a preference for universal channels over regional ones. In other words, a moderate international system, or one in which there exist compelling reasons why even deep and lasting ideological and power conflicts must be kept under control, creates opportunities for international organization, but these opportunities may be meager and difficult to exploit (cf. the nineteenth century international system).

It is impossible here to provide a thorough analysis of the international system or of the United Nations. I have tried to be more analytic elsewhere. I would like only to sketch briefly first the relations between the United Nations and the international system in recent years and second some of the possible relations in the future.

I. A Sketch of the Past

The image of the United Nations which guided the founding fathers of Dumbarton Oaks and San Francisco suffered from the huge discrepancy between the international system it postulated and the international system that emerged from World War II. The Charter assumed and required a pluralistic yet controlled world that never came into being. First, it was supposed to be managed and regulated by the concert of the Great Powers, a modern version of the European Concert. Secondly, it was supposed to be a moderate international system partly because that concert would keep it so, partly because of an optimistic evaluation about regimes (they would be "democratic"), economic conditions, and international legitimacy. Hence the primary responsibility for peace and security placed on the Big Five in the United Nations. Hence the famous provision of article 2, paragraph 7, about the respect for domestic jurisdiction—a precondition for moderation in past international systems—and the procedures of chapter VI which are traditional procedures of mediation and conciliation suitable for moderate conflicts. Hence, finally, the vague provisions about international economic affairs, inspired by "the free enterprise vision of the international economy,"[1] by the hope that there would be no fundamental imbalance between rich and poor, and by the expectation that, as in the past, economic development would be promoted essentially by private means.

The bipolar world of the late 1940's did not resemble this idyll any more than the Greek world before the Peloponnesian War resembled the international system after 1815. The Charter had created an international organization that was irrelevant to the revolutionary world in which two fierce ideological conflicts—East versus West and colonial versus anticolonial—seemed to destroy both the chances of any great-power consensus and the chances for moderation.

Facing a choice between permanent paralysis and transformation, a majority of the members of the United Nations opted for the latter even though it meant a drastic de facto revision of the Charter. Despite the legal primacy of the Security Council the UN, confronted with the breakdown of the great-power consensus, overhauled the system of the Charter through General Assembly Resolution 377A (V) of November 3, 1950 (the "Uniting for Peace Resolution") which appeared to reopen the road to collective security. Faced with life and death disputes, many of which originated within what the colonial powers claimed to be their domestic jurisdiction, the organs of the United Nations disregarded article 2, paragraph 7, tried to blur the differences between colonies and trusteeships, and innovated far beyond traditional diplomatic procedures by methods of collective intervention and the establishment of UN presences. When economic development emerged as a major problem in world politics, the United Nations multiplied agencies for technical assistance and development.

[1] Ernst B. Haas, *Tangle of Hopes: American Commitments and World Order* (Englewood Cliffs, N.J.: Prentice-Hall, 1969), p. 120.

This de facto transformation of the United Nations was based on an image of the world that was at least as far removed from reality as had been the image of the original UN. It was the image of a fictitious world community able and willing to make of the UN a force that would represent and expand the common interest of mankind. It could be useful as a kind of Sorelian myth thanks to which one of the superpowers would rally a majority against its rival and enlist the UN behind its own policies, but it was once again bound to create illusions and disillusionment. For at the basis of these changes one finds two postulates. One was majority rule—a neat reversal from the days of the great-power unanimity principle and from the sober but paralyzing realism of those who had deemed international organization incapable of imposing the will of a majority, especially against a Great Power or its allies, in matters such as collective security or race relations. (And yet the only powers that were explicitly charged with aggression by UN organs turned out to be the Democratic People's Republic of Korea [North Korea], the ally of the Union of Soviet Socialist Republics; then the People's Republic of China [Communist China] after its intervention in Korea; and later the Soviet Union after its invasion of Hungary.) The second postulate was the capacity of the secretary-general to play a kind of executive role, carrying out mandates given to him by the General Assembly but also filling gaps, interpreting ambiguities in these delegations, taking political initiatives, enlarging, so to speak, the bridgehead toward one world, and defending the common interest of mankind.

Illusions have their virtue when they inspire action. The fiction of a world community has made it possible for the organs of the United Nations to concern themselves with most of the important political and economic issues that agitate the international system and to promote that equalization of concern which is a rudimentary, first factor of homogenization in a highly diverse and uneven world. Yet, as a result, a gap between attempts and achievements, resolutions and resolution, motions and motion appeared—a gap no smaller nor less frustrating than the original Charter's gap between legal possibilities and political aspirations. The majoritarian illusion has been short-lived. An obvious discrepancy between votes and compliance developed almost as soon as the Uniting for Peace Resolution was adopted. Thus the resolution was never to be fully put into effect insofar as collective security was concerned. Moreover, after the increase in UN membership since 1955 the art of obtaining sufficient majorities became subtle, arduous, and uncertain, and the hazards of such consensus building revealed all too often that numerical majorities in organs without weighted voting may breed as many disadvantages as the paralyzing vetoes of the Security Council. The hope for a largely autonomous secretary-general, executor or even shaper of the majority, was crushed twice: once when Trygve Lie had to resign because of Soviet obstruction, once

when Dag Hammarskjöld, who after a cautious beginning in office and behind the misty screen of deliberately fuzzy language had become a bold man-
ager and theorist of the "new United Nations," died in the midst of the most
serious constitutional crisis of the organization.

 And yet the demise of fictions has not meant a verdict of complete impotence and paralysis. The UN has been able to play a limited role as "universal actor" in the system because of certain favorable features that reintroduced
a modicum of moderation into the international system. These features were
quite different from those the founding fathers had expected. They have not
obliterated either the revolutionary characteristics of the elements of the system (bipolar distribution of power; heterogeneity of the basic unit, of regimes,
ideologies, and levels of development) or the revolutionary aspects of relations
between units in the system (immoderate ends and means). But they have
imposed certain limits on those means, thereby contained the inflation of ends
within practical (if not verbal) limits, and restored some flexibility. It is the
existence of these features which explains why in the UN in the 1950's even
the minority went along (despite protests and filibusters) with the de facto
revision of the Charter. The reason why the search for more elastic procedures
of discussion and intervention, despite its excessive ambition, has allowed
the United Nations to develop is the evolution of the international system. It
is still an interstate system of competing units, but it is no longer the bipolar
system of the late 1940's and early 1950's—neither "tight" nor "loose"; new
features have emerged.

 I have analyzed elsewhere[2] the nature of the present system in terms of three
different layers: the fundamental, latent bipolar stratum; the manifest layer
of polycentrism; and an emergent layer of multipolarity. Insofar as the relations between states which develop in this system are still revolutionary, the
impact of the UN on world affairs continues to be severely limited. Thus, on
the one hand, the bipolar contest has constantly reduced UN effectiveness:
The UN has been timid and ineffective whenever one of the Big Two was
determined to act freely with force or threats of force in its sphere of domination (the Soviet Union in Hungary and Czechoslovakia, the United States
in the Caribbean). Also, serious rifts between the superpowers have continued
to result in UN impotence. There have been no attempts at organizing collective security in a world in which the mobilization of one camp against the
other could all too easily mean world war III and in which those minor conflicts that find both superpowers determined not only to remain uninvolved
but even to restore peace can be handled in less ponderous ways—ways which
also do a better job of concealing the collusion of the otherwise hostile superpowers. When serious disputes have broken out between the United States

[2] Stanley Hoffmann, *Gulliver's Troubles, or the Setting of American Foreign Policy* (Atlantic Policy
Studies) (New York: McGraw-Hill [for the Council on Foreign Relations], 1968), chapter 2.

and its allies on one side and members of the now splintered Communist world on the other, the role of the United Nations has been either nil (as during the second Berlin crisis of 1958-1962, the Vietnam war, and the Quemoy and Matsu incidents of 1955) or minimal (as during the Berlin blockade of 1948, the war in Laos, the Cuban missile crisis of 1962). When moderation was observed or restored, it was not through the UN. Whenever the Great Powers were at odds over a conflict that, even though it did not involve them or their allies directly, nevertheless greatly affected their interests, the effectiveness of UN peacekeeping operations suffered an eclipse, as in the Congo in the fall of 1960, or even collapsed, as in the Middle East in May 1967. The financial crisis which has affected UN peacekeeping ever since 1961 and has never been resolved is the direct result of a continuing constitutional conflict between the superpowers.

On the other hand, quite apart from cold-war situations, the prevalence of life and death conflicts between states or within states and the formidable challenge of the poor nations in the economic and social realms have left the UN incapable of finding remedies in the absence either of any substantive consensus of the superpowers or of any joint determination on their part to enforce such a consensus and in the presence of all the obstacles raised by state sovereignty. In major political crises the United Nations has sometimes been absent when it was obvious that intervention would meet with fierce resistance from one party (Algerian war) or else when an attempt at intervening risked escalating, rather than resolving, a local conflict (Biafra). More often, the General Assembly or the Security Council have adopted resolutions that have not been effective. A considerable difference has emerged between attempts at peacekeeping (or peace restoration)—successful for reasons to be discussed below—and attempts at solving the disputes that had led to violence —unsuccessful because of the resistance of some or all parties in matters which seemed to them to affect their essential interests; hence the long record of UN disappointments in Kashmir, Palestine, Cyprus, and in the cases of Southern Rhodesian and South African apartheid. In economic affairs there has been no massive transfer of funds from the rich to the poor through UN channels. The story of efforts at creating agencies for capital development has been depressing, and the results of the UN Conference on Trade and Development (UNCTAD) have been disappointing. The bulk of aid to the underdeveloped countries continues to be handled by bilateral agreements. However huge the majority behind a resolution, if those who are asked to make a sacrifice, a gamble, or a move remain deaf, the majority will remain frustrated and the crises will stay unresolved in a world of states where the superpowers are often among the deaf and, even when they are not, they distrust each other too much to establish a condominium.

However, there has been a dampening of the superpowers' contest and a reintroduction not only of restraints but even of cooperation in multiple forms in the international system. I have stressed two factors as the main causes for these developments: the new legitimacy of the nation-state and the new conditions of the use of force in a nuclear world. A third factor deserves equal recognition: the heterogeneity of the system, which has made it impossible for the superpowers to engulf the whole planet into their rivalry (whereas Athens and Sparta had absorbed all of the Greek world into theirs). It has also made it possible for the lesser powers, protected by the legitimacy of nationalism and by the superpowers' fear of collision, to impose various restrictions on the Big Two duel. It has given to this duel and to the other contests in the system a variety of configurations depending on local and regional circumstances, and it has reintroduced—in what is the first worldwide international system in history—broad opportunities for balancing within and between regions. The second and third layers of the system—polycentrism and multipolarity—have thus appeared as a consequence of the muting of the bipolar conflict and as a reaction against the astringency of bipolarity. It is the combination of these three factors and of these changes in the international hierarchy which has given to the United Nations its chances and its role in postwar political and economic affairs.

The United Nations has reflected those features but also contributed to, exploited, and magnified them. Thus, the change in the balance of forces within the UN organs and the increasing need for bargaining and compromise in order to get resolutions passed reflects the shift from a bipolar world to the new, more complex system. In the bipolar one there could perhaps be thumping majorities piled up by one camp against another, but at the cost of effectiveness and with a purely symbolic meaning. In the present world, within the limits set by latent bipolarity (i.e., the exclusion of those issues over which an irreconcilable rift between the superpowers still condemns the United Nations to impotence) the lesser powers can play a conspicuous role on the world stage largely because of another kind of impotence: that of the superpowers which owe their dominant position to a kind of material might which they cannot freely use (i.e., weaponry). The relative deference with which the United Nations, even in colonial affairs, has treated France and the United Kingdom, its prudence toward Communist China, and the importance of India reflect the tendency toward multipolarity, i.e., the rise of secondary or potential nuclear powers. But the United Nations has also contributed to polycentrism because of the role which the voting procedures give to small states, each one of which counts as much as any large power and must be courted and coaxed for the requisite majority to be attained. Thus, the new balance of forces that has emerged in the 1960's (both in a much larger General Assembly where no single bloc has any more the control of the requisite two-thirds majority and, more recently, in the broadened Security Council) has allowed the UN to mitigate somewhat the importance of bipolarity. What matters is not the positive agreement of the Big Five but the absence of deep disagreement of the Big Two. The enlargement of the membership gives an opportunity to third parties, whose votes are indispensable to the Big Two, to appeal to the common or convergent interests of the superpowers and thus to coax through their initiatives the kind of consensus which the original Charter had seemed to leave almost exclusively to the initiative of the superpowers themselves. In some instances it is the prodding of the smaller powers, dissatisfied with the gap between them and the superpowers, which produces a kind of defensive rapprochement of the Big Two qua superpowers, determined both to protect their superiority and to disarm the lesser powers' drive by occasional concessions that do not threaten their own position as top dogs (cf. the Treaty on the Nonproliferation of Nuclear Weapons, various votes on economic development; cf. also the recent tendency to return to the Security Council its primary role).

Similarly, the United Nations reflects—indeed is based on—the principle of state sovereignty. But it has made quite a contribution to the legitimacy and sanctification of the nation-state. The increase in the importance of the General Assembly has heightened the attraction of statehood, and the ease with which the United Nations has, after 1955, given its blessing and opened its doors to new nations has been largely responsible for the huge rise in the number of new states: The United Nations, and especially its General Assembly, has been the matrix and target of new nation-states. Moreover, in the excolonial area as well as in economic affairs the organs of the United Nations have given a solemn endorsement to the nation-state (even to the mini-state) and have wrapped the rights and privileges of the Charter around the frail and shivering new nations, thus promoting a kind of pluralist and equalitarian legitimacy which inhibits considerably the more blatant moves the superpowers could be tempted to make in their relations with weaker states.

No one will doubt that the organs of the United Nations reflect the heterogeneity of the international system: In every major crisis submitted to the organization, such as the Congo or the Middle East, the diversity of regimes, ideologies, levels of development, regional concerns, allegiances, etc., engenders a drama of conflicting purposes and a process of painful negotiation. It is the combination of national legitimacy and fragmentation which accounts for the failure to establish an international police force and for the glaring weaknesses of past peacekeeping forces, for they have been crippled both by the nations' jealous defense of the principle of consent, as applied to the stationing and financing of those forces, and by the bloc conflicts that have shaped the composition of the forces and that led in May 1967 to the disintegration of the United Nations Emergency Force (UNEF). The more fragmented the international system, the less likely the establishment of a permanent force based on universally applicable principles and the more likely the reliance on ad hoc procedures and local balances. But the United Nations has also contributed to this fragmentation. The Sisyphean approach of its major organs, with their tendency to sacrifice precedents and legalism to flexibility and political expediency, has meant that each issue would be considered on its merits with due respect for the configuration of political forces at the moment and in the area. The attempt by Hammarskjöld and, more quietly, by U Thant to engage in what the former had called "preventive diplomacy" so as to avoid the spread of the Cold War to all parts of the globe has strengthened heterogeneity by reinforcing all those specific, sometimes parochial, forces that resist the absorption of local conflicts into the cold-war mäelstrom. The frequent reliance on, or deference to, regional organization has had the same effect.

Finally, the United Nations has of course reflected the new conditions of the use of force. Had the fear of nuclear war and the desire to prevent an escalation of major head-on collisions between the superpowers not dominated their policy and strategy, the United Nations would not have had the chance to become a test of coexistence. Had conquest and the subjugation of determined, well-organized peoples in revolt not become prohibitively costly, the United Nations would not have had the opportunity to intervene so often in wars of national liberation. The United Nations has been effective whenever there has been a sufficient consensus (explicit or tacit) between the superpowers to curtail third-party violence. If one examines the cases in which the Security Council or the General Assembly have been able to adopt resolutions which were put into effect by the organization or its members, one finds that they fall into three groups, all of which entailed such a consensus. First, there are the cases in which a concert of the superpowers developed for the restoration of peace in a troubled area in which they were not directly involved (Indonesia, Middle East crises of 1948 and 1956, Kashmir, Yemen). Secondly, there are the instances of resolutions adopted after a balancing process in which groups of states other than the two camps of "cold warriors" played a major role but succeeded in formulating an effective text only because of the explicit or tacit consent of the superpowers (Congo crisis in the summer of 1960 and after Hammarskjöld's death, Middle East crisis of 1958, Cyprus, Middle East crisis during the first week of June 1967 and later in November 1967; however, the superpowers' disagreement about the meaning of the Security Council resolution of November 22, 1967, deprived the initial consent in the latter case of its effectiveness). Thirdly, there is a case involving both a concert and a balancing process: that of the nonproliferation treaty.

But the United Nations has, once again, gone beyond this: It has skillfully exploited what I have called the upper and the lower limits of the usefulness of applying force. It has buttressed the lower limit not by simply condemning the resort to force against peoples in revolt for their independence but by actually giving its blessing to the use of force toward the acquisition of statehood—much to the indignation of the colonial powers and despite the creation thereby of an apparent double standard toward violence (cf. India's attack on Goa): Wars of national liberation are legitimate, other resorts to force or threats of force are not (unless in case of self-defense). Also, the United Nations has done its best to strengthen the one barrier that is decisive for world peace—the upper limit on the use of force—through its practices of international neutralization in those military conflicts that it can handle. Its long record of cease-fires, military observers, and peacekeeping forces expressed both the determination of the superpowers not to let world peace be upset by moves of (or conflicts within) the lesser powers and the determination of the small states to maximize the restraints on great-power intervention in such disturbances. The United Nations has thus provided indispensable devices for all-round face saving, making it possible, not only for belligerents to put an end to hostilities without humiliation, but also to install some impartial, if fragile, checks on peace once the fighting has ended. The result is original: Even though the stopping of armed conflicts through international pressure (including the tacit or explicit consensus of the superpowers) is an old practice of balance-of-power systems, the fact that UN peacekeeping mechanisms have kept aside the Great Powers contributes to the atrophy of the latter's coercive power.

A final judgment on the *role* of the United Nations in the system and on the *impact* of the UN on the system must, once again, be balanced. Concerning its role, the change in legal practices and the emergence of new voting groups in the United Nations have increased the flexibility, maneuverability, and scope of interests of UN organs without drastically transforming the limits imposed by the international system. On the one hand, as an instrument of international cooperation and conflict resolution the United Nations appears as a kind of residual category. It is effective in the sense of having both authority and legitimacy in cases which prove to be neither too divisive (as are the cold-war conflicts, substantive disagreements in the Middle East or Asia, racial issues in southern Africa, etc.), nor too huge to be handled by the limited means of the organization (as was Algeria), nor capable of being treated primarily by or shunted to a regional organization (cf. the Organization of American States [OAS] for Guatemala and the Dominican Republic, the Organization of African Unity [OAU] for Biafra). The only exception to this has been the Korean war, which turned out to be neither a precedent nor a model.

On the other hand, as a residual instrument the United Nations has been extraordinarily resilient. As an arena and a stake it has been useful to each of the competing groups eager to get not only a forum for their views but also diplomatic reinforcement for their policies, in the Cold War as well as in the wars for decolonization. As an institution able to discharge various executive responsibilities in peacekeeping or technical assistance or economic development the United Nations has proven to be necessary almost to all. It has been necessary to those states that were the beneficiaries of efforts whose absence would have exposed them to greater poverty, more debilitating defeats, or more overt great-power pressure. It has also been necessary to major states which, had the United Nations not existed, would have had a difficult choice between direct, undisguised and trouble-making involvement on behalf of their national interests and possibly damaging abstention. What has kept the United Nations afloat in a stormy world has been, and remains, the need for all states to find some form of deterrence against the most formidable of those storms (large-scale wars, major economic disasters) and the impossibility for even the superpowers to count exclusively on their own individual efforts or on direct agreements (ruled out by their contest) for such protection.

Concerning the impact of the UN on the system, the United Nations has both contributed to defusing it by restoring elements of moderation and management and helped to subvert the international hierarchy. There are other, powerful reasons for this subversion, for the relative "impotence of power" of the Great Powers and the greater freedom of maneuver of the small states. But the United Nations, by its procedural practices as well as by the way in which it has exercised its legitimizing function, has reinforced the importance of the lesser powers. In this respect its contribution to world order is mixed, for while it was and remains necessary to curtail the predominance of the superpowers in a world in which force is too blunt a tool and most of the tasks have to be performed through consent, too radical a reversal of the hierarchy can be pretty unhealthy. The UN propels on the world scene states or statesmen whose performance rests more on showmanship than on realities and thus divorces posture from responsibility. It also prepared a potentially excessive reaction of middle powers, some collusion of the Great Powers, determined to restore or protect their supremacy, and a symbolic insurrection of the smaller powers against their own actual ineffectiveness, as shown by various resolutions of the 24th session of the General Assembly. The role played by the United Nations in legitimizing the nation-state helps safeguard national independence and integrity, but it also perpetuates all the obstacles which the traditional state of nature has accumulated on the road to peace and cooperation. The United Nations' contribution to heterogeneity has moderated and fragmented the relation of major tension between the United States and the Soviet Union, but it has also made calculations of deterrence and control more difficult and complicated the search for worldwide solutions to major problems. The UN approach to the use of force has added to the inhibitions on conventional and nuclear war, but, combined with repeated UN failures in solving disputes and with the encouragement to wars of liberation, it has also helped the generalization of violence at lower levels, favored the "internalization" of war, and encouraged further trends toward balkanization. Success in extinguishing fires has not prevented, indeed it has facilitated, the freezing of underlying conflicts and the incitation of troublemakers to resort to subversion, infiltration, psychological warfare, etc.

Thus, one can conclude that while the United Nations has been a significant factor in establishing a world order based on the nation-state and possessing a distorted, rather equalitarian hierarchy, considerable flexibility, and severe taboos on the traditional ways of using force, it has also perpetuated the drawbacks of sovereignty and bought moderation at the cost of making the resort to limited or subliminal violence endemic and the recurrent explosion of unsolved disputes inevitable. Only utopians will find this mixed balance sheet distressing. Historians will recognize in this picture many (but not all) of the features of balance-of-power systems, in which the code of legitimacy was far less equalitarian and resort to force less inhibited but in which large conflicts used to be avoided or moderated at the cost of multiplying lesser ones.

II. A Query for the Future

The future relations between the United Nations and the international system and the role the United Nations could play in it depend essentially on what this system will be and this, in turn, depends much less on UN actions (given their limited effectiveness and the fact that they reflect state policies more than they affect them) than on other factors to be mentioned below.

A. The Evolution of the International System

We are living in what might be called the world political system, an international system which differs from past ones not only through its scope but also through features that deserve a theoretical and empirical study. The nature of this system is original, its future unclear.[3]

It is marked, in the first place, by increasing interpenetration between domestic politics and international politics. The conceptualization of the latter as a "state of war," in contrast with the ideal type of the former as a community with central power, remains valid at the level of ideal types (there is still no central power in the international system, and given its radical heterogeneity consensus either about ends or about the means toward generally accepted ends is as far away as ever). There are however two new and important qualifications. On the one hand, there is a *rapprochement* in practice between the two kinds of politics. In many nations (new and old) there is

---

[3] For a formulation both very close to and more detailed than this one see Karl Kaiser, "Transnationale Politik," *Politische Vierteljahresschrift*, 1969 special issue, pp. 80–109.

little consensus, central power is more a stake than a force, and there is a potential and even endemic state of war. At the same time international politics has become more moderate. This is partly due to the new conditions of the use of force. There is another cause; for a variety of reasons (including those new conditions as well as economic enmeshment in an age dominated by the expansion of science and technology) the competition between states takes place on several chessboards in addition to the traditional military and diplomatic ones: for instance, the chessboards of world trade, of world finance, of aid and technical assistance, of space research and exploration, of military technology, and the chessboard of what has been called "informal penetration." These chessboards do not entail the resort to force. On most of them competition is based, not on the traditional kind of strategic-diplomatic interaction in which each player remains a separate unit following the logic of diversity, but on an interdependence which, to be sure, often covers relations of domination and dependence yet creates a logic of integration which restricts considerably the theoretical freedom of choice of each actor. Thus, "winning" presupposes the acceptance and mastery of considerable constraints. These constraints result either from the player's own entanglement in the web or (as, for instance, in the case of attempts at "playing domestic politics" abroad by manipulating foreign political movements or interest groups) from the hazardous nature of the game on this chessboard over which the actor rarely has adequate control. International politics thus becomes much more complex. Not only does each chessboard have rules of its own which have often not been adequately studied, but there are complicated and subtle relations between chessboards: For instance, depending on the national situation a state may be able to offset its weakness on one chessboard thanks to its strength on another or else be prevented from exploiting its strength on one because of its weakness on another.

On the other hand, there is a tight *interconnection* between the two kinds of political systems: While international politics still consists largely of interstate moves, a fourfold "internalization" of world politics is going on. Foreign policy entails increasingly attempts at influencing domestic affairs, i.e., at operating within rather than across borders. Major changes in the system result from revolutions rather than wars: Internal upheavals and crises short of all-out war (i.e., breakdowns which reflect the greater moderation of international politics) are now the two chief agents of change. Major shifts in rank in the international system result from domestic achievements or failures rather than from interstate contests. Finally, the international system of today is not one of cool, somewhat interchangeable, cabinet diplomats but one of "socially mobilized" polities which project on the world scene their domestic conceptions, experiences, and fantasies instead of following some external and objective national interest. Thus international politics becomes a kind of confrontation of domestic political systems in action (with an alternation of periods in which international politics is a frenzied clash of national designs or phobias and quieter periods in which the national systems "turn inward" and give priority to domestic demands, with a corresponding shift in priorities on and between the chessboards).

In the second place there is also a growing interpenetration between transnational society and world politics (defined as interstate politics). The *logic* of the "game" of world politics, so well analyzed by Raymond Aron, is shaped by the nature of the international milieu. But the *scope* and the specific *rules* of the game at any given time are determined, on the one hand, by the type of international system in existence (characterized mainly by the number of major powers, the presence or absence of major ideological cleavages, and the technology of conflicts) and, on the other hand, by the nature of the relations between state and society in the main competing units. Today, there is a world political system but no worldwide transnational society: There is still little contact between Communist China and much of the rest of the world at the level of society (whereas Communist China is definitely part of the international political system), and great discontinuities persist between the non-Communist transnational society and the Eastern world. Especially, but not only, in the latter there is—by comparison with the world of economic liberalism—a considerable politization of transnational society: The states control, directly or indirectly, the international economy and communications, international monetary relations, and the development of technology. The large socalled multinational corporations, due to their control, size, and wealth, cannot be considered either purely private or genuinely cosmopolitan. Their activities do affect the chips with which states play on several of the chessboards of international politics (hence the frequent resistance of states to their penetration by "private" foreign companies).

But, conversely, despite such politicization there is in much of the world a semiautonomous transnational society in the sense that it too has rules of its own, determined by its functions, which the state players must respect or can disregard only at prohibitive costs given the degree of interdependence. One can speak of additional chessboards such as that of industrial technology, on which the actors are both states (either as clients or as initiators) and private groups (corporations, banks), or that of scientific research, on which the actors are states, universities (public or private), foundations, industries, etc. Thus the interstate competition of today, while it has reached an unprecedented scope geographically and functionally, must observe a variety of restraints which contribute to making the world political system look more like domestic polities (a term which refers both to the narrow political sector, i.e., the state, and to the state's relations to society).

In what direction is this world political system going? It is easy to predict that the two interpenetrations will persist. But, far from limiting the number of possibilities this prediction actually increases them. If one examines the international system of today, one can state that some of its features are irrevocable. Nuclear weapons will not be disinvented, "social mobilization" (or the decline of apathy, or the growth of communications) will continue, and technological innovation will probably be accelerated. Other features are likely to persist but not with the same degree of certainty: the nuclear stalemate between the superpowers (yet who can be sure that there will be no unilateral breakthrough?), the military gap between the superpowers and other states, the relative fragmentation of the system and its basic heterogeneity. All the rest—including the present balance between its three layers and its ad hoc restraints on force—is dubious. Moreover, the irrevocable or likely features are all ambiguous in their effects from the viewpoint of world order, i.e., cooperation and the moderation of conflict. Nuclear weapons have so far had a stabilizing and restraining impact. But in the long run the very fear of nuclear war may increasingly force the superpowers to do battle through proxies and thus to play Russian roulette with their interests: This could be destabilizing, as one observes in the Middle East. The other powers are caught between the unsettling attraction of nuclear diffusion and the recurrent crises which the freeze on the large-scale use of force engenders. Social mobilization has also had a stabilizing impact by making foreign penetration into internal political systems more difficult and total domestic concentration on foreign policy less likely; but it can be disruptive by making foreign policy too rigidly bureaucratic or on the contrary by exposing it to internal instability and passions. The fragmentation of the international system makes it possible to isolate local conflicts and limits the scope and significance of superpower gains or losses. But it also makes for more uncertainty in the mechanism of escalation and complicates the superpowers' dilemmas in maintaining world order.

Thus there is a broad range of choices for the future. One can only say that international relations in the world political system will be the manipulation of interdependence by the separate, competing units. This formula suggests the growing awareness by states of the limits of their freedom of action and of its risks on the military as well as on the other chessboards: i.e., it suggests the new dimensions of prudence, the triple safety net of nuclear deterrence, economic solidarity, and domestic priorities under the tightrope of competition. But it also suggests that world order remains precarious, since the name of the game is still manipulation and contest: The desire to preserve *a* world system is not synonymous with a desire to preserve *any* existing system or exclusive of the desire to establish a radically different one on the ruins of the present one. There will therefore remain a tension between, on the one hand, the states' tendency to manipulate interdependence for their own benefit, as well as the explosive consequences of big internal disruptions, and, on the other hand, the need to turn the world political system into more of a society, i.e., to tame the independence of its members, to provide for more cooperation, and to keep violence within limits.

In a world which knows no political and psychological mutations (and short of the kind of mutation that might take place if there were a holocaust large enough to convert those not directly affected, yet not so huge as to annihilate us all) the establishment of world order means the achievement of a moderate international system. This rules out a return to an intense bipolar conflict. It does not rule out either a bipolarity of condominium (or collusion) or the prolongation of the present international system; yet I do not believe (for reasons described elsewhere) that either formula is either likely or capable of assuring moderation.[4] A moderate system will have to be a "multihierarchical" one. It is impossible to predict whether the latter will emerge sooner rather than later (there is considerable resilience in the present international system); nor is it possible to predict whether a multihierarchical system will be moderate or not. The answer to both questions depends essentially on three factors. First, there is the behavior of the superpowers, their degree of competition and cooperation and their degree of involvement in other parts of the world (on those factors depend, in turn, the degree of autonomy of subsystems and the degree of superpower resignation to domestic changes abroad). Second, there is the behavior of the present and potential middle powers, with its impact on the relations between the superpowers as well as on the degree of moderation, coherence, and autonomy of the subsystems. Third, there is the scope, rate, and location of nuclear diffusion (and, perhaps, nuclear control). It is obvious that there are countless configurations, and it would be depressing to try to list them all or to give degrees of probability to each.[5] Let us therefore abandon empirical forecasting for normative political analysis and see what role international organization *ought* to play if a moderate international system is to prevail, i.e., if the present world political system were to become a true society.

B. *The Role of International Organization in a Moderate International System*

My assumption—which will not be accepted by all—is that there will be no institutional mutation; i.e., sovereignty, anything but absolute and probably emptied of much of its erstwhile meaning and sting, will remain a claim and a foundation for the states' foreign policies. Even though there may be a considerable development of international and regional institutions, including a successful pursuit of integrative policies in some parts of the world, there will be no "superseding of the nation-state" (whatever its devaluation) at the

---

[4] Hoffmann, chapter 10.

[5] For a sobering example of what happens when one tries, see Herman Kahn and Anthony J. Wiener, *The Year 2000: A Framework for Speculation on the Next Thirty-Three Years* (New York: Macmillan Co., 1967), chapters 5, 7, and 9.

global level. It is my contention, first, that such a mutation is unlikely; second, that a world political system based on the nation-state can procure world order as long as (and as soon as), on the one hand, its most important members adopt certain kinds of attitudes and policies and, on the other hand, the traditional state insistence on total freedom of decision and from outside interference is curbed on behalf of international institutions and procedures. In other words, a moderate world political system will require an expansion and strengthening of international organization, but, in my opinion, it does not require the kind of centralization of power that world federalists have envisaged. It requires that international organizations, while continuing to be arenas and stakes, be allowed to develop greater autonomy, not in the sense of ceasing to be "expressions of the interests of particular states or other international actors,"[6] but in the sense of also expressing what might be called systemic interests, those long and short-term interests of states which aim, if not at maintaining the system (for it is futile to hope for a world of status quo powers), at least at maintaining moderation.

It is necessary to examine separately the conditions for the establishment of a moderate international system and the conditions of its maintenance. In each instance I will try to list the tasks which international organization ought to perform as well as its limits.

The establishment of a moderate international system requires three broad sets of conditions. First, such a system will emerge (or, if one prefers, continue to develop out of the original bipolar Cold War) only if certain kinds of crises are avoided. There ought to be no resort to nuclear weapons. The taboo that has prevailed since Nagasaki has become psychologically and politically essential (even though tactical nuclear weapons might conceivably be used without political and military disaster, the psychological effects could well prove deeply disruptive). In this respect the role of international organization will probably remain modest yet useful in a variety of ways: by providing what one might call a code of illegitimacy through resolutions and treaties; by establishing a legal framework for measures to restrict or slow down nuclear proliferation (which, if it became too widespread and especially if it reached certain countries with pressing grievances or fears, would strain the present taboo intolerably); by giving an international sanction to superpower agreements on arms control in the field of nuclear weapons and missiles; by lending the appearance of an international mandate to what might otherwise look like superpower collusion with respect to guarantees to third powers; by creating sufficiently objective or depoliticized mechanisms of inspection as soon as the refusal of one superpower has vanished (for internal as well as external reasons) and thus has ceased to justify the reticence of other states. To be sure,

---

[6] See Robert Keohane, "Institutionalization in the United Nations General Assembly," *International Organization*, Autumn 1969 (Vol. 23, No. 4), p. 862.

one can argue that a small nuclear war between lesser powers could take place without destabilizing the whole system; only a nuclear war involving a superpower or middle state would disrupt it. However, any violation of the nuclear taboo, even if it is restricted and contained when it first occurs, could have repercussions in the subterranean world of attitudes and expectations. The same considerations apply to biological and chemical warfare.

For similar reasons there ought to be no large-scale conventional war. The imperative of limitation—in geographical area (the number of states participating in a conflict) and in intensity—must be maintained, both because of the danger of escalation if a superpower is or becomes involved and because of the fact that the control of violence requires a kind of progressive "ritualization" or routinization of strictly limited wars. Here the United Nations will have to play a very important role. It will have to continue to practice "preventive diplomacy" and preventive peace restoration so as to keep local conflicts between nations (other than those between superpowers and their allies) from becoming superpower confrontations; the United Nations may well be aided here by the superpowers' increasingly strong unwillingness to be dragged into such confrontations by third parties. Also, in the future the United Nations will have to find more effective ways than it has found in the past of limiting conflicts in which a superpower or a middle power (such as Communist China) is or becomes involved. Even though—as before—the capacity to resolve such a dispute may be lacking, the willingness to apply some of the techniques of peace restoration and peacekeeping to these kinds of conflicts will have to develop; for whereas there can be no world order that fails to recognize the special position and responsibilities of the superpowers, there can also be no world political society if these states, while playing an important role in defining political legitimacy and the rules of the game, nevertheless insist on being above the latter and outside the former. To be more precise and blunt, in the long run there can be no moderate international system with a United Nations and a United States behaving as they have done during the war in Vietnam.

However, it will be impossible to curtail violence if its causes and opportunities remain unchecked. Despite past failures the United Nations (and regional organizations) have no alternative to trying even more persistently to solve or attenuate those disputes between states which the restraints on force have perpetuated and brought to periodic bloodshed. What is needed is a permanent engagement of all these organizations in diplomacy. This is the area in which the greatest efforts of imagination on the part of these agencies' secretariats will be needed and the most constant amount of gentle pressure by their bodies on states engaged in potentially destructive conflicts will have to be maintained. It would be wrong to say that past fiascoes are due to the sporadic, sputtering quality of the efforts made: The reasons go much deeper.

It would also be wrong to believe that more persistent efforts could ever succeed if the member states, particularly the major powers, fail to provide support and pressure on behalf of such attempts. But moderation will require, here again, ritualization: Such disputes should be under constant mediation, not merely under a mixture of occasional mediation and preventive yet superficial or belated injunctions against force; international agencies often appear better centers for such mediation than specific groups of states. In a world in which, for many reasons, there may not be a permanent police force the development of diplomatic techniques may be the best hope and greatest challenge. (In this respect, as in few others, one might look back at the practices of the League of Nations.)

Since explosions remain nevertheless likely, a last contribution of international organization in this area should be helping to make the costs of military operations prohibitive, although the greatest obstacle to successful wars will undoubtedly remain the solidity and resistance of each party to a conflict. To the extent to which international agencies can participate in what has been called "nation building" (an ugly expression for a muddy concept) they will strengthen the two current limits to the usefulness of the resort to force.

This brings me to the last kind of crisis that will have to be avoided: large-scale economic disruptions, either in the relations between the rich and the poor or, more generally, in international financial mechanisms and through balance-of-payments problems. This is an area in which the chances for order and the development of international organization—as the framework of interstate cooperation, as a center for executive action on behalf of the states, and as the place in which a code of conduct for multinational corporations can be defined—are synonymous. There have been remarkable beginnings among the industrial nations (primarily in the non-Communist world). But enormous progress remains to be made both with respect to the regulation of transnational activity there and in relations between advanced and underdeveloped countries, particularly in order to protect the latter from balance-of-payments and commodity price fluctuations.

Such progress requires a change of attitude among the industrial nations. Here we come to a second set of conditions for the establishment of a moderate international system: superpower restraint. This is not the place to describe in detail the perils of superpower activism; the experiences of Nikita Khrushchev and Lyndon Johnson are eloquent enough. The more active and involved the superpowers, the greater the perils of imbalance—through confrontation or disequilibrium between the superpowers and their protégés or tension between their external commitments and their internal troubles. Now, restraint will be incompatible with the pursuit and protection of their policies and interests and therefore acceptable to the superpowers only under certain circumstances; here again, international and regional agencies will have a

role to play. There will have to be a restraint on arms races that could lead
to superpower confrontations. This means, of course, first of all, a limitation
of their own arms race. Such a limitation is beginning to appear to them as
being in their own interest despite their security fears. Also contributing to
this new sense of urgency is the superpowers' fear of arms race contagion to
middle powers, a contagion inspired by the superpowers' example and by their
determination not to be immediately outdistanced by the Big Two. If the
superpowers want to stop their challengers, they will have to make concessions to them: Reciprocity operates here, as the long negotiations over the nuclear nonproliferation treaty have shown, and a cumulative mechanism (somewhat comparable to that which, within limits, works in the European Communities) may have been set in motion—in an area in which the prohibitive
economic and financial imperatives of the arms race may fortunately overtake
and overturn the traditional logic of competition and diversity. The United
Nations and regional organizations provide the best framework (and face-
saving facade) for such bargaining and balancing. Restraint also means curb-
ing arms races among third parties whose conflicts might engulf the superpowers in their role as providers of weapons and supporters of clients. Here
again, international and regional organizations can serve as arenas for negotiation, sources of inspection, and concealers of superpower collusion.

Restraint will also mean adopting a kind of residual, or reserve, position
with respect to peacekeeping: The enforcement of peace by the superpowers
in every conflict between third parties could only either exacerbate their differences or also lead to a breakdown due either to third-party resistance or to
opposition within the superpowers' own political systems. And yet, the Great
Powers will continue to want local armistices and settlements to reflect their
own views and to satisfy their own ambitions. Again, in a world in which
traditional military alliances have lost much of their advantage, both for the
superpowers, scared of being too deeply entangled, and for their allies, afraid
of being either abandoned or subjugated, only international and regional organizations can perform at the same time three important functions. They
can provide the procedural battlefield in which the Great Powers' views and
ambitions can be expressed and pressed; they can offer the channels of bargaining in which the lesser powers (without whose participation there can be
no world order other than the dangerously activist one of superpower imperialism) can both amend the designs of the superpowers and be courted
by them; and they can be the source of legitimacy once a solution has been
adopted. In other words, insofar as crises break out in various parts of the
world (whether they involve a superpower or not), the large states, in order
to establish a moderate international system, will have to resort to international and regional agencies, first so as to end hostilities and restore peace,
second so as to supervise and execute settlements (whether those settlements

will have been negotiated directly by the parties, achieved through the efforts of the international or regional agencies themselves, or obtained through other procedures of mediation).

Finally, restraint by superpowers will mean a considerable change in their attitudes toward underdeveloped countries—both a willingness to separate economic aid from expectations of political advantage in the Great Powers' contest and (in the case of the United States) a resignation to inevitable manifestations of economic nationalism at the expense of American private interests deemed nefarious for the development of a national economy. Once more, recourse to international and regional agencies will be essential. The shift from bilateral to multilateral aid and the settlement of disputes arising out of expropriations through the efforts of such agencies and according to guidelines laid down by them (instead of a vicious cycle of mutual reprisals) should allow for the kind of superpower restraint that would not amount to neglect of the needs of the poorer nations and for the sort of superpower retreats that would not amount to a dangerous humiliation of the rich.

Global and regional agencies will be able to play such roles, however, only if a third condition of moderation is met: the gradual ending of quarantines in the world political system. This system will obviously be moderate only if it is worldwide. States excluded or quarantined remain the most dangerous sources of crises because of their very psychological or ideological isolation. They are least likely to accept as impartial international or regional agencies which either do not admit them as members or treat them as pariahs within their organs and which can therefore not expect to be allowed to play any significant role in peacekeeping, in the working out or in the carrying out of settlements involving such states. At this time, the very code of legitimacy developed by international organizations justifies the quarantine of states which refuse to conform to their code and whose ideological aggressiveness or racial policies are repugnant to a great majority of nations. But moral indignation and political or even economic boycotts are not the most effective forms of disapproval, the most likely ways of influencing behavior, nor the kind of practices most capable of creating a moderate world political system. Those who have disapproved of the isolation of Communist China are often supporters of the quarantine of South Africa or Southern Rhodesia; but, on balance, and for the purpose of establishing a system of cooperation and management of conflict among interdependent but drastically diverse states, no quarantine ought to be perpetuated. For if one wants all states to adopt certain rules of conduct, they all have to be brought into the game and caught in its grip.

This does not mean that they will immediately accept those rules and play by them or be caught in the web at once. But the chance that this will eventually happen is greater if they are in than if they are out. The decision not to play, the decision to stay in splendid isolation, ought to be theirs. There are different ways of achieving moderation. The best is that which results from ideological homogeneity, from the convergence or parallelism of national practices and policies. But given the nature of the present world this remains a utopian vision. An international organization that would try to achieve it by verbal thunderbolts would only get farther away from it: Diversity would be inflamed instead of being made manageable. There remains only one other way to moderation. It consists of combining (regretfully perhaps) the toleration of, or resignation to, repugnant internal religions and relations with the prevention and repression of efforts by such regimes to spread their gospels and export their venom. Changes in their domestic beliefs and behavior will have to result from the frustration of such efforts, from domestic upheavals, and from the gradual effects of entanglement in the world political system.

This brings us to the conditions for maintaining a moderate international system, established thanks to the observance of the imperatives discussed above. Some of these conditions concern the elements that make up the system, others concern relations between the actors. A moderate system will have to be endowed with a fairly complex hierarchy of superpowers, middle powers, and small states or rather with a number of functional hierarchies that will overlap but be much more diversified than the traditional hierarchy based essentially on military might. It will also, given the complexity and continuing heterogeneity of the world, require considerable regional decentralization. Despite (or because of) the multiplicity of regimes it will need an attitude of competitive coexistence on their part instead of one of mutual exclusiveness. And it will require strong transnational links, i.e., a broad transnational society that will provide the states with new areas of cooperative goals or with goals that cannot be reached through violent conflict. Thus, the elements of the system will by themselves require, and allow for, a multiplicity of regional as well as universal organizations (the latter consisting largely of functional agencies). Each one will have its own bargaining process and its own balancing mechanism, based on the specific hierarchy of power that corresponds to its region or to its function. Each one will contribute therefore to decentralization and functional specialization in the system and to the diversification of power; each one will come close to what Ernst Haas has called a self-contained negotiating universe.

The relations within the world political society, or the rules of the game, will consist both of the imperatives for the establishment of a moderate system, which will continue to be indispensable, and of further developments in two directions. First, a new international legitimacy will have to emerge, as in every past moderate system. The world political society of the future, if it wants to avoid becoming a jungle, will have to meet two requirements. On the one hand, even though there appears at first sight to be a contradiction between the interpenetration of domestic and world politics, as well as that of transnational society and international politics, and a gradual extinction of foreign policy efforts at manipulating domestic politics in other countries, such a withdrawal from manipulation will have to take place. It would be facilitated by the increasing impermeability of consolidated societies to foreign intervention in a world in which the overt use of force becomes the exception and by statesmen becoming increasingly aware of the risks and uncertainties of such attempts at controlling others. This does not mean that the old principle of nonintervention will become more sacred than in the past. It means that the scale and scope of interventions must shrink and that attempts at influencing the behavior of a state must aim primarily at its *external* behavior on the various old and new chessboards of international affairs instead of being aimed at *internal* control. This will require on the part of international and regional agencies both continuity and change. They would continue to defend their members' sovereignty against outside intrusion and to be prudently ready to intervene through "preventive diplomacy" or for humanitarian reasons in large-scale civil wars so as to deter more interested and selfish interventions by cunning or greedy powers. But they would change, insofar as it would become more difficult for certain states to utilize regional or international agencies as a cloak behind which they resort to the manipulation of domestic affairs, under the pretext provided by collective statements condemning certain kinds of regimes or endorsing certain kinds of domestic practices. Such a change will occur only if the elements of the system meet the requirements listed, i.e., if the international hierarchy and the panoply of power available to any given state are sufficiently complex and diversified to allow for the types of balancing and bargaining that would curtail such instrumental uses of regional or international bodies by a handful of dominant actors.

On the other hand, the nature of the new chessboards and the need to dampen conflict on the old ones will require in a shrinking world, if not an increasing transfer of sovereignty to international organization (which would gradually receive some of the attributes of statehood), at least an increasing pooling of sovereignties for the exercise of cooperation in the various economic, monetary, and technical fields; in communications; in scientific research and exploration, etc.; and even in peacekeeping. Thus, progressively, overt conflict and all-out competition would be replaced, not by harmony, but by competition in a framework of cooperation and by muted conflict, i.e., by bargaining (which is not at all, as labor negotiators know, necessarily a mild, easy, and brotherly activity). It is obvious that only regional and universal institutions can provide the framework, incentives, expertise, and rules of security and predictability required.

Second, along with the new legitimacy of nonmanipulation and competitive cooperation, the procedures for the maintenance of order will have to be fortified in two areas discussed in connection with the emergence of a moderate system. On the one hand, insofar as peacekeeping is concerned, there is obviously in the long run no substitute for international measures of arms control with a growing network of supervision, inspection, and enforcement. Transfers of sovereignty of the kind envisaged once by the Baruch plan or by the Clark-Sohn scheme remain improbable; but complex third-party procedures and balanced (one dare hardly say objective or impartial) safeguards going beyond unilateral limitations and contractual promises will be necessary. And even if no permanent world police force emerges, ad hoc forces in readiness for the policing of violent conflicts other than those involving major powers will be needed (even if the deterrence of nuclear war or of conventional aggression by secondary nuclear powers remains the preserve of the superpowers themselves). On the other hand, beyond the strengthening of the techniques of diplomacy for the settlement of disputes, international and regional bodies will have to develop regular procedures of peaceful change if the avoidance or limitation of the resort to force is to become a ritual; for there will always be tensions and pressures for change, and the more one insists on keeping them under control, the more one will need to develop mechanisms of review and nonviolent adjustment. This is the realm in which the outlines of the future are dimmest and in which the role of international organization may be greatest, especially by comparison with its past failures and present pallor.

A moderate world society will have to be based on two principles. One is the universalization of concern. This does not mean that (as in the theory of collective security) every conflict should be escalated to the world level rather than localized. Universal concern does not require universal involvement: Actual participation in the management of troubles ought often to remain within the boundaries of subsystems, and the need for superpower restraint has been stressed before. But in a worldwide political system the real alternative to universal concern is unilateral action, especially by a superpower within or even outside its self-proclaimed sphere of vital interests. If this recipe for immoderation is to be discarded, and although (or because) there can be no ironclad guarantees of security and there neither is nor should be any possibility for constant, worldwide policing by the superpowers, there will have to be collective intervention for peacekeeping and settlement so as to increase the disutility of the resort to force. Superpowers at the world level and middle powers in their regions will themselves find it necessary to obtain collective sanction for their interventions in interstate disputes or collective participation in the enforcement of peace or of settlements. The other principle is the need for safety valves for change, the more the uses of force are repressed. Hence, the requirement that states both stop manipulating internal affairs and accept broad, even violent, domestic change and regimes hostile to their own conceptions or to private foreign interests, as long as the external behavior of these regimes or revolutionary forces is nonviolent and nondisruptive; hence also the necessary development of collective procedures of peaceful change for interstate relations.

At this stage in world affairs it is difficult to foresee whether a world society built on those principles will emerge. The listing of conditions and requirements provides a better critique of the present than a prophecy of the future. Whether such a society emerges depends only for a very modest part on what international organization initiates, even though, as we have seen, international organization will have many important roles to play if states allow this society to emerge. What can be stated is that such a society would afford the greatest opportunities and the widest need for international and regional organizations without which it would be crippled. We noted earlier that not every moderate system has a procedural consensus that makes of such agencies the legitimate channels for controlling conflict and for promoting cooperation; but it is obvious that a worldwide international system with a complex hierarchy of power and a formidable range of tasks and chessboards can have no other legitimate channels: The scope and intensity of interstate and transnational relations leave no alternative. It can also be stated, in turn, that such organizations—which today remain epiphenomena rather than prime movers—will not develop fully as long as the international system has not found more organic forms of moderation than the rather mechanical or tactical ones which have appeared in recent years. And it is perfectly possible to conceive of a diversified world society with a network of such agencies even though a (much tamer) nation-state would still, in theory and practice, be the highest form of social organization and center of allegiance.

PART II

INTERNATIONAL ORGANIZATION AND THE STRUCTURE OF INFLUENCE

BLOC VOTING IN THE GENERAL ASSEMBLY

M. Margaret Ball

The spectre of bloc voting has haunted the United Nations since the Charter was first debated at San Francisco. Since then, the influence of certain groups of states in affecting the outcome of elections has occasioned considerable comment, and it has been suggested that the same groups have been inordinately powerful in deciding substantive issues. Some highly tentative conclusions as to the validity of these contentions may be drawn from a study of certain matters which have come before the Assembly during its first five sessions.

Assuming that a bloc is any group which consistently votes as a unit on all or particular kinds of issues, the point of departure has been the voting records of states which might conceivably be expected to vote together because they constitute "regional groups" within the meaning of the Charter (Organization of American States, Arab League), or because they simply inhabit the same geographical area (Asia, Latin America, middle east), or because they have a common ideology (communist states), or common interests (colonial powers), or because they have some machinery for consultation in matters of foreign policy (Benelux, Scandinavian states, British Commonwealth). The first objective, of course, is to see whether these groups actually operate as blocs in the Assembly, and if so, on what kinds of issues. Other objectives are to obtain additional light on the extent to which the course of any group is determined by its most powerful member; to discover the extent to which specific groups may be expected to combine forces, and whether such combinations may be regarded as representative of the bulk of the opinion of "We the peoples of the United Nations." Last, but not least, it is of interest to attempt to discover whether bloc voting in the General Assembly amounts to more than a normal political phenomenon which may be expected to occur in any national parliament or international conference. Bloc voting was widely regarded as a defect of the League of Nations. Is it to be so considered in the United Nations?

Apart from the electoral process, the questions to be studied have been selected with a view to covering: 1) the approximate time span of

M. Margaret Ball is Professor of Political Science at Wellesley College, author of *Post-War German-Austrian Relations, 1918–1936* and *Problems of Inter-American Organization* and has recently returned from a Guggenheim fellowship in Europe.
From Volume 5, No. 1 (1951), pp. 3–31.

the first five sessions; 2) a broad range of subject matter; and 3) questions in which particular groups might be expected to have a strong interest, as well as questions in which they might not.

I

It is in the area of elections that the most is known of the effects of bloc voting, and the least can be proved, since Rule 92 of the Rules of Procedure provides that all elections shall be held by secret ballot and without nomination. Nevertheless, it is common knowledge that a good deal of caucusing goes on prior to elections, and that something analogous to "Senatorial courtesy" is practiced in the election of the General Committee as well as in elections to other posts where the principle of geographical representation is deemed to hold. The latter principle does hold, of course, not only for the General Committee (by virtue of Rules 31 and 38 of the Rules of Procedure), but also for the election of non-permanent members of the Security Council (under Article 23 of the Charter), and for ECOSOC (by common agreement). It is too early to discover the extent to which it applies to the Trusteeship Council, but it clearly does hold for a number of lesser bodies (as the Assembly's own subcommittees, special committees, etc.), within the Assembly's power of appointment.

The election of the Assembly President precedes that of the committee chairmen; that of the seven vice-presidents follows both, in order to assure the "representative character" of the General Committee. Despite the absence of roll calls, it would seem that bloc voting sometimes, but not always, plays a part in the election of the Assembly President. At the second session, for example, Aranha of Brazil received 26 votes on the first ballot (this may well have represented a combination of the Latin American and Arab League votes); Evatt of Australia received 23, and Masaryk of Czechoslovakia received 6 (doubtless from the Soviet bloc).[1] In contrast, however, at the first special session, Aranha was elected on the first ballot by 45 votes, while five other candidates received only one each.[2] Committee chairmanships appear to be allocated after considerable negotiation, as are the vice-presidential posts. At the first session, before the no-nomination rule went into effect, the Netherlands proposed a slate of candidates for vice-president which was adopted at the suggestion of Mexico without a ballot,[3] thus indicating that it was generally

---

[1] General Assembly, *Official Records* (2d session), p. 9.

[2] *Ibid.* (1st special session), p. 2–3.

[3] *Ibid.* (1st session, 1st part), p. 69–70.

acceptable as rounding out the geographical distribution of the committee. Later elections appear to indicate, however, that despite widespread caucusing, general agreement has sometimes been difficult to achieve.[4] Whatever the extent of lobbying for General Committee posts, it has not yet resulted in monopolizing the seats of any geographical region by a particular group of states within it. Thus the middle east has been represented not only by Syria, Lebanon and Egypt (Arab League states), but also by Iran and Turkey. Similarly, the Pacific and Asiatic areas have been represented by New Zealand, Australia, India, Pakistan, Thailand, the Philippines and China.

Bloc voting has had particularly important effects for the Security Council. The Charter provisions on elections (given general agreement to subordinate the criterion of "contribution . . . to the maintenance of international peace and security . . . " to that of "equitable geographical distribution"), have made it seem logical, once the areas to be represented were agreed upon, to leave the choice of candidate to the area concerned. Indeed it was asserted by the USSR at the fourth session—and denied by the United States—that a gentleman's agreement existed to this effect. The record would seem to indicate that such a "gentleman's agreement" was generally, but not unanimously, subscribed to. At the first session, part one, for instance, the massing of ballots on five of the candidates makes it evident that the Latin American, Arab League, and east European candidates had been nominated by the respective regional groups and concurred in by the rest of the Assembly, while there was no such prior arrangement on the part of the Commonwealth and the Assembly itself was divided on the Commonwealth representative.[5] The replacement of Egypt, Mexico and the Netherlands by Colombia (51 votes), Syria (45) and Belgium (43) on the first ballot at the first session, part two,[6] on the other hand, is further evidence of basic agreement on both geographical representation and the right of the regional group to nominate. That the agreement was not unanimous, however, was again demonstrated at the second session, in which Argentina and Canada were elected on the first ballot to replace Australia and Brazil, but the Ukrainian SSR replaced Poland only on the twelfth ballot, after India had withdrawn,[7] and after Vyshinsky had appealed to the Assembly to elect

[4] For example, the election of vice-presidents at the third session, part I resulted in the selection, on the first ballot, of China (46 votes), France (44), USSR (41), United Kingdom (41), United States (41), Mexico (29) and Poland (28). Nevertheless, the Philippines received 25 votes, and 23 other states received from 8 to 1 votes each (*ibid.*, p. 25–26).

[5] Brazil received 47 votes, Egypt 45, Mexico 45, Poland 39, Netherlands 37, Canada 33, Australia 28, Iran 6, Norway 5, Czechoslovakia 4, Denmark 2; a number of other states received 1 each (*ibid.* [1st session, 1st part], p. 82–84).
[6] *Ibid.* (1st session, 2d part), p. 975–976.
[7] *Ibid.* (2d session), p. 320–749.

the Ukrainian SSR on the ground that the selection of a Slav country was necessary to fulfill the requirements of the Charter.[8]

The issue of the right of the regional group to nominate was brought into the open, of course, at the fourth session, at which Ecuador and India replaced Argentina and Canada on the first ballot, and Yugoslavia was elected to replace the Ukrainian SSR on the second ballot over strong Soviet opposition.[9] It will be recalled that Czechoslovakia was the Soviet bloc candidate on this occasion, and that it received 20 votes to Yugoslavia's 37 on the first ballot (39 votes were necessary to elect). There was division of opinion among the great powers on this matter (the United Kingdom supported Czechoslovakia; the United States, Yugoslavia), as well as among the membership of the Assembly as a whole. Although Vyshinsky vociferously alleged that the election of Yugoslavia violated both the Charter and the "firmly established tradition that candidates for non-permanent membership were always nominated by the States belonging to the geographical areas concerned,"[10] it was evident that a two-thirds majority rejected the USSR contention—and either took the view that a country which had been excluded from consultation about the regional nomination had not lost its right to be elected to the Security Council, or voted for Yugoslavia out of a simple desire to weaken the influence of the USSR.

One of the most serious effects of bloc voting for Security Council members was the reservation of the middle east seat for members of the Arab League during the first four sessions. This monopoly was broken at the fifth session on the fourteenth ballot, when Lebanon withdrew and Turkey was elected by a vote of 53–4–3 to fill the seat vacated by Egypt.[11] Since certain non-permanent members of the Security Council appear to regard themselves as speaking for geographical regions (witness the extent to which the Latin American and Arab League countries caucus on substantive issues, as Korea), any monopoly of a seat allocated to a whole region by only some of the states within it would appear to create a highly unrepresentative situation.

In ECOSOC elections, while the record shows some scattering of votes, and in some cases, several ballots,[12] the general tendency appears to have been to accept the nomination of the regional group. There has been no attempt comparable to that successfully undertaken during the first four

---

[8] *Ibid.*, p. 323, 327. One of the problems here, of course, was the fact that six non-permanent seats were not sufficient to permit representation of all the areas that desired to be represented.
[9] *Ibid.* (4th session), p. 102–103.

[10] *Ibid.*
[11] *New York Times,* October 8, 1950.
[12] General Assembly, *Official Records* (1st session, 2d part), p. 976–1231; *ibid.* (2d session), p. 329–333.

sessions with respect to the Security Council to reserve the middle east seats for the Arab League.

It is more difficult to ascertain the extent to which bloc voting has played a part in Trusteeship Council elections, and it is perhaps premature to speak of a fixed geographical pattern in this connection. It is probable, however, that the numerous votes of the Arab League, Latin American and Asiatic states (themselves formerly subject to imperialism), and the Soviet bloc (professionally anti-imperialist), have been cast for states which might be expected to protect the interests of indigenous populations rather than those of administering powers.

The most active voting combination in elections is that of the Arab League and Latin American states. With Europe still seriously underrepresented in the United Nations, the 26 votes held by these two groups constitute very nearly a majority of the 60 member states. By picking up five additional votes (not a very difficult feat), this combination could dictate elections to Assembly posts. The combined votes of the two groups (or even the 20 Latin American votes plus 1), are sufficient to veto unacceptable candidates to the Security, Economic and Social, or Trusteeship Councils. The two groups have not been slow to realize their power. That they have not seriously misused it, except in the case of the Security Council monopoly mentioned above, is to their credit.

II

On substantive issues, the action of blocs is easier to demonstrate than in elections, although the effects are perhaps more difficult to evaluate, as will be seen from the following case studies.

Franco Spain. The resolution of the first session, part I, endorsing the San Francisco and Potsdam statements on Franco Spain, was adopted 46–2, with three states absent. The two dissenters were El Salvador and Nicaragua (Honduras was not present);[13] even at this early date, Latin America was not undivided on the Spanish question. The near-unanimity of this action broke down at the first session, part II, and was never subsequently restored.

At part II of the first session, there was a strong division of opinion between those desiring that stronger action be taken (Mexico, Poland), and those which did not. The issue was not a clear-cut fascist-anti-fascist one, but was complicated by the fact that a number of states considered that stronger action against Franco's regime would constitute an un-

---

[13] *Ibid.* (1st session, 1st part), p. 361.

warranted intervention in the domestic affairs of another state. A number of important votes illustrate this division (see Chart I). The first committee rejected the paragraph of a draft resolution[14] calling for the breaking of diplomatic relations with Spain by a vote of 20–20–10 in which only the Soviet bloc voted as a unit.[15] The compromise paragraph calling for the withdrawal of heads of mission was adopted by the first committee 27–7–16 in a vote on which Latin America continued to be split three ways, and the Commonwealth (except for South Africa's abstention), the Scandinavian states, the Soviet bloc, and the Arab League, voted as units.[16] On the votes on the resolution as a whole in committee (23–4–20) and in the plenary session (34–6–13), Latin America continued to be split three ways, the Commonwealth was divided between pro and abstention, both the Arab League and the Soviet bloc voted as units, and western Europe was solid except for the Netherlands, which abstained.[17]

The crucial votes at the second session pertained to the reaffirmation of the 1946 resolution contained in paragraph 2 of document A/C.1/265. This paragraph was accepted by the first committee by a vote of 30–14–11, but was rejected by the narrow margin of 29–16–8 by the plenary session.[18] In both cases, the bulk of the opposition votes came from Latin American powers; the Commonwealth was also divided, while the Arab League, the Soviet bloc, and all of western Europe except the Netherlands, were solid. While ten states changed position between the committee and plenary sessions, the deciding factor on both votes was the split within Latin America itself. It is probable that the United States, which opposed the reaffirmation and was responsible for the paragraph-by-paragraph roll call in the plenary session, used its influence to defeat the paragraph to which it objected. In any case, Resolution 114 (without the former paragraph 2) was adopted 36–5–12, without a roll call.[19]

At the third session, the Arab League and Soviet blocs remained solid, and western Europe and Latin America were divided (although the latter was somewhat less divided than at the previous session). While the Soviet bloc sought sanctions against Spain, the more important controversy related to a draft resolution presented by Bolivia, Brazil, Colombia and Peru,[20] which provided for the restoration of freedom of action to Members in their diplomatic relations with Spain. The operative para-

[14] Document A/C.1/128.
[15] General Assembly *Official Records* . . . *First Committee* (1st session, 2d part), p. 301. Throughout this article the first figure refers to votes in favor, the second to negative votes and the third to abstentions.
[16] *Ibid.*, p. 303.

[17] *Ibid.*, p. 304; *ibid., Official Records* (1st session, 2d part), p. 1222.
[18] *Ibid., Official Records* . . . *First Committee* (2d session), p. 430; *ibid., Official Records* (2d session), p. 1095–1096.
[19] *Ibid.*, p. 1096.
[20] Document A/C.1/450.

graph was passed by the first committee 25–16–16, but the resolution was rejected 26–15–16 by the plenary session.[21]

The resolution of the fifth session rescinding that part of the 1946 resolution which barred Franco Spain from the specialized agencies and recommended the withdrawal of heads of mission, was passed by a 38–10–12 vote of the plenary session.[22] The core of the majority consisted of the United States, sixteen Latin American states, and the Arab League. The Soviet bloc, Benelux and Scandinavia voted as units; other groups were divided.

The action on Franco Spain during the first five sessions was characterized by the division of the Latin American states (although the dissenters from the position taken by the majority of these states became fewer as time went on), and the solidarity of the Arab League and the Soviet bloc. The Arab League tended to maintain a neutral position until the third session; at the third and fifth sessions, it sided with the majority of the Latin American countries. The Soviet bloc pursued throughout a policy consistent with its antipathy for fascism. Some of the western European nations and the United States seemed to be less concerned with ideological than strategic considerations, and with their interpretation of the jurisdiction of the United Nations on this question. The Latin American countries found that common language, common religion and common origin (of eighteen of them, at least), were less important in reaching common policy than differing political beliefs and varying conceptions of non-intervention and its requirements in this case.

Spanish as a Working Language. At the third session, the fifth committee, having received reports from the Advisory Committee on Administrative and Budgetary Questions, as well as from the Secretary-General, opposing the adoption of Spanish as a working language of the Assembly, voted 21–20–5 that the step not be taken.[23] The slight majority supporting the negative committee recommendation consisted of the Commonwealth, Turkey, the Soviet bloc, all of the western European countries voting, China and the United States. The opposition included Egypt, Saudi Arabia and Syria (of the Arab League), the Philippines, and all of the Latin American powers voting (sixteen) except Brazil. Afghanistan, Brazil, Burma, Ethiopia and Greece abstained. Before the plenary session, the Philippines and the Latin American countries mobilized the total membership of the Arab League and all of the Latin American votes

[21] General Assembly, *Official Records . . . First Committee* (3d session, 2d part), p. 239; *Ibid., Official Records* (3d session, 2d part), p. 501.

[22] *New York Times,* November 5, 1950.
[23] See documents A/624, A/657 and A/704.

in support of an amendment[24] to the committee report which would attain their objective. These 27 votes, plus those of Greece, Iran, Turkey, Ethiopia and Liberia, passed Resolution 247 by a vote of 32–20–5,[25] thus adding considerably to the United Nations budget and causing exactly the kind of administrative and technical problems foreseen by the Secretary-General.

This is a case where the combined votes of the solid Latin American and Arab League blocs, with the support of a few other countries, overrode all opposition. It should be noted, of course, that as far as the Latin Americans and the Philippines were concerned, it was a matter of cultural pride and national prestige upon which all could agree (even the Brazilians and the Haitians, out of solidarity with their fellow Latin Americans); unanimity is harder to achieve on other types of issues, as illustrated in the case of Franco Spain. It should also be noted that in this case, a small-power majority, on a procedural vote, successfully opposed all of the larger powers. Furthermore, the Latin American, middle east, and African states, Greece and the Philippines outvoted the United States, China, three of the Dominions, and all of Europe (including the United Kingdom). The possibility (inherent in the present voting rules) that decisions will be taken by majorities representing a minority of the populations of the Member states was realized in this case. It remains to be seen, however, whether this possibility is likely to be realized in the future except in such unusual circumstances as existed here.

Palestine Partition. The inability of the Arab League to muster sufficient support to defeat partition—a matter of vital interest to its members —is evidence of the weakness of this bloc. The League had the backing of India, Pakistan, Afghanistan, Iran, Turkey, Thailand and Cuba in committee; it was supported in the plenary session by these states (except Thailand) and Greece.[26] (Chart II.)

The vote in the *ad hoc* committee was 25–13–17—an insufficient margin to assure passage in the plenary session. Bloc lines were drawn by the Arab League, the Soviet bloc (except for Yugoslavia's abstention), the Scandinavian states and Benelux, but not by Latin America. The large number of abstentions in committee gave ample opportunity for lobbying before the final vote. That the opportunity was not neglected is indicated by the vote in the plenary session (33–13–10).[27] Of the states which

---

[24] Document A/742.

[25] General Assembly, *Official Records* (3d session, 1st part), p. 757. The following voted against the amendment: Australia, Canada, New Zealand, the United Kingdom, the Soviet bloc, Benelux, Scandinavia, France, Iceland, China and the United States; the following

abstained: India, Pakistan, South Africa, Afghanistan, Thailand.

[26] General Assembly, *Official Records . . . Ad Hoc Committee on the Palestinian Question* (2d session), p. 222–223; *Ibid., Official Records* (2d session), p. 1424.

[27] *Ibid.*, p. 1424–1425.

changed position between the committee and plenary sessions (see Chart II), the three most remarkable were Chile, Haiti and the Philippines. The change in the Chilean position from pro to abstention was not explained, but may conceivably have represented a revolt against American pressure tactics. The Haitian and Philippine votes in favor of partition were clearly the result of pressure, since both delegations had categorically stated only two days before that their delegations would vote against it.[28]

The victors comprised part of the Commonwealth, the Soviet bloc (solid except for the Yugoslavian abstention), western Europe (solid) and a considerable number of Latin American states, the Philippines and Liberia. The nucleus of the opposition was the Arab League, which was supported by the middle east, Greece and Cuba. A "deal" with Latin America was not on the cards on this question, however closely the two groups may cooperate in the electoral process.

Admission of Israel. The Arab League was even less successful in its attempt to deny membership in the United Nations to Israel (Chart II). Supported by other middle eastern powers, it was opposed by most of the rest of the world. Bloc lines held firmly in this case for the Arab League, the Soviet bloc and Latin America, but again the Arab League and the Latin American powers were in opposite camps.

Internationalization of Jerusalem. The alignment of states on this fourth session issue differed materially from that on partition and the admission of Israel (Chart II). Both in committee (35–13–11) and in the plenary session (38–14–7)[29] support for internationalization came from the Arab League, some of the other near and middle eastern states, some western European and Asiatic states, the Soviet bloc (except Yugoslavia), and a number of Latin American states. The opposition was scattered and without geographical significance. Two elements in this case were of particular importance: the religious issue and the implementation question. The religious issue, while important, did not result in the formation of a Catholic, Protestant or Moslem bloc; the Catholic powers, for example, while desiring protection of, and access to, the Holy Places, were divided on internationalization of the whole city as a method of securing it. For other states (United Kingdom, New Zealand, Sweden, Netherlands, Canada, etc.), the difficulty of implementation in the absence of consent by Israel and Jordan, and the lack of provision in the resolution for implementation, were determining. These states either voted against the resolution or abstained.

[28] *Ibid.*, p. 1313, 1353–1354.

[29] Document A/1222; General Assembly, *Official Records* (4th session), p. 607.

In the plenary session, only Benelux and the Arab League voted as units; this is one of the few cases where the Soviet bloc was divided, and where Yugoslavia went so far as to vote against the position adopted by the other communist states instead of abstaining. Latin America, which might have been expected to pursue a common policy because of its common religious heritage, was again divided. The Arab League was on the winning side, but the victorious combination was essentially an Arab League-Soviet bloc-Latin American one (with only five Soviet bloc and thirteen Latin American states involved), rather than a simple Arab League-Latin alignment.

Italian Colonies. The handling of this question at the third session, part II, makes it one of the most interesting cases on record. It was clear from the beginning that a solution would be difficult to reach: the United States and United Kingdom favored British trusteeship for Cyrenaica, Italian trusteeship for Somaliland, and the division of Eritrea between Ethiopia and the Sudan; the Latin Americans concurred in British trusteeship for Cyrenaica and were willing to cede a part of Eritrea to Ethiopia, but insisted on Italian retention of most of its former colonies; the Arab League wanted a united, independent Libya either at once or after a brief period of trusteeship, and opposed a return of any of the Italian colonies; the Soviet bloc advocated United Nations trusteeship for all of the colonies, except a part of Eritrea, which it was willing to cede to Ethiopia.[30] Under the circumstances, a certain amount of lobbying was to be anticipated. The fundamental difference of view between the Arab League and the Latin American states made it impossible for the two groups to agree, although it has been stated that the attempt was made.[31] The Latin American countries, however, not only caucused extensively on this question, but also entered into negotiations with France, the United States and the United Kingdom in an effort to reach a satisfactory solution. The impressive size of the Latin American vote made it imperative for that group to be satisfied if a decision was to be reached. The Bevin-Sforza agreement of May 6, 1949 satisfied the Latin American demands, and enabled subcommittee 15 of the first committee to propose a draft resolution which provided that: Libya was to become independent in 10 years, with Assembly approval; meanwhile Cyrenaica, Fezzan, and Tripoli (beginning in 1951) were to be placed under the trusteeship, respectively, of Britain, France and Italy; Italy was to be given a trusteeship for Somaliland; all of Eritrea except the western

[30] For a more extensive discussion of these viewpoints, see Benjamin Rivlin, "The Italian Colonies and the General Assembly," *International Organization*, III, p. 459–470.
[31] *Ibid.*, III, p. 466–467.

province was to be incorporated into Ethiopia, subject to minorities guarantees, etcetera; and the western province of Eritrea was to be incorporated into the Sudan.[32]

The fact that the Latin Americans regarded this as a package deal is on record. Mr. Castro (El Salvador), during the vote in the first committee, and before the paragraph-by-paragraph roll call on the Libyan provisions, stated that: "he would abstain from voting on sub-paragraphs (a) and (b) [relating to Cyrenaica and the Fezzan respectively]. If the question of Tripolitania were decided favorably in accordance with sub-paragraph (c), his delegation, which in principle did not oppose trusteeship over the Fezzan for France nor over Cyrenaica for the United Kingdom, would vote in favor of the entire resolution."[33]

In committee, the subcommittee's proposals, except that pertaining to the incorporation of the western province of Eritrea into the Sudan, were approved (Chart III); the provision with respect to Italian trusteeship for Tripoli, however, received less than the two-thirds majority necessary to carry it in the plenary session. The committee vote on the resolution as a whole (without the provision relating to the western province of Eritrea) was 34-16-7.[34]

In the plenary session, the success of the deal rested upon the fate of the Tripoli paragraph—but after acceptance of the Cyrenaica and Fezzan paragraphs, the Tripoli provision was rejected by one vote (33-17-8).[35] The nucleus of the opposition to this paragraph in the plenary session, as it had been in committee, was the Arab League and the Soviet bloc; supported by Burma, India, Pakistan, Philippines and *Haiti*, the two groups were able to defeat the paragraph, and as a a result, the entire resolution—for, as noted above, Latin American acceptance of the resolution depended upon the adoption of *all* of its provisions, and especially those relating to Tripoli and Somaliland.

The elimination of the Tripoli paragraph was followed by the rejection of the provisions relating to Somaliland (35-19-4),[36] and the acceptance of the Eritrea paragraph. The resolution as a whole (without the para-

[32] Document A/C.1/466.

[33] General Assembly, *Official Records . . . First Committee* (3d session, 2d part), p. 391. This is further substantiated by the statement of Mr. Arce (Argentina), after Italian trusteeship for Somaliland had been voted down by the plenary session. He "recalled that, with the purpose of reaching a concrete and positive solution, a group of Latin-American Republics, upholding their principles and granting concessions on certain points, had reached an agreement concerning the draft resolution which had been submitted to the General Assembly by the First Committee. He was sure that all delegations were aware that if a single one of the points of that compromise resolution failed, the entire proposal would fail, since a whole group of Latin American Republics was prepared to vote against the draft resolution in its entirety" (*ibid.*, *Official Records* [3d session, 2d part], p. 590.)

[34] *Ibid.*, *Official Records . . . First Committee* (3d session, 2d part), p. 391-395.

[35] *Ibid.*, *Official Records* (3d session, 2d part), p. 587.

[36] *Ibid.*, p. 593.

Chart I

FRANCO SPAIN

First Sess., Pt. I, A/BUR/25, excluding Spain from UN, approved 46–2; 1st Sess., Pt. II, First Comm. rejected 20–20–10 proposal to break diplomatic relations with Spain; approved 27–7–16 proposal to withdraw Heads of Mission; plenary vote 34–6–13; 2nd Sess., First Comm. reaffirmed 1946 res. by vote of 30–14–11; reaffirmation rejected by plenary 29–16–8; 3rd Sess., Pt. II, proposal for freedom of action approved First Comm. 25–16–16; rejected plenary, 26–15–16; 5th Sess., res. restoring freedom of action and admitting Spain to specialized agencies adopted plenary 38–10–12. In this and in following charts, P = pro, C = con, A = abstention.

	1st Sess., Part I			1st Sess., Part II — Committee — Break Rels.			1st Sess., Part II — Committee — Withdraw Heads			1st Sess., Part II — Plenary			2nd Sess. — Comm. (Reaffirm. 1946 Res.)			2nd Sess. — Plenary (Reaffirm. 1946 Res.)			3rd Sess., Part II — Comm. (Freedom of Action)			3rd Sess., Part II — Plenary (Freedom of Action)			5th Sess. — Plenary (Freedom of Action)		
	P	C	A	P	C	A	P	C	A	P	C	A	P	C	A	P	C	A	P	C	A	P	C	A	P	C	A
Commonwealth																											
Australia	x				x		x			x				x			x		x			x				x	
Canada	x			x			x					x	x				x			x			x		x		
India	x			x			x			x			x			x			x			x				x	
New Zealand	x				x		x			x			x			x			x			x			x		
Pakistan															x			x	x			x			x		
So. Africa	x			x					x	x			x			x		x	x			x			x		
UK	x			x			x			x			x			x				x			x				x
Near & Middle East																											
Arab League																											
Egypt	x					x		x		x				x		x			x				x		x		
Iraq	x			x			x			x				x		x			x			x			x		
Lebanon				x			x			x				x		x			x			x			x		
Saudi Arabia	x			x			x			x				x		x			x			x			x		
Syria	x			x			x			x				x		x			x			x			x		
Yemen														x		x			x			x			x		
Other																											
Afghanistan						x		x		x						x			x				x		x		
Greece	x					x		x		x			x			x				x		x			x		
Iran	x									x			x			x			x			x			x		
Israel																					x			x	x		
Turkey	x			x			x			x			x			x			x			x			x		
Eastern Europe																											
Byelorus. SSR	x			x			x			x			x			x			x			x			x		
Czechoslovakia	x			x			x			x			x			x			x			x			x		
Poland	x			x			x			x			x			x			x			x			x		
Ukrainian SSR	x			x			x			x			x			x			x			x			x		
USSR	x			x			x			x			x			x			x			x			x		
Yugoslavia	x			x			x			x			x			x			x			x			x		
Western Europe																											
Benelux																											
Belgium	x			x			x			x			x			x				x		x		x	x	
Luxembourg	x			x			x			x			x			x				x		x		x	x	
Netherlands	x					x			x			x	x			x				x		x		x	x	
Scandinavia																											
Denmark	x				x		x			x			x			x			x				x				x
Norway	x			x			x			x			x			x			x			x		x			x
Sweden	x			x			x			x			x			x				x			x				x
Other																											
France	x			x			x			x			x			x			x			x			x		
Iceland						x			x	x			x			x			x			x	x		x		
Asia																											
Burma																			x			x					x
China	x			x			x			x			x			x			x			x		x	x	
Philippines				x					x	x			x			x			x			x			x		
Thailand																			x			x			x		
Indonesia																											x
Org. of American States																											
Argentina	x											x	x			x			x			x			x		
Bolivia	x			x			x			x			x			x			x			x			x		
Brazil	x				x		x			x			x			x			x			x			x		
Chile	x			x			x			x			x			x			x			x		x	x		
Colombia	x				x			x				x	x					x	x			x			x		
Costa Rica	x				x			x				x	x			x			x								x
Cuba	x				x			x		x					x	x			x			x			x		
Dominican Repub.	x				x		x					x	x			x					x	x			x		
Ecuador	x				x		x					x	x					x	x			x			x		
El Salvador			x		x		x					x	x			x			x			x			x		
Guatemala	x			x			x				x		x			x			x				x		x		
Haiti	x										x		x			x			x				x		x		
Honduras					x			x				x	x					x	x			x			x		
Mexico	x			x			x			x			x					x	x			x			x		
Nicaragua			x		x				x	x					x	x			x			x			x		
Panama	x			x			x			x					x	x			x			x			x		
Paraguay	x				x				x	x				x				x	x			x			x		
Peru	x				x				x	x				x				x	x				x		x		
USA	x				x				x	x				x				x	x			x			x		
Uruguay	x			x			x			x			x			x			x				x			x		
Venezuela	x			x			x			x			x			x			x			x			x		
Others																											
Ethiopia	x			x			x			x			x			x			x			x			x		
Liberia	x									x			x			x			x			x			x		

Chart II

PALESTINE PARTITION—ADMISSION OF ISRAEL—INTERNATIONALIZATION OF JERUSALEM

Partition, 2nd Sess., passed Committee 25–13–17, plenary 33–13–10; Israel admitted, 3rd Sess., Part II, 37–12–9; res. 303 (IV) on internationalization of Jerusalem adopted in *Ad Hoc* Political Committee, 35–13–11; adopted plenary 38–14–7.

	Partition Comm.			Partition Plenary			Admission of Israel			Jerusalem Comm.			Jerusalem Plenary		
	P	C	A	P	C	A	P	C	A	P	C	A	P	C	A
Commonwealth															
Australia	x			x			x			x			x		
Canada	x			x			x					x		x	
India		x			x			x				x	x		
New Zealand			x	x			x					x			x
Pakistan		x			x			x		x			x		
So. Africa	x			x			x				x			x	
UK			x			x			x		x			x	
Near & Middle East															
Arab League															
Egypt		x			x			x		x			x		
Iraq		x			x			x		x			x		
Lebanon		x			x			x		x			x		
Saudi Arabia		x			x			x		x			x		
Syria		x			x			x		x			x		
Yemen		x			x			x		x			x		
Other															
Afghanistan		x			x			x		x			x		
Greece			x		x				x	x			x		
Iran	x				x		x			x			x		
Israel											x			x	
Turkey		x			x				x		x			x	
Eastern Europe															
Byelorus. SSR	x			x			x			x			x		
Czechoslovakia	x			x			x			x			x		
Poland	x			x			x			x			x		
Ukrainian SSR	x			x			x			x			x		
USSR	x			x			x			x			x		
Yugoslavia			x			x	x				x			x	
Western Europe															
Benelux															
Belgium		x		x					x	x			x		
Luxembourg		x		x						x			x		
Netherlands		x		x			x					x			x
Scandinavia															
Denmark	x			x					x	x				x	
Norway	x			x			x				x			x	
Sweden	x			x					x		x			x	
Other															
France		x		x			x			x			x		
Iceland	x			x			x				x			x	
Asia															
Burma						x	x			x			x		
China		x				x	x			x			x		
Philippines				x			x					x	x		
Thailand		x							x			x			x
Org. of American States															
Argentina		x				x	x			x			x		
Bolivia	x			x			x			x			x		
Brazil	x			x					x	x			x		
Chile	x					x	x				x				x
Colombia		x				x	x			x			x		
Costa Rica	x			x			x			x				x	
Cuba		x			x		x			x			x		
Dominican Repub.	x			x			x					x			x
Ecuador	x			x			x			x			x		
El Salvador			x			x			x	x			x		
Guatemala	x			x			x				x			x	
Haiti		x		x			x				x		x		
Honduras		x				x	x			x					x
Mexico		x				x	x					x	x		
Nicaragua	x			x			x			x			x		
Panama	x			x			x					x			x
Paraguay				x			x			x			x		
Peru	x			x			x			x			x		
USA	x			x			x				x			x	
Uruguay	x			x			x				x			x	
Venezuela	x			x			x					x	x		
Others															
Ethiopia		x				x		x				x	x		
Liberia		x		x			x			x			x		

Chart III   ITALIAN COLONIES

Res. on Somaliland adopted by show of hands 36–17–5; first roll call on Eritrea on incorporation of all but Western Province into Ethiopia adopted 36–6–15; incorporation of Western Province into Sudan defeated 16–19–21. Third Sess., Part II, Doc. A/C. 1/466 as amended adopted First Comm. 34–16–7; Doc. A/873 rejected by plenary 14–37–7.

| | First Committee | | | | | | | | | | | | Plenary | | | | | | | | | | | | | | | | | |
| | Cyrena-ica | | | Fezzan | | | Tripoli | | | Res. as Whole | | | Cyrena-ica | | | Fezzan | | | Tripoli | | | Soma-liland | | | Eritrea | | | Res. as Whole | | |
	P	C	A	P	C	A	P	C	A	P	C	A	P	C	A	P	C	A	P	C	A	P	C	A	P	C	A	P	C	A
Commonwealth																														
Australia	x					x			x				x			x			x			x			x			x		
Canada	x			x			x						x			x			x			x			x			x		
India			x			x			x			x			x			x	x			x			x			x		
New Zealand	x			x			x			x			x			x			x			x			x			x		
Pakistan		x			x			x			x			x			x			x			x			x					
So. Africa	x			x			x			x			x			x			x			x			x			x		
UK	x			x			x			x			x			x			x			x			x			x		
Near & Middle East																														
Arab League																														
Egypt		x			x			x			x			x			x			x			x						x		
Iraq		x			x			x			x			x			x			x			x						x		
Lebanon		x			x			x			x			x			x			x			x	x					x		
Saudi Arabia		x			x			x			x			x			x			x			x		x				x		
Syria		x			x			x			x			x			x			x			x					x	x		
Yemen		x			x			x			x			x			x			x			x					x	x		
Other																														
Afghanistan															x															
Greece	x			x			x			x			x			x			x			x			x			x		
Iran															x			x			x			x	x					x
Israel		x				x			x			x			x			x			x			x			x			x		
Turkey	x				x			x			x		x					x			x	x			x			x			
Eastern Europe																														
Byelorus. SSR		x			x			x			x			x			x			x			x			x			x		
Czechoslovakia		x			x			x			x			x			x			x			x			x			x		
Poland		x			x			x			x			x			x			x			x			x			x		
Ukrainian SSR		x			x			x			x			x			x			x			x			x			x		
USSR		x			x			x			x			x			x			x			x			x			x		
Yugoslavia		x			x			x			x			x			x			x			x			x			x		
Western Europe																														
Benelux																														
Belgium	x			x			x			x			x			x			x			x								x
Luxembourg	x			x			x			x			x			x			x			x						x		
Netherlands	x			x			x			x			x			x			x			x			x					
Scandinavia																														
Denmark	x			x			x			x			x			x			x			x			x					
Norway	x			x			x			x			x			x			x			x			x					
Sweden			x			x			x			x			x			x			x			x			x			x
Other																														
France	x			x			x			x			x			x			x			x			x			x		
Iceland	x			x			x			x			x			x			x			x			x			x		
Asia																														
Burma		x		x			x			x			x			x			x			x			x			x		
China			x			x			x			x			x			x			x			x			x			x
Indonesia																														
Philippines			x	x			x			x			x			x			x			x			x			x		
Thailand	x					x			x			x	x					x			x	x			x			x		
Org. of American States																														
Argentina	x			x			x			x			x			x			x			x			x			x		
Bolivia	x			x			x			x			x			x			x			x			x			x		
Brazil	x			x			x			x			x			x			x			x			x			x		
Chile	x			x			x			x			x			x			x			x			x			x		
Colombia	x			x			x			x			x			x			x			x			x			x		
Costa Rica	x			x			x			x			x			x			x			x			x			x		
Cuba	x			x			x			x			x			x			x			x			x			x		
Dominican Repub.	x			x			x			x			x			x			x			x			x			x		
Ecuador	x			x			x			x			x			x			x			x			x			x		
El Salvador			x	x			x			x			x			x			x			x			x			x		
Guatemala		x		x			x			x			x			x			x			x			x			x		
Haiti		x				x			x			x		x			x				x			x			x		x		
Honduras	x			x			x			x			x			x			x			x			x					
Mexico	x			x			x			x			x			x			x			x			x			x		x
Nicaragua	x			x			x			x			x			x			x			x			x			x		
Panama	x			x			x			x			x			x			x			x			x			x		
Paraguay	x			x			x			x			x			x			x			x			x			x		
Peru	x			x			x			x			x			x			x			x			x			x		
USA	x			x			x			x			x			x			x			x			x		x			
Uruguay	x			x			x			x			x			x			x			x					x	x		
Venezuela	x			x			x			x			x			x			x			x					x	x		
Others																														
Ethiopia	x			x					x	x			x			x						x			x			x		
Liberia	x					x						x	x			x					x	x			x			x		

Chart IV   Non-Self-Governing Territories

Fourth Sess.: Czech amendment to make the Special Committee a permanent subsidiary organ rejected by 4th Comm. 13–23–12; res. to re-create the Special Committee for 3 years adopted 4th Comm. 41–4–2; res. on Territories to which Chapter XI of the Charter Applies adopted 4th Comm. 30–10–7; plenary 30–12–10.

South West Africa

Res. 141 (II) adopted 41–10–4; Para. of res. 227 (III) reiterating previous res. adopted 32–14–5; 4th Sess. USSR draft res. condemning So. Africa for Charter Violation rejected by 4th Comm. 12–17–17; 4th Sess. reiteration of previous res. adopted by plenary 33–9–10; 4th Sess. res. calling for Advisory Opinion adopted by 4th Comm. 30–7–9.

	Czech. Amend. Perm. Organ (Comm.)			Re-estab. Sp. Comm. (Comm.)			Terr. to Which Chapt. XI of Charter Applies — Comm.			Plenary			2nd Sess. Res. 141			3rd Sess. Para. 2 Res. 227			Rus. Draft			Re-it. Prev. Res.			Ad. Op.		
	P	C	A	P	C	A	P	C	A	P	C	A	P	C	A	P	C	A	P	C	A	P	C	A	P	C	A
Commonwealth																											
Australia		x			x			x			x			x			x			x			x			x	
Canada		x			x			x			x			x			x			x			x			x	
India			x	x			x			x			x			x				x				x			x
New Zealand		x				x	x			x			x					x		x		x			x		
Pakistan	x			x			x			x			x			x				x		x					x
So. Africa		x				x	x			x			x				x			x			x		x		
UK		x			x			x			x		x				x		x				x				x
Near & Middle East																											
Arab League																											
Egypt	x				x		x			x			x			x						x			x		
Iraq			x		x		x			x			x							x		x			x		
Lebanon			x		x		x			x			x							x		x			x		
Saudi Arabia		x			x		x			x			x							x		x			x		
Syria		x			x		x			x			x			x			x			x			x		
Yemen		x			x		x			x			x			x				x		x			x		
Other																											
Afghanistan			x	x			x			x			x			x			x			x			x		
Greece	x					x		x			x		x			x				x		x			x		
Iran		x		x			x			x			x			x				x		x		x			
Israel			x	x			x			x			x			x				x		x			x		
Turkey									x				x			x			x			x			x		
Eastern Europe																											
Byelorus SSR	x			x			x			x			x			x			x			x				
Czechoslovakia	x			x			x			x			x			x			x			x				x
Poland	x			x			x			x			x			x			x			x				x
Ukrainian SSR	x			x			x			x			x			x			x			x				x
USSR	x			x			x			x			x			x			x			x				x
Yugoslavia	x			x			x			x			x			x			x			x				x
Western Europe																											
Benelux																											
Belgium	x				x		x				x		x				x		x				x			x
Luxembourg											x		x				x		x				x				
Netherlands	x			x			x				x		x				x		x				x		x		
Scandinavia																											
Denmark	x			x					x				x			x			x			x			x		
Norway	x			x			x			x			x			x			x			x			x		
Sweden	x			x			x			x			x			x			x			x			x		
Other																											
France	x				x		x			x			x			x			x			x			x		
Iceland									x	x			x			x			x			x			x		
Asia																											
Burma							x			x			x			x			x								
China	x			x			x			x			x			x				x		x			x		
Indonesia																											
Philippines	x			x			x			x			x			x				x		x			x		
Thailand	x			x			x			x			x			x				x		x			x		
Org. of American States																											
Argentina		x		x					x	x			x			x			x				x		x		
Bolivia									x	x			x			x			x				x				
Brazil	x			x			x			x			x			x				x		x			x		
Chile	x				x		x				x	x			x				x		x		x		x		
Colombia		x		x			x			x			x			x			x		x		x		
Costa Rica												x		x				x								
Cuba	x			x			x			x			x			x		x			x			x		
Dominican Repub.		x		x			x			x			x		x			x			x			x		
Ecuador		x							x			x		x			x		x			x			x		
El Salvador							x			x			x			x		x			x			x		
Guatemala	x			x			x			x			x		x				x		x			x		
Haiti	x			x			x			x			x			x		x			x			x		
Honduras										x			x				x		x			x			x		
Mexico	x			x			x			x			x				x		x		x		x		
Nicaragua												x	x			x			x					x		
Panama													x			x											
Paraguay													x		x												
Peru	x			x								x	x			x			x			x				
USA	x			x						x			x			x			x			x					x
Uruguay			x	x			x			x			x			x			x		x			x			x
Venezuela			x	x			x			x			x			x			x			x		x		
Others																											
Ethiopia	x			x			x			x			x				x										
Liberia			x	x			x			x			x			x		x			x			x		

91

Chart V · EAST-WEST ISSUES

Res. giving Interim Committee indefinite tenure (4th Sess.) passed Ad Hoc Political Committee 41–6–6; final part of res. 292 (IV) on "Threats to the . . . independence of China" passed 29–7–20; Russian draft res. on condemnation of war (4th Sess.) defeated in Committee 5–52–2 (para. 1); res. on Essentials of Peace (4th Sess.) adopted 53–5–1; Eight Power res. on Korea (5th Sess.) adopted 47–5–8; res. on United Action for Peace (5th Sess.) adopted as a whole in plenary 52–5–2.

	Interim Comm. P	C	A	China P	C	A	Condemn. of War (Para. 1) P	C	A	Essentials of Peace P	C	A	Korea P	C	A	Uniting for Peace (Plenary) P	C	A
Commonwealth																		
Australia	x					x	x			x			x			x		
Canada	x					x	x			x				x				
India		x				x	x			x								x
New Zealand	x			x			x			x			x			x		
Pakistan		x		x			x			x			x			x		
So. Africa	x				x		x			x			x			x		
UK	x					x	x			x			x			x		
Near & Middle East																		
Arab League																		
Egypt	x			x			x			x					x	x		
Iraq	x						x			x				x		x		
Lebanon	x			x			x			x				x				
Saudi Arabia	x			x			x			x				x				
Syria	x					x				x				x		x		
Yemen	x					x			x	x						x		
Other																		
Afghanistan		x				x	x			x			x			x		
Greece				x			x			x			x			x		
Iran	x			x			x			x			x			x		
Israel		x				x	x			x			x			x		
Turkey	x			x			x			x			x			x		
Eastern Europe																		
Byelorus. SSR		x			x		x				x			x			x	
Czechoslovakia		x			x		x				x			x			x	
Poland		x			x		x				x			x			x	
Ukrainian SSR		x			x		x				x			x			x	
USSR		x			x		x				x			x			x	
Yugoslavia			x		x				x			x		x		x		
Western Europe																		
Benelux																		
Belgium	x			x			x			x			x			x		
Luxembourg	x			x			x			x			x			x		
Netherlands	x					x	x			x			x			x		
Scandinavia																		
Denmark	x					x	x			x			x			x		
Norway	x					x	x			x			x			x		
Sweden	x					x	x			x			x			x		
Other																		
France	x			x			x			x			x			x		
Iceland	x						x			x			x			x		
Asia																		
Burma																		
Burma			x	x			x			x			x			x		
China	x			x			x			x			x				x	
Indonesia																		
Philippines	x					x	x			x			x			x		
Thailand	x					x	x			x			x			x		
Org. of American States																		x
Argentina	x			x			x			x			x			x		
Bolivia	x			x			x			x			x			x		
Brazil	x					x	x			x			x			x		
Chile	x			x			x			x			x			x		
Colombia		x		x			x			x			x			x		
Costa Rica				x			x			x			x			x		
Cuba	x			x			x			x			x			x		
Dominican Repub.				x			x			x			x			x		
Ecuador	x			x			x			x			x			x		
El Salvador	x			x			x			x			x			x		
Guatemala							x			x			x			x		
Haiti	x			x			x			x			x			x		
Honduras	x			x			x			x			x			x		
Mexico	x					x	x			x			x			x		
Nicaragua	x			x			x			x			x			x		
Panama	x			x			x			x			x			x		
Paraguay	x			x			x			x			x			x		
Peru	x			x			x			x			x			x		
USA	x			x			x			x			x			x		
Uruguay	x					x	x			x			x			x		
Venezuela						x	x			x			x			x		
Others																		
Ethiopia						x	x			x			x			x		
Liberia							x			x			x			x		

Chart VI

	Trusteeship Agreements 1st Sess.			South West Africa: 2nd Sess.			South West Africa: 3rd Sess.			South West Africa: 4th Sess. Reiteration Prev. Res.			Sp. Com. on Non-Self-Gov. Terr., 4th Sess.		
	P	C	A	P	C	A	P	C	A	P	C	A	P	C	A
Brussels Treaty Powers															
Belgium		x			x			x			x			x	
France		x		x				x			x			x	
Luxembourg		x		x				x			x				
Netherlands		x		x				x			x		x		
UK		x			x			x			x			x	
Other Members Council of Europe															
Denmark		x		x			x			x			x		
Greece		x			x			x			x				x
Iceland		x		x				x							
Norway		x		x			x				x		x		
Sweden		x		x			x				x		x		
Turkey		x			x			x		x			x		
Asiatic & Southwest Pacific Powers															
Australia		x			x			x				x	x		
Burma							x			x					
China		x		x			x			x			x		
India			x	x			x			x			x		
Indonesia															
New Zealand		x				x			x			x			x
Pakistan				x			x			x			x		
Philippines			x	x			x			x			x		
Thailand				x			x			x			x		
Big Five															
China		x		x			x			x			x		
France		x		x				x			x			x	
USSR	x			x			x			x			x		
UK		x			x			x				x		x	
USA		x		x			x				x		x		

	Palestine Partition 2nd Sess.			Admission of Israel 3rd Sess., Pt. II			Internat. of Jerusalem 4th Sess.			Italian Colonies: 3rd Sess. Comm., Res. as Whole			Italian Colonies: 3rd Sess. Plenary Res. as Whole		
	P	C	A	P	C	A	P	C	A	P	C	A	P	C	A
Brussels Treaty Powers															
Belgium	x					x	x			x					x
France	x			x			x							x	
Luxembourg	x			x			x			x					x
Netherlands	x			x					x	x			x		
UK			x			x		x		x			x		
Other Members Council of Europe															
Denmark	x					x		x		x			x		
Greece		x				x	x			x					x
Iceland	x			x				x		x			x		
Norway	x			x				x		x			x		
Sweden	x					x		x				x			x
Turkey		x				x		x				x	x		
Asiatic & Southwest Pacific Powers															
Australia	x			x			x			x			x		
Burma					x		x				x			x	
China			x	x			x					x			x
India		x			x		x				x			x	
Indonesia															
New Zealand	x			x					x	x			x		
Pakistan		x			x		x				x			x	
Philippines	x			x			x				x			x	
Thailand						x			x			x			x
Big Five															
China			x	x			x					x			x
France	x			x			x			x				x	
USSR	x			x			x				x			x	
UK			x			x		x		x			x		
USA	x			x				x		x			x		

	Franco-Spain: 1st Sess. Pt. I			Franco-Spain: 1st Sess. Pt. II Plenary			Franco-Spain: 2nd Sess. Plenary			Franco-Spain: 3rd Sess. Plenary			Spanish as Working Language 3rd Sess., Pt. I		
	P	C	A	P	C	A	P	C	A	P	C	A	P	C	A
Brussels Treaty Powers															
Belgium	x			x			x					x		x	
France	x			x			x							x	
Luxembourg	x			x			x					x		x	
Netherlands	x					x		x				x		x	
UK	x			x			x					x		x	
Other Members Council of Europe															
Denmark	x			x			x					x		x	
Greece	x					x		x		x			x		
Iceland				x			x			x				x	
Norway	x			x			x				x			x	
Sweden				x			x					x		x	
Turkey	x					x		x		x			x		
Asiatic & Southwest Pacific Powers															
Australia	x			x				x			x			x	
Burma												x			
China	x			x								x		x	
India	x			x			x				x				x
Indonesia															
New Zealand	x			x			x				x			x	
Pakistan									x	x					x
Philippines				x				x		x			x		
Thailand				x						x					x
Big Five															
China	x			x			x					x			
France	x			x			x					x			
USSR	x			x			x				x				
UK	x			x			x					x			
USA	x			x				x				x			

	China 4th Sess.			Interim Comm. 4th Sess.			Condemnation of War 4th Sess.			Essentials of Peace 4th Sess.			Korea 5th Sess.		
	P	C	A	P	C	A	P	C	A	P	C	A	P	C	A
Brussels Treaty Powers															
Belgium	x			x				x		x			x		
France	x			x				x		x			x		
Luxembourg	x			x				x		x			x		
Netherlands			x	x				x		x			x		
UK			x	x				x		x			x		
Other Members Council of Europe															
Denmark			x	x				x		x			x		
Greece	x							x		x			x		
Iceland				x				x		x			x		
Norway			x	x				x		x			x		
Sweden			x	x				x		x			x		
Turkey	x			x				x		x			x		
Asiatic & Southwest Pacific Powers															
Australia			x	x				x		x			x		
Burma			x			x		x		x			x		
China	x			x				x		x			x		
India			x			x		x		x					x
Indonesia															
New Zealand	x			x				x		x			x		
Pakistan	x				x			x		x			x		
Philippines			x	x				x		x			x		
Thailand			x	x				x		x			x		
Big Five															
China	x			x				x		x			x		
France	x			x				x		x			x		
USSR		x			x		x				x			x	
UK			x	x				x		x			x		
USA	x			x				x		x			x		

graphs relating to Tripoli and Somaliland), was defeated 14–37–7,[37] on a roll call in which Haiti voted for the resolution, eighteen Latin American countries opposed it, and Nicaragua abstained.

Bloc voting was of the greatest significance in this case. Had Haiti voted with the rest of the Latin Americans on Tripoli, the resolution would have had a good chance of passage (depending upon what happened to the Somaliland provision in the light of that fact). Latin America, the United States and western Europe were defeated on this issue. The victors, however, were two other blocs (Arab League and Soviet bloc), which were able to gain the support of five additional states to prevent the resolution from passing and to hold the question over for the fourth session.

Trusteeship Agreements. In dependent areas cases, one might expect to find a somewhat different alignment than in other types of cases, and this seems to be substantiated by the facts. During the first session, part II, the USSR, on the ground that the agreements presented by the United Kingdom, France, Belgium, Australia and New Zealand had been drafted without consulting "the powers directly concerned," submitted a draft resolution rejecting the agreements and recommending that new ones be substituted. The Soviet bloc was alone in its support of this resolution; it was opposed by the other members voting except India, Egypt, Iraq, Saudi Arabia, Iran, Philippines, Colombia, Ecuador, Guatemala, Ethiopia and Liberia, which abstained.[38] While the Commonwealth, Arab League and Latin America were all divided on this resolution, and while those disapproving of the agreements abstained rather than hold up the establishment of the Trusteeship Council, the beginnings of a new alignment were manifest: colonial powers and their sympathizers against doctrinaire anti-imperialists and countries which, themselves formerly subject to imperialism, tended in principle to take the part of the dependent areas and to support a liberal interpretation of the Charter powers of the Assembly in that regard.

South West Africa. The refusal of the government of the Union of South Africa to place South West Africa under trusteeship has called forth a number of resolutions which are interesting not only because they offer a means of studying bloc voting on a trusteeship issue, but also because it is a case where the members of the Commonwealth might be expected to vote together (if ever), since the interest of one of its members is directly involved.

[37] *Ibid.,* p. 595–596.   [38] *Ibid.* (1st session, 2d part), p. 1286.

The second session reiterated the invitation extended in Resolution 65 (I) to place South West Africa under trusteeship. The vote on Resolution 141 (II) was complicated by a marked difference of view as to whether South Africa had a legal, purely moral, or no obligation at all, to submit an agreement. It was this factor, rather than regional interest, which was determining in the final vote, in which only the Soviet bloc, the Asiatic states, and the Arab League were solid (Chart IV). The Commonwealth was divided, with India and Pakistan in favor, Australia, Canada, South Africa and the United Kingdom opposed, and New Zealand abstaining. Latin America was divided, as were also the colonial states and administering authorities. The final vote was overwhelmingly in favor of the resolution (41–10–4).[39]

The crucial vote at the third session was on the second paragraph of Resolution 227, in which the Assembly reiterated its earlier recommendations. This paragraph was carried 32–14–5[40] by a vote in which the Commonwealth was divided as before, the Soviet bloc, the Asiatic states and Scandinavia were solidly in favor and Benelux solidly in opposition. The vote on the resolution as a whole was carried without a roll call, 43–1–5. (A number of states which had opposed the disputed paragraph voted for the resolution as a whole, doubtless because of its appeal to South Africa to continue to administer South West Africa in the spirit of the mandate and to continue to supply information to the Trusteeship Council.)

Opposition to South Africa's announced course of sending no further reports to the Trusteeship Council and of developing a still closer union between South Africa and the mandate took the form of three draft resolutions submitted to the fourth session. The most radical was that of the USSR, which accused South Africa of violating the Charter.[41] This draft resolution was voted down 12–17–17 by the fourth committee (Chart IV), in a vote in which only the Soviet bloc, western Europe and Asia were solid, and the Commonwealth, Latin America and the Arab League were divided.[42] A number of states indicated their sympathy with the Soviet evaluation of South Africa's conduct by abstaining on the resolution, although they were unwilling to support it.

The more moderate Indian draft resolution, adopted as Resolution 337 by a vote of 33–9–10, reiterated the previous resolutions and requested South Africa to continue to report to the Trusteeship Council.[43] The third draft resolution requested an advisory opinion of the International Court

[39] Ibid. (2d session), p. 650–651.
[40] Ibid. (3d session, 1st part), p. 592.
[41] Document A/C.4/L.61.

[42] General Assembly, Official Records . . . Fourth Committee (4th session), p. 272.
[43] Ibid., Official Records (4th session), p. 536.

of Justice. Approved by a roll call vote of the fourth committee 30–7–9, this draft became Resolution 338 without a roll call by the plenary session, which passed it 40–7–4.⁴⁴ The Commonwealth was divided on Resolutions 337 and 338 between Asiatic and non-Asiatic members. The Arab League and the Soviet bloc were solid on both (Yugoslavia abstained on Resolution 338). Western Europe was nearly solid (with the notable exception of the United Kingdom, which abstained on both resolutions), and Asia was entirely so. Latin America was fairly solid, but a number of states either abstained or did not vote at all.

Considered as a whole, the important thing about these votes seems to be less the degree of solidarity of the individual blocs, but the combinations of votes which passed the resolutions. And here it is apparent that the alignment is essentially one of the proponents of the widest possible extension of the principle of international accountability against states which take a more limited view of what can or should be achieved in this direction. As far as the Commonwealth is concerned, this has resulted in India and Pakistan (newly independent countries), consistently calling South Africa to account, while Australia, Canada, New Zealand and the United Kingdom followed a more conservative course.

Non-Self-Governing Territories. The issue of the extension of the principle of international accountability was similarly raised in three of the resolutions of the fourth session on non-self-governing territories. The first involved the question of reporting on political developments in these territories (pressed by the USSR, India, China, Brazil, etc. and opposed by the United Kingdom, France, Belgium, New Zealand and Australia). The final text of Resolution 327, which expresses the hope that political information will be submitted, was adopted without a roll call vote, 33–9–11.⁴⁵ The second related to the future status of the special committee on non-self-governing territories. In the fourth committee, the significant votes on this question were on an Indian draft resolution which called for the re-creation of the special committee for three years, and a Czech amendment which would have made it a permanent "subsidiary Organ" of the United Nations. The Czech amendment was rejected 13–23–12,⁴⁶ (see Chart V) in a vote on which only the Soviet bloc and western Europe were solid. The vote on the Indian draft resolution was 41–4–2, with only Belgium, France, South Africa and the United Kingdom opposed, and Greece and New Zealand abstaining.⁴⁷ While the line-up here was not strictly one of colonial against non-colonial powers (the

⁴⁴ *Ibid.*, p. 537; *ibid., Official Records* . . . *Fourth Committee* (4th session), p. 282.
⁴⁵ *Ibid., Official Records* (4th session), p. 461.
⁴⁶ *Ibid., Official Records* . . . *Fourth Committee* (4th session), p. 170.
⁴⁷ *Ibid.*, p. 171.

United States, Netherlands and Denmark, for example, were willing to accept the compromise), that factor appears to have been of greater importance than regional considerations. There was no roll call in the plenary session; Resolution 332 was adopted by a vote of 44–5–4.[48] The third draft resolution, introduced by Egypt, was designed to give the Assembly a voice in determining the point at which an obligation to report on former non-self-governing territories should cease to exist. Resolution 334 (Territories to Which Chapter XI of the Charter Applies) was adopted by the fourth committee 30–10–7, and by the plenary session 30–12–10.[49] The alignment here was again basically one of colonial powers and administering authorities against the rest, although the United States and Denmark, less antagonistic to the principle of international control than other colonial powers, abstained. These three cases form part of an effort of anti-colonial powers (including the Soviet bloc) to increase the United Nations control over non-self-governing territories. It was clearly the feeling of the United Kingdom, France and Belgium, in particular, that these powers were going beyond the bounds of the Charter, and were attempting to interfere with matters strictly within the domestic jurisdiction of the metropoles. The United Kingdom, France and Belgium firmly resisted what they considered an attempt to make virtual trusteeships of the non-self-governing territories.[50]

Interim Committee. Despite the absence of roll call votes, it is clear that the negative votes on Resolution 111 (II) (establishing the Interim Committee) and Resolution 195 (III) (re-establishing it for a further year), were cast by the Soviet bloc. There is not sufficient evidence to determine the identity of the six abstainers on the first resolution, or the single abstainer on the second. The vote in the plenary session on Resolution 295 (IV) (giving the Interim Committee indefinite tenure) was also taken without a roll call, and resulted in a 45–5–4 decision.[51] The roll call in the *Ad Hoc* Political Committee (Chart V), however, indicates the probable distribution of votes. In that committee, the draft resolution was opposed by five communist states and Pakistan; the abstainers were Afghanistan, Burma, Colombia, India, Israel and Yugoslavia.[52]

On the east-west issue, it should be noted that the Arab League made no effort to adopt a neutral attitude, although other middle eastern states did so. The Arab League, like many other middle and smaller powers, was more interested in increasing the power of the Assembly (as it had

[48] *Ibid., Official Records* (4th session), p. 461.
[49] *Ibid.,* p. 461; *ibid., Official Records . . . Fourth Committee* (4th session), p. 188.
[50] *Ibid., Official Records* (4th session), p. 453–458.
[51] *Ibid.,* p. 312.
[52] Document A/1049, p. 2.

hoped to do from San Francisco on down), than it was in avoiding the appearance of supporting the west at the expense of the east.

Threats to the Political Independence and Territorial Integrity of China. Action on Chinese allegations against the USSR at the fourth session took the form of the adoption of Resolution 292. The first part of the draft resolution, which authorized the Interim Committee to study the question and report its recommendations to the fifth session, was passed without a roll call, 31–5–16. The latter part of the draft resolution, which authorized the Interim Committee alternatively to report to the Security Council, passed on a roll call vote, 29–7–20.[53] In this roll call (Chart V), the negative votes were cast by the Soviet bloc and South Africa, while a number of Commonwealth, middle east, Latin American, western European and Asiatic powers abstained. Bloc lines were without significance; neither were all of the western powers lined up against the communist states. A number of the western states refused to support the resolution, but indicated their dissent by abstention rather than a negative vote.

Condemnation of War, Essentials of Peace. At the fourth session, before considering a draft resolution on Essentials of Peace submitted by the United States and the United Kingdom, the first committee considered a Soviet draft resolution,[54] paragraph 1 of which condemned the United States and the United Kingdom for preparing a new war. The committee vote on this paragraph (Chart V) reflected a distinct east-west alignment, with only the five east bloc members in good standing voting in favor, 52 states opposed, and Yemen and Yugoslavia abstaining.[55] The draft resolution on Essentials of Peace (Resolution 290), in contrast, was adopted by a roll call vote of 53–5–1 by the first committee, after a paragraph-by-paragraph vote.[56] The non-communist states comprised the 53 proponents; Yugoslavia was the sole abstainer. The vote in the plenary session duplicated that of the first committee.[57]

Korea. The most important vote on Korea at the fifth session was on the draft resolution submitted by the United Kingdom, Australia, the Philippines, Brazil, Pakistan, the Netherlands, Norway and Cuba—a cross-section of all areas but eastern Europe and the middle east. This resolution, calling for the establishment under the United Nations supervision of a united, stable, independent and democratic Korea, and containing implicit authorization for the crossing of the 38th parallel by the United

[53] General Assembly, *Official Records* (4th session), p. 571.
[54] Document A/996.
[55] Document A/1150, paragraph 5 (*a*) (i).

[56] *Ibid.*, paragraph 5 (*b*) (xvi).
[57] General Assembly, *Official Records* (4th session), p. 438.

Nations forces, was adopted in the first committee and in the plenary session by votes of 47–5–8 (Chart V). The negative votes on both occasions were those of the Soviet bloc, except Yugoslavia, which abstained. Other abstainers in committee were India, Egypt, Lebanon, Syria, Afghanistan and Yemen. In the final vote, Indonesia joined the abstainers. The Soviet draft resolution calling for withdrawal of the United Nations' troops, to be followed by elections organized by the existing north and south Korean governments, preceded the vote on the eight-power resolution, and was defeated in the first committee 5–46–8, with Indonesia not voting.[38] The sole proponents of the draft resolution were the Soviet bloc, minus Yugoslavia; the abstentions comprised the Arab League (minus Iraq, which voted against the resolution), Afghanistan, India and Yugoslavia.

On this clear-cut issue, the tendency of the Arab League states, certain other middle eastern powers, and India, to retain a neutral position is again manifest. The defection of Iraq from the Arab League group does not alter the general tendency—particularly since Iraq is regarded by other members of the League as too closely aligned with Britain for comfort.

United Action for Peace. Again at the fifth session, the most important committee vote on the draft resolution sponsored by the United States, Canada, France, Philippines, Turkey, United Kingdom and Uruguay, and opening the way for effective Assembly action in the event of future Security Council paralysis, was on the paragraph which asked the Members to ear-mark national contingents for use on Assembly recommendation. This paragraph was adopted by a vote of 45–5–6, on which the Soviet bloc (except Yugoslavia) voted against, and India, Indonesia, Sweden, Argentina, Yemen and Iceland abstained. The resolution as a whole was adopted at the plenary session by a vote of 52–5–2,[39] in which Yugoslavia voted with the majority, the Soviet bloc voted con, and India and Argentina abstained. While this is again primarily an east-west issue, it is noteworthy that the Arab League joined the majority in favor of the resolution. As in the resolution on the Interim Committee at the fourth session, the League appeared to be motivated more by a desire to make the Assembly effective than to preserve neutrality as between east and west. The contrast between its position and that of India is significant.

III

From the above cases, three things are clear at a glance. First, the unanimity of the great powers does not hold. Second, the Commonwealth

[38] *New York Times*, October 5, 1950.   [39] *Ibid.*, November 4, 1950.

almost never votes as a unit. Whatever prior consultation may take place on substantive issues, it does not result in a general pattern of Commonwealth solidarity. India and Pakistan appear to have a distinct tendency to vote with the Arab League on issues on which the latter are solid—particularly on trusteeship or non-self-governing territories questions, or on other questions of particular interest to the middle east. Both Commonwealth countries are evidently anxious to retain a position of neutrality on east-west issues. This has, of course, been especially evident with respect to India, which abstained on the resolutions on Korea and United Action for Peace at the fifth session. Both appear to be motivated more by conviction than political opportunism, and neither has been deterred from standing by its anti-imperialist convictions by the fact that its vote happened to coincide with those of the Soviet bloc.

Third, the solidarity of the Soviet bloc is striking. Before Poland and Czechoslovakia were as fully dominated by Moscow as they are today, vestiges of independence and dissent were occasionally manifest, but in all of the major votes on the cases studied, these two states were on the same side as the USSR, Byelorussia and the Ukraine.[60] Yugoslavia, which consistently voted with this group until the Stalin-Tito rift, abstained on the votes on the partition of Palestine in the second session, on a number of votes at the fourth session, and on the Korean resolution at the fifth session. It has rarely gone so far as to oppose the group outright, although it did so on the internationalization of Jerusalem and on the committee vote on United Action for Peace (fifth session). In view of the unfriendly relations between Yugoslavia and the Cominform, there is some question whether the former should be considered a member of the Soviet bloc. Nevertheless, Yugoslavia's character as a communist state appears in general to determine its conduct in the assembly (see, for example, its vote on the resolutions on Franco Spain at the fifth session).

The Arab League states caucus on important issues before the Assembly, and agree to follow a common policy on issues regarded as vital to the group (as Palestine, the admission of Israel, the internationalization of Jerusalem, the Italian colonies). In addition, the group generally votes as a unit on most, but not all, resolutions having to do with dependent areas. Caucus decisions are evidently not binding on questions of more remote concern, as Korea and China. It is perhaps of interest that disagreement among these states appears to be indicated more by absten-

[60] In several cases of minor amendments at the fourth session, the Soviet bloc did not vote as a unit. In one such case, in the fourth committee, the bulk of the Soviet bloc voted in favor, while Poland abstained. In another, Bye-lorussia, Czechoslovakia, the Ukrainian SSR and Yugoslavia voted in favor, and Poland and the USSR abstained. (General Assembly, *Official Record . . . Fourth Committee* [4th session], p. 240–241).

tion than by a for or against division. There would seem to be a desire on the part of these states (shared by India, Pakistan, and perhaps Burma) to remain neutral on what are regarded as east-west questions. This was demonstrated, for example, by four of the six countries of the League in the Korean case. The fact that the League voted against the Soviet draft resolution on Condemnation of War, and in favor of the rather mild resolution on Essentials of Peace, does not invalidate this point. The votes in favor of indefinite tenure for the Interim Committee and on the Resolution on United Action for Peace, indicate a desire to increase the powers of the Assembly at the expense of the Security Council rather than to align the group with the west as opposed to the east.

Other states of the middle east fail to conform to a fixed pattern. It may probably safely be said that more of them generally tend to vote on the same side as the Arab League than otherwise.

Western Europe does not approach the solidarity demonstrated by eastern Europe. On the partition of Palestine, the approval of trusteeship agreements, strictly east-west issues, and Spanish as a working language, there was complete solidarity. There was considerable solidarity ·on certain votes on South West Africa, and on most of the votes on the Italian colonies. On the other hand, there was a good deal of division on the final vote on the Italian colonies at the third session, on the internationalization of Jerusalem, on certain votes on South West Africa, and on the future status of the special committee on non-self-governing territories. There is no evidence of prior consultation comparable to that of the Arab League and the Latin American states.

The Benelux states vote together on a number of issues, including most votes on dependent areas, non-self-governing territories issues, and east-west questions, but they also split on a number of votes. It is perhaps of interest that Luxembourg does not always vote with Belgium. The Scandinavian states vote together on a larger number of issues than does Benelux, but also sometimes differ on important questions. It should be noted that in the cases studied, with few exceptions, dissent was indicated by abstention rather than an opposed vote. In instances in which the three Scandinavian states were not unanimous, Iceland sometimes voted with Denmark, and sometimes with Norway or Sweden.

It is too early to attempt to establish a pattern of voting for Brussels Treaty powers or members of the Council of Europe. Chart VI gives some indication of the positions of these powers in the cases studied. Certainly these states tend to vote together on east-west issues, but considerable divergence is to be found on other votes.

There does not appear to be a consistent voting bloc in the southwest

Pacific or Asiatic area, as is illustrated in Chart VI. A higher degree of solidarity would seem to have been reached on some east-west issues and dependent areas cases than on other questions.

An analysis of voting on the part of the twenty-one American republics that comprise the Organization of American States indicates that in the majority of cases studied, two-thirds or more of the states voting were in the same camp. This held for the resolution on trusteeship agreements at the first session, part II, the proposal at the fourth session to re-establish the special committee on non-self-governing territories, all of the votes on the Italian colonies at the third session, the votes on South West Africa, the votes on partition and the admission of Israel, the resolutions on Franco Spain at the first session, part I and the fifth session, the vote on Spanish as a working language, and the votes on the independence and territorial integrity of China, the re-establishment of the Interim Committee, the Condemnation of War and the Essentials of Peace at the fourth session, and Korea and United Action for Peace at the fifth session. In only four of the votes tabulated, however, were all of the Latin American states voting to be found in the same column; in six or seven more votes, dissent from the main Latin American position was indicated by abstention rather than an opposed vote. On the other hand, there was a rather wide-open split in the following cases: the establishment of a permanent organ on non-self-governing territories (3–5–6); the Soviet draft resolution on South West Africa at the fourth session (4–5–7); the internationalization of Jerusalem (12–5–4 and 13–4–4), and most of the votes on Franco Spain. This would seem to indicate that despite a strong tendency to caucus, the Latin Americans do not always consider themselves bound by a caucus majority. The Latin American nations do not always stand together on dependent areas cases; they do tend to unite in support of greater authority for the General Assembly (Interim Committee and United Action for Peace). They are not always unanimous on east-west issues, but there is not the same tendency to maintain neutrality on these questions as the Arab League displays.

On the question of leadership within the various groups, several things emerge. The United Kingdom clearly does not control the Commonwealth votes. The USSR, in contrast, is the undisputed leader of the orthodox communist group. Within the Arab League, Egypt exercises a good deal of influence, but its leadership is not always followed by the other members (see, for example, its isolated position on the proposal to establish a permanent organ on non-self-governing territories at the fourth session, and on the proposal at the first session, part II, to break diplomatic relations with Franco Spain). The question of the influence of the most powerful member does not arise in connection with Benelux or Scandinavia. It is, however, of very great importance with respect to the members of OAS. The number of Latin American delegations voting with the United States in the cases studied ranges from zero (on Spanish as a working language and the reiteration of the previous resolution on South West Africa at the fourth session) to 19 or 20 (on Condemnation of War, Essentials of Peace, United Action for Peace). Although the United States delegation includes a full complement of liaison officers, it does not control, or seek to control, the Latin American votes on all issues. Indeed, it occasionally follows a strong Latin-American consensus as a matter of policy. The best available criterion of the actual number that the United States can control is evidently the result in cases where the United States has used pressure to influence the decision. One such case was that of the partition of Palestine, and there the United States, despite all its efforts, was able to gain the support of only thirteen nations on the final ballot. On strictly east-west issues, of course, the western position is normally supported by a larger number of Latin American states. In dependent areas cases, the influence of the United States is apt to be somewhat less than in other cases. The support which the United States received from Latin America is enough, in any case, to make the USSR, with its four sure supporters, feel at a considerable disadvantage.

The rather general impression that the Arab League and Latin American votes wag the dog is not entirely substantiated by the facts. Unquestionably, their combined total of 26 votes gives them the possibility of preventing decisions on which a two-thirds vote is required (including elections to the Security, Economic and Social, and Trusteeship councils). Actual experience indicates, however, that while these blocs tend to remain solid in the electoral process, they do so to a much less degree on substantive issues. Where the blocs are solid, and in agreement, they are in a position to exercise an influence out of proportion to their combined populations. While the combination has been highly influential in elections, in none of the substantive cases studied was it the determining factor. In the Italian colonies case, the two groups were on opposite sides of the fence, and action at the third session was defeated by a combination which did not include a solid Latin American bloc. On the vote to re-establish the special committee on non-self-governing territories, the two blocs were on the same side, but so were most of the other members of the Assembly. In the resolution on Franco Spain at the fifth session, Latin America was not solid; moreover, the resolution would have passed even without the votes of the Arab League. Latin American and Arab League votes did, however, constitute the nucleus of the majority vote.

In cases where a simple majority is required, the position of the two groups is much more favorable. The importance of the two blocs in elections of Assembly officers derives from the fact that it is a simple majority which is involved. This fact also explains the ability of the two to put through the adoption of Spanish as a working language. Here again, however, the actual power of the groups in combination depends upon their ability to reach agreement both within and between the blocs. The difficulty of achieving the latter would seem to indicate that the actual power of the combination is less than its potential power.

Theoretically, other combinations are potentially as influential as that of the Arab League and Latin America—for example, a Latin American–western European combination, or a Latin American–Soviet bloc combination. What prevents these potentialities from being realized is, of course, the fact that the interests of these groups do not consistently coincide, nor have they common interests which are consistently opposed to the interests of other groups. What does happen, however, is that a number of Latin American states, in combination with the Arab League and the Soviet bloc, forms the nucleus of the required majority—as was the case in the vote at the plenary session on the internationalization of Jerusalem, where these states accounted for 24 of the 38 votes in favor of the resolution, or in the case of the reiteration of the previous resolutions on South West Africa at the fourth session, where this combination cast 22 of the 33 votes which passed the resolution. Similarly, the nucleus of the votes in favor of a number of resolutions on Franco Spain was the Soviet bloc, most of western Europe, and some of the Latin American states.

On substantive issues, more important than any theoretically possible combination of blocs, is the weight of the Latin American votes, even when divided. Taken together, the 20 Latin American votes far outweigh those of any other regional group. Even divided, eleven Latin American votes are more than the Commonwealth, the entire near and middle east, the communist states, or western Europe (including the United Kingdom), possess, and are equal to the combined total of the Arab League and the five sure Soviet bloc votes. Latin America alone, if solid, could until the fifth session prevent action on matters requiring a two-thirds vote; an Arab League–Soviet bloc combination could not. Even after the admission of Indonesia as the 60th Member of the United Nations, Latin America need find only one additional vote to prevent action on this kind of question. That Latin America is a factor to be reckoned with on substantive issues as well as in elections, is an axiom of the United Nations politics.

The General Assembly, like the Security Council, is a political body, and politics will inevitably be played therein. Groups of states will vote together, or differ, depending upon their individual interpretation of principle and national and international interest. When there is a high coincidence of interest or common belief among the members of a regional or other organized group, bloc voting may be anticipated. And where there is a high coincidence of interest or belief as between regional or other groups, combinations of blocs may be anticipated—and log rolling is not precluded. However, these voting combinations appear to be not immutable; and, in important cases, the combinations may break down before a resolute opposition—as indicated by the election of Turkey to the Security Council at the fifth session.

The Political Framework of the United Nations' Financial Problems

INIS L. CLAUDE, JR.

It has frequently been asserted that the financial problem of the United Nations is, in reality, a political problem. This proposition contains enough truth to serve us well, provided it is used not to dispose of the problem but to introduce serious consideration of it. Properly conceived, the political emphasis does not entail the denial of the meaningfulness and significance of the financial issue, but rather suggests the nature of the context within which that issue must be examined, and proposed solutions must be evaluated. Without an understanding of the political background of the fiscal difficulties of the United Nations and the political determinants of its future role in world affairs, one cannot deal intelligently with the problems and prospects of the Organization's treasury.

This view of the matter stems directly from the recognition that the United Nations is an agency of the multi-state system, owned and operated by states which undertake, cooperatively and competitively, to use it to affect the working of the system and to influence their fortunes within the system. It does not stand above or outside the international political system, but is clearly *in* and decidedly *of* that system. Serving as both a workshop for collaboration and an arena for conflict, the Organization is inexorably involved in the political relationships of states and is affected by political developments within states. A United Nations insulated from world politics and working undisturbed to promote global welfare is neither possible nor desirable. Political involvement is

INIS L. CLAUDE, JR., is Professor of Political Science at the University of Michigan, and is a member of the Board of Editors of *International Organization*.

This paper was prepared in connection with a research project of the Brookings Institution on financial problems of the United Nations, and will be substantially incorporated in a forthcoming volume deriving from that project, under the general authorship of John G. Stoessinger.

From Volume 17, No. 4 (1963), pp. 831–59.

the price of relevance; only a world organization which is subject to the buffeting of political forces is in a position to contribute significantly to the solution of the critical problems of international relations.

This study is concerned with the present financial predicament and the future financial requirements and prospects of the United Nations. Before coming to grips with the political aspects of these problems, however, we would do well to note that the history of general international organizations has been marked by the tendency of states to invest only the most meager financial resources, and those grudgingly, in such institutions. If poverty is a perennial virtue of international agencies, it is one born of necessity imposed by tight-fisted states. In short, there is ample precedent for the World Organization's condition of financial stringency. Viewed in historical perspective, the budgets of the United Nations and the specialized agencies have been more, not less, generously supported than might have been expected. This is not to minimize the financial difficulties encountered by the international organizations of the present generation, but to note that these agencies are not unique in having troubles of this sort.

The general tendency of states to starve international institutions reflects the limited character of their commitment to the process of international organization. Despite the fact that multilateral institutions have become an essential part of the apparatus for conducting inter-state relations in an era of impressive and increasing interdependence, the attitudes of national leaders toward such agencies are still marked by a certain tentativeness. Thus, the notion that the United Nations is "on trial" is frequently expressed, and the question whether one is "for" or "against" the United Nations is widely regarded as a meaningful issue. In all probability, general international organizations have passed from the status of optional experiments to that of firmly established requirements of the multi-state system, and it is unlikely that many responsible statesmen are really prepared to contemplate the effort to operate the international system without such mechanisms. Nevertheless, the verbalization of the view that the maintenance of the United Nations is still something of an open question indicates a basic indecisiveness in the commitment of states to international organization.

In any case, general international organizations continue to occupy a peripheral rather than a central position in the conduct of foreign relations for many if not most states, and this political fact is expressed in the reluctance of members to provide adequate financial backing for such organizations. In some instances, statesmen doubtless hope to get something for nothing; they expect, or at least demand, substantial benefits from multilateral organizations, but are disinclined to contribute significantly to their resources. In other cases, the level of financial support may be an accurate measure of the importance which statesmen expect, or are willing to permit, international organizations to develop. Money may express more truly than words the significance attributed to international institutions and the commitment to promote or permit the growth of their capabilities. For whatever reason, the policies of states toward international institutions have typically kept those agencies in straitened financial circumstances. In the light of this background, the present predicament of the United Nations is revealed as the product of a failure to achieve a decisive breakthrough, not as evidence of a disastrous breakdown, in the support of international institutions.

THE POLITICAL PROBLEM OF THE ROLE OF THE UNITED NATIONS

The cost of the United Nations is a function of the uses to which it is put. This is not to say that the most important activities of the Organization are necessarily the most expensive ones; the correlation of price and value is quite as imperfect in this realm as in many others. Nevertheless, it is certainly true that the world may have a cheap institutional system or an expensive one, and that the determination of financial requirements is dependent upon political decisions regarding the activities to be undertaken by the United Nations. The initial linkage between political and financial considerations is thus expressed in the question: what, in functional terms, is the United Nations to be?

A minimal consensus has emerged since World War II, to the effect that the United Nations should exist as a continuously operating center for the diplomatic interplay of representatives of most, if not literally all, of the world's governments. The Organization should serve as a kind of global diplomatic headquarters, providing occasions and facilities for debate and consultation, speech-making and vote-taking, declaration and resolution. This concept of the United Nations as a "static conference machinery," as the late Secretary-General Hammarskjöld put it,[1] has enjoyed remarkably widespread and steady support among governments, as evidenced by the facts that virtually every state in the world has assumed the privileges of membership at the earliest opportunity and that none has yet, however frustrating and embittering its experience as a participant may have been, seen fit to withdraw from membership. Whatever reservations one may have about the value of this sort of international forum, it is clear that the leaders of most governments believe that it is eminently worthwhile—or, at the least, that their states cannot afford to be excluded from it so long as it exists.

---

[1] "Introduction to the Annual Report of the Secretary-General on the Work of the Organization, June 16, 1960–June 15, 1961," General Assembly *Official Records* (16th session), Supplement No. 1A, p. 1.

This political consensus has been manifested in the relative lack of difficulty and controversy concerning the regular administrative budget of the United Nations. This is not to say that Members have displayed unquestioning generosity with respect to this aspect of the Organization's financial requirements. The Secretary-General has had to carry on the housekeeping functions within a rapidly expanding establishment under the pressure of severe budgetary limitations; representatives of Member States have frequently voiced alarm at growing budgetary requests; and the notion of a rigid budgetary ceiling has been advanced by the Soviet Union. The inclusion of particular items in the regular budget has sometimes given rise to political controversy. For instance, the Soviet Union has persistently objected to appropriations for subsidiary organs which it has regarded as "illegally" established or constituted, and has recently declared its intent to give effect to its opposition to certain budgetary items by withholding a portion of its annual assessment. This tends to confirm the general proposition that the financial support of the routine administration of the United Nations has not been a notably contentious issue, for objection to particular items has usually been grounded upon the claim that controversial expenditures were being smuggled into an uncontroversial budget. In principle, no state has objected to the view that Members should provide the funds necessary for keeping the United Nations in business as a conference center and a supplier of essential services for international meetings. So far as the regular budget of the Organization is concerned, there is no major financial crisis, and none is in prospect. States evidently recognize the need for and the utility of a broad international forum, and they are, by and large, willing and able to pay for it. It is a reasonably safe prediction that the routine administrative cost of the United Nations will gradually increase, and that Member States will, while grousing about this trend and attempting to check it, continue to make the necessary payments.

Significant political issues arise only when the question is posed as to what, if anything, the United Nations is to do beyond the agreed minimum of providing a setting for multilateral or parliamentary diplomacy. The alternative to an Organization which is *merely* "a static conference machinery" is one which additionally serves as "a dynamic instrument of Governments," carrying out "executive action."[2] This view of the United Nations suggests an operational role for the Organization in programs within two fields, which may be roughly defined as the political and security area and the economic and social area. The Organization has in fact ventured into both these realms, and the central questions for the future are whether, and how far, it shall continue

[2] *Ibid.*

thus to move. It is in connection with these operational functions that major financial and political problems may arise and become entangled with each other. In the first place, the execution of programs in either of these fields tends to be, by the normal standards of international organizations, an extraordinarily expensive proposition; in the second place, such programs tend to be politically contentious, partly but by no means entirely because of their unusual financial implications.

To be sure, there is a middle ground between the two extremes of a world organization providing inexpensive and politically uncontroversial conference services, and an organization operating substantive programs at great cost under conditions of intense political disagreement. Expensiveness is a relative concept, as is political sensitivity. Indeed, the record shows that the United Nations has never been restricted literally to the minimal conference-supporting role, that it has frequently undertaken executive tasks, some of which involved quite minor budgetary implications, and that some of its operational ventures have not stirred political opposition within the Organization. It is doubtful that any state is really committed, on either financial or political grounds, to the rigidly circumscribed conception of the Organization's function implied in the notion of "a static conference machinery." The United Nations has persistently exceeded that role, without consistently encountering financial or political difficulties.

Nevertheless, it is clear that the present financial crisis of the United Nations is the direct result of the Organization's involvement in large-scale, relatively expensive, and politically contentious executive activities. If the specter of bankruptcy now hovers over the United Nations, it is because alarming deficits have appeared in the special accounts established for the sustenance of major operations, undertakings which are quite incompatible with the concept that the Organization should be limited to the provision of conference facilities. While there is no effective political demand for the United Nations to remain strictly within the confines of that minimal concept, the farther the Organization is pushed beyond those limits, the greater is the risk of stirring up political conflict over its proper role.

Political and Security Operations

Specifically, the ventures which have precipitated the present crisis in the United Nations are the peace-keeping operations in the Middle East and the Congo, particularly the latter, involving the maintenance of two groups of military units assembled under United Nations direction (United Nations Emergency Force [UNEF] and the United Nations operation in the Congo

[ONUC]) and, in the case of the Congo, the effort to provide a substantial civilian assistance program as well. The lack of adequate voluntary support and, in particular, the failure or refusal of many Member States to pay their allotted shares of the costs of these activities have created grave difficulties for the Organization in meeting its financial obligations, called into question the capability of the Organization for completing the tasks which it has assumed, and raised the issue of whether the United Nations can, or should, undertake similar ventures in the future. Past, present, and future are involved; default on obligations already incurred, discontinuance of present activities, and rejection of a peace-keeping executive role in emergencies yet to come are the possibilities which these delinquencies have thrust upon the United Nations.

Fundamentally, the deficits relating to UNEF and ONUC, which are the only significant elements in the Organization's present fiscal imbalance, represent political rather than economic considerations. While a number of states presumably are in default because of financial difficulties, the greater part of the deficit is attributable to states which are unwilling, not unable, to pay. In short, the United Nations finds itself over-committed in political terms, which explains the fact that it is under-supported in budgetary terms.

This would suggest that there is inadequate political consensus within the United Nations on the utilization of the Organization as an instrument of what Dag Hammarskjöld called "preventive diplomacy"—at any rate, when this involves the mustering and maintenance of significant peace-keeping forces. Since financial support presumably implies approval, and refusal of support may be taken as evidence of some degree of disapproval, it seems clear that only a dangerously narrow political basis exists for United Nations operations of the type undertaken in the Middle East and the Congo. What are the implications of this conclusion?

One alternative is to insist upon a functional retrenchment for the United Nations—to argue that the current quasi-military ventures should be terminated as promptly and as gracefully as possible, and that the idea of launching new ones in the future should be abandoned. Shifting from advocacy to prediction, this position might suggest that the policy of retreat from executive action in the political-security sphere is likely to be adopted; like it or not, one must anticipate that the Secretary-General and representatives of Members will shy away from such initiatives. Both of these formulations reflect an attitude of caution, a conviction that prudent concern for the effectiveness of the United Nations requires or suggests that the Organization not court financial disaster by undertaking activities that are not firmly supported by the bulk of its membership, including, most importantly, the major powers. Indeed, financial embarrassment is not the only peril; the record of the Soviet Union in the Congo case is one of several indications that dissenters may express their opposition to executive actions in a variety of ways, all of which damage the foundations of the Organization and imperil its usefulness. It is unreasonable, so the argument might run, to jeopardize the modest attainments and potentialities of the Organization by setting the United Nations to ambitious tasks which it cannot hope to complete successfully. In these terms, financial crisis is a warning signal which prudent men cannot afford to ignore; if it is not heeded, the United Nations may be destroyed by those who value it most.

A variation on the theme just stated would be to propose not that the United Nations should never again be given assignments similar to those in the Middle East and the Congo, but that new projects of this type should be weighed with the utmost care and undertaken only if there is firm evidence of broad support, including that of the major powers. Perhaps this should be described as a "hardly ever" rather than a "never again" position. The mood is essentially the same: disinclination to wreck the United Nations on the rocks of political conflict over its proper function. The assumption of this variant position is that political and security operations may *sometimes* command the necessary "critical mass" of support and, therefore, enjoy adequate financial backing; on this basis, it is argued that the United Nations should be put to such uses when, but only when, these conditions prevail.

It should be noted that this position conforms quite closely to the original conception of the Organization's possibilities, as stated and implied in the United Nations Charter. The veto provision embodied in Article 27, paragraph 3, reflects the view that the United Nations cannot successfully perform significant political or security functions in the absence of unanimity among the major powers, that its existence will be imperiled if it is pushed into such futile ventures, and that constitutional safeguards are needed to prevent its being maneuvered into dangerous and unpromising situations of this sort. In essence, the position under discussion is one which expresses belief in the political wisdom of the concept of the veto and advises adherence to the policy of restraint in the use of the United Nations under circumstances of major political dissension.

Moreover, Secretary-General Hammarskjöld had appeared to espouse this position in his classic statement of the theory of preventive diplomacy, issued in 1960.[3] Considering the issue of "the possibilities of substantive action by the United Nations in a split world," he virtually discarded the idea that the Organization could usefully or safely intervene in "problems which are clearly

[3] "Introduction to the Annual Report of the Secretary-General on the Work of the Organization, June 16, 1959–June 15, 1960," General Assembly *Official Records* (15th session), Supplement No. 1A, pp. 4–5.

and definitely within the orbit of present day conflicts between power blocs."
In such instances, he feared, it would be "practically impossible for the Secretary-General to operate effectively with the means put at his disposal, short of
risking seriously to impair the usefulness of his office. . . ." Hammarskjöld
drew the conclusion that "the main field of useful activity of the United
Nations in its efforts to prevent conflicts or to solve conflicts" should be defined
as that of taking action to fill vacuums in areas of conflict outside of, or marginal to, the zones already involved in the Cold War struggle, so as to minimize
the tendency or diminish the incentive of great powers to move competitively
into those situations. Thus, he hoped, the Organization might prevent the
widening and aggravation of the bloc conflicts. Hammarskjöld seemed to acknowledge that this kind of operation was dependent upon the approval of the
major Cold War contestants, asserting:

> There is thus a field within which international conflicts may be faced and solved
> with such harmony between the power blocs as was anticipated as a condition for
> Security Council action in San Francisco. Agreement may be achieved because of
> a mutual interest among the Big Powers to avoid having a regional or local con-
> flict drawn into the sphere of bloc politics.

Writing specifically of the Congo operation, he held that this was "rendered
possible by the fact that both blocs have an interest in avoiding such an extension of the area of conflict because of the threatening consequences, were
the localization of the conflict to fail." He stressed the UN's role in "providing
for solutions whenever the interests of all parties in a localization of conflict
can be mobilized in favour of its efforts."

What emerges from this analysis of Hammarskjöld's essay is that the father
of the theory and practice of preventive diplomacy was wary of executive action
by the United Nations in opposition to the will of a major power, but hopeful
that the Organization could carry out successful and useful operations in the
political and security field, whenever the primary contestants in the Cold War
were agreed that they had a common interest in having the United Nations
interposed as a neutral force to prevent their direct confrontation. While he
was not absolutely explicit on this point, he clearly implied that the United
Nations could not perform this function in the absence of such agreement and,
presumably, should not attempt it in such circumstances. Ironically, the final
chapter of Hammarskjöld's life seemed to confirm the views he had stated in
1960; the Congo operation *became* one which aroused bitter Soviet opposition,
and Hammarskjöld's efforts to maintain it in the face of that attack brought a
fundamental challenge to the usefulness of his office. The Soviet rejection of
the concept of the Secretary-General as executive leader of the United Nations

occurred as Hammarskjöld sought to carry on the Congo action in the context of a disintegrating political consensus.

While some may read the Congo record as a warning against attempting to use the United Nations as an executive agency for political and security operations in any future case, or in any case where such use is or appears likely to become a subject of political disagreement among the major powers, others react by insisting that the Organization's development of executive functions must not be interrupted. Political opposition to the operational role of the United Nations in this field, whether expressed in financial non-support or otherwise, must be overridden if necessary; somehow, the Organization must be enabled to perform this function, even in the face of the determined objections of powerful states or blocs.

This position represents a refusal to accept the philosophy of the veto as originally incorporated in the Charter. Concretely, it is an expression of the insistence, most notably on the part of the United States, that the Soviet Union must not be permitted to block the the development of the United Nations along lines acceptable to a sufficient number of other states. The argument that it is essential to have the Organization maintain and expand its operational role in cases like the Congo crisis is sometimes pressed so vigorously that its proponents appear to challenge the minimal consensus on the role of the United Nations; if the Organization cannot go well beyond the mere provision of conference machinery, so they seem to say, it is hardly worth having at all. It may be that this devaluation of the minimal function of the United Nations is simply a tactic adopted in the campaign to achieve the maximization of its function. If this is not the case, the political issue of the role in which the United Nations is to be cast may become doubly complex. Conceivably, there may be no possibility of attaining general agreement either to the proposition that the United Nations should function as more than a static conference machinery, or to the view that it should function as less than a dynamic instrumentality of executive action. In specific, but oversimplified terms, this might mean that the Soviet Union would refuse to tolerate a maximal United Nations, while the United States would refuse to support a minimal United Nations. The difficulty of achieving consensus on executive activity by the Organization may be matched by the difficulty of achieving consensus on executive inactivity. Either difficulty could be disastrous; Soviet opposition might wreck an Organization which was pushed to excessively ambitious functions, and withdrawal of support by the United States might wreck an Organization restricted to an excessively modest role.

The problems posed by states which espouse the minimalist view—those which generally resist the expansion of United Nations activity beyond the conference-serving function—are weighty indeed, and they appear to be taken too lightly by the maximalists—those who insistently advocate that expansion. It is true that the Soviet Union has confined its opposition to some of the minor peace-keeping ventures to verbal protests, and has, in the past, gone ahead to pay its share of the regular budgets which have included expenditures for these operations. Nevertheless, it is a fact of experience that states opposing the international programs in the Middle East and the Congo have, by refusing to contribute funds, precipitated the grave financial troubles which afflict the United Nations. The bitter Soviet attack upon the Secretary-General and the Soviet threat to demolish the institution of the Secretary-General's office in its evolved form serve as vivid reminders of the possibility that powerful opponents of United Nations executive action could and might inflict upon the Organization damage other than, and more serious than, financial damage. A realistic view of the behavior of states would suggest that no state is likely to give active financial or other support to a collective enterprise to which its policy is opposed, and that no major power can be expected passively to tolerate the use of an international institution for purposes which it regards as inimical to its vital interests. In such instances, neither a judicial ruling that a state is obliged to contribute funds nor a moral insistence that a state should respect majority decisions is likely to prove effective.

In the final analysis, the crucial question is how to react to the evidence that major powers are not agreed upon the role which should be assigned to the United Nations in political and security affairs. From one point of view, consensus is essential; either the activities of the Organization must be restricted to fit the consensus, or the consensus must be broadened to support the developing range of activities. Financial difficulty is but a symptom of the deeper political crisis which is almost automatically precipitated by miscalculation of the limits of the prevailing consensus, or by deliberate efforts to push the Organization beyond those limits. This position suggests that it is imprudent to push the United Nations, and unrealistic to expect that the Organization can succeed in such ambitious enterprises or survive to perform more modest but still important functions, if it is used in this manner. The immediate necessity is to trim functional concepts to fit consensus; the longer-term ideal is to expand consensus to support more ambitious activities. In these terms, the primary political question is how to produce agreement among most members of the United Nations, including particularly the Soviet Union, on the assignment to the Organization of an executive role in cases threatening the maintenance of international peace.

From the other point of view, the lack of consensus may be deplored, but it must be essentially ignored. The problem of enabling the United Nations to operate in cases of the Congo type is defined, not as the task of expanding consensus, but as the task of carrying on successfully despite the limitation of consensus. Financial crisis does not mean that the United Nations has gone too far; it means that resources must be found for equipping the Organization to continue and even to deepen its probes in the functional area beyond the limits of the minimal consensus. This mood calls for the discovery of effective means for defiance of opposition, not for concessions to the obstructive capability of opponents of the expanding executive role of the United Nations. It is not concerned with avoiding financial crises, but with surmounting them.

Clearly, the issue of whether the United Nations is to have a continuing series of such crises depends largely upon which of these two viewpoints prevails. If the latter is dominant, financial difficulties may be expected to become a recurrent feature of the history of the United Nations. It may prove possible to deal with them—but it ought not to be assumed that states which object to the maximal concept of the political and security role of the Organization can be brought to assist in the solution of these problems.

There is, of course, a middle ground of acquiescence between support for and opposition to an expanding executive role for the United Nations in political and security matters. Many states are simply willing to permit this development of the Organization's function. Such states may support the initiation of operations with their votes, but they probably will not support the operations with their funds. Thus, while they may not contribute to the political controversies, they are likely to contribute to the budgetary deficiencies. On balance, then, states exhibiting a permissive attitude probably tend to exacerbate rather than to aid in the solution of the financial crises which may result from the effort to conduct politically contentious peace-keeping activities.

Another middle ground must be pointed out—one which lies between the cautious insistence on executive inactivity, unless general agreement on a line of action is clearly in evidence, and the audacious urge for action even in the face of formidable opposition. The limits of consensus are not always either clearly visible or absolutely rigid. In a given case, it may be desirable to initiate United Nations action despite uncertainty as to those limits; the risk of damaging the Organization by pushing it beyond the limits which some important Members will tolerate must be balanced against the risk of failing to exploit its potentialities by exercising undue restraint. There is a strong case for probing the limits of consensus in the hope of discovering that restrictive views of the Organization's role are not firmly held, or that opposition in principle to

United Nations executive action is qualified in the particular instance by appreciation of its potential contribution to political stability. If this probing goes too far, the precipitation of financial crisis may result, as one aspect of the political overextension of the United Nations. If it does not go far enough, the United Nations will be doomed to the underdevelopment of its capabilities for service to Member States.

The decision as to how far to go should not necessarily be determined by considerations related to the financial health of the United Nations. One may cite excellent reasons for pushing the United Nations as far as possible in the direction of executive activity in the political realm, but, in so doing, one must confront the fact that the farther the Organization exceeds the discernible bounds of consensus, the greater becomes the probability of running into serious financial difficulties. This is a risk which cannot be denied and should not be ignored; if one opts to subject the United Nations to the risk, one should do so advisedly.

Actually, financial non-support is the least serious manifestation of opposition to a United Nations executive action. If a given action, supported by the United States, arouses only this passive kind of resistance by the Soviet Union (as in the case of UNEF), it is open to the United States to prevent the involvement of the United Nations in financial crisis by accepting the responsibility for paying most of the expenses. This may be sound policy; if the United States regards a United Nations undertaking as desirable, it should perhaps be less disturbed by the fact that the Soviet Union refuses to share in the cost than gratified that the latter power permits the United States and other Members to use the Organization, at their own expense, for that undertaking.

The case is different when a United Nations program stirs the active opposition of a major power or a significant group of Members. As we have noted, the Congo operation (after its initial phase) became one which the Soviet bloc was not only unwilling to support but also determined to obstruct. Soviet opposition went beyond financial deprivation to an attack upon the executive mechanism of the United Nations, which indicated an urge to prevent the Organization's being used, at anybody's expense, for the conduct of such operations. When opposition takes this active form, it is clear that the United Nations has gone well beyond the limits of consensus. In such a case, the Organization incurs not only the risk of bankruptcy, which can be alleviated by subsidies provided by states favoring the operation, but also the risk of political disruption, which cannot be disposed of so handily. In the Congo case, the vigor of Soviet obstructionism ultimately subsided. In agreeing to the election of U Thant as Secretary-General, first on an acting basis and then as full-fledged holder of the office, the Soviet Union expressed the modification of its attitude toward the Congo operation from one of active opposition to one of passive opposition, or reluctant acquiescence. In this instance, the threat of the disruption of the United Nations seems to have been lifted.

Economic and Social Operations

The issue of the operational role to be assigned to international institutions arises in the economic and social realm as well as in the sphere of politics and security. In the case of the United Nations and its affiliated agencies, this is fundamentally a question of the degree to which emphasis will be placed upon programs designed to promote economic growth in the developing countries. From the beginning, the organizations of the United Nations system have been involved in this kind of activity, and their commitment to such programs has steadily increased. There appears to be no significant opposition, in principle, to this phase of their operations. The involvement of international agencies in technical assistance and economic development activities is firmly established, and the prospects are for mounting political pressures in support of the launching of more ambitious—and more expensive—programs. In this realm, the political issue is not whether the United Nations should effect a retreat, but whether it should undertake major advances. The line of political division is not essentially the East-West boundary, as in the issue of political and security operations, but the North-South boundary; the debate is not conducted among rival great powers so much as between the states seeking international economic assistance and the industrially advanced states which are the primary suppliers of economic aid, actual and potential. The United Nations is, and seems certain to continue to be, the major setting for the confrontation of the political demand of the underdeveloped states and the political reluctance of the highly developed ones.

In the literal sense, there is no financial crisis in the United Nations with respect to economic and social operations. That is to say, the Organization has not become involved in spending money that it does not have; it has not incurred financial obligations that it appears incapable of meeting; it has not been embarrassed by a rash of delinquencies on the part of Members. In a different but more basic sense, however, there is a financial crisis in this realm. The Organization may be able to meet its commitments, but it cannot meet the needs and opportunities with which it is confronted; the crisis, in short, is that of the inadequate budget rather than the unbalanced budget. The problem lies not in excessive delinquencies, but in too meager commitments.

In the future development of the economic and social work of the United

Nations and the specialized agencies, financial problems of this variety seem likely to persist. What is relevant to the political debate is not that there is great objective need for economic development programs, but that there is increasingly effective political demand for such programs, expressed particularly in speeches and votes within international institutions. There is every reason to assume that operational activities in this field will continue and, to some degree, expand; the real question is how much the states most capable of supplying resources for this work will be willing to contribute through international channels. The central political issue has to do with the nature of the response these states will make to the insistent demand of the less affluent countries.

There is a significant reversal of the identity of suppliers and consumers of international services, as between the operations of the United Nations in the political-security and the economic-social areas. While the greater part of the financial burden falls upon the major powers in both instances, it is nevertheless true that these powers are the primary recipients of direct benefit in the former instance, and that this position is assumed by the weaker and less developed states in the latter. This is not to deny that such an operation as ONUC has immense political value to the Congo and its neighbors in helping to prevent their region from becoming the focus of great-power competition. Nevertheless, its central aim is to enlist the service of lesser states in helping the major powers to avoid a mutually—and, perhaps, globally—disastrous confrontation. In activities falling under the rubric of preventive diplomacy, weaker states are called upon to do something for the great powers which the latter cannot do for themselves; in economic and social programs, the more advanced states are called upon to do something for the developing countries which these could not do for themselves. Presumably, the entire world will benefit if the great powers are assisted in avoiding a catastrophic showdown and if the less advanced states are helped toward economic development, but direct benefits are differently allocated in these two types of enterprise. Consumer demand is not the same in both instances. As we have seen, the great powers are not agreed in wanting, or even in being prepared to accept, the services which other states may be able to render through participation in operations of the Congo type, while the underdeveloped states display an almost unanimous urge to secure the greatest possible expansion of United Nations activities on their behalf. In the one case, the basic political problem is to develop a consensus among the consumers; in the other, it is to promote agreement between consumers and suppliers. In both cases, the financial problem derives from and draws its distinctive nature from the underlying political considerations.

The Political Problem of the Distribution of Cost
of United Nations Operations

It would be misleading to suggest that political controversy concerning the role of the United Nations turns exclusively on differing conceptions of the nature and scope of the international activities which should be encouraged, supported, or permitted. It is true that some states are more favorably disposed than others, in principle, to the growth and strengthening of international institutions. However, the most significant differences regarding the operational evolution of the United Nations system derive less from such abstract considerations than from concrete political interests. One of the points at issue is the distribution of cost. The question is not simply what kind of activity the United Nations should undertake, on what scale of expense, but, among other issues, who should pay for it, on what basis of apportionment.

This issue has been avoided in the financing of most of the non-security operational programs involving relatively high costs by the device of building them upon voluntary contributions. Member States have been left free to decide whether, and to what extent, to participate in the financial support of international enterprises. States opposed to or critical of particular programs have not been expected to support them, but, at most, to tolerate their being conducted under United Nations auspices with the support of other states; the operating agencies have tailored their programs to fit the budgetary resources which states have been willing to provide. If these resources have sometimes been disappointingly meager, at least over-commitment and political controversy over the effort to extract funds from unwilling governments have been avoided. The history of major economic and social programs in the United Nations system conforms largely to this pattern.

The story is quite different when the attempt is made to require all Members to share in the support of programs, regardless of their attitudes toward the activities in question, and to establish a scale of assessment. The first really substantial programs in which the effort was made to cover a major portion of costs by this method were the quasi-military ventures, UNEF and ONUC—precisely the programs, be it noted, that precipitated the present grave financial crisis. When the principle of compulsory financial support is adopted, two categories of questions arise: those relating to the criteria for equitable distribution of cost, and those relating to the mechanism for authoritative determination of assessments.

With regard to the question of "fair shares," several alternative criteria should be noted. States may be expected to contribute in proportion to their ability to pay. While precise computation of this factor may be impossible to achieve, this is the basis used for distributing the costs of the normal administrative budgets of the United Nations and various other agencies, and experience indicates that a rough approximation of equity can be achieved on this basis. This scheme has the merit of dramatizing the international quality of programs and the collective responsibility of states—large and small, rich and poor—for maintaining the work of the organized community.

Other devices for cost-sharing tend to move away from the principle of universal participation by Member States. It may be argued that all, or virtually all, of the expense of a given operation should be borne by the major powers, with lesser states bearing at most a nominal part of the burden; such, for instance, was the import of some proposals regarding the support of UNEF and ONUC. Behind this lies the view that the special status of the great powers in the United Nations should carry with it special obligations, and perhaps the view that the great powers, having been exempted from the policing duties contemplated for them when the Charter was formulated and thus having become the beneficiaries of policing functions carried out by other states, should offer financial compensation for this shift of the peace-keeping burden. Another suggested criterion is that of guilt: the state or states which created the necessity for a given enterprise in preventive diplomacy should be required to pay most if not all of the cost. This slogan, "make the aggressors pay," has been advanced notably, but not exclusively, by the Soviet Union in the Middle Eastern and Congo cases. Finally, the criterion of benefit has figured in discussions of the issue. It has been applied in the sense that states receiving technical assistance and other economic aid under international programs have customarily been required to combine substantial local resources with those externally supplied. There are obvious limits, however, to the feasible application of the principle that recipient states should pay for international assistance—since, at the extreme, it would lose altogether the character of assistance.

The problem of defining fair shares seems certain to be a major political issue in the United Nations for the indefinite future. States which oppose programs will insist that their proper share is zero. States which merely tolerate programs will argue that the actively interested states should bear all, or virtually all, of the cost. States which favor programs will differ as to who should pay how much. Small states will argue that the great powers, having the status symbol of the veto, should carry most of the burden. Great powers, noting the regime of formal equality in the General Assembly, will think that the smaller fry may be saved from the temptation to vote irresponsibly if they are sufficiently burdened with financial responsibility for the programs which they may press upon the Organization. From the standpoint of functional effectiveness, the United Nations needs to lay a foundation of obligatory financial support by all, or appropriately designated groups, of its Members under the programs which it may undertake. From the political standpoint, however, disharmony is likely to result from the attempt to apply any of the criteria which have been suggested for the compulsory allocation of expenses. While individual states may take a different position on particular occasions and with respect to specific projects, it can be asserted as a general proposition that the principle of cost-distribution which is most acceptable to members of international organizations is that embodied in the scheme of voluntary contributions: i.e., financial support should be correlated with political support; a state should give financial backing to an international activity only if and to the extent that it regards that activity as compatible with, and conducive to, the interests and purposes expressed in its national policy. States may endorse the principle that all members should share in the cost of all programs, but this really means that *others* should pay, even for programs of which they disapprove; no state wishes itself to provide backing for a program that it regards as unfavorable to its interest. The task of developing the United Nations as an effective agency involves the problem of resolving the tension between the urge of some states to achieve that end, and the urge of all states to maintain the criterion of national interest as the measure of their individual contributions to international projects. It may prove possible to resolve this tension, but it should not be imagined that it can be done without serious political difficulty.

As we have suggested, the principle of compulsory financial support for United Nations operations involves not only questions relating to the criteria for the equitable distribution of cost, but also issues concerning the manner in which the determination of national assessments is to be made. Clearly, this principle can be given effect only by vesting in some international organ the competence to decide upon allocations of financial responsibility. Ultimately, the question of what criteria should serve as bases for allocations is overshadowed by the question of what organ, acting in accordance with what procedure, should have authority to make these decisions.

Given the political and structural evolution of the United Nations, as well as the assignment of functions provided in the Charter, it appears that only one organ is in line for this role—the General Assembly. For all practical purposes, to say that major United Nations operations must be supported by obligatory rather than voluntary subscription is to say that the authority to legislate in regard to assessments must be exercised by the Assembly. This body, of course, already possesses this competence with respect to the normal budget, and it has gained the support of the International Court of Justice for its assertion of the capacity to assign financial responsibilities for support of extraordinary political and security operations as well.[4] Technically, it may not be necessary to confer additional authority upon the Assembly; politically, it is essential to secure general recognition and acceptance of the Assembly's authority to determine assessments in support of all United Nations programs, if the principle of compulsory financing of those programs is to be given effect. This does not mean that the Assembly must necessarily be authorized to carry out this legislative function under its existing procedural rules, which assign equal voting power to all Members and require a two-thirds majority for important decisions. Conceivably, a modified decision-making process might be established by Charter amendment, although it would be unrealistic to assume that the political barriers to this accomplishment could easily be surmounted.

Taking the Assembly as it now is, with its one-state, one-vote procedure, there is little possibility of achieving general agreement to its exercising the function of defining obligatory assessments for the support of all United Nations action programs. The current financial crisis is a striking manifestation of the unwillingness of many Member States to accept the exercise of this kind of legislative competence by the Assembly. The Soviet Union, viewing the Assembly from the perspective of a permanent minority position, is clearly not inclined to accept the broadening of that organ's capacity to impose financial obligations. Instead, the Soviet Union, joined in this matter by France, insists that only the Security Council, the organ designated in the Charter as the bearer of primary responsibility for the maintenance of international peace and security, is competent to provide for the financing of peace-keeping operations. For great powers, equipped with the veto in the Security Council, this stand obviously represents a refusal to subject themselves to the assessment of budgetary obligations without their consent. If this position implies an unreasonable constriction of the Assembly's general control over the apportionment of the expenses of the Organization, stated in Article 17, paragraph 2, it may be argued that the opposite position, which attributes to the Assembly the authority to vote binding assessments for the support of peace-keeping operations, implies the excessive expansion of the Assembly's competence. It can no longer be maintained that the Assembly is limited to the recommendation of peace-keeping actions if it is empowered to obligate states to provide financial support for such actions; in such circumstances, there arises the phenomenon, familiar to veterans of the military service, of compulsory voluntarism.[5]

[4] *Certain Expenses of the United Nations (Article 17, paragraph 2, of the Charter), Advisory Opinion of July 20, 1962: I.C.J. Reports 1962,* p. 151.

[5] See Leo Gross, "Expenses of the United Nations for Peace-Keeping Operations: The Advisory Opinion of the International Court of Justice," *International Organization,* Winter 1963 (Vol. 17, No. 1), pp. 5–6.

The position of the United States with respect to the exercise of legislative competence in the matter of financial assessments by the Assembly is a study in ambiguity. Focusing on the financial troubles of UNEF and ONUC, the United States condemns the refusal of the Soviet Union and other states to acknowledge their obligation to pay the shares determined by the Assembly, and insists that the Assembly's authority should be upheld and respected. However, the generalization of this position would hardly be attractive to the United States. Despite the ostensible support of the United States for the proposition that the Assembly is entitled to launch whatever operations it pleases for the realization of the purposes stated in the Charter and to bind Member States to pay whatever sums it decrees for their support, there is every reason to believe that the United States would balk at the application of that rule in cases involving programs to which its policy was opposed. It is one thing to assert that the Soviet Union should pay its designated part of the Congo expenses, but it would be quite a different thing to admit that the Assembly is competent to establish, say, a massive capital fund, over American objections, and to obligate the United States to bear a specified portion of its cost. There is a keen awareness in the United States of the shift in the balance of voting power which is taking place in the Assembly. Correctly or not, the United States fears increasing "irresponsibility" on the part of the Assembly. Hence, the trend of United States policy may well run against, not toward, acceptance of an expanded legislative role for that organ as it is presently constituted.

For some states, the acceptability of the Assembly as the authoritative agency for defining financial obligations of Members with respect to all operations would be enhanced by the adoption of an appropriate weighted voting procedure. The political demand for abandoning the procedural expressions of the fiction of the equality of Members of the Assembly is mounting, although it is not clear that political resistance to any move toward weighted voting in the Assembly is likely to undergo a corresponding decline, or that political agreement on any specific scheme for reallocating voting power is in prospect. Even if the smaller states were prepared to sacrifice their disproportionate influence in the operation of the Assembly, it seems improbable that any arrangement could be devised which would enable the Assembly to inspire the confidence equally of all the great powers, or of both the Soviet Union and the United States. Two competing powers cannot *both* be given the assurance of control over the decisions of the Assembly; without that assurance, neither the Soviet Union nor the United States is likely to make a genuine commitment to accept and respect that body's competence to implement the principle of compulsory financial support for all activities which may be initiated under the auspices of the United Nations.

Even if the competence of the Assembly in this respect were universally acknowledged, there would still remain the formidable political problem of giving practical effect to that theoretical competence. How could or would binding decisions of the Assembly be enforced? What sanctions might be brought to bear in cases of delinquency? It was not a cynical communist leader, but the Prime Minister of the United Kingdom, who said with respect to the financing of the Congo operation:

> There is the compulsory subscription and the voluntary subscription. The only difference between them is this. The compulsory is the one that you do not pay if you do not want to, and the voluntary is the one that you need not pay unless you wish to.[6]

The Charter provides, in Article 19, that Members falling into arrears equaling or exceeding assessments due for two years shall be deprived of their vote in the Assembly, unless that body waives the penalty. This might prove to be a sanction of more than negligible importance, but it can hardly be argued that it provides an adequate guarantee that United Nations operations will in fact receive the financial backing that they may require, or that budgetary decisions of the Assembly will command respect. Institutional sanctions of this general variety, possibly culminating in the expulsion of recalcitrant Members from the United Nations, would seem to be the only feasible measures for backing the Assembly in its exercise of financial authority. Such measures might be self-defeating, however. While the threat of expulsion might stimulate some states to pay their assessments, the carrying out of that threat would not enrich the treasury of the United Nations, and it might damage the usefulness of the Organization as an international meeting point and forum. Again, we are confronted with the question whether it is politically desirable to press for the functional maximization of the United Nations at the risk of undermining its capacity to play its minimal role in world politics. Conceivably, the attempt to lay a financial foundation for executive actions by the United Nations might destroy the political foundation for the Organization's doing anything at all. The consideration of sanctions for failure to pay assessments should not proceed without due attention to the proposition that no state—and, particularly, no great power—will accept compulsion to support activities which it regards as detrimental to its national interest.

---

[6] Speech by the Rt. Hon. Harold Macmillan in the House of Commons, December 14, 1961. Official text, mimeographed, supplied by the British Information Services, New York, December 19, 1961.

The Political Problem of the Control of United Nations Operations

A further point at issue in the debate concerning the development of the United Nations is the matter of direction and control of international executive actions. The question is not simply what kind of programs the Organization should undertake or who should bear the resultant financial burdens, but how they should be managed and what ends they should be made to serve.

Concretely, the Soviet Union is not so much opposed in principle to the ONUC operation or disturbed by the portion of the operational budget assigned to itself, as it is dissatisfied with the policy direction of the United Nations intervention in the Congo and the place allotted to the Soviet Union in the control mechanism. This is clear from the record. The Soviet Union approved the beginning of the Congo operation, turned against that operation only when it concluded that ONUC was being used for purposes unfavorable to Soviet interests, and expressed its concern by demanding an arrangement—the troika—which would give itself a powerful position in the executive mechanism of the Organization. This effort to extend the veto power into the "office of the chief executive" represented the insistence of the Soviet Union that it should have, if not the power to control policy in the positive sense, at least the power to block policy developments which it disapproved. The Soviet Union later relinquished its demand for the troika, presumably because of the realization that this constitutional alteration was unattainable, but it had made its point: the Soviet Union was capable of preventing the installation of a Secretary-General with full claim to legitimacy and with unimpaired ability to exercise the functions of the office. In withdrawing its threat to exercise this capacity, the Soviet Union presumably expressed the mitigation of its dissatisfaction with the conduct of the Congo operation. Nevertheless, the entire episode leaves as its residue the clear revelation of the unwillingness of the Soviet Union to tolerate United Nations operational policies which it regards as incompatible with its interests.

It should not be imagined that the American attitude is fundamentally different from this. If the United States has valued the veto less highly than the Soviet Union, this is essentially because the United States has had less occasion to believe that the United Nations was, or to fear that it might be, dominated by forces inimical to its national interest. If the United States has been less suspicious than the Soviet Union of the Congo operation, this is basically because the United States has had the expectation that the officers in charge would direct it in a manner acceptable to the West—if not favorable to the West, at least not unneutral in a pro-Soviet sense. American reaction to a

United Nations operation, like ONUC, which the United States believed to be dominated by a pro-Soviet policy, would not be substantively different, though it might be stylistically different, from Soviet reaction to the Congo operation. The record of debate concerning the establishment of a Special United Nations Fund for Economic Development (SUNFED) suggests quite strongly that the question of policy control arrangements has figured significantly in the negative position of the United States; the positive attitude of the United States toward the World Bank and the cluster of financial institutions which have grown up around that agency is presumably not unrelated to the favorable position of the United States and its Western allies in the mechanism for policy determination.

In short, Members of the United Nations are not clearly and permanently divisible into those which oppose and those which favor an executive role for international agencies. Those which might be listed in the former group oppose United Nations operations *unless* control arrangements acceptable to themselves are made; those which might be listed in the latter group favor United Nations operations *only if* control arrangements acceptable to themselves are made.

Regardless of the formal provisions that may be made for political direction of a given United Nations operation, of either the peace-keeping or the economic variety, the dependence of such an operation upon the financial backing of Member States confers upon states—particularly the great powers—a considerable capacity to influence policy. The act of withholding payment of funds can be used by any state as an informal vote against prevailing policy, or a vote for change of policy. The power of a major state or a bloc of states to deprive a program of a large portion of the necessary financial resources is virtually the power to veto the policy being followed or considered; it can be used as a threat to destroy a program unless policy demands are met. This is the phenomenon of the "financial veto," the capacity of the state whose financial support is indispensable to dominate policy in a negative sense. The financial method of influencing policy is available, in varying degrees, to all Members of the United Nations, as a substitute for or supplement to a more formal status in the mechanisms for controlling the conduct of programs.

To accept the principle that a state can be legally bound to pay an authoritatively determined assessment in support of a given United Nations program is to relinquish this capacity to use the financial weapon as an instrument of control. At this point, a major political question arises: are states prepared to abandon this instrument? Many states, of course, play such a minor role in financing the United Nations that the effect of their individual financial dissents is insignificant—although this does not necessarily mean that they do not value such capacity to influence policy as they possess. Other states and groups of states are aware of the fact that their importance as budgetary contributors gives them a highly effective, if not a decisive, voice in the management of United Nations operations, and they may be most reluctant to give up this basis for control. For instance, the Soviet bloc has indicated quite clearly that it values the power of financial deprivation as a partial compensation for the weakness of its formal voting capacity in the General Assembly. The United States deplores the use of the "financial veto" by other Members of the United Nations, complains about the proportion of the financial burdens which is left for itself to carry, and worries about the effect upon the Organization of excessive dependence upon United States support. It should not, however, be lightly assumed that the United States would happily relinquish the prominent role in direction and control of programs, which is an accompaniment of its decisive importance as a contributor. At the present time, of course, the United States supports the effort to establish the competence of the General Assembly to require Member States to provide financial backing for the UNEF and Congo operations; thus, it appears to be willing to give up its financial veto. However, it must be noted that this policy of the United States relates to particular programs which this country strongly supports. The policy is designed to overcome the reluctance or unwillingness of other states to provide backing for these programs. If the situation were different, the policy of the United States might well be different; if, for instance, it were a matter of securing funds for an operation to stabilize the Castro government in Cuba, an operation which the United States believed was being conducted for a purpose and in a manner unfavorable to its own national interest, it seems quite likely that the United States would be inclined to exercise, not to relinquish, its power to hinder through financial non-support. The supposition that the United States is prepared to extend the policy adopted in the present financial crisis to the problem of securing financial support for any and all operations which the United Nations might undertake in the future is open to doubt.

So long as policy-making organs are not so constituted as to satisfy the aspirations of major powers for directive capacity, the latter may be expected to value the possibility of using the financial veto. Even if, by some miracle of statesmanship, control arrangements acceptable to all the major powers and political blocs were devised, it is probable that the retention of the capacity to exercise financial pressure upon policy would be regarded by at least some of the powers as a desirable expedient for strengthening their position.

The problem of the unpredictable future looms large in the attitudes of states toward international institutions and their operations, making them wary of setting precedents which might later prove embarrassing. It is one thing for a government to accept a share of financial responsibility for a program already in operation, but quite a different thing to contract to support future programs without foreknowledge of their budgetary scope, their purposes, or their control mechanisms. Bluntly, states have a deep-seated reluctance to buy a pig in a poke; the urge not to do this is a fundamental expression of the sense of sovereignty—which is, above all, the freedom of the state to set its own policy as situations arise. This reluctance is a formidable political obstacle to the acceptance of the obligation to follow the budgetary dictates of the General Assembly in the indefinite future. While the Members of the United Nations voted, 76 to 17, with 8 abstentions, to acknowledge this obligation in adopting General Assembly Resolution 1854 A (XVII) on December 19, 1962, it is doubtful that this action represented, in political terms, a genuine commitment to accept the obligation in all circumstances. To retain discretionary power to lend or withhold financial support is to maintain some degree of control over the future activities of the United Nations. Since no Member or group of Members can be certain of dominating the United Nations in the years that lie ahead, it is understandable that great political value should be attached to this method of influencing the development of the Organization's functions. Many states, of course, give high priority to the project of making the United Nations a stronger and more reliably effective Organization; this political objective is, in some degree, an offset to the political urge to retain the sovereign right of financial opposition to United Nations operations. However, it is doubtful that pretensions of unconditional commitment to the abstract ideal of a strong and active United Nations have much real depth. Underneath, one is likely to find that the degree of commitment depends upon the issue of the political control of the Organization. The right to withhold financial support is for every state a political hedge against the possibility that the United Nations may come under the domination of the "wrong" elements of the international community. For the great powers, it is a reserve capacity to exercise a veto over operational policies objectionable to themselves.

POLITICAL IMPLICATIONS OF A FINANCIALLY INDEPENDENT UNITED NATIONS

Thus far, operations of the United Nations and the specialized agencies (except for the International Monetary Fund, the World Bank, and the agencies associated with the latter) have been based upon either voluntary contributions of states or purportedly binding assessments levied upon states or some combination of the two. Neither scheme for providing funds has proved wholly satisfactory or successful. Programs dependent upon voluntary contributions have seldom enjoyed a genuinely adequate level of support. The two major operations based upon assessments, UNEF and ONUC, have failed so abjectly in gaining the support demanded of states that they have thrown the United Nations into an acute financial crisis.

There is, however, a third alternative which must be considered: the United Nations might be enabled to obtain its major financial support from sources other than states. The Organization might, in short, achieve financial independence. This is not a totally new proposition, for revenues from nongovernmental sources have played a supplementary role of some importance in the financing of several international projects under the auspices of the United Nations. Nevertheless, the suggestion that such an organization as the United Nations should derive the bulk of the funds needed for large-scale operations from sources other than governments, thus emancipating itself from dependence upon either the voluntary or the compulsory support of governments, is essentially a new and untried idea.

If this plan were successfully applied, it would appear likely to reduce or eliminate some of the political difficulties which have affected the development of the executive role of the United Nations. For instance, there would be no controversy over "fair shares," if states were not called upon to provide budgetary sustenance. Moreover, under such a system the implications of a neutral, or permissive, attitude of states toward United Nations programs would be more favorable to the success of those programs. When an operation is based upon voluntary contributions, a state which merely acquiesces in the launching of the activity offers it no substantial support; the program may fail for lack of positive support from some of the more affluent states. Typically, a United Nations program cannot be carried out unless it inspires a more positive attitude than permissiveness on the part of the United States. In contrast, a financially independent United Nations would be able to function on the basis of the consent of states, without requiring their active support. Mere acquiescence by a state would amount to a vote *for,* not *against,* a program. When United Nations operations are based upon compulsory assessment, the middle ground of permissiveness is, in effect, eliminated. A state which regards a program with indifference is not allowed simply to stand aside; it is pressed to act as if it supports the program—and if it refuses, it is put into the position of opposing the program and hindering its operation. On the other hand, a United Nations which could draw upon its own treasury would have no need to press indifferent states to lend active financial support and, thereby, to risk shoving them into the ranks of the opponents of its action. In any given case, there are likely to be many states which are neither determined to hinder the Organization in carrying out a proposed international project nor willing to help it; if the United Nations is in a position to undertake the project without the financial help of its Members, it can treat such an attitude as a positive resource.

However, the political difficulty posed by the definite opposition of states to United Nations operations would not be eliminated by making the Organization financially independent. It must be remembered that states do not in every case oppose United Nations programs because they do not want to pay for them; on the contrary, in the most significant instances they are unwilling to pay for them because they oppose them. In such instances, the removal of the issue of financial support would not alter the opposition. The expression of opposition would necessarily take a new form, but it must be assumed that states which were determined to block or hamper United Nations activities would be able to contrive substitutes for the weapon of financial deprivation. The record of the Congo case indicates that the Soviet Union is willing and able to attack United Nations programs in more than one way; the personal attack upon Dag Hammarskjöld and the attack upon the office which he held were significant supplements to the refusal of the Soviet Union to meet its assessments. United Nations operations which made no financial demands upon states would still raise the possibility of contention regarding the purposes to which they were directed and the mechanisms of policy control under which they were conducted. Indeed, a United Nations which had become financially independent might tend to inspire greater mistrust on the part of some states, for it would appear to be less responsive to the will of its Members. Such a development would no doubt be welcomed by any state insofar as it felt confident that the Organization would always act in accordance with the state's own interest; equally, it would be viewed with misgiving by any state insofar as such confidence was lacking. A world organization capable of functioning as an autonomous factor in world affairs would not be attractive to the Soviet Union if it seemed likely to exhibit a pro-Western bias in its operations, nor would it be acceptable to the West if it seemed likely to operate in a pro-Soviet manner. Again, the issue of control is the central political concern, and this issue would probably be more, rather than less, acute in the case of a financially independent United Nations.

Assuming that general agreement might be reached among Members of the United Nations that the Organization should, in principle, be permitted and enabled to acquire financial resources without resort to governmental contributions or assessments, the problem of securing political agreement on the specific measures for implementing this principle would remain. This would pose many difficulties, ranging from the reluctance of states to permit the United Nations to take over valuable economic resources which they might otherwise appropriate for themselves, to the fear that a world organization vested with the power of taxation might become a kind of superstate challenging the sovereign status of its members.

If these difficulties were overcome and the United Nations became an agency able to conduct major operations in the peace-keeping and economic fields without dependence upon the financial support of states, what would be the probable results? From one point of view, the situation would be ideal. The Organization would be equipped to meet many of the basic needs of the world. It could undertake to deal with emergency situations such as the Congo case, unimpeded by uncertainty regarding financial support. It could move decisively into the realm of economic development, providing large-scale and long-term programs offering promise of genuinely constructive results. In short, the United Nations would have the prospect of doing much more of what needs to be done, of rendering increasingly valuable service to the world. States should welcome this result—as well as their emancipation from the necessity of carrying the financial burden of the United Nations. Thus runs the argument in favor of a financially independent United Nations.

There is another view, however, which deserves careful examination. A financially independent Organization might be thrust by general agreement into a position of political irrelevance; instead of provoking arguments about how to use it for important political purposes, the United Nations might inspire a consensus to the effect that it should be treated as an innocuous international philanthropic agency. Its Members might restrict it to operations so little related to the central issues of international relations that those operations would be as unlikely to arouse vigorous political opposition as to stimulate spirited political support. The United Nations might tend to become a sort of global "Foundation," investing its funds in worthy projects but, precisely because of its financial autonomy, declining in significance as an instrument of states in their relations with each other. Losing its status as a creature of states, dependent upon their sustenance, it might cease to be a center of political controversy—at the high cost of becoming an object of political indifference. According to this point of view, the aim should be not to shift the United Nations to the periphery of world politics, where it can operate unaffected by political conflicts, but to move it ever closer to the center, where it can be used to affect the critical struggles taking place in our time. To change the figure, the danger of wrecking the United Nations on the rocks of political conflict is not to be met by anchoring the Organization in a quiet apolitical harbor, but by attempting to develop a channel of political consensus which it may successfully—and usefully—navigate. This position suggests that the dependence of the United Nations upon the financial support of states may be essential to its being taken seriously by states; this dependence may weaken its executive effectiveness but enhance its political meaningfulness.

Conclusions

The United Nations is an international—which is to say, an *intergovernmental*—organization. What it can become and what it can do are ultimately determined by the governments of Member States. Particular governments may adopt an attitude of positive support, permissiveness, or opposition to a given program of the Organization. Regardless of how it is financed, a program requires a certain level of support from the membership of the Organization, if it is to be carried out successfully. Within limits, indifference and opposition can be tolerated; these limits cannot be stated precisely, or defined in terms applicable to every situation, but they are nevertheless very real. Much depends upon the identity of the state or states declining to give active support or registering determined opposition. The most critical difficulties arise when one of the two major powers, the Soviet Union or the United States, offers strenuous objection to a given program; in actual experience, the Soviet Union has functioned as the crucial dissenter from United Nations activities, although it is conceivable that the United States might assume that position in future contingencies. The present financial crisis of the United Nations is a manifestation of the difficulty of sustaining an international operation against the opposition of one of the major powers.

When a United Nations operation arouses the hostility of one of these powers, either before or after it has begun, there are two immediate alternatives: the operation may be abandoned in deference to that opposition, or the effort may be made to carry it on, despite the opposition. As we have noted, the continuation of the Congo operation in the face of active Soviet opposition appears to have been vindicated by the subsequent tempering of the Soviet attack upon the operation and upon the office of the Secretary-General. However, this experience provides no assurance that a similar tactic would produce equally satisfactory results in every case. The choice between defying and deferring to the opposition of a major power is a difficult one, and it is not possible to prescribe a general rule as to what should be done under such circumstances.

Shifting from the concrete situation to the problem of the long-run development of the United Nations, we might suggest that neither of these alternatives should be adopted, but that a third course is in order: to expand, so far as possible, the consensual basis for United Nations operations. The constructive political approach, combining the best elements of realism and idealism, is to explore and exploit the possibilities of convincing the dissident power that its own best interest requires an effectively operational United Nations and that the Organization can be relied upon to render impartial service, furthering the common interest in the stabilization of international relationships and the advancement of the general welfare. If the great powers can reach agreement on their mutual need for this kind of service, and can develop confidence in the capacity of the United Nations to render it in a spirit of political impartiality, the World Organization will have an increasingly useful role to play in the future. Presumably, this development will not come as a sudden and dramatic transformation. One ought not to expect a joint communiqué in which the great powers proclaim their definitive acceptance of the principle that the United Nations should move uninhibitedly toward the fullest expansion of its operational competence. Rather, one might hopefully anticipate a gradual enlargement of the area within which executive active by the Organization will be tolerated, valued, and supported. Obstructive opposition might be progressively changed, through the stages of passive opposition and reluctant acquiescence, to positive and responsible support for executive action. One might hope for the growth among all states of confidence in the United Nations and awareness of its potentiality for serving the real interests of all in achieving a viable world order, and for the evolution of a general recognition of the need to give the Organization the resources essential to the realization of that potentiality. If this sort of consensual foundation can be laid for its operations, the United Nations may expect from time to time to encounter financial problems that offer real challenges, but not financial crises that threaten its very existence.

The Study of Political Influence in the General Assembly

ROBERT O. KEOHANE

THE student of the United Nations General Assembly faces a "level of analysis" problem of his own. He can concentrate in his research on one of three aspects of the Organization: 1) the results of its deliberations; 2) the voting patterns within the Assembly; or 3) the political process which produces both the results and the voting patterns. Traditional analyses often adopt the first approach; statistically oriented political scientists have recently concentrated on the second. Very little systematic work has been done, however, on the political process: the exercise of political influence in the service of national policies.

A principal reason for this gap in our understanding is that the overwhelming emphasis of major works on the General Assembly has been on the analysis of voting patterns. Important as the understanding of individual and group voting behavior undoubtedly is, such analysis does not provide us with comprehensive knowledge of General Assembly politics. A sophisticated and accurate statistical analysis will indicate alignments and may provide clues to bargaining processes underlying them, but it does not yield detailed and relevant information about those processes. After statistical techniques have indicated the nature of the Assembly's political structure, the law of diminishing returns sets in rather quickly. If voting data are overused to the exclusion of other less accessible and quantifiable sources of information, the transition from traditional analysis to the investigation of voting behavior can merely substitute a new for an old formalism. The turtle's shell may now be exam-

ROBERT O. KEOHANE is Assistant Professor of Political Science at Swarthmore College, Swarthmore, Pennsylvania. The author wishes to express his appreciation to the Social Science Research Council for a summer grant, which facilitated research and thought on this subject. An earlier draft of this article was presented to a Conference on Research in International Organization, arranged by the Committee on International Organization of the SSRC in Berkeley, California, January 6–8, 1967. The author is grateful for the useful comments and criticisms offered by participants in that conference.

From Volume 21, No. 2 (1967), pp. 221–37.

ined, often in meticulous detail, but the existence of the turtle is hardly recognized, much less understood.

POLITICAL PROCESS AND POLITICAL INFLUENCE

By the "political process" in the General Assembly, I mean the interactions between delegations and Secretariat members through which General Assembly decisions are reached. This process can be viewed as primarily a struggle for influence, where influence is defined in terms of effect on *outcomes* rather than control over individual states. Who shapes the results is the relevant question rather than who has the most satellites. The Union of Soviet Socialist Republics (Soviet Union) in the early 1950's must be regarded as having had very little influence in the General Assembly although it could control the behavior of a number of delegations. Thus, we will regard a state as influential in the General Assembly insofar as it is able to affect the decisions of the General Assembly so that they accord with its wishes. Two questions are therefore crucial in deciding how influential any state is in the Organization: 1) To what extent did General Assembly decisions accord with its wishes? 2) In what ways and with what effects did the state affect those decisions?

Three types of influence can be distinguished, the most important of which is influence over outcomes by affecting the policies of individual Members. If the effect on delegations' policies contributes to producing an effect on the outcome, influence, in our definition of the term, has been exercised. This process may be bilateral or multilateral; it may take place within, between, or without respect to caucusing groups. The relationship may be reciprocal, on a single issue ("compromise"), an artificially linked set of issues ("log rolling"), or a broad range of General Assembly business ("mutual understandings," "patterns of cooperation"). If the relationship in the Assembly is not reciprocal—that is, the behavior of one state *in the General Assembly* is influenced by the other but not vice versa—this may be accomplished through argument ("persuasion"), by positive inducements ("promises"), or by negative inducements ("pressure" or "threats").

Prestige or power outside the Assembly can therefore be translated into influence within. For example, a state with high "moral stature" may be able to deny legitimacy to a resolution by opposing it. If the sponsors are aware of this situation in advance, they may find it desirable to consult with that state before formally presenting their resolution. Thus, Scandinavian states have sometimes derived political influence from their moral authority, particularly with respect to African resolutions attacking apartheid. On the other hand, a state may gain influence within the Assembly by sheer economic or political power. If the cooperation of the United States is required to implement a resolution, it can usually be expected that before adoption the American delegation's views will be important within the Assembly as well as outside. Explicit threats or "pressure" are frequently not necessary. For instance, in the twentieth session the American delegation was able to exercise influence on the United Nations Relief and Works Agency for Palestine Refugees in the Near East (UNRWA) resolution by letting it be known that the United States was strongly opposed to the draft that had emerged from the Special Political Committee. Not only was it likely that the United States could have mustered a "blocking third" of the votes in the Assembly on this issue; equally important was the fact that American funds provide most of the revenues for the refugee program. The Arab delegations that favored the Committee draft were forced, therefore, to negotiate a compromise with the United States.

Group formation and coalition management in the Assembly provide examples of influence over outcomes through influence over individual Members. Like-minded states may cooperate in order to increase the influence of each over outcomes; at the other extreme a coalition may be formed through the threats and promises of one Member. In the former case gains and losses from the action are shared relatively equally by the coalition members. In the latter instance, however, the organizing power (a "political entrepreneur") expects to reap the gains if his coalition succeeds and to take the losses if it fails: He has already "purchased" the support of his coalition partners, who may have little stake in the outcome. Thus certain members of the coalition opposing the seating of the People's Republic of China (Communist China) probably care little about the outcome but vote as they do because the United States has provided inducements to do so.

Secondly, a state may be able to affect the choices with which the General Assembly is faced, quite apart from its influence over the policies of Members. Thus, a state may exercise influence by proposing an item for the agenda that no other state would be willing to propose but that no state is willing to oppose. Even if all governments have unchangeable positions on an issue, the form in which alternatives are presented to the Organization can affect the outcome of the process. Since a large legislative body such as the General Assembly must work with a limited number of specific alternatives, the proposals that the Organization takes most seriously usually form the basis for the final result. Much negotiation in the General Assembly, as well as most parliamentary maneuver, is designed to alter the situation with which the Organization's Members are faced rather than to affect the policies of any delegation. If the Assembly's decisions are thereby favorably affected, delegations that take initiatives, make successful compromise suggestions, or raise relevant procedural points can be said to have had influence even though they may not have been able to alter the policies of any states. Here the context within which national policies are applied, rather than the policies themselves, is affected.

A third form of influence is a function of the formal procedures of the Assembly: Each state has one vote. Thus, in a purely formal sense, before attempts by states to influence the situation or each other begin, each state has influence equal to $1/n$, where n is the number of states represented in the organization.[1] As lines begin to be drawn between members, states in a "pivotal" position can be said to have the greatest influence since their decisions— although intrinsically no more important than those of any other states—will "decide" the issue. Not only will these states tend most often to be on the winning side, but their votes will presumably be sought by the activists on either side. Moderation or indecision may therefore create something of value, an undecided vote.

This focus on political influence within the Assembly does not imply that states always act to increase their influence in that body. On the contrary, political maneuvers may be taken for domestic political reasons, to please a particularly important ally, or to satisfy the personal ambitions of a foreign minister. The Republic of China, for instance, could probably increase its influence in the Assembly by being more independent of the American delegation, but it would not be likely to do so if this involved seriously antagonizing the United States. This merely points to the truism that General Assembly politics are subordinate to world politics generally. Broad national policies and the goals for which influence is sought necessarily limit the search for influence and the "pure politics" that might result.

THE MEASUREMENT OF INFLUENCE

Statistical techniques for determining how influential an actor is in a committee or parliament usually rest on an implicit model of the political system being studied; if this model is faulty, the techniques become rather useless. It has been proposed, for instance, that influence ratings be compiled on the basis of the percentage of the time a member of a legislative body votes with the majority of the group.[2] The larger a member's majority-support score, the more influential he would be said to be. Similarly, Shapley and Shubik suggest that influence ratings be compiled by comparing the probability that an actor was "pivotal" on any given series of votes, with his a priori probability of being "pivotal." Thus, in a nine-member committee each member has a hypothetical influence value of $1/9$; however, on a decision taken by a 5-4 majority, each majority member is assigned an influence value of $1/5$ (that is,

[1] See L. S. Shapley and Martin Shubik, "A Method for Evaluating the Distribution of Power in a Committee System," *American Political Science Review*, September 1954 (Vol. 48, No. 3), pp. 787–792.

[2] See Robert A. Dahl, "The Concept of Power," *Behavioral Science*, July 1957 (Vol. 2, No. 3), pp. 201–215; and Donald R. Matthews, "Patterns of Influence in the U. S. Senate: Five Approaches" (unpublished paper prepared for delivery at the 1960 annual meeting of the American Political Science Association), for discussions of this technique.

$1/n+1$, where n is the number of actors voting in the majority with him) whereas each member of the minority is assigned a value of zero.

The difficulty with these indexes, whose results are likely to approximate one another, is that they implicitly assume an atomistic assembly in which each member is presented with an issue from outside the system and makes his voting decision without being influenced by others. Thus, the results exaggerate the influence of members whose ideological positions are near the center of the legislative body. If the act of voting constituted the whole of politics, this objection would be irrelevant: Actors in the political center of an assembly would indeed exercise the greatest control over outcomes and would therefore be the most influential. Thus, in the fifteenth session of the General Assembly, according to the majority-voting test, Somalia, Iran, Malaya, and Pakistan were the most "influential" states; in the eighteenth session, these computations discover Malaysia, Gabon, Haiti, and Liberia to have been of decisive importance. In both sessions the United States, the United Kingdom, France, and the Soviet Union were at or near the low end of the scale: In the eighteenth session, out of 111 states, the United States ranked 96th, the United Kingdom 97th, France 99th, and the Soviet Union in a seven-way tie for 103rd in majority support. The implausibility of these results as clues to relative political influence renders further comment superfluous.

Alker and Russett have applied Donald Matthews' concept of "legislative effectiveness" to groups in the General Assembly with useful and interesting results.[3] The index of legislative effectiveness simply measures the proportion of resolutions introduced by an actor that are passed by the legislative body. Although valuable for indicating who initiates action, this index cannot be used effectively to indicate the relative influence of individual states since to do so would be to equate political influence with acceptance of proposals that one formally sponsors. In reality, however, the sponsors of resolutions are often not its most important supporters; furthermore, the influence of states that successfully oppose initiatives is not taken into account by this technique. Using this technique to measure state influence in the fifteenth and sixteenth sessions, an investigator would find that Yemen, Nepal, Afghanistan, Somalia, and Togo were among the most "influential" Members of the General Assembly whereas the United States and the Soviet Union were less important.

The common problem with the legislative-effectiveness and majority-support tests is that one must infer the extent of a state's influence from the results of Assembly action with no way of determining the impact of that particular state on those results. The first question posed above can in some measure be answered by these tests: That is, to what extent did General Assembly

[3] Hayward A. Alker, Jr., and Bruce M. Russett, *World Politics in the General Assembly* (New Haven and London: Yale University Press, 1965), Chapter 9. Alker and Russett make it clear that they are aware of the limitations of this technique in measuring political influence.

decisions accord with the expressed wishes of a particular state? To answer the second question, however—in what ways and with what impact did the state affect those decisions—the researcher must investigate the process as well as the results. His technique must rest on a model of the political process that is complex rather than simple.

A RESEARCH PROPOSAL

It is clearly necessary, therefore, not to limit our research on the General Assembly to roll-call voting and other easily accessible and quantifiable material. Such a shift from the study of votes to that of processes may require that we relax, temporarily at least, our standards of quantitative precision to fit the complexity and ambiguity of our data. In particular, I suggest that it is necessary to undertake intensive and insofar as possible systematic analysis of General Assembly politics on a range of issues, concentrating on the question of political influence but not attempting at first to specify in quantitative terms the precise amount of such influence. This approach requires extensive interviewing of national representatives as well as careful analysis of the official record and the clues it provides, to discover who was active, in what ways, and with what effect. Beginning with an understanding of the normal patterns of behavior in a given session or set of sessions, we can then inquire into specific issues of particular interest.[4] On questions such as the Article 19 crisis and Cyprus the case study method may be appropriate; for less unique events composite issue-categories may be useful as focal points for analysis.[5]

This approach is disturbingly specific and therefore poses obvious problems for systematic comparison and analysis of Assembly politics generally. It is hard to see, however, how we can construct large-scale generalizations or complex and detailed models at this point without doing violence to our subject matter.[6] The political process of the Assembly is varied, complex, and relatively poorly understood. Influence and communications patterns, as well as alignments and interests, vary from one issue to another; at this point we understand differences in alignments better than variations in political processes.

The first requirement, therefore, is to make necessary empirical distinctions between the various types of political processes operating in the Assembly. If we ask systematically about influence in particular situations, certain patterns

---

[4] A preliminary attempt to use this approach can be found in Robert Keohane, "Political Influence in the General Assembly," *International Conciliation*, March 1966 (No. 557).

[5] For example, see the discussion of procedural questions below, p. 233.

[6] In his comments on an earlier draft of this article Hayward Alker, Jr., proposed simulation as a superior alternative method. I do not deny that simulation may be a valuable approach; however, it seems to me to depend upon, rather than to negate the value of, close empirical analysis. As Karl Deutsch has written, "Simulation at best cannot be much better than our understanding of the processes which we imagine we are simulating." ("Recent Trends in Research Methods in Political Science," in *A Design for Political Science: Scope, Objectives and Methods* [Philadelphia: American Academy of Political and Social Science, December 1966].)

may appear that can later be tested more thoroughly. This search for patterns must be carried out with the aid of a set of theoretical questions centering on the problem of political influence. What are the sources of influence, how is it exercised within various relationships, what constraints exist on its use?[7] Although such a theoretical framework has not yet been constructed, the following pages may suggest, in a limited and unsystematic way, how some of these questions might be investigated.

THE INFLUENCE OF SMALL POWERS: CYPRUS

Politics in the General Assembly can be categorized not only "vertically"—in terms of the subject matter of the issues—but also "horizontally"—according to the level at which the most significant interactions take place. Thus, a controversy may revolve primarily around the two superpowers, or it may focus on relationships between great and small states, or it may be fought out among small powers. These levels are not neatly separable; many questions are considered on several levels simultaneously.

The crisis over the application of Article 19 of the UN Charter to the Soviet Union, France, and several other states illustrates the first two levels of General Assembly politics: The important relationships were those between the protagonists, particularly between the Soviet Union and the United States, and those between the protagonists and small states holding a majority of General Assembly votes. Small-power/great-power relationships were clearly marked by mutual dependence: Small states dared not take initiatives themselves beyond making suggestions to the Great Powers involved, yet the outcome for the Great Powers depended on the attitudes of small states. After the reluctance of many states to vote sanctions against the Soviet Union had wrecked the American plans, nothing could be done until a compromise was reached or one Great Power capitulated. Small states could prevent a solution to which they did not wish to become committed; but, particularly in the absence of unity, they could not dictate the outcome.

The limitations on the influence of small states in the Article 19 crisis raise the question of small-state influence in the General Assembly when the Great Powers are not intimately involved. For the student of political influence and political technique, interactions between relatively powerless states have a special significance: How is influence exercised, if it is, without a physical power capacity to buttress it? Do the relationships between states that would otherwise come into little or no contact with each other diplomatically indicate anything about the nature of international leadership, and how it is gained

---

[7] Donald J. Puchala suggested in his comments on this article at the SSRC conference that public opinion polls might constitute a useful analogy for such a set of questions. A case study of an issue in the General Assembly would roughly correspond to an individual respondent in the public opinion polls; that is, a systematic set of questions would be asked with regard to each.

and exercised apart from physical power capacity? For the student of contemporary world politics, also, the study of small-state interaction and influence is important, both in providing information about the newly emerging patterns of relationships between developing states and in indicating the influence that small states may have over Great Powers in certain situations. To understand great-power relationships with small states it is necessary not only to investigate the influence of the former over the latter but also the converse; not only how effectively the United States can affect Greek policy on questions vital to American national interests but how successful Greece can be vis-à-vis the United States where Greek interests are paramount.

The twentieth session of the General Assembly provided a superb example of small-power conflict over a discrete issue: the question of Cyprus. Since two of the major contestants, Greece and Turkey, are members of the North Atlantic Treaty Organization (NATO), political alignments were not formed from the outset on "East-West" or "North-South" lines. Faced with civil war on the island, the Security Council had, in March of 1964, established the United Nations Peacekeeping Force on Cyprus (UNFICYP), which had reduced the level of violence without being able to effect a reconciliation between Turkish and Greek Cypriots or the respective national states. Both sides requested that the question of Cyprus be placed on the Assembly's agenda for the twentieth session, the first regularly operating session since UNFICYP had been created.

Cyprus and Greece worked for a resolution emphasizing the "full sovereignty and complete independence" of Cyprus and stressing that there should be no foreign interference in its affairs whereas Turkey hoped for a purely procedural resolution supporting Security Council action. Turkey, with considerable support from the Great Powers and with regional military superiority, could be content with a neutral General Assembly; Cyprus, on the contrary, desired active Assembly support for its cause. As a result the Cypriot objective in the Assembly was to engineer a Turkish defeat or to force Turkey to change its position in important ways. In the view of Cyprus a compromise that was really acceptable to Turkey would not represent a satisfactory outcome in the General Assembly. The Cypriots wanted a weapon for use against the Turks, not a formula for reconciliation.

Cyprus pursued its objectives through a series of complicated procedural maneuvers. Priority was granted to the Cypriot-favored draft, which was adopted by the First (Political and Security) Committee by a vote of 47 in favor, 6 opposed, with 51 abstentions. Success was not yet assured, however, since the possibility remained that the Committee would also adopt a superficially similar draft proposed by friends of Turkey, thus creating an ambiguity about the intentions of the body. This possibility was foreclosed by the tabling of amendments that would have made the second draft resolution into almost a carbon copy of the first: When these amendments had been accepted for consideration by the Chairman of the Committee, the states friendly to Turkey withdrew their resolution. Several last-minute attempts at compromise failed, and Cyprus achieved its immediate political objectives when the General Assembly adopted the resolution, 47–5–54.

ARGUMENTS AND POSITIONS OF STATES

The most interesting aspect of these developments relates to the extent to which Cyprus gained support for its self-interested and very specific objectives through the exploitation of quasi-idealistic and universal principles. Of the 29 states voting consistently with Cyprus on all roll-calls involving the question of Cyprus seventeen were non-Arab African: No non-Arab African states supported Turkey's position more often than that of Cyprus. According to a wide variety of United Nations delegations the Cypriots gained this strong African support by appealing to the principle of self-determination. As a memorandum of Cyprus stated the issue:

> The problem of Cyprus appears exceedingly complicated and involved but in essence it is very simple. It stems from a virtual denial to the people of Cyprus of its fundamental right to self-determination and from an effort to deprive the Republic of Cyprus of the substance of its sovereignty and independence.[8]

Cyprus reinforced this general point with more specific references to Africa and, in particular, Southern Rhodesia. As the Cypriot representative put it in the First Committee, according to the official summary:

> The Turkish government's policy was to divide the people into two separate and equal communities, irrespective of numbers and the question of majority or minority, which he had dismissed outright. In the present age, however, the majority rule was generally accepted and a situation could no longer be tolerated in which a small class of persons, irrespective of their origin, whether they were civilized or uncivilized, whether or not they were a historic people, could hold a privileged position in a unitary, unified State. The dedication of the African peoples to true democracy was an example to be proud of and to follow.[9]

This point was made even more explicitly in private. If special privileges for the Turkish minority on Cyprus were permitted by the Assembly, under cover of treaty rights, could not the analogy be used to justify a similar status for the white residents of Southern Rhodesia? With arguments such as these Cyprus used general principles as means by which to connect two separate situations and to persuade newly independent African countries that *their* interests, as well as its own, were involved. Thus, the general principles did

---

[8] UN Document A/5934/Add.1, September 22, 1965, p. 2.
[9] General Assembly *Official Records . . . First Committee* (20th session), 1408th meeting, p. 340.

not stand on their own in the Cypriot appeal but were woven into an argument that rested on considerations of specific national interests.

Turkey could counter the Cypriot arguments with appeals to international
legality and the sanctity of treaties that were attractive to Western states. Unfortunately for the Turks, however, those states that supported its position
and agreed with the legal principles that it espoused were for various reasons
disinclined to take strong stands. Six of the seven states providing troops for
UNFICYP abstained on the crucial votes in the interest of "neutrality." This
decision having been made, it was no longer possible for Turkey to avoid
parliamentary defeat; thus, other states that might have supported Turkey
apparently decided to abstain on the final vote rather than find themselves
in a tiny and conspicuous minority. Abstention was the safe course of action.
Since the outcome was determined, to oppose the majority would be to court
trouble. The result was therefore paradoxical: Many of the UNFICYP contributors apparently favored a mild procedural resolution, which would have
been acceptable to Turkey, but their self-conscious "neutrality" helped Cyprus
to put through a strong substantive measure, calling for a change in the legal
status quo.

This was an interesting development since it indicates more clearly the
difficulties in taking a stand on the "merits" of an issue in the General Assembly. Just as the nonaligned states pursue the goal of nonalignment, so the
UNFICYP contributors pursued the goal of neutrality; in both cases, one
motive is to preserve the status of an "objective" potential mediator. Paradoxically, however, the result is often the opposite of objectivity: Mechanical adherence to a rule allows one's behavior to be manipulated or taken advantage
of by whichever contesting party is in a favorable position to do so.[10]

It should not be concluded that the behavior of all states was decisively
influenced either by general arguments or principles of "objectivity": In fact,
many states' attitudes appear to have been shaped primarily by considerations
of parochial or regional interests and loyalties. Thus, regional solidarity was
certainly a major factor in producing a sharp and unusual cleavage between
nonaligned Asian and Arab states such as Afghanistan and Iraq, which supported Turkey, and their usual allies in Africa. Of the thirteen Arab states in
the General Assembly eight tended to favor Turkey, four backed Cyprus,
while one was neutral. The four Arab supporters of Cyprus were the United
Arab Republic, Syria, and Yemen, along with Lebanon. In the Middle East,
the three contiguous non-Arab Islamic states—Afghanistan, Iran, and Pakistan
—also supported the Turks. In view of the "cross-pressures" to which Middle
Eastern states were subject from the general tendency of nonaligned states to
support Cyprus, this voting record provides significant evidence of the impact
of regional and cultural loyalties.

[10] The behavior of African and Asian neutrals in the Article 19 crisis provides another example of
this phenomenon; see Keohane, *International Conciliation*, No. 557, especially pp. 57–64.

Antagonisms as well as loyalties were played upon by the participants. India, for instance, is widely regarded by delegates as having supported Cyprus so strongly (it was one of three pro-Cypriot "floor leaders") partly because Pakistan was pro-Turkish. Cyprus, for its part, did its best to attract India by immediately taking the Indian side in the Kashmir conflict of 1965; Cyprus knew that Pakistan, being tied so closely to Turkey, would provide no support in return for Cypriot help but hoped that India would. The clearest example, however, of antagonisms taking precedence over other considerations—even ideology—is provided by Albania. Although Albania is the most intransigent opponent of the United States, NATO, and neocolonialism in the General Assembly, as well as being a small state vulnerable to intervention from without, it voted *against* the pro-Cypriot resolution, standing with the United States, Iran, and Pakistan in supporting Turkey. The consensus of delegates on this point seems to be that Albania's vote was an anti-Greek gesture, expressing opposition to Greek "imperialism" and reflecting strained Albanian-Greek relations and territorial disputes. Thus, Albania voted with the chief "imperialist" state against a resolution that purported to protect a small, nonaligned state from neocolonialist intervention!

Techniques of Influence

The Cyprus case suggests strongly that the first rule for states wishing to construct majorities is: Court the "nonaligned." In this endeavor, Cyprus had an initial advantage since it was generally considered to be a nonaligned state and had compiled a voting record close to the political center of the Assembly whereas Turkey's voting was heavily influenced by its NATO membership. Both states, however, attempted to gain support from the nonaligned states by using nonaligned states as leaders in the fight. Thus, Sierra Leone, Guinea, and India served as "floor leaders" for Cyprus—not Greece, a NATO member, which stayed for the most part in the background. On the other side, Afghanistan and Iraq led the pro-Turkish forces, rather than Iran and Pakistan, which were actually somewhat more strongly committed to Turkey's cause.

Both Cyprus and Turkey, however, went beyond simple persuasion and used both promises and "pressures"; that is, they offered rewards for help and indicated to other states that retaliation might be the consequence of antagonistic actions. Interestingly enough, three Security Council members seem to have been the chief recipients of such attention: China, the United States, and the Soviet Union. China, which sympathized with Turkey, was induced to abstain by Greek and Cypriot threats to support Communist Chinese admission to the General Assembly if the Nationalists voted against the Greek-Cypriot draft. The Soviet Union, on the other hand, despite its early support for Cyprus, was "brought over" to neutrality on the issue by intensive Turkish efforts.

The position of the United States, which consistently supported the Turkish position, was more complex. As far as Greece and Cyprus were concerned it was less important how the United States voted than how it acted behind the scenes: Although its votes with Turkey were "unacceptable," the exercise of American influence on behalf of Turkey could have been disastrous. Thus, twice during the twentieth session, when the Greek delegation thought that the United States was attempting to persuade Latin American states to support Turkey, it made strong representations with the United States mission. These representations were generally successful; the United States did not engage actively in the struggle.

This last example particularly indicates the leverage that a committed small state may possess with respect to a less involved Great Power; it also illustrates how limited are the influence resources of the superpowers. The United States must husband its influence so that it can gain votes where it needs them most. Pressure exercised on behalf of Turkey would not only have dangerously antagonized Greece but would also have incurred costs of other kinds. Influence resources used on the Turkish issue might not be available for a future struggle over Chinese representation. Every successful exercise of influence creates a corresponding political liability: a political debt that must be discharged in the future, a commitment of one sort or another. Thus, even American influence cannot be exercised effectively on more than a small fraction of the issues before the General Assembly.

The Cyprus issue may have some interesting implications for the future course of General Assembly politics. In an international system of over 120 states, local and regional quarrels, often lacking real ideological content, are likely to occur frequently. These conflicts may be settled bilaterally or in regional organizations, but insofar as they come to the United Nations General Assembly, the patterns of action there may resemble those on the Cyprus issue. National interests will be pursued through an interplay of ideology and concrete interests, by using new dogmas and old antagonisms and loyalties. As one delegate put it, "the *quid pro quo* is served up on a tray of abstract principles." It may be suggested, however, that as states become more sophisticated, the ideological aspect of the respective arguments may be seen as less applicable, and the General Assembly may increasingly become an arena for the more explicit pursuit of national goals. The still serviceable "tray of abstract principles" may therefore become less useful if international ideologies give way increasingly to particularist nationalisms. If this were to happen, political alignments in the Assembly, at least on many issues, would become less rigid. There would be more "cross-cutting solidarities"—and also a greater variety of conflicts.

Parliamentary Procedure and the General Assembly

The United Nations General Assembly is no exception to the rule that political organizations necessarily become involved in procedural disputes. As an organization of states without extensive common interests or sentiments to bind its Members together the General Assembly confronts formidable problems in developing normative standards that will be respected regardless of considerations of immediate advantage. As a highly experienced permanent representative remarked privately, "It is a general principle that whoever can take advantage of the rules of procedure will do so." Thus, the struggle for influence in the Organization often turns on disputes over the application of procedural rules, and votes on procedural questions are frequently more crucial than votes on the substantive issues with which they are associated.

The importance of procedure is emphasized by the closeness of roll-call votes on procedural questions in the twentieth session. Fifteen roll-call votes were taken on such issues; on only two of these was either side able to gain a two-thirds majority. The mean cohesion index (that is, the difference between the sum of majority votes and the sum of minority votes, divided by the total number of votes cast, and multiplied by 100) was only 16.2. Thus, a vote of 47 to 31, with 22 abstentions and 17 absences, could be considered roughly typical. In every case except that of Chinese representation, in which later votes were taken on the chief issue at stake, the crucial votes on parliamentary procedures were more closely contested than the substantive votes.

Political Uses of Procedure

Procedural disputes in the twentieth session centered primarily on two types of questions: attempts to establish either a majority or two-thirds decision-making rule in plenary session and attempts to reduce opportunities for modifying resolutions, either by denying separate votes on controversial paragraphs or by preventing votes on amendments or counterresolutions. The Cyprus issue illustrates the latter tactic. Such a maneuver may permit a cohesive majority or near-majority to impose its will and still emerge with a final resolution that is opposed by few states. This result occurs because many delegations that oppose particular parts of a resolution may nevertheless be reluctant to oppose the entire measure because of the universally accepted shibboleths that compose its major portion. Thus, the parliamentary battle in the General Assembly, as in the Cyprus case, often takes the form of an elaborate ritual in which supporters of a resolution attempt to bury controversial passages in layers of rhetoric to which few states can object and then attempt to manipulate procedure so that the resolution must be considered *in toto*. After the resolution has been safely adopted, the controversial passages are sure to be resurrected by their sponsors.

The most delicate type of procedural controversy arises when a state, fearing to be a minority on the issue, attempts to have it ruled an "important question" requiring two-thirds support for passage. The delicacy of the situation arises from the fact that successful use of the ploy requires that states not willing to support one's position on the major question will provide support on the preliminary procedural issue. United States actions in the twentieth session on the Chinese representation question provide good illustrations of this tactic.

The United States position in this issue was that regardless of one's view of Communist China's relationship to the United Nations it was necessary for any honest man to agree that the issue was an "important question" within the meaning of Article 18 of the Charter,[11] particularly since it had been so considered by the sixteenth session of the General Assembly. Thus, states with respect for legality and the Charter would side with the United States on this issue, even if they differed on the question of Chinese representation itself. This argument, however, was subject to criticism. As technically a question of representation rather than admission or expulsion of Members the issue did not clearly fall under the mandatory provisions of Article 18, paragraph 2, requiring two-thirds support for passage of a resolution. It could well be argued, on the contrary, that it fell under Article 18, paragraph 3, stating that "additional categories" of questions subject to the two-thirds decision rule could be created by a majority of Members present and voting. If this were so, the decision of the sixteenth session to treat the Chinese representation problem as an "important question" could be interpreted as creating an additional category under Article 18, paragraph 3, rather than as affirming the applicability of paragraph 2. In this case the validity of the precedent from the sixteenth session would be open to doubt: According to Goodrich and Hambro's interpretation of Article 18 the precedent would not be binding.[12]

<hr>

[11] Article 18 reads as follows:

    1. Each member of the General Assembly shall have one vote.

    2. Decisions of the General Assembly on important questions shall be made by a two-thirds majority of the members present and voting. These questions shall include: recommendations with respect to the maintenance of international peace and security, the election of the non-permanent members of the Security Council, the election of the members of the Economic and Social Council, the election of members of the Trusteeship Council in accordance with paragraph 1 (c) of Article 86, the admission of new Members to the United Nations, the suspension of the rights and privileges of membership, the expulsion of Members, questions relating to the operation of the trusteeship system, and budgetary questions.

    3. Decisions on other questions, including the determination of additional categories of questions to be decided by a two-thirds majority, shall be made by a majority of the members present and voting.

[12]

    A question which the Charter does not expressly answer is whether the General Assembly, once it has determined by a majority vote additional categories of questions to be decided by a two-thirds vote, can reverse its actions by a majority vote. Although categories established by Article 18 (2), cannot be abolished except by the method specified for amending the Charter, it is clear that "additional categories" established under paragraph 3 can be abolished or modified by the Assembly by a majority vote of the members present and voting since a session of the General Assembly cannot bind future sessions.

(Leland M. Goodrich and Edvard Hambro, *Charter of the United Nations: Commentary and Documents* [2nd and rev. ed.; Boston: World Peace Foundation, 1949], p. 190.)

Thus a plausible argument could be made for the view that voting against treating the Chinese representation issue as an important question did not imply disrespect for the Charter or international legality.[13]

Although the American legal position was at least open to doubt, semantic advantage lay with the United States: Since the problem of Chinese representation was obviously important in the ordinary usage of the term, it was a small step to the conclusion that it was "important" in the technical language of Article 18. This ambiguity may have helped the American delegation achieve its political objectives: Seven states voted with the United States on the "important question" issue while abstaining or voting against the United States on the question of representation. Thus, the United States-backed procedural resolution was adopted, 56–49–11, whereas the vote on seating Peking's representatives ended in a 47–47–20 tie. American legal and semantic arguments may have been sufficient to persuade some of the states in this category, but the situation of the Netherlands and the United Kingdom, at least, was probably more complex. As close American allies that had recognized Communist China, these states were in a particularly embarrassing political position. Thus, they faced a cruel dilemma from which they were saved by the complexity of the "important question" issue.

Here an interesting parallel is evident between the General Assembly and the United States Congress where procedural votes are sometimes used to decrease the visibility of Congressmen's behavior, thereby increasing the influence of the party leadership, which understands procedural complexities better than the electorate.[14] In the Chinese representation case the United States acted similarly: By complicating the issue it allowed Britain and the Netherlands to maintain their "principles" without really opposing the American position. Thus, procedural complexity, plus legal and semantic ambiguity, may allow governments to assist an ally—perhaps in return for an implicit or explicit *quid pro quo*—without being castigated effectively at home or by other states for subservience. This tactic is probably particularly useful to Great Powers, which have the resources to provide inducements to friendly behavior in such situations. When the French representative in the twentieth session commented that the legal problem was "obscured by a wave of confusion which is more or less deliberately maintained,"[15] he paid implicit tribute to the American delegation's political skill as well as its capacity for semantic legerdemain.

Contrasting with the nimble manipulations of the United States were the

---

[13] This position—that the General Assembly was free to decide in each session what the voting procedure should be on the Chinese representation question—represents a middle ground between the views of the United States and many of its opponents which held that the Assembly was violating the Charter by considering this question of representation "important."

[14] Lewis A. Froman, Jr., and Randall B. Ripley, "Conditions for Party Leadership: The Case of the House Democrats," *American Political Science Review*, March 1965 (Vol. 59, No. 1), pp. 52–63.

[15] General Assembly *Official Records* (20th session), 1399th plenary meeting, December 17, 1965, p. 16.

heavy majoritarian tactics of the anticolonial powers on several twentieth-session issues. The new "mechanical majority" was particularly evident on a resolution that called on the "colonial Powers" to dismantle military bases located in colonial territory and requested the Special Committee on the Situation with Regard to the Implementation of the Declaration on the Granting of Independence to Colonial Countries and Peoples (Special Committee of Twenty-Four) to "apprise the Security Council of developments in any Territory examined by it which may threaten international peace and security.... "[16] Despite the obvious fact that this resolution made "recommendations with respect to the maintenance of international peace and security," the Assembly decided that it should be subject to adoption by majority vote. On colonial and neocolonial issues the intensity of feeling in the Assembly leads to a loosening of procedural restraints: Since the Assembly itself interprets the Charter, rampant majoritarianism is a continual possibility.

LIMITATIONS ON THE POLITICAL USES OF PROCEDURE

Normative limitations on the abuse of procedure in the General Assembly are obviously weak. All states attempt to manipulate procedure; many are willing to approve quite radical deviations from Charter specifications. This raises the question, therefore, of limitations on the exercise of influence by procedural means. Are there any tactics that are ruled out because they are considered "unfair"?

It is clear that in some situations, particularly where emotional involvements are high, many states will be willing to use whatever tactics may bring success. Nevertheless, three kinds of limitations on the ruthless manipulation of procedure can be suggested. In the first place, the interests of some states and the ethical standards of some representatives would bar outright violation of the Charter for political objectives. The sanctity of the Charter may be considered more important than any Assembly victory, for moral, legal, or political reasons.

Secondly, the abuse of procedure by a majority tends to create more bitterness in the Assembly than factional domination on substantive issues: It is less infuriating merely to be defeated than to feel that the "rules of the game" have been changed to one's disadvantage.[17] To the extent, therefore, that ruthless procedural tactics create bitterness that hinders future success in the Assembly by damaging working relationships such tactics may become dysfunctional and be less frequently used. For the United States in the twentieth session, for example, the adoption of the resolution on colonialism referred to above caused much less bitterness than the procedural finding that the issue

[16] General Assembly Resolution 2105 (XX), December 20, 1965.

[17] For a contrasting view on the significance of procedural votes for consensus, see Alker and Russett, p. 158.

was not an "important question." If the United States were to respond to such procedural abuses by being less cooperative toward African states, the use of these tactics might be discouraged.

Related to this is a third point, that anticipation of problems involved in implementing a resolution may limit ruthless procedural tactics. Particularly if these tactics are used against the wishes of a Great Power or a state with control over the situation, they can easily backfire. Thus, the Assembly's resolution on Cyprus has been lightly regarded by Western powers, whose representatives considered its enactment an example of "smart small-time manipulating," to use the words of one delegate. A resolution adopted in a more open fashion, with less recourse to procedural devices, might well have received more thorough consideration by the important powers involved. An unwillingness to implement resolutions adopted through the use of questionable tactics may on occasion perform similar functions to those of international norms in restraining future recourse to such expedients.

Conclusion

This article has presented an argument for detailed empirical research on political influence as one approach by which we can investigate important aspects of General Assembly politics. Such research will put flesh on the skeletal description provided by voting studies while preparing the way for more advanced forms of descriptive and explanatory analysis. As long as the General Assembly itself is politically significant scholarly work of this type will require no further justification.

Yet inquiry along these lines is significant in two other ways. As an international assembly the General Assembly is relevant to the study of international assemblies and quasi legislatures generally. Secondly, and perhaps more important, the study of General Assembly politics necessarily raises crucial questions about present and future patterns of world politics.[18] Even from the few cases discussed in this article insights can be gained into great-power/-small-power relations, the interaction of national interests and ideology, and the problem of international norms. Neglect of the political process of the General Assembly not only hinders our understanding of the United Nations and international organizations in general; it also prevents us from exploring international politics from a different perspective.

---

[18] Relying primarily on their analyses of votes and other official data, Hayward Alker, Jr., and Bruce M. Russett have used the General Assembly to raise important and interesting questions about world politics. See *ibid.*; and Bruce M. Russett, *Trends in World Politics* (New York: Macmillan, 1965), especially Chapters 4–6.

The Executive Head:

An Essay on Leadership in International Organization

Robert W. Cox

The quality of executive leadership may prove to be the most critical single determinant of the growth in scope and authority of international organization. Now sufficiently long and varied to allow a comparative approach, the history of international organization may provide elements for a theory of leadership. This essay is but a preliminary effort in that direction. It is concerned not only with how the executive head protects and develops his position as top man but also with how, by doing so, he may be the creator of a new (if yet slender) world power base.

The origin of the comparative study of executive heads of international organizations was the observation that Albert Thomas was a very different kind of man from Sir Eric Drummond and had very different ideas about how to carry out his job. From this observation stemmed a number of speculations. The failure of the League of Nations in the late thirties was contrasted with the apparent success of the International Labor Organization (ILO). Would the story have been different had a Thomas been Secretary-General of the League? Or would—as seems to have been Sir Eric Drummond's view—the nature of the job have led a Thomas to fail in the League? Whatever disagreement surrounds this speculation there is a greater measure of agreement that with the Drummond approach ILO would have become nothing more than a technical information bureau.[1]

Robert W. Cox is Director of the International Institute for Labor Studies (which was created by the International Labor Organization) as well as Professor at the Graduate Institute for International Studies, Geneva. The views expressed by him do not, of course, in any way commit ILO. The article is a development of a paper presented to the Sixth World Congress of the International Political Science Association, Geneva, September 1964.

[1] The fact that ILO, particularly under the leadership of its first Director-General, Albert Thomas, has been held up as a model of dynamic leadership in international organization may excuse the promi-

From Volume 23, No. 2 (1969), pp. 205-30.

The interest of the comparison is not confined to curiosity about the consequences of different styles of leadership. It lies also in the possibility that the executive head may be the explanatory key to the emergence of a new kind of autonomous actor in the international system. If we want to answer the question "Are international organizations merely the instruments of national foreign policies or do they influence world politics in their own right?" then we must take a closer look at the executive head.

This question has both ontological and systemic implications. The ontological implication may be illustrated by a second question: "What is the United Nations going to do about it?" (e.g., as applied to Hungary, Suez, apartheid, Cuba, Czechoslovakia); or, alternatively, "What can the United Nations do about it?" The form of the question itself behooves us to define the meaning of "United Nations" in it. Political analysts will usually take the nominalist position that "United Nations" is just a name, not a real essence. Instead of saying "United Nations" the questioner should specify what persons, what procedural processes, what committees or assemblies he has in mind. Yet by the very fact that he puts the question the questioner protests against such nominalism. The questioner is a realist, a believer in real essences. For him the United Nations either actually or potentially is more than just a name covering a multitude of exogenously determined activities. He knows why the Security Council does nothing: because the states represented on it have conflicting interests, because of a big-power veto. But he still thinks, as a realist, that there must be some fundamental essence in the United Nations that ought to receive expression. Most probably he expects the executive head —the Secretary-General—to express this latent reality. A few years ago it would have been bad form to put a problem in political analysis this way. But Professor Herbert Marcuse has taught us we are wrong to continue to discount the realists.

The "systemic" implication of the original question concerns how an international system based upon nation-states may become transformed in the direction of greater integration. Since it is common in literature about systems to find diagrams, the following is offered as an outline of the hypothetical process of integration:

International system composed exclusively
of nation-states

↓

Multilateral diplomacy

|

nence of the ILO case in this article. Of Thomas' leadership the best account is still E. J. Phelan, *Yes and Albert Thomas* (London: Cresset Press Limited, 1949). More recent is B. W. Schaper, *Albert Thomas: Trente ans de réformisme social* (Assen, Netherlands: Van Gorcum & Comp. [1959]).

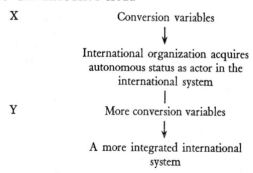

The hypothesis within the hypothesis is that among possible conversion variables at X and Y the executive head is especially important. It may be through his leadership that an international organization is transformed from being a forum of multilateral diplomacy into something which is more than the sum of its inputs and that this new potency continues to take on more common tasks and make more decisions on behalf of the whole community of nation-states, thereby gradually bringing formerly anarchic interstate relations under a common regulatory power.

The ontological and systemic implications become joined if we regard the emergence of a new and more integrated world order as the culmination of a dialectical process in which conflicts between nations are resolved through the discovery of higher common interests and the creation of international agencies to promote and regulate them. The real essence of international organization then becomes not a commitment to the performance of specific tasks but a commitment to bring about the new, more integrated world order. The executive head, in this vision, is cast in a role comparable to that of the proletariat in a better-known dialectical proposition—a heavy load of historical expectations for a rather lonely figure to bear.

These are not points of view to be defended in what follows. They are some of the reasons why the study of executive heads may be found interesting. Now, how to go about it?

Until recently the literature about executive heads could have been divided according to three characteristic emphases: legal-institutional, idiosyncratic (personality or leadership style), and ethical-normative.

The legal-institutional studies stress the formal constitutional powers of the executive head and how these have been contained or enlarged by practice and interpretation. Specific constitutional references to the executive head's powers and functions reflect whether the constitution-makers intended him to be solely an administrative officer, the limit of whose responsibility is to provide services for the deliberations of national representatives, or whether some opportunities for independent initiative by the executive head were clearly anticipated. Linked with this is the question of how far the executive head has in fact used whatever constitutional opportunities he had in order to expand his own *de facto* sphere of initiative and influence. For example, Drummond's annual reports were self-effacing administrative accounts of League activities, whereas Thomas used his opportunity of laying an annual report before the International Labor Conference to express his views on major issues of social and economic policy—an opportunity for initiative which his successors in ILO have continued to exploit.[2]

The opportunity for political initiative by the Secretary-General of the United Nations is seen as founded upon Article 99 of the Charter, which empowers the Secretary-General to "bring to the attention of the Security Council any matter which in his opinion may threaten the maintenance of international peace and security." Studies of the legal-institutional kind have been particularly interested in the apparent expansion of the Secretary-General's executive functions, particularly in regard to peacekeeping activities but also in the administration of economic and technical aid to developing countries. Michel Virally has buttressed a legal argument concerning an enlarged interpretation of Article 99 with an analysis of the different types of political activity undertaken by the Secretary-General and of the doctrine concerning his role elaborated by Dag Hammarskjöld.[3]

The weakness in the legal approach is its tendency to be unilinear and cumulative, arguing from precedent to precedent toward the steady expansion of the Secretary-General's role and his emergence (in Virally's terms) as a *gouvernant* rather more than a *fonctionnaire*. The idea of cumulative institutional development is, however, of doubtful application to the history of the UN. More evident has been the impact of the major shifts in the configuration of world power and in the pattern of cleavages on salient world issues which have changed the balance within the United Nations Organization among its major organs—the Security Council, the General Assembly, and the Secretary-General. Every such shift has changed their respective roles and practical powers. The difference between Trygve Lie's role in the Korean conflict and Hammarskjöld's in the Congo conflict is to be explained more by reference to the Organization's changed relationship to the two big-power blocs and the emergence of a better-articulated neutralist group than by differences in the interpretation held by the respective incumbents of the institutional responsibilities of the Secretary-General. Throughout the history of the Organization the world pattern of conflict and alignment appears as the independent variable and the institutional development of the United Nations as the de-

[2] Phelan, pp. 124–127.
[3] Michel Virally, "Le role politique du secrétaire-général des Nations-Unies," *Annuaire français de droit international* (Vol. 4) (Centre National de la Recherche Scientifique: Paris, 1958), pp. 360–399.

pendent variable. The weakness of the legal approach has been its implicit assumption (a natural consequence of a lawyer's preoccupation with institutional machinery) that the relationship is reversed.

A second emphasis in the literature has been upon the personality of the executive heads themselves. The implicit assumption here is that it is the man who makes the institution. One might call it the "great-man theory of international organization."[4] Much discussion in this connection has revolved about the point of an executive head's origins. Was he, before his appointment, a national political figure of some stature or was he primarily a diplomat, an administrator, or a technician? Another point of discussion concerns his style of leadership.

In the case of both the League and the United Nations early thoughts turned in the direction of a forceful role for a prominent statesman, and in both cases the governments in the end settled for something a little less ambitious (in the case of the League rather more explicitly than in the case of the United Nations).[5] In the Organization for European Economic Cooperation (OEEC) and in the North Atlantic Treaty Organization (NATO) cases United States representatives advocated a more demonstrative role for the executive head and the appointment of a prominent political personality while the United Kingdom's policy was to confine the international secretariat's role to something like that of the cabinet secretariat at home.[6]

Yet despite the controversy this ground of comparison does not always seem to have been very significant. Dag Hammarskjöld entered the UN with the public image of an administrator who would keep the United Nations' house in order and avoid rash political initiatives—on both grounds probably contrasting with his predecessor in the minds of those who appointed him. Yet it was Hammarskjöld, responding to the opportunities thrown up by world events following his appointment, who gave effective political content to the office of the Secretary-General.

ILO has had Directors-General of both the "political" and the "administrative" background. Edward Phelan might be considered the archetype of the civil servant. Yet while he never attempted to cut a public figure in the more flamboyant style of Thomas, it was in no small measure his diplomatic skill and political understanding which enabled ILO to traverse the war period and to survive as part of the new system of international organizations linked

---

[4] This is a natural bias in most biographical studies, for example those on Albert Thomas, and would seem to be the central idea in Stephen M. Schwebel, *The Secretary-General of the United Nations: His Political Powers and Practice* (Cambridge, Mass: Harvard University Press, 1952).

[5] Jean Siotis, *Essai sur le secrétariat international* (Publications de l'Institut Universitaire de Hautes Etudes Internationales, No. 41) (Geneva: Librairie Droz, 1963), pp. 60–64, 135ff; and Leon Gordenker, *The UN Secretary-General and the Maintenance of Peace* (New York and London: Columbia University Press, 1967), pp. 5–6, 18ff.

[6] Max Beloff, *New Dimensions in Foreign Policy: A Study in British Administrative Experience 1947–59* (London: George Allen & Unwin, 1961), pp. 39, 58–59.

with the United Nations, despite considerable political disadvantages, e.g., ILO's prewar Geneva associations, the hostility of the Union of Soviet Socialist Republics, and competition for influence within the new UN system from the newly organized World Federation of Trade Unions (WFTU).

The executive leadership of an international organization is preeminently a political task—but of a special kind, requiring particular aptitudes and knowledge on the part of its exponents. A background in national politics may be an advantage, but the contrast between the civil servant and "political" types is not in itself a valid indicator of leadership potential in the international sphere. The individual's interpersonal and "cross-cultural" sophistication and his access to the highest levels in diplomacy and government are better criteria.

An executive head who behaves in the manner of a local politician may lack capacity for leadership in an arena of larger and more variegated dimensions. On the other hand, executive heads who have conceived their roles primarily as technicians have not been notably successful. Their projects, for all the intrinsic merit they may possess, may fail either because of bad judgment on timing or because they have not taken sufficient account of effective opinion among the Organization's membership: Sir John Boyd-Orr's scheme for a world food board was a case in point.

On styles of leadership the classic contrast is between charismatic and bureaucratic types. ILO during the interwar period became identified with Thomas' personality and the doctrine he preached even though much of what he proposed was never consecrated formally by the votes of the ILO Conference. He infused his staff with a sense of devotion to a cause of which he appeared to them as a world leader. He traveled widely, not only to talk with the official political and diplomatic representatives of member countries but even more to contact workers' leaders and to speak to the people. Yet for all that it warms the heart, the charismatic style seems out of fashion in international organizations of the postwar period. Mainly, this is because of the heterogeneous world in which executive heads have to operate. The responsibility they have for preserving and continually reconstructing a slender basis of consensus among the members of their organizations has encouraged "quiet diplomacy" and discouraged a policy of continuous self-assertion.

There are, however, moments when the executive head can effectively give verbal leadership: when, for example, major powers are known to be prepared to accept a course of action though unable or disinclined themselves to advocate it. The creation of the United Nations Emergency Force (UNEF) in the Suez crisis is an example. (Whether the idea originated with the executive head is not so important as that he became identified with it and his office with its implementation.) The leadership of the executive head may, in such rather exceptional circumstances, lead to the creation of a new consensus among the powers. This rational use of personal initiative may be distinguished from cultivating charisma as a political style.

Personality is in this as in all spheres of politics a significant variable. But it would be a distortion to regard it as the independent variable, just as it would be wrong so to regard legal-institutional forms and practices. The problem we are left with is to formulate better the relationship of the personality and style of the executive head with other possibly weightier variables.

A third current of literature concentrates upon the concept of the international character of the role and responsibilities of the international secretariat and its executive head. Much of it welled out over the *troika* controversy of 1960 when the Soviet Union attacked Hammarskjöld over his handling of the Congo situation and proposed his replacement by a three-man executive composed of representatives of the three main divisions of world politics (at least as they appeared to Soviet viewers): Socialist, Western, and nonaligned. The controversy revolved about two doctrinal positions: the first, conveyed by the statement Nikita Khrushchev, Chairman of the Council of Ministers of the Soviet Union, is supposed to have made to Walter Lippmann that "there are neutral nations but there are no neutral men"—a statement which greatly incensed Hammarskjöld who saw it as a personal attack upon his integrity; and the second, defended by Hammarskjöld and most Western participants, of an exclusively international Secretariat whose actions are guided by the principles of the Charter, a Secretariat which can be developed as a neutral executive instrument of the Organization and whose international character, in the words of Hammarskjöld, "is not tied to its composition, but to the spirit in which it works and to its insulation from outside influences. . . . "[7] The Hammarskjöld argument immerses the executive head within the larger concept of the international secretariat which it views in monolithic and moral terms.

In historical perspective the two opposing arguments lose their absolute character and will be seen as ideologies buttressing particular sides in a global conflict; but both are very inadequate descriptions of actual behavior and are of very little use to the analyst.

A different perspective on this particular conflict results from considering the UN as one case of a broader trend in modern political institutions. This is the tendency in international organization as in national government for bureaucracies to expand their functions, which is accompanied by a growing difficulty for the parliamentary or representative organs holding formal power

[7] Dag Hammarskjöld, *Introduction to the Annual Report of the Secretary-General on the Work of the Organization, 16 June 1960—15 June 1961* (General Assembly *Official Records* [16th session], Supplement No. 1A), p. 6; also Dag Hammarskjöld, *The International Civil Servant in Law and in Fact* (Oxford: Clarendon Press, 1961), *passim;* a study written in the same context is Sydney D. Bailey, *The Secretariat of the United Nations* (United Nations Study No. 11) (New York: Carnegie Endowment for International Peace, 1962).

to supervise and control in detail many of these functions. In national affairs this is particularly true in connection with the broadening intervention of the state in economic life, for example, in the recent attempts of government in many industrialized countries to control or influence prices and incomes. In response to this problem new types of bodies are being created which are neither bureaucracies in the old sense of "civil service" nor are they representative in the old sense of elected. They are appointed by governments but composed in such a way as to be considered representative of significant segments of national opinion. The efficacy of these new agencies (such as prices and incomes boards) depends upon the confidence they inspire in their representative character.

The analogy applies to international secretariats. Specifically, the UN had, through the agency of the Secretary-General, taken on peacekeeping functions and broad executive functions for economic and social development. The representative organs of the UN—in particular the Security Council with respect to peacekeeping—were unable to control or direct these tasks. The abortive *troika* proposal was an expression of the lack of confidence of one major segment of world power opinion in the way the job was being done and a warning that a condition for reestablishing consensus was to make the new locus of decisionmaking more representative.

These three approaches, which reflect traditional scholastic analyses of political leadership, do not exhaust the subject. Richard Neustadt in his *Presidential Power*[8] has studied the actual extent and limitations of the influence of a political executive in decisionmaking. From the direction of organization theory, stimulated in particular by Chester Barnard in *The Functions of the Executive*,[9] another current of analysis throws light on executive leadership. These approaches, in contrast with those just discussed above, put emphasis on the informal rather more than the formal, on process rather more than norm, and on role rather more than idiosyncrasy.

Among studies of international organization a great step beyond the three traditional approaches to executive leadership was made by Ernst Haas in *Beyond the Nation-State*.[10] Haas views an international organization as a structure within a world environment. The inputs to the structure come from the demands and expectations of the states and other organized forces in the environment. It is the configuration of these input pressures—the elements of

---

[8] Richard E. Neustadt, *Presidential Power: the politics of leadership* (New York: John Wiley and Sons, 1960). The author describes his book as a contribution to analysis of "the classic problem of the man on top in any political system: how to be on top in fact as well as in name." (P. vii.) Arthur M. Schlesinger, Jr., *The Coming of the New Deal* (Boston: Houghton Mifflin, 1959), especially Part 8, "Evolution of the Presidency," adopts a similar approach. Gordenker follows Neustadt's approach in his stress on process and influence.

[9] Chester Barnard, *The Functions of the Executive* (Cambridge, Mass: Harvard University Press, 1946).

[10] Ernst B. Haas, *Beyond the Nation-State: Functionalism and International Organization* (Stanford, Calif: Stanford University Press, 1964), especially pp. 119ff.

overt and potential conflict and consensus among them—which defines opportunities for action through the organization. The executive head is in the key position to maximize these opportunities, in other words to interpret the input pressures in such a way as to bring about an expansion of the tasks and of the authority of the organization. Haas is thus concerned with executive leadership as a politically adaptive function, not about its legal bases, personal styles, or ethical principles.

How does the executive head fulfill this role? According to Haas he makes use of conflict in the environment to propose actions which were not part of the contestants' original intentions but which they can be persuaded to acquiesce in as at any rate less harmful than a continuation of conflict. These actions, undertaken by the international organization, expand its task and enhance its authority. The classic illustrations are the creation of UNEF in the Suez conflict and the mounting of the Congo operation by Hammarskjöld. In both cases the Secretary-General interpreted the conflict in the environment in such a way as to expand the task of the UN and more specifically to expand his own executive functions. At the same time Hammarskjöld elaborated a doctrine to explain and justify this expansion: the doctrine of the UN as an actively neutral intervening force or interposing force in situations of potential big-power conflict, a doctrine in which the concept of an actively neutral international secretariat was an essential element. Another example can be taken from ILO: The two major program expansion areas of ILO in the postwar era, human rights and manpower, grew out of the ILO leadership's interpretation of the cold-war pressures and the opportunities they offered.

Haas distinguishes three critical variables in the executive head's strategy for maximizing opportunities for task expansion. First, the executive head must define an ideology which gives clear goals to the organization and prescribes a method for attaining these goals. This ideology must respond to a wide range of demands and expectations from the constituents. He must not be satisfied with a program which is a mere accumulation of odds and ends of projects, some appealing to one, some to another, group of constituents. Pursuit of such subgoals may be useful in retaining support in specific quarters; but the organizational ideology, in order to perform its function of expanding the task and enhancing the authority of the organization, must point to a few clear and overriding objectives with which the executive head is identified. Second, he must build a bureaucracy committed to this ideology and having a sense of its own independent international role. Third, he must make coalitions and alliances—which of their nature will be more implicit than formalized—to ensure support from a sufficient proportion of the constituents. Building a supporting coalition is a difficult business. International organizations work by separating issues. Quite different majorities may be formed on different issues. But to be assured of the kind of support he needs for attainment of his major goals the executive head must be able to retain over a period of time—perhaps throughout his tenure of office—the support of the same basic coalition. The requirements of ideology and of coalition-building coincide here: The executive head can and probably should refrain from involvement in lesser issues in order to concentrate on those which link with the major goals he has defined. Hammarskjöld again serves as proto-type: He concentrated his attention on a limited range of issues to do with peacekeeping and related functions—a reserved area which he dealt with helped by a small personal staff—leaving the many other functions of the UN under the care of undersecretaries.[11]

For any concrete application theory has to be placed in a historical context. The utility of a theory lies in the extent to which it draws attention to the significant explanatory factors in a particular historical situation. The Haas model of executive leadership is in this respect a big advance over earlier thinking. Its weakness may lie in encouraging on the part of the researcher who uses it a presumption that the executive head has more effective initia-tive than in fact he often does have. By presenting almost a formula for inte-grative leadership it may lead to an underestimation of the constraints which are inherent in the set of relationships of which the executive head is a part. It is the purpose of this article to complement the Haas model by trying to specify and to begin to analyze the key relationships in executive leadership.

The three relationships analyzed here are those of the executive head with:
1) the international bureaucracy;
2) the member states (and especially the most powerful among them); and
3) the international system.

LEADERSHIP AND CONTROL OF THE INTERNATIONAL STAFF

The first problem of the executive head is to establish his leadership of the staff of the organization. In doing this he has to deal with two related sets of problems. The first concerns the relationship of the staff to outside pressures from the constituents of the organization. The second concerns the executive head's relationship to the top officials of his own staff. It is convenient to deal with these separately.

The Staff and the Constituents

Out of the interwar experience of international organization grew a set of opinions broadly accepted among international officials concerning the ideal of an international civil service. Alexander Loveday's *Reflections on Inter-national Administration*,[12] for example, embodies this orthodoxy. The staff

---

[11] Bailey, pp. 57–58; Gordenker, p. 103.
[12] Alexander Loveday, *Reflections on International Administration* (Oxford: Clarendon Press, 1956).

of an international organization, in this conception, should be an autonomous entity having no links with national administrations, and its members should cultivate a distinct "international" viewpoint. In order to achieve this the international civil service must be a career service; and a career service can be built securely only on the basis of individual merit and uniformly fair treatment under regulations which allow for no arbitrary intervention. This orthodoxy exalted the notion of a eunuch-like detachment from "politics." A major concern was to protect the staff from political intervention; and in this connection Loveday views the head of an international administration with some suspicion. "There is no *a priori* reason," he warns,

> for assuming that the head of an international organisation will prove competent and judicious. In all probability he will have been appointed as a result of a political compromise and will not be the strongest candidate available.

And further:

> When the organisation is a reflection of a divided world . . . he may endeavour to ingratiate himself with one camp or another, and the staff may suffer. . . . *The more politically minded the Secretary-General, the greater the danger.*[13]

The attitude betrayed by these lines is worth stressing because it has been characteristic of many international civil servants.

The career service thesis has not, however, had a monopoly. The NATO international staff was composed largely of officials on short-term secondment from national administrations.[14] This practice may increase the intensity of intergovernmental cooperation by familiarizing a growing number of national officials with the workings of NATO. It is clearly more appropriate to an organization in which there is a relatively great commonness of purpose among its members than to one more heterogeneous. It also produces the least permanent organizational effect since it creates no institutional interest concerned exclusively with the perpetuation and development of the organization itself.

In a more broadly based international organization with greater diversity among its members this secondment system would tend to produce an unmanageable cacophony. It is in this more universal context that the development of a career service cultivating a distinct loyalty to the organization seems most necessary. Short-term secondments are not conducive to this concept of international loyalty since each temporary official would naturally be influenced by his own long-term career prospects in national service. Thus, the universal organizations have introduced the practice of permanent contracts of employment for international staff and of career development in international service as a means of strengthening the staff's capacity to resist outside pressures.

[13] Loveday, pp. 118–119. Author's italics.
[14] Cf. Lord Hastings Ismay, *NATO: The First Five Years, 1949–1954* (Paris, 1954), p. 64.

A long period of gradual growth under dynamic leadership can enable an organization to assimilate officials of widely diverse origins into a common pattern of behavior and outlook. ILO officials in the immediate postwar period sometimes exhibited a distinct feeling of their own Organization's superiority in this respect to the newly established United Nations whose larger staff had perforce been quickly assembled. Indeed, strong organizational tradition seems to be a more potent influence toward staff discipline and conformity than is a marked degree of ideological homogeneity among the membership. The relatively strong sense of unity within the early postwar staff of ILO (which was working in a world of sharp ideological divisions, especially prominent among the labor movements with which it had to deal) contrasts with the internal divisions present now within the secretariats of the European Communities, divisions which follow national, political party, and pressure group lines.[15] The narrower range of ideological divergency within the Europe of the Six seems to have encouraged a franker policy of representation of interests within the secretariat with a consequently greater measure of diversity than exists where an established tradition exercises its formative power in the education of newcomers in conformity.

The concept of loyalty to the international organization calls for some further comment. It is a general principle enshrined in the regulations governing international staffs that no international official should seek or accept instructions from any authority external to the organization. That is the law, and every official is bound to it by oath of office. But there is a political reality which modifies the law. Appointments are made so as to effect a certain balance within the staff between different nationalities, geographical areas, and sectional interest groups. This applies both at the very top level of officials and at lower levels as well. Each member country (and in some cases major interest groups as well) considers itself entitled to "representation" on the staff. An executive head will normally try to give satisfaction to these pressures (and sometimes a government may impose its choice of officials upon him). In part he is motivated by a desire not to alienate by a negative attitude any important segment of opinion within the organization. But in a more positive sense part of the value to the executive head of a diversified staff is as a sounding board for national, regional, or sectional reactions to his policy ideas.

The "representative" function of the staff normally does not take the form of a crude violation of the pledge not to seek or accept outside instructions though sometimes it must come very close to that. Certain officials will enjoy the confidence of the official national representatives of their country or of pressure groups such as international trade-union organizations. They may

<hr />

[15] Jean Siotis, "Some Problems of European Secretariats," *Journal of Common Market Studies*, March 1964 (Vol. 2, No. 3), especially pp. 245ff.

have access to information of a confidential or semi-confidential nature from two sources: the internal network of the international organization and the external national or pressure group network. The way in which they adjust their conduct in the light of what they know, and the extent to which they reveal information from one network to the other, measures the balance of their loyalties. Even officials from the most monolithic of states acquire some degree of commitment to the organization; and even the most disciplined of loyal international officials has to give some small change to retain the confidence of his outside contacts.

Thus "conflict of loyalties" is rarely nowadays a drama of personal conscience. At one time perhaps it was: in the case, for example, of League officials of German or Italian nationality confronted with Nazi or Fascist reaction to the League. Yet in more recent years one can sense a tendency of the universal organizations of the United Nations system to abandon gradually their normative content. Staff members are more easily able to espouse a variety of personal ideologies, knowing that each has the degree of respectability conferred upon it by some national or regional interest represented in the organization while none has an imperative universal sanction.

The Loveday conception cited earlier represents the secretariat as an automatically functioning and self-regulating machine in which attempts by an executive head to assert leadership are to be discouraged. Once the problem of adaptation of the secretariat is posed, however, it is the executive head who must give the leadership and direction. And his efforts toward redefining the ideology of the organization and toward adjusting its political base will encounter the resistance of bureaucratic *immobilisme*. The executive head faces a problem which is typical in any bureaucratic situation: His orders will not be carried out in the way he intends them; they will be twisted in the course of execution to conform with the prior intentions of subordinate officials. The executive head may take special precautions in particular instances, but his personal influence cannot be everywhere all the time.

The very factors which are supposed to strengthen the international character of the staff—long-term tenure of appointment, judicially interpreted administrative regulations, etc.—reinforce this *immobilisme*. The executive head has very little latitude to dismiss officials who are patently undisciplined; he will often be reluctant to take any sanctions against them for fear of displeasing particular member states or pressure groups. His only recourse is to place recalcitrant officials as far as possible in positions where they can do little harm to his plans and to maneuver them out of the effective circuit of communications within the bureaucracy; but even in doing this he must often be careful to avoid arousing the protests of outside interests.

A direct consequence is the great difficulty of dislodging special limited goals and programs (what Haas calls "subgoals") once they have been incorporated into an organization's regular activities. Such limited goals are served within the bureaucracy by technical specialists and are supported outside by particular pressure groups. This combination of paired internal resistance to changes and external pressures for the maintenance of existing goals and activities makes it very difficult for the executive head to effect real adjustments in the work of an international organization in line with his redefinition of major goals and priorities. The changes he makes in the ideology tend to remain verbal only; and the "back-scratching" tendency of international conferences makes delegates reluctant to oppose individual projects which are dear to the hearts of others for fear of a hostile attitude toward their own. Thus it is rarely advisable or profitable for an executive head to risk a confrontation with the membership and with a segment of his own staff in order to eliminate redundant activities. These activities tend to continue but to atrophy slowly to the extent the executive head is able to deny them the impetus of fresh and renovating thought. This is one reason why international agencies carry so much deadwood.

Thus, if stability and conformity in outlook among the staff are elements in strengthening its international loyalty to the organization, these same qualities are in latent antithesis with the desire of the executive head to lead in new directions, redefining the major objectives of the organization and readjusting its political base. This is an instance of a more general conflict between innovators and established bureaucracies. In national settings radically new policies usually have been put into effect by an influx of new administrators. This was, for example, the case of the New Deal in the United States in the 1930's. It is also the case today of countries initiating the new policies of economic planning where conflict develops between the established bureaucracies and those seeking to put into effect the new policies. The same type of conflict is to be anticipated in international bureaucracies led by innovating executive heads.

The only practical way an executive head can combat these tendencies toward stabilization of programs and inertia of policy is to surround himself with new staff committed to his objectives and to give this new staff as far as possible the initiative for program innovation within the bureaucracy. In practice, therefore, he will inject conflict within the bureaucracy and throw the weight of his influence, to the extent the political constraints upon him permit, behind the innovating group.

Relations with Top Officials

The second set of problems referred to concerns the executive head's relations with the top officials within the organization. Two difficulties arise from a tendency toward "feudalism" characteristic of international secretariats: There are conflicting poles of authority at the top level of staff and a corresponding division of loyalties into clusters of informal groups within, converging on top staff members. While these may be factors in any large organization, they are given special weight in international bureaucracies when senior officials base their position upon support from outside constituencies.

Internal opposition or passive resistance to new policies by the executive head may thus originate within the bureaucracy. Such internal opposition will be fortified by the ability of the top officials concerned to activate a group of the organization's constituents to put pressure on the executive head. Conflict within the bureaucracy can thus spread to the constituency. Within the staff it is based not only upon the fact that the "opposition" is hierarchically in command of a sector of the staff; even more it is based upon informal networks of communications and personal loyalties which top officials can build up around themselves. (Apart from the nobler sentiments of identification with specific policies or goals subordinate officials look to the top officials to advance their own careers.)

Now it is in the nature of the political position of these top officials to be closely identified with subgoals. There are occupational and political reasons for this. Occupationally, each top official is responsible for a limited sector of the organization's activity; his interests will be inclined into this sector and his contacts will be with those most concerned with the subgoals characteristic of that sector. He may come subjectively to consider these sectoral subgoals as the main purposes of the organization. Politically, he will look for support to a limited group of the organization's constituents and must therefore give special prominence to satisfying the expectations of these constituents.

There are legal-institutional differences among organizations in the relationship of the executive head to his top level subordinates. Formally, in the United Nations and the specialized agencies each organization has one executive head—the Secretary-General or the Director-General—and other officials usually have status only as his appointees. In fact, procedures have normally become established and accepted whereby the executive head consults formally or informally with a politically representative body before making top appointments, and understandings exist as to the regions or pressure groups to be given satisfaction in such appointments.[16] The executive head's freedom in such appointments is always limited. Sectors of the bureaucracy's work will have to be allocated to these top officials.

At the other extreme, in the legal sense, are the executives of the European Communities which are collegial bodies on which provision is made for the representation of separate national and political interests. In fact, these executives cannot work on all questions as a collegial body and so they operate on the principle of a division of labor, each member of the executive body being responsible for a sector of work.[17]

---

[16] Concerning the arrangements for top appointments in the UN see Gordenker, pp. 91ff.

[17] There is a "written procedure" in force in the European Commission whereby files with decisions

Thus, underlying differences in legal form there appears to be a common resemblance in the internal political processes of international bureaucracies.

There are three ways in which the executive head may seek to control the top staff so as to maintain his political initiative. These are:

1) *Complete domination and centralization of power in his own hands.* This would mean effectively overcoming the "feudal" tendencies by reducing the top officials to a position in which they would be dependent on the executive head, holding their appointments at pleasure and carrying out subordinate technical functions. Albert Thomas seems to have aimed at something like this when he first refused to accept Harold Butler as Deputy Director, offering him instead an appointment as a chief of one of the divisions he intended to create. But Thomas was soon convinced that the confidence and support of important member governments—and in particular of the British government —depended upon his appointing Butler as Deputy Director.[18] It is doubtful whether any executive head has or could achieve a position in which his top subordinates hold their posts at pleasure; but one means of preventing them from developing a power base within the bureaucracy is to make frequent changes of responsibilities and to prevent the emergence of well-defined continuous sectors within the bureaucracy. While this may achieve the political objective of preventing the identification of top officials with major bureaucratic sectors, the costs in administrative inefficiency may be high.

2) *Presiding over a cabinet of top officials.* Usually an executive head will want to meet with his senior staff periodically to discuss matters of general concern to the organization. This will be a means of pulling individual top officials out from under their preoccupation with subgoals by keeping them informed about important matters outside their own particular sphere. It will also oblige conflicting elements among the top staff to have at least a minimum of contact with each other. And it may help the executive head— if he is skilled at this—to smoke out differences among his staff about which he is not adequately informed. Collective discussion can be used as an instrument favoring a certain conformity of policy. But it would be an unwise executive head who did not take his major decisions on policy *after* consultation rather than *in* consultation with his top officials. The cabinet technique is, at best, an instrument of communication and of limited control over the top-level officials. It has not proven to be an effective instrument of decision-making.[19]

by each member are circulated to all the others. Anyone with experience of official bodies would assume that the principle of nonintervention would become the rule. Rarely would any member of the executive college interfere in the work of another member for fear of others crossing his own jurisdictional boundaries.

18 Phelan, pp. 28–33.

19 The parallel with President Franklin D. Roosevelt's use of the cabinet is evident from Schlesinger: The meetings evidently retained some obscure usefulness for the President. The reaction he got from this miscellany of administrators perhaps gave him some idea of the range of public opinion.

3) *The "reserved area" of policy.* By this is meant that the executive head reserves certain types of decisions to himself and equips himself with a personal staff so as to be able to act within this area of policy. Following from the prescriptions implicit in the Haas model the questions which an executive head would reserve in this way include:

(a) those relating to the definition of the major goals and policy orientation (including program priorities) and the development of organizational ideology; and

(b) matters of direct concern to the executive head's base of political support and his coalition policy for the construction of alliances to support his program.

Everything else he would delegate to his top officials and interfere as little as possible with them; but to the extent that he allows top officials to encroach upon the reserved areas he would undermine his own capacity for leadership. This is the most usual method for executive heads to follow, using it in some combination with the cabinet system, as described, for communications and general supervision.

The "reserved area" implies that the executive head acquires his own staff distinct from the staff controlled, in fact, by his senior officials (while the latter staff is formally under the executive head's supreme control, in fact he is inhibited from exercising his authority over it). This personal staff can provide an executive head with several essential, effective components to his job:

(a) a few people in whom he has virtually complete confidence, with whom he can talk frankly about all the issues arising within the organization. With his top officials, because of their political position, he is usually in a posture of negotiating;

(b) channels of intelligence providing accurate assessment of the expectations and demands from the membership of the organization. His top officials provide a sounding board for sectional reactions, but in addition the executive head needs his own research and intelligence network to assess the possibilities and limits presented by the world situation in terms of the policy objectives which he determines to pursue;

(c) competent advisers to help him redefine as necessary the major aims which the organization is to pursue and to explain these in such a way as to gain the necessary political support. In other words, the staff would effectively command program and policy development and avoid determination of the pro-

It also helped him to measure the capacity of his subordinates. . . . But, like all strong Presidents, Roosevelt regarded his cabinet as a body of department heads, to be dealt with individually—or, sometimes, as a group of representative intelligent men, useful for a quick canvass of opinion—not as a council of constitutional advisers.

(P. 504.) The similarity of UN practice under Lie, Hammarskjöld, and Thant is pointed out by Gordenker.

gram by specialists committed to subgoals and subject to the special influence of particular outside pressure groups.

RELATIONS WITH MEMBER STATES

The executive head's relationship with the bureaucracy determines his capability for action and initiative. His relationship with the national constituents determines the political support he will have for his action and thus the limits to which it can go. Some of the analytical features of this relationship emerge from a comparison of cases involving the executive heads of ILO during a period of almost 50 years.

Albert Thomas came to the directorship of ILO with the acquiescence, though not with the wholehearted political support, of the French government. The French government wanted a Frenchman as Director; it could hardly have desired Thomas who was politically in opposition to it. Thomas' appointment was secured on the initiative of the Western European trade unions, supported by Employer representatives, at a time when the governments had no concerted policy on the directorship. Thomas identified ILO with his ideology of reformist socialism, stressing educational action among workers, the development of trade unions, and reforms such as worker participation in management, social insurance, and nationalization. He made the trade unions of the International Federation of Trade Unions (IFTU) (Amsterdam) his political base.

Thomas soon became embroiled in a controversy with the French government before the Permanent Court of International Justice (PCIJ) in the course of which he appeared in person to contest the French government's position. This conflict between the Director and the government of his country has to be seen within the context of French domestic politics. Thomas never gave up the intention of returning to active political life in France. He maintained his political affiliation with the Socialist Party, the Section Française de l'Internationale Ouvrière (SFIO), and, more particularly, retained the support of Léon Jouhaux and the Confédération Générale du Travail (CGT). It was this domestic political support which gave Thomas his freedom to criticize his political opponents who were occupying the seats of power in the government.

Harold Butler, Thomas' successor, contributed to the development of the organizational ideology of ILO in the 1930's. He redirected ILO thinking along lines similar to those of the American New Deal, advocating a broader role for ILO in the field of international economic policy particularly as regards measures to fight the depression. This major contribution to ILO ideology prepared and solidified his principal political success: the acquisition of United States membership.

Nevertheless, Butler's position had political weaknesses. To some extent these may have been a question of personality. Temperamentally he was an intellectual and a civil servant, closer to the men of government—particularly to upper-middle-class reformers such as the New Deal brought to the fore—rather than to the trade unions, closer, indeed, in many ways to some of the employers than to the trade unions.

Butler's last ILO battle, concerning an apparently trivial matter of an appointment to the ILO staff, brought out these weaknesses. Four consecutive French governments during the period from the autumn of 1937 through the spring of 1938—the Camille Chautemps popular front government, the Chautemps radical government, the short-lived Léon Blum government of March 1938, and the Edouard Daladier government of national union—pressed Butler to appoint as his representative in the Paris Office of ILO a person in whom Butler had no confidence. Butler, in this situation, had no political leverage within France, such as Thomas had enjoyed through the favor of the CGT. The French employers, who appeared to share Butler's views, either could not intervene to change the official position or did not consider it worth their while to do so when they had more vital interests at stake. Butler's only weapons were the threat to resign and the possibility of mobilizing outside pressure. He tried both and both failed to change the French position.[20] Butler first threatened to resign over this issue in March 1938 at a time when on the broader international scene Hitler was menacing Austria. Though Butler himself might not have come so well out of it, the French government might equally have been implicated in a blow at the remains of the Geneva edifice of international cooperation. Butler was persuaded to withdraw his resignation at this time on the understanding he would be supported by the officers of the Governing Body and by the British government in resolving the issue which had brought him into conflict with the French government. This attempt to "internationalize" a conflict between the Director and a major member state was resented in French circles. Butler again pressed his resignation, advancing personal grounds, as the only way out for him. His purely diplomatic position, lacking a solid base of political support, left him powerless in a crisis with a member state.

John Winant, Butler's successor, was a leading American political personality, having been Governor of New Hampshire and holding the respect and confidence of President Franklin Roosevelt. Winant was only for a brief period Director of ILO, but he had to handle the major crisis into which the outbreak of war plunged the Organization. Winant was determined, contrary to the decision taken by the League, to remove ILO from the threat that its

[20] It is, of course, difficult to disentangle at this distance in time the personal motives of Butler as regards his resignation. But these motives do not materially enter into the political analysis of the use of resignation as a weapon.

resources might be seized or its capacity for action destroyed by the Axis powers; consequently, he decided to transfer the Organization to North America. Indeed, destiny seemed to have given him this role to play. In June 1940, as the Nazis advanced into France, Winant appealed to Secretary of State Cordell Hull, and through him to Roosevelt, to permit the removal of ILO to the United States. He met with their refusal; ILO was low on their list of preoccupations and they were unprepared to face isolationist, anti-League hostility in Congress. As things worked out, the result was politically satisfactory for ILO, which went to Canada with the support of Prime Minister Mackenzie King and thus became located in a belligerent country from the very earliest phase of the war—a major factor in ILO's survival into the postwar world. But the refusal of the Roosevelt Administration was a blow for Winant, who resigned shortly thereafter. It underlines the point that personal relationships of confidence between a Director and the head of the government of a major state are not a sufficient guarantee of support when domestic political currents, to which national leaders will be more sensitive, are working against the policy of the Director.

David Morse, the present Director-General, has had to deal with a series of crises, in all of which ILO's relationship to the United States was crucial. Shortly after he assumed office an anti-ILO campaign became active among right-wing business circles in the United States allied with the forces advocating the Bricker amendment to the Constitution of the United States.

This attack reached its critical phase in 1956–1957. ILO had the sympathy of the Dwight D. Eisenhower Administration; yet the White House, while taking a position against the Bricker amendment, did not risk antagonizing a large body of Congressional opinion by actively supporting ILO, e.g., on the question of the ceiling fixed by Congress on the United States' contribution to the ILO budget.

Morse had, however, the support of certain domestic forces which could independently influence Congress. These included liberal businessmen (David Zellerbach, Paul Hoffmann, and others), certain Catholic groups (e.g., the National Catholic Welfare Conference), and, above all, the American Federation of Labor–Congress of Industrial Organizations (AFL-CIO).

The domestic attack on ILO within the United States became accentuated in reaction to the Soviet Union's reentry into ILO after 1954. The fact that Morse was able to arouse sufficient domestic support for ILO within the United States enabled him not only to counter the threat of reduced participation or even withdrawal of the United States from the Organization but also to maintain personally the confidence of both the United States and the Soviet governments. The key factor in the situation was the support Morse had, not from the United States Administration (which while favorable would not actively support ILO in the face of any major challenge from public opinion or influential pressure groups) but from the domestic groups, principally the trade unions.

This position has certain inherent difficulties, particularly that of a possible conflict between the primary aims in the international sphere of AFL-CIO and those of ILO as articulated by its executive head. During the United States domestic crisis on ILO matters in 1956–1957 the policies advanced by Morse conformed with those of the AFL-CIO: notably, the abolition of forced labor and the promotion of freedom of association for trade unions, both of which were seen at that time primarily in terms of a challenge to the Communist world. However, the gravity and extent of the problems confronting an international organization and the perspective from which an executive head has to deal with them makes it increasingly difficult for him to maintain a firm doctrinal alliance with particular domestic interests in a major member state. Yet lacking such domestic support, the executive head may find himself defenseless in a major crisis since governments will be far less responsive to the appeal of an executive head than they will to powerful domestic pressure groups.

From this outline of the relationships between executive heads and member states the following propositions may be drawn:

1) The issues which are most important to the executive head are seldom of the same order of importance to national governments;

2) strong local pressure groups or local political factors are more likely to influence a government's attitude toward an international organization than any sense of commitment to the personality at the head of the organization;

3) the interests of international organizations have to be advanced within the domestic context of its major member states by making use of such favorable currents of domestic opinion as present themselves, i.e., the executive head must exercise the sailor's skill in using available winds and currents to advance in the direction of his choice;

4) thus, the executive head needs to fortify his position by alliance with domestic pressure groups. He must not limit himself to "foreign" politics but know how to make domestic politics work in favor of his policies.

In order to be able to work in this way the executive head must have great political skill. He needs also a personal confidential intelligence network reaching into domestic politics of key countries. Of necessity these networks of contacts will be limited for any single individual to a very few countries; and taking this into account, the ideal executive head is one who is able to engage in political confrontation in those countries which at the particular time are crucial in the evolution of the organization.

Finally, the executive head, because this is inherent in political confrontation, must be able when necessary to compromise on nonessentials in his program and his definition of the aims of the organization. This is a difficult matter of judgment since he must be able to reconcile any compromise with the need for ideological clarity in his leadership of the bureaucracy and the organization's constituents. When compromising he must appear to be acting on principle, consistent with his professed organizational aims. He must not appear to be too much of a bargainer.

The International System

The basic personal qualification for effective leadership is clear perception of what action and initiative the state of the international system at any time permits. The definition of organizational ideology and the establishment of the political base for an organization's action have to be determined in the light of the executive head's reading of the constraints imposed and the opportunities opened by the world political situation. His perception will determine the balance between an executive head's role as a negotiator in "quiet diplomacy" and as a taker of personal political initiatives.

The oldest and most regularly recurrent political function of an executive head is to be a mediator in negotiating agreement among different constituent interests. In order to do this effectively the executive head must:

1) acquire and maintain the confidence of all major segments of opinion;

2) be identified with a definite, though to some extent flexible, ideology representing a consensus within the organization, i.e., his suggestions must be seen as conforming with the aims and purposes of the organization and not as seeking merely agreement for its own sake and at any price; and

3) have an adequate intelligence at his disposal so that he can make constructive suggestions and avoid pitfalls.

These conditions are not easy to combine. There is a potential conflict between maintaining the confidence of major powers or interests and standing forth as spokesman of a clear organizational ideology. Furthermore, adequate intelligence cannot easily be acquired solely through the services of an international organization. Thus, the executive head will have to rely on supplementary intelligence from the diplomatic services of major powers or other sources outside the organization. The extent to which he has to rely on particular outside sources may adversely affect confidence in his impartiality on the part of those powers to which he is less close.

Much greater difficulty arises when the executive head is in the position of taking political initiative for which he and the organization will bear the full responsibility. Such was the initiative of 1956 to create UNEF in the Suez crisis. At this point the Secretary-General emerged dramatically from the role of chief administrator and "quiet diplomat" to take on that of an independent actor in world affairs. The Suez initiative was carried through successfully, with considerable enhancement to the prestige of his office. It was the kind of initiative which met with a broad degree of support or acquiescence. In the Congo, by contrast, attempting a second time to bear the same kind of political responsibility, the Secretary-General was not able to maintain the same degree of consensus behind his actions. He became a political casualty before his tragic death in the air crash of September 1961.

Hammarskjöld had a keen sense of the risks of his position. Five years before his death he had written in a personal letter to Max Ascoli:[21]

> It is one thing that, in the vacuum which suddenly developed in the Suez crisis, I had, for what it was worth, to throw in everything I had to try to tide us over; it was one of those irrational and extremely dangerous situations in which only something as irrational on a different level could break the spell. But it is an entirely different thing, every time the big powers run into a deadlock, to place the problem in the Secretary-General's hands with the somewhat naive expectation that he can continue to turn up with something. It is a matter of course that a continued use of the office of the Secretary-General in that way sooner or later leads to a point where he must break his neck, politically. If, as in the Suez situation, the very facts, as established by the policy of the various big powers, force the Secretary-General into a key role, I am perfectly willing to risk being a political casualty if there is an outside chance of achieving positive results. But if the Secretary-General is forced into a similar role through sheer escapism from those who should carry the responsibility, there is a place for solid warning. Politically, the Secretary-General should be, and is, most expendable, but he should not be expended just because somebody does not want to produce his own money.

An initiative-taking Secretary-General cannot become a substitute for a Security Council that does not work because no consensus exists. When the major powers are deadlocked, the Secretary-General may try to play a role. In fortuitous circumstances, such as the Suez crisis, he may succeed, but it is a risky formula. The Secretary-General can be the most significant contributing factor toward building up a working consensus within the United Nations, but his success in this depends upon maintaining the confidence of all the major powers and groups of countries. Once a risky action has led to this confidence being withdrawn by any major party, then—even though the others may feel honor-bound to support him—the Secretary-General's ability to be the architect of consensus is expended.[22]

[21] Letter from Hammarskjöld, quoted in Max Ascoli, "The Future of the U.N.—An Editorial," *Reporter* (New York), October 26, 1961, p. 12.

[22] Leland M. Goodrich, "The Political Role of the Secretary-General," *International Organization*, Autumn 1962 (Vol. 16, No. 4) stresses the Secretary-General's role as consensus-builder and concludes that dangers to the UN might be avoided

> if governments assume their responsibilities in the General Assembly and Security Council and do not place upon the Secretary-General or make it necessary for him to assume responsibilities beyond his powers and of such a nature as to expose him to serious political attack.

(Pp. 734–735.)

The executive head needs to be able to count upon a working majority of the organization's constituents in support of his policies. In order to build majorities he may, as suggested earlier, have to engage quietly in domestic politics in key countries. But he cannot afford either to appear as the spokesman of a coalition of countries or as the supporter of domestic factions. He has to limit his coalition policy at the point where he risks alienating a major power or interest within the organization, and he has to limit his personal political initiative at the same point. Once he becomes the prisoner of any particular coalition which divides the organization, he can no longer perform his primary function of consensus formation. The potential conflict between his function as catalyst of consent and his personal political initiative constitutes the executive head's most troublesome dilemma and that most likely to lead to his downfall.

In his introduction to the Secretary-General's report to the 1961 session of the General Assembly Hammarskjöld set forth ideas which appeared to suggest the political base for UN action would be the emerging nations of Asia and Africa.[23] He attempted subtly to reconcile the notion of a universal rule of law in international relations with a notion of the will of the international community reminiscent of Rousseau. This ideology—though one should not impute to Hammarskjöld personally what is not explicitly stated by him— could lead to the use of Assembly majorities as a means of putting pressure upon the industrialized countries. The United Nations would become the gadfly of the Great Powers, an international pressure group of the poor used to secure concessions from the rich.

An alternative political strategy would be to rest the political base of the system upon the industrial powers, using it as an instrument of building consensus between Western countries and the Soviet Union. The corresponding ideology would stress functional areas of common interest between East and West and move from broadening functional cooperation toward a concerted policy of industrialized powers to facilitate economic development of the poorer nations. It is a less demagogic policy, more skeptical of majorities unless they are majorities which represent negotiated agreement.

Within international organizations there is now some evidence of disenchantment with majoritarianism although it is difficult to discern a consistent alternative strategy. In the UN Conference on Trade and Development (UNCTAD) the "77," realizing that majority votes could not compel real concessions from the rich countries, accepted a conciliation procedure in case of division between blocs on substantive issues. Retreat from majoritarianism would imply a reversal of the doctrine espoused by United States administrations from the late 1940's which could bring the United States closer to So-

23 Hammarskjöld, *Introduction to the Annual Report of the Secretary-General on the Work of the Organization, 16 June 1960—15 June 1961.*

viet and French views on the UN system. But the distinction to be brought out in the context of this article is that while the policy of alignment with the emerging nations calls for continued use of initiative on the part of the Secretary-General at the risk of a growing impatience of the industrialized countries of both East and West and a growing disillusionment of the emerging nations at the hiatus between aims and results, the policy of East-West reconciliation would give the primacy in the Secretary-General's role to quiet diplomacy and consensus formation.

*   *   *

In the foregoing the executive head has been used as a focus for the study of some problems of international organization and as a means to sketch out a framework of analysis for the purpose. It is now useful to turn back to the notions enunciated at the start. The first of these is that the executive head plays a key role in converting an international organization conceived as a framework for multilateral diplomacy into one which is an autonomous actor in the international system. The Haas strategy (organizational ideology *plus* committed bureaucracy *plus* supporting coalition) offers valid guidelines, but in seeking to follow them the executive head must be conscious of and work within constraints. The first of these constraints is bureaucratic *immobilisme* which is to some extent amenable to effective leadership. The second, less amenable, is the limitation on the executive head's control which comes from institutionalizing client interests within the bureaucracy. As the executive tasks of international organization expand, client control will come to depend more and more upon an intrabureaucratic balance of influences, and thus issues of representation within the bureaucracy are likely to become more salient and the primacy of the executive head more hemmed in. The third constraint—and the most determining in the short run—is the world pattern of conflicts and alignments. In a tight bipolar situation, such as prevailed during the early 1950's, the executive head may try to play a role of intermediary between rival blocs but is most likely to become aligned with one of them. This may give the illusion of strength to the organization (as to the UN in the Korean conflict) but in the perspective of the system as a whole the international organization appears as the instrument of the bloc which succeeds in dominating it. In a looser system the executive head may be able to mobilize uncommitted supporters in order to follow a line independent of the rival blocs, the limits of which will be fixed by big-power tolerance or willingness to acquiesce. In a system characterized by several, e.g., five or six, concentrations of more equally balanced effective power it is conceivable that an executive head might play an important brokerage role. The personal idiosyncratic dimension enters both in the form of the executive head's ability to maintain himself as top man in bureaucratic politics and in the clarity of his perception of the significance for international organization of the prevailing pattern of conflicts and alignments.

The second notion advanced earlier was that the executive head may be a key factor in bringing about a transformation of the system in the direction of greater integration. The test of whether he can do this lies in his ability to bring about changes in national policies so that they conform more with the decisions and interests of the international organization. A diplomatic go-between or brokerage role, useful as it may be for helping to preserve peace within the system, does not meet this test because it does not bring about change in the system. In performing it the executive head acts as the instrument of the powers for reaching their own accommodation.[24] In this article only a limited number of crisis situations in the relations between an executive head and member states have been examined, admittedly not a representative or typical sample. Yet the tentative conclusion seems indicated that an executive head's ability to bring effective influence to bear on government policy depends upon his ability to exert influence through actors *within* the domestic political system. The requisites for this are: 1) access to domestic groups having influence; 2) adequate intelligence concerning their goals and perceptions; and 3) ability to manipulate international action so that these groups can perceive an identity of interest with it. The cases cited all involve pluralistic polities, in respect of which the requisites might conceivably be met. But what about noncompetitive and especially ideological polities which succeed in subjecting internal groups to a common political direction and in insulating the polity from external influences? The prospects of system change through the agency of international organizations and their executive heads would seem to be linked with the progress of pluralism in polities. The long-term possibilities of penetrating ideological regimes may, if we follow David Apter's reasoning, lie through the scientific elites, a group likely to lose patience with political orthodoxies which cramp the search for new knowledge, to demand free access to information necessary for scientific work, and to see advantages in contacts with scientists abroad.[25] The potentiality of scientific elites as a channel of penetration depends not only on their receptivity to external influences but also on whether they have real influence upon the political leadership at home, and in this last respect recent events suggest that the long term may be quite long indeed.

---

[24] Perceptive executive heads have realized this, as, for example in former ILO Director-General Edward Phelan's comment to Schwebel:

> The Secretary-General's activity behind the scenes is useful. But multiple consultations decide nothing. They keep the Secretary-General informed and they exercise a gentle influence. This is not the same as influencing an international, collective decision.

(Schwebel, p. 211.) Nor is it the same as influencing a government to change its policy.

[25] David E. Apter, *The Politics of Modernization* (Chicago and London: University of Chicago Press, 1965), pp. 432–463.

PART III

INTERNATIONAL ORGANIZATION AND POLICY OUTPUTS

CONCEPTS AND REALITIES IN INTERNATIONAL POLITICAL ORGANIZATION

William M. Jordan

The heading under which these observations are brought together may well seem presumptuous. The request made to me was to deal with the subject: "collective security"—a phrase which I am hesitant to use, for it has come to cover the most diverse international political arrangements. The title adopted provides a convenient umbrella under which to bring together a number of general observations on the approach to the problem of maintaining peace.

Just forty years have passed since Leonard Woolf brought together in his two studies, *International Government* in 1916 and *The Framework of a Lasting Peace* in 1917, the proposals which were then being put forward for the maintenance of peace and the body of experience available at that time regarding the working of international institutions. The range of relevant experience was then slender. Thought on the subject had to be based on analogy from the working of national institutions, on the traditions and practices of international law, and on the operation of a few, mainly technical, international agencies. In the past forty years, a vast range of experience has been accumulated, and our problem is now largely one of devising means to view this extensive experience as a whole.

Clarity of thought is made all the more difficult by the great variety of approaches. Numerous case histories of the handling of specific political problems are now available. They have the great merit of facilitating the study of the working of international political organs within the broad framework of conflicting national policies. But concentration on the detail of an individual case tends to preclude the formulation of generalizations valid for the working of international political organs as a whole. So the endeavor has been made to discern reasonably constant elements in the functioning of international political organs regarding both their internal procedures and their expedients for dealing with problems, and to classify and expound the range of experience under headings indicative of characteristic types of activity. This mode of analysis was commenced in masterful fashion by T. P. Conwell-Evans some thirty years ago,[1] and has been applied in Leland Goodrich and Anne Simons' work, *The United Nations and the Maintenance of International Peace and Security*.[2]

Side by side with these empirical studies are the works concerned with the constitutional instruments under which international political organs operate. But the meticulous study of the texts

William M. Jordan is Acting Director of the Political Affairs Division of the UN Secretariat. This article is based on an address given at the annual meeting of the American Political Science Association, September 5, 1957. It reflects the personal views of the author, and is in no way official.

From Volume 11, No. 4 (1957), pp. 587–96.

[1] T. P. Conwell Evans, *The League Council in Action*, London, Oxford University Press, H. Milford, 1929.
[2] Leland M. Goodrich and Anne P. Simons, *The United Nations and the Maintenance of International Peace and Security*, Washington, Brookings Institution, 1955.

gives rise only too readily to the defect, so aptly described by M. Geny—that "the idea, completely detached from its object, finds its own release and leads a life of its own, deprived of all contact with the living reality".[3] In works prepared by the Secretariat, such as the *Repertoire of the Practice of the Security Council* and the *Repertory of Practice of United Nations Organs,* the attempt has been made to relate the living reality of the work of the organs to the provisions of the Charter. But the study of the working of essentially political institutions requires a freedom of analysis and exposition which cannot be attained within a framework of constitutional commentary. The utility of such works is limited by reason of the necessary formalism of their approach.

Then there are those whose minds have ranged freely over the realm of experience, either on the basis of actual participation or on the basis of wide study, and who have sought to formulate by intellectual processes which we but dimly understand—we call it reflection, judgment, or intuition—counsels of wisdom which give guidance for the present and future. The diversity of approaches applied to the wide range of experience accentuates the difficulty of any one mind bringing within its focus the extensive knowledge and reflection which has been directed to the subject of international political institutions.

Many new theoretical approaches are being devised for the study of international politics and international political institutions. The advance in modes of political analysis cannot but be of special interest to an international secretariat which increasingly needs to bring to bear a body of corporate thought on the development of the organs which it serves and the political problems which those organs face. Within an international secretariat the great problem is not so much the conflict of national loyalties, but rather the great diversity of mental habits which men and women of different countries bring to their work. We have to strive toward some unity of analytical approach if a corporate body of work is to emerge. Economists have seemingly built up agreed modes of analysis which transcend national boundaries, and the world has come to accept the tradition of current economic analysis by its international servants. In the political field, we are still almost wholly dependent on individual wit and wisdom. I recall that some thirty years ago Graham Wallas, reflecting on the political differences which arose through the devotion of Englishmen to intuitive processes of thought and of Frenchmen to logical reasoning, made a prophecy which might appropriately be quoted:

" . . . I find myself hoping that some day an art of thought may prevail— perhaps after the horrors of a new Thirty Years' War—in which the psychological truths implied in both types of thinking may be recognized and combined, and the errors of both may in some measure be avoided. If the psychologists ever create such an art, it may be that, a century hence, in gratitude for escape from some world disaster which had seemed to be 'logically' inevitable, a statue will be set up in New York or Paris or Pekin, not to the Goddess of Reason, but to

[3] Quoted in Charles de Visscher, *Theory and Reality in Public International Law,* Princeton, New Jersey, Princeton University Press, p. 67.
[4] *Repertoire of the Practice of the Security Council,* 1946–1951, New York, 1954; *Repertoire of the Practice of the Security Council, Supplement, 1952–1955,* New York, 1957; *Repertory of Practice of United Nations Organs,* Vol. I–V, New York, 1955.

'Psyche', the goddess who presides over the wise direction of the whole thinking organism. . . .

"Sometimes I hope that an art of thought which makes full use of every factor in the human organism may first be developed in America."[5]

In much writing on collective security I find myself puzzled by what appears to me a sometimes bewildering combination of logical and empirical thought. The temptation seems inescapable to define collective security, and thereafter to proceed by an exploration of the logical implications of the definition. But collective security is not a term of law which requires definition. The term is not, I think, to be found in the Charter or in the Covenant of the League of Nations. The process of definition and logical exposition is by no means identical with, and not always reconcilable with, the task of envisaging concretely— almost in physical form—the problem which confronts us and the manner of dealing with it. "De quoi s'agit-il?" was the question which Marshal Foch insistently demanded that his officers pose to themselves when lost in the labyrinths of their own reasoning.

The problem is that of ending the institution of war, of establishing arrangements to achieve that goal, and of estimating the prospects of their successful working in practice.

In the inter-war period, the conviction developed that war could most assuredly. be brought to an end if a system were established whereby wrongful recourse to war was met by the application of collective counter-measures of overwhelming strength. The essential and indispensable feature of such a system had

to be certainty in the operation of sanctions; for without certainty, deterrence could not be assured. The quest for certainty gave rise to long debate concerning the scope of the acts to be included in the definition of wrongful recourse to war and the means whereby the application of the definition to circumstances as they arose could be made automatic. Only in this way could the application of sanctions become an inexorable consequence of the commission of the wrongful act of war.

Such were the arrangements for which the term collective security was coined. That at least is my impression. The Covenant of the League of Nations was not itself a system of collective security in this sense. The Covenant prescribed procedures of pacific settlement which states were required to observe before having recourse to force for the protection of their interests. The sanctions to be applied by Member States were designed to ensure the observance of procedures of settlement.

The conviction that peace might be maintained most surely by establishing machinery for the automatic application of coercive measures against any state which broke the peace arose primarily from the endeavor of France and her allies to convert the League into a system which would provide them with a guarantee of the maintenance of the territorial settlement in Europe. Their thesis was simple. You ask us to disarm. We hold that if we disarm, we shall be unable to defend our frontiers and to maintain the territorial settlements concluded in 1919. In so far as we reduce our national armaments, we must obtain a corresponding degree of protection by the organization of international mili-

[5] Graham Wallas, *The Art of Thought*, London, J. Cape, 1926, p. 185.

tary assistance. That assistance must be as efficacious for purposes of national defense as national military organization. It must be certain in its application against the disturber of the peace. It must be brought into operation without delay. It must be provided to a degree and in a manner made known in advance, since common plans of defense cannot be devised at a moment's notice. The temper of the time precluded the possibility of discussing the defense of France simply and purely as a problem of checking the resurgence of German power. The immediate preoccupations of France in relation to Germany were translated into general terms such as the defining of aggression and the designation of the aggressor.

The world was left with the conviction that the road to peace lay through the organization of collective security in the sense of automatic application of sanctions against aggression. The success which attended the intellectual effort of France is indicated by the conviction which arose that the urgent problem was to solve the so-called gap in the Covenant. In fact, there was no gap in the Covenant. The Covenant was simply the Covenant. The gap existed only on the assumption that the Covenant was intended to be a system of collective security complying with the logical French criteria of adequacy. The failure to meet the threat of Hitlerism until it involved the world in a Second World War appeared to confirm the thesis that the road to peace lay in the assured mobilization of collective measures against the aggressor. That failure has led to a state of mind in which the ability of an international organization to take effective measures against aggression tends to

be regarded as the primary criterion of its utility and success.

But neither experience nor reflection provides grounds for believing that any system of collective security organized between independent states could provide the certainty which was premised of collective security in the inter-war period. Even the discharge of an obligation is, when the time comes, an act of will. The final decision to apply sanctions must be taken when the occasion arises, in circumstances of discouragement. For the objective of collective security is the maintenance of peace, not ultimate victory. When the moment comes to apply sanctions, the primary purpose of collective security has already been defeated. Participants are in the position of those called upon to pay for the horse after it has left the stable. The legal obligation to apply sanctions is therefore an imperfect measure of the probability of their application. A complete system of sanctions against aggression would indeed seem to require sanctions against those who fail to apply sanctions. When war breaks out, each state is prone to balance the degree of the menace presented to it by the initial outbreak, against the risks involved in joining in collective repression of the wrongdoer. When war breaks out, too, the response of other states is likely to be decisively influenced by the view taken of the soundness or justice of the situation which precipitated it. In the theory of automatic collective security, the obligation arises to engage in coercive action against the state which has placed itself in the position of committing aggression within the definition, without account being taken of the element of provocation, of the surrounding circumstances, or of the natural affinities of feelings between peoples. This is not unjust, it is urged, providing procedures are available for peaceful change. Yet, in fact, in moments of crisis, the course of action followed by a state will be largely swayed by the feelings of sympathy entertained at that moment and by attention to the consequences of immediate action on future relations.

There is then, I think, general agreement that collective security as it was understood would need to be preceded by a conviction on the part of men and women throughout the world that recourse to armed force in any part of the world is a threat to them individually and collectively; and this conviction must be held with sufficient compelling force to enable them to join in common action, whatever the cost to themselves and to their individual countries.

It would be premature to say that these psychological conditions exist. Even if and when these psychological conditions prevail, it would be hazardous to forecast that they will find expression in institutions of collective security automatic in their application. Police action against individuals in communities wedded to the observance of law is no precedent for automatic coercive sanctions against states. This conclusion has been cogently expressed by Oliver Lissitzyn:

"It does not appear that peace has ever been successfully maintained, over appreciably long periods of time, by the application of coercive sanctions to political entities alone. This fact was well known to the framers of the United States Constitution. Federal force has never been used in the United States to enforce a judgment against a state of the

Union, and at least one such judgment remained unexecuted. Yet in most federal unions courts have compulsory jurisdiction in disputes between the states and their decisions are usually obeyed. This is attributable to the transfer of the primary allegiance of the individuals from the subordinate entities to the federal Union and to the growth of respect for law."[6]

I should stress that these observations apply only to collective security in the sense of the automatic application of sanctions against aggression. Those who framed the Charter in 1945 wisely avoided any element of automatism. In the Charter the decision to apply enforcement measures was made the prerogative of the Security Council, and was subjected to a voting procedure which would ensure that no such decision would take place against the will of a permanent member. The so-called "veto", at least in relation to Chapter VII, was designed to afford protection as much to lesser states as to the great powers. For it ensured that membership in the UN would not entail for lesser states the burden of a binding obligation to participate in the application of sanctions in circumstances which might involve them in conflict with a great power. Since 1945 the development of nuclear weapons has accentuated the difficulties attending the exercise of coercive power by an international authority.

Should we therefore conclude that the sense of personal identification on the part of men and women with their national communities is so exclusive and unassailable as to render vain the effort to channel the political forces of our time along peaceful lines through the

[6] Oliver James Lissitzyn, *The International Court of Justice*, New York, Carnegie Endowment for International Peace, 1951, p. 108.

agency of international political institutions? Such would seem to be, if I understand aright, the conclusion of Percy Corbett. He sees a more promising line of advance in the re-orientation of international organization around the focus of human rights. An area of human life should, he proposes, be selected for study, report, and eventually supervision by a super-national agency, and he has pointed to racial discrimination as the most promising area. "The important thing", he comments, "is the development of effective procedures to which men may increasingly repair in matters which concern them individually and deeply. This is the way to bring international organization out of the high clouds of diplomacy and to win for it the common loyalty which is the firm foundation for authority."[7]

"The common loyalty which is the firm foundation for authority" may command our assent as a statement of the goal, without committing us to the road we are invited to travel. I wonder whether Corbett does not underestimate the impact of the principles of the UN Charter. This is not a matter on which we can make confident assertions. Yet we cannot but seek to assess the degree to which the political precepts of the Charter are becoming an element in the structure of thought of men and women throughout the world. The formulation of purposes and principles as obligations to govern the conduct of Member States and to guide the functioning of UN organs was perhaps the outstanding innovation of the Charter as compared with the Covenant of the League. I would feel that there is good reason to hold that within the framework of the UN—

granted amidst much contradiction and many conflicts of national interest—the representatives of its Members have in fact striven to translate into practice the general principles of the Organization. The working of the Organization has been shaped not so much by adherence to prescribed procedures as by concern to move, amidst the tense and baffling conflicts of national interest, toward conditions closer to the Charter's standards which command at least verbal homage. These unifying standards are general in scope yet compelling in appeal: the dignity of the human personality, the promotion of economic development, the principle of self-determination, and above all, the renunciation of the use of force.

The maintenance of international peace and security was given priority among the purposes of the Organization. In the service of this objective, two related conceptions were written into the Charter: first, the renunciation of the use or threat of force by Member States,[8] and second, the exercise of force by the Security Council under the provisions of Chapter VII of the Charter. The provisions for placing force at the disposal of the Security Council have not been fulfilled largely because the creation of a powerful international force does not eliminate the problem of the rivalry of great states for predominant influence within it. Yet the very inability of the Organization to develop as an instrument of coercion would seem to have focused attention on Article 2(4) as an anchorage of the Organization's authority.

The text of Article 2(4) runs:

"All Members shall refrain in their international relations from the threat or

[7] P. E. Corbett, *Law and Society in the Relations of States*, Institute of International Studies at Yale University, New York, Harcourt, Brace, 1951, p. 298.

[8] Article 2(4).

use of force against the territorial integrity or political independence of any State, or in any other manner inconsistent with the Purposes of the United Nations."

The fear was expressed at San Francisco that this phraseology would leave it open to a Member State to use force in a manner which it claimed to be consistent with the purposes of the UN, but without securing the Organization's assent to such use of force. The Committee of the Conference responsible for the drafting of Chapter I sought to dissipate all doubt by stating in its report: "The unilateral use of force or other coercive measures is not authorized or admitted."[9] Subject to the explicit reservation of the right of self-defense, this interpretation has been ratified in commentaries, notably in the United Kingdom and United States commentaries issued in 1945, and has been markedly fortified by more recent events. Doubt has been expressed whether the renunciation of force can be maintained in practice unless other means are organized for ensuring the protection of the just interests of states. It seems unlikely that this dilemma will receive a solution in general terms; it is a problem likely to demand solution in situations as they arise. Meanwhile, in moments of crisis, Article 2(4) in isolation remains the focal point. For men and women are well aware that national states can now only in limited degree perform their historic function of affording the individual peace and security. These changing political conditions at present express themselves in an undercurrent of anxiety rather than in any modification of traditional social attitudes.

Yet it is significant that, despite the strains and stresses of the post-war years, no nation has yet cared to challenge the existence, nor in a sense the lasting authority, of the UN. We might do well to think of the UN not so much as an institution or organization, but rather as the process of defining the relation of each state to the totality of other states. In recent events do we not discern a deepening conviction that each state is accountable to all for any exercise of force?

A moment ago I referred to the authority of the UN. I did so advisedly, for I feel that the analysis of international relations in terms of power runs into difficult waters in the matter of international institutions. The conception of power politics has played and will continue to play a valuable role in the realistic probing of a wide range of problems in the relations of states, but there is little reason to believe that it can serve to explain the totality of the relations between organized social groups, of which the state is one category. At a further remove, the relations of men and their social groupings are governed by the mental conceptions which command obedience by virtue of the structure of their personalities. The conception of power as the dominating element gives way before the more elusive conception of authority in the general, non-legal sense of that term. It may well be that our preoccupation with considerations of power constitutes a hindrance to the formulation in general terms of the role which the UN plays in the processes of international relations. Must it not be a main objective of the Organization to give the stamp of approval to social attitudes consonant with the needs of our generation?

[9] *United Nations Conference on International Organization*, Vol. VI, p. 459.

From the character of the Charter it-self it follows that the Organization is both an instrument for the pursuance of broad social objectives and an agency for the continuous adjustment of the rela-tions of established and nascent political groupings. A variety of descriptive phrases may be employed to depict the net effect of the voluminous debates and formal recommendations through which the Organization expresses itself. They afford an outlet for national tensions and a means whereby assurance may be given by governments to their peoples that steps are being taken for the remedying of national grievances without recourse to force. They furnish a plane on which negotiations may be conducted over and above direct exchanges between states through diplomatic means, and they af-ford an opportunity to Member States for clarifying the attitudes and intentions of other states on specific problems and their reactions to varying lines of policy. They constitute a forum within which broad considerations of international in-terest can be formulated and pressed. They are a device whereby vexed prob-lems can be dealt with against the back-ground of a changing concert of powers rather than by a fixed alignment of states. In the process of collective con-sultation, rigid lines of opposition be-tween defined groups are at least miti-gated. Even in circumstances of chronic conflict, they afford the occasion for ex-change of views and for negotiations. The scene of these deliberations is now a diplomatic center without parallel. De-vices and expedients for the adjustment of the relations of states which defy any standardized approach are formulated according to the exigencies of the mo-ment. The relations of states are by these means rendered more calculable in a world in which these relations are gov-erned by considerations more complex and uncertain than in the past. While it is true that within the arena of the UN efforts are made to win support for national policies and interests, it would be hazardous to contend that national policies remain unmodified by the influ-ence of the generality of states and the precepts of the Organization within whose framework they meet.

The transaction of the multifarious po-litical business which comes before the UN may well be differentiated from its functions on those occasions when the peace of the world as a whole appears to stand in the balance. The courses open to states on the verge of conflict were formulated by Sir Alexander Cadogan when he submitted the so-called Berlin Question to the Security Council in 1948. He recalled briefly the courses of action which appeared to be open to his gov-ernment: it could passively yield to ef-forts to deprive it of its authority in Berlin; or it could agree to continue dis-cussions under the conditions of duress established by the Soviet Union. "It is inconceivable," he observed, "that His Majesty's Government, for its part, could consent to either of these courses." "Thirdly," he continued, "His Majesty's Government could themselves resort to force as the only possible way of defend-ing and maintaining their legitimate rights." To do so would be equivalent to adopting the methods of duress of which it complained, and might give rise to unknown consequences. "In all the circumstances," he concluded, "the only step which His Majesty's Govern-ment . . . can now take is to bring this matter to the attention of the Security Council as a clear threat to the peace.

. . . "[20] In such circumstances the UN is simply the ultimate political council available to the states of the world.

Inquiry as to common elements in the processes whereby the UN has contributed to or was instrumental in maintaining general international peace on the main occasions on which it has been endangered since 1946 seems to yield little harvest. Each occasion has its special history to add to the fund of experience and demands examination in all its particularity. Consider the example of the Uniting for Peace Resolution. It was designed to codify experience in dealing with the attack on the Republic of Korea. Yet the Uniting for Peace Resolution has repeated the experience of the Charter. Its effective contribution has been the provision of an instrumentality through which the purposes of the Charter may be pursued, in this instance, the emergency session of the General Assembly. The detailed provisions of the Uniting for Peace Resolution have remained in large degree inoperative. In October–November 1956, new expedients were devised appropriate to the exigencies of the situation: the establishment of the United Nations Emergency Force (UNEF); the utilization of the services of the Secretary-General for the establishment of the Force, the assignment to him of responsibility for the supervision of its operations, and reliance on him for negotiation with the states concerned regarding the implementation of the Assembly resolutions; and, finally, the institution of an Advisory Committee for consultative purposes. UNEF was a novel conception. The forces of the permanent members were excluded. Its chief responsible officer was appointed by the UN itself and was responsible ul-

timately to the General Assembly; his authority was so defined as to make him independent of the policies of any one nation. But the creation and operation of the Force was dependent on the attitude and interests of the states directly concerned in the specific circumstances. The applicability of such a device in the future would similarly depend on the special aspects of the crisis which arises.

From the experience of the UN some have concluded that the Organization would be well advised to concentrate exclusively on its function as an arena of international debate and on its role in the peaceful settlement of disputes, and wholly to eschew the application of coercive measures. Doubtless in practice the emphasis has been on stimulating the will of states to settle disputes peacefully and on providing ways and means of settlement not otherwise available. But it is questionable whether the effort to organize force through the agency of an international political organ could be wholly abandoned without the most detrimental repercussions on arrangements for the settlement of disputes. At any time states are open to the temptation to seize possession or to enforce their will by recourse to force, and to calculate that a situation once so created will not be reversed. Uncertainty as to the eventual reaction of the Organization constitutes a factor making for restraint, especially in circumstances where the immediate problem is to arrest the outbreak of hostilities or to prevent their spread. The events of the past twelve months leave somewhat incalculable both the degree of political authority exercisable by or through the UN and the manner of its exercise.

It will, I think, be felt that we are

---

[20] Security Council *Official Records* (3d year), 364th meeting, October 6, 1948, p. 35–36.

experiencing a great modification in the conditions governing the relations of states and the methods of conducting those relations. Between the wars it was the common assertion that armaments were the backing of diplomacy, and that war was the conduct of diplomacy by other means. The correlation between the armed power of a state and the feasible objectives of its foreign policy was not difficult to discern. That correlation is now more obscure. Our conception of the state in international politics has been that of a sharply defined entity dealing with other similar defined and enduring entities exclusively through the authorized agency of its foreign minister. This conception by no means corresponds to reality as closely as in the past. It is not only that the concept of self-determination has rudely challenged the integrity of many existing states—a challenge which would have involved the UN in far greater difficulties had the guarantee of territorial integrity been written into the Charter. It is also that issues which arise in international relations tend to transcend national boundaries. The relations of states tend to be defined—for better or for worse— through a process of international public debate of which the UN is a focal point, but which spreads far beyond its walls. It is in the light of such changing circumstances—the incalculability of force in relation to the achievement of political objectives and the attuning of domestic opinion to views entertained in other lands—that the role of international political organization must be estimated.

We are in no position at present to translate the outcome of such changes into precise institutional forms. Instead, the maintenance of peace remains dependent on restraint and wisdom in the formulation of policy both within and without the formal framework of the UN. The situation which confronts us has been aptly summed up by Mr. Menzies in a recent speech in London:

> "Every nation, and particularly every great nation, whatever its natural resentment may be at some actions of the United Nations, must face up to the fact of the Assembly and give to the work of that Assembly a very high authority, threshing out its own policy with great care, presenting it with the greatest authority and force, taking the diplomatic opportunities provided by Assembly meetings for securing the widest measure of support for that policy."[11]

May I conclude that an official will necessarily have difficulty in discerning to what extent his appraisal is an objective examination of the institution which he serves and to what extent it is colored by being viewed through official spectacles. That I have wholly escaped the temptation to move from detached analysis to partisan advocacy is more than I would expect. International political organization is the microcosm of the realm of international politics. The detail and the vastness of the canvas may well defeat the effort to see it clearly and to see it whole.

11 *The Times* (London), July 9, 1957.

THE UN SECURITY COUNCIL

Leland M. Goodrich

It has been the unfortunate fate of the United Nations to have been most conspicuously unsuccessful in performing that task which was to be its major responsibility and for which it was supposed to be best equipped. Naturally this has also been the fate of the Security Council upon which the Members of the Organization, by the terms of Article 24, conferred "primary responsibility for the maintenance of international peace and security". Against this background of failure and consequent dissatisfaction, many have been asking whether the Security Council is fated to become like the human appendix, an atrophied organ with no useful function to perform or whether the present condition is not one that can and should be remedied or that perhaps will be changed in any case by an improvement in the state of international relations. To form a judgment on these possibilities it is necessary to recall the original conception of the Security Council, to review its record, and to analyze the causes of its decline and the likelihood of their elimination or counterbalancing by other forces.

I.

The peace and security provisions of the Charter appear to have been based in part on conclusions that were drawn by their authors with respect to the causes of the failure of the League system.

First of all, it was rightly believed that a major cause of the failure of the League system was its lack of universality, and particularly the absence of the United States. Consequently, the first concern of the Charter-makers was to have as members all the major powers in the Organization, and above all the Soviet Union and the United States. Secondly, it was believed that a weakness of the League system was its provision that sanctions should be applied against every aggressor, irrespective of whether or not it was a major power, and whether or not all the major powers joined in applying them. Consequently the authors of the Charter stressed the need of agreement among the permanent members of the Security Council as a condition of enforcement action, thus returning to the principle underlying the European Concert in the nineteenth century. Thirdly, it was believed that an important reason for the failure of the League system was the absence of any effective provision for the use of military force and the unwillingness of states under a voluntary system to take such extreme measures for defeating aggression. Therefore, the authors of the Charter were concerned with placing effective military force at the disposal of the Organization and making certain that it would be used when necessary. Finally, it was apparently believed, by some at least, that the League system

LELAND M. GOODRICH is a member of the Board of Editors of *International Organization* and Professor of International Organization and Administration at Columbia University. The author is indebted to Mr. Yasushi Akachi, a former Fulbright Scholar and at present member of the Department of Security Council and Political Affairs of the United Nations Secretariat, for assistance in the preparation of this article.

From Volume 12, No. 3 (1958), pp. 273–87.

was weakened by the failure of the Covenant clearly to delimit the respective responsibilities of Council and Assembly. Therefore the Charter-makers sought to define the limits of the responsibilities of the UN counterparts of these two organs. As written at San Francisco, after a lengthy process of elaboration in which the United States government played a leading role, the Charter set the maintenance of international peace and security as the first purpose of the Organization. It prescribed two principal approaches to the achievement of this purpose: collective measures for preventing or removing threats to the peace and suppressing acts of aggression or breaches of the peace, and adjustment or settlement of international disputes or situations by peaceful means. The regulation of armaments was made a subsidiary approach with emphasis upon agreements to make armed forces and facilities available to the Security Council and upon achieving "the least diversion for armaments of the world's human and economic resources"[1] consistent with the assured maintenance of international peace and security.

The primary responsibility for doing these things was placed on the Security Council, an organ so constructed and with voting procedures so defined that no decision other than a procedural one could be taken except with the concurrence of the five permanent members.[2] This gave assurance that no action could be taken against a permanent member or without its consent. The powers given to the Security Council were such as to give assurance that once the permanent members were in agreement and had the support of two other members—which would in all likelihood not be difficult to

achieve—effective action could be taken to maintain peace and security. The requirement of unanimity, moreover, was regarded as assurance that the coercive power vested in the Council would not be abused. Thus, in effect, the maintenance of international peace and security was to be made the responsibility of a "concert of the permanent members".

It was assumed that the members of this concert would each have an interest in the maintenance of peace and security, following a war which had imperilled them all. Furthermore, the members of the Council were required to act in accordance with the Purposes and Principles of the Organization, as set forth in Chapter I, in discharging their responsibilities. But it was also recognized that the concert might not always materialize in fact.

The underlying theory, however, was that if one of the major powers were to prove recalcitrant, or were to refuse to abide by the rules of international behaviour that were being inscribed in the Charter, a situation would be created in which the recalcitrant nation might have to be coerced; and it was apparent that no major nation could be coerced except by the combined forces of the other major nations. This would be the equivalent of a world war, and a decision to embark upon such a war would necessarily have to be made by each of the other major nations for itself and not by any international organization.[3]

There was no disagreement among the major powers at San Francisco or in previous discussions on the principle that unanimity of the major powers should be required. There was disagreement as

[1] Article 26 of the Charter.
[2] The one qualification was that a permanent member must abstain from voting when a decision was being taken under Chapter VI or Article 52, par. 3.

[3] Leo Pasvolsky, "The United Nations in Action," Edmund J. James Lectures on Government, Fifth Series, Urbana, University of Illinois Press, 1951, p. 80-81.

to how far the principle should be applied in disputes involving one or more of the major powers. The view of the United Kingdom was that no one, even a permanent member of the Council, should be allowed to vote in its own case. The Soviet view was that the unity of the major powers was the important consideration and no provision should be included in the Charter which would tend to encourage disagreement. At Yalta, however, Stalin accepted President Roosevelt's proposal that a member of the Council, party to a dispute, even though a permanent member, should not be allowed to veto a decision which the Council might take in the performance of its function of peaceful settlement or adjustment. The agreement reached at Yalta did not fully hold at San Francisco, however, when it became evident that it was not interpreted in like manner by all the parties to it. Extensive further discussions among the four sponsoring governments were necessary before final agreement was reached on the scope of the unanimity requirement.[4] By the San Francisco agreement, accepted by France, it was made clear that the requirement of unanimity of the permanent members did not apply to Council decisions to consider and discuss matters brought to its attention, or to decisions inviting parties to disputes to be heard. On the other hand, the "chain of events" theory as elaborated in the Statement was interpreted as preventing the Security Council from deciding to conduct an investigation or take any subsequent non-procedural decisions save with the concurrence of the permanent members, the one exception to the rule being that above

indicated. Furthermore, the Statement asserted that the question whether or not a particular matter was procedural was itself non-procedural. While the Statement contained no commitment not to use the right of veto excessively or unreasonably, it did contain the statement that it was

not to be assumed . . . that the permanent members, any more than the non-permanent members, would use their "veto" power wilfully to obstruct the operation of the Council,

and representatives of the permanent members reaffirmed their sense of responsibility in Conference discussions.

With respect to the division of powers between the Security Council and the General Assembly, there was even less disagreement among the permanent members up to the time of the San Francisco Conference. The Tentative Proposals of July 18, 1944,[5] which the United States submitted to the other participants in the Dumbarton Oaks Conversations gave the executive council (Security Council) the "primary responsibility for the peaceful settlement of international disputes, for the prevention of threats to the peace and breaches of the peace, and for such other activities as may be necessary for the maintenance of international peace and security". They empowered the General Assembly "to take action in matters of concern to the international organization which are not allocated to other organs by the basic instrument", and specifically

a. to make on its own initiative or on request of a member state, reports on and recommendations for the peaceful

---

[4] See Dwight E. Lee, "The Genesis of the Veto," *International Organization*, February 1947 (Vol. 1, No. 1), p. 33–42. For text of Statement by the Delegations of the Four Sponsoring Governments on Voting Procedure in the Security Council, see United Nations Conference on International Organization, *Documents*,

XI, p. 710–714, and Goodrich and Hambro, *Charter of the United Nations: Commentary and Documents*, rev. ed., Boston, World Peace Foundation, 1949, p. 216–218.
[5] *Post-War Foreign Policy Preparation*, Department of State Publication 3580, p. 595–606.

adjustment of any situation or controversy, the continuance of which it deems likely to impair the general welfare;

b. to assist the executive council, upon its request, in enlisting the cooperation of all states toward giving effect to action under consideration in or decided upon by the council with respect to:

    1) the settlement of a dispute the continuance of which is likely to endanger security or to lead to a breach of the peace;

    2) the maintenance or restoration of peace; and

    3) any other matters within the jurisdiction of the Council.

This proposed delimitation of the respective responsibilities of the two organs was substantially accepted at Dumbarton Oaks and incorporated into the Dumbarton Oaks Proposals.[6] This not only represented Department of State thinking, but it was in line with Soviet reluctance to permit extensive participation by the lesser powers in the activities of the Organization in the maintenance of international peace and security.

At San Francisco, a variety of pressures —the insistence of the lesser powers on a larger measure of participation, growing skepticism regarding the likelihood of cooperation among the major powers, and the insistence of Republican leaders and Congressional members of the United States delegation[7]—led to the broadening of the powers of the General Assembly, particularly by the inclusion of Articles 10 and 14, and the consequent blurring of the line dividing Security Council and General Assembly responsibilities and powers. Thus the Charter

foundation was laid for the subsequent development of the role of the General Assembly in the field of action originally reserved to the Security Council.[8] The primary role of the Security Council was further jeopardized by the inclusion of Article 51 recognizing explicitly "the inherent right of individual or collective self-defense" in case of an armed attack upon a Member, until such time as the Security Council has taken measures necessary to the maintenance of international peace and security.

II.

The most striking trend in the practice of the UN since its establishment has been the increasing inability of the Security Council to serve the purposes for which it was intended and the growing preference of Members to make use of the General Assembly. This trend has been accompanied by the gradual breakdown of the lines of functional separation between the Security Council and the General Assembly, drawn up at Dumbarton Oaks and preserved, though with important modifications, at San Francisco, and by the gradual assumption by the General Assembly of an active role in the maintenance of international peace and security.

A quantitative measurement of the trend, though obviously inadequate, provides us with an indication of the changing role of the Security Council within the UN machinery. The declining frequency of the meetings of the Security Council in a world beset with conflicts, together with the increasing number of political questions considered by the General Assembly in comparison with the number considered by the Council,

[6] Department of State *Bulletin,* October 8, 1944 (Vol. 11, No. 276), p. 368 and following.
[7] See John Foster Dulles, *War or Peace,* New York, Macmillan, 1950, p. 36–41.

[8] See Goodrich and Hambro, *op. cit.,* p. 150–163 and 178–181 and H. Field Haviland, Jr., *The Political Role of the General Assembly,* New York, Carnegie Endowment for International Peace, 1951, p. 5–28.

underscores the diminishing role of the Council. The figures are extremely illuminating:[9]

Period	Meetings of the SC	Substantive Political Questions Considered by the	
		SC	GA
Jan. 17, 1946–July 15, 1946	50	5	2
July 16, 1946–July 15, 1947	108	8	4
1947–1948	180	8	5
1948–1949	92	8	11
1949–1950	46	6	10
1950–1951	72	7	19
1951–1952	43	6	12
1952–1953	26	1	14
1953–1954	59	4	11
1954–1955	22	3	15
1955–1956	32	1	11
1956–1957	52	6	13

Since the peak reached in the period from July 1947 to July 1948, there has been a general decline in the number of meetings. Even in the period comprising the crises which simultaneously arose in the Middle East and Hungary in the fall of 1956, the frequency of Council meetings registered merely a moderate reversal of the trend. The provision of Rule I of the Provisional Rules of Procedure of the Security Council that "the interval between meetings shall not exceed fourteen days" was fairly well observed during the first three years, when there were only three instances in which the interval between meetings exceeded fourteen days. The situation began to deteriorate in 1949, and has not been remedied since.

Although the decline in the number of meetings of the Security Council and the number of new questions submitted to it would appear to be indicative of a decline in the importance attached to the work of the organ, one would not be justified in drawing conclusions regarding the effectiveness of the Council from these figures alone. Before passing final judgment upon the degree to which the Council has been effective in performing its Charter responsibilities, it is necessary to examine in some detail the Council's actual record of performance in the principal fields of its activity. These can be roughly defined as four in number: 1) the taking of collective measures to keep or restore international peace and security in case of threat or actual violation; 2) the peaceful settlement or adjustment of disputes and situations; 3) the regulation of armaments; and 4) the performance of certain organizational functions, including the recommendation of new members and the recommendation of a Secretary-General.

In the performance of the first function, the Council has achieved a considerable measure of success in dealing with those situations where its permanent

---

[9] Substantive political questions are those designated "Political and Security Questions" in the Annual Reports of the Secretary-General on the Work of the Organization and which do not relate to constitutional, organizational or procedural matters, including the admission of new Members or the representation of Members. For detailed information, see the Secretary-General's reports and the Reports of the Security Council to the General Assembly.

members, for whatever reasons, have had a sufficient interest in the maintenance of restoration of international peace and security to agree on a common course of action. Thus in dealing with the situation in Indonesia created by Dutch "police" action to re-establish the authority of the Netherlands in Indonesia, the Security Council was able eventually to get the parties to agree to the cessation of hostilities leading to an acceptable political settlement. It must be recognized, however, that Security Council action alone might not have been effective without strong supporting action of an economic nature by the United States and certain Asian states. The major powers were unwilling, however, to use military force to achieve their purpose.

In dealing with the Palestine question during the initial period of crisis, the Security Council achieved considerable success. Although it was not willing to undertake the enforcement of the partition plan recommended by the General Assembly in its resolution of November 29, 1947, it did exercise steady and increasing pressure on the parties to the hostilities which broke out after the Israeli declaration of independence of May 14, 1948, to cease fighting and agree to permanent armistice arrangements. Largely as a result of this pressure, the armistice agreements were concluded, and a system of international supervision under the general oversight of the Council was established. Until the Israeli attack of late October 1956, this system was effective in preventing a resumption of general hostilities, notwithstanding the failure of the UN to achieve a peaceful settlement of outstanding issues, occasional incidents of violence, and the deterioration of relations between the Soviet Union and the western powers.

The Security Council also achieved a considerable measure of success in dealing with hostilities involving India and Pakistan over Kashmir. The parties acceded to the proposal made by the Council's commission that a ceasefire be concluded under a system of international observation established with the consent of the parties, and a condition of nonfighting has since been maintained, even though efforts to settle the dispute have failed.

Only under exceptional conditions, has the Council been at all effective in dealing with threats to or breaches of the peace where the vital interests of permanent members have been directly in conflict. When, following the Communist *coup* in Czechoslovakia in February 1948, the complaint of Soviet intervention in that country was brought before the Council, any action, even the appointment of a committee to study the situation, was prevented by Soviet vetoes. It is difficult to see how any effective action could have been taken in any case, even if the right of veto had not existed, unless the western powers were willing to risk the unleashing of a general war.

In September 1948, the Council was asked to consider the situation resulting from the Soviet blockade of Berlin. The Soviet Union, by its veto, prevented any action from being taken. Again it is difficult to see what the Council could have done, even without the veto, without risking a general war, other than provide, as it did, the occasion for representatives of the interested parties to meet and negotiate.

When north Korean forces attacked the Republic of Korea on June 25, 1950, the Security Council was presented with a unique opportunity to take action in a situation involving the conflicting vital interests of permament members, since the Soviet representative was absent in protest against the seating of the Chinese representative appointed by the Nationalist government. This condition of affairs proved to be temporary, and when the Soviet representative returned to the Council at the beginning of August, the possibility of making further use of the Council to guide and determine UN action ceased.

It was this situation which led to the adoption by the Assembly of the "Uniting for Peace" resolution of November 3, 1950,[10] by which the Assembly asserted for itself, under a liberal interpretation of Charter provisions, the right to consider any threat to the peace, breach of the peace, or act of aggression, if the Council, because of lack of unanimity of its permanent members, had failed to discharge its primary responsibility, and to make appropriate recommendations, "including in the case of a breach of the peace or act of aggression the use of armed force when necessary". While the General Assembly was to exercise this "residual responsibility" only after the Council had failed to take action and had removed the item from its agenda, the fact that this could be done by a procedural vote made it impossible for a permanent member by its veto to prevent Assembly consideration. Thus, the relationship between Council and Assembly which had been spelled out in the Department of State proposal of July 18, 1944, and in the Dumbarton Oaks Proposals and maintained in principle in the Charter was explicitly redefined to permit a majority of seven in the Council, in the face of opposition by as many as four of the permanent members, to transfer the consideration of an alleged threat to or breach of the peace to the General Assembly. Thus the way was prepared for making the Council's "primary responsi-

[10] General Assembly Resolution 377 (V).

bility" largely nominal, unless the permanent members were in full accord, and for making the Assembly's "residual responsibility"—based on extremely liberal Charter interpretation—major in fact, at least for as long as the cold war continued.

The Hungarian and Middle East crises in October 1956 again demonstrated that the Council was incapable of acting in a situation involving the conflicting vital interests of the major powers, though in the latter case it was not the cold war that was mainly responsible. In both cases, action was taken by the General Assembly, in the first case with no visible effect on the actual course of events and in the second case effectively. This experience tended to show that even when the General Assembly acts, the chances of successful action are small unless the United States and the Soviet Union are on the same side.

In discharging its second function, the peaceful settlement or adjustment of international disputes and situations, the Security Council has had very limited effectiveness. The disputes and situations that have been brought to its attention have, almost without exception, fallen into one or the other of two main categories: 1) disputes and situations resulting from the cold war—the ideological-power conflict between the communist powers and the western powers; and 2) disputes and situations resulting from the conflict of interests between the more advanced western powers, including particularly the colonial powers, and the states, mainly of Asia and Africa, which had recently emerged from colonial domination or have strong attachments to the cause of Asian-African nationalism.

In dealing with disputes and situations

in the first category, the Council has only exceptionally had some measure of success. Pressure brought to bear through the Council appears to have influenced the Soviet Union to withdraw its military forces from Iran in 1946 after that country had complained of their illegal presence. Following a Council recommendation, the dispute between the United Kingdom and Albania over damage to United Kingdom ships in the Corfu Channel was submitted to the International Court of Justice for decision. However, Albania did not accept the award of damages. The Council was not able to agree on the appointment of a governor of the Free Territory of Trieste. It was unable by its own action to bring about a settlement of the dispute leading to the Berlin blockade. It was unable to take decision on various complaints submitted to it at the time of the Korean conflict. For the most part, the parties initiating UN consideration of cold war questions have considered the General Assembly better suited to their purposes.

In handling disputes and situations in the second category, the Council has not been much more effective. Only in the Indonesian case did it play a major part in bringing about an agreed settlement. The fact that the Soviet Union has generally aligned itself with the Asian and African states in their differences with the West and that some of the other permanent members have taken a rigid stand in opposition has largely eliminated the possibility of agreement among the permanent members of the Council on any course of action. Even the major western powers themselves have often been in disagreement, largely due to the unwillingness of the United States to go as far as the United Kingdom and

France in opposing Asian and African claims. Generally speaking, the Asian and African Members have preferred to bring the questions involving claims against the West before the General Assembly where their voting strength is proportionately greater. When the western powers find it in their interest to bring a question before the Security Council, as in the case of the Anglo-Iranian oil dispute or the Suez Canal dispute, any effective Council action is likely to be prevented by a Soviet opposition or by disagreement among the western powers themselves.

The disputes between the Arab states and Israel and between India and Pakistan over Kashmir do not completely fit into either of the above categories. Here, too, the Council has failed as an organ of peaceful settlement. And one of the decisive factors in these cases, as in the ones previously considered, has been the failure of the permanent members to agree, as the result of their conflicting interests in the cold war. Without this agreement, not only may the Council be prevented from taking a decision, but even if it is able to take a decision as the result of one or more abstentions by a permanent member, the authority of the Council is greatly weakened.

In the performance of its third function, the achievement of agreement on the regulation of armaments, the Council has a record of complete failure. In the first place, it has been unable to conclude any agreement with Members by which they would undertake to place military forces and facilities at the disposal of the Council. This has been due to the inability of the permanent members, the members of the Military Staff Committee, to agree on the principles to be applied in the conclusion of these agreements.[11] As a result, the Council has not had available to it the military forces essential to the full discharge of its responsibility for the maintenance of peace. Without these forces it can only recommend military measures, as it did in the Korean case. Secondly, all efforts that the Security Council has made to prepare proposals for the regulation of national armaments, whether atomic or conventional, have ended in complete deadlock due to the inability of the major powers to agree. Nor has the Assembly, which has taken the leading initiative in disarmament discussions, been more successful.

In discharging its functions relating to membership and the internal organization of the UN, the Security Council has had a mixed record. Because of vetoes cast by the Soviet Union, a deadlock developed over the admission of new members with the result that from 1950 to 1955 not a single new member was admitted. Indicative of the seriousness of the situation was the fact that in 1953 21 applications for membership were listed by the UN as not having been favorably acted upon by the Council. Down to December 14, 1955, the UN admitted only nine new members. The log-jam was broken in December 1955 when, under the terms of a "package deal", sixteen new members were admitted and since that time, six other new members have been taken in. At the present time, only the Republic of Korea, the Mongolian People's Republic, the Democratic People's Republic of Korea, the Democratic People's Republic of Vietnam and Vietminh stand outside because of refusal of the Council to act favorably on their applications, and of

these only two are outside solely because of the use of the veto in the Council.[12] It would be highly subjective to attempt any evaluation of how well the Security Council has performed its membership function. Probably the UN is nearer universality of membership at the present time as the result of the deadlock in the Security Council and the resulting necessity of a "package deal" than it would have been if the Assembly alone had controlled admissions. On the other hand, many qualified states were kept out for years, when the Assembly stood ready to admit them, solely because the use of the veto prevented favorable Council action.

In performing its recommending function in connection with the appointment of a Secretary-General, the Council has probably contributed to strengthening the role of that official in the work of the Organization. The requirement of agreement of the major powers increases the likelihood that the Secretary-General will have their confidence, which in turn is helpful, if not essential, to the full and most effective use of his powers. While the Council, due to the Soviet veto, did prevent the reappointment of Trygve Lie in 1950, the use of the General Assembly to break the deadlock did not produce very satisfactory results. In 1953 the Council recommended, and the Assembly appointed, Dag Hammerskjöld as Lie's successor. Experience since then has demonstrated the advantage of having a Secretary-General who commands the confidence of the major powers.

III.

Clearly the Security Council has failed to discharge its Charter responsibilities in the manner and with the degree of ef-

[11] See Goodrich and Simons, *The United Nations and the Maintenance of International Peace and Security*, Washington, Brookings Institution, 1955, p. 397–405.

[12] The Federal Republic of Germany undoubtedly would have applied and been admitted before now if it had not been for the knowledge that its application would be vetoed by the Soviet Union.

fectiveness which the authors of the Charter envisaged. Furthermore, there can be little doubt that the Council has declined greatly in prestige and has seemed to most Members of the UN less useful than in the beginning. This decline has been accompanied by a corresponding increase in the prestige and use of the General Assembly. What have been the reasons for the Council's decline?

The one reason upon which most people would seem to agree is the "veto". It is common to cite the number of vetoes cast and to draw the conclusion that the excessive use of the veto has been the cause of the Council's failure. Eighty-nine vetoes were cast in the Security Council up to May 2, 1958. The number of vetoes cast, however, does not tell the whole story regarding the influence of the veto on the work of the Council. It is necessary, first of all, to consider the nature of the proposals that have been vetoed. Of the total number, 48 vetoes were cast on proposals to admit new members, and in some instances the same country was "vetoed" four times.[12] Thirty-nine were used to defeat proposals made in connection with the discharge by the Council of its responsibility for the maintenance of international peace and security. Two vetoes have been cast in connection with the appointment of the Secretary-General.

If we consider only the vetoes that fall into this second category, we find a number of cases where the majority of the Council's members appear to have maneuvered to force the minority permanent member to repeat its veto on substantially the same issue for the record. For example, during the consideration of the Greek complaint against its northern neighbors in August 1947, the Soviet

[12] Italy's application was vetoed 6 times.

Union cast two vetoes consecutively, first on the Australian draft resolution and then on the United States draft resolution. The second veto must have been anticipated since the United States resolution was stronger than the Australian and therefore more objectionable to the Soviet Union.

The veto of a proposal has not necessarily prevented its substance from being put into effect. In the Syrian and Lebanese case, for example, the United States draft resolution expressing the confidence of the Security Council that the United Kingdom and French troops would be withdrawn "as soon as practicable" was not adopted due to the negative vote of the Soviet Union, which wanted a stronger resolution urging the immediate withdrawal of foreign forces. Nevertheless, the representatives of France and the United Kingdom declared that their governments were willing to give effect to the majority opinion, and the withdrawal of forces was carried out to the satisfaction of all concerned.

On the other hand, in those situations where the cooperation of the vetoing power is necessary to the carrying out of the proposal, the veto simply registers a factual situation. Even if the right of veto did not exist and the proposal were adopted by the required majority, there would be little likelihood that the dissenting major power would back down, if a vital interest was at stake, except under compulsion that might risk general war. Thus, if the Security Council had been able to take a decision in the Czechoslovak and Hungarian cases notwithstanding Soviet opposition, there is little reason to believe that the results would have been different since the majority members were not prepared to take those measures of coercion which alone had any chance of influencing Soviet action.

Concentration of attention upon the voting procedure of the Council as an explanation of Council weakness seems somewhat misplaced, since the real cause lies deeper than a mere organizational or procedural defect. The veto, when used, reflects the schism in the relations among the permanent members of the Council. It is a symptom, rather than the cause, of a disunited world.

The primary cause of the decline of the Security Council and especially of its role in relation to the General Assembly must be sought in the breakdown since 1945 of the wartime alliance of the Soviet Union, the United Kingdom, and the United States—the alliance whose continuation was the assumption upon which the idea of the Security Council as the guarantor of peace was constructed. The rivalry among the major powers induced them in many cases to use the Security Council as a tool for propaganda purposes to advance their divergent political objectives rather than to harmonize the action of nations in the attainment of common purposes, as intended by the authors of the Charter. Furthermore, these same powers discovered that for purposes of appealing to world opinion, and gaining support for their respective policies and programs in the cold war the General Assembly provided a more effective forum than the Security Council.

The work of the Security Council has been hampered by the conflicts among former Allied powers over the peace settlements. The authors of the Charter had remembered the onus attached to the Covenant of the League because of its close association with the settlements after the First World War. Accordingly, they provided a separate machinery for the making of the peace treaties with the Axis powers after the Second World War. Contrary to their hopes, however, the Allied unity broke down soon after the disappearance of the common enemies, and from the outset the Security Council had to carry burdens beyond its capacity, to deal with questions arising from the differences among the major powers concerning the peace settlements, such as the questions of Greece, Iran, and Czechoslovakia, the status of the Free Territory of Trieste, and the Berlin and the Korean questions. Deadlocks over the terms of the major peace settlements, moreover, were bound to make agreement on other issues more difficult to achieve.

Another cause contributing to the diminishing role of the Security Council has been the post-war emergence of numerous new nations in Asia and Africa, their crucial role in the world's balance of power, and their general preference for the Assembly rather than the Council for bringing their influence to bear in connection with the issues of colonialism, human rights, and disarmament. The anxiety of the major powers to win resounding political victories by the support of these newly independent states has helped the Assembly to gain further importance.

In addition, the advance in the use of mass media of communications and the increasing role of public opinion in the governmental process have tended to revolutionize traditional views on the relative merits of public discussion and participation in foreign policy making on the one hand, and quiet diplomacy and private negotiations on the other. The result has been that the attention of the strategists of national policy has turned to the manipulation and exploitation of the General Assembly as a world forum.

Doubtless the Assembly provides a more spectacular arena to wage the "war of ideas" than a small body like the Council.

IV.

It would seem likely that any amelioration of the relations among the major powers would bring about an improvement in the effectiveness of the Security Council; it would also reduce the desire of the major powers to turn to the General Assembly for political propaganda reasons. Amelioration of the major power relations does not, however, appear to be a sufficient condition to bring about the complete revival of the Security Council as the predominant organ for the maintenance of international peace and security as envisaged by the authors of the Charter, because the newly independent, non-western nations would be most reluctant to relinquish their power of effectively influencing political developments in the world through the General Assembly rather than through the Security Council, unless the composition of the Security Council is revised to meet their objections to its west-slanted membership. With the world situation as it is, it seems probable that the major questions of political adjustment, of the cold war as well as of the liquidation of colonialism, will remain the primary concern of the General Assembly rather than of the Council. The Security Council is more likely to confine itself to dealing with specific disputes or situations related to the maintenance of peace and security, which require swiftness of action and continuity of study and surveillance by the international organization, and about which the permanent members are able to achieve some measure of agreement.

The inclination of the western states to clarify and bring to the fore the residual responsibility of the Assembly in matters related to peace and security, as exemplified by their support for the "Uniting for Peace" resolution, appears to have been checked as a result of their realization of the new situation brought about by the increase in the voting power of the Asian and African states, often unsympathetic to the West. In fact, the Asian and African states have come to possess a potential veto over Assembly decisions. In consequence, the passage of west-sponsored resolutions through the Assembly can no longer be taken for granted. It was noteworthy that when the Syrian-Turkish question (1957) was brought before the Assembly, the representatives of Australia, France, the Netherlands, the United Kingdom, and the United States raised the constitutional issue that the proper place to deal with a threat to the peace under the Charter was the Security Council, not the Assembly.[14] This was in marked contrast to the Soviet silence regarding the competence of the Assembly in connection with the question. The seeming reversal of the positions of the western and communist states on the respective roles of the Security Council and the General Assembly on questions of peace and security is indicative of the fluidity of Members' preferences for one organ over another, stemming from the changing political configuration of these organs, caused partly by the addition to the Asian and African group of recently admitted states and partly by the trend of some members of this group of nations towards neutralism.

[14] Documents A/PV.706 (October 18, 1957); A/-BUR/SR.116 (October 21, 1957); and A/PV.708 (October 22, 1957).

Setting aside broad political considerations which would ultimately determine the relative roles for peacemaking of the Security Council and the General Assembly, several advantages which the Council possesses over the Assembly, from an organizational point of view, are worth noting. The Security Council is an executive committee of a small size in a state of constant alertness. Its members, even non-permanent members chosen for two year periods, can accumulate considerable knowledge and skill with respect to disputes and situations brought to its attention. It is able to act at a moment's notice, continue its supervisory functions without intermission, and serve as an effective negotiating body. In comparison, the size and lack of continuity of the General Assembly, together with the publicity attendant on its consideration of questions and the deficiency of experience of some of the delegates to the Assembly, suggest that it is primarily a forum of the nations for the discussion of questions of a general character, rather than an organ suited to perform intricate diplomatic functions of negotiation and conciliation. The establishment of subsidiary organs like the Interim Committee, the United Nations Commission on Korea, and the Advisory Committee on the United Nations Emergency Force, may overcome some of the organizational deficiencies of the Assembly. But an effective use of the Security Council would have several advantages not possessed by the subsidiary organs of the Assembly. It would also avoid an unnecessary duplication of functions.

Proposals have been made for the strengthening of the Security Council to enable it to perform more effectively the functions assigned to it by the Charter.[15] These may be divided into two categories: those calling for revision of the powers and voting procedures of the Council, and those involving some change of the Council's composition.

The frustration resulting from the frequent use of the veto has led to the following suggestions[16]: 1) abolish the veto completely and accord equality in voting to all members of the Security Council; 2) substitute for the requirement of the absolute unanimity of all permanent members that of a qualified unanimity by which the favorable votes of three or four of the permanent members would be necessary for a decision; 3) restrict the use of the veto to clearly defined areas and eliminate it from the pacific settlement of disputes and the admission of new members; 4) alter the fundamental nature of the Security Council by substituting powers of recommendation for its present enforcement powers; and 5) strengthen further the role of the General Assembly by giving it enforcement powers. Suggestions 1) and 2) seem unacceptable at the present to any of the permanent members. Suggestion 3) has been espoused by the United States since the Vandenberg Resolution of June 1948. This was confirmed by President Eisenhower in his letter to Premier Bulganin dated January 12, 1958.[17] Formal adoption of suggestion 4) would mean a retrogression of international organization, although it is not more than an acknowledgment of the existing state of affairs in the Security Council arising from the failure to implement provisions of Article 43. It is also unlikely that the major

[15] See Francis O. Wilcox and Carl M. Marcy, *Proposals for Changes in the United Nations*, Washington, Brookings Institution, 1955, Chapts. X and XI.
[16] U. S. Senate Committee on Foreign Relations, Subcommittee on the United Nations Charter, *The Problem of the Veto in the United Nations Security Council*, Staff Study No. 1, Washington, 1954.
[17] Department of State *Bulletin*, January 27, 1958 (Vol. 38, No. 970), p. 125.

powers would agree to the expansion of the powers of the Assembly, unless they have a share in the voting commensurate with the responsibility which they have to assume. A prerequisite to such agreement would be solution of the complicated question of weighted voting in the General Assembly. In short, suggestion 3) appears to be the only proposal which has some hope of acceptance by the powers constituting the permanent members, although there is no indication that the Soviet Union has changed its view on the "chain of events" theory by which it justified extension of the veto to the peaceful settlement of disputes.[18] Thus, even the adoption of suggestion 3) would have to await substantial relaxation of tensions between the western powers and the communist bloc, and this relaxation would make it largely unnecessary.

The question of change of composition of the Security Council has two facets, namely, the increase in the number of the non-permanent members of the Council, and additions to or elimination of the permanent members. The former question has already arisen in the Assembly and is probably easier to solve than the latter. Though an informal "gentleman's agreement" was reached among the major powers in London in 1946 on the allocation of non-permanent seats, the increase in the number of Member States, in particular from Asia and Africa, has brought about intensified pressures for a reconsideration of the original allocation. It has also given rise to contests for non-permanent seats, as evidenced in the Yugoslav-Philippine rivalry of 1955 and the Japanese-Czechoslovakian competi-

tion of 1957. In its eleventh and twelfth sessions the General Assembly had before it a proposal by Latin American states and Spain to increase the number of non-permanent members of the Security Council, but decided to postpone consideration until the following session.[19] The Latin American proposal for an increase of two non-permanent seats in the Council was favored by the western powers, but was opposed by many Asian and African nations who felt that the allocation of merely one of the two proposed seats to their region and the other to Europe was not proportionate to their increased number.

The question of the expansion of membership of the Council must be carefully weighed in the light of the aspirations of various regions of the world to be justly represented on the Council and the requirement to preserve the advantages inherent in a small, compact Council. The rise of India as a spokesman of the neutral nations and the recovery of west Germany, Italy, and Japan as influential powers, though west Germany is not yet a Member of the UN, may give rise to the question of their permanent—or semipermanent—membership in the Council. There is no doubt that the question of the representation of China also has a crucial importance for the revitalization of the Council as an organ reflective of the reality of the power in the world.[20]

Of more importance than formal changes for the immediate future of the Security Council would be the improvement of the Council proceedings by the use of informal techniques not requiring revision of voting procedure or composi-

[18] See Premier Bulganin's letter to President Eisenhower, February 1, 1958, *ibid.*, March 10, 1958, p. 378.
[19] General Assembly *Official Records* (eleventh session), Annexes, Agenda items 56, 57, and 58; A/SPC/SR.74 and 75 (December 1957); A/PV.728 (December 12, 1957).
[20] See Herbert W. Briggs, "Chinese Representation in

the United Nations," *International Organization*, May 1952 (Vol. 6, No. 2), p. 192–209; and an address given by the Secretary-General at a recent meeting of members of the British Houses of Parliament held under the auspices of the British group of the Inter-parliamentary Union, *United Nations Review*, May 1958 (Vol. 4, No. 11), p. 9.

tion. Among such techniques, mention might be made of the following: an effective use of private, as against public, meetings of the Council, depending on the nature of the problem, as illustrated by the three private Council meetings held in connection with the question of the nationalization of the Suez Canal in October 1956; the vitalization of the provisions of Article 28 (2), which have remained dormant, regarding periodic meetings of the Council attended by foreign ministers or heads or other members of government;[21] the appointment of a rapporteur or conciliator for a situation or dispute brought to the Council, who would make efforts at conciliation before the Council enters into the consideration of the substance of the question, along the lines of the Assembly resolution 268 B (III); and other measures of private diplomacy within the framework of the Security Council, making use of the good offices of the Secretary-General, as exemplified by his repeated trips to the Middle East since the spring of 1956 at the request of the Security Council.

The Security Council may indeed have an increasingly important role to play in the task of keeping the peace, provided that a discriminating choice is made by its members of the various instruments and techniques of diplomacy at its disposal. As part of the "evolution of emphasis and practice"[22] of the over-all United Nations machinery, it may yet become an active and vigorous guardian of the peace, though it is not likely to achieve the stature envisioned by the architects of the Charter.

---

[21] Proposals dealing with the periodic meetings of the Security Council have been made by the Secretary-General in the past. Cf. General Assembly *Official Records* (sixth session) Supplement No. 15 (A/1902), "Development of a Twenty-Year Programme for Achieving Peace Through the United Nations"; General Assembly *Official Records* (tenth session), Supplement No. 1 (A/2911), "Annual Report of the Secretary-General on the Work of the Organization, 1 July 1954 —15 June 1955".

[22] General Assembly *Official Records* (twelfth session), Supplement No. 1A (A/3594/Add.I), "Introduction to the Annual Report of the Secretary-General on the Work of the Organization, 16 June 1956—15 June 1957".

Collective Legitimization as a Political Function of the United Nations

Inis L. Claude, Jr.

As the United Nations has developed and as its role in world affairs has been adapted to the necessities and possibilities created and the limitations established by the changing realities of international politics, collective legitimization has emerged as one of its major political functions. By this I mean to suggest that the world organization has come to be regarded, and used, as a dispenser of politically significant approval and disapproval of the claims, policies, and actions of states, including, but going far beyond, their claims to status as independent members of the international system. In this essay I shall undertake to refine and elaborate this rough definition of collective legitimization and to discuss the performance of this role by the United Nations. It is essential in the beginning, however, to provide a foundation by offering some observations about the general problem of political legitimacy.

THE PROBLEM OF POLITICAL LEGITIMACY

The history of political theory offers ample evidence of the perennial interest of philosophers in the problem of legitimacy, an interest which more often than not has been intimately linked with the highly practical concerns of rulers or rebels, intent upon maintaining or challenging the political status quo. The urge for formally declared and generally acknowledged legitimacy approaches the status of a constant feature of political life. This urge requires that power be converted into authority, competence be supported by jurisdiction, and possession be validated as ownership. Conversely, if we look at it from the viewpoint of those who attack the status quo, it demands that the *de facto* be

Inis L. Claude, Jr., a member of the Board of Editors of *International Organization*, is Professor of Political Science at the University of Michigan. This article was adapted from Professor Claude's forthcoming book *The Changing United Nations*, copyright by Random House, 1966.
From Volume 20, No. 3 (1966), pp. 367–79.

denied or deprived of *de jure* status, that the might of their antagonists not be sanctified as right. The principle is the same whether we are dealing with those who want the *is* to be recognized as the *ought* or with those who are setting out to convert their *ought* into a newly established *is*. Politics is not merely a struggle for power but also a contest over legitimacy, a competition in which the conferment or denial, the confirmation or revocation, of legitimacy is an important stake.

To assert this is in some sense to deny the proposition that the behavior of political leaders, on either the domestic or the international plane, must be interpreted as a purely power-oriented phenomenon. This ancient viewpoint, which flourished in modern Europe as *realpolitik* and has achieved great influence in contemporary America under the label of political realism, is always easier to entertain in the abstract than in the particular instance. The American "realist" who likes the ring of the generalization is not likely to insist that it rings true in the case of a national hero like Abraham Lincoln or of a contemporary whose human characteristics are readily visible—Dwight D. Eisenhower or Lyndon B. Johnson, for instance. When one turns from generalization about rulers to consideration of individual cases, one is struck by the observation that the urge to possess and exercise power is usually qualified by concern about the justification of such possession and exercise. Among statesmen, the lovers of naked power are far less typical than those who aspire to clothe themselves in the mantle of legitimate authority; emperors may be nude, but they do not like to be so, to think themselves so, or to be so regarded.

In part, this reflects the fact that power holders are burdened, like other human beings, by the necessity of satisfying their own consciences. By and large, they cannot comfortably regard themselves as usurpers or tyrants but require some basis for convincing themselves of the rightness of their position.

In a larger sense, however, this argument confirms rather than denies the power-oriented character of politics. Power and legitimacy are not antithetical, but complementary. The obverse of the legitimacy of power is the power of legitimacy; rulers seek legitimization not only to satisfy their consciences but also to buttress their positions. Legitimacy, in short, not only makes most rulers more comfortable but makes all rulers more effective—more secure in the possession of power and more successful in its exercise. Considerations of political morality combine with more hardheaded power considerations to explain the persistence of concern about legitimacy in the political sphere.

Two fundamental concepts figure prominently and persistently in the history of the problem of political legitimacy: law and morality. Lawyers tend simply to translate legitimacy as *legality,* capitalizing upon the derivation and literal meaning of the word. Similarly, moralists are inclined to claim a monopoly, treating political legitimacy as a problem of moral justification. Law and morality are both well-established and important legitimizing principles, but neither singly nor in combination do they exhaust the field. Each of them requires its own legitimization; the legitimacy of the positive law, or of the prevailing moral code, is sometimes the precise issue at stake in a political controversy. Moreover, relations between law and morality are variable. They sometimes reinforce each other, as when morality enjoins obedience to law or law codifies and sanctions the demands of morality. However, they may also come into conflict, as when morality condones disobedience to an unjust law or the law commands citizens to fulfill their public duty rather than follow the dictates of their private moral convictions. In the final analysis, the problem of legitimacy has a political dimension that goes beyond its legal and moral aspects. Judges and priests and philosophers usually make themselves heard, but they do not necessarily have the last word; the process of legitimization is ultimately a political phenomenon, a crystallization of judgment that may be influenced but is unlikely to be wholly determined by legal norms and moral principles.

While different principles of legitimacy and agents of legitimization may be simultaneously operative within a given political unit and among the constituent units of the global political system, there is nevertheless a tendency for a single concept of legitimacy to become generally dominant in a particular era, to achieve widespread acceptance as the decisive standard. Indeed, the existence of such a consensus may be regarded as the essential characteristic of a cohesive and stable political system at either the national or the international level. Like most fashions, fashions in legitimization change from time to time, and the crucial periods in political history are those transitional years of conflict between old and new concepts of legitimacy, the historical interstices between the initial challenge to the established concept and the general acceptance of its replacement. Thus, the era of modern European politics was ushered in by the substitution of the Voice of the People for the Voice of God (a change thinly concealed by the myth that the Voice of the People *is* the Voice of God) as the determinant of political legitimacy. The democratic principle has achieved widespread acceptance as the criterion of legitimate government within the state, however far short of general applicability it may have fallen as an operative political principle; the democratic pretensions of undemocratic regimes do not detract from, but lend support to, the proposition that popular consent is broadly acknowledged as the legitimizing principle in contemporary political life. The modern era has also seen the establishment of national self-determination as the basis of legitimate statehood, and the global extension of the reach of this legitimizing principle has been one of the most significant developments of recent decades.

At any given time the operative significance of the dominant principle of legitimacy tends to be less than that of the agency of legitimization. This means that the crucial question is not *what* principle is acknowledged but *who* is accepted as the authoritative interpreter of the principle or, to put it in institutional terms, *how* the process of legitimization works. There is, of course, a correlation between the nature of the legitimizing principle and the identity of its applicator. For instance, the principle of divine right tends to call for an ecclesiastical spokesman, and the consent theory implies reliance upon a democratic electoral process. In the long run, perhaps, the principle may be decisive; a secular change in the ideology of legitimacy can be expected ultimately to bring about the repudiation of the old and the recognition of a new agency or process of legitimization. Thus, over time, papal decrees have lost, and plebiscite results and public opinion surveys have gained, influence in the legitimizing process. Nevertheless, in the short run, a paraphrase of the maxim that "the Constitution means what the judges say it means" can be generalized. Principles of legitimacy are necessarily rather vague and uncertain in their applicability, and the nature of the process by which their application is decided or the means by which legitimacy is dispensed can be of the greatest importance.

LEGITIMIZATION IN INTERNATIONAL RELATIONS

Against this background I should like to discuss these two propositions: 1) that the function of legitimization in the international realm has tended in recent years to be increasingly conferred upon international political institutions; and 2) that the exercise of this function is, and probably will continue to be, a highly significant part of the political role of the United Nations.

The first proposition implies that the current fashion of legitimization of the status and behavior of states in the international arena emphasizes the *collective* and the *political* aspects of the process. While statesmen have their own ways of justifying their foreign policies to themselves and their peoples, independently of external judgments, they are well aware that such unilateral determinations do not suffice. They are keenly conscious of the need for approval by as large and impressive a body of other states as may be possible, for multilateral endorsement of their positions—in short, for collective legitimization. Moreover, it is a political judgment by their fellow practitioners of international politics that they primarily seek, not a legal judgment rendered by an international judicial organ.

This is not to say that international law has no place in the contemporary procedures of legitimization. States do occasionally resort, and even more frequently propose to resort, to the International Court of Justice (ICJ) or to *ad hoc* arbitral tribunals, and still more often they invoke legal arguments in justification of their positions or denunciation of those of their opponents. One might argue that states should rely predominantly or exclusively upon judicial interpretation of international law for the handling of issues concerning legitimacy, and one might expect that in a more settled period of international relations a heavier reliance upon adjudication might develop. But my present concern is with what *is*, not with what should be or might be, and it is a fact of present-day international life that, for whatever reasons of whatever validity, statesmen exhibit a definite preference for a political rather than a legal process of legitimization.

The explanation lies partly in the fact that the legitimacy of international law is widely challenged—that is, there is a defective consensus concerning the acceptability of the standards of legitimacy incorporated in the law. Moreover, the International Court is inhibited in the development of a more prominent role in the legitimizing process by the fact that it can assume jurisdiction in a case only with the consent of both sides, given *ad hoc* or by previous acceptance of the optional clause of its Statute, while international political organs are not restricted in this way. More broadly, it must simply be said that this is a highly politicized era, not a legalistic one. Collective legitimization has developed, for better or for worse, as essentially a political function, sought for political reasons, exercised by political organs through the operation of a political process, and productive of political results.

Even when states resort to the International Court of Justice, they often appear to seek a judicial contribution to the success of their cause in the political forum rather than to express a preference for the legal over the political process of legitimization. Thus, the request for an advisory opinion concerning certain aspects of the United Nations financial crisis, addressed to the International Court in 1961, was designed to strengthen the case for a reassertion by the General Assembly of its competence to assess Members for support of peacekeeping operations. Somewhat similarly, the South West Africa case, brought before the Court in 1960, was undoubtedly initiated by Ethiopia and Liberia with the hope of obtaining judicial support for an intensified prosecution of South Africa in the General Assembly. The use of the Court in these instances clearly reflects the intention to pursue the issue of legitimacy in the political forum, not to transfer it to the judicial forum. Moreover, the Court's ruling in favor of South Africa in the latter case can be expected to stimulate many states to respond that the South African position, while possibly legal, is certainly not legitimate.

The function of collective legitimization is not, in principle, reserved exclusively to the United Nations. The United States has placed considerable reliance upon the Organization of American States (OAS) as an instrument for justifying its policy in various cases involving Latin American states, and the anticolonial bloc has used special conferences, beginning with the Asian-African Conference at Bandung in 1955, to proclaim the illegitimacy of continued colonial rule. However, the prominence of the United Nations in the pattern of international organization and its status as an institution approximating universality give it obvious advantages for playing the role of custodian of the seals of international approval and disapproval. While the voice of the United Nations may not be the authentic voice of mankind, it is clearly the best available facsimile thereof, and statesmen have by general consent treated the United Nations as the most impressive and authoritative instrument for the expression of a global version of the general will. The notion that the United Nations gives expression to "world public opinion" is largely a myth, propagated by the winners of diplomatic battles in the Organization in order to enhance the significance of their victories. It would be more accurate to say that the judgments of the Organization represent the preponderant opinion of the foreign offices and other participants in the management of the foreign affairs of the governments of Member States. However, the issue of what the United Nations actually represents is less important than the fact that statesmen have conferred the function of collective legitimization primarily upon that Organization.

This function has been given relatively little attention in analyses of the political role of the United Nations. Most studies have tended to focus upon the operational functions of the Organization—its programs, interventions, and peacekeeping ventures. Our action-oriented generation has concentrated on the question of what the United Nations can and cannot *do,* on the issue of its executive capacity, rather than on its verbal performance. When forced to pessimistic conclusions regarding the possibilities of United Nations action, the typical analyst or editorialist falls back upon the dismal assertion that the Organization is in danger of being reduced to a mere debating chamber, a contemptible talk-shop. Given this negative attitude toward the verbal function, it is small wonder that serious efforts to analyze its significance have been rare. When such efforts have been made, they have usually focused upon the concept of multilateral diplomacy or that of lawmaking by multilateral processes. In the case of the former emphasis, the function relating to collective legitimization has been too readily deplored to be seriously explored; it tends to be summarily dismissed as a propagandistic abuse, an activity inimical to meaningful negotiation and alien to genuine diplomacy, multilateral or otherwise. The emphasis upon lawmaking is closer to the point, but it nevertheless misses the central point that the legitimizing function performed by United Nations organs is less a matter of purporting either to apply or to revise the law than of affixing the stamp of political approval or disapproval.

Collective legitimization is an aspect of the verbal rather than the executive functioning of the United Nations, and in some sense it is a result of the Organization's incapacity for decisive intervention in and control of international relations. One might argue that the United Nations has resorted to saying "thou should" because it is in no position to say "thou shalt" and to saying "thou may" because it cannot say "thou must." It authorizes and endorses in compensation for its inability to effectuate commands, and it condemns and deplores in compensation for its inability to prohibit and prevent. However, the mood expressed in a *New York Times* editorial which, noting the danger that financial difficulties would prevent the United Nations from undertaking further peacekeeping operations, warned that "the end result would be abandonment of its Charter obligation to enforce peace and suppress aggression and a consequent slump into the status of a debating society"[1] is neither realistic nor conducive to a perceptive appraisal of the actual and potential capabilities of the Organization. It reflects an exaggerated conception of what the United Nations might have been; surely, no one who had consulted the Charter and the expectations of its framers in preference to his own hopes and ideals could ever have believed that the United Nations promised to be a dependable agency for enforcing peace and suppressing aggression in an era of great-power division. Even more, it reflects an exaggerated contempt for international debating societies and a disinclination to examine the question of what it is possible for the United Nations to do when it cannot do the impossible.

If we can learn to judge the United Nations less in terms of its failure to attain the ideals that we postulate and more in terms of its success in responding to the realities that the world presents, we shall be in a better position to analyze its development. Approaching the Organization in this spirit, we find that its debating-society aspect is not to be deplored and dismissed as evidence of a "slump" but that it deserves to be examined for evidence of the functional adaptation and innovation that it may represent. My thesis is that the function of collective legitimization is one of the most significant elements in the pattern of political activity that the United Nations has evolved in response to the set of limitations and possibilities posed by the political realities of our time.

The development of this function has not been, in any meaningful sense, *undertaken* by the United Nations, conceived as an independent institutional actor upon the global stage. Rather, it has been thrust upon the Organization by Member States. Collective legitimization is an answer not to the question of what the United Nations can *do* but to the question of how it can be *used*.

Statesmen have been more perceptive than scholars in recognizing and appreciating the significance of this potentiality for utilization of the Organization. They have persistently, and increasingly, regarded the United Nations as an agency capable of bestowing politically weighty approval and disapproval upon their projects and policies. As will be illustrated in the following section of this article, the General Assembly and, to a lesser degree, the Security Council have been used for this purpose. The debates within and negotiations around these political organs have largely concerned the adoption or rejection of resolutions designed to proclaim the legitimacy or the illegitimacy of posi-

[1] *The New York Times*, September 16, 1963.

tions or actions taken by states. Governments have exerted themselves strenuously to promote the passage of resolutions favorable to their cause and the defeat of unfavorable resolutions. In reverse, they have attempted to block resolutions giving approval and to advance those asserting disapproval of their opponents' positions.

The scale of values developed by Members of the United Nations may be represented schematically by the following device in which states A and B are assumed to be engaged in a dispute:

1) Approval of A's position
2) Disapproval of B's position
3) Acquiescence in A's position
4) Acquiescence in B's position
5) Disapproval of A's position
6) Approval of B's position

In this scheme A's preferences would run in descending order from the top of the list, and B's from the bottom of the list. Parliamentary battles over the endorsement, the acceptance, and the condemnation of positions taken by states are a standard feature of the proceedings of the United Nations.

One may question whether proclamations of approval or disapproval by organs of the United Nations, deficient as they typically are in both formal legal significance and effective supportive power, are really important. The answer is that statesmen, by so obviously attaching importance to them, have made them important. Artificial or not, the value of acts of legitimization by the United Nations has been established by the intense demand for them. One may question whether great importance should be attributed to such acts and contend that the political organs of the United Nations are inappropriately cast as dispensers of legitimacy. But a fact is no less a fact for being deplored, and it *is* a fact that governments have tended more and more to treat those organs as agencies of legitimization.

I do not mean to suggest that states are willing to accept in principle or to follow in consistent practice the proposition that the collective judgment of the General Assembly or any other international body is decisive. While states vary in the degree to which they display respect for the function of collective legitimization, this variation appears to reflect differences in experience and expectation rather than in commitment to the principle of the validity of collective evaluation. Any state can be expected to assert the validity of acts of legitimization that support its interests and to deny that acts contrary to its interests are worthy of respect. However, the vigorous effort that states customarily make to prevent the passage of formal denunciations of their positions or policies indicates that they have respect for the significance, if not for the validity, of adverse judgments by international organs. While states may act in violation of General Assembly resolutions, they evidently prefer not to do so, or to appear not to do so, on the ground that collective approbation is an important asset and collective disapprobation a significant liability in international relations. A state may hesitate to pursue a policy that has engendered the formal disapproval of the Assembly not because it is prepared to give the will of that organ priority over its national interest but because it believes that the adverse judgment of the Assembly makes the pursuit of that policy disadvantageous to the national interest. This is simply to say that statesmen take collective legitimacy seriously as a factor in international politics; the opinions and attitudes of other states, manifested through the parliamentary mechanism of the United Nations, must be taken into account in the conduct of foreign policy.

Clearly, statesmen do not attach identical importance to all judgments of legitimacy pronounced by political organs of the United Nations but weight the significance of resolutions according to the size and composition of the majorities supporting them and the forcefulness of the language in which they are couched. This variation in the impressiveness of formal resolutions was anticipated in the Charter provisions requiring a two-thirds majority for decisions on important questions in the General Assembly (Article 18, paragraph 2), and unanimity of the permanent members of the Security Council in decisions on nonprocedural matters in that body (Article 27, paragraph 3). In practice, it is evident that a Security Council resolution supported by all the permanent members is taken more seriously than one on which three of them abstain, that the support or opposition of India is treated as more significant than that of Iceland in evaluating a resolution of the General Assembly, and that a unanimous decision of the latter body deserves and receives more attention than a narrowly passed resolution. Moreover, a clear and firm act of approval or disapproval carries more weight than a vague and ambiguous pronouncement, and a series of resolutions, pointing consistently in the same direction, is more impressive than an isolated case. While states value even narrow parliamentary victories, achieved by garnering votes wherever they may be found and diluting the language of resolutions as much as may be necessary, they obviously recognize that the most convincing legitimization is provided by the cumulative impact of repeated and unambiguous endorsements of their positions, supported by massive majorities that include the bulk of the most important and most influential states.

Some Instances of Collective Legitimization

The United Nations has been heavily involved in matters relating to the question of the ratification and solidification of the status claimed, as distinguished from the policies followed, by political entities. Generally, this can be subsumed under the heading of membership business; admission to or seating in the Organization has tended to take on the political meaning, if not the legal implication, of collective recognition. New states have been inclined to regard the grant of membership as the definitive acknowledgment of their independence. Nonadmission of the segments of divided states appears to have been motivated in part by the conviction that admission would somehow sanctify existing divisions, thereby diminishing the prospects for future reunification. West Germany, for instance, has been particularly sensitive to the danger that East German membership would have the effect of legitimizing, and thus helping to perpetuate, the division of Germany. The continued acceptance of the Chinese Nationalist regime and rejection of the Peking regime have been championed as a device for strengthening the hold of the former upon Taiwan and denying to the latter the advantage of an important international status symbol. The prompt admission of Israel to the United Nations was clearly regarded, by both friends and foes of the new state, as a major contribution to its capacity to survive in a hostile neighborhood. The issue of conferment of status arose in a different way when Malaysia was elected to a Security Council seat by the General Assembly. Indonesia's subsequent withdrawal from the Organization, ostensibly in protest against that action, can be interpreted as a tribute to the potency of collective legitimization, for Indonesia evidently felt that the United Nations had given an intolerably valuable boost to Malaysia's international stock.

A major campaign has been waged in the United Nations to delegitimize colonialism, to invalidate the claim of colonial powers to legitimate possession of overseas territories—in short, to revoke their sovereignty over colonies. This movement culminated in the overwhelming adoption by the General Assembly of sweeping anticolonial declarations in 1960 and subsequently. The implication of this anticolonial triumph became clear in late 1961 when India was cited before the Security Council for its invasion of Goa. India's defense was, in essence, the assertion that the process of collective legitimization had operated to deprive Portugal of any claim to sovereignty over Goa and thus of any right to protest the invasion—which, by virtue of the same process, had become an act of liberation, terminating Portugal's illegal occupation of Goa.

This case illustrates the proximity of the political and the legal aspects which is frequently implicit and occasionally explicit in the operation of the process of collective legitimization. India was accused in legal terms, and it responded in similar vein. The rejoinder by and on behalf of India proclaimed, in effect, that an accumulation of multilateral denunciations of colonialism had effectively abrogated the legal right of European states to rule non-European territories; these acts had created a new law under which colonialism was invalid. Despite this exchange of legal arguments, it appears that India's real concern was not so much to clear itself legally as to vindicate itself politically. It regarded the political approval or acquiescence of the United Nations as a more important consideration than any legal judgment. In a basic sense, India won the case. Although it obtained no formal endorsement of its position, it carried through its conquest of Goa without incurring formal condemnation, and its Western critics, by declining to take the issue to the Assembly, conceded that they could not expect to win, in that organ, a political verdict unfavorable to India. Obviously, the doctrine of the invalidity of colonial sovereignty has not achieved universal support, and its claim to legal status is most tenuous. But that is beside the point; it has been established by the political process of collective legitimization, and, while lawyers are free to brush it aside, statesmen are bound to take it into account as one of the facts of international political life. If the doctrine is illegal, its supporters would claim that this only convicts the law of illegitimacy. In this respect at least, they attach greater weight to the political consensus of the Assembly than to the established provisions of international law. Thus, in one of its aspects, collective legitimacy represents a political revolt against international law.

It should be noted that ex-colonial states have not confined themselves to using the United Nations for legitimization of the campaign for definitive liquidation of the colonial system. In the economic sphere they have undertaken, in concert with other underdeveloped countries, to use the Organization to secure the establishment and general acceptance of the doctrine that they have a right to receive, and advanced states have a duty to provide, assistance in promoting economic development. Toward the same end they have invoked the support of the Organization for policies designed to free themselves from obligations and arrangements that they regard as exploitative and inimical to economic progress, including foreign ownership or control of their basic natural resources. In an era of rising economic expectations, intensive effort on the part of many new states to establish solid economic foundations for their national structures, and extreme sensitivity to vestiges of the old system of colonial domination, the legitimizing function of the United Nations has had particular significance for the realm of economic policy.

The Goa case is by no means the only one in which the use of military force, either in overt invasions or in more subtle interventions, has been at issue. The United Nations was used to characterize as aggression North Korea's attack upon South Korea in 1950 and, subsequently, Communist China's collaboration in the assault; conversely, the United States sought and won endorsement of a collective military response and gave convincing evidence throughout the Korean War of its high valuation of the United Nations stamp of legitimacy. In the Suez crisis of 1956 the adverse judgment of the Assembly was invoked against the attackers of Egypt, as it was also against Soviet intervention to suppress the Hungarian revolt. In the Congo crisis of

1960 the function of collective legitimization was performed, negatively with respect to Belgian intervention, Katangese secessionist efforts, and unilateral Soviet intrusions, and positively with respect to interventionists organized under United Nations auspices.

The United States, like India in the Goa case, has in some instances profited from collective legitimization in its minimal form: United Nations acquiescence or avoidance of United Nations condemnation. In some of these cases the United States has pioneered in the development of the strategy of involving a regional organization in the process. When the United States became involved in the overthrow of the Guatemalan government in 1954, it vigorously asserted the claim that the United Nations should disqualify itself from considering the case in favor of the Organization of American States. This tactic, which clearly reflected American respect for the potency of United Nations disapprobation, was practically, though not technically, successful. In the Cuban crisis of late 1962 the United States altered its strategy, opting to combine the functioning of the OAS and the United Nations rather than to set them off against each other. On this occasion the American scheme, successfully executed, was to secure the legitimizing support of the regional organization and then to use this asset in the effort to obtain the approval, or avoid the disapproval, of the Security Council with respect to the measures taken against Soviet involvement in Cuba.

More recently, the United States has been conspicuously reluctant to press the United Nations for formal consideration of the situation in South Vietnam in which American forces have become heavily engaged. This restraint has no doubt derived from lack of confidence that a United Nations organ would endorse the claim of the United States that its military commitment constitutes a legitimate counterintervention against illegitimate intrusions by Communist states. Policy makers in Washington have evidently given greater weight to the risk of an adverse judgment than to the hope of obtaining a favorable verdict. The implication is not that the American cause is illegitimate but that political calculations have suggested that it might be branded as illegitimate— and not that the United States has denigrated the value of collective legitimization but that it has dreaded the effect of possible collective delegitimization. When, in early 1966, the United States did move to place the Vietnam issue before the Security Council, it evidently sought assistance in promoting a negotiated settlement rather than a judgment on the merits of its position. However, the fact that the Soviet Union opposed this move suggests the possibility that Soviet leaders believed that the United States was seeking, and might conceivably obtain, United Nations endorsement of its stand in Vietnam.

Conclusion

This account of selected instances in which the United Nations has been involved in the process of collective legitimization suggests that there is great variation in the effectiveness of the positions taken by the Organization. It is seldom possible to make confident estimates of the degree of influence upon state behavior exerted by United Nations resolutions, although the intensity of the concern exhibited by states about the outcome of votes in the Organization indicates that the seal of approval and the stigma of disapproval are taken seriously.

There is also room for disagreement and uncertainty concerning the merits and demerits of collective legitimization. The entrusting of this function to such an organization as the United Nations is pregnant with both valuable and dangerous possibilities, as the cases discussed may suggest. The endorsement of a United Nations organ can strengthen a good cause, but it can also give aid and comfort to a bad cause—and we can have no guarantee that international political institutions, any more than national ones, will distribute their largess of legitimacy in accordance with the dictates of justice or wisdom. Habitual utilization of the United Nations as an agency for pronouncing on the international acceptability of national policies and positions may inspire statesmen to behave with moderation and circumspection; their concern regarding the outcome of deliberations by the Organization may stimulate them to make compromises designed to improve their chances of securing collective approval or avoiding collective disapproval. On the other hand, this use of the United Nations may promote its exploitation as an arena within which propaganda victories are sought, to the detriment of its role in promoting diplomatic settlements. Collective legitimization may stimulate legal changes that will make international law more worthy of respect and more likely to be respected, but it may also encourage behavior based upon calculation of what the political situation will permit rather than consideration of what the principles of order require. In short, the exercise of the function of collective legitimization may be for better or for worse, whether evaluated in terms of its effect upon the interests of a particular state or upon the prospects for a stable and orderly world. The crucial point is that, for better or for worse, the development of the United Nations as custodian of collective legitimacy is an important political phenomenon of our time.

United Nations Peace Forces and the Changing United Nations:

An Institutional Perspective

BRIAN E. URQUHART

Aᴛ its founding one of the UN's most publicized advantages over its predecessor, the League of Nations, was the fact that it was a peace organization "with teeth." This somewhat unattractive phrase referred to Chapter VII of the Charter and the possibility of military force being put at the disposal of the Security Council. In fact this provision of the Charter was one of the first victims of East-West disagreement, and, although the Military Staff Committee met regularly for many years and in the early years held voluminous discussions, the actual military arrangements foreseen in Chapter VII never became a reality. The assumption of the continuing unanimity of the great powers, which particularly affected this part of the Charter, proved to be illusory almost at once, while the idea that the Organization could not and should not take collective action against one of the great powers has continued, with the partial exception of Korea, to be respected. Thus it has become increasingly clear that the United Nations can neither deal with an aggression arising from a great-power conflict nor use the military resources of the great powers directly in dealing with other breaches of the peace, since such a use might all too easily project the great-power struggle onto the situation being dealt with. The development of new forms of peace-keeping machinery have in part been the response of the Organization to this dilemma.

The difference between the present reality of great-power relationships, at

Brian E. Urquhart is Principal Officer in the Office of the Under-Secretary for Special Political Affairs of the United Nations.

From Volume 17, No. 2 (1963), pp. 338–54.

223

least in the context of the United Nations, and what was foreseen at San Francisco has made new developments in the United Nations not only possible, but desirable. In 1945 the great powers were the victors over Germany and Japan, the custodians of peace in an exhausted world, the arbiters of destiny; and on this image some vital parts of the Charter were based. Very soon, however, their own virulent rivalry and the development of weapons of mass destruction by both sides in the East-West conflict showed this image to be a hollow one. What was to have been the leadership and inspiration of the reconstructed world turned out to be a vacuum, in which the most powerful countries of the world tended to be increasingly immobilized by rivalry, suspicion, and fear. For some years this vacuum persisted, and it seemed likely that because of it the United Nations might be doomed to play at best a peripheral role in an essentially hopeless situation.

But with the growth of the membership of the Organization and the emergence of new forces and alignments, it now seems possible that the United Nations and the vast majority of its members are in the process of establishing a collective influence and authority in the affairs of the world—an influence and authority which they might never have achieved if the great powers had behaved as was foreseen by the authors of the Charter. No one would deny that the persistence of East-West rivalry, the inability to reach agreement on disarmament, and the failure to bridge ideological differences still rank as dominating problems in the world, and that so far the United Nations as such seems to have been able to make little progress with them. But other activities have shown a very promising potential in the Organization and a solidarity, as well as a vitality, which bodes well for its future growth. It is perhaps of some significance that those on the extreme right and left who used to criticize the United Nations for its ineffectiveness in the days of great power domination now tend to complain more of its new vitality and activity in peace-keeping operations.

The Korean action in 1950 gave rise to a temporary enthusiasm for and renewed belief in the possibility of the classical type of collective action against aggression. It was also realized that the freak conditions which had allowed the Security Council to take action on the Korean question without a veto were unlikely ever to recur. The result was the adoption by the General Assembly in 1950 of the "Uniting for Peace" resolution, which has had a fundamental effect on the capacity of the Organization for taking action in dangerous situations. The object of the resolution was, in President Truman's words, to prepare the United Nations "for quick and effective action in any future case of aggression." The original hopes of the authors of the resolution, however, were never fully realized, nor did the new enthusiasm for collective security survive the disillusionments and confusions of the latter part of the Korean operation. Regional pacts thus came more than ever to be regarded as the maximum practical basis for collective action, and the Collective Measures Committee and the Peace Observation Commission set up by the resolution have had little or no practical impact on events.

Nevertheless, the other main feature of the resolution, which provides for the General Assembly to move quickly into a critical situation if the Security Council is paralyzed by the veto, has had extremely important consequences—even if they are not precisely the ones envisaged by the original authors. It has been the basis upon which the consideration of matters affecting peace and security have come within the purview of the whole membership of the United Nations and upon which quite new methods of resolving crises, such as the extension of the role of the United Nations as mediator and the use of the United Nations' peace-keeping forces, have been built up.

While this part of the "Uniting for Peace" resolution provides a quasi-constitutional device for liberating questions of peace and security from the dead hand of the unanimity rule in the Security Council, other practices and precedents have grown up which have, over a period of sixteen years, extended the capacity of the United Nations to deal with emergencies and have evoked from the Organization a practical response to such situations very different from that envisaged in the Charter. The demands of dangerous situations, and the obvious need for some effective method of dealing with them without involving them in the ultimate stresses and strains of the East-West struggle, have been one motivating force in this process. Another and very important factor was certainly the leadership, diplomacy, and political imagination of the late Secretary-General, Dag Hammarskjöld. A third has been, in spite of criticism and occasional disillusion, an increasing reliance on the United Nations in situations of real emergency, especially by the smaller powers, and, resulting from this, their firm support of its efforts. A corollary of this last development has been the tendency of the great powers to neutralize each other in situations of emergency through fear of getting involved to the extent of atomic war, thus leaving a certain freedom of action for the smaller powers and the international Secretariat. In fact, in certain situations of intolerable stress the United Nations has become a way out both for the great powers and the small from the ultimate consequences of a great-power clash.

In the early years of the United Nations, before its membership was more than doubled by the advent of new nations, there was a tendency among the major powers toward extreme distrust of any initiative on the part of the Secretariat. Some overtly and others tacitly made it clear that the Secretariat was basically a servicing staff which, except in very unusual circumstances, had little or no freedom of action of its own. Even the smallest show of initiative or independence on the part of the Secretariat tended to be greeted with raised eyebrows or letters of protest. When one thinks back to the first four or five years of the United Nations, a most significant development is the change in this attitude. Before the Secretary-Generalship of Dag Hammarskjöld it was very unusual for a Secretariat official to enjoy executive powers. Such powers were very occasionally delegated to someone of distinction and known reliability, as, for example, Count Bernadotte or Dr. Bunche in the Middle East, but normally situations were handled, or were supposed to be handled, by intergovernmental commissions set up by one of the organs of the United Nations and serviced by members of the Secretariat. When in doubt delegations tended to invoke the name of Sir Eric Drummond and the League of Nations Secretariat as the ideal of discreet Secretariat behavior.

In these early years, while the use of military personnel on a large scale and under the exact terms of the Charter was being discussed with diminishing prospect of agreement in the Military Staff Committee, methods of using military personnel productively on a far smaller scale evolved almost by accident. In Greece the military attachés of the members of the United Nations Commission proved themselves invaluable as an observer group in checking on infiltration into Greece from her northern neighbors. In Kashmir an observer group of military officers was formally set up by the Security Council and is still operating, its success being vouched for perhaps most eloquently by the fact that one scarcely ever hears about it.

The first truce agreements in the Palestine war in July 1948 were enforced on the ground by some 700 United Nations military observers working under the United Nations Mediator and Chief of Staff. This team developed into the United Nations Truce Supervision Organization (UNTSO) after the armistice agreements between Israel and her Arab neighbors were concluded in the period from February to July 1949. This organization of officers from many countries has played a vital role in keeping peace in the Middle East, in umpiring frontier incidents, and in giving time for tempers, grievances, and historic disagreements to cool off.

Such ventures have resulted in the gradual creation of an officer cadre in many countries with international experience of peace-keeping operations; to that extent, the armies of many countries are being indoctrinated in the peace-keeping process. In a turbulent world it is pleasant to reflect that the professional soldiers of Brazil, Canada, Denmark, Ethiopia, Ghana, India, Indonesia,

Ireland, Malaya, Morocco, Nigeria, Norway, Pakistan, Sierra Leone, Sweden, Tunisia, and Yugoslavia—to name only a few—are performing every day the functions of controlling and mitigating frictions in several regions, and by example creating a new role for military discipline and common sense.

The Suez situation of 1956 was complicated by the heavy involvement of two great powers and by the ominous threats of a third. It was a situation in which traditional alliances fell apart and where everyone seemed to have been caught unawares by an action as ill-advised as it was ill-planned. Even if the surprised indignation generated by the Suez action had not demanded recourse to the United Nations, the UN was undoubtedly the only place left in which there was a hope of sorting out such a confusion with the minimum loss of life and face. Almost everyone concerned was to some extent in a state of shock, and the gravity of the situation called forth a completely new form of international institution, the United Nations Emergency Force (UNEF) in the Middle East. That such an institution could come into being so fast in a situation in which two great powers were directly involved was a token both of the baffled anxiety of the world community and of the then almost universal confidence in Hammarskjöld. Even five years before, it would have been inconceivable that one of the great powers would meekly accept a cease-fire and a face-saving device of such an entirely novel kind. It would also have been inconceivable for the General Assembly to ask the Secretary-General to write his own plan for such a novel venture and entrust him completely with the negotiations and executive action required. Now, on the contrary, the Assembly did this with enthusiasm, while many of its members also volunteered troops and all sorts of assistance in the most expeditious and informal way. This was not a force designed actively to counter aggression. Rather, it was a security force designed to allow common sense to prevail and the armies of the parties concerned to disengage and return to their own soil.

The force was assembled in a few days, and United States aircraft flew them to a staging point at the Capodicino airport at Naples (made available by the Italian government), whence Swiss aircraft would take them into Egypt as soon as agreement for their arrival was received from the Egyptian government. An agreement with the Egyptian government was negotiated by the Secretary-General, which was based very much on the concept of "good faith" and which has not been subjected to a serious breach or disagreement for over six years. The Israelis, British, and French, once they had agreed to being replaced on the soil of Egypt by the international force, also cooperated, sometimes almost with enthusiasm. The British, for example, made over the United Nations vehicles and supplies for the use of UNEF in Egypt.

It is idle to speculate whether such an experiment could have succeeded as well as it did without the skill and indefatigability of Hammarskjöld. In the growth of an institution the genius of a great man is one very important factor among many factors, a thread in history which, combined with other threads, can produce great developments or, if it is missing at a crucial time, great disasters. Personality, skill, and the inspiration of confidence are likely to be more important initially in the creation of historical precedents and in dealing with crises of a new order of complexity than in conscious institutional development.

It was not only the creation of UNEF that liquidated the Suez crisis. Under Hammarskjöld's executive planning and direction, the clearance of the Canal was negotiated and completed. He thus silenced those critics in France and England who had originally greeted with derision his acceptance of responsibility for this vital operation, which their own misjudgment had largely made necessary.

For over six years UNEF has watched over the borders of Israel with the United Arab Republic in the Gaza Strip and through Sinai. Ships now pass freely through the narrows at Sharm-el-Sheik to the port of Elath, and in Gaza the crops grow right down to the border from both sides, and the area has never been so prosperous. UNEF has not been in the news for years, nor have the provocative actions of extremists, which used to make that frontier a permanent trouble spot. UNEF provides politicians on both sides a reason for resisting extreme counsels and avoiding useless mischief, just as it initially provided a useful face-saver for the British and French. The one serious problem it poses is how to terminate its existence without generating new and dangerous instabilities.

When the problems of an international force are discussed in theory, numerous problems are raised which often prove in the event to be illusory. It used to be said, for example, that problems of language, diversified equipment, and differences in training and tradition would make an international force very difficult to operate. In UNEF such problems have turned out to be minor, negligible, or, in the case of different customs and traditions, a positive advantage. Such differences provide an interest during the long dull terms of duty in the desert, and on Christmas Day the Indians take over duty from the Christian contingents, who reciprocate during Indian festivals.

But, as in most affairs, the unexpected problems are the hardest. They must be met as they appear, unless a sufficiently all-embracing international military establishment can be founded and supported to meet every conceivable contingency. Such an establishment is obviously impossible in the present complex state of world affairs and the present stage of development of the United Nations. For this basic reason the late Secretary-General was lukewarm to the idea of establishing a permanent international force at so early a stage in the practical development of the idea. In 1958 he summarized the lessons learned from the UNEF operation[1] and concluded that the special circumstances surrounding UNEF did not justify the projection in detail of its organization onto unknown situations in the future, as had already been shown by the differing requirements of the situations in 1958 in Lebanon and Jordan. He therefore proposed that stand-by arrangements for future action should for the time being be limited to the approval of certain general principles, which would provide a framework for mounting future operations without delay and in accordance with the demands of the actual situation. These principles were later to provide the basis for Hammarskjöld's proposals on the Congo force.

By the autumn of 1958 the United Nations had been involved in another crisis of another kind in the Middle East. In Lebanon a domestic political struggle in the 1958 election campaign had become the basis for accusations of foreign infiltration and interference which had been taken up in earnest by interested powers. The Security Council set up a three-man observer group and left the Secretary-General considerable latitude in the arrangements to make this group effective. A mobile team of 600 officers was quickly organized to police the frontier of Lebanon by road and air against the possibility of infiltration across the border, while the scene was set for the necessary negotiations and discussions to reduce the temperature and resolve the crisis. Although the United States landed a division of marines in Beirut, and the British at another juncture sent a parachute brigade to the airfield of Amman, the storm finally blew out and both of these forces were withdrawn, the latter with the assistance of the United Nations officers in Lebanon and Jerusalem. The United Nations observer group was also withdrawn by the end of 1958. There was some pressure at the height of the crisis for sending another UNEF to Lebanon and, had a standing international force existed, the pressure might well have succeeded and involved the United Nations most embarrassingly in a conflict that was very largely domestic.

The emergence of the new African countries and the twilight of colonialism in Africa became a dominating feature of the United Nations after 1959. The Organization, as well as stimulating this development, has provided, and still provides, it with a place where the leaders and officials of these new countries can get a quick education in the ways of world politics, learn for themselves what motives and what realities lie behind the policies of other states, and

[1] UN Document A/3943.

establish their own views on the world situation as it affects them. Not least important, the United Nations allows them to see themselves and each other more sharply within the context of world affairs. The new nations of Africa were destined very soon to play an important part, notably by the provision of troops, in the most critical and unprecedented United Nations peace-keeping operation.

Although the United Nations was already much concerned with the emergence of Africa and with the help to be given to the new countries, it was in 1960 suddenly confronted with the problem in a form so ugly and urgent as also to involve its ultimate responsibilities for the maintenance of peace and security. This emergency arose from the chaotic events immediately following the independence of the former Belgian Congo on June 30, 1960.

No one realized better than Hammarskjöld what a tremendous risk the Congo operation represented for the Organization and for himself as Secretary-General. But he also realized vividly the intense danger of the Congo situation —the imminent possibility of great power interventions and clashes, the exacerbation of rivalries among African states, and the explosive mixture of big money, tribalism, adventurism, inexperience, and susceptibility within the Congo itself. Weighing the relative risks and foreseeing all too clearly the appalling difficulty of the task ahead, he knowingly accepted the danger to the Organization and to himself rather than countenance the consequences which would almost certainly ensue from inaction.

Both external and internal factors add to the extraordinary complication of the Congo affair, and even without them it would be difficult to deal with the basic situation resulting from the total unpreparedness and lack of experience of the Congolese government. The position of the United Nations itself is also of necessity a very delicate one. It is present in the Congo at the request of the central government (a government, incidentally, which was not legally constituted for almost a year from September 1960 to August 1961), and also because in the judgment of the Secretary-General and the Security Council the situation is a potential threat to international peace and security. It is there to assist the government in all ways, including the maintenance of law and order, until the government can fully exercise its functions itself. It is precluded from interfering in the internal political dissensions of the country, and yet it is held responsible for the protection of life and property and the maintenance of normal services. It has a force (18,000 strong in the fall of 1962) which is in fact the mainstay of order in the country, but whose right to use force is limited by directives of the Security Council to self-defense, to the prevention of civil war, and, in the last resort, to the apprehension of foreign military personnel. Because the Congolese National Army (now about 30,000 strong) tends to be split among the rival factions and was until very recently on terms of active hostility with the Katangese *Gendarmerie* (about 20,000 strong but with a slightly superior military performance), the work of the United Nations force has been anything but easy. It is further complicated by the facts that large sections of public opinion in the world hold the United Nations responsible for almost everything that happens or does not happen in the Congo, and that different political factions in the Congo each have their passionate supporters in the world outside.

In 1960 and early 1961 opinion at the United Nations itself was divided on almost diametrically opposed lines as to the correct course of action in the Congo, and this division made the lives of officials dealing with critical situations on the spot very difficult indeed. One school of thought, which had supporters among the governments furnishing essential logistical and financial support, was averse to anything which might be interpreted as a forceful solution. Both sides had their own decided views as to the acceptability or nonacceptability of certain Congolese leaders, and the murder of Patrice Lumumba added to the already overheated situation a tragic and violent element. Perhaps fortunately, the remarkable illogic and inconsistency of the internal Congolese situation has by now blurred these lines of disagreement, and there is presently some recognition that the situation cannot be judged by normal standards and must be dealt with more at its own level within a broad interpretation of the principles underlying the United Nations action. This does not mean that the task of the United Nations in the Congo is any easier, only that its difficulties are more generally recognized.

In its more than two and a half years in the Congo, the United Nations force, predominantly composed of soldiers from African and Asian states, has been confronted with a series of situations more varied and eccentric than anything the armies of the old colonial powers had to face, and it has not had any of the freedom of action which those armies used to enjoy in meeting emergencies. It was put together overnight and precluded from using, except for transport and supply outside the Congo, the military resources of those great powers whose military establishments were the only ones in the world designed for such far-flung operations; it was deployed with bewildering speed into obscure and totally unpredictable situations, while being constantly restrained by political directives which make a mockery of established military principles. Nonetheless, it has met its responsibilities in such a way that the situation is certainly far calmer and more promising than it was two and a half years ago. In so doing, it has suffered numerous casualties as well as occasional humiliations and failures. It has been the target of both ill-informed and malicious criticism annd propaganda from the left and the right, criticism which is often curiously similar in its terms and clichés. It has received very little gratitude or appreciation from those—and there are many—who abuse the United Nations in good weather and are the first to run to it for protection when a storm blows up. It not only has to moderate the consequences of Congolese political and tribal rivalries but also to keep calm in a situation where secessionist movements, especially that of Katanga, have produced incessant threats of civil war and are supported by a bewildering variety of outside interests and adventurers.

Few peacetime military tasks can be less enviable than the one to which the Members of the United Nations have committed the officers and men of the UN force in the Congo. The necessity for calm under provocation, insult, and violence; the need to comply with political directives which must inevitably often be incomprehensible to the soldier on the spot; the variety of other tasks, including assistance to refugees, civilian protection, and all sorts of assistance to the civil authorities; the prevailing attitude of resentment, especially by the European population, except when protection or help are needed; and the interminable machinations of a raffish crew of military and civilian adventurers in pursuit of money are not the conditions which an ordinary national army would accept. The high morale of the soldiers, their enthusiasm, and their astonishingly few complaints (for an army) can only result from a job that is challenging and responsible and which the soldiers think is worth doing. Those armchair critics of international organizations who say, as they often do, that the UN people, military and civilian, are in the Congo for the money or the power should view for themselves the conditions of service there, or study the fate of the Ghanaians at Port Francqui, the Irish at Niemba, the Sudanese at Matadi, the Italians at Kindu, or the Indians manning a roadblock in Elisabethville, then try to make an honest reappraisal. The thousands of soldiers from some twenty countries who accepted this challenge in the Congo have begun to learn to apply the arts of war to the infinitely subtle and difficult problem of maintaining the peace—this may be a development of more lasting importance than what eventually does or does not happen in the Congo itself.

The involvement of United Nations troops in three episodes of actual fighting in Katanga has raised in many quarters the question of the appropriateness of the use of force by a peace-keeping international force. The question has been obscured and inflated by a great deal of misrepresentation both deliberate and unintentional.

The conditions under which a resort to force by the United Nations force in the Congo is permitted by the Security Council are three: ultimate self-defense, the prevention of civil war, and, in the last resort, the apprehension of foreign military personnel. In September 1961 the United Nations force in Elisabethville came under attack when it tried, on September 13, to continue the rounding up of the mercenaries which had started peacefully with the cooperation of Mr. Tshombe on August 28 and had then been suspended at the request of various consuls, who undertook to carry out the task themselves but proved unable to do so. The fighting, by any normal military standard, was on a very small scale and the casualties were light. This has not stopped various people and groups, with various motives, from alleging that the September 1961 episode was an effort to suppress the secession of Katanga by force. This was neither the intention nor the result. Had it been the intention, which it could not have been under the Security Council mandate, the preparations and arrangements would have been very different and the military and civilian action of an entirely different kind.

In December 1961 the Katangese *Gendarmerie* was under the control of a group of former Secret Army Organization (OAS) officers who conceived the notion of eliminating the United Nations force in Elisabethville at a time when it was at its weakest due to the rotation of units. A prelude of this operation, in which a number of European civilians were also involved, was a series of incitements to violence, harassments, kidnappings, and murders of United Nations personnel in the best OAS style. After a week of intensive effort to persuade Mr. Tshombe and his ministers to abandon this plan, the United Nations was compelled to protect the safety of its force and personnel by removing the roadblocks put up by the *Gendarmerie* and by re-establishing its freedom of movement and access to the airport in Elisabethville. As soon as this was done the action stopped. Once again Katangese propagandists raised the cry that this was an attempt to end secession by force. The simple fact is that such a course, including the arrest of Mr. Tshombe and his ministers, would have been by far the simplest for the United Nations. It could not and did not take it because it had no right to take it.

After Mr. Tshombe had signed, on December 21, 1961, the declaration of Kitona, which reaffirmed his intention of cooperating with the central government, a year passed in intensive talks and negotiations designed to make this declaration a reality. In December 1962 the *Gendarmerie* in Elisabethville again got out of hand and attacked the United Nations force, which, after accepting attacks for six days without firing back, finally dealt with the Elisabethville *Gendarmerie*. This precipitated a move which Mr. Tshombe and the world had long since been warned to expect—namely, the assertion by the United Nations of its right, under the basic agreement with the government of the Congo, to freedom of movement throughout the Congo, including Katanga. This freedom established, all military action ceased. Mr. Tshombe remained in his residence at Elisabethville as provincial president of Katanga. Again the cry has been raised that this was forceful ending of secession, while from the other side came the counter-cry that the United Nations had failed to deal with the traitor Tshombe. By the law of most countries there would be at least an arguable case for accusing Mr. Tshombe of treason, armed rebellion, murder, sabotage, and genocide against a state which he himself played an active part in creating and whose territorial integrity the United Nations is pledged to protect. These are internal questions for the government of the Congo, which has granted an amnesty. Thus Mr. Tshombe continues to be unmolested by the United Nations as long as he conducts himself as provincial president. The complaint of United Nations over-severity therefore seems rather hard to maintain.

It would be silly to pretend that there is nothing in the United Nations operation in the Congo (ONUC) to criticize. If there were not, it would be unique in history. There have, from time to time, been mistakes and failures and errors of judgment at various levels, and the problems, though less acute than formerly, are still anything but solved. But criticisms should be made within the framework of the real and the possible. ONUC is an operation comparable in novelty with the first voyage to the moon. It is a multinational effort to keep the peace, to help an important and large new country get on its feet, and to moderate violence and strife, which has both internal and external origins, so as to keep it from spreading disastrously to the community of nations. The difficulty and novelty of such an effort becomes apparent when one realizes that many of the hundred or so Member States who support the operation have particular interests in the affair which are by no means always directly served by the United Nations operation, or else, for widely differing reasons, refuse to have anything to do with it at all. That ONUC has worked and exists at all in these circumstances is something of a miracle in itself.

Institutionally UNEF and ONUC, although involving the service of some 5,000 and 18,000 soldiers respectively, as well, in the latter case, as of some 1,200 civilians, are supposedly temporary additions to the Organization rather than new and integrated parts of the structure of the Secretariat. While UNEF virtually runs itself under the general supervision and logistical backing of New York, the Congo operation is politically so complicated and delicate that it is still very closely controlled by the Secretary-General, and the original idea that it might become a semi-independent operation has never been realized. For different reasons it is hard to envisage a firm date for the termination, or even for the scaling down, of either of these operations, which, at $20 million and $110 million a year respectively, are by far the most expensive items on the United Nations budget.

The progress and development of the idea of peace-keeping forces has so far been pragmatic rather than institutional. Precedents have been set and experience has been gained, but the structure of the Secretariat largely does not reflect this progress. UNEF and ONUC are essentially emergency operations, although their actual duration may seem to make the word "emergency" inappropriate. Although there is a small military staff at United Nations Headquarters to deal with Congo affairs and there is now a permanent military adviser, there is still no permanent military staff to plan in detail for future emergencies or contingencies; nor is there any permanent system of a general kind for the selection of troops for future situations. For both UNEF and ONUC there are advisory committees basically composed of representatives of the countries supplying troops, and these have proved an admirable device for bringing governments into the problems which the Secretary-General faces as the executive authority for these two operations. The logistical support of the two forces is still a function of the normal civilian services of the Secretariat, temporarily expanded for the purpose. Their other needs—legal advice, public information, etc.—are also supplied by the normal departments of the Secretariat. In fact, apart from the military adviser's small staff and a very small civilian affairs unit, also in the Secretary-General's office in New York, there is no United Nations military or special organization outside the actual areas of operation to backstop the United Nations forces in the Congo, Middle East, and now West New Guinea.

There are undoubtedly strong arguments for some institutional development of a permanent kind. The present system means, in any emergency, a degree of unpreparedness and improvisation which would be considered crazy in a normal army. In both the Middle East and the Congo the initial moves of troops have been to a very large extent dependent on the magnificent cooperation of the United States Military Air Transport Service. The logistical apparatus in particular presents vast and expensive problems, especially in the early stages of an operation before a supply pipeline can be established. Transportation of United Nations forces in a large area of operations like the Congo, especially as regards aircraft and suitable vehicles, is an abiding problem under the present improvised system. Since the participation of the permanent members of the Security Council in the actual area of operations is precluded, the

aircraft and air organization available for service in the Congo have been anything but ideal for the task.

However excellent their performance, the troops made available, being predominantly infantry, are very often not ideally suited by training to the kind
of job they have to do. For example, the value of trained riot police in the
Congo, when they have been available to the United Nations, has proved to be
out of all proportion to their numbers. Nor does the United Nations have the
equipment or the men to form highly mobile units for immediate dispatch to
critical points. Communications and suitable signals personnel also present a
major problem for both language and technical reasons, and planning and
execution are complicated by these difficulties. The formation of integrated and
experienced military staffs has also proved difficult, while the lack of an intelligence organization, such as is normally available to a national army or police
force, has proved at times to be a serious handicap. There is also a serious problem of continuity in a force based on units from national armies serving only
for short terms in the Congo.

It is a mistake, however, in stating these shortcomings to compare an international peace-keeping force with a national army or police force, just as it is
misleading to compare the international Secretariat with a national civil service.
The very possibility of objectivity in world affairs on the part of international
officials is denied by one group of powers, and, while not denying it in the
same categorical way, there are always those in other camps who question it
in particular situations. The whole idea of international institutions is in its
infancy, an infancy complicated by worldwide political and ideological divisions. At the best of times the development of such institutions would have
profound effects on such doctrines as national sovereignty and the rights of
nations. The institutional addition at this time of a permanent international
police force would in all probability worsen the state of international politics,
and it might, by its very existence or through precipitate and inappropriate
use, complicate the very situations it was designed to solve. This in itself is a
strong argument for the pragmatic approach, whatever its practical disadvantages. There will, of course, be muddling and difficulty, but, on the evidence to
date, something at least gets done to avoid the worst disasters, and in the process
many people learn a lot and think a lot, which is a good investment for the
future.

There is also of course the burning question of money. Although the United
Nations, so often piously referred to by statesmen as "the world's best hope for
peace," has a budget which is chicken feed by comparison with the defense
budgets of a number of powers, the fact is that the Organization is constantly

on the brink of bankruptcy, from which only its indispensability and the far-sightedness of a few powers somehow usually rescue it. A permanent international force would greatly increase its expenses, an addition which could probably only be accepted by governments after many more years of acclimatization to the idea and the practice of such activities.

Until such a development occurs, some interim measures may be developed to improve the efficiency of the present improvisational system. Various forms of training for international service could probably quite easily be fitted into the normal training programs of national armies. UNEF, ONUC, and the UN Truce Supervision Organization in the Middle East have already provided a long list of officers from many countries with previous experience in and proven suitability to international peace-keeping tasks. On the logistical side too, experience with equipment and supplies can be used to prepare for future emergencies.

In the meanwhile the precedent exists when the emergency is grave enough to demand it, and in spite of the complications under which United Nations forces operate, the performance of their constituent units is encouraging. With virtually no exceptions the soldiers have been admirably loyal to United Nations directives and have remained aloof from politics, either national or local. They have shown themselves to be objective professionals with a considerable capacity for adaptation and improvisation in difficult circumstances, and by their bearing and discipline they have shown how much professional soldiers have to contribute to the keeping of the peace. Any mistake by a United Nations force is of course triumphantly seized on by critics all over the world and magnified out of all proportion. Tragedies have on occasion occurred, and they too are used to give a popular idea of incompetence or worse. This is to be expected in a venture which is both new and extremely difficult.

The Congo operation on its bad days has frequently been hailed triumphantly by its detractors as the last time when any country will ever call upon a United Nations force to help it in its difficulties. It is therefore interesting that the Dutch and Indonesians agreed to ask for a United Nations force (a small one, admittedly, and provided by one nation only, Pakistan) to provide security during the interim period in West New Guinea, prior to the Indonesian takeover from the Dutch.

From this rather cursory survey of the theory and practice of UN peace-keeping operations, a number of points emerge. The first and most obvious is that the original plan laid down in the Charter soon proved to be unworkable and is unlikely to prove workable in the foreseeable future. The natures of war and of peace have changed too fast for it. Even the secondary plan, the

"Uniting for Peace" resolution of 1950, which was produced in the period of enthusiasm for collective security engendered by the Korean War and in the realization that some way round the paralysis of the Security Council had to be found, has been used only in its procedural part for the transfer of issues involving peace and security from the Council to the Assembly.

Instead emergencies have been met in the heat of crisis by developments of a more pragmatic kind and by the gradual evolution of new confidence in and use of the international staff and machinery of the Organization as such. It is not only the leadership and commanding objectivity of Hammarskjöld that pointed the way to and made possible developments which would have been considered revolutionary and dangerous even ten years ago. The very relationship of the great powers to each other in the nuclear age has meant that much responsibility and potential for useful activity in the maintenance of peace has passed to the smaller powers, and the new forms of peace-keeping machinery in the Middle East and the Congo are very largely dependent upon them for their personnel and support. Thus international responsibility has been diversified in an unexpected way, and, with this diversification, support for and understanding of the United Nations has been strengthened and widened. This development is the product of necessity, for there are new situations in which the intervention of any one power or group of powers is too dangerous for anyone to contemplate.

This development has as yet produced no sweeping institutional change. There has, however, been a steady development of thinking and experience and a widening circle throughout the world of military personnel and units with experience of United Nations activities, and this may prove in the long run to be of lasting value. There is also a growing recognition, except in one quarter, that the United Nations in its objective way can, as the mediator of historic change, play a role which can be played by no other agency, and that, despite its manifest imperfections, this role is an irreplaceable one, to which all nations can contribute in good faith and in their own ultimate interest. There is also a growing recognition that the role requires on occasions the use of peace-keeping forces of one kind or another.

The development of an international institution of over 100 members must inevitably be a slow and delicate business. Provided that the United Nations can respond to challenges when they appear—and it has shown already that in many cases it can—it will maintain and enhance its usefulness as an institution and slowly strengthen the basis of confidence on which alone, in the absence of overwhelming material power, it can operate. In the atmosphere of suspicion and rivalry in the world this will be a long and arduous process, but it is already under way and has shown results. If it can be maintained and developed, the necessary institutional changes will come about eventually almost of their own accord, having been already proved and tempered in practice. This pragmatic development, if subject occasionally to muddle and imprecision, has tended historically to produce the strongest and most enduring institutions.

International Agencies and Economic Development:

An Overview

ROBERT E. ASHER

I

UNCTAD I, the United Nations Conference on Trade and Development held in Geneva in the spring of 1964, marked a major milestone in international concern with and approaches to the problems of less developed countries. The principal achievements of this mammoth, contentious, allegedly economic gathering, however, were in the political realm. Economic issues of great importance were raised but not resolved. Instead they were consigned for study and consideration to the elaborate continuing machinery born at Geneva, as well as to various previously established agencies, and eventually to the agenda for UNCTAD II, convened in New Delhi in early 1968.

Will UNCTAD I and II prove to be milestones on the road to a global partnership of rich and poor countries, to a revolution of rising frustrations, or to an uneasy federation of regional and ideological blocs? The evidence is mixed. In 1945, according to the Preamble of the United Nations Charter, "the peoples of the United Nations" proclaimed their determination "to promote social progress and better standards of life in larger freedom" and "to employ international machinery for the pro-

ROBERT E. ASHER is a member of the Senior Staff of The Brookings Institution, Washington, D.C., and Vice-President of the Society for International Development. The author notes his considerable indebtedness to the other contributors to this volume and would gladly acknowledge each borrowing but for the very nature of an overview and the exigencies of space. The interpretations and conclusions contained in this essay are the author's and do not necessarily represent those of collaborators in the present undertaking, of fellow members of the Brookings staff, or of administrative officers of The Brookings Institution.

From Volume 22, No. 1 (1968), pp. 432–58.

motion of the economic and social advancement of all peoples." Whatever its feasibility at the time—when more than half of the people presently alive and more than half the nations now in the UN had not yet
been born—the problems facing mankind today, the political will and
economic capacity to deal with them, and the institutional framework
for doing so have changed drastically since the closing days of the Second
World War.

The ground rules for international economic cooperation that were
drawn up in the 1940's under the leadership of the United States were
aimed primarily at preventing actions found harmful by the major powers
during the 1930's, not at promoting practices helpful to the emerging
nations. Since about 1950, however, the international community has
devoted an enormous amount of attention to the manifold problems of
the low-income countries, gradually modifying the original ground rules
and introducing many innovations, including various forms of development assistance. The spokesmen for the less developed countries nevertheless continue to think they are condemned to live in a world they never
made under arrangements designed to perpetuate their underdog status.

In their view, the time for a "new international division of labor" is
overdue. In economic terms, they mean by this more domestic processing
of the primary products they have to date been exporting; more rapid
industrialization, with opportunities for specialization in certain types of
manufacturing; and greater assurance of the wherewithal to help them
meet their development goals. Their aspirations, however, are not confined to the economic sphere; they are also profoundly political.

No government, least of all that of the United States, thinks of itself
as insensitive to the needs of others or wedded to the status quo. The
United States has been instrumental in launching a bewildering array of
intergovernmental agencies, institutions, commissions, programs, and
campaigns. These have been endowed with sufficient resources to do some
good (by stealth, it has been said), to get in each other's way, and to make
it difficult for all but the most persevering of analysts to discover what is
really happening. Some of this machinery fits neatly into the UN system,
some fits loosely, and some is totally outside.

The less developed countries—"the fraternity of the impatient," they
have been called by Harlan Cleveland—appear, however, to regard the
United States as a principal defender of the status quo.[1] They consider

[1] See "The Fraternity of the Impatient," U.S. Department of State Press Release 335, July 22,
1964, subsequently published in the Department of State *Bulletin*, August 17, 1964 (Vol. 51,
No. 1312), pp. 241–248. Assistant Secretary Cleveland included the United States in the fraternity. Noting that the post-UNCTAD joint declaration of the 77 developing countries expressed
great impatience, he said to the UN Economic and Social Council (ECOSOC): "For our part,
we not only honor and applaud their impatience—we share it. Welcome to the 'fraternity of the
impatient,' we say." (*Ibid.*, p. 246.)

the major innovation of the postwar era—the extension of grants, loans, and technical assistance on a modest scale from more developed to less developed countries—as little more than a "token effort." They are much more aware of what remains to be done than of the steps already taken.

The situation is strikingly similar to the civil rights struggle in the United States, but with two significant differences. The challengers in the development arena, though they inhabit the same rapidly shrinking planet as the challenged, are not subjects of one specific government and cannot be accommodated through established political processes. Secondly, and more important, they are not a minority group. On the contrary, they constitute the overwhelming majority of mankind. They seek an end to second-class citizenship, a better chance to acquire dignity and status, to earn a livelihood and educate their children, to speak up and be heard as persons and nations rather than as petitioners. This means not only heroic efforts at self-help but also cooperation with others in obtaining real integration instead of token integration in a wider, more humane, more forward-moving community of nations.

A "new international division of labor" can benefit the more developed as well as the less developed countries. Mutual education is needed; instant development is impossible, but a century of imperceptible gradualism will be unacceptable. Time is a critical factor. As Americans should have learned from the civil rights struggle in their own country, measures that would be hailed with joy at one moment in history will be attacked as inadequate, ineffective, and insulting a few years later—if the psychological moment for adopting them has passed. Feelings of frustration can cause the frustrated to abandon integration as a goal and nonviolence as a technique.

Attitudes are more important than machinery. The problem at the international level is surely not the lack of machinery but of sufficient fuel, committed engineers, and an agreed itinerary. More specifically, multilateral efforts to promote development are predicated upon the notion that the national interests of the participating governments, though not identical, overlap sufficiently to permit each nation to benefit in its own peculiar way from cooperation with others. It is thus conflicting conceptions of these national interests that prevent the machinery from more quickly fulfilling its high-sounding purposes.

Despite the solidarity of the less developed countries at UNCTAD I and other evidences of international cooperation, the sense of international community is not particularly potent as of this writing. Nationalism continues strong, and on every continent country after country has grown more inward looking, more nationalistic, more assertive about its rights, and more reticent about its responsibilities. The communications gap between rich and poor, notwithstanding all the talk, is as wide as the income gap. The Cold War is no longer an automatic stimulus to action by the more affluent nations on behalf of the less affluent. The intransigence of the development process itself, which makes a mockery of "development decades" and early "take-offs" into self-sustaining growth, is discouraging. The evidence that development does not necessarily lead to peace, stability, and goodwill toward men is plentiful.

While circumstances have thus conspired to complicate incredibly the tasks of the organizations whose activities have been reviewed in this volume, their achievements are far from negligible. The object of their solicitude—the less developed world—has not been standing still. Its record is in many respects remarkable. An adequate foundation for further progress has been built.

How, in brief, has this come about? What machinery is in place? What problems have been tackled? What successes and failures should be noted?

II

Today, no development problem can be permitted to surface without an accompanying demand that an agency be established to "solve it" or, as a minimum, "to give the problem the importance it deserves." No previously established international agency can afford to admit that it is not primarily a development agency. The Universal Postal Union (UPU) and the Intergovernmental Maritime Consultative Organization (IMCO) will doubtless consider complaining to our editors about the insufficient attention given to them in this study of international organization and economic development.

In 1958, in a review of international economic cooperation since the close of the Second World War, I urged that the main (though not the sole) goal of the UN system be a much more vigorous pursuit of the

> vitally necessary job of concentrating additional resources from both developed and underdeveloped countries on raising levels of living among peoples no longer resigned to poverty, hunger, disease, and subordinate status.[2]

I was aware of certain lacunae in the panoply of international machinery—most notably, an agency of the stature and breadth of the International Trade Organization (ITO) called for by the Havana Charter of 1948 and a financial agency able to provide grant aid to less developed countries and truly long-term loans at nominal rates of interest. However, I sounded no clarion call for the creation of a series of new agencies.

[2] Robert E. Asher, "Economic Co-operation Under UN Auspices," *International Organization*, Summer 1958 (Vol. 12, No. 3), p. 300.

Reporting to the Economic and Social Council (ECOSOC) were four regional economic commissions and a number of functional commissions dealing with transportation and communication, social problems, human rights, statistics, narcotic drugs, and other matters. There were specialized agencies in the fields of manpower, health, education, food and agriculture, civil aviation, telecommunications, postal services, meteorology, international investment, and monetary policy. An International Atomic Energy Agency (IAEA) and the already-mentioned Intergovernmental Maritime Consultative Organization had just come into being.

The General Agreement on Tariffs and Trade (GATT) was operating as a partial substitute for the stillborn ITO and making encouraging progress in reducing tariffs and liberalizing trade. The International Bank for Reconstruction and Development (IBRD) had made lending to low-income countries, especially for electric power, transportation, and economic overhead projects, respectable. The United Nations itself was firmly engaged in operational activities through its Expanded Program of Technical Assistance (EPTA). The vigorous campaign of the less developed countries for a capital assistance fund under the aegis of the United Nations had not been successful but had already led to such important by-products as the creation of the International Finance Corporation (IFC) as an affiliate of the World Bank which would invest in private industrial enterprises in the less developed countries, and the UN Special Fund to finance "preinvestment" undertakings in those countries.

Some notable multilateral initiatives had been taken outside of the UN framework. The Organization for European Economic Cooperation (OEEC) had greatly liberalized trade and payments within Western Europe. Three European "communities"—the European Economic Community (EEC) or Common Market, the European Coal and Steel Community (ECSC), and the European Atomic Energy Community (Euratom)—had been created. The Colombo Plan, however, remained one of the few such initiatives that involved developing as well as developed countries. To summarize, there appeared in 1958 to be no dearth of intergovernmental machinery.

Since then, as even the most casual reader of this symposium will have noted, the creation of international machinery has continued unabated. In global terms UNCTAD is politically the most important addition, for reasons well set forth in the essay by Richard N. Gardner. At the regional level the Alliance for Progress which is a multilateral undertaking but not an agency (though it embraces certain agencies described elsewhere in this study) is politically and economically highly significant. So, too, are the establishment of the International Development Association (IDA) as a second affiliate of the World Bank, the creation of the European Development Fund (EDF) and the Inter-American Development Bank (IDB), and the opening of regional development banks in both Asia and Africa. In promoting development, financial institutions have an asset—money—which enables them to launch productive projects as well as to recommend policies, make studies, run seminars, negotiate agreements, and engage in the more costless international activities to which other agencies are perforce limited.

Other new machinery worthy of mention in this incomplete catalog includes:

The extensive substructure of UNCTAD, comprising, *inter alia,* a 55-member Trade and Development Board which meets twice a year, a 55-member Committee on Commodities, 45-member Committees on Manufactures, on Shipping, and on Invisibles and Financing Related to Trade, and a secretariat of several hundred people in Geneva under Dr. Raúl Prebisch of Argentina;

The United Nations Industrial Development Organization (UNIDO), like UNCTAD an organ of the General Assembly, which has a 45-member Industrial Development Board, an "action-oriented" mandate that stresses operational activities rather than research, and a relatively autonomous secretariat in Vienna under Dr. I. H. Abdel-Rahman of the United Arab Republic;

A World Food Program (WFP) in Rome set up in 1963 under the joint sponsorship of the United Nations and the Food and Agriculture Organization (FAO) to use food surpluses, cash contributions, and services such as shipping for both emergency relief and economic and social development;

"Centers" within UN Headquarters such as the Center for Development Planning, Projections, and Policies and the Center for Housing, Building, and Planning and centers elsewhere such as the joint International Trade Center being established by GATT and UNCTAD;

Institutes galore, among them the UN Research Institute for Social Development in Geneva; the UN Institute for Training and Research (UNITAR) in New York; Institutes for Economic Development and Planning in Latin America, Africa, and Asia set up with the help of the Special Fund in cooperation with the regional economic commissions of the UN; an International Institute for Labor Studies established by the International Labor Organization (ILO); and an International Institute for Educational Planning spun off by the UN Educational, Scientific and Cultural Organization (UNESCO);

The Advisory Committee on the Application of Science and Technology to Development;

Last and as yet least, the capitalless UN Capital Development Fund.

The sole notable move toward consolidation has been the merger, effective January 1, 1966, of the Expanded Program of Technical Assistance and the Special Fund into the United Nations Development Program (UNDP).

Although the creation of new development agencies dominated by the less developed countries has been a major pastime of the international community during the 1960's, the bulk of the real work, insofar as the international promotion of economic growth and social change is concerned, continues to be done by the previously established agencies. Those agencies, moreover, have undergone profound changes in response to the pressures and needs of the low-income countries and new attitudes on the part of the high-income countries. Though the old stereotypes live on in the debates, the machinery established in the 1940's and the 1950's is focused as never before on current problems of the low-income countries.

The World Bank Group (the International Bank for Reconstruction and Development, the International Finance Corporation, and the International Development Association) has increased the annual level of its commitments to less developed countries from under $300 million in 1956 to about $1.2 billion in 1966. Formerly concentrating its resources heavily in electric power and transportation and inclined to remain aloof from other international agencies, the World Bank Group has stepped up its financing of agricultural and industrial development and exhibited a new and timely willingness to lend for educational development. It has worked out cooperative and fruitful relationships with FAO and UNESCO, overcome the misgivings it once had about technical assistance and soft lending, and, through the consortia and consultative groups it has convened and serviced, raised a multilateral umbrella over a sizable volume of bilateral assistance.

The International Monetary Fund (IMF), long regarded by many of the less developed countries as a citadel of economic orthodoxy rather than a source of short-term assistance, has become a much more flexible instrument. Gross drawings by less developed countries, which amounted to only $420 million during the years 1947–1955, exceeded $1 billion in 1956–1960 and more than $2.5 billion during the years 1961–1967.[3] Of special interest to less developed countries is the provision made by the

---

[3] For details see Edward M. Bernstein's lucid essay elsewhere in this volume.

IMF in 1963 and substantially liberalized in 1966 for the compensatory financing of foreign exchange deficits due to shortfalls in export proceeds below the level of the medium-term trend and beyond the control of the exporting country.

GATT, particularly since its innovative report, *Trends in International Trade,* published in 1958, has become acutely conscious of the need to maintain and expand the export earnings of the less developed countries through measures other than the reciprocal reduction of tariff barriers. A new Part IV of the General Agreement, entitled "Trade and Development," entered into force in 1966 and, as John W. Evans reports, brought to an end the period during which the GATT contained neither

> textual recognition of the role of exports in economic development nor a constitutional framework for many of the activities in which the Contracting Parties had been engaged

since 1958.

The contributions of the International Labor Organization and the United Nations Educational, Scientific and Cultural Organization to the conventional wisdom of the mid-1960's about the supreme importance of investment in human resources are delightfully described by Robert W. Cox. The Food and Agriculture Organization, a club in which the less developed countries have long felt more at home than in most of the pre-1960 intergovernmental agencies, has been serving them more relevantly and diligently since launching its Mediterranean Development Project in 1958. It has been moving away from the provision of technical assistance on an uncoordinated, retail basis and become deeply concerned with the strategy of agricultural development.

The heavy emphasis in multilateral agencies, old as well as new, on problems of the less developed countries might appear to provide a basis for the charge that the international economic machinery has somehow been stood on its head and is now neglecting the problems of the industrialized nations in order to concentrate exclusively on those of the low-income countries. Closer scrutiny, however, would show that the charge is false.

The principal protagonists and beneficiaries of the recently completed Kennedy Round of tariff negotiations which preoccupied GATT for four exhausting years (1963–1967) are the major trading areas of the non-Communist world, especially the United States and the European Economic Community. Real benefits will accrue to the less developed countries, benefits more substantial than many of us expected, but the deepest cuts were made in tariffs on items of most interest to the principal negotiating partners.[4]

[4] "Although such concessions were, of course, extended by the MFN [most-favored-nation] rule to developing countries as well, they were in general irrelevant to the latter." "Tariff Averages for

Similarly, the equally protracted negotiations on international monetary reform involving the creation of a new reserve asset, the SDR or special drawing right, have been of paramount interest to the major industrial countries, in this case the so-called Group of Ten in the IMF. The gross drawings of the more developed countries on the Fund during the years 1947–1967 exceed $9 billion, of which nearly $7 billion has been drawn during the 1960's. However, all IMF members, including the 81 less developed countries, can benefit from the new arrangement.

The World Bank continued until quite recently to be used by Australia, Finland, Japan, and other developed countries as a source of long-term credit. It has promoted and protected the interests of private international investors, most of whom are in high-income nations. The intergovernmental machinery in the fields of civil aviation, telecommunications, meteorology, and shipping is obviously not neglectful of the interests of developed countries.

The Organization for European Economic Cooperation, launched during the Marshall Plan period, has been transformed into the Organization for Economic Cooperation and Development (OECD) in which the United States, Canada, and Japan have joined the former OEEC states as full members. Only a small part of the far-flung program of this organization—primarily work of the Development Assistance Committee (DAC), the Trade Committee, and the semiautonomous OECD Development Center—is devoted directly to expediting growth in the less developed world.

The more developed countries, it seems to this observer, have all the machinery they want, plus the ability to create more when they feel so inclined. They suffer primarily from division in their ranks, an ailment from which no group of nations is immune.

III

Reverting to our main theme, multilateral efforts to promote growth and change in the low-income world, and reviewing the present array of machinery, it is reasonable to ask: What has it accomplished? What accounts for the proliferation? What trends are discernible? Who, if anyone, is minding the store—in other words, exercising some overall control? Let us postpone for the moment consideration of the first and most fundamental of these questions and address ourselves briefly to the others.

Insofar as the proliferation of machinery is concerned one must bear

Products of Interest to Developing Countries as Compared with Other Products" (United Nations Conference on Trade and Development Research Memorandum No. 13/2, August 4, 1967 [provisional draft, mimeographed], p. 8.)

in mind the low base from which it all started. Development was hardly recognized as an international problem two decades ago although it was deemed worthy of the attention of the newly established International Bank for Reconstruction and Development—*after* the necessary priority had been given to reconstruction. Almost every national government now has a much more complicated, disorderly panoply of agencies for dealing with economic and social problems than it had ten years ago. No one is happy about this, least of all congresses, parliaments, and treasuries, but expansion at the national level tends to be accepted with greater equanimity than expansion at the international level.

Most of the growth at the international level is a perfectly normal response to increased need. As one after another of the "keys" to development fails to open the door, as the infinite complexity of the unlocking process is revealed, as the interrelationships between economic, social, attitudinal, and institutional changes become better understood, and as new stages of development are attained, revised strategies and different pinpointings of effort are required. The desired objectives can sometimes be achieved by modifying the terms of reference or work programs of agencies already in being. At other times new machinery will be needed.

The balance in favor of new machinery has been massively tipped by the great increase in the number of sovereign states, their voting strength in intergovernmental forums, their self-evident qualification for the label "less developed," and their discontent with the agencies they have inherited. As Professor Gardner has reminded us, the less developed countries are not concerned about organizational neatness but about immediate results. When existing machinery appears to them to be inadequate, their response tends to be a vote for new machinery in which they will have greater control.

The establishment of an organization, moreover, creates the illusion of an attack on a problem and thus tends to satisfy demands for action without really answering the question of what should be done to solve the problem. Unfortunately, illusions too must now be bigger and better than they used to be; demands that could once have been satisfied by setting up a small committee today require as a minimum response the establishment of a sizable agency.

Does it do any good to set up machinery by a majority vote that does not include the votes of the nations expected to provide, in the form of money and expertise, most of the muscle and at least part of the brain? Not much good, but some. Governments that stand aloof grow uncomfortable when they could be sitting in chairs awaiting them at conference tables. The prospect that the machinery will be run entirely by others—without their own steadying hand at the helm—is too dreadful to contemplate. Once their participation is obtained, funds and good works may follow.

Furthermore, the more developed countries, which frequently oppose the initiatives of the less developed countries for new machinery and a voice more nearly commensurate with the share of the low-income countries in world population, have themselves exhibited ingenuity in adding workrooms and dormer windows to the organizational structure. They cannot blithely blame the less developed countries for all of the proliferation.

The prospect of rival machinery is often the best way to jog existing agencies out of well-worn ruts. The trouble is that by the time the substantive objective has been achieved and the proposed new functions have been more or less subsumed by existing agencies the propagandists for a new agency have become convinced by their own propaganda and insist on carrying through their threat. Given the good performance of the International Development Association, it is almost shocking that the less developed countries have continued to devote so much energy to establishing a UN Capital Development Fund and so little to keeping IDA alive and growing. The recalcitrance of the developed countries whenever the resources of IDA require replenishing highlights even more revealingly the present state of international economic cooperation.

Multilateral machinery grows and evolves not only in response to genuinely pressing needs, to needs that once were pressing but have already been substantially met, to the desires of vocal delegates, to the ambitions of secretariats and prospective members of secretariats, and to the hope that more machinery for development will result in more resources being devoted to development; it proliferates also because machinery begets machinery. The establishment of an Economic Commission for Europe (ECE) leads almost inevitably to economic commissions for every other major region. The existence of a worldwide organization to promote agricultural development requires in fairness to industry the establishment of a worldwide organization to promote industrial development. The justification that originally helped to support the creation of a Food and Agriculture Organization—that three-fourths of the people in the world derive their livelihoods from agriculture—can later be turned around to support the establishment of an Industrial Development Organization on the ground that there are too many people in agriculture and not enough in industry.

The success of a global preinvestment fund managed by Paul Hoffman has helped bring into being a Preinvestment Fund for Latin American Integration under the aegis of the Inter-American Development Bank. A regional development bank for Latin America, coming to fruition after a 70-year history, promptly gives rise to agitation for regional development banks in Asia and Africa.

The converse of the foregoing is also true: Established bureaucracies fight to preserve their empires and their policy standards and to protect them from invasion or subversion. The World Bank was not always hospitable to the idea of regional development banks; ILO saw no need for UNIDO; the specialized agencies for the most part opposed the merger that brought the UN Development Program into being.

The greater the number of international organizations the more hazardous it is to generalize about them. Exceptions can be cited, but the most noteworthy features of the organizational situation today, as compared with the situation ten or fifteen years ago, seem to me as follows:

1) The less developed countries have a much stronger voice in the policymaking bodies, often at the cost of transforming those bodies into organs too unwieldy to make policy. The less developed countries (like the Communist countries) are also more strongly represented in international secretariats. The obligation to distribute appointments over a wider geographic area has, at least for the time being, lowered the average technical competence of the secretariats and in some cases made them more partisan in their work.

2) Understandably enough, there continues to be enthusiasm among the less developed countries for machinery that can provide aid or strengthen the case for material assistance, and resistance to machinery geared to enforce standards or criticize poor performance. The history of the rise and fall of the Panel of Experts of the Alliance for Progress (the Nine Wise Men) and the subsequent effort to create a strong Inter-American Committee on the Alliance for Progress (CIAP) show how unwilling the Latin Americans have been to commit themselves to multilateral decisions on the allocation of aid among competing claimants.[5]

3) Regional machinery is sprouting up on every continent, much of it outside the UN framework, and regional economic integration is beginning to replace investment in human resources as the latest panacea for development. Insufficient attention, it can be argued, is being given to potential conflicts between the goals of regional and global integration.

4) The original notion under which within the UN framework certain broad fields of functional or technical specialization could be assigned to permanent, global specialized agencies related to the central political agency (the United Nations) but operating under their own constitutions and charters has been further eroded. The shortcomings of

---

[5] See the essay by Raúl Sáez elsewhere in this volume. Nevertheless, by comparison with present arrangements in Asia, Africa, or the Middle East the Alliance for Progress constitutes a long step toward a multilateral approach to development.

the functional approach (particularly its deleterious effects on development programming and execution at the country level) and the current tension between the functionalism of ILO, UNESCO, and FAO and the newer functionalism of UNCTAD or UNIDO are well brought out in Robert W. Cox's perceptive contribution to this symposium. UNCTAD and UNIDO are specialized agencies in everything but name, with charters that deliberately overlap those of older organs but with less protection from the political winds that rock the General Assembly.

5) The expenditures of international agencies for development purposes are still rising, but no progress has been made in endowing them with independent sources of revenue. Nongovernmental groups periodically pass resolutions urging that the United Nations be given title to the mineral resources of the oceans and ocean beds or the right to levy a surcharge on postage or a tax on international trade, but governments are not that eager to build a financially strong UN. The result has been a significant increase in the number of programs to be financed, like the budget of UNDP, by voluntary pledges with all the uncertainty inherent in that procedure.

6) The whole picture is a lot untidier than it used to be and no one is really minding the store. There once was a hope—it never was more than a hope—that the Economic and Social Council would become the economic and social "general staff" of the United Nations and that economic analysis of the kind not done by the secretariats of the specialized agencies would be provided by the Department of Economic and Social Affairs (of which the secretariats of the regional economic commissions were integral parts). The Economic and Social Council has been enlarged, as a result of a 1963 amendment to the UN Charter, from eighteen to 27 members, thereby giving the less developed countries a comfortable majority. In the Council representatives of the less developed countries have cooperated encouragingly in refurbishing its image as a coordinator and supervisor but in the General Assembly and elsewhere have furthered the fragmentation and decentralization that make orderly supervision by either the Council or the UN Secretary-General impossible.[6]

7) The novelty of the commitment to development, the complexity of the process, and the fact that there is no one best way to develop provide justification for a variety of functional and geographic approaches and for agencies of different size, scope, ideology, and autonomy. A real directorate-general for international economic affairs is not in the cards

---

[6] Walter M. Kotschnig in his essay calls attention to the newly revived and strengthened Committee for Program and Coordination and strikes a more hopeful note concerning the prospects for coordination.

within the foreseeable future. The sense of international community is too feeble, understanding of the strategy of development is too rudimentary, and revolutions, whether of rising expectations or rising frustrations, are too disorderly.

IV

There are several reasons for caution in speaking of the accomplishments and shortcomings of multilateral efforts. The word "multilateral" itself has come to embrace very much more than a project, program, or research undertaking directed, financed, and executed by a single intergovernmental agency. Distinctions between multilateral and bilateral, and national and international, have been blurred as a result of experiments in cooperation and conscious efforts to take advantage of the favorable connotations of the term "multilateral." In consequence the multilateral effort is sometimes only the wagging tail of a bilateral dog. Sometimes it is the dog, but with a bilateral tail and more bark than bite. Occasionally, it reveals itself as a pedigreed thoroughbred.

This study is replete with examples difficult to classify. The World Bank convenes government representatives from selected countries in consortia and consultative groups to review the development prospects and aid requirements of designated nations and to see what can be done about meeting agreed needs. Although a portion of the necessary financing will be provided multilaterally by the World Bank family, another, usually larger portion, will be provided by participating governments in accordance with arrangements worked out bilaterally between lender and borrower.[7] The Inter-American Development Bank, a multilateral institution with its ordinary capital resources subscribed to by all of its members, now finances social development projects from its expanded Fund for Special Operations but previously financed them from a separate Social Progress Trust Fund of more than $500 million contributed entirely by the United States.

The United States Agency for International Development (AID) on occasion joins the World Bank and the Inter-American Development Bank in financing a Latin American project. Private foundations and corporations may also participate in the effort. At other times two or more aid-giving governments join in financing a project in an aid-receiving country and refer to the undertaking as multilateral, even though no intergovernmental agency is involved.

[7] For perceptive accounts of the problem of aid coordination see Michael L. Hoffman, "The Co-ordination of Aid," in *Effective Aid* (London: Overseas Development Institute, 1967), pp. 65–84; and Seymour J. Rubin, *The Conscience of the Rich Nations: The Development Assistance Committee and the Common Aid Effort* (New York: Harper & Row [for the Council on Foreign Relations], 1966), especially pp. 12–20.

A further ground for caution is that even when the multilateral agencies appear to be operating independently, they are not autonomous forces divorced from the governments that create and maintain them. What Roger Revelle refers to as the "dismal record" of the World Health Organization (WHO) in family planning is not in any real sense a commentary on the efficacy of the agency, as he would be the first to admit, but a reflection on the state of public and governmental opinion in different areas of the world. In malaria control the record of WHO is excellent.

Bearing in mind these caveats and turning now to the substantive side of development, we may ask: What problems have been tackled multilaterally? What are the principal successes and failures of the multilateral approach? What has it contributed to popular and expert understanding of the problems of development and to the resolution of recognized problems?

The publications of international organizations and *ad hoc* expert groups have contributed significantly to the slowly emerging, as yet far from complete comprehension of the process of development. The annual *World Economic Report* and regional economic surveys, the biennial *Report on the World Social Situation,* published by the UN, the annual review of *International Trade* by GATT, the *State of Food and Agriculture* by FAO, the annual reports of the IMF and IBRD, the reports of the UN and OECD on the flow of financial resources to the less developed countries, and innumerable special reports on land reform, community development, commodity problems, and human rights provide essential basic data and interpretive analyses of recent trends. Various experts' reports—such as the 1951 report by a panel of experts appointed by the UN Secretary-General, *Measures for the Economic Development of Under-Developed Countries, Trends in International Trade* published by a GATT panel of experts, *Towards a New Trade Policy for Development* by the Secretary-General of UNCTAD, and *Development Assistance Efforts and Policies* by DAC's Chairman—have also been influential and in some cases are virtually classics.

Reports by international agencies and international committees tend to stress the need for international measures. It can be argued that debate and discussion have "overinternationalized" the development problem and exaggerated the degree to which success depends on international action, especially on more liberal trade, aid, and investment policies on the part of the industrialized, high-income countries.

With due allowance for agency loyalties and the primacy each professional accords to his profession as compared with all other professions a slowly growing consensus about the nature of the revolution politely called "development" or "modernization" is detectable. Development is not a stage reached when per capita incomes attain some specified level or after a particular list of "obstacles" has been overcome. It is a process—dynamic, pervasive, never ending, destructive as well as constructive. The essence of the process is the inculcation of new attitudes and ideas, of states of mind eager for progress, hospitable to change, and capable of applying scientific approaches to an ever wider range of problems.

The rapidity with which the process unfolds depends on the will and capacity of the people of the underdeveloped country far more than on natural resources or imported equipment and supplies. It depends on leaders who educate as well as agitate and on followers who teach as well as learn. Communication between them needs to be a two-way exchange with a meaningful feedback from the people to their leaders. Popular participation in development programs appears to be essential to facilitate the learning process, to prevent unbridgeable urban-rural gaps, and to enable inherited institutions to be transformed rather than to be replaced abruptly by unfamiliar, and therefore perhaps unworkable, transplanted institutions. As yet the wish to develop is more widespread than the will, and not enough is known about how to translate the wish into the will.

Although gross national product (per capita as well as total), savings and investment rates, earnings from exports, and other economic indexes should move upward, modernization consists of more than maximizing these. A decent sharing of the increased wealth, the elimination of discrimination based on race, color, or creed, higher literacy rates, broader and better-informed participation in political life, and efficient and humane administration—these, too, are vitally important objectives of development.

The term "economic development" is therefore being superseded by the more generic term "development" (without any qualifying adjectives) or "modernization" and is understood to mean economic, social, and political growth. For countries in the very early stages of development—traditional societies where more than 70 percent of the people are still on the land, where fewer than 30 percent are literate, where the birth rate runs from 40 to 50 births per 1,000 inhabitants per year, where life is truly at the margin of subsistence and man is at the mercy of the elements—modernization involves a top-to-bottom transformation of society. It means fundamental changes in traditional values, motivations, institutions, and patterns of behavior. It is a long-term job. At best it will be an erratic, two-steps-forward, one-step-backward, one-step-sideways movement.

Nevertheless, the journey toward self-sustaining growth need not be as drawn-out and costly in human terms as was the comparable journey for the now high-income, better-integrated nations of Western Europe and North America. Their experience, some of their resources, and other more recent experiences can be drawn on to shorten the time span. On the other hand, higher rates of population increase, greater difficulty in favoring investment over consumption, rising aspirations, and better-equipped competitors make the job more difficult than it was a century ago. Political exigencies demand speed, but how rapid the modernization process can become without destroying its organic nature and internal balance remains unknown. It will differ from area to area.

In addition to increased consensus regarding the general nature of the modernization process there is greater understanding than there was in 1950 of the vast differences between the 80-odd less developed countries. Each nation is to an important extent in a class by itself, dubiously aided by broad-brush policy prescriptions designed to cover simultaneously Brazil and Burundi, Costa Rica and Nepal, Libya and India.

Many new techniques have been devised in the economic and social field during the last two decades. It is easy to forget that in the early 1950's the World Bank was firmly opposed to soft lending, that in the late 1950's a publicly financed preinvestment fund seemed to many a questionable way to promote investment, and that until UNCTAD I non-discriminatory treatment in international trade was an overriding objective of international trade policy. Today, soft lending, like technical assistance or national banks for industrial and agricultural development, is an established technique for promoting growth in the low-income world. A preinvestment fund for financing resource surveys, training institutes, and market analyses, it is readily admitted, can evoke substantial sums for subsequent productive investment. In trade policy, discrimination in favor of the less developed countries is openly advocated by most of the developed countries and is being seriously considered by the rest.

Development planning, like development lending, has been made respectable. Low-income countries have been helped to formulate national development plans and 50 or more countries now have partial or comprehensive programs.

> Some of this planning has been faulty and, at times, even useless. But behind these weaknesses lies a truly remarkable phenomenon—the acceptance of the planning technique.[8]

[8] Irving S. Friedman, *International Problems of Economic Development,* Address to the Canadian Political Science Association, Ottawa, Canada, June 7, 1967 (Washington: International Bank for Reconstruction and Development, 1967), p. 8. Mr. Friedman goes on to say,

> By planning technique . . . I do not mean a detailed control and regulation of economic activity. Rather, it is the method by which governments make commitments to future actions and policies, thus extending the time horizons within which economic calculations

The effective execution of a few fundamental policies and programs is at least as important as the preparation of an elaborate, internally consistent, five-year plan based—all too frequently—on statistical data of doubtful validity and in any event unlikely to be carried out because of the absence of machinery and procedures linking the plan to the actual investment decisions of the government and the private sector. More attention is consequently being given to 1) better sector programming and project preparation in agriculture, education, transportation, and other fields; and 2) the formulation of integrated regional or area development schemes which seek to direct all the necessary inputs simultaneously (so that they will reinforce each other) into a single, manageable, geographic region within a developing country.

International agencies have been helpful in selecting promising regions, providing teachers and supplies, and, at the national level, advising on policies, assisting in the drafting of sectoral as well as overall development programs, and making long-range supply-and-demand projections for particular commodities. FAO is engaged in drawing up an ambitious Indicative World Plan for Agriculture. Jan Tinbergen looks forward to the day when there will also be an indicative overall economic plan for the world and in his essay suggests both a rationale and some guidelines for the undertaking.[9]

The key role of the agricultural sector is currently better appreciated, thanks in part to FAO. Increased food production in developing countries is at last beginning to receive the priority it deserves. Whether large-scale famines during the 1970's and 1980's can be averted remains questionable, but the Secretary-General of the United Nations, without being accused of seeking to keep the less developed countries in rustic subservience, can now warn that:

> Unless production on the farms . . . begins to go up, there is no surplus for saving, no surplus to feed the towns, no surplus to keep pace with rising population and keep down costly imports of food, no agricultural raw materials to feed into industry and, above all, no rise in farm income to provide an expanding market for the nascent industrial system. There is no conflict between the priorities of farming and industry, and the need to re-emphasize farming springs not from any desire to "keep developing economies dependent" but simply to counteract the glamour of factory chimneys which may all too often be smoking above products which no one in the community can afford to buy.[10]

based on objective criteria can play a greater part. The planning technique then becomes an important instrument for coordinating development activity on a number of different fronts, and for maintaining some sort of continuity in the pace of development.

[9] See Jan Tinbergen, "Wanted: A World Development Plan," elsewhere in this volume.

[10] "The United Nations Development Decade at Mid-Point: An appraisal by the Secretary-General" (UN Document E/4071, June 11, 1965), p. 32.

The distinguished UN Advisory Committee on the Application of Science and Technology to Development has identified a number of problems that merit concerted attack by means of scientific research and has made recommendations for mounting the attack. The provision of adequate food supplies heads its list of problems.

Doctrinal fights over the role of private foreign investment are being resolved pragmatically. Endless hours have been spent in futile efforts to develop acceptable multilateral codes for the treatment of private foreign investment. Meanwhile, unilaterally adopted investment guaranty schemes have been successful in safeguarding and perhaps enlarging the flow. There is a possibility that these will be complemented and supplemented by a multilateral scheme.[11] Nevertheless, the flow remains modest (only about half the level of public grants and loans) and is heavily concentrated on extractive industries in a handful of countries. The line between public and private, like the distinction between multilateral and bilateral, is not always clear. The World Bank engages in joint operations with investment banking houses, floats bond issues in the capital markets of industrialized countries to obtain resources for its public loans, and sells to institutional investors the early-maturity portions of previously made loans.

Recognition of the complexity of the development process should not obscure the elemental fact that an inflow of capital for investment purposes remains immensely important. The flow of public grants and loans to less developed countries rose encouragingly during the last half of the 1950's but stabilized in the early 1960's at a level considered grossly inadequate by the less developed countries and by most of the contributors to this volume. The stable absolute level of total aid since 1961 has in reality been a declining level because: 1) In the receiving countries population growth has reduced the amount available per inhabitant while in the donor countries rising incomes have reduced the fraction of the gross national product devoted to economic aid; 2) the terms of aid have been hardening and increasing sums have been needed by the less developed countries to pay interest charges on loans already received; 3) the cost of every kind of assistance has been rising; and 4) the proportion of aid tied to particular sources of supply and therefore not available for purchases wherever the goods are cheapest has also been climbing. The proportion of public grants and loans moving through multilateral channels has risen slightly but remains less than 15 percent of the total.

The population explosion, like the weather, is a phenomenon everyone talks about, but the international agencies are well behind the procession in doing anything about it. The private foundations and some of the

[11] See Stanley D. Metzger's trenchant analysis of investment issues elsewhere in this volume.

smaller bilateral programs (e.g., that of Sweden) have pioneered. The
United States aid program has recently overcome its taboos, but the
World Health Organization has been prevented by certain of its mem-
bers from playing an effective role.[12]

The role of international trade in development, skillfully summarized
by Isaiah Frank for readers of this symposium, is now much better understood by the international community than it was a decade ago. The
focus has shifted from import substitution (i.e., producing at home, almost regardless of cost, items that previously were purchased abroad) to
export promotion.

> The shift of focus from imports to exports as the important trade fac-
> tor in economic development has occasioned a parallel policy shift from
> measures applied by an individual country to international action. There
> is a new general awareness that the problems of expanding exports of
> developing countries, except for temporary and unusual circumstances,
> can be tackled only as a cooperative venture. . . . [13]

About 85 percent of the export earnings of the less developed countries
still comes from primary products. With some exceptions among the
minerals and metals, however, the market for these exports is sluggish
and subject to considerable price fluctuations. Moreover, most of the
primary products exported by the low-income countries must compete
with commodities produced and exported by the rich countries.

Agriculture in the developed countries until quite recently has been
virtually exempt from the trade liberalization movement of the postwar
years. Domestic producers of sugar beets and sugar cane, cereals, and
many other primary products are sheltered from foreign competition.
Elimination of agricultural protection in the highly developed countries
could be an enormous stimulant to the exports of the less developed countries. Full elimination during the foreseeable future is unlikely, but a
prompt follow-up on the beginning made in connection with the Kennedy Round would be helpful.

Pending genuine diversification of production and exports by the less
developed countries—i.e., pending development—one of the remedies they
have sought most persistently is a series of international commodity agreements to stabilize and step up earnings from those primary products that
they do export in quantity—coffee, cocoa, tea, bananas, rubber, tin, copper, lead, and zinc, among others. The list of commodity agreements in

---

[12] Richard N. Gardner finds "the ratio of talk to action . . . still distressingly high" and concedes
that the UN got off to a slow start insofar as family planning assistance is concerned. He regards
1962–1967 as the years of the breakthrough, however, and calls attention to the record of the
UN Children's Fund (UNICEF) and agencies bolder than WHO. See his essay "Toward a World
Population Program" elsewhere in this volume.

[13] Margaret G. de Vries, "Trade and Exchange Policies for Economic Development," *Finance
and Development*, June 1967 (Vol. 4, No. 2), p. 116.

operation is very short; sensible arrangements are inordinately hard to work out and seldom very successful after having been put into effect. The difficulties and divergencies of interest are distressingly formidable. The International Coffee Agreement with its proposed fund for diversification does represent something of a breakthrough, however. (The International Cotton Textiles Arrangement, negotiated to prevent "market disruption" from imports in countries such as the United States, is a backward step, disadvantageous to the developing countries that export textiles and to consumers in the importing countries. At the same time it is illustrative of the fact that many inherent technical difficulties in working out agreements vanish when powerful countries are determined to surmount them.[14])

The limited role for commodity agreements has underscored the need to move ahead in other ways to promote the export earnings of less developed countries. Pursuant to a request made by the 1964 UNCTAD the staff of the World Bank devised a scheme that would help to relieve commodity agreements of the responsibility they have been least successful in meeting, namely, the maintenance of the total export earnings of producing nations. The scheme, subsequently reviewed by an intergovernmental group of experts, would provide less developed countries with an accessible source of assistance to enable them to maintain internationally approved development programs in the face of unforeseen adverse export movements that are beyond their control and beyond their ability to offset from reserves or to finance on a short-term repayable basis. The plan is predicated on the vital assumption that it would be supplementary to, and not a substitute for, existing forms of aid.

The less developed countries are determined not to be confined to the role of producing and exporting primary products. They want to get into the manufacturing business. Their comparative advantage, initially at least, lies in industries requiring relatively large amounts of unskilled labor and relatively little capital or highly skilled labor.[15] Japan and Italy among the developed countries and Hong Kong, the Republic of China (Nationalist China), and the Republic of Korea (South Korea) among the developing areas have already shown the way.

However, the present tariff structure of the United States and of most other nations as well is rigged against the labor-intensive manufactures that less developed countries are or can become best equipped to supply.

[14] Because it deals with processed rather than primary products, the Cotton Textiles Arrangement is not a commodity agreement in the usual sense of the term.

[15] This should not be construed as an argument against the establishment of heavy industries. A number of less developed countries have passed the "initially at least" stage to which I refer or can justify capital-intensive undertakings on other grounds. See, for example, Hla Myint, *The Economics of the Developing Countries* (New York: Frederick A. Praeger, 1965), pp. 136–142, 157–159.

Tariffs generally escalate in accordance with the amount of processing done abroad. Noncompetitive raw materials get the best treatment, semimanufactures the second best, while manufactured products pay the highest duties. Those particularly discriminated against include not only textiles, carpets, clothing, and accessories but also footwear, glassware, china, and pottery; toys, sporting goods, and bicycles; various processed foodstuffs; and furniture and other simple wood products.

As a result of protracted tariff negotiations held under the auspices of GATT tariffs on manufactured goods have been reduced enormously since 1947. The average nominal or legal tariff in now somewhere between 10 and 15 percent, depending upon how it is calculated. Publicizing the average, however, tends to conceal the fact that many individual rates, including those in which the less developed countries are particularly interested, are well above the average. Moreover, the nominal tariff rates usually understate substantially the true protective effect of the tariff structure.

Zealous protection of labor-intensive lines of production from foreign competition is both a disservice to the less developed countries and to the general public in the industrialized countries. Development means a steady rise in average labor income and should be accompanied by a gradual transfer of resources out of the less sophisticated, low-income-yielding lines. In an economy willing to use adjustment assistance to facilitate the transfer process and enjoying relatively full employment the hardships should be few and the benefits many. The low-cost producers in less developed countries could fill the resulting breach.[16]

In summary, as aid has leveled off, pressure for fresh action on the trade front has increased. Changes that will allow the less developed countries to earn from exports more of the foreign exchange that they need will affect their self-respect, their need for foreign aid, and their integration into the international community. The trade proposal that has evoked the most enthusiasm in the low-income world is for temporary tariff preferences in the industrialized countries for manufactured products from less developed countries. If, for example, the duty on bicycles were 10 percent, it might for a decade be reduced, for less developed countries only, to half of the regular rate or to zero.

A scheme of generalized preferences for less developed countries would sanction a form of discrimination but in my view would not constitute a retrograde or disastrous step. The path to a policy goal like nondiscrimination is usually a zigzag course. Nevertheless, a preference scheme for less developed countries could at best make only a modest contribution

[16] See Harry G. Johnson, *Economic Policies Toward Less Developed Countries* (Washington: Brookings Institution, 1967), especially pp. 78–110.

to a new international division of labor. The greatest potential trade contribution to a better-integrated world enocomy would be much easier access for everyone to the rich markets of the high-income countries. If the low-income countries in turn maintained realistic exchange rates and otherwise equipped themselves to take advantage of the enlarged opportunity, the potential benefit would become real.

V

Judged by historical standards the progress of the less developed countries since the close of World War II has been quite remarkable. But man does not live by historical standards alone. Frustration and foreboding are rife.

India, the largest less developed nation in the non-Communist world, has suffered from two years of unprecedented drought, from tired and undynamic leadership, and from centrifugal forces of ominous strength. The People's Republic of China (Communist China) has been a threat, and the peace with Pakistan is fragile. Nigeria, most populous of the African countries and groomed to be a showcase of purposeful development on that restive continent, has been rent by civil war. The Democratic Republic of the Congo, site of a heroic effort by the international community to build in short order the foundations for a sovereign state, is foundering. Indonesia took itself to the very brink of disaster, hovered, and seems at last to be turning around. In the western hemisphere Brazil and Argentina—for all their promise—have performed indifferently.

The smaller nations are in many cases too small to survive as sovereign entities, yet federations embracing several such states have so far proved unviable. The future of Hong Kong, a genuine success story, has been placed in jeopardy by externally inspired rioting and nearby hostile forces. With one or two exceptions the members of the Arab League have devoted more energy to seeking the destruction of Israel than to emulating the Israeli record in building a nation and making the desert bloom. Everywhere, armaments exact their unholy toll on available resources.

The behavior of the so-called "more developed" or "advanced" countries offers little inspiration to the less developed countries. Their grand designs are petty, self-serving, or nonexistent. Their economies exhibit signs of slowdown. Their commitment to help develop other continents is wavering. Their preoccupation with domestic problems—and, in the case of the United States, with a costly, divisive, interminable war in Vietnam—is all too apparent. Indications that the Union of Soviet Socialist Republics will cooperate in making the world "safe for diversity" are hard to find.

The list of portents could be lengthened and the reasons for disenchantment—which include totally unrealistic expectations in both developed and less developed countries—could be dealt with in more detail. International machinery draws attention to disasters and quite properly removes from its agenda problems that no longer cry for action. Crop failures or falling raw material prices trigger debate; rising earnings and dramatic agricultural achievements such as the increase in the Mexican wheat yield and the phenomenally productive rice strains developed at the International Rice Research Institute receive, at most, two brief cheers.

The postwar record itself consequently deserves mention, if only to offset the widespread impression of stagnation, disintegration, and worse.

In terms of gross domestic product the less developed countries have been growing at a respectable rate since 1950. The rate exceeds the growth rate of the more developed countries during the same period as well as for earlier periods of comparable duration. However, because of the much faster rates of population growth in the less developed countries—almost twice those of the developed countries—the rate of improvement per person has been less in the low-income part of the world than in the high-income part despite the fact that its overall rate of growth has been slightly greater. Moreover, because of the low level from which they started, per capita incomes in the less developed countries in dollar terms have risen only modestly. Although the average rise in per capita income has been small for the less developed world as a whole, there are a number of areas with records that are distinctly encouraging—for example, Israel, Nationalist China, South Korea, Hong Kong, Malaysia, Mexico, Peru, Jamaica, Central America, Tunisia, Ivory Coast, and Pakistan. Some of the current pessimism about India is as naïve as was the optimism of the early 1950's; India has made measurable progress without sacrificing its democratic institutions and has laid a foundation for better-balanced growth in the years to come.

The export earnings of less developed countries grew slowly during the 1950's. But they were in reality high to begin with, partly because of the Korean War boom. Their slow expansion was responsible for much of the gloom about trade prospects during the 1960's. The export proceeds of the developing countries, however, rose at an impressive annual rate of 6 percent during the first half of the Development Decade. Exports of manufactured products, despite the obstacles they encounter, grew at a thumping 14 percent per year—from an admittedly low base.

Significant social progress has also been made, particularly in the fields of education and health, where the payoff is slow but cumulative. School enrollment has risen spectacularly at every level. Literacy rates are up significantly. Maternal and child mortality have been reduced. Successful campaigns against malaria, yaws, smallpox, tuberculosis, and other scourges have been conducted. In the field of health the gap between the more developed and the less developed countries has probably narrowed.[17] Housing has remained thoroughly inadequate, urban problems are accumulating, and industrial production, though it has doubled in the last decade, has provided far fewer jobs than had been expected of it.

There is no UN report on the world political situation and, as yet, we know even less about political development than about economic and social development. Furthermore, the political record of the last quarter century has not been adequately appraised. In many respects the liquidation of vast colonial empires has been astonishingly orderly. The number of nation-states is about two and one-half times what it was in 1945. The new nations have produced a respectable number of remarkable leaders. Heartening examples of democratic development at the grass roots can be cited, but democracy, alas, is not a form of government acquired automatically as levels of living improve; military take-overs, coups, and revolutions continue to occur. The foreign policies pursued by the less developed countries are, except for a few cases of rampant nationalism, readily understandable from the point of view of their own immediate interests and least threatening to the rest of the international community where development itself is most obviously taking root. The new states have hastened to join the United Nations and other international organizations and on the whole have played responsible roles in them.[18]

One can concede that significant progress has been made by the less developed countries since the end of World War II while wondering how much, if any of it, should be attributed to multilateral efforts. Unfortunately, the multilateral contribution to the substantial but unevenly distributed gains noted above cannot be isolated and measured. It has assuredly been important and, equally assuredly I suspect, been minor for most of the major countries though major perhaps for some of the minor countries.

Instructive and influential as the publications of international agencies have been, they constitute a small segment of the burgeoning literature on development. Much appreciated as the multilateral technical assistance programs are, they are not demonstrably superior to bilateral programs and they probably account for less than 10 percent of the technical as-

[17] *1963 report on the World Social Situation* (United Nations Publication Sales No: 63.IV.4 [UN Document E/CN.5/375/Rev.1]) (United Nations, 1963), Chapter I.

[18] This summary of the postwar record of the less developed countries draws heavily on Robert E. Asher, *International Development and the U.S. National Interest* (Washington: National Planning Association, 1967), pp. 21–24.

sistance provided. As already noted, only a small fraction of the capital assistance comes directly through multilateral channels, though the indirect total is considerably larger. The improved export earnings of the less developed countries are attributable to a much greater extent to full employment policies and attendant higher levels of demand in the high-income countries than to the trade programs of multilateral agencies.

Had there been no United Nations, the formation of a political bloc of less developed countries might have been delayed a few more years. Pressures to pursue sensible economic and social policies would have been weaker and more intermittent. Progressive forces in less developed countries would have felt more isolated and ignorant. Without the United Nations and related agencies the emphasis given to the special difficulties of the less developed countries would have been less universal, the analysis less searching, and the incentives to action less compelling. The problems would nevertheless have worked their way to the center of the world stage, for their solution is by almost any standard the major economic and social challenge of the day.

VI

The foundations for more rapid growth in the 1970's are present if governments have the wit and the will to build upon them. National integration, I think, is almost a prerequisite for regional or global integration, and many of the new nations have a long way to go before achieving a genuine sense of national identity and mission, a fusion of tribal and parochial loyalties, and a lasting measure of internal social integration. Backsliding and disorder are to be expected. They will more often reflect differences of opinion about the pace of progress than about the need for modernization.

As the nations of the world modernize and more of them move into a middle-income group, interdependence will assume new meaning. Foreign trade will grow, people will immigrate to as well as emigrate from developing areas, ideas will circulate more readily, and technology will be more easily shared. "The very process of modernization within societies tends to foster international integration without the assistance of formal outside institutions."[19] Nevertheless, international institutions and the consultations, confrontations, and cooperative practices that they institutionalize can speed the process.

International integration can be regional or global. Greater integration at the regional level, now being pursued with enthusiasm, may be a

[19] C. E. Black, *The Dynamics of Modernization: A Study in Comparative History* (New York: Harper & Row, 1966), p. 154.

prerequisite for integration on a wider scale. The larger the number of countries involved and the greater their differences in size, wealth, history, and cultural heritage the harder it is to weld effective international machinery. Concentration on the creation of regional machinery without a concurrent strengthening of interregional bonds, however, can produce powerful, intransigent regional blocs that will make integration on a wider scale, or even peaceful coexistence, much more difficult.

The nations of the world have had very little experience in seeking accommodation on the basis of the welfare of all. They cling tenaciously to obsolescent concepts and tend to support international programs only if they can explain to their inhabitants that national sovereignty remains unimpaired. The building of international community must be, so to speak, undetectable to those involved. A gossamer net of imperceptible weight has to be woven a thread at a time.

Weaving without a master pattern on looms at different locations, with numerous hands on each shuttle, is not conducive to efficiency. During the immediate future the increased political strength of the less developed countries is likely to be reflected in more machinery to deal with specific problems and to overlap or submerge machinery in which the less developed countries lack confidence. A good deal of it will be outside of the universal framework of the United Nations. Some of the industrialized nations that have been the major providers of development assistance may decide to rely more heavily on multilateral machinery. Their motive will be to limit their bilateral commitments rather than to fortify the multilateral approach.

So long as the international machinery remains dependent on voluntary contributions and pass-the-hat exercises, its capacity to mobilize resources and promulgate policies favoring development will be limited. International ownership of a revenue-producing resource or possession of the power to tax would represent a real breakthrough in national versus international relations. Such authority is more likely to develop as a corollary than as a forerunner of unremitting commitment to the brotherhood of man.

In the perspective of human experience the twenty-odd years since the end of World War II constitute a fleeting moment. One hundred years from now, if nuclear holocaust has been avoided, people everywhere may look with pride upon the sturdy, flexible, efficient network of international institutions catering to their needs. Ignorant of the patchwork of yesteryear, forgetting how wary and recalcitrant they were at every turning point, they may, with their customary disdain for history, say in all sincerity, "We planned it that way."

PROSPECTS FOR A FUTURE WHOLE WORLD

Philippe de Seynes

PHILIPPE DE SEYNES is United Nations undersecretary-general for economic and social affairs. This article is based on a speech made by de Seynes on May 6, 1971, at the Institute of International Studies, University of California, Berkeley.

I.

The notion of the "world as a whole" is becoming increasingly prominent in the thinking and pronouncements of international prognosticators. Yet "globalism," its functional expression, is a relatively new approach in the United Nations. In fact, it has hardly arrived. This statement is not paradoxical or even surprising. Globalism is not the same thing as internationalism as we have known it up to the present. There is more involved here than a matter of semantics. Traditional internationalism is derived from the dictates of political wisdom and a sense of human solidarity in a world of growing interdependence but of unlimited horizons opened up by technology. Globalism is associated today with the ambivalence of technology, its negative effects on the degradation of the environment, the destruction of ecological balances, the limited capacity of the biosphere, the possible depletion of natural resources, the population explosion, the finiteness of the planet, and perhaps even the finiteness of knowledge.

None of this thinking was instrumental in the founding of the UN. In fact, the word "technology" does not even appear in the Charter of the United Nations, and the early years of the organization were strongly shaped by the emergence of new states and the process of their political and economic emancipation which did not postulate a global approach.

This is not to say that the charter and the fundamental practices developed in the organization are in need of drastic revision. On the contrary they provide an instrument sufficiently flexible to encompass a new vision of the world and to stimulate the new institutional arrangements required. Nevertheless, as it is only recently that the "spaceship earth" has been spoken of, we have been slow and even remiss in developing some of the functions which should now impera-

From Volume 26, No. 1 (1972), pp. 1-17.

tively be associated with it, namely, long-term forecasting — a measure of central planning and management, new regulatory machinery, and the definition of more international policies and norms, which may, or may not, come into conflict with national aspirations.

The reluctance of the United Nations polity to accept long-term projections as a basis for policymaking was only gradually eroded during the 1960s and then only in the demographic and economic fields. It is, of course, quite true that *direct predictability* of the future, even in the most classical economic terms, seems further off than ever in spite of the progress made in technological forecasting, operational research, and other tools of modern analysis. This does not mean that nothing can be done. In fact, forecasting is taking place on a national basis on a large scale, but, under the present predicament of the world economy, governments are left with too many uncertainties for comfort in regard to important aspects of their forecasting if no attempt is made internationally to project a number of global quantities. In any planning done without a comprehensive — even if rudimentary — long-term perspective short-term decisions run the risk of being misconstrued. The rigidity observed in short-term and medium-term developments leads to the assumption of stable relationships and leaves little room for the unexpected. Long-term studies can at least aim at a presentation, in a broad and general background, of desirable and feasible developments, at the identification of those decisions which are committing the society to an irreversible course, and at the highlighting of sectors and areas in which performance levels must be changed. Such thoughts, however, are often suspected in international circles of amateurism or of bias, and this has made it difficult to establish the necessary disciplines as a fundamental piece of United Nations decisionmaking. The Economic Commission for Europe (ECE) has been concerned for some years with the momentous mutation from the industrial to the postindustrial society and has felt the need for a very thorough analysis and examination of the consequences of imperceptible changes which have been taking place. Yet, it is only recently that the ECE has set up the necessary machinery to assist countries in this effort.

II.

How optimistic can one be about the prospects of global planning, central management, and international regulations within the UN, the only universal institution in which such an attempt would seem plausible? In seizing the opportunities and responding to the challenges, whether in the traditional field of international cooperation or in new endeavors, the organization's record has recently been mixed. One potentially successful attempt was made in respect of the seabeds, which remain largely unappropriated despite extreme national claims. In this case the chances of collective action were recognized and investigated in time, that is, at a sufficiently early stage of technological development so that there could be adequate and orderly preparation for the institutional arrangements required. But in outer space, another unappropriated area, the organization was not so prompt and left the field of satellite communications to be explored and controlled under other jurisdictions although it is not inconceivable that a measure of initiative might be regained if the existing UN instrumentality, the International Telecommunications Union (ITU), were to be reinforced.

In the more traditional areas of internationalism the urge for action has neither been very great nor very productive. There is a long practice of cooperation in monetary matters, but in 1958 the world returned to convertibility without developing a central machinery for the control of capital movements or the coordination of monetary policies. When such coordination is indispensable, it has been achieved in the most pragmatic and haphazard way on the basis of ad hoc arrangements which may have prevented catastrophies but on balance have done no more than maintain the system on a very precarious course. In this vacuum a large "floating market" of currencies has developed unchecked and uncontrolled; it is prevented from generating large disequilibria only through repeated improvizations.

In the last 25 years a new type of social organization, full of promises but also of threats and conflicts, has developed — the multinational corporation — and with it the new phenomenon of international production under the decisionmaking power of a corporate brain which may at any time come into conflict with national aspirations and policies. Yet no system of international policing, no forum or institution for the resolution of conflicts or the investigation of grievances was created although the principle of such a system was embodied as far back as 1948 in the Havana charter of the International Trade Organization (ITO). Here also long-term thinking is of great importance for it would be useful to have a working hypothesis to separate out that part of this spectacular movement toward international production which corresponds to a once-and-for-all phenomenon and that part which reflects a durable trend. Both of those problems, that of the control of capital movements and that of the policing of the international corporations, should be high on the agenda of the 1970s. They should be tackled with vigor and engage the efforts of the best brains.

On the other hand, long-term thinking and a measure of forecasting and planning has been carried on in the United Nations in the area of economic development. At the beginning it met with skepticism, if not derision. But models have been built, initially with the aim of calculating foreign exchange and savings gaps. These crucial quantities have been recognized as being of great importance in the assumption of collective responsibility for development and were later refined to embrace a number of other factors. The development model built by the United Nations Center for Development Planning, Projections, and Policies followed efforts started in the 1950s, first in the Economic Commission for Latin America (ECLA), then in the World Indicative Plan of the Food and Agriculture Organization (FAO) and in the debates of the first United Nations Conference on Trade and Development (UNCTAD I) on the trade gap. It aimed at a more comprehensive coverage than earlier models and won wide acceptance, as exemplified by the work of the Commission on International Development (Pearson commission) and by the debates of the UN General Assembly during its 25th anniversary. Yet, it remains sketchy. There are no provisions for technological changes, changes in demand elasticity, and many other elements. It is also quite true that crucial policy parameters referring to some of the burning problems of the day, such as employment, education, nutrition deficiencies, distribution of income, and agrarian structures, are enunciated in only the most general terms reflecting the insufficiency of statistical evidence and the inadequacy of analytical tools. Yet, with all its defects, the proposal for the Second United Nations Development Decade (DDII) has some of the characteristics of a strategy: a ten-year perspective, a model of coherence with some 69 elements, a feedback process embodied in a systematic monitoring mechanism to check performance against established benchmarks and to allow revisions in the whole model in response to changes in the socioeconomic environment or in human knowledge. The adjustment and integration of the various assessments to be undertaken at the national, regional, and sectoral levels as well as in the global framework will also lead to a gradual evolution — and hopefully an improvement — in the functioning of a rather disjointed institutional system and in the development of its relationship with its constituent 127 national governments. This embryonic attempt at collective management of one of the great problems of the day should result in a new instrument of cooperation which can enhance the influence of the organization and encourage the mobilization of political will.

III.

But globalism, as it is advocated today, means that a far greater degree of stewardship must be exercised in respect of the "spaceship earth" if we are to avoid impending catastrophes or ensure the survival of the human species. It is important to realize that the planning and collective decisionmaking required to handle these problems, while even more necessary than for development problems, may be even more forcefully resisted.

The development strategy does pit one set of countries against the other — North versus South — in a process of negotiation and sometimes of confrontation, but the resulting action could, at least in the long run, be viewed as favorable to both. It has never been suggested that economic self-interest of developed and less developed states alike could not work in the same direction as the broader humanitarian imperatives and the counsels of political wisdom. The disagreements therefore have been on means, not on goals: the nature of the commitments entered into, the volume for capital transfers and official donations, the scope of the preferential treatment offered to less developed countries in commercial transactions, the type of adjustments required from the rich countries in their industrial structure, and the degree of accountability involved in the monitoring and assessment process. But it was always assumed that changes required from the rich countries for the improvement of the lot of the poor would also serve the best interests of the former, that such changes might even lead them more rapidly to beneficial transformations such as the deployment of their resources in activities either of greater productivity or of greater social benefit, and that these changes would help in relieving the rich of a sense of guilt toward the two-thirds of mankind living in poverty, disease, and ignorance. Even technology is viewed in this context as a thoroughly benevolent factor which would on the whole help the poorer countries in their development process — notwithstanding the difficulty of adapting certain processes to different conditions — and would help the richer countries in sustaining economic growth, thereby giving them additional elbow room for pursuing liberal trade and aid policies.

On the other hand, when we come to the concept of the "spaceship earth" with its problems of environmental degradation and the possible depletion of resources, we are in a situation which is potentially conflictual or at least is frequently so regarded. Philosophically these new concepts are a direct challenge to the assumption of linear progress which underlies the development strategy and much international cooperation up to now. Practically they suggest that in a world far more interdependent and vulnerable than we have assumed changes in any place at any time may adversely affect the whole and that to avoid this difficulty national jurisdiction may have to be severely restricted, even in the choice of objectives.

It is therefore not surprising that the eager proclamation of these new basic assumptions and the consequences which are drawn from them for the international system and for the day-to-day action of the United Nations organization are being received with mixed feelings. The planning which is implied here and which is so emphatically advocated by some is suspected by others as being a diversionary tactic. It should come as no surprise that the two-thirds of mankind struggling with hunger, poverty, and disease should not be very much concerned with a planetary ideal or with the idea of a single world. How can we hope to arouse ignorant and poorly fed masses by the now almost ritual evocation of the concept of the quality of life when they barely possess the quantity of goods necessary for their subsistence? How can we talk about a planetary outlook to those whose horizon is, throughout their life, limited to the elementary needs of the survival of their families?

The sad fact is that we must now face these new and challenging problems of collective organization before we have made much progress toward achieving a better equilibrium, before we can confidently assert that the intolerable inequalities existing between the different regions of the world will be remedied, before a soundly structured international development policy has been irreversibly accepted and strictly adhered to, and before the reflexes, habits, and disciplines inherent in it have truly passed into our daily behavior.

The prevailing background of social stratification on a worldwide basis is inevitably reflected in the structure of power as it is expressed in the United Nations organization in spite of the formal equality of the voting procedures, and this explains the resistance of many governments even to mild forms of international planning. Planning may reduce uncertainties in an already integrated community with a high degree of group loyalty and with checks and balances which may at times be paralyzing but at least afford a measure of protection to most sections of the community. But in an almost anarchical world community with a mosaic of states as yet bound together only by the most general notion of solidarity and with an international system in which the area of clearly recognized common interests is still small the possibility of central planning immediately conjures up new uncertainties, specifically the fear of manipulation by the powerful. The evocation of guidelines for an international policy in the development of natural resources, which could perhaps be justified by the possible danger of depletion, by the need to protect the environment, or by considerations of equity in extreme situations of rent and monopoly, has been castigated as neo-colonialism. Another graphic illustration of such attitudes may be found in the attempts made, up to now in vain, to introduce into the organization a more rational system of budget programming with a measure of medium-term planning, an effort at more rationality in budgetary choices. Both savers and spenders have, for a long time, resisted any change lest their relative position might be altered to their disadvantage.

Problems of the environment cannot, it is assumed, be dealt with in the same way as problems of development strategy, i.e., within a context of converging long-term interests and short-term frictions or conflicts of interest. In fact, certain accepted objectives, those of rapid economic development, are presumably threatened with being displaced. Less developed countries suspect that public funds will be diverted from development aid to cure the ills of the industrial countries. They fear that international antipollution standards or norms will be established — or at least attempted — which will burden their own development. They speculate that preoccupation with the environment will slow down, if not arrest, the growth of their exports to rich countries or unfavorably affect the composition of these exports. These apprehensions, admittedly, are at present more emotional than rational, to the point that less developed countries sometimes overlook certain comparative advantages which may result for them from the strict control of environment in presently industrial regions. But it must be recognized that the emotions — and random speculations — are not all on one side. They are, on the contrary, characteristic of many of the pronouncements relating to the "spaceship earth." There is not as yet an organized body of knowledge which could be the foundation of rigorous and disciplined thinking leading to collective action and the setting up of institutions. The first and most urgent need is for conceptualization and elucidation.

IV.

In this respect we cannot dismiss certain schools of thought which enjoy only a small and specialized audience and do not seem as yet greatly to influence the policymakers. Those ideas represent an important product of academia and evoke a sympathetic response from wider circles; therefore they may yet find their way into the "technostructure." The central role of economic growth is being challenged. Zero growth, the stationary state, stasis, these are a few names which are used to formulate a concept which is at times a prediction, at times a prescription. The concept is not without credentials for it was probably, explicitly or implicitly, an underlying presupposition of the major protagonists of economic science in the classical age. In fact, the great thinkers, from physiocrats to David Ricardo, Thomas Malthus, Karl Marx, and Joseph A. Schumpeter, have postulated the advent of a stationary state, some viewing it as a desirable condition, others as an apocalyptic prospect. Only the development of modern science and technology changed this perspective and opened the way to the idea of indefinite and linear progress overcoming the constraints of factors presumed to limit the development of both production and knowledge. Going back to the "steady state" would not therefore seem implausible but might even be regarded as a natural hypothesis since it was held for so long and by such distinguished men. We can also wonder whether we have not already witnessed in at least one or two of the industrial European countries an unconscious acceptance of, or preference for, a society in which growth would not figure as a primary objective or a necessary condition of other objectives, i.e., a society which would carry out a transition from growth to equilibrium. This may have happened during the last 25 years, first through the wave of welfare reforms of the postwar period and now through the overwhelming concern for the pollution of the human and natural environment and the yearning for a better quality of life.

Given the preoccupations of the United Nations and the analyses which it has produced, it is not likely that any collective action or any institutional innovation could be accepted if it were based on the theory that in the foreseeable future growth would cease to be an indispensable impetus of progress. Nobody of course has said as yet that growth should stop in the less developed world. The prescription is confined to those countries which have gone through the various phases of the industrial revolution. But it is doubtful that even in the case of these countries a policy tending toward zero growth by the end of the twentieth century would be acceptable; such a policy would probably be expected to produce results so serious that by comparison the increase in pollution and other dangers to the "spaceship earth" would appear secondary. Growth is still an indispensable factor in the social progress of the most advanced countries of the world. Indeed, when presenting their forecasts to the Organisation for Economic Co-operation and Development (OECD) or when discussing them in the ECE, governments of industrial states assert quite clearly that sustained economic growth is the indispensable precondition for every concept of long-term development, whatever the stage of development reached and whatever the system of socioeconomic institutions. There remain in the most advanced countries pockets of poverty and squalor, groups whose horizon is still blocked by the stringency of their limited incomes (reflecting a glaring insufficiency in collective services and equipment), new aspirations toward more equality and security, all requiring deep structural changes which cannot be contemplated except under conditions of sustained growth if one wants to avoid catastrophic distortions or severe depression of the living standards of large sections of the population. Even corrections of the negative side-effects of growth, if they are to be achieved, require the stabilizing influence of continuing economic growth.

This is not to say that the pattern of growth should not change. Indeed, the pattern has changed considerably to reflect the increasing role of education, knowledge, and management. It is even more obvious that the behavior of consumers must change; indeed it is already changing. Above certain income levels there is a growing realization that the quality of life cannot be equated with the quantity of goods; there is an emerging trend, for example, toward more symphony orchestras and fewer automobiles. But such desirable changes require the elbow room generated by growth. This is true even if we do not take into account the factor of personal freedom which is certainly subject to new interpretations and should absorb a greater content of collective discipline but which at times is ignored by some of the more recent utopias.

More relevant to the preoccupation of the United Nations would be the creation of an international economic climate which would encourage the accelerated development of the less developed countries; this would require, under the present structure of world relationships, the stimulus of economic growth in industrial countries. This is not to say that such growth in itself would resolve inequalities and narrow the gaps in production and living standards between rich and poor countries. But sustained economic growth in the industrial countries is necessary to create conditions for expanding foreign trade and also for increasing transfers of capital from the advanced to the less developed countries. Sluggish conditions in the industrial economies breed attitudes of protectionism, exclusiveness, "beggar-my-neighbor" policies, "Cartierism," and the like. There is a very strong link, documented by numerous studies, between a less developed country's capacity to import and its growth rate; this capacity to import in turn depends very largely on exports to developed countries as well as on the capital transfers received from them. However desirable the schemes of regional integration, in particular, and the development of trade between countries of the third world, in general, and however convincing the striving for more self reliance, these factors will not significantly reduce the interactive relation between the growth of the industrial and the less developed countries.

It is quite true of course that a number of economists have discerned some negative elements and even harmful effects in the interrelations between the growth of richer and poorer countries. They have underlined the polarization of capital and other factors of growth in already developed areas. They have stressed the damage of an indiscriminate transfer of technology unsuited for conditions in the third world, the brain drain from less developed countries, the demonstration effect of modern luxury consumption, and other problems. These are real difficulties which we encounter every day. But few economists except the more extreme advocates of complete self-reliance — who may perhaps be prompted more by ideology than by analysis — would contend that high rates of growth in the richer countries have not been immensely helpful to the poorer areas of the world and have not enabled them to maintain a rate of progress which by historical standards is remarkable. There is not at present, nor in the foreseeable future, any real substitute for interaction in growth rates, no new ethic of sharing on a worldwide basis which could suddenly replace it and could stimulate new patterns for the world community as a whole; there is therefore an intrinsic flaw in any model proposed for the present or near future which does not give this interaction a central place.

Insistence on the need for growth as a fundamental ingredient of progress does not imply acceptance of the present scheme of things. Radical changes are needed to correct the negative externalities which have accompanied economic growth in the industrial period. But the would-be stewards of the "spaceship earth" would be well advised to recognize that they will gain no real credibility in the universal political forums if they apply the concept of "benign neglect" to the imperative of development; if they remain content to give it only lip service; if they fail to incorporate it organically and meaningfully into the models they build; if they refuse to recognize conflictual situations between various objectives; or if they rely on some form of natural harmony or invisible hand to effectuate the necessary reconciliations.

It is quite typical of the primitive state of knowledge and conceptualization that so many brilliant minds, because of their anxieties and irritations about pollution of the biosphere, because of their fear of exhaustion of natural resources, because of their yearning for less congested cities, clean rivers, and a more contemplative life, seem to be espousing with so much alacrity the concept of zero growth without fully recognizing some of the problems involved in such a choice, namely, the radical changes amounting to a cultural mutation which it would entail. It is quite puzzling to find among the promoters of this school of thought groups with a progressive ideology, with an acute sense for the injustice and immorality of the world. But it must be said that they show — at times — considerable provincialism in pursuing this trend of thought in the face of the effects which its application would have on the impoverished and disinherited of this planet.

One can, of course, take refuge in utopias. Utopias are mushrooming today as in most eras of rapid change. Utopias can be quite useful, and we can learn something of how they work by reverting to the experience of the past, notably the first half of the nineteenth century in France. There were utopias of the "greening," "golden-age" type, telescoping the process of cultural change which their ideals postulated; for example, there was the utopia of Francois Fourrier who hinted at women's liberation and advocated unbridled sexual freedom. There were utopias of the functional or technocratic type, such as that of Claude Saint-Simon and his republic of bankers. Both types were forerunners of socialism, but, since they overlooked the organization of power, they never really provided the emerging working class with an ideology designed to help it find a place in society. On the contrary, they probably were instrumental in promoting the advent of capitalistic industrial society. Karl Marx, on the other hand, precisely because he focused on the structure of power as well as on the inevitable historic sequences inherent in cultural patterns, did provide the working class with an ideological instrument, one so powerful that for many people it retains today a nostalgic appeal even though the circumstances which gave birth to it have been radically altered.

V.

We stand very far from an integrated thinking on global matters which could be the basis of international decisions in regard to the "spaceship earth." The need to fill this gap is urgent. Planning for linear progress was difficult enough, but planning for the complex systems of tomorrow will present more technical as well as political problems. The UN has as yet only a minimum of coordinating power, but it is already a very useful, indeed unique, center for collective reflection. The need for research and education created by the notion of the "spaceship earth" is enormous, and it is not suggested that the organization should assume the whole burden of it. The convergence of efforts of universities, research agencies, individuals, and think tanks is needed. A new intellectual movement analogous to the eighteenth-century encyclopedists adapted to the modern ways of research and teaching must emerge. But ultimately the consensus must emerge in the United Nations for this is the only place where "globalism" would be politically plausible. The organization should rapidly develop its own instrumentality for evaluation, prediction, and stimulation of thinking as these processes relate to the "spaceship earth."[1]

In fact a rapid development of thinking and knowledge is a prerequisite to even the most elementary new planning. At present "spaceship earth" has all the appeal of a new catchword and also

[1] Interesting proposals were heard in this respect at a symposium on human survival held at the United Nations headquarters which are now being followed in the United Nations Institute for Training and Research (UNITAR).

much of the vacuity implied in such a phrase. There is no real basis for the emergence of a consensus. Since so much, especially of that which human beings consider to be worthy and good, is predicated on economic growth, it is essential that scientists come to an early agreement on the matters which will affect the debate on the "steady state" idea. There is no agreement between scientists on the capacity of the biosphere, nor is it easy to make a clear distinction between the real hazards to health and those aspects of an aesthetic or hedonistic nature which no doubt cover quite legitimate aspirations but which have to be seen in relation to other, often more compelling, imperatives. It is essential also that economists throw more light on the costs and benefits of alternative courses so that choices may be made with a better knowledge of the economic parameters involved. When these investigations develop, it will probably be found that quite a number of the problems which are highlighted today can be viewed in terms of tradeoffs rather than in terms of collision courses, in terms of planetary priorities rather than in terms of human survival. It may also be found that technology, though often maligned, has a capacity for finding new, cleaner ways of doing things.

In one area highly relevant to these problems the UN has already been a pioneer. Population is obviously one of the crucial parameters in global planning. Most students of the problem would contend that in the long run zero population growth (as distinct from zero economic growth) is the only acceptable hypothesis, and they would also agree that this point of equilibrium is not likely to be reached by the end of the century. There is perhaps a slight chance that the population growth rate will decline faster than the projections imply; this depends on a number of factors including the effectiveness of policy measures now being planned or implemented. But the stark outlook is the high probability that the population of less developed countries will double during the next 30 years. Even this estimate is based on a 27 percent decline of fertility rates, equivalent to a reduction in the gross reproduction rate from 2.7 to 1.7, or from a family size of over five children to under 3.5 children. The point of near equilibrium in population growth, namely 0.3 percent, might come, with a total world population of 9.7 billion, in the year 2070 for less developed countries and, of course, earlier for other states. These projections help in narrowing the range within which thought about the future must take place and societal changes will have to occur for the new age pyramid resulting from equilibrium or near equilibrium in population will require considerable changes in the pattern of social organization as well as of individual behavior. Such matters as old-age care, the organization of leisure, the very notion of work or of education, and the role of young people would have to be viewed in a completely new light. Time of course will be an important element in facilitating the needed adjustments, but any estimate would suggest that these adjustments would have to be drastic. These elements should from now on be more intensely analyzed.

Forecasting is far less advanced in the field of natural resources in which some experts predict early exhaustion of supplies. Experts in the United Nations would dispute assumptions made in this respect, except in the case of water supplies. They believe that technology has developed to a point at which vast amounts of minerals as well as new sources of energy such as geothermy will be discovered; they suggest that such developments, together will alterations in price structures and appropriate recycling, would take care of impending shortages. But these arguments do not as yet carry the degree of conviction which would be necessary for a consensus on these lines to emerge. Vast investigations and presumably even some continuing system of surveying and forecasting would be required. Some measure of planning and of forecasting may become necessary in the not-too-distant future on grounds of overabundance rather than depletion; this would be the case if the vast resources of the seabeds are going to be exploited under an international authority. The establishment of such an authority is in itself a difficult matter because of the problem of trying to place limits on national sovereignty. Exploitation of seabed resources, such as manganese, might seriously upset international markets. The proximity of areas in which exploitation will be determined by a central entity and of areas subject to national sovereignty will raise problems of equilibrium, equity, organization of markets, and protection of existing interests which will call for some type of conscious planning process.

The present concern for the environment will be the most immediate challenge to the planning capacity of the UN system. Monitoring, early warning, and regulations will have to be established. It is not yet very clear how these matters will ultimately be settled. New institutional arrangements, perhaps modest initially, will no doubt be required if the totality of the problem is to be kept in perspective and related to other problems. It is not certain that this will emerge even from the United Nations Conference on the Human Environment, to be held in Stockholm in 1972, because a sufficient conceptual consensus may be lacking. One of the great difficulties is that under the pressure of public opinion in certain countries governments have to act rapidly, sometimes through measures which might be difficult to reverse, when it might be better to seek action on a multinational and carefully planned basis. It will take a great deal of persuasion to fix standards on an international or even on a regional basis. The cooperation of the less developed countries is very necessary and is likely to be forthcoming in spite of initial resistance. There is a need for these countries to anticipate and prevent the deterioration of their environment; this requires a realization that prevention rests above all on careful planning and may not be costly. Moreover, international regulations, if well conceived, might turn to the advantage of the less developed countries by encouraging decentralization of industries to new places where the environmental requirements may be less drastic. But above all, these countries should realize that some forms of standards and regulations will be established in one context or another and that they should not pass up the chance to influence the establishment of a reasonable pattern under United Nations auspices. The existence of complex, ambivalent systems resulting from technological developments now confronting the international community cannot be wished away just because we have previously believed in the concept of linear progress.

VI.

The intrusion of ecological considerations into the United Nations presents a great challenge — and opportunity — which should gradually lead to a meaningful discussion of planetary priorities on the basis of human needs, thereby giving "globalism" its full operational meaning. Such discussion — and with it the possibility of conflict between development and environment — would presumably reveal the necessity of introducing some form of international cooperation and coordination for the control of technological development on the basis of some international assessment. It is finally becoming apparent that too rapid a pace of technological innovation involves enormous waste due to early obsolescence, regardless of the damage to the environment, and that it will at some point be necessary to come to an understanding about an optimum path of technological progress. We already find ourselves speculating somewhat nostalgically that the task of development in the third world would have been much easier within the context of more gradual technological change. But the traumatic experience of the supersonic transport, and more generally of the aerospace industry, marks a turning point in this respect, revealing crudely the inadequacies of a decisionmaking process which is not adapted to the present phase of advanced technology. Joint multinational planning rather than international competition, particularly when the latter involves such a strong and unhealthy element of national prestige, is called for in projects in which huge investments in research and equipment as well as masses of highly skilled manpower are required. The supersonic transport was canceled in the United States on the grounds that it constituted an environmental threat. What is involved is not simply a question of whether a particular technological development should be put to use; rather, the whole process by which such decisions are reached is on trial. Gross waste is sure to occur if technological innovations develop autonomously, stimulating private enterprise and almost forcing public authorities to subsidize them on the basis of necessarily vague cost-benefit calculations without any appropriate ecological assessment or reference to human needs. International competition, even peaceful, in certain of the most advanced areas of technology is thwarting, not helping, efforts to discover a true order of priorities related to human needs. Gross waste of resources should be as potent a motivation for central planning as the protection of the environment. The recognition of the value of international cooperation in certain technological endeavors as a substitute for international competition is one of the motives which underlie the link established in the UN between disarmament and development, an idea which unfortunately has not gone beyond the stage of studies. United States President John F. Kennedy had sensed the need for such cooperation when he suggested in 1961 at the United Nations that the space efforts of the United States and the Union of Soviet Socialist Republics should be pooled. Yet, when in 1969 the first astronauts landed on the moon at the very time when the UN Economic and Social Council (ECOSOC) was holding its summer session, the only effect felt in the council was a moment of collective pride and intense emotion. No resolution was proposed indicating that this historic event and the cost of it had to be viewed in a perspective wider than that of an act of human and technological prowess.

The United Nations Advisory Committee on the Application of Science and Technology to Development has attempted to relate technological development to human needs and has produced a plan of action, a minimum program to redress some of the imbalances resulting from the development of modern technology. But it was not given the mandate to look into the wider problem of controlling technology through international coordination. This has still to be developed at the conceptual level.

It is highly encouraging that the United States and the Soviet Union are already exchanging information on some aspects of nuclear fusion and space technology. The astronomical cost of research should lead them much further on that path. The pooling under some joint or international organ of at least part of the resources devoted to advanced technology could help in orienting research and development toward the most useful endeavors and in permitting many countries to participate in it. The major technological powers may at this stage hesitate to vest such responsibility in the UN. The process of agreement may have to be pursued elsewhere. But the organization has a natural vocation to contribute to the creation of a new value base which would gradually command the allegiance of the world community, including that of the technological superpowers.

The problem is of course that a proper methodology is not really at hand for the establishment of a value base, a system of planetary priorities corresponding to the hierarchy of human needs, in a world in which the marketplace has become inadequate to indicate a true schedule of preferences. New methods of ascertaining preferences and of highlighting human needs, particularly in relation to the so-called external economies, would have to be thought out and developed on a very large scale. Experiments to this effect have not been attempted beyond the municipal framework; they may, nevertheless, show the way to some of the processes which could help our "global village" to make a better use of its vast resources.

Given the present stage of our knowledge, the conceptual uncertainties and the lack of intellectual consensus, the imbalances in the distribution of power in the world, and the potentialities and weaknesses of the only institutional system capable of handling the minimum of global planning which circumstances require, the advent of a globalist philosophy within the United Nations cannot be taken for granted. But without such a philosophy new or modified institutional arrangements will not be operative. This point is often missed by the advocates of reform.

The situation is different from what it was twenty years ago when a strong majority of new states pushed the problem of development to the forefront of the world stage and formulated an ideology to which other countries could hardly object. One should welcome this interest in global problems. The new philosophy and its institutional implications may help even at this stage combat the incipient signs of sclerosis discernible in the United Nations system, such as an inability to mobilize new resources, the concept of budget stabilization which is accepted as a revealed truth, resistance — hidden under tranquilizing statements — to embarking on adaptive changes required by new pluridisciplinary problems, and above all a certain lack of thirst for knowledge and discovery. But if some of the major implications of the new concept are to be implemented, including those related to the environment, the whole United Nations system should be seen to move more rapidly in certain directions.

First, the unfinished tasks of implementation and adaptation of the development strategy should show rapid, even spectacular, progress. This should have been the business of the 1960s. Unless the strategy for DDII becomes operational as a normative as well as an adaptive system and is rapidly translated into a number of individual and collective decisions, as well as a heightened sense of accountability on the part of all concerned, it will be difficult to elicit fully from the vast majority of governments the interest needed for the planning of new and difficult tasks. An evolution must also be registered in the real distribution and exercise of power within the United Nations. The organization must be seen to be moving toward more international democracy. Acceptance and effectiveness of planning are predicated on a minimum of democratic participation. Against the background of formal equality in the voting process a large number of countries today feel frustrated in their desire to participate in the most important decisions. There is also a degree to which democracy is indivisible. Everybody recognizes the special responsibilities of certain powers in the peacekeeping process, and it is also accepted that coordination of decisions cannot always take place on a worldwide basis. The charter as well as the procedures and machinery established in the early days of the UN in fact cover such problem in many subtle ways. But it is not always the most democratic interpretation of charter provisions that prevails.

From its awareness of pervasive and major inequalities in economic, social, and power status the United Nations has derived a powerful impulse to act. This sense of inequalities should not be allowed to dissolve in a planetary perspective which would not bring them out with sufficient clarity. Such a risk can be avoided if the UN itself assumes a responsibility at an early stage for the shaping of the new philosophy, as it did in the case of development. Globalism will take the United Nations to as yet uncharted territories of greater coordinating power necessary in order to arbitrate planetary priorities, negotiate the tradeoffs, and devise the regulations. Some may feel that this is beyond its strength. One should rather reason that from the exercise of these new functions, however timid or clumsy at the beginning, the organization might gain considerable impetus which would redound on the implementation of its other tasks, political, economic, and humanitarian. Such a development will enhance the acceptance of collective international decisionmaking as a natural method of handling human affairs and promote its extension to ever-widening areas.

THE UNITED NATIONS AND COLONIALISM:
A TENTATIVE APPRAISAL

Harold Karan Jacobson

I.

Colonialism, at least as it is generally defined in the United Nations as Western rule of non-metropolitan areas, is rapidly being brought to a close. As a consequence, within a few years some of the activities of the United Nations will be reduced to almost insignificant proportions. Seven of the eleven territories that were once included within the trusteeship system have already achieved self-government or independence,[1] and another, Ruanda-Urundi, will soon attain that goal. Unless new territories are added, only Nauru, New Guinea, and the Pacific Islands will remain under trusteeship. The list of territories which according to the General Assembly are subject to the provisions of Chapter XI of the Charter has not been cut as drastically, but in terms of the number of people involved, the reduction is equally impressive. Even with the high rate of population growth and the addition of the Spanish and Portuguese dependencies, the number of people living in such areas is about one-fifth of the 1946 figure of 215,000,000. With a few important exceptions such as Kenya, Uganda, Nyasaland and the Rhodesias,

and Angola and Mozambique, the territories which in the UN's view "have not yet attained a full measure of self-government" are small and have populations of less than one million. It has already been recommended that the future of the Department of Trusteeship and Information from Non-Self-Governing Territories[2] and the possibility of allocating its duties to other departments be reviewed in the light of these developments. Although colonial disputes will probably continue to occupy prominent places on the agendas of the Security Council and the General Assembly for a time, the number of possible controversies of this nature is quickly diminishing. On the other hand, the passing of colonialism has also confronted the United Nations with new problems and tasks, as the Congo dramatically illustrates. Thus, an important chapter in the history of international organization is almost concluded, while another is just beginning.

It may be an appropriate time therefore to attempt a tentative appraisal of the work of the United Nations with regard to colonialism: to consider the manner in which the UN has performed its tasks

Harold Karan Jacobson is Associate Professor of Political Science and Research Associate in the Law School at the University of Michigan. The author began to examine this topic while he was the World Affairs Center Fellow, and subsequently received assistance from the Rockefeller Foundation to support his work.

From Volume 16, No. 1 (1962), pp. 37–56.

[1] British Togoland elected to join Ghana, which became independent in 1957. The French Cameroons, French Togoland, and Italian Somaliland

attained independence in 1960. The trusteeship for the British Cameroons was terminated in 1961 when the Northern Cameroons became part of the Federation of Nigeria on June 1 and the Southern Cameroons joined the Republic of Cameroun on October 1. Tanganyika became independent December 9, 1961. Western Samoa gained that status January 1, 1962.

[2] See the report of the Committee of Experts on the Activities and Organization of the Secretariat: Document A/4776, p. 61–62.

and to ponder the effects of its actions. Since there is a definite connection between earlier events and some of the problems of the post-colonial era, an analysis of the UN's work in this field must necessarily extend beyond the actual period of colonial rule; to a limited extent a review of the last chapter must also include a preview of the next.

II.

Before examining the substantive aspects of the UN's activities with regard to colonialism, it may be useful to consider the institutional and political framework within which these activities have been carried on. From reading the Charter, one might expect that most of these functions would have been conducted within the Trusteeship Council, and, in the case of colonial disputes, within the Security Council. This has not been the case. The General Assembly, for reasons which are common to nearly all aspects of the UN's work and others which are especially related to this field, has overshadowed both organs. The Assembly has set up its own subordinate bodies to deal with colonial problems: the Committee on Information from Non-Self-Governing Territories and the Committee on South West Africa. It has belabored the Trusteeship Council and has in a sense reversed some of that organ's decisions and recommendations. It has considered colonial disputes which the Security Council has refused to view and has acted when that body would not.

Since the broad reasons for the development and enhancement of the General Assembly's role are well known, we need only consider those which are especially related to colonial problems. Here, the basic reason for the Assembly's becoming the most important center of activity is that the advocates of change—the side really interested in involving the UN—have been in a stronger position in this body. Mustering support for anticolonial actions has always been easier in the Assembly than in either the Trusteeship Council or the Security Council. In terms of the UN's total membership, the colonial powers have constantly been overrepresented on the two Councils, and as the membership has grown, so has the disparity between the political composition of these organs and the Assembly. Moreover, the two most important colonial powers have held veto rights in the Security Council, and while they have seldom used this privilege, it no doubt has had a deterrent effect. Another important factor, given the nature of the power of the United Nations, is that the Assembly has been more productive of world headlines and a world-wide audience.

There are also other explanations for the Assembly's prominence. Had South West Africa been put under trusteeship, the Assembly probably would not have become so deeply and persistently involved in that question. Had the colonial powers given meaning to the provisions of Article 77c of the Charter by voluntarily putting some of their colonies under trusteeship, the pressure to develop the Committee on Information might not have been so great. To be sure, the movement to develop Chapter XI began before it was certain that this sub-paragraph would be a dead letter, and it would have been a potent force as long as any dependent territories remained outside of the trusteeship system. Perhaps few, if any, seriously expected that the colonial powers would make extensive use of Article 77c. As it was, however, the anticolonial forces could take the position, trenchantly expressed by the study group which analyzed India's role in the UN, that:

> . . . the division of dependent areas into non-self-governing territories and trust territories was merely an accident of history; the former were the possessions of the victors of the two world wars and the latter those of the defeated.[3]

This attitude nourished the already existent desire to provide the same degree of international supervision for both types of territories.

Nor would one gain a sense of the importance of the Secretariat in this phase of the United Nations work from reading the Charter. Nevertheless, in routine matters, although not in crises, the Secretariat has been extremely influential. The Secretariat's expert knowledge concerning some of the more technical issues in the colonial field has caused many delegates to rely heavily on it as a source of advice. They have also been willing to allow it considerable discretion in handling day-to-day colonial issues. Moreover, the UN's procedures for dealing with such matters have enhanced the Secretariat's influence. Reports have figured prominently in this phase of the UN's work. Members of the Secretariat usually draft these reports, and then the delegates amend and approve them. When the pressure of time is great and little national staff assistance is available, as in the case of visiting missions, the power to draft verges on the power to commit. By and large, the Secretariat's

influence has benefited the anticolonial forces. For one thing, although the Secretariat's knowledge has been available to all, it has been more useful to these delegations, for their national staffs could hardly match those of the colonial powers. More importantly, the sympathies of the UN Secretariat appear generally to have tended in this direction.

Turning from international institutions to states, we find that both major protagonists in the Cold War have played distinctive roles in the UN's activities concerning colonialism.

Many commentators have attributed an obstreperous and obstructive quality to the Soviet Union's participation in this phase of the UN's work.[4] Without question the USSR and the Soviet bloc have been the most outspoken critics of colonialism in the United Nations. Vyacheslav M. Molotov, in a press conference at San Francisco, gave a forecast of this when he stated: "We must first of all see to it that dependent territories are enabled as soon as possible to take the path of national independence."[5] Soviet policy has not deviated from this line; it has granted the colonial powers no quarter.

One effect of this has been to encourage the development of more extreme positions on both sides and thus to constrict the possibilities of agreement. In this sense, the adjective "obstructive" can accurately be applied to the USSR's conduct. Soviet behavior has had a demonstrably inflationary effect on the actions of the anticolonial forces.[6] Extreme Soviet proposals could

[3] *India and the United Nations* (New York: Manhattan, 1957), p. 101.
[4] See for example: Annette Baker Fox, "International Organization for Colonial Development," *World Politics,* April 1951 (Vol. 3, No. 3), p. 340–368, p. 353–354; and, Sherman S. Hayden, "The Trusteeship Council: Its First Three Years," *Political Science Quarterly,* June 1951 (Vol. 66, No. 2), p. 226–247, p. 229–230.

[5] *New York Times,* May 8, 1945.
[6] For a few examples see Elliot R. Goodman, "The Cry of National Liberation: Recent Soviet Attitudes Toward National Self-Determination," *International Organization,* Winter 1960 (Vol. 14, No. 1), p. 92–106.

not be ignored. The advocates of change have been forced either to support them, or to introduce alternative proposals. Then too, the Soviet bloc has usually supported anticolonial initiatives made by others. Western commentators have sometimes characterized this Soviet support as a "mixed blessing," but the record gives little indication that the beneficiaries have been seriously bothered. To the contrary, in parliamentary situations support is generally welcomed, regardless of the source, and by taking the most extreme positions, the USSR has allowed others to appear fairly moderate in comparison. On the other side, the colonial powers have recoiled before the Soviet accusations, becoming more and more defensive and less willing to submit their colonial affairs to international scrutiny. One unfortunate consequence of all this has been the occasional tendency of the administering authorities summarily to dismiss as propaganda any criticism voiced by the USSR. As a result, valid points have sometimes been obscured.

Viewed in a somewhat different perspective, it is striking how little the Soviet bloc has been involved in the UN's activities relating to colonialism. By virtue of Article 86 the USSR has always held a

seat on the Trusteeship Council, but no member of the Soviet bloc has ever been elected to this organ. The Soviet Union has always been a member of the Standing Committee on Petitions, but beyond that it has held few positions on the Trusteeship Council's subsidiary organs. No Soviet national has ever been a member of a visiting mission or of a plebiscite or election inspection team.[7] Soviet bloc representation on the body now known as the Committee on Information has been limited to the membership of the USSR from 1946 through 1952.[8] No member of the Soviet bloc has ever been a member of the Committee on South West Africa or of any of the *ad hoc* bodies concerned with this territory. One of the most important factors in the decisions concerning the Italian colonies was a desire to preclude Soviet influence. The Soviet bloc (although not Yugoslavia after its break with the bloc) has been excluded from all of the committees and commissions which have been established to deal with colonial disputes. Despite its determined efforts, the USSR was unable to gain a seat on the Economic Commission for Africa (ECA), a body of potential importance for the immediate post-colonial era.[9]

[7] On the one occasion when the question of the USSR's participating in a visiting mission was formally raised, the Soviet representative immediately replied that "his delegation would be unable to take part . . . " (Trusteeship Council *Official Records* [5th session], p. 257). The discussion occurred in July 1949. It concerned the composition of the mission which would visit the trust territories in the Pacific in the late spring and early summer of 1950.

[8] In the 1952 election the USSR was defeated by China, 27–24, on the second ballot. In 1955 China won a place over the USSR again, this time on the first ballot. Three years later, the Soviet Union again seriously offered its candidacy, but withdrew at the last moment in favor of Ghana so as not to split the vote against China. Tactically the move was successful as China was not elected.

[9] The Sudanese draft resolution defining the terms of reference of the Economic Commission

for Africa (Document E/L.780 and Rev.1) gave membership to both the United States and the USSR. The African states which were then in the UN strongly supported this provision. The USSR was eager to serve on the Commission. The United States, however, argued that membership on the Commission should be limited to the states of Africa and the relevant metropolitan powers. The Council finally rejected the paragraph in question by a vote of 5 (Indonesia, Poland, Sudan, USSR, and Yugoslavia) to 12 (Brazil, Canada, Chile, China, Costa Rica, France, Greece, Mexico, Netherlands, Pakistan, United Kingdom, and the United States) with one abstention (Finland) (ECOSOC *Official Records* [25th session], p. 86). ECOSOC Resolution 671 (XXV) April 29, 1958, provides that membership on the Commission is open to independent states in Africa and to states which have responsibilities for territories in Africa as long as these responsibilities continue.

These facts give some point to the Soviet Union's insistence at San Francisco that the Charter should require that the five Great Powers be represented on the Trusteeship Council. Indeed, it might be argued that one of the central themes running through all of the activities of the United Nations with regard to colonialism has been an attempt to minimize possibilities for Soviet influence in the process of decolonization and to exclude the USSR from the colonial settlement. Sometimes this has been done under the guise of keeping the Cold War out. It should be remembered, however, that excluding the two major protagonists, as in ECA or the United Nations Emergency Force, or even the members of the two alliance systems, does not necessarily exclude Western influence. Interestingly, hardly any noncommunist states have objected to the Soviet bloc's exclusion, except in the case of the Economic Commission for Africa.

These comments are not made to pass judgment on the justice of the situation. The Soviet bloc generally did not have historical interests in or connections with the areas which were the object of this aspect of the UN's work. From the point of view of the West, there have been sufficient reasons for excluding the USSR and its allies. Nor are these comments intended to indicate that the USSR's participation has been unimportant or without influence. Their purpose is merely to delineate more precisely the impact of Soviet policy.

In contrast to the USSR, the United

States has been deeply involved in most aspects of the UN's work concerning colonialism, and it has been extremely influential. The United States has occupied a key position in the Trusteeship Council and consequently has often been able to mold this body's actions. American proposals have provided the basis for much of the work of the Committee on Information. Countless General Assembly resolutions have been shaped so that they could gain American approval. In crisis situations, such as that involving Indonesia, the United States has frequently exercised a determining role.

The UN has been a useful instrument in this respect for the United States. It has provided an access to problems which might otherwise have been beyond the realm of American influence.[10] For one thing, the United States had few intrinsic reasons for becoming involved in unextraordinary developments in Africa. Furthermore, advice from an international organization is sometimes more acceptable and more effective than advice from an ally.

Of course, membership in the United Nations has also forced the United States to take stands when it might have preferred to remain silent. In short-range and tactical terms, actions in the UN obviously have often placed the United States in a difficult dilemma.[11] If the United States were to side with the anticolonial majority in the UN, it would anger the colonial powers, several of which were important allies of the United States.[12] On the other

[10] Annette Baker Fox foresaw this at an early date and urged the United States to take advantage of it. See "International Organization for Colonial Development," p. 340–341.

[11] The best treatment of the way in which the United States has met this dilemma is Robert C. Good, "The United States and the Colonial Debate," in Arnold Wolfers (ed.), *Alliance Policy in the Cold War* (Baltimore: The Johns Hopkins Press, 1959), p. 224–270.

[12] For a detailed description of several instances in which allies put pressure on the United States see Senator Wayne Morse's supplementary report to the Committee on Foreign Relations on his experiences as a delegate at the fifteenth session of the Assembly: *The United States in the United Nations: 1960—A Turning Point* (Washington, D. C.: Government Printing Office, 1961).

hand, if the United States were to support
the colonial powers, it would violate the
much vaunted American tradition of anti-
colonialism, disappoint the anticolonial
group, and leave the field open for the
Soviet Union. Moreover, the problem
which the United States has faced has not
simply been a matter of deciding which
side to support. Americans too frequently
forget that the United States is a colonial
power, of however modest proportions,
and that it has been unwilling to take
some of the actions which have been demanded by the anticolonial forces.[13] Further, at times the anticolonial pressures
have almost taken the form of a campaign
against foreign investment, which has
definitely put the United States on the
defensive. Military considerations have
also posed problems for the United States,
and it has been hesitant to support independence for territories which might not
be able to maintain internal stability or be
impervious to communist pressures. Some,
of anticolonial persuasion, regard the
United States as the foremost neocolonial
power.

Frequently the United States has sought
to resolve its dilemma through refuge in
a kind of neutralism, and the record contains a large number of American abstentions on colonial issues. However, neither
side has regarded abstention as a neutral
course, and in fact it has not been without
political significance. Among other things,
it has affected the number of votes required to achieve a majority, since according to the UN's rules of procedure, abstentions are not included within the
meaning of the phrase "Members present
and voting."

But even in these short-range terms
"the dilemma" has not been the only
aspect. The United States position as a

"progressive" administering power, which
it sometimes flaunts to the discomfort of
its allies, has had its compensations. Although being placed in the middle may
have been painful, it has also frequently
resulted in unusual opportunities to influence the outcome: for instance, in the
Indonesian and Suez crises and in the decisions relating to the Committee on Information. Whether one emphasizes the
problems which the UN has created for
the United States by its actions in this field
or the opportunities that it has offered
depends at least partially on one's estimate
of the inevitability of the changes which
have occurred in the colonial field during
the past two decades.

There is some justification for dividing
the remaining Members of the UN into
two groups; for putting the western European states, the older members of the
Commonwealth, Iceland, and Israel in one
category, and the Latin American, African, and Asian states (often including
Nationalist China) in another. In broad
terms, the activities of the United Nations
concerning colonialism have been characterized by a struggle of the latter group—
the anticolonial forces or the advocates of
change—against the former. On this level
the Soviet bloc must be added to the anticolonial forces, and the United States to
the West. However, a division on exactly
these lines has prevailed only occasionally,
on such issues of principle as the question
of including the right of self-determination in the draft covenants on human
rights and the passage of Resolution 637
(VII) of December 16, 1952, "The Right
of Peoples and Nations to Self-Determination." Thus, although this gross distinction may describe the tenor of the UN's
proceedings, it has little meaning beyond
that. Even on general issues the two

[13] See Harold Karan Jacobson, "Our 'Colonial' Problem in the Pacific," *Foreign Affairs*, October 1960
(Vol. 29, No. 1), p. 56–66.

groups have not been completely unified, and on more specific questions their internal divisions have been pronounced.

Within the West, the states which are, or previously were, responsible for dependent territories have formed a special subcategory. The colonial powers have often felt beleaguered in the United Nations. Several of them have charged that the United Nations has exceeded its proper jurisdiction in this sphere. As a group, they have felt that the UN has unfairly scrutinized their colonial practices in detail, while it has given much less attention to what they have considered the more serious offenses of others in different areas. They have resented criticisms of conditions in their dependent territories by delegates from states which may not have had even equal standards of economic, political, and social life. They have often regarded the UN's recommendations as utopian schemes, untempered by concern for reality.[14]

However, there have been differences among the colonial powers. The Union of South Africa, Portugal, and Belgium have been the least sympathetic to the United Nations activities concerning colonialism. The Union of South Africa has refused to place South West Africa under trusteeship. It has bitterly criticized the UN's work with regard to this territory, and on occasion has boycotted the Assembly in protest. Portugal has refused to admit that it is a colonial power and

to transmit data to the Committee on Information. Belgium ceased participating in the Committee on Information in 1953. If a continuum were drawn with these three states, in the order listed, at one extreme, moving toward the other end, an appropriate rank order would be: France, Spain, Italy, the United Kingdom, the Netherlands, Australia (after the Liberal-Country Party gained power in December 1949) and, close together, the United States, New Zealand, and Denmark. There have been occasions, though, when this ranking would not apply. For example, during the early years France submitted political information on Morocco and Tunisia as well as the required economic, educational, and social data, and from time to time France has voted for resolutions concerning non-self-governing territories which the United Kingdom opposed.

The other Western countries, particularly the Scandinavian states, Greece, Turkey, Iceland, Ireland, and Israel, have been much more willing to go along with, or at least not to oppose, the Assembly's anticolonial majority.

On the anticolonial side, there has been a basic distinction between the Latin American states and the African-Asian group. The Latin American states have usually supported and have sometimes even led the anticolonial forces. However, this group has contained a wide range of views.[15] Some Latin American states, such

[14] For a sample of this opinion see Sir Alan Burns, *In Defense of Colonies: British Territories in International Affairs* (London: George Allen and Unwin, 1956). Sir Alan served as the delegate of the United Kingdom to the Trusteeship Council for nine years and also participated in the General Assembly. Even Sir Alan's more moderate successor, Sir Andrew Cohen, has occasionally shown signs of similar feelings. See his *British Policy in Changing Africa* (Evanston: Northwestern University Press, 1959).

[15] This has been graphically illustrated by two

statistical analyses: Thomas Hovet, Jr. *Bloc Politics in the United Nations* (Cambridge: Harvard University Press, 1960), p. 141; and, Leroy N. Rieselbach, "Quantitative Techniques for Studying Voting Behavior in the UN General Assembly," *International Organization*, Spring 1960 (Vol. 14, No. 2), p. 291–306, p. 300–306. For a more detailed analysis of the position of the Latin American states see: John A. Houston, *Latin America in the United Nations* (New York: Carnegie Endowment for International Peace, 1956), p. 162–221.

as the Dominican Republic, have consistently taken positions which were very close to those of the colonial powers, while others, for example, Haiti, Mexico, and Guatemala, have been among the UN's most rabid anticolonialists. Furthermore, as a group, the Latin American states have generally been somewhat less extreme than the African-Asian group. Since they had few direct ethnic and cultural ties with the peoples of the dependent territories, and since their own colonial experiences and revolutions were different from those being considered by the UN, the anticolonialism of the Latin American states has not had quite the same emotional content as that of the African and Asian states. At times the Latin American states have even acted as if they felt closer ties with the metropolitan powers.[16] Perhaps because of their own emphasis on the doctrine of nonintervention, some Latin American states have paid greater attention than the African and Asian countries to the legal niceties which were involved in colonial issues. The Latin American states have generally been more sensitive to the Cold War implications of the UN's actions in this field and more responsive to United States leadership. Since the Latin American states were not uniformly and unalterably committed to the most extreme anticolonial position, and because of the political composition of the United Nations, this group has occupied a key role in the UN's decisions concerning colonialism. The support of some members of this group has been a virtual requirement for the adoption of any reso-

lution, and this has frequently served as a moderating influence.

Although the African-Asian group has generally taken a more extreme anticolonial position, this group has not been a solid unit either. Among the Asian states, those which have alliances with the West have often taken a somewhat less demanding stand. The African group has also been divided.[17] The relatively moderate position of several of the former French sub-Saharan territories has been well documented.

Just as many in the West have become critical of the UN's activities concerning colonialism, and some have even grown embittered, similar reactions, although with different content, have developed among the anticolonial states. On this side, the criticism is not that the United Nations has violated the terms of Article 2, paragraph 7, by intervening in essentially domestic matters, but rather that this article has illegitimately been used to frustrate the Organization and to preclude constructive action. The anticolonial forces have been as distressed about the slowness with which the United Nations has become involved in colonial disputes and the limited extent of this involvement as the colonial powers have about the fact of the UN's involvement. To those of anticolonial persuasion, Chapter XI has been "given meaning" through the activities of the Committee on Information, not "amended." This view has it that the colonial powers, rather than having magnanimously cooperated with an enterprise of dubious legality, have dragged their

[16] Latin American concern for Italy was an important ingredient in the decisions relating to the Italian colonies. The sympathy which some of these states felt for France appears to have been a major factor in the General Assembly's decision, at its sixth session in Paris in 1951, not to discuss the Moroccan dispute. In 1956 the Latin American relationship with Spain and Portugal apparently was the key factor in the General Assembly's

reinstitution of the requirement that certain categories of decisions regarding non-self-governing territories required a two-thirds majority for adoption.

[17] See the interesting analysis of the reactions of the African states to the UN's actions concerning the Congo: Robert C. Good, "Four African Views of the Congo Crisis," *Africa Report*, June 1961 (Vol. 6, No. 6), p. 3–4, 6, 12, 15.

feet and have violated the spirit, if not the letter, of Article 73 by not supporting the work of the Committee on Information more fully.

III.

The first task of the United Nations in this field was that of providing a measure of international supervision of colonial regimes. Chapters XII and XIII of the Charter gave the UN an elaborate mechanism for this work. With provision for annual reports from the administering authorities, petitions from the indigenous inhabitants, and visiting missions to the field, the system was well designed to maintain a close relationship between the World Organization and dependent territories. Its application, however, was limited to the eleven territories which were voluntarily put under trusteeship. Counting the dependencies of Portugal and Spain, there were more than eight times as many non-self-governing territories outside the trusteeship system, and they contained over ten times as many people. For these, with the exception of South West Africa which was given special treatment, the UN's machinery was the much looser and less substantial structure derived from Chapter XI.

The differences between the two principal systems have been analyzed in detail elsewhere.[18] The continual drive of the anticolonial forces to endow the Committee on Information with the attributes of the Trusteeship Council is proof that these differences exist and are significant. Granting this, it is important not to become so engrossed in the legal and formal distinctions that decisive similarities between the two systems are obscured.

Probably the most significant proce-dural difference between the two main sets of machinery has been that through the acceptance of petitions, the dispatch of visiting missions, and the attendance of special representatives from the territorial administrations at Trusteeship Council sessions, the United Nations has been able to have direct contact with the trust territories. This has not been the case with the other territories, or in UN parlance, the non-self-governing territories.

Governments are required to supply more data to the Trusteeship Council, but there is a relationship between the Council's Questionnaire and the Committee on Information's Standard Form. Although Article 73e does not require political information, five of the ten (if Portugal and Spain are included in the total list) administering powers have transmitted such data regularly. In addition, as mentioned above, France also did this for a limited time with respect to two territories, and in 1961 the United Kingdom announced that it would henceforth submit political information for all dependent territories which remained under its administration. Moreover, at one of the most important points, the termination of dependent status, the United Nations has required and obtained political data concerning non-self-governing territories.

The Committee on Information is not formally authorized to make recommendations concerning political matters, but as one delegate with strong anticolonial views put it in private conversation, "we

[18] See James N. Murray, Jr., *The United Nations Trusteeship System* (Urbana: University of Illinois Press, 1957); Emil J. Sady, "The United Nations and Dependent Peoples," in Robert E. Asher and others, *The United Nations and the Promotion of* *the General Welfare* (Washington, D. C.: The Brookings Institution, 1957), p. 815–1017; and Charmian Edwards Toussaint, *The Trusteeship System of the United Nations* (New York: Frederick A. Praeger, 1956).

have gotten around that." To some extent he was right. There is a difference between recommending that the number of unofficial representatives on the Tanganyikan Legislative Council should be increased and recommending that there should be greater participation by indigenous populations in the formulation of economic plans in non-self-governing territories, but the difference is not one of kind. Perhaps the most important distinction is in the degree of specificity. This probably accounts for the intense opposition of the colonial powers to the suggestion, which was made in 1955, that the Committee on Information should be given the right to make recommendations concerning regional groups of territories.[19]

The substantive recommendations of the Trusteeship Council and the Committee on Information have been strikingly similar. Because of its composition and method of operation the Trusteeship Council could generally only pass judgment on actions which had already been taken and adopt exhortations.[20] This is also what the Committee on Information has done, albeit in more general terms. Both bodies have advocated the same things: increased educational facilities for the indigenous inhabitants; enlarged social welfare programs with emphasis on community development; more extensive and compre-

hensive economic programs which would aim at diversification; and, greater opportunity for the indigenous inhabitants to participate in decision-making. Although the colonial powers have been asked to take steps to preserve (or discover) traditional cultural values in the dependent territories, basically the UN's recommendations have been directed toward encouraging social, economic, and political change. When the General Assembly has adopted resolutions concerning colonial practices it has underscored these themes. In the case of the trust territories the basic themes have been embroidered with such things as expressions of hope that the administering authority would take steps to develop a national consciousness in the territory under scrutiny. But at their core the recommendations concerning trust territories and non-self-governing territories have been the same.

The most salient motive force underlying the UN's recommendations seems to have been a feeling that all racial discrimination should cease and that the indigenous inhabitants of dependent territories are entitled to a position of full equality.[21] The anticolonial forces appear to have been convinced that in almost all instances logically, and as a practical matter, full equality could be achieved only through independence.

---

[19] The United Kingdom threatened to withdraw from participation in the committee if it were given this power (General Assembly *Official Records*, Fourth Committee [10th session], p. 108–109). The UK and other colonial powers have also used this threat to block proposals that the committee be given permanent status.

[20] Or as Annette Baker Fox put it: "The Trusteeship Council tends to ventilate existing practices rather than to analyze alternative solutions for problems perplexing conscientious administrators." ("International Organization for Colonial Development," p. 347.) One wonders, though, whether the administering authorities would have been willing to accept a different role for the Council.

[21] It can be expected that the anticolonial forces will continue to advance similar demands even after colonialism as such passes. The resolution that the International Labor Organization adopted in the summer of 1961, on the prompting of Nigeria, which recommended that the Union of South Africa withdraw from membership (ILO Conference, *Provisional Record*, 1961 [45th session], No. 38, p. vi. The resolution was adopted by a vote of 163 to 0, with 89 abstentions), and the actions against this country at the sixteenth session of the General Assembly are surely an indication of things to come. To the anticolonial forces, it will be a continuation of the same battle.

They have also taken the position that "good government is no substitute for self-government." Thus, most of the UN's recommendations have been aimed, directly or indirectly, at hastening the transfer of power to the indigenous inhabitants. The opponents of colonialism have rejected the thesis that certain minimum economic and social standards are a prerequisite to independence. They have buttressed their case by citing data submitted to the UN showing the slow pace of progress by dependent territories in these fields. They have argued that progress will be accelerated when the indigenous population has control. However, they have never allowed this contention to be scrutinized. After a brief attempt, the Secretariat was in effect forbidden to compare conditions in non-self-governing territories with those in neighboring independent states.[22]

It is not going too far to state that the majority in the United Nations has viewed the task of supervising colonial administrations principally in terms of bringing these regimes to a close. Nowhere is this more evident than in the long-standing and acrimonious debate concerning the establishment of intermediate and final target dates. In this sense, General Assembly Resolution 1514 (XV) of December 14, 1960, The Declaration on Colonialism, could well be read as a capstone to the UN's attempt to supervise colonial regimes.

There is little reason for believing that this conception will change with the contraction of colonialism. On the contrary, the anticolonial powers seem determined to push for the final liquidation of colonialism in the shortest possible time. With their strength augmented by the UN's new Members, they are in a better position to advance their cause. Now the African,

Asian, and Latin American states by themselves constitute a two-thirds majority. Further, the states which have been admitted to the UN since 1959 have not tempered the position of the anticolonial forces. Indeed, some of them—Mali for instance—seem to favor even more extreme stands.

Since the majority in the United Nations has taken this view, it is inappropriate to compare the work of the Trusteeship Council and the Committee on Information with that of the Permanent Mandates Commission, for the League defined its role in quite different terms. The League was chiefly concerned with improving standards of colonial rule, while the UN's aim has been to liquidate colonialism. Political bodies, like the Trusteeship Council and the Committee on Information, are probably better suited for the latter task than groups of experts, such as the Permanent Mandates Commission. The two concepts also call for different types of recommendations.

In the UN's drive to liquidate colonialism the nature of the post-colonial political regimes has largely been ignored. This has been true even with regard to trust territories where there have been no constitutional barriers to the discussion of political issues. The UN has championed a few democratic precepts, such as universal suffrage and majority rule, but in practice this has generally amounted to urging that a plebiscite should be held to accept or decide the method of terminating dependent status and to approve the successor government. Illiteracy has been held to be no barrier to the right of suffrage. Assessing the effects of the UN's attempt at supervision is difficult. In the case of the trust territories, there appear to have been a few instances when UN

[22] General Assembly Resolution 447 (V), December 12, 1950.

recommendations had a direct and immediate effect. The UN's involvement was apparently a factor in New Zealand's revision of its regime in Western Samoa in 1947.[23] To meet Council criticisms, Australia changed certain provisions in the law which provided for the administrative union of Papua and New Guinea.[24] But it is hard to find many cases in which the correlation between UN recommendation and action by the administering authority was so clear-cut.[25] More often, the UN's function, lacking all but moral sanctions, seems to have been to affect the climate of opinion: to create and support attitudes favoring change.[26] It has exposed the actions of the administering authorities and has made colonial officials more aware of the implications of their actions. Progressive forces have sometimes used the UN to buttress their case in arguing for liberal colonial policies. In these respects the World Organization has occasionally been a counterbalance to settlers and old-style imperialists. The UN has also been used as a scapegoat for actions which were unpalatable to certain groups. Finally, the UN has provided a measure of support and protection for indigenous nationalists by focusing attention upon them and by giving them a forum in which to expound their views.[27]

The UN's general proclamations concerning self-determination and its actions with regard to South West Africa and other non-self-governing territories have obviously been designed with the hope of achieving the same effects. The difference has been that in the case of the trust territories the UN has had immediate access to both colonial administrators and the indigenous population. Since the issues involved generally have not commanded wide public attention, this access has been extremely important. No doubt, this explains why the anticolonial forces have argued so persistently that the administering powers on the Committee on Information should include in their delegations representatives of the indigenous population and functional specialists.

A system of the type that the United Nations has developed for supervising colonial regimes depends for its effectiveness in large part on a fundamental agreement on values: those affected by recommendations must concede the premises on which they are based. That the UN's system has had as much success as it has reflects the fact that the anticolonial and nationalist demands were derived mainly from the intellectual tradition of the West.[28]

[23] See Lawrence S. Finkelstein, "Trusteeship in Action: The United Nations Mission to Western Samoa," *International Organization*, May 1948 (Vol. 2, No. 2), p. 268–282.

[24] See Norman Harper and David Sissons, *Australia and the United Nations* (New York: Manhattan, 1959), p. 193–196.

[25] For analyses of this issue see the Secretariat study concerning the implementation of UN recommendations concerning trust territories (Document A/1903 and Adds.1 and 2); Margaret L. Bates, "Tanganyika: The Development of a Trust Territory," *International Organization*, February 1955 (Vol. 9, No. 1), p. 32–51; and B. T. G. Chidzero, *Tanganyika and International Trusteeship* (London: Oxford University Press, 1961).

[26] See the interesting discussion of this matter in Annette Baker Fox, "The United Nations and

Colonial Development," *International Organization*, May 1950 (Vol. 4, No. 2), p. 199–218.

[27] Certainly the 1954 visiting mission to East Africa which suggested, *inter alia*, that Tanganyika should become self-governing or independent in less than 20 years (Trusteeship Council *Official Records* [15th session], Supplement No. 3, "Report on Tanganyika," p. 67–68) had a profound effect on the Tanganyika African National Union (see Thomas R. Adam, "Trusteeship and Non-Self-Governing Territories," in Clyde Eagleton and Richard N. Swift (ed.) *Annual Review of United Nations Affairs, 1955–1956* [New York: New York University Press, 1957], p. 117–140, p. 125 ff.).

[28] See Rupert Emerson, *From Empire to Nation: The Rise to Self-Assertion of Asian and African Peoples* (Cambridge: Harvard University Press, 1960).

The UN's system of supervision has also had secondary effects and by-products which so far remain largely unexplored.[29] Developments in one territory have probably affected other areas. One writer (a British official in Tanganyika) has speculated that the greatest impact of the trusteeship system "is likely to flow from its progressive disintegration."[30] So far as by-products are concerned, observers have noted that some petitioners seem to have used their opportunity to appear before the United Nations primarily to advance their political fortunes at home, and that certain states have tried to structure internal political developments in trust territories to the advantage of more or less radical forces.[31] The Soviet Union has sought to use its position on the Trusteeship Council's Standing Committee on Petitions to create the impression that it alone fully supported the demands of the downtrodden in the trust territories. One suspects that fear of neocolonialism was not the only factor which prompted Ghana and several Latin American states to press for studies of the effects of the European Economic Community on the trust and non-self-governing territories; their own commercial interests were deeply involved. Nor is it overly Machiavellian to think that some offers of scholarships and fellowships for students in dependent territories have been made in the hope that this would be a way of molding future elites. It is far from clear, however, what these efforts have achieved.

IV.

A second task of the United Nations has been that of officiating at the liquidation of colonialism. In most instances this has meant participating in the birth of states. Articles 83 and 85 of the Charter made it clear that the Organization would have this function with respect to trust territories. Article 73e has been interpreted as giving the United Nations a similar role with regard to non-self-governing territories; the majority has asserted that the UN has the right to determine whether or not a colonial power is justified in deciding to cease transmitting data concerning the economic, educational, and social conditions in a given territory. In the case of the Italian colonies, the United Nations became involved by default when the Great Powers could not agree. Finally, despite the protestations of several colonial powers, the UN has assumed a role in colonial disputes, such as those involving Indonesia, the French North African colonies, Cyprus, and Angola.

In performing this task the United Nations has first of all provided support for nationalist forces. It did this by demanding and supervising elections at crucial points in French Togoland and Ruanda-Urundi. When the Assembly decided in 1949 that Libya should become independent no later than January 1, 1952, and

[29] Among other things we know very little about the reactions of the inhabitants of dependent territories to the United Nations. The only detailed analysis of this question is: Camilla Wedgwood, "Attitudes of the Native Peoples of Papua and New Guinea to the United Nations 1945–1954," Appendix D in *Australia and the United Nations*, p. 384–400.
[30] John Fletcher-Cooke, "Some Reflections on the International Trusteeship System, With Particular Reference to its Impact on the Governments and Peoples of the Trust Territories," *International Organization*, Summer 1959 (Vol. 13, No. 3), p. 422–430, p. 430.
[31] See *ibid.*, p. 427; and Ernst B. Haas, "Dynamic Environment and Static System: Revolutionary Regimes in the United Nations" (paper read at the 1961 Convention of the American Political Science Association), note 47.

that Somaliland should also gain that status by the end of 1960, it must have given encouragement, as the French feared that it would,[32] to nationalist forces everywhere and especially in the neighboring territories. Probably these decisions relating to the former Italian colonies were among the most significant of the UN's actions in this field.

In the case of Indonesia the support was more direct and tangible. At several key points in the struggle the United Nation's role was decisive, and its influence generally redounded to the benefit of the Republicans.[33] It might be argued that the United States played the crucial role—for example, its decision to cut off Marshall Plan aid to the Netherlands East Indies and apparent willingness to go even farther had a telling effect—but it is hard to see how the United States could have become as aroused as it did or as involved as it was without the UN. The point is not that traditional forces ceased to be operative, but rather that the United Nations became an important new ingredient.

The United Nations has played the same role, although with much less intensity, in the cases of Morocco, Tunisia, Cyprus, Algeria, and Angola. Although brief, ambiguous, and sometimes innocuous resolutions may seem to be of minor importance, the strenuous efforts of both sides to influence the outcome provide evidence that at least the parties which are most immediately concerned think that

they are significant. An interesting pattern of events has developed over the years with respect to the UN's discussions of the French North African colonies. First there is increased tension and violence; next, a new French proposal for settlement; and finally, the Assembly debate. The same sequence was repeated when Cyprus was considered. Rupert Emerson explained it this way:

At least until the unlikely event of the creation of an international organization empowered to decide when and how each colony should attain self-government, the dependent peoples who receive an international hearing will usually be those who have resorted to self-help.[34]

Those who allege that action by the United Nations has complicated negotiations are in a sense correct in that UN support has probably made nationalist elements more potent and demanding. On the other hand, when the UN failed to support the nationalists, the colonial powers occasionally became more intransigent.[35] The broader point, though, is that the United Nations has provided an arena which has been used to mobilize pressure and in that way has contributed to the liquidation of colonialism.

Secondly, the United Nations has performed a validating function. UN membership has become an important symbol of national independence.[36] Each time that a new state is admitted to membership,

[32] See Peter Calvocoressi, *Survey of International Affairs, 1949–1950* (London: Oxford University Press, 1953), p. 545.

[33] See the fascinating study by Alastair M. Taylor, *Indonesian Independence and the United Nations* (Ithaca: Cornell University Press, 1960).

[34] *From Empire to Nation*, p. 399. The nationalist forces clearly recognized this. In 1952 the French censorship disclosed two letters which were allegedly written by Dr. Habib Bourguiba in 1950 (*Le Figaro*, April 7, 1952). In them Dr. Bourguiba told Mr. Abed Bouhafa, a representative of

the Arab League in the United States, among other things, that violence alone would force the United Nations to consider Tunisian affairs.

[35] France certainly acted this way in 1952. See Richard P. Stebbins, *The United States in World Affairs, 1952* (New York: Harper, 1953), p. 362.

[36] See the place accorded to it in General Assembly Resolution 742 (VIII), November 27, 1953, "Factors Which Should Be Taken Into Account in Deciding Whether a Territory Is or Is Not a Territory Whose People Have Not Yet Attained a Full Measure of Self-Government."

the World Organization acknowledges that the colonial tie has been broken. Presumably, this action also endows that state with a degree of legitimacy and enhances its status as an entity. Further, UN membership has importance for the domestic prestige of the new governing elite. In many cases this is all that the United Nations has done.

In others, however, its involvement has been more extensive. By approving the termination of the trusteeship agreements for the French Cameroons and Tanganyika, the United Nations formally sanctioned the grant of independence. In the Indonesian case, its involvement was even deeper, for the UN played a major part in shaping the settlement. It has also done this, although not to the same degree, with respect to French Togoland and Western Samoa by its supervision of plebiscites or elections which will have immediately preceded independence, and it will have performed the same role in the case of Ruanda-Urundi. With regard to Somaliland, the United Nations helped to keep a messy border situation from becoming explosive by providing a mechanism for settlement and meanwhile more or less endorsing the provisional line.

The UN's validation may have been even more important when colonial status was ended through the union of a dependent territory with an independent state. In Eritrea, British Togoland, and the British Cameroons, the UN-supervised plebiscites were essential elements in the solutions. However much one might deplore the gyrations of the Assembly in the last two instances,[37] the plebiscites did provide acceptable solutions to what otherwise might have been very troublesome issues.

The United Nations has also given its approval when a non-self-governing territory became fully integrated into the political structure of the metropolitan state. While this action with regard to Greenland and Alaska and Hawaii may not have had too much significance, it established a standard. Having granted approval, the Assembly presumably could refuse to do so in other cases. Given these precedents, the United Nations may well be in a better position to dispute the Portuguese contention that its "overseas provinces" are not non-self-governing territories.

The United Nations also gave its approval to the status of Puerto Rico and to that of Surinam and the Netherlands Antilles. But in these cases it did something beyond validating the liquidation of colonialism. Here, in the discussions of the "factors," and in the debates which occurred in 1956 and 1957 concerning the future of French Togoland, the UN began to explore ways of ending colonial rule which involved neither full independence nor full integration with an independent state. In the case of French Togoland, the United Nation's involvement was clearly a factor in the alteration of the territory's status, and the subsequent grant of full independence. The UN's action may also have had some impact on the formulation of the constitutional provisions for Surinam and the Netherlands Antilles.[38] What the UN has done in these cases is to attempt to define a new and internationally approved status to substitute for colonial rule when it was impossible to apply either of the two more obvious solutions. Such a status is not easy to construct, and the skepticism which was expressed in the debates is warranted, at

---

[37] For a detailed description of the UN's involvement in one of these cases see James S. Coleman, "Togoland," *International Conciliation*, No. 509, September 1956, p. 1–91.

[38] See Emil J. Sady, "The United Nations and Dependent Peoples," p. 914.

least in general terms if not in the cases which were discussed. On the other hand, many of the remaining dependent territories will probably require such a solution. Many of them are relatively minute and have small populations; they are hardly economically viable in modern terms. Independence, therefore, is not a realistic alternative, unless the concept is changed.[39] Nor will the metropolitan states be willing—rightly or wrongly—to integrate all of these territories into their own political structures on equal terms.

Clearly the United Nations has not progressed very far in defining this new status. The relevant part of the List of

Factors contained in General Assembly Resolution 742 (VIII) is far from an adequate set of criteria for it.[40] However, a start has been made, and the concrete cases have provided some experience with the problems of the practical application of broad principles. As the fate of the major dependent territories becomes more and more clear, it may be easier to consider this issue again in the UN. Since precedent will not be so important, the anticolonial powers may be less doctrinaire. On the other side, the colonial powers will have no ulterior motives, if they ever did have.

V.

The third task of the United Nations has consisted of providing assistance to newly independent states and facilitating their participation in the world community. This task has been regarded as a logical and necessary extension of the UN's activities concerning colonialism. One reason for this view is the awareness that the liquidation of colonialism inevitably left a void which had to be filled. Whatever its faults, colonialism performed a number of useful functions.[41] It frequently provided the motive force for processes of social, economic, and political change. It was always a source of some technical assistance, and it was often a source of financial aid as well. Colonialism provided a system for managing relation-

ships both between the dependent territories and metropolitan states and among the dependent territories themselves. Another reason is the general recognition that not all of the newly independent states have been as well prepared for their new status as might have been desirable. The nature of this third task is still evolving; much will depend on the outcome of the UN's involvement in the Congo. Although it is therefore far too early for a detailed appraisal of the UN's performance of this third task, the record of events so far is not without significance.

The United Nations has helped the newly independent states in developing their economies. In most instances, however, the Organization's greatest contribu-

---

[39] It may well be though if Western Samoa is a harbinger. Certainly independence does not mean the same thing for Western Samoa—an area with 1,130 square miles of land and a population of about 106,000—as it does for larger and more populous territories, such as Tanganyika.

[40] For example, the list mentions eligibility for UN membership as one criterion. It is hard to believe, however, that full membership would be appropriate. More thinking needs to be done along the lines of Lincoln P. Bloomfield's sugges-

tion of associate membership. See *The United Nations and U.S. Foreign Policy: A New Look at the National Interest* (Boston: Little, Brown, 1960), p. 199–200.

[41] See Rupert Emerson, *From Empire to Nation;* Max F. Millikan and Donald L. M. Blackmer, *The Emerging Nations: Their Growth and United States Policy* (Boston: Little, Brown, 1961); and Reinhold Niebuhr, *The Structure of Nations and Empires* (New York: Scribner's, 1959).

tion has not been in directly providing concrete aid; the UN has been more important as a catalytic agent. It has provided means of publicizing the needs of the newly independent states and of the less developed countries generally. It has also provided a mechanism which could be used to put pressure on the more wealthy countries. This pressure appears to have been a factor in the expansion of both multilateral and bilateral aid programs.[42] The Economic Commission for Asia and the Far East has served as a catalytic agent in a different fashion. Through its advocacy and support of the Mekong River Project it has provided an important stimulus for national development efforts and cooperative endeavors. In time, the Economic Commission for Africa may also perform this function.

The United Nations has recognized an obligation to provide concrete assistance to newly independent states. This was first done in the case of Libya in 1950. Since 1959, both the General Assembly and the Economic and Social Council (ECOSOC) have proclaimed that the UN has a special responsibility with respect to former trust territories and a more general obligation to all newly independent states.[43] ECOSOC has completed a study of the available international assistance, and both the Council and the Assembly have urged that this be supplemented. However, on the basis of results thus far, the outlook is not promising. Libya's experience gives little reason for optimism, and although the general aid programs of the UN and the specialized agencies have been enlarged in response to the process of de-

colonization, they are still greatly overshadowed by programs which are conducted bilaterally or through agencies with restricted membership. Realistically, there is little reason to expect that the liquidation of colonialism will make either the West or the Soviet bloc significantly more willing to channel their aid to underdeveloped countries through the UN and the specialized agencies. Also, the debates on the resolutions which have been adopted in the Assembly and ECOSOC indicate that if too much preference is given to newly independent states, other underdeveloped countries will certainly object.

There is, of course, one extremely important exception to these generalizations. In the Congo the United Nations has launched an unprecedented program of technical and financial assistance.[44] As of June 30, 1961, the Civilian Operations of the United Nations in the Congo had an international staff of 750. There were 100 medical specialists alone. In addition, the United Nations had granted the government of the Republic of the Congo $15,000,000 to meet its urgent requirements for foreign exchange. However, the circumstances which led to a program of this magnitude were also without parallel. Few states have been as ill-prepared for independence as the Republic of the Congo, and the situation there could easily have sparked a major conflagration. Even if an analogous case were to arise in the future, in view of the difficulties which the United Nations is having in financing its activities in the Congo, it is an open

[42] See John G. Hadwen and Johan Kaufmann, *How United Nations Decisions are Made* (Leyden: A. W. Sythoff, 1960), p. 109–111.

[43] See particularly General Assembly Resolutions 1414 (XIV) and 1415 (XIV), December 5, 1959.

[44] For general descriptions of the UN's Civilian Operations in the Congo see General Assembly *Official Records* (16th session), Supplement No. 1, "Annual Report of the Secretary-General on the Work of the Organization, 16 June 1960—15 June 1961," p. 47–51; and "Chaos Averted in the Congo," *United Nations Review*, September 1961 (Vol. 8, No. 9), p. 29–31.

question whether such extensive operations could be undertaken again.

The UN's task of aiding newly independent states has also included significant political functions. So far the UN has done three things in this realm.

First, it has played a role in the relations among the new states. The liquidation of colonialism can result in difficult and explosive situations, as it did when the British rule was ended in India and Palestine. The UN's peacekeeping activities with respect to Kashmir and the Arab-Israeli dispute are well known; presumably they could be repeated. Moreover, imperialistic desires are found not only in the West. By its actions with regard to Lebanon and Jordan, Cambodia and Thailand (the Beck-Friis mission), the Sudanese-Egyptian border, Laos, and Kuwait, the United Nations has attempted to provide security for newly independent states. The existence of the UN may well have been a deterrent in other cases. The United Nations has also facilitated contacts among the representatives of the new states. This is a significant, natural outcome of the processes of parliamentary diplomacy.

Secondly, the United Nations has played an important role in the relations between the new states and their former metropoles. The debates concerning West Irian, Suez, and the Tunisian-French imbroglios are examples. Wherever justice may lie in the controversy between Indonesia and the Netherlands over West Irian (or the Netherlands New Guinea), the UN has provided a channel for airing the

dispute peacefully. Whatever views may be in the West, the UN's role in the Suez case was widely interpreted by anticolonial forces as the frustration of an attempt to reassert colonial rule. Similarly, Tunisia has regarded its appeals to the UN as efforts to protect its sovereignty. It can be expected that the new states will continue to attempt to enlist the assistance of the United Nations in cases of this nature. Given the almost paranoic fear of neo-colonialism in many of the newly independent states, the colonial powers might find it useful to involve the UN frequently in their relationships with their former dependencies.

Finally, in the Congo, the UN's role has been to buttress the internal structure of the state and to bring some stability to a chaotic political situation.[45] Although it is impossible to tell how successful this endeavor will ultimately be, even the achievements so far are significant. However, the difficulties involved in the UN's playing this role are also apparent. Efforts to achieve internal stability cannot be neutral, for they inevitably have far-reaching domestic and international consequences. Moreover, since the United Nations was created with international disputes primarily in mind, it has been difficult to define the basis for the Organization's actions in the Congo. Initially, there appears to have been some hope that such Western concepts as federalism and parliamentary rule would provide helpful guidelines for the UN's operations,[46] but the inapplicability of these principles soon became apparent. Thus far the United Nations has

[45] See Inis L. Claude, Jr., "The United Nations and the Use of Force," *International Conciliation*, No. 532, March 1961, p. 325–384, p. 376–379; and John Holmes, "The United Nations in the Congo," *International Journal*, Winter 1960–61 (Vol. 16, No. 1), p. 1–16. For a discussion of some of the legal aspects of the UN's playing this role see E. M. Miller, "Legal Aspects of the United

Nations Action in the Congo," *The American Journal of International Law*, January 1961 (Vol. 55, No. 1), p. 1–28.

[46] See especially Document S/4417, "Second Report by the Secretary-General on the Implementation of Security Council Resolutions S/4387 of 14 July 1960 and S/4405 of 22 July 1960."

successfully surmounted these obstacles, and hopefully, it will continue to do so. It would be rash, however, to expect that the UN could again easily undertake political responsibilities similar to those which it has assumed in the Congo.

The record is mixed, but it indicates that serious attempts have been made in the United Nations to deal with many of the problems of the post-colonial era, and at this stage, a summing up would show relative success in several areas.

VI.

Evaluations of the activities of the United Nations with regard to colonialism will vary, depending as they do on personal values. Final judgments will be impossible until the outcome of events still in process is clearly known. Nevertheless, some conclusions can be stated without entering the debate over the merits of the UN's role and without going beyond the bounds imposed by the available evidence.

It is clear that the UN's part in the revolution which has occurred in the colonial system in the last two decades was modest. Many of the most important motive forces were at work before the Organization was established. The British Parliament adopted the Colonial Development and Welfare Act in 1940, and the independence movement in such places as the Indian subcontinent and Indonesia was already under way by the end of the Second World War. Even after it was established, the UN played no part in some important developments concerning colonialism—for instance the settlement in Indo-China—and was only peripherally involved in others.

It is equally evident, though, that the United Nations has contributed to raising standards of colonial rule and to hastening the liquidation of colonialism. For various reasons, the UN was constitutionally

committed to become involved in the struggle.[47] Once engaged, it inevitably altered the balance of forces and thereby affected the outcome. On balance, the colonial revolution has probably been more peaceful because of the UN's involvement. A case can also be made to the effect that the UN has contributed to international stability through its activities at the time of the accession of dependent territories to self-government or independence and in the post-colonial era. It would be going too far to state that the United Nations has provided adequate substitutes for the colonial system or that it has devised wholly effective measures for bringing what some have termed "teen-age states" to responsible maturity, but the Organization has made significant progress in these areas.

Establishing a connection between the activities of the United Nations and the nature of the emerging states is more difficult. The UN has generally favored modernizing over traditional elements. It has upheld the goal of racial equality and advanced the concept of the plebiscite, but beyond that it has done little to implant concepts of democratic rule. This is understandable. There is certainly no agreement among the UN's Member States that democracy as practiced in the West is the most desirable form of government. More-

[47] See Inis L. Claude, Jr., *Swords into Plowshares: The Problems and Progress of International Organization* (New York: Random House, 1959, 2d ed.), p. 341–371; and, Ernst B. Haas, "The Attempts to Terminate Colonialism: Acceptance of the United Nations Trusteeship System," *International Organization,* February 1953 (Vol. 7, No. 1), p. 1–21.

over, democratic concepts (again as understood in the West) may have little applicability in primitive contexts where
national unity is not even established.[48]

Some scholars and statesmen have de-
cried the fact that in its activities concerning colonialism, the United Nations has
been more an arena for combat than a
focal point for international cooperation.
Perhaps this view overstates the facts. But
even if the allegation were correct, it
would not necessarily be a cause for despair. Peaceful cooperation requires consensus, which was clearly lacking in this
case. Any observer of the San Francisco
proceedings could see the deep dichotomy
between the views expressed by Lord
Cranborne of the United Kingdom on one
side and those voiced by Fadhil Al-Jamali
of Iraq, Carlos Romulo of the Philippines, and Professor Awad of Egypt on
the other.[49] Lord Cranborne argued the
necessity of empire; he maintained that
liberty could not have been preserved in

the Second World War without it. He
regarded independence as an appropriate
goal for only a few territories, and even
for these, he felt that it was a distant
objective. To the others, imperialism was
an evil which should be terminated with
haste. In their view, the best solution,
almost without exception, was national independence. What is significant is the
extent to which such a deep and important
struggle has been carried on within an
international organization.

From the perspective of those of anticolonial persuasion and of those whose
prime interest is the achievement of a
combination of international stability and
orderly processes of change—including
most Americans—the results of the UN's
involvement in this struggle have generally been beneficial. In the end, probably
even many of the colonialist critics of the
United Nations will admit that the outcome was in their best long-run interests.

---

[48] See Rupert Emerson, *From Empire to Nation*,
p. 272–292; and Max F. Millikan and Donald
L. M. Blackmer, *The Emerging Nations*, p. 68–90.

[49] UNCIO *Documents* (Vol. 8), p. 143–146 (see
also the milder revision, p. 155–159), 133–134,
137–142, and 147–149 respectively.

The Politics of Decolonization:

The New Nations and the United Nations Political Process

DAVID A. KAY

I

THE fifteenth session of the General Assembly of the United Nations which convened in New York in September 1960 marked an important turning point in the history of the Organization. The United Nations had been created primarily through the efforts of states with a European or European-derived political and social culture possessing a common history of political involvement at the international level. During its first ten years the Organization was dominated by the problems and conflicts of these same states. However, by 1955 the process of decolonization which has marked the post-1945 political arena began to be reflected in the membership of the United Nations. In the ten years preceding the end of 1955 ten new nations devoid of experience in the contemporary international arena and struggling with the multitudinous problems of fashioning coherent national entities in the face of both internal and external pressures joined the Organization. By 1960 the rising tide of decolonization had reached flood crest with the entry in that one year of seventeen new Members—sixteen of which were from Africa.

The growth in the proportion of Members which have achieved independence since 1945 is impressive. Whereas in 1955 only 13.2 percent of United Nations Members fell in this category, by the end of 1966 this figure had leaped to 45 percent. Equally important in terms of their impact on the Organization was the fact that the size of the influx of new nations in 1960-1961 was largely unexpected as late as 1958.[1]

DAVID A. KAY is Assistant Professor in the Department of Political Science, University of Wisconsin, Madison, Wisconsin.

From Volume 21, No. 4 (1967), pp. 786–811.

[1] The movement towards self-government in Africa proceeded much more quickly during 1960

Despite all the discernible distinctions between the new nations—and there are many—they possess a common core of characteristics that vitally affects their participation in the United Nations' political process. These new nations are generally ex-colonial, nonwhite—in the 1960 influx predominantly black—and possessed of a compelling desire to eradicate speedily the remaining bastions of European colonialism. Closely associated with their demands for an end to colonialism is their personal commitment to eradicating that variant of racialism which maintains white superiority over black. In terms of social and economic criteria many sectors of their societies are premodern, a fact that is only thinly disguised by the polite diplomatic euphemism "developing countries" which is currently in vogue to describe this aspect of their condition. In terms of the lodestar of post-1945 international relations, the East-West conflict, the preponderant majority of these new nations, with varying degrees of consistency, attempt to follow the lesson of the African proverb, "when two elephants fight, it is the grass that suffers."[2]

II

In the hierarchy of priorities of the new nations no issue exceeds in importance their commitment to securing a speedy and complete end of Western colonialism. While their drive in the United Nations to advance this goal is certainly less important to its achievement than the underlying surge of nationalism in Africa and Asia, it has been the central focus of the diplomacy of the new Members in the United Nations. This study sets out to examine the United Nations' political process from the point of view of the demands in the decolonization area that the new nations have made upon the system, their degree of success in achieving their demands, and, finally, the general nature of the political process as it has evolved under the impact of the new nations.

The Charter of the United Nations offers a two-pronged approach to colonial problems. First, in Chapters XII and XIII the trusteeship system, the direct successor of the League of Nations' mandate system, is set forth. This system, which was to cover

    a. territories now held under mandate;

    b. territories which may be detached from enemy states as a result of the Second World War; and

than even the most informed observers would have anticipated in 1959, let alone in 1958 or earlier. In a very real sense, therefore, the large influx of new members in 1960 to the United Nations came as something of a surprise to the U.N. as an institution and, in many ways, as something of a surprise to the new members themselves.
(John G. Hadwen and Johan Kaufmann, *How United Nations Decisions Are Made* [2nd ed. rev.; Dobbs Ferry, N.Y: Oceana Publications, 1962], p. 128.)

   2 Cecil V. Crabb, Jr., *The Elephants and the Grass: A Study of Nonalignment* (New York: Frederick A. Praeger, 1965), p. 2.

    c. territories voluntarily placed under the system by states responsible for their administration.[3]

offered the maximum amount of direct United Nations supervision. A Trusteeship Council, operating under the authority of the General Assembly and composed of governmental representatives, was set up to exercise the functions of the Organization with respect to trust territories. It was given the power to consider reports submitted by the administering power, to accept petitions without prior submission to the administering authority, and to make periodic visits to the trust territories.[4]

    As a counterpoint to the trusteeship system the Charter in Chapter XI, the Declaration Regarding Non-Self-Governing Territories, embodied a commitment by the Members controlling territories not placed under the trusteeship system to "accept as a sacred trust the obligation to promote to the utmost . . . the well-being of the inhabitants of these territories."[5] Further, to achieve this goal these Members agreed to develop self-government, to assist in the progressive development of free political institutions, and to transmit regularly to the Secretary-General information on the economic, social, and educational conditions in these territories. The assumption by the Member States of international responsibilities for all of their colonial possessions was an important departure from the traditional order. In retrospect it is in the Declaration of Chapter XI that one can most clearly glimpse the fundamental forces that were at work to change the colonial order. It embodied the first assertion, admittedly inchoate, of an international responsibility for the management of colonial territories outside the mandate or trusteeship system. It is from this acceptance of international responsibility that the assertion of institutionalized international accountability has developed.

    In terms of the scope of application the task of applying the elaborate provisions of the trusteeship system met with only limited success. In only eleven territories were the provisions of Chapters XII and XIII ever applied.[6] At its height there were more than eight times as many non-self-governing territories, containing over ten times as many people, outside the trusteeship system as in it.[7]

    For reasons partly related to the small number of countries under the trusteeship system and more directly related to the strength of anticolonial forces in the Assembly the period 1946–1960 was marked by a steady shift of active

---

[3] Charter of the United Nations, Article 77 (1).

[4] *Ibid.,* Article 87.

[5] *Ibid.,* Article 73.

[6] These territories were: Cameroons (British); Cameroons (French); Nauru; New Guinea; North Pacific Islands; Ruanda-Urundi; Somaliland; Tanganyika; Togoland (British); Togoland (French); and Western Samoa. As of 1967 all but three—Nauru, New Guinea, and the North Pacific Islands—have become independent states.

[7] Harold Karan Jacobson, "The United Nations and Colonialism: A Tentative Appraisal," *International Organization,* Winter 1962 (Vol. 16, No. 1), p. 45.

concern with colonial problems from the Trusteeship Council to the General Assembly. The Assembly during this period often took the Trusteeship Council to task for its timidity in dealing with the colonial powers. The Assembly also did not hesitate to consider colonial disputes which the Security Council dodged. Thus, by the start of 1960 the Assembly through a decade and a half of active, probing concern with colonial problems had established for itself a dominant position in the Organization with respect to these problems.

The systematic decolonization campaign of the new Members can be dated from their efforts in 1960 to secure Assembly adoption of their draft declaration on colonialism. Only a very little political acumen would have been required in the spring and summer of 1960 to foresee that the fifteenth session of the General Assembly convening in September 1960 would be decisively affected by the increased tempo of the disintegration of the colonial empires of Africa. Seventeen colonial territories were scheduled to gain their independence in time for admission to the Organization at that session; of this prospective batch of new Members only Cyprus was a non-African country, and it was in Africa that the colonial revolution was then at its acme. From past experience with newly independent states it was easy to guess that these states would be almost totally mesmerized by the compulsion to hasten the total end of colonialism in the underdeveloped world. In a body as politically oriented as the United Nations the shifting voting balance in the Assembly resulting from this rush to independence of a whole continent could not go unnoticed.

This, then, was the political context in which the Union of Soviet Socialist Republics decided to seize the initiative on September 23, 1960, by requesting that an additional item, a "declaration on the granting of independence to colonial countries and peoples," be added to the agenda of the fifteenth session.[8] The Soviet draft declaration stridently proclaimed that in the colonial territories "the swish of the overseer's lash is heard; there heads fall under the executioner's axe."[9] In order to remove the multitude of injustices which the Soviets saw as flowing from the Western colonial system the Soviet declaration went on to proclaim that all colonial countries "must be granted forthwith complete independence" and that all foreign bases in other states must be eliminated.

There was no reticence on the part of the Soviet Union in divulging to the General Assembly the strategy that underlay the formulation of its draft declaration. Nikita Khrushchev, Chairman of the Council of Ministers of the Soviet Union, who was in personal attendance at the fifteenth session, explained the strategy very concisely when he said,

> I very much like the words of August Bebel, the social-democrat and leader of the German workers, who said, more or less, this: If the bourgeoisie praises you,

[8] UN Document A/4501, September 23, 1960.
[9] UN Document A/4502, September 23, 1960.

Bebel, think, in that case, what a stupid thing you must have done. If the bourgeoisie reviles you, it means that you are truly serving the working class, the proletariat! If the colonialists now revile me, I am proud of it, because it means that I am truly serving the peoples which are struggling for their independence, for their freedom.[10]

And the Soviet declaration was indeed formulated according to this precept. The operative paragraphs of the Soviet draft, phrased as "demands," were not in the bland diplomatic language of the Assembly which is best suited to encompass the widest divergency in views and garner the largest number of affirmative votes.

Once the decision had been taken to place the Soviet item on the agenda, informal talks began within the Afro-Asian group which at that time included all the new nations in the United Nations except Israel. In spite of a wide range of opinion on the Soviet draft a consensus was reached that the Afro-Asian group should try to formulate, without prejudice to the Soviet draft, its own draft resolution on this item. There was a general fear among the Afro-Asian states that Soviet sponsorship would result in a "cold-war" vote in which the Latin Americans would join the West in opposing the Soviet draft with the result that the draft might fail to achieve the votes in the Assembly necessary for adoption. Also there was an emotional belief that as the nations with the most direct concern and experience with colonialism they should be the ones to introduce and sponsor any Assembly resolutions on colonialism.

Having decided to propose its own draft resolution on colonialism, the Afro-Asian group was next faced with the task of coming up with a text which would encompass the diversity of opinion within its own membership.[11] During this period in which the struggle over a provisional text was taking place no attempt was made to consult groups outside the Afro-Asian group as to their views on the alternative texts, the feeling being that such consultations would only tend to splinter the Afro-Asian group itself. On the whole, the newer nations of Africa, the majority of which favored a draft close to the Soviet proposal, lost more battles than they won during the intragroup negotiations. For example, the specific mention of Algeria's right to independence was deleted from the final version. As one of the more moderate members of the group explained it later,

> There is no doubt, for example, that many of the co-sponsors of this draft declaration who have suffered greatly from the ravages of colonialism would have preferred a more expressive text, including clauses condemning colonialism in its

[10] General Assembly *Official Records* (15th session), 902nd plenary meeting, October 12, 1960, p. 687.
[11] This account of the negotiations leading to the adoption of the declaration on colonialism draws on contemporary press reports in *The New York Times* of November 1960 and the many revealing remarks made by the delegates during the debate on the question.

most culpable aspects. However, in order to rally all currents of opinion in the Assembly in favour of a text acceptable to all the Members of the United Nations, they have, in a spirit of conciliation, accepted certain phrases of a much more moderate nature.[12]

The final Afro-Asian draft in its preamble drew heavily upon the resolutions previously approved by the Afro-Asian conferences at Bandung in 1955, Accra in 1958, and Addis Ababa in 1960 because they represented previously agreed-upon phraseology which could be accepted without extensive negotiation. The operative paragraphs of the final draft fluctuated between easily accepted platitudes and ambiguous phrases into which each sponsor could inject its own interpretation. First an example of the former:

> The subjection of peoples to alien subjugation, domination and exploitation constitutes a denial of fundamental human rights. . . .

Of the latter:

> Inadequacy of political, economic, social or educational preparedness should never serve as a *pretext* for delaying independence. . . . [13]

This Afro-Asian draft differed from its Soviet counterpart in both tone and substance. Whereas the Soviet draft was both anticolonial and anti-Western, the Afro-Asian text was only anticolonial and strenuously avoided attacks on specific Western countries. The tone was as measured, although slightly shrill, as the platitudes were general. Instead of proclaiming "the following demands" as in the Soviet draft, this draft only "declares." The substance of the operative paragraphs also differed. While the Soviet text had demanded that all colonial territories "be granted forthwith complete independence and freedom," the Afro-Asian draft spoke of "immediate steps" to be taken to transfer power, implying that the transfer could proceed according to an orderly timetable. In contrast to the Soviet draft no mention is to be found in the Afro-Asian draft of any prohibition upon foreign bases.

During the debate on the drafts which opened on November 28 the Western states in their effort to depict the more constructive aspects of colonialism received considerable support from Latin America. Appealing to the new nations to take a more balanced account of their colonial past, the Latin American representatives pointed to the constructive cultural and educational benefits of the system. They aptly noted that in many cases it was the language of the excolonial power which provided a major bond uniting the new nations.

Neither the West nor the Latin Americans found a willingness among the new nations to concede the possibility of some beneficial effects resulting from colonialism. Almost as one the new nations depicted the colonial era as

---

[12] Mehdi Vakil (Iran), General Assembly *Official Records* (15th session), 926th plenary meeting, November 28, 1960, pp. 995–996.
[13] UN Document A/L.323, November 28, 1960. Emphasis added.

nothing other than a stormy succession of wars and expeditions waged by Powers intoxicated by their economic and military potential, seeking to gain strategic positions and hankering for wealth and prestige.[14]

Although the Latin Americans had presumed to speak on colonialism as fellow products of the system, the new nations would not accept this relationship and defended their exclusive right to speak as experts on colonialism. As the delegate from Mali said,

> The delegations which speak in this Assembly of their colonial experience or proclaim the benefits of colonialism can unfortunately only speak of the empire of their fathers' day; they speak of it as a heritage.
>
> If their countries were colonized at some time in history, they know it only from history books. Therein lies the fundamental difference between those delegations and ours, who have personal experience of colonial rule. Our knowledge is not based on hearsay or on what we learnt in school; we were for decades the living embodiment of that system.[15]

The Soviet bloc was far from silent during the debate on the agenda item that it had proposed. The Soviets maintained a withering fire against all forms of Western colonialism. Foreign military bases and North Atlantic Treaty Organization (NATO) assistance to countries engaged in colonial wars were favorite subjects of this often vitriolic attack. However, despite the ferocity of this attack the Soviet bloc was able to avoid incurring the odium of the new nations for injecting cold-war politics into the debate because it shared with those nations a common target, Western colonialism. The Soviets continued to press publicly for the adoption of their own draft resolution. The Afro-Asians were quite happy to have the Soviet Union continue to urge its own more far-reaching resolution rather than publicly embrace their milder resolution. This happy configuration, which has been repeated often on colonial issues since 1960, enabled the new nations to appeal to their Western and Latin American colleagues as a voice of reason and restraint which if not supported would result in the victory of the more odious Russian draft.

When the General Assembly on December 14 turned to voting on the drafts before it, the Soviet text as well as two Soviet amendments to the Afro-Asian draft were quickly defeated.[16] By this time there was certainly no doubt as to the vote's outcome, and the only element of suspense was provided by the uncertainty as to how the United States would vote. During the Assembly debate the United State delegation had displayed a disquieting ambivalence. It had only the strongest praise for the struggle of the colonial areas toward

---

[14] General Assembly *Official Records* (15th session), 945th plenary meeting, December 13, 1960, p. 1250.

[15] General Assembly *Official Records* (15th session), 931st plenary meeting, December 1, 1960, p. 1065.

[16] General Assembly *Official Records* (15th session), 947th plenary meeting, December 14, 1960, pp. 1272–1273.

nationhood and was most solicitous toward their problems, but a strange reticence prevailed as to how it would finally vote on the resolution.[17] It was common knowledge in the Assembly that the United Kingdom and Portugal, two NATO allies of the United States, were exerting great pressure on the United States not to vote in favor of this draft. Thus, on the final vote more than on any of the minor decisions preceding it the United States was being asked to choose between its old ally, the United Kingdom, and the new nations of Africa and Asia.

By a roll-call vote of 89 in favor, none against, and with 9 abstentions the Afro-Asian draft became General Assembly Resolution 1514 (XV), the Declaration on the Granting of Independence to Colonial Countries and Peoples.[18] Those abstaining were Australia, Belgium, the Dominican Republic, France, Portugal, Spain, the Union of South Africa, the United Kingdom, and the United States.

The disquietude of the United States delegation at finding itself in the company of this group of colonial powers was not helped by the fact that the only Negro member of the delegation, Mrs. Zelma Watson George, stood up and applauded the adoption of the draft. In explaining its vote the United States justified its abstention on the grounds that the resolution was "completely silent on the important contributions" which the administering powers had made in the colonial areas and was so "heavily weighted towards complete independence as the only acceptable goal."[19] While this was the formal explanation given for the United States abstention, the actual reason appears to have been a direct appeal from British Prime Minister Harold Macmillan to President Dwight D. Eisenhower to avoid placing the United Kingdom in an awkward position. The final decision that the United States should abstain was made by Eisenhower against the advice of the entire United States delegation.[20]

An important element contributing to the success of the new nations in obtaining Assembly adoption of the Declaration on Colonialism was the strong feeling in the Assembly that the victory of the decolonization movement was

17 For the views of the United States delegation see Senator Wayne Morse (Oregon), "The United States in the United Nations: 1960—A Turning Point," *Supplementary Report to the Committee on Foreign Relations, United States Senate* (Washington: U.S. Government Printing Office, 1961), pp. 20–21.

18 General Assembly *Official Records* (15th session), 947th plenary meeting, pp. 1273–1274.

19 *Ibid.*, p. 1283.

20 *The New York Times*, December 16, 1960, p. 4; Thomas J. Hamilton, "Colonialism at the U.N.," *The New York Times*, December 18, 1960, Section IV, p. 9; and Morse, pp. 20–21. According to Arthur Schlesinger,

Our delegation even had the concurrence of the State Department in Washington in its desire to vote for the resolution. But the British were opposed, and Harold Macmillan called Eisenhower by transatlantic telephone to request American abstention. When an instruction to abstain arrived from the White House, James J. Wadsworth, then our ambassador to the UN, tried to reach Eisenhower to argue the case. Eisenhower declined to accept his call.

(Arthur M. Schlesinger, Jr., *A Thousand Days: John F. Kennedy in the White House* [Boston: Houghton Mifflin Co., 1965], pp. 510–511.)

inevitable and the accompanying unwillingness to sacrifice developing relations with the new nations in defense of a system which most states admitted was doomed. And while the principal colonial powers did abstain, that in itself was a form of victory in that the draft in question, *inter alia*, proclaimed "the necessity of bringing to a speedy and unconditional end colonialism in all its forms and manifestations." This unwillingness to be clearly stigmatized as being against the lofty principles enunciated in the draft is testimony of sorts to the political influence of the new nations. Few had supposed in any case that the new nations had a great deal of influence on Portugal, Spain, and the Union of South Africa. The United Kingdom, probably the most progressive of all colonial powers, had again demonstrated its testiness on the issue of international responsibility for the administration of colonial possessions. It was really only with the United States that the new nations could have been disappointed with the results of their exercise of political influence. When the issue came down to a choice between fidelity to the principal ally of the United States and support for the new nations on an anticolonial declaration in the United Nations, the Eisenhower Administration supported Britain. But the loss was not without profit for the Afro-Asian states. The abstention of the United States had focused attention on the nature of the choice and made clear that many even within the Administration would have preferred to support the new nations. And, perhaps most hopeful from the standpoint of the new nations, a new Administration that spoke eloquently of a new role for the United States in support of the national aspirations of the colonial and former colonial parts of the world was about to assume power in Washington.

III

In 1961 with the initial push again coming from the Soviet Union but with the major source of influence being supplied by the new nations the General Assembly established a special committee on colonialism to examine the implementation of the Declaration passed the previous year.[21] Whereas nine countries had abstained on the 1960 Declaration, four of these states, the United States, Belgium, Australia, and the Dominican Republic, voted in favor of the establishment of the Special Committee. The ranks of those willing to stand against overwhelming Assembly majorities on the question of a general commitment to end colonialism had substantially dwindled since the Charter was written in 1945. Concerned as the new nations were with accelerating the final demise of colonialism and possessed of sufficient votes in the Organization to make this national concern the concern of the United Nations, they

[21] General Assembly Resolution 1654 (XVI), November 27, 1961. In the idiom of the UN the formal title of this body is the Special Committee on the Situation with Regard to the Implementation of the Declaration on the Granting of Independence to Colonial Countries and Peoples, often referred to as the Special Committee on Colonialism or the Special Committee of Twenty-Four (after 1962).

were able in 1960 and 1961 to move all but a remnant of colonial powers to join publicly in singing the funeral dirge of colonialism.

Considerable political sophistication was shown by the new nations in pushing in 1961 for a subsidiary organ with a predominant anticolonial bias as a means of achieving their aims. Though cloaked in moderate terms, General Assembly Resolution 1654 (XVI) which established the Special Committee on Colonialism provided the new nations with a vehicle to push for the end of colonialism without any necessity of kowtowing to the administering powers as in the Trusteeship Council or the Committee on Information from Non-Self-Governing Territories. Both of the latter bodies were organized on the basis of parity of membership between the colonial powers and the noncolonial states. From its beginning, however, the Special Committee on Colonialism had an automatic anticolonial majority with initially eight of its seventeen members being Afro-Asian states, two being from the Soviet bloc plus Yugoslavia, two from Latin America, and two from Western Europe plus the United States and Australia. In 1962 the Special Committee's membership was given an added anticolonial bias with the addition of seven members: four Afro-Asian states, one Soviet bloc state, one Latin American state, and one Scandinavian state.

The first task faced by the Special Committee was to decide exactly what its broad General Assembly mandate meant in terms of operational procedures.[22] In the context of parliamentary diplomacy the Special Committee's operation would be governed by rules of procedure "subject to tactical manipulation to advance or oppose a point of view,"[23] hence the determination of its operating procedures could decisively affect its future role. Over the objections of its Western members the Special Committee decided to resort to voting procedures "whenever any member felt that procedure was necessary" and that territories should be considered on a country-by-country basis with priority given to the territories of Africa.[24]

The Case of Rhodesia

Rather than attempting to cover the Special Committee's activities with regard to the more than 60 territories which it has considered between its first meeting on February 10, 1962, and the middle of 1966 the case of Rhodesia will be used to illustrate the use to which the new nations have put the Special Committee in their drive to abolish colonialism. As the first territory

---

[22] General Assembly Resolution 1654 (XVI), operative paragraph 5, under which the Assembly directs the Special Committee to carry out its task by employment of all means which it will have at its disposal within the framework of the procedures and modalities which it shall adopt for the proper discharge of its functions. . . .

[23] Dean Rusk, "Parliamentary Diplomacy—Debate vs. Negotiation," *World Affairs Interpreter*, July 1955 (Vol. 26, No. 2), p. 122.

[24] UN Document A/5238, October 8, 1962, p. 18.

considered by the Special Committee and the one which has received the most sustained attention of this body Southern Rhodesia is particularly suited to this purpose.

Situated in south central Africa, Rhodesia is the northern bastion of the white-dominated third of Africa. With the Zambezi River as its northern frontier it sprawls over 150,000 square miles populated by approximately 3,600,000 Africans and only about 222,000 Europeans. Although first seized as a private venture by Cecil Rhodes in the late nineteenth century, Rhodesia passed in 1923 to the United Kingdom as a self-governing territory with control of the territory's foreign relations resting with Britain. From 1953 until 1963 white-dominated Southern Rhodesia was part of an uneasy federation with Northern Rhodesia and Nyasaland. This British-sponsored federation broke up in 1963 partly over the antagonistic racial policies of the Southern Rhodesian government. With the dissolution of the federation Northern Rhodesia continued as a self-governing but nonindependent British territory. The Southern Rhodesian constitution of December 6, 1961, which had eliminated most of the residual powers formerly held by the United Kingdom while holding only the most tenuous of promises for any meaningful African participation in the government, served as the constituent document of the territory until its unilateral declaration of independenec in 1965.

After devoting fifteen of its first 26 meetings to Southern Rhodesia the Special Committee established, with Western acquiescence, a Subcommittee on Southern Rhodesia. This Subcommittee, composed of India, Mali, Syria, Tanganyika, Tunisia, and Venezuela, immediately undertook to establish contact with the United Kingdom government to discuss the future of the territory. After holding talks in London with the British government between April 7 and April 14, 1962, the Subcommittee recommended that "the situation in Southern Rhodesia should be considered by the General Assembly . . . as a matter of urgency."[25] The Special Committee, over the objections of Australia, Italy, the United Kingdom, and the United States, not only endorsed this recommendation but also recommended Assembly adoption of a draft resolution which declared Southern Rhodesia to be a non-self-governing territory within the meaning of Chapter XI of the Charter and requested Britain to take immediate steps to set aside the 1961 Rhodesian constitution, to restore civil liberties in Rhodesia, to immediately apply there the 1960 Declaration on Colonialism, and to repeal all Rhodesian laws which sanctioned racial discrimination.[26]

Over sustained Western objections the Assembly in June 1962 took up the Special Committee's recommendations. The United Kingdom's position, which had been placed previously before the Subcommittee and the Special Com-

[25] UN Document A/5124, May 21, 1962, Annex I.
[26] Ibid., Annex III.

mittee, was reiterated before the Assembly. Resting on the nuances of the
United Kingdom's constitutional practices, the British contended that they
had no power to annul the Rhodesian constitution and that because of its
status as a self-governing territory neither the United Kingdom nor the United
Nations had a right to discuss its internal affairs. A 39-power Afro-Asian draft
was offered to the Assembly as a moderate alternative to the more sweeping
draft recommended by the Special Committee. While this draft affirmed that
Southern Rhodesia was a non-self-governing territory within the meaning of
Chapter XI of the Charter, it avoided calling directly upon the United Kingdom to annul the Rhodesian constitution. However, the 39-power draft did
request Britain

> to undertake urgently the convening of a constitutional conference . . . which
> would ensure the rights of the majority of the people in conformity with the
> principles of the Charter of the United Nations and the Declaration on the grant-
> ing of independence to colonial countries and peoples. . . . [27]

The Assembly debate revealed that a clear majority of the membership felt
that Britain had a moral obligation which should transcend any constitutional
limitations to protect the African majority from the white-dominated government of Southern Rhodesia. The compromise draft was overwhelmingly approved by a vote of 73 in favor to 1 against, with 27 abstaining, and Portugal
and the United Kingdom present but not voting.[28]

Neither the British nor the Southern Rhodesian whites were moved to
change their previously announced positions by the Assembly's action. Faced
with this intransigence, the anticolonial forces decided upon seeking another
Assembly resolution before the first elections could be held at the end of
1962 under the 1961 constitution. In a display of power that both angered
and awed many delegates the Afro-Asian states forced a closure of Fourth
(Trust and Non-Self-Governing Territories) Committee debate on their draft
on October 31, 1962, only one day after its introduction and before all states
had had an opportunity to speak, and brought the draft before the Assembly
that night. This draft called upon the United Kingdom to secure "the immediate suspension of the enforcement" of the 1961 constitution, "the immediate convening of a constitutional conference," and "the immediate extension
to the whole population without discrimination of the full and unconditional
exercise of their basic political rights. . . . "[29] In both its tone and substance
this draft went further than the resolution on the same subject approved by
the Assembly four months earlier, but the Assembly approved it on the same
evening it was brought before the plenary session. In fact, the vote this time

[27] UN Document A/L.386/Rev.1 and Add.1-4, June 18-19, 1962.
[28] General Assembly *Official Records* (16th session), 1121st plenary meeting, June 28, 1962, p. 1549.
The draft was adopted as General Assembly Resolution 1747 (XVI), June 28, 1962.
[29] UN Document A/C.4/L.753, October 31, 1962.

was even more lopsided, with 81 in favor, 2 opposed, 19 abstaining, and the United Kingdom not participating. Again there was no response from the United Kingdom other than the standard reply that Southern Rhodesia had been self-governing since 1923 and neither Britain nor the United Nations had a right to intervene in its internal affairs.

In March 1963 the Special Committee returned to the question of Southern Rhodesia and again dispatched a subcommittee to London for talks with the British. On the basis of its London visit this subcommittee, composed of Mali, Uruguay, Syria, Sierra Leone, Tanganyika, and Tunisia, recommended consideration of the question of Southern Rhodesia at a special session of the General Assembly, drew the attention of the Security Council to the deteriorating situation in Southern Rhodesia, and requested the Secretary-General to draw the attention of the United Kingdom to the seriousness of the situation.[30] On June 23, 1963, the Special Committee, with Australia, Denmark, Italy, and the United States abstaining and Britain not participating, approved its subcommittee's report and recommendations and also requested Britain to abrogate the 1961 constitution.[31] The Chairman of the Special Committee transmitted its report to the Security Council, and this was quickly followed by the request of 32 African states for an urgent meeting of the Security Council on the grave threat posed to the peace and security of the African continent by Southern Rhodesia.[32] When the Security Council convened on September 9, 1963, Ghana, Morocco, and the Philippines submitted a draft resolution which requested the United Kingdom not to grant independence to Southern Rhodesia until a fully representative government had been established.[33] This draft was vetoed by the United Kingdom—France and the United States abstained—and the Security Council was forced to adjourn without adopting any resolution.

Having failed to obtain Security Council approval of their demands, the new nations brought them before the eighteenth session of the Assembly and quickly obtained their adoption.[34] With the Assembly decisions in hand the Special Committee—minus the Western states—on March 23, 1964, drew the Security Council's attention to "the explosive situation" in Southern Rhodesia.[35] At the same time the Special Committee asked the United Kingdom to declare that independence would not be granted to Southern Rhodesia except on the basis of universal adult suffrage and also requested all states to voluntarily refrain from supplying arms and ammunition to Southern Rhodesia. In May 1964 the Special Committee decided to send to London a third subcom-

[30] UN Document A/5446/Add.3, July 30, 1963, Appendix.
[31] Ibid.
[32] UN Document S/5409, August 30, 1963.
[33] UN Document S/5425, September 11, 1963.
[34] General Assembly Resolutions 1883 (XVIII), October 14, 1963, and 1889 (XVIII), November 6, 1963.
[35] UN Document A/AC.109/61, March 23, 1964.

mittee, composed of Ethiopia, Mali, Sierra Leone, and Yugoslavia, to discuss with the British the implementation of the previously adopted United Nations resolutions. This subcommittee concluded that further discussions with the United Kingdom were "unlikely to yield fruitful results" and called upon the Security Council to again consider the question of Southern Rhodesia "as a matter of urgency."[36] After considering its subcommittee's report the majority of the Special Committee adopted a resolution on June 26, 1964, deploring "the persistent refusal" of Britain to cooperate in the implementation of the United Nations resolutions on Southern Rhodesia.[37] This resolution also endorsed the conclusions and recommendations of the subcommittee and reiterated the call for Security Council action. On October 27, 1964, the Special Committee drew "once again . . . the attention of the Security Council to the question of Southern Rhodesia."[38] The Special Committee on November 17, 1964, authorized its subcommittee to keep the situation under review and to maintain close contact with the United Kingdom with a view to achieving the implementation of the United Nations resolutions.[39]

The Rhodesian case illustrates vividly the circuitous policy that the new nations have followed in attempting to influence the course of events in the remaining colonial areas. Secure in their control over the Special Committee of Twenty-Four, the new nations have used it and its subcommittees as originating points for new initiatives and as organs of constant surveillance of these colonial areas.[40] Subcommittees, which lack even the token Western representation of the parent body, have borne the main burden of conducting initial investigations and formulating recommendations. Usually over Western opposition the Special Committee endorses the reports of its subcommittees, although sometimes toning down their draft resolutions. Next, the Special Committee's recommendations are forwarded to the General Assembly. Within the Assembly, as the case of Rhodesia illustrates, the dominant anticolonial majority ensures a sympathetic hearing for the Special Committee's recommendations although some modification is usually introduced in order to obtain the largest possible majority. Simultaneously the Special Committee has called for Security Council action on its reports. In 1964 three separate pleas were addressed to the Security Council for action on Southern Rhodesia. The Special Committee has not been altogether successful in obtaining even a hearing, much less action, from the Council on its proposals. This circuitous policy has been most successful in maintaining continuous United Nations

36 UN Document A/AC.109/L.128, June 17, 1964.
37 UN Document A/AC.109/88, June 26, 1964.
38 UN Document A/5800/Add.1, Part II, December 22, 1964.
39 UN Document A/AC.109/SR.315, November 19, 1964.
40 For example, during the period 1962–1964 Southern Rhodesia was considered at the following meetings of the Special Committee: 9, 11, 13–26, 37, 44, 45, 47–49, 53, 71, 107, 130–140, 143, 144, 146, 168, 171–177, 223–233, 245–249, 252, 254, 255, 258, 259, 262, 263, 268, 269, 271–273, 278, 286, 294–296, 315.

involvement with the colonial areas and increasing the verbal intensity of the resolutions adopted. It had been successful by the end of 1964 in obtaining broad and repeated censure of the remaining recalcitrant colonial regimes. However, this circuitous policy had not yet produced any change in the policy of these hard-core regimes or any operational role for the Organization in bringing about some change in this area.

Ironically, through their threats of a unilateral declaration of independence from the United Kingdom and finally with such a declaration on November 11, 1965, the Rhodesian government brought about the direct involvement of the United Nations which the new nations had been unable to achieve. In the early autumn of 1965 as the signs of an early unilateral declaration of independence multiplied, 40 Afro-Asian states rushed a draft resolution through the Fourth Committee and the General Assembly condemning any attempt by the Southern Rhodesians to seize independence and calling upon the United Kingdom to use all possible means to prevent a unilateral declaration of independence.[41] The Assembly again appealed on November 5, 1965, for British action to prevent a Rhodesian declaration of independence.[42] This resolution was in stronger terms than the October resolution and, in fact, called upon the United Kingdom "to employ all necessary measures, including military force" to prevent a unilateral declaration of independence. In reaction to the Rhodesian declaration of independence on November 11 the Assembly in near unanimity adopted a resolution which condemned "the unilateral declaration of independence made by the racialist minority in Southern Rhodesia" and recommended that the Security Council consider the situation as a matter of urgency.[43] This resolution, sponsored by 36 African states, was adopted by 107 in favor, 2 against, and 1 abstaining. As was the case with the October resolution only Portugal and South Africa voted against this resolution while France abstained.

At the behest of the United Kingdom the Security Council met on November 12, 1965, to consider the Rhodesian situation. With this meeting the principal locus of United Nations' concern with Rhodesia shifted from the General Assembly to the Security Council where it remains at the time of this writing, the fall of 1967. In requesting a Security Council meeting on Southern Rhodesia the British were finally abandoning their position that neither the United Kingdom nor the United Nations had the right to interfere in the territory's internal affairs. During November 1965 the Security Council passed resolutions which condemned the unilateral declaration of independence, called upon all states to refrain from recognizing or assisting the regime, requested all states to break economic relations with Southern Rhodesia, and

[41] General Assembly Resolution 2012 (XX), October 12, 1965.
[42] General Assembly Resolution 2022 (XX), November 5, 1965.
[43] General Assembly Resolution 2024 (XX), November 11, 1965.

requested the establishment of an embargo on oil and petroleum products to Southern Rhodesia.[44]

In defiance of the Security Council's request for an embargo on the shipment of oil and petroleum products to Southern Rhodesia two oil tankers were discovered in April 1966 to be nearing the port of Beira in Portuguese Mozambique with cargoes rumored for transshipment to Rhodesia. At the request of the British government the Security Council met, declared that the "situation constitutes a threat to the peace," and authorized the British to prevent "by the use of force if necessary" oil from reaching Rhodesia through the port of Beira.[45] This marked the first time that a specific state had been authorized to carry out a decision of the Security Council.

The tempo of United Nations action against Rhodesia was again increased in December 1966 after the collapse of renewed negotiations between London and the Ian Smith regime. Under strong African pressure the United Kingdom asked the Security Council to approve for the first time since its founding selective, mandatory sanctions against a regime.[46] During a week of discussion the African states made a concerted attempt to alter drastically the British draft to include more commodities and to provide enforcement provisions to ensure that the Council's edict was carried out. The African states also sought to have the Security Council deplore the British refusal to use force against Rhodesia and to call upon the United Kingdom to withdraw all previous offers to the Rhodesian regime and to declare flatly that it would grant independence to Rhodesia only under majority rule.[47]

In this attempt the African states largely failed although the final resolution contained eight African amendments, including a ban on the supply of oil and oil products to Rhodesia.[48] On December 16, by a vote of 11 to 0, with Bulgaria, France, Mali, and the Soviet Union abstaining, the Security Council approved a ban on the purchase of twelve of Rhodesia's chief exports and the supply to Rhodesia of oil and oil products. Not only did this mark the first use of mandatory sanctions by the Security Council, but the Council itself emerged as a new instrument in the politics of decolonization. The success or failure of these developments will, moreover, have a profound effect upon the Organization's relations with the remainder of southern Africa.

Thus, by the beginning of 1967 the Rhodesians by their own actions had provided the occasion for the United Nations to initiate mandatory sanctions against the regime. This was an action long desired by the new nations but one which even their adroit use of political influence had been unable to obtain prior to the Rhodesian unilateral declaration of independence.

[44] Security Council Resolutions 216 (1965), November 12, 1965, and 217 (1965), November 20, 1965.
[45] Security Council Resolution 221 (1966), April 9, 1966.
[46] *The New York Times*, December 9, 1966, p. 22.
[47] *The New York Times*, December 17, 1966, p. 9.
[48] Security Council Resolution 232 (1966), December 16, 1966.

IV

For the new nations the traditional concern of the United Nations with human rights has been but another vehicle for advancing their attack on colonialism and associated forms of racial discrimination. Traditionally, the promotion of human rights has been viewed from the perspective of protecting the citizens in the fullest possible exercise, compatible with organized society, of those rights which flow from the dignity and worth of the individual. For this perspective, centered as it is on the individual, the new nations have substituted a perspective centered on the evils of Western colonialism with its domination of black by white. As Louis Henkin has aptly noted,

> The struggle to end colonialism, also swallowed up the original purpose of co-operation for promotion of human rights. The gradual elimination of dependent areas and their admission to the UN meant an ever increasing Assembly majority with some agreed attitudes, particularly a determination to extirpate the remnants of white colonialism and white discrimination. These attitudes impinged on the human rights program as well. Of course, they assured the sharpest scrutiny of human rights in dependent areas. . . . But it was a championship of anticolonialism, designed to accelerate "self-determination." It was not an assertion of general standards which other nations, including the champions, were prepared to accept in their own countries.[49]

The extent to which the new nations' concern with eliminating all vestiges of colonialism dominated the perspective from which they viewed the human rights activity of the Organization was pointedly demonstrated at the Assembly's seventeenth session. In preparation for the fifteenth anniversary in 1963 of the adoption of the Universal Declaration of Human Rights the United States joined with six other states at the seventeenth Assembly in requesting the Secretary-General to appoint a special committee to draft plans for the anniversary.[50] During the Third (Social, Humanitarian, and Cultural) Committee's consideration of this draft Guinea, Mali, and Mauritania joined in offering an amendment expressing the hope

> that all States will implement General Assembly resolution 1514 (XV) [Declaration on the Granting of Independence to Colonial Countries and Peoples] so that the fifteenth anniversary of the Universal Declaration of Human Rights may be celebrated in an atmosphere of independence and freedom.[51]

For the new nations self-determination and national independence, rights of political groupings and not of individuals, head the list of human rights which the Organization should promote. This redefinition of the traditional individ-

---

[49] Louis Henkin, "The United Nations and Human Rights," *International Organization*, Summer 1965 (Vol. 19, No. 3), p. 512.
[50] UN Document A/C.3/L.991/Rev.1, October 15, 1962.
[51] UN Document A/C.3/L.1002/Rev.1, October 25, 1962.

ual-centered concept of human rights has gained acceptance with the entry of the new nations into the Organization, and both the Third Committee and the Assembly adopted this amended version of the draft.[52]

At the seventeenth session the Assembly approved a draft sponsored by 34 states requesting the Commission on Human Rights to prepare a draft declaration and a draft convention on the elimination of all forms of racial discrimination. Using the draft declaration prepared by the Commission as a basis for discussion, the eighteenth Assembly proceeded to draft the final text of the Declaration on the Elimination of All Forms of Racial Discrimination. During the course of the Third Committee's consideration of the draft Declaration three of the nine paragraphs were successfully amended by various new nations. One new paragraph each was added to the preamble and the operative paragraphs.[53] The net effect of these successful maneuvers of the new nations was to impose a sense of stridency on the draft and sharpen its application to the remaining white colonial regimes of Africa and particularly South Africa. It declared that

> an end shall be put without delay to governmental and other public policies of racial segregation and especially policies of *apartheid*, as well as all forms of racial discrimination and separation resulting from such policies.

And finally, every state

> shall fully and faithfully observe the provisions of the present Declaration, the Universal Declaration of Human Rights and the Declaration on the granting of independence to colonial countries and peoples.[54]

With seventeen states abstaining the Third Committee approved the amended draft which the Assembly adopted unanimously.[55]

In assessing the role played by the new nations on human rights questions Henkin's appraisal seems sound.

> The anticolonial atmosphere of the Assembly and the increasing and confident majorities of "new nations" led to the injection of anticolonial issues into the human rights covenants. Self-determination was added to the roster of human rights as an additional weapon against colonialism although there was no suggestion that this was a right of the individual, that the individual could claim it against an unrepresentative government, or that minorities could invoke it to sup-

[52] General Assembly Resolution 1775 (XVII), December 7, 1962.

[53] General Assembly *Official Records . . . Third Committee* (18th session), 1213th–1233rd, 1237th, 1242nd, 1244th–1250th, and 1252nd meetings.

[54] The draft declaration is contained in UN Document A/5603, November 12, 1963.

[55] General Assembly *Official Records . . . Third Committee* (18th session), 1245th meeting, October 28, 1963, p. 2.

The seventeen states abstaining in Committee were Australia, Belgium, Canada, Denmark, Finland, France, Greece, Iceland, Ireland, Italy, Luxembourg, the Netherlands, New Zealand, Norway, Sweden, the United Kingdom, and the United States. South Africa remained absent from both the Committee and plenary meetings because of the specific mention of apartheid. The draft was adopted as General Assembly Resolution 1904 (XVIII), November 20, 1963.

port secession. . . . Human rights was being used as a political weapon against colonialism or economic imperialism, not to enhance the rights of all persons against all governments.[56]

V

A systematic analysis of the Assembly's voting record is a significant tool in measuring the success with which the new nations have wielded political influence on colonial issues. Such an analysis is particularly well suited to determining publicly acknowledged shifts in positions and the number of battles won or lost.[57] For the purpose of this study 23 roll-call votes on colonial issues taken during the sixteenth, seventeenth, and eighteenth plenary sessions of the General Assembly have been selected for analysis. Selection was based on the importance of the issues involved and was designed to provide as representative a grouping as possible.[58] Where multiple votes, i.e., paragraph-by-paragraph votes, were taken on a draft, an attempt was made to select the vote which best represented the issue involved. In general, the plenary vote was used in this analysis. However, in a few cases where the only roll-call vote on a draft resolution was in committee or where the committee vote reflected an element not present in the plenary vote the committee vote was selected.

One indication of the extent of influence exercised by the new nations on colonial issues can be provided by determining the extent of their concurrence with the United Nations majority on these issues. While it is true that frequent concurrence with the majority cannot prove that effective influence

[56] Henkin, *International Organization*, Vol. 19, No. 3, p. 513.

[57] However, a caveat is owed the reader as to the shortcomings of voting analysis in elucidating the workings of the political process of the United Nations. First, the number of votes taken in the Organization each year has soared to such an extent that it even has become onerous using modern high-speed computers to encompass every vote taken. In their recent study Alker and Russett, in fact, found that it was no longer practical to include every main committee and plenary roll call when they dealt with only one session, the sixteenth, of the Assembly. (Hayward A. Alker, Jr., and Bruce M. Russett, *World Politics in the General Assembly* [New Haven and London: Yale University Press, 1965], p. 27.) While there are guidelines, there are no hard-and-fast rules as to which votes should be selected for analysis and which ones rejected. This is a hazardous process; but to pretend that any guarantee exists as to proper selection other than the skill of the observer would be misleading. Although it does not lessen the subjective content of the selection process, the guidelines used in determining which votes to include in this study are set forth later. Another important limitation on the use of voting analysis in a study of the United Nations derives from the nature of the Organization's political process in which so much negotiation takes place behind the scenes. If voting analysis is coupled with extensive qualitative analysis of the political system, the limitation is not so acute. Voting analysis, properly undertaken, is only one tool among many available to the political scientist in probing the nature of a given political system. When used in conjunction with the other tools of the profession, it is a valuable aid in examining those decisions in which states are forced to publicly take sides. Like any of the other tools of the profession when used alone voting analysis all too often presents at best a limited and somewhat facile picture of the system and at worst a picture of another system entirely.

[58] Of course, one important criterion in the selection of votes was the availability of the voting records in a form usable for analysis. If one considers all the votes taken in any one session of the Assembly, in both plenary and main committee, it is found that the great majority are not recorded on a country-by-country breakdown as they are not roll-call votes. This inherent limitation in selection is somewhat mitigated by the general rule of thumb that the most important votes are those taken on a roll call.

was exercised—it may only indicate a slavish following of the majority—the lack of such agreement would demonstrate the absence of effectively applied influence.[59] The certainty with which a high degree of concurrence with the majority can be used as one index of effectively applied political influence increases when the states concerned are found to have actively engaged in initiating and pushing the proposals voted upon. Such intimate involvement with the issues of parliamentary diplomacy is largely incompatible with a blind desire to be always on the winning side regardless of the merits of the question at stake. As the central focus of the diplomacy of the new nations in the United Nations colonialism certainly qualifies as an area in which they have been actively engaged. Thus, if it is found that the new nations have a high majority agreement voting score on the colonial questions analyzed, it would be at least presumptive evidence of the effective exercise of political influence on their part.[60]

On those colonial votes analyzed for the sixteenth through the eighteenth sessions in which 50 percent or more of the new nations voted together they were in agreement with the Assembly majority on 87 percent of the votes.[61] A majority of the new nations found it necessary to oppose the Assembly majority on only 4.3 percent of these votes and abstained on 8.7 percent of them. The two issues on which the majority of the new nations abstained were rejected by the Assembly. This majority agreement score is particularly impressive as an index of the effective exercise of political influence when it is noted that 91.3 percent of the votes were on items initiated and sponsored in whole or in part by the new nations. The possibility of servile fellowship yielding a specious index is considerably reduced by this intimate involvement with the issues.

A telling demonstration of the effectiveness of the new nations' influence on colonial issues is provided in Chart 1. This chart presents an analysis of the number of negative votes cast by France, the United Kingdom, and the United States on 97 decolonization issues between the fifth and eighteenth sessions of the General Assembly. The chart clearly shows a steady, though somewhat irregular, decline in the percentage of negative votes cast by these three states commencing with the eleventh session in 1956. This decline in negative voting coincides with the accelerated entry of new nations into the Organization and their opening of an intensive campaign against colonialism. More significant as evidence of the effective influence of the new nations than the decline of negative voting by these three states is that it occurred during

[59] Robert E. Riggs, *Politics in the United Nations: A Study of United States Influence in the General Assembly* (Urbana: University of Illinois Press, 1958), p. 170.

[60] A majority in plenary sessions of the General Assembly is actually a two-thirds majority on "important questions." (See Article 18 of the UN Charter.)

[61] By comparison, the majority agreement scores of the Soviet Union, the United States, and the United Kingdom were as follows: Soviet Union, 82.6 percent; United States, 47.8 percent; United Kingdom, 34.8 percent.

CHART I

PERCENTAGE OF "NO" VOTES CAST BY FRANCE, THE UNITED KINGDOM,
AND THE UNITED STATES ON SELECTED DECOLONIZATION ISSUES,
FIFTH–EIGHTEENTH SESSIONS OF THE GENERAL ASSEMBLY

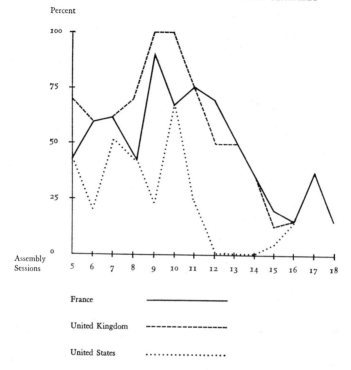

Percent

100

75

50

25

0

Assembly
Sessions

5 6 7 8 9 10 11 12 13 14 15 16 17 18

France ——————————

United Kingdom – – – – – – – – –

United States · · · · · · · · · · · ·

a steady escalation in the severity of the resolutions being voted upon. For
example, at the seventh session of the Assembly France and the United Kingdom voted against and the United States abstained on the question of establishing a commission to study the question of race conflict in South Africa,
but at the eighteenth session all three states voted in favor of a resolution condemning the government of South Africa for its policy of apartheid. At the
seventh session of the Assembly France, the United Kingdom, and the United
States voted against a draft resolution upholding the right of all peoples and
nations to self-determination, yet at the fifteenth session these states failed to
vote against a much more far-reaching draft resolution calling for immediate
steps to be taken "to transfer all powers" to the peoples of colonial territories.

The records are replete with many similar cases in which France, the United Kingdom, and the United States have since 1956 either acquiesced in or supported anticolonial resolutions far stronger than these three states voted against in earlier years. However, it should be noted that for the British and the French the compulsion to vote negatively probably dropped as their empires were dismantled. In addition, before the rush of new nations into the Organization a negative vote by these three powers on a colonial question carried the possibility of blocking action, while it now does not.

Also of significance in measuring the effectiveness of the political influence wielded by the new nations is the extent to which the other Assembly groupings have supported or opposed the new nations. Chart 2 clearly shows the extent to which the new nations have gained the support of the other nations on colonial issues. As might be expected the original members of the Afro-Asian group have been the most consistent in their support while the Western European nations have failed more often than not to support the new nations.

CHART 2

COMPARISON OF VOTES ON COLONIAL ISSUES OF THE MAJORITY
OF OTHER ASSEMBLY GROUPS IN RELATION TO THE NEW
NATIONS, SIXTEENTH–EIGHTEENTH SESSIONS OF
THE GENERAL ASSEMBLY

Percentage	0	20	40	60	80	100

Groups[a]

Afro-Asian — 100 (With the new nations)

Communist — 100 (With the new nations)

Latin American — 76.2 (With the new nations) | 23.8 (Abstained or nonparticipating)

Western European — 36.3 (With the new nations) | 41 (Abstained or nonparticipating) | 22.7 (Against the new nations)

▨ With the new nations

☐ Abstained or nonparticipating

▥ Against the new nations

a All groups are exclusive of any new nations which might normally be considered members of them.

However, the most striking fact revealed in this analysis is the extent to which it has become exceedingly unfashionable to oppose the anticolonial thrust of the new nations. While the majority of the Latin American nations supported the new nations on 76.2 percent of the 23 analyzed colonial votes, not once did a majority of the Latin American Members oppose the new nations on these issues. Even the Western European states have found the sanctuary of abstention more alluring than outright opposition to the new nations on colonial issues. On only 22.7 percent of the analyzed roll-call votes did a majority of the Western European states vote in opposition to the new nations. The extent to which states are unwilling to publicly record through the medium of a roll-call vote their opposition to the anticolonial measures advanced by the new nations in the United Nations is a convincing demonstration that at least with respect to this issue category the new nations have successfully used their political influence to delegitimize colonialism. It is no longer respectable or politic to vote against such measures, and the only prudent means of registering opposition in the Assembly has become abstention.[62]

Certainly one element of the success of the new nations in regard to colonial issues is the cohesion of the group on this issue. Of the 23 votes analyzed for the sixteenth through the eighteenth sessions of the Assembly there are only six instances in which states voted in an opposite direction from that of the group and all six of these instances were on the two roll calls where a majority of the group abstained.[63] On the other 21 votes there was not a single case of a state voting in the opposite direction from that of a majority. Even more impressive as an index of cohesion is the failure of any of the new nations to resort to abstention on any of the twelve votes from the seventeenth and eighteenth sessions. At least on colonial issues the new nations form a cohesive group that has an impressive record for initiating and obtaining the adoption of a wide range of anticolonial measures.

VI

One must view as an outstanding achievement of the new nations their successful forging between 1960 and 1966 of an international moral consensus against the continuation of Western colonialism. By 1966 the impropriety of any defense of the continued existence of colonialism was apparent to all except the retrograde regimes of southern Africa. Within the United Nations itself the new nations succeeded during this period in making their own uppermost concern, colonialism, the uppermost concern of the Organization.

[62] Of course, this says nothing about the types of measures adopted, the compromises made, or the ultimate goals sought, but these are questions most suitable for descriptive techniques and are so handled in other sections of this study.

[63] The states which voted in opposition to the majority of the new nations on the 23 votes analyzed were Tunisia, Malaysia, Pakistan, the Philippines, and Israel.

At the behest of the new nations the Assembly has moved from general pronouncements of moral and legal rights, such as the 1960 Declaration on Colonialism, to condemnations of specific nations accompanied by requests for diplomatic and economic sanctions and threats of military sanctions. The Special Committee of Twenty-Four has maintained a constant surveillance of the remaining colonial areas while its anticolonial directorate has kept up a steady stream of reports and recommendations to other organs of the United Nations. As frustration grew over the recalcitrant attitude of the remaining colonial powers, the new nations sought Security Council endorsement of mandatory enforcement programs designed to eliminate these regimes. By the end of 1966 such sanctions had been adopted only with regard to Rhodesia, and in that case the precipitous action of the Rhodesian regime played a large role in forcing the Security Council to take such a course. The greatest success of the new nations' wielding of political influence during these years remained the success in shifting their concern and outlook on colonialism over to the Organization.

Much of the success of the new nations in effectively exercising political influence in the United Nations in the decolonization process is owed to a propitious world political situation. One product of the Cold War has been the creation of an environment in which either of the two major antagonists, the United States and the Soviet Union, views a gain in support for the other as a defeat for itself. This attitude on the part of these two Great Powers has been reflected in active campaigns on their part to cultivate the support of the new nations. This great-power competition for support provided the new nations with numerous opportunities to advance their interests by playing off the East and the West against each other. Well aware of the bargaining advantages offered by the circumstances of the Cold War, the new nations have not hesitated to employ this advantage to the fullest. Repeated warnings were issued by the new nations that the obstinate attitude of the West on colonial questions was rapidly diminishing its influence with these new states and aiding the East in its courting of these states.

Another advantageous aspect of the political situation facing the new nations during this period was that their major goal, the independence of the remaining colonial areas, was largely under the control of the West. Most of the Western nations were more sensitive to public pressure than many other states and also found the role of colonial master a profoundly disturbing one to play. Reinforcing the disquietude of the West over its role as colonial master were the remarkably successful indigenous nationalist movements which were threatening if not to evict the colonial powers at least to make their continued rule extremely expensive in both blood and treasure.

The extent to which the new nations were able to make their own perspective of the proper concerns of the Organization the perspective of the Organization itself decisively demonstrates its hyperdependency upon the Member States.[64] At least at its present stage of development the United Nations is more an arena than an actor in the international scene. It provides a convenient forum for the assertion of conflicting national policies and demands and even in some instances for multilateral collaboration in the settlement of disputes. One consequence of the ease with which the dominant concern of the United Nations can be altered by a shift in the concern of a significant group of Member States or the entry of new Members is the disillusionment and bitterness that such shifts cause among the advocates of the previous dominant concern. Witness, for example, the melancholy remarks of the Earl of Home upon the rise of decolonization as the major concern of the United Nations.

> Resolutions have been persistently passed by the Assembly in particular on colonialism, which could only be described as reckless and careless of peace and security. Everyone has seen the chaos in the Congo and knows that it derives from a premature grant of independence to a country whose people were totally unprepared for their new responsibilities. Yet many Delegates were instructed by their Governments to sponsor and vote for resolutions which could only multiply and magnify that chaos in other places.

. . . .

> Such a resolution [the Declaration on Colonialism] and others like it reveal an almost total lack of responsibility, and certainly pay no heed to the main purpose of the United Nations which is to ensure order and security of peace.

. . . .

> One of the main causes of the present troubles is an apparent difference of aim and purpose between the fifty-one founder members and many of the fifty-three newly independent countries which were elected to membership subsequently to the United Nations' foundation . . . the founder members laid the whole emphasis on the organization of peace through collective security.

. . . .

> A large number of new countries are putting their campaign for acceleration of independence for colonial territories before the main purpose of the Charter which is to provide peace and security. They are more concerned to impose their views on "colonialism" on others than to fulfill their primary duty which is to "harmonize the actions of nations."[65]

The severity of such resulting "crises of confidence" could perhaps be lessened

[64] Ernst B. Haas, "Dynamic Environment and Static System: Revolutionary Regimes in the United Nations," in Morton A. Kaplan (ed.), *The Revolution in World Politics* (New York: John Wiley & Sons, 1962), pp. 267–309.

[65] Speech by the Earl of Home, December 18, 1961, to the Berwick-on-Tweed branch of the United Nations Association, reproduced in Raymond A. Moore, Jr. (ed.), *The United Nations Reconsidered* (Columbia: University of South Carolina Press, 1963), pp. 128–130.

if there were a general realization that at its present stage of development the United Nations is primarily an arena for the interaction of conflicting national policies. This is not to deny that it may perform valuable tasks in areas of peace and security, decolonization, or economic development but rather to argue for a realization that the performance of such tasks rests on the approval or acquiescence of the Member States and does not have a significant life apart from their attitudes. Thus, the shift after about 1955 in the primary emphasis of the Organization away from collective security and toward decolonization efforts is a natural result of its hyperdependency on the attitudes of the Member States.

In connection with this phenomenon it seems also to be a characteristic of United Nations politics that secondary concerns either are recast in terms similar to the predominant emphasis or else gradually atrophy. Thus, the traditional human rights activities of the Organization have lost their individual-oriented perspective and have become to a considerable extent only an adjunct to the decolonization struggle. On the other hand, collective security has ceased for the present to be a meaningful concern of the Organization. As is strikingly indicated in the activities of the new nations the politics of the United Nations is a politics of successive approximation toward goals involving a variable mix of private negotiations, public oratory, and voting. The circuitous tactics of these nations in regard to Rhodesia have demonstrated the extent to which the patient application of such tactics can gradually lead to a desired goal. Of course, compromise is the very heart of this political process of successive approximation. The compromises are intra- as well as inter-group accommodations and often involve issues remote from the immediate concern of the negotiations. Thus, the United States during the 1960's was forced to balance its support for its European allies in the military-political confrontation with the East against hoped-for influence with the new nations.

The Role of International Organization in Ocean Development

Daniel S. Cheever

THE 22nd session of the United Nations General Assembly was unexpectedly enlivened by a late addition to its agenda when Malta, a newcomer even by UN standards, sought to demilitarize the ocean floor "beyond the limits of present national jurisdiction" and to internationalize its "resources in the interest of mankind."[1] Ambassador Arvid Pardo, Malta's Permanent Representative to the United Nations, sought immediate steps to draft a treaty that

> should envisage the creation of an international agency . . . to assume jurisdiction, as a trustee for all countries, over the sea-bed and the ocean floor, underlying the seas beyond the limits of present national jurisdiction. . . .

In advancing his proposal, in a surprise move thought to be premature by some governments, Ambassador Pardo accelerated and intensified the consideration of national and international interests in "ocean space." How is the last earthbound frontier to be explored and exploited? Is it to be assigned to international jurisdiction or taken over by national authorities? A disconcertingly rapid rate of technological advance emphasizes the urgency of a decision. This article will first consider the disposal of the Malta proposal by the 22nd session of the General Assembly and then attempt to consider its significance as a challenge to the development of international organization.

DANIEL S. CHEEVER, Professor of Political Science and Professor of International Affairs in the Graduate School of Public and International Affairs at the University of Pittsburgh, is on leave of absence during 1967-1968 as the Visiting Research Scholar at the Carnegie Endowment for International Peace. The research assistance of Margaret Galey, graduate student at the University of Pennsylvania, is gratefully acknowledged.

[1] Malta's UN membership dates from December 1964. The Maltese *note verbale* requesting the inclusion of a supplementary item on the agenda of the 22nd session of the General Assembly was distributed with an explanatory memorandum as UN Document A/6695, August 18, 1967.

From Volume 22, No. 3 (1968), pp. 629-48.

I

The Maltese request was first entitled:

Declaration and Treaty Concerning the Reservation Exclusively for Peaceful Purposes of the Sea-Bed and the Ocean Floor, Underlying the Seas Beyond the Limits of Present National Jurisdiction, and the Use of Their Resources in the Interests of Mankind.

The accompanying memorandum expressed concern that new techniques developed by the technologically advanced countries would result in the national appropriation and militarization of the ocean floor "beyond present national jurisdiction" resulting "in the exploitation and depletion of resources of immense potential benefit to the world, for the national advantage of technologically developed countries." The declaration sought to establish the principles that the seabed should be reserved as a common heritage of mankind to be used exclusively for peaceful purposes and that any financial benefits derived from its exploitation should be used primarily to promote the development of poor countries.

The Assembly's General Committee recommended the acceptance of Malta's proposal as an additional agenda item and its assignment for consideration to the First (Political and Security) Committee. When the Assembly met to consider this recommendation, however, Malta's representative moved to delete the reference to a "declaration and treaty" owing to certain delegations' concerns about a premature emphasis on "legal objectives." Although the General Committee had agreed unanimously to the inscription of the item, he explained, "divergent views were expressed about its correct allocation in committee."[2] Some delegations thought it should be assigned to the First Committee as a political matter. Others thought it should go to the Sixth (Legal) Committee. This discussion drew attention to the fact that corridor diplomacy and General Committee debate had uncovered considerable disagreement on both the merits of the proposal and the procedure to be followed. A number of governments were unready to consider a treaty or even a declaration of principles that might compromise their future interests in "ocean space." Subsequent discussion in the First Committee disclosed the reasoning for the recommended word change and the assignment to the First Committee, both of which the Assembly accepted quickly and without debate.

The Peruvian delegate, for example, explained that he and certain other Latin American delegates opposed the reference to a "declaration and treaty" as premature. It would involve the Sixth Committee before there was sufficient study of the scientific, political, legal, and economic implications to permit

[2] Victor J. Gauci spoke for Malta on this occasion. His comments appear in UN Document A/PV.1583, October 6, 1967, pp. 82–83.

agreement on treaty provisions.[3] Several Latin American governments, he went on to note, sought successfully, in addition, to persuade the Maltese delegate to change the word "jurisdiction" to its plural form so that the item would refer to the seabed and ocean floor beyond the limits of national "jurisdictions," only to be rebuffed by the Secretariat "for technical and bureaucratic reasons . . . which no doubt form part of the mechanical grammar of the Secretariat. . . . " The Chilean delegate clarified this latter point. Because several Latin American governments claimed exclusive sovereignty over wide bands of the coastal sea, the sea bottom, and its subsoil they insisted on a change in syntax and the allocation of the Maltese proposal to the First Committee.

Ambassador Arthur J. Goldberg, on behalf of the United States, urged that the First Committee be assigned responsibility for the Maltese proposal because in seeking to reserve the ocean floor exclusively for peaceful purposes the topic was inevitably concerned with armaments regulation. He urged the Assembly to follow the precedent of the Committee on the Peaceful Uses of Outer Space and establish a committee on the oceans to consider all proposals before the Assembly on marine questions and to make recommendations in promotion of long-term international cooperation in marine science. It was quickly evident that the United States was unwilling to accept new international commitments for the control of ocean space without further study and deliberation. Ambassador Goldberg explained that his government was still in the throes of formulating a "coordinated long-range program in marine science [and] developing a comprehensive program of international cooperation." He was, however, able to cite one authoritative policy guideline, a statement by President Lyndon B. Johnson on July 13, 1966, at the commissioning of the research vessel, *Oceanographer*. The President declared:

under no circumstances, we believe, must we ever allow the prospects of rich harvests and mineral wealth to create a new form of colonial competition among the maritime nations. We must be careful to avoid a race to grab and to hold the lands under the high seas. We must ensure that the deep seas and the ocean bottoms are, and remain, the legacy of all human beings.[4]

Despite this ringing statement the road to a United States policy decision will be rocky. The introduction of the Maltese proposal in the General Assembly gave rise to nearly two dozen resolutions introduced in the House of Representatives from early August through October opposing the vesting of

[3] See the Peruvian statement in UN Document A/C.1/PV.1529, November 15, 1967, p. 56, and the Chilean statement in UN Document A/C.1/PV.1526, November 13, 1967, pp. 22 and 23. Both governments were seeking to support the 1952 "Declaration of Santiago" in favor of a 200-mile seaward limit for national jurisdiction.

[4] President Johnson's statement and Ambassador Goldberg's speeches before the General Assembly's General and First Committees are respectively on pp. 231–232 and pp. 57 and 287 of the *Interim Report on the United Nations and the Issue of Deep Ocean Resources together with Hearings by the Subcommittee on International Organizations and Movements of the Committee on Foreign Affairs* (Washington: U.S. Government Printing Office, 1967) (hereinafter cited as *Interim Report*).

control over deep ocean resources in an international body. Four resolutions, however, favored the development of international cooperation and new sources of revenue for the United Nations and the developing countries. The Senate, evidently less concerned than the House that hasty action contrary to national interests would be taken at the United Nations, considered only three resolutions. One by Senator Norris Cotton expressed opposition to vesting title to the ocean floor in the United Nations "at this time." Two by Senator Claiborne Pell, however, went far to support the objectives of the Maltese proposal. One urged the President "to place before the General Assembly of the United Nations a resolution endorsing basic principles for governing the activities of nations in ocean space."[5] These principles would seek to limit national appropriation of ocean space, promote the peaceful exploration and exploitation of ocean resources "by all nations without discrimination of any kind on a basis of equality of opportunity and in accordance with international law," fix limits to the continental shelf, and establish a UN sea guard under the control of the Security Council to enforce international compliance.

The Assembly's political processes blunted not only Ambassador Pardo's attempt at a "declaration and treaty" but also Ambassador Goldberg's plea for a "committee on the oceans." After speeches by 57 delegates and three representatives of international organizations in twelve sessions of the First Committee, plus several meetings by members of a working group, the General Assembly opted unanimously for an *ad hoc* committee, rather than a permanent committee, to study the peaceful uses of the seabed and the ocean floor beyond the limits of national jurisdiction.[6] This Committee was requested to prepare in cooperation with the Secretary-General a study for the 23rd session of the Assembly to include a survey of past and present activities of all intergovernmental bodies and international agreements dealing with the seabed. The Committee was also instructed to provide "an indication regarding practical means to promote international co-operation in the exploration, conservation and use of the sea bed. . . . " The Secretary-General was asked to assist the *Ad Hoc* Committee by seeking the views of Member States and submitting the results of studies already under way to implement two previous resolutions dealing with ocean resources, one by the Assembly and one by the Economic and Social Council (ECOSOC).[7]

  [5] The House resolutions are on pp. 1, 36, and 77–78 of the *Interim Report*. The Senate Resolutions are on pp. 1–7 of U.S. Congress, Senate, Committee on Foreign Relations, *Hearings, Governing the Use of Outer Space*, 90th Congress, 1st session, 1967.
  [6] General Assembly Resolution 2340 (XXII), December 28, 1967. Thirty-five countries were named to the *Ad Hoc* Committee, none of them developing landlocked countries from Asia, Africa, and Latin America, as was noted regretfully by the Nepalese and Paraguayan delegates.
  [7] General Assembly Resolution 2172 (XXI) of December 6, 1966, requested the Secretary-General to survey activities in marine science and technology undertaken by the UN family of organizations and member governments and to formulate proposals for an expanded program of international cooperation in the exploitation and development of marine resources. Economic and Social Council Resolution 1112 (XL) of March 7, 1966, requested the Secretary-General, in cooperation with the Advisory Committee

Why an *ad hoc* committee? A full answer to this question cannot be wrung from the verbatim record. Important discussions on the Maltese proposal were carried on out of earshot by an "open-ended" working group appointed by the Chairman of the First Committee. This group reached a total of 43 members whose hard labors were rewarded by the unanimous adoption of the resolution they sponsored. It considered several drafts which, it can be inferred, covered the spectrum from a permanent Assembly committee on the oceans to a mere request to the Secretary-General to prepare a report for the Assembly's consideration. The Union of Soviet Socialist Republics opposed the creation of a permanent committee on the oceans by the 22nd Assembly and even had "specific doubts" about an *ad hoc* committee which might be the "foundation for a future permanent organization." The Soviet delegate noted that other international organizations, particularly the Intergovernmental Oceanographic Commission (IOC) under the aegis of the United Nations Educational, Scientific and Cultural Organization (UNESCO), were already considering various aspects of the ocean floor. He preferred to ask the Secretary-General and IOC to report on current international organization activities and on the coordinating arrangements that had been made or should be made than to take "over-hasty action" on a complex problem. Clearly, the *Ad Hoc* Committee was a compromise between those governments seeking immediate agreement on principles and new institutions to regulate the exploitation of ocean resources for the particular benefit of developing countries and those anxious to rely on IOC. The latter had moved already to stake its claim by passing a resolution in October to create a working committee on legal questions related to the scientific investigation of the ocean.[8] Unlike the Assembly's *Ad Hoc* Committee, the IOC working committee's attention is limited to "the legal principles" which should guide scientific investigation of the oceans and ocean resources, including "the effect of the sea on scientific research . . . and . . . the contribution of scientific knowledge to the development of the law of the sea. . . . "

The Secretariat also responded to the Maltese challenge. During the First Committee's deliberations the Secretary-General submitted a note drawing attention to the activities of the Secretariat "under previous resolutions of its governing bodies."[9] In addition, he noted his conclusion from preliminary

on the Application of Science and Technology to Development and the specialized agencies, to survey the present state of knowledge of the resources of the sea, excluding fish, beyond the continental shelf and to identify those "now considered to be capable of economic exploitation, especially for the benefit of developing countries." The Assembly resolutions called for reports to the 23rd session.

[8] The views of the Soviet delegate, L. I. Mendelevich, may be found in UN Documents A/C.1/1525, pp. 8–21, and A/C.1/1544, pp. 31–32. The Soviet Union introduced the IOC resolution (v-6) promulgated as UN Document SC/CS/150 (1) which carried in October 1967. The Secretary of IOC is a Soviet national who serves also as the Director of UNESCO's Office of Oceanography.

[9] UN Document A/C.1/952, October 31, 1967. The most important previous resolutions are General Assembly Resolution 2172 (XXI) and Economic and Social Council Resolution 1112 (XL), both adopted in 1966.

work on the task assigned him. The legal status of deep sea resources and ways and means of ensuring that the exploitation of these resources would benefit the developing countries "constitute[d] two major gaps." Consequently the Secretary-General indicated his intention to:

> examine various alternatives, including the advisability and feasibility of entrusting the deep sea resources to an international body. The General Assembly may consider it advantageous for the Secretary-General to prepare a more comprehensive report which would include a study of the legal framework which might be established for the deep sea resources, the administrative machinery which may be necessary for effective management and control, the possible system of licensing and various possible arrangements for redistributing and/or utilizing the funds which would be derived therefrom, including those earmarked for the benefit of the developing countries.[10]

The UN Office of Legal Affairs had been assigned the reponsibility of bringing up to date its legislative series on the law of the sea. All these activities, he noted, required the active cooperation of Member governments, the specialized agencies, and his own staff.

Suggestions preceding the Maltese proposal had already come from other sources. The Commission to Study the Organization of Peace urged in its seventeenth report that the United Nations take title to the sea beyond the twelve-mile limit and the seabeds beyond the continental shelf and that there be established a special United Nations marine resources agency to administer international marine resources, hold ownership rights, and grant, lease, or use these rights in accordance with the principles of economic efficiency.[11] Resolution 15 of the Geneva World Peace Through Law Conference of July 1967 recommended that the General Assembly of the United Nations proclaim that the nonfishery resources of the high seas outside the territorial waters of any state and the bed of the sea beyond the continental shelf "appertain to the United Nations and are subject to its jurisdiction and control."[12] The question of fisheries was referred back to committee for more study. United States Senator Frank Church had already suggested that the United Nations be better equipped to keep the peace by having "some degree of financial independence" by receiving title to mineral resources on the ocean floor beyond the continental shelf. The Committee on Oceanography of the National Academy of Sciences (NASCO) recommended as early as 1959 the establishment of a world oceanographic organization within the United Nations "to provide a single home

10 UN Document A/C.1/952, p. 4.

11 See *New Dimensions for the United Nations,* seventeenth report of the Commission to Study the Organization of Peace, Clark M. Eichelberger, Chairman (Dobbs Ferry, N.Y: Oceana Publications, 1966), pp. 39–41.

12 Resolution 15 of the Geneva World Peace Through Law Conference is cited in *Interim Report,* p. 8.

for the various marine scientific and technological activities now lodged in several United Nations specialized agencies."[13]

Although these suggestions from international and national officials and from intergovernmental and nongovernmental organizations present a wide spectrum of alternatives, all of them require in some degree the use of international institutions. To what degree will depend in part on the past roles played by international organization in ocean management.

II

The most startling developments in ocean floor exploitation have required little assistance from international organization. Oil and gas in the North Sea are being tapped by national companies, private or public, licensed by national authorities to exploit the subsoil, which has been divided by median lines for national jurisdiction and exploitation. These lines, to be sure, are drawn on the basis of principles established by the United Nations Conference on the Law of the Sea.[14] The number of oil rights in the Gulf of Mexico is already close to 2,000. The United States Department of the Interior has issued leases for oil and gas exploration at depths of 1,500 feet (500 meters) as far from the West Coast as 22 miles.[15]

Although international organization has so far had only minor significance in exploiting resources on or under the ocean floor, international law has been crucial. By defining the limits of the continental shelf as

> The seabed and subsoil of the submarine areas adjacent to the coast but outside the area of the territorial sea, to a depth of 200 meters or, beyond that limit, to where the depth of the superjacent waters admits the exploitation of natural resources of the said areas . . .

the "elastic" clause in Article I of the 1958 Geneva Convention on the Continental Shelf encourages national governments to exercise "sovereign rights" over "adjacent" seabed resources in phase with their industrial capacities. As a consequence the supply of important minerals has been increased. There is no certainty that international agencies would do the job more equitably or more efficiently than national agencies working under international rules. This should not be taken to mean that international organization has played a negligible role in facilitating the use of ocean resources as a whole. The

---

[13] Frank Church, *The UN at Twenty-One*, report to the Committee on Foreign Relations, U.S. Senate 90th Congress, 1st session, February 1967, p. 25; and *Oceanography, 1966: Achievements and Opportunities*, National Academy of Sciences and National Research Council publication 1492 (Washington, 1967), p. 183 (hereinafter cited as *Oceanography, 1966*).

[14] W. Langeraar, "The North Sea," *U.S. Naval Institute Proceedings*, January 1967 (Vol. 93, No. 1), p. 20 ff. See also Article 6 of the Convention on the Continental Shelf (contained in UN Document A/CONF.13/L.55).

[15] *Interim Report*, p. 164. See also remarks by L. F. E. Goldie in Louis M. Alexander, ed., *The Law of the Sea* (Columbus: Ohio State University Press, 1967), pp. 273–279.

General Assembly, ECOSOC, the International Law Commission, the Food and Agriculture Organization (FAO), and UNESCO's IOC, to name only a few of the more influential bodies, have all played their part in fostering agreement on ground rules for ocean management. The international regulation of ocean fishing by conventions, commissions, and advisory scientific bodies has a long history. International cooperation has included also nongovernmental endeavors as ocean scientists in all countries have increased their professional collaboration.

Ten years ago when NASCO, working concurrently with the Scientific Committee on Ocean Research (SCOR) of the International Council of Scientific Unions (ICSU), recommended a world oceanographic organization, the United States was reluctant to see a further proliferation of specialized international agencies as semiautonomous centers of operational activities and political influence. Coordination of the activities of such agencies, nationally by the State Department and internationally by the Secretary-General, the Assembly, and the Administrative Committee on Coordination (ACC), was thought to be already awkward and inadequate.[16] Instead, the oceanographers were told that an existing international agency would be preferable from the foreign policy point of view. There were few plausible candidates. Although FAO has a Department of Fisheries, its work tends to be dominated by ministers of agriculture. The interest of the World Meteorological Organization (WMO) in ocean management is limited principally to serving national weather bureaus. The Intergovernmental Maritime Consultative Organization (IMCO) deals principally with navigation and maritime safety. The choice in 1960 was to exploit UNESCO's role in international scientific cooperation by establishing its Office of Oceanography and its semiautonomous Intergovernmental Oceanographic Commission.

This Commission is for the moment the most comprehensive and active international body dealing with marine affairs. While it has produced some results in international scientific cooperation, however, it is a far cry from the international institution that would be needed to control and manage ocean resources in a fully effective manner. IOC's role is coordinative in the main rather than operational. Its Secretary, a Soviet scientist, reports that it has helped to plan and coordinate three large-scale international expeditions.[17] Probably the most noteworthy of these is the International Indian Ocean Expedition (IIOE) of 1959–1966, involving 40 research vessels from fourteen countries, 2,000 scientists from 23 officially participating countries, and the

16 These problems are discussed by Nathaniel M. McKitterick in *U.S. Diplomacy in the Development Agencies of the United Nations* (Washington: National Planning Association, 1965) and by W. Mcl. Chapman in several addresses, notably "The State of Ocean Use Management" at the second session of the Food and Agriculture Organization's Committee on Fisheries, Rome, April 24, 1967.

17 K. N. Fedorov, "International Oceanography—The Way Scientific Cooperation Develops," *UN Monthly Chronicle,* March 1966 (Vol. 3, No. 3), pp. 29–37.

cooperation of FAO and the World Health Organization (WHO) as specialized agencies. The data collected are being stored and catalogued, it is significant to note, in two world data centers established during the International Geophysical Year in Washington and Moscow and are to be available to all member countries of the expedition. IOC has helped also to plan and coordinate oceanographic research studies in the South Atlantic, the Kuroshio current near Japan, and the Gulf of Guinea.

In Cochin, India, IOC has approached operational responsibility by establishing the Indian Ocean Biological Center by agreement between India and UNESCO. This Center, staffed with Indian scientists under the supervision of an international coordinator, maintains the first international collection of zooplankton. It is open to all marine biologists for study. National ships contribute their share of oceanographic observations to such world data centers—some national and some international—so that new information is available to the world's oceanographic community if national governments and research agencies are willing to share it.

There are other operational and coordinative activities in the oceans that are indicative of international organization's potentialities. WMO is planning a "World Weather Watch" dependent heavily on internationally organized ocean research. Activities related to radioactive pollution are the responsibility of the International Atomic Energy Agency (IAEA). The UN Development Program (UNDP) funds ocean resources research conducted by FAO. What is particularly needed, in NASCO's judgment, whether or not there is to be a single world oceanographic organization, is to make better use of existing agencies, especially as there is no adequate means of liaison among them. The nearest approximation is provided by the Subcommittee on Oceanography of the Administrative Committee on Coordination of ECOSOC.[18]

The NASCO report implies that international coordination is difficult without national coordination and that the latter can be helped by the former. United States relations with FAO are often dominated by the Department of Agriculture even when ocean matters are at issue. An Interagency Committee on Oceanography (ICO), established early in 1960 by the Federal Council for Science and Technology, had little influence even though its principal task was "to develop an annual national oceanographic program" by opening channels of communication between 22 federal bureaus and agencies.

To provide clearer national goals and a more coordinated program than was possible under the weak authority of ICO the 89th Congress passed the

---

[18] *Oceanography, 1966*, p. 180. See also a similar recommendation for "long-term action" in *International Ocean Affairs*, a special report prepared by a joint working group appointed by the Advisory Committee on Marine Resources Research of the Food and Agricultural Organization of the United Nations, the Scientific Committee on Oceanic Research of the International Council of Scientific Unions, and the Advisory Committee of the World Meteorological Organization (La Jolla, Calif: September 1967).

Marine Resources and Development Act in 1966 calling on the President to develop a comprehensive, long-range, and coordinated program in marine science with the assistance of a National Council on Marine Resources and Engineering Development and a Commission on Marine Science, Engineering, and Resources. ICO has been replaced by the Committee on Marine Research, Education, and Facilities, one of the National Council's five committees whose chairmen are appointed by, and report to, the Vice President. The Council's first report, *Marine Science Affairs—a Year of Transition*, emphasizes that it is not a rival of existing departments because it is not an operating agency:

> Its purpose is to assist the President in identifying Government-wide goals, in developing alternative strategies for their achievement, in identifying issues, and in reaching an informed decision. Helping the operating agencies to do their jobs is a prime objective of the Council, but the agencies must rely on their own budgetary resources to carry out programs called for in their organic legislation.[19]

By listing the marine sciences and technology programs of eleven major federal agencies and the major purpose of each the report suggests, perhaps unintentionally, the complexity of the interface between national and international administration. For fiscal year 1966, for example, over 50 percent of all federal funding for marine sciences was spent for national security by the Department of Defense. The program plans for marine science and technology for the remaining departments and agencies are listed in descending order of magnitude: Interior, The National Science Foundation, Commerce, Transportation, Atomic Energy Commission, State, Health Education and Welfare, and the Agency for International Development (AID). In fiscal year 1968 civilian activities will increase more rapidly than defense activities, reflecting the increasing emphasis on utilizing marine sciences to meet industrial, economic, and social goals.[20]

This allocation of national marine science resources among government agencies implies a restricted role for international organization because ocean technology, including mineral extraction and deep submergence transportation and communications, has a high military value. It also suggests the vested interests of some national agencies in existing international bodies. The Marine Resources and Engineering Development Act (PL 89–454) hedges on international collaboration in a traditional manner by stating that cooperation will be sought "with other nations and groups of nations and international organi-

---

[19] *Marine Science Affairs—A Year of Transition* (Washington: National Council on Marine Resources and Engineering Development, February 1967), p. 24. The Assistant Secretary of the Navy for Research and Development heads the Committee on Marine Research, Education, and Facilities. The Undersecretary of State for Political Affairs heads the Committee on International Policy in the Marine Environment. The five committees report to the Vice President as Chairman of the National Council on Marine Resources and Engineering Development.

[20] *Ibid.*, p. 28.

zation . . . when such cooperation is in the national interest." That interest, for many countries, is rapidly creeping out on the ocean floor. Cooperation in some matters will not seem to be in the national interest.

The Council has recognized this danger. Its first report emphasizes that intensified use of the sea could very well "stimulate national rivalries and conflict" defeating the very purpose of national policy—the efficient use of ocean resources for human ends. The report highlights a dilemma by emphasizing that a sea-based force is essential for a deterrence strategy intended to reduce the danger of armed conflict. The oceans, moreover, are not as susceptible as outer space to self-denying arms agreements. A complex weapons balance depends on waterborne weapons which governments are not likely to abandon for some time to come. Arms control to date has been successful to the extent it has *not* required international inspection by *international authority*. The 1963 test-ban treaty is acceptable largely because it required no inspection or control beyond national capabilities. Even with this self-enforcing feature France and the People's Republic of China (Communist China) denounce the test-ban treaty and the nonproliferation treaty as well. If it is to be used exclusively for peaceful ends, the ocean floor will require more highly developed forms of arms control than have yet been acceptable to all the major powers.

Security problems limit the utilization of international organization. So does the fragmentation of political power and authority in world politics. So does ocean exploitation as opposed to ocean research which, in comparison, has benefited from international organization. In planning the future control of the oceans military uses, for the present at least, predominate over economic uses despite the possible advantages of exploiting "common resources" by common ownership.

Other considerations bode poorly for Ambassador Pardo's proposals. Foreign aid programs in all major donor countries, particularly the United States, are declining steadily as percentages of both national and per capita incomes. There is as yet no major shift from bilateral aid (approximately 90 percent) to multilateral aid. Both points suggest that it will be difficult to agree on the allocation of "net financial benefits derived from the use and exploitation of the sea-bed . . . to promote the development of poor countries."[21] Despite some significant regional developments there is little evidence of the worldwide political cooperation that would be required to create and control an international agency "to assume jurisdiction, as a trustee"[22] over as large and important an area as the seabed. The United Nations and its agencies are as much cockpits of conflict as they are instruments of cooperation. Regional organizations are often rivals. National governments, in sum, have developed their

---

[21] UN Document A/6695, p. 2.
[22] *Ibid.*, p. 3.

interests too narrowly and intensively to permit international organizations in the near future to be really significant agents to cope with world hunger and international insecurity. The burden will continue to rest most heavily on national governments. But this need not mean that the baby must be thrown out with the bath water. Some international organization is better than no international organization. It can perform roles to complement those carried on by national governments. The extent to which the latters' actions can be restrained by international law and organization depends on the imperatives of national interest and the utility of international agencies.

III

The first imperative is international security. Efforts to reserve the ocean floor "exclusively for peaceful purposes," in Ambassador Pardo's words, could well run afoul of nationally perceived military necessities. The countries best equipped to exploit the ocean's resources for all mankind are the countries most urgently concerned with ocean space as their first line of defense.

The second is the urgency of increased food production. The control and management of the oceans will ultimately involve regulating the deep sea as well as the seabed and its subsoil because the space above the bed is potentially a plentiful source of protein for an increasingly large and hungry world population.

A third is the danger, if not the likelihood, that the developed countries will appropriate the resources on the ocean floor by taking advantage of the permissiveness of Article I of the 1958 Geneva Convention on the Continental Shelf. Because it promises exploitation in all but the greatest depths underwater technology has demonstrated that the existing definition of the shelf no longer limits national claims effectively. As a consequence, there is a danger of international disagreement and even conflict unless governments are restrained in advancing their claims to the shelf, the continental slope, and the depths beyond. The ocean floor presents more of a problem than the sea above. International law and international organization are currently developed sufficiently to enable men to traverse the oceans and fish peaceably. On the bottom, however, there is already a frontier, potentially more active than outer space, where homesteaders are moving farther out and deeper every year.

A fourth imperative is the need to control the world's environment for human benefit. Marine science provides the knowledge and marine technology the means. Weather control, irrigation, and power production are but three examples of ocean use capable of contributing to the control of man's environment.

A fifth imperative is the improving of communications and transportation systems by greater utilization of the ocean's depths. The comparative tranquillity of the deep ocean offers many advantages over the sea surface.

Major difficulties in the control problem, in short, stem from the multiple uses of the oceans. Indeed, the list can be lengthened to include recreation and waste disposal (including atomic waste) among many others. Whatever uses have priority, administrative regimes must assume that the earth's oceans constitute a single biological "system."

Derivative factors in the control problem are the relevance, utility, and limits of international organization. Despite potentially significant exceptions in the direction of supranational authority international organizations serve to strengthen rather than to displace national governments. To date they have played minor though useful roles in furthering the exploitation of natural resources on the continental shelf and in the sea. They can be expected to play similarly minor, though important, future roles in the exploitation of the ocean bottom and its subsoil beyond the continental shelf. Their major function has been to harmonize or, in some instances, coordinate the policies and operations of national governments. Because only the advanced industrial countries are equal to the task of exploiting deep ocean resources for the foreseeable future the role of international organization in regulating the oceans and their resources may well magnify rather than diminish the most salient feature if not the hallmark of mid-century international politics, the disparity in political and military power and in living standards between industrial and preindustrial countries.

Can international organization assume sufficient authority and operational responsibility in the regulation of ocean resources to break away from traditional patterns? Is the United Nations simply to continue its role of facilitating and harmonizing national action when there is agreement enough to do so? Can international agencies be expected to develop further so as to coordinate national efforts by assigning responsibility and allocating resources? To some extent they already do in the cases of the International Bank for Reconstruction and Development (IBRD) and the International Monetary Fund (IMF) where authority is derived from the alignment of voting power with economic power sufficiently to elicit the grudging acceptance of rich and poor alike. Can international agencies go further in controlling and exploiting seabed resources? The most tantalizing question of all is whether mankind is faced with a never-to-be-repeated opportunity to internationalize important resources before they are inevitably and irretrievably nationalized.

To ask these questions is to suggest the importance of distinguishing between short-run and long-run factors. To do so helps to prevent assigning to national governments authority that cannot be revoked or to international organizations tasks so impracticable for the short run as to weaken their utility for the long run. An understanding of the long-range consequences of short-range actions should assist national governments in avoiding actions today that would compromise irreparably their interest in developing new forms of international cooperation tomorrow. It is possible, for example, that the oceans, the air space above them, and their subsoils, if weather and minerals are taken into account, can be exploited best to meet human needs in the short run by national programs regulated by international treaties prescribing not only the rights and duties of member governments but also assigning harmonizing roles to international institutions. There might as a result be an increase of international cooperation of the kind that has taken place in the International Indian Ocean expedition, or a world oceanographic organization or marine science organization within the United Nations might be established to match the increasing coordination and centralization of oceanographic activity that are taking place, or soon will take place, in national governments. Short-run moves in this direction, rather than toward the premature granting of title over the high seas or ocean bottom beyond national limits either to the United Nations or to national governments, would preserve important options for the long run. What is needed now is a dependable treaty regime to facilitate the use of ocean resources by licensing and regulating exploitation and by settling disputes.

There are precedents for this conservative approach in the short run. Sovereign claims to Antarctica have been frozen without being granted to the United Nations or any other international body.[23] No "international sovereignty" was created to make space the "province of mankind." Rather, the United Nations has been the political forum which facilitated the preservation of outer space as a common resource.

Despite international organizations' emphasis on consultative, advisory, and coordinative functions they also play political or policy roles. This has often been called "parliamentary diplomacy" and is thought to assist member governments to define their interests more broadly and press them more effectively than can be done in bilateral diplomacy. It increases governments' abilities to share information, mobilize support, conduct joint operations, and seek to isolate countries pursuing unwelcome lines of action. While governments are prepared to adjust their policies and actions as a consequence of these processes, they are careful in most instances to limit international institutions' freedom of action and to supervise their international operations carefully.

The role of international organization, regional or universal, specialized or multipurpose, is suggested by the prevalence of "multilateral bilateralism" and "multilateral unilateralism." Member states through these practices continue to conduct their foreign relations and international operations, such as foreign

[23] John G. Stoessinger and Associates, *Financing the United Nations System* (Washington: The Brookings Institution, 1964), *passim* and, on revenue from Antarctic exploration and ocean resources, pp. 281–289.

aid and ocean research, on a bilateral or unilateral basis. They do so, however, under the influence and oversight of international bodies that scrutinize national policies in multilateral confrontation and review.

Exceptions to the voluntary, nonoperational character of international organizations exist and will increase. They are rather limited in number and in degree of obligatory authority, however, and reflect the particular needs of influential governments, or particular groups of members, in special circumstances. These exceptions suggest some of the conditions that will be required if deep ocean resources are to be reserved for peaceful use and regulated by an international authority. Only when its permanent members agree, for example, may the Security Council take enforcement action or impose economic sanctions binding on all governments including nonmembers of the United Nations.

IBRD is noteworthy as an agency that conducts important operations, particularly in developing countries, drawing on the services of a qualified international staff. Although it floats bond issues on national money markets, it is a surprisingly autonomous organization, autonomous with respect to its member governments and, compared with almost all of the specialized agencies, autonomous of the United Nations itself. In reaching decisions, moreover, its statute frees it from the sacred cow of "one state, one vote." It is for this reason in large measure that the United States has sufficient confidence in the Bank to acquiesce in its conducting operational activities. With its weighted vote and its friends among the industrial nations the United States can influence if not control the Bank's operations. Equally significant for the emerging problems of the oceans, nearly all Communist governments, despite a few signs of awakening interest, continue to shun the Bank. Whether national or international interests in ocean management will be served by international organizations boycotted by significant ocean powers is debatable. The authority and functions assigned to an organization have much to do with the membership it attracts and holds.

The UN Development Program (UNDP), while strictly voluntary, is "operational" in character and therefore suggestive of the role international organization may play in ocean management. Indeed, some of its preinvestment surveys are in ocean fisheries. More of such organized international activity can be expected since ocean exploitation is simply beyond the means of most national capabilities individually applied or is inefficient at best without international coordination.

The major economic powers, however, have as a general rule been reluctant to see powerful, autonomous, economic organization develop in the United Nations or in most regional systems of international organization. They delayed for a long time the efforts of the great majority of developing countries (the group of 77 in the UN Conference on Trade and Development

[UNCTAD]—now considerably more) to persuade them to discriminate in favor of the 100 or so poor countries in trade or monetary policies. They have also resisted the development of international mechanisms that might obligate, or put pressure on, the rich to undertake unacceptable economic policies to help the poor. Thus the United Nations Capital Development Fund was established by the General Assembly only after ten years of persistent efforts by the developing countries. With the establishment of UNCTAD on a permanent basis this political tension between rich and poor provides much of the political dynamism of United Nations bodies under conditions increasingly favorable for the poor. The world's industrial giants are targets for the poor countries convinced that the rich rig the world's economic and trading patterns against them. Despite ideological and political differences the two superpowers have reason to regard with skepticism any increase in the power and autonomy of international organizations, which already exert discernible influence. By institutionalizing the rich-poor confrontation, for example, UNCTAD has established a new frame of reference for the discussion of world trade and development problems. It has focused attention on issues that hitherto had been diffused through a multiplicity of international organizations. It has nudged governments to reconsider traditional policies and principles.

Although the achievements of economic organizations at times may seem to threaten the interest of the wealthy countries, they are not sufficiently important to sustain the notion that international organization will be sturdy enough for some time to come to take title to the ocean floor or distribute its resources in an equitable and efficient manner. Nor do they provide much ammunition for the "functionalists" who in varying degrees envisage political boundaries withering away under the impact of a spreading web of international activity organized along functional (economic and social) lines. They assume that international organization, as an institutional reflection of functional cooperation and integration, can and will replace the national state as the primary unit of authority, power, and administration. They assume that the functional (economic) day-to-day life of manifestly interdependent nations will depoliticize their international relations.

In fact, twentieth century experience implies that functionalism as a path to world peace through world law and government is as much a "pipe dream" as were interwar efforts toward disarmament. Functional relations have become permeated with politics more than political relations have been cleansed by functional cooperation. International cooperation in the International Labor Organization (ILO) on a pluralistic basis, representing the interests of states, owners, and workers, for example, has proved very contentious since the Soviet Union joined it and other specialized agencies after 1953.

Perhaps the functionalists will have the last word. Perhaps the challenge of ocean management, involving as it must 71 percent of the earth's surface, will so exceed the capacities of the international system's mechanisms that more powerful and integrated world institutions will become acceptable. There is no early prospect of such an eventuality, however, on a world scale. Regionally, the prospects are better but not markedly so. While functional cooperation continues and will grow under the European Economic Community (EEC), the Common Market is slower in becoming a political community than its European (and American) fathers had hoped. The EEC Council of Ministers is still more powerful than the European Assembly or, for that matter, the Commission of the three Communities (the European Coal and Steel Community, the EEC, and the European Atomic Energy Commission). The negative vote of *one* power in the Council is still sufficient to control European policy despite weighted voting in a parliament where the delegates sit by political party rather than by *patrie*.

IV

What steps, then, can be sought with some hope of success to realize the laudable goals of the Pardo proposal?

First, the world's nations should agree to modify the elastic clause of the Continental Shelf Convention so as to extend their renunciation of *exclusive* sovereign rights over the high seas and the ocean depths to the sea bottom and its resources. They could do this by setting aside the exploitability test in favor of finite limits to exclusive national jurisdiction over seabed and subsoil resources measured from the territorial sea, or by depth, or by some combination of both. Progress toward national renunciation could well be furthered by the adoption in the General Assembly of a declaration of principles to guide the revision of the Continental Shelf Convention and the drafting of new treaties dealing specifically with the exploitation of the ocean floor beyond agreed limits of national ownership.

Secondly, governments should agree to the Pardo principle that the resources of the seabed beyond the limits of national jurisdiction are to be used as a "common good" in the interest of mankind. This interest should be defined and acted upon so that developing countries will be benefited. The common-good principle is already accepted in the international law of the sea to regulate transportation on the surface and "hunting" in the depths below. Mineral rights, as opposed to title, might be granted to private firms or national agencies, as the case may be, either by national or international licensing authorities, depending on the arrangements specified in the treaties regulating the exploitation of seabed resources. Governments, it should be noted parenthetically, are not now prevented by the Continental Shelf Convention as it stands from undertaking obligations in a separate treaty or preferring as a matter of policy to share with the less developed countries a given percentage of their take from the ocean floor. Under such circumstances the developing countries themselves may prefer national appropriation of seabed resources if the advanced countries are influenced to exploit quicker, further, and deeper because national jurisdiction seems more certain than international jurisdiction as a protection for mineral rights.

Thirdly, the ocean floor beyond agreed limits of national jurisdiction should be reserved exclusively for peaceful uses. On the basis of published sources the ocean's principal military use stems from its role as an opaque transportation and communications system for highly mobile weapons. This use could be expected to continue even if the ocean floor were off-bounds for weapons. If fixed installations on the ocean floor were thought to have technical superiority over mobile carriers in the sea, they might nonetheless be renounced by military powers choosing to demilitarize the ocean bottom as they did Antarctica and celestial bodies. A serious problem in the case of the ocean floor, however, would be the probable necessity of an inspection system.

Fourthly, a new international agency should be created eventually to deal with the oceans as a whole. It would be useful in harmonizing or, if it succeeded in eliciting confidence, coordinating national ocean programs in the fashion of IOC. Its jurisdiction, of course, would be broader than that of IOC to include "exploitation" as well as (scientific) "exploration" of ocean resources. Until further study the extent to which it would assume operations or would simply coordinate existing international operations by the specialized agencies can only be surmised.

Despite uncertainties, some of the functions the new agency might perform can be set forth. In whatever way ocean resources are to be exploited in the future, by national or international instrumentalities, or by a combination of both, the common-good principle will require coordinated data gathering and dissemination. This function is being performed already to some extent by several international agencies. The NASCO report cited above suggested that it can be performed better.

The data will need to be analyzed on a multilateral basis. Since discovery in the ocean depths by a single country has great importance for all, opportunity should be provided for a multilateral review of unilateral operations and achievements. Despite military considerations there is considerable incentive for governments to organize and institutionalize international scientific collaboration.

Planning is a function that will be assisted by international organization because it will be required at both national and international levels. Even those decisions made primarily for domestic purposes will be influenced by pressures and information brought to bear in international conferences. Most uses of the sea are already impossible or at least difficult without international planning.

Another function typically performed by international organization is treaty negotiation to establish international norms. Such areas of concern as pollution control, conservation, and regulation of the ocean floor for peaceful uses come to mind.

An international agency will be needed to coordinate ocean operations conducted by national and international agencies much as IOC seeks to coordinate a large part of the world's oceanographic research. Governments can be expected to encourage such developments for the same reason they subscribe to international treaties—for their mutual advantage. This will be the case particularly with the far-ranging and often simultaneously conducted investigations necessary to map the ocean floor and the currents above.

Regulatory functions will be performed in all probability, including licensing, the enforcement of internationally agreed regulations, and possibly the collection of royalties. It seems reasonable to suppose that such regulation can be carried out by an international agency without granting it actual title to the resources being exploited. If the wealthy countries should ever become really determined to narrow the income gap between them and the developing countries, the agency might be authorized to collect and distribute income from deep sea exploitation in agreed proportions.

The agency may very well be assigned operational responsibilities such as monitoring ocean pollution, managing an undersea laboratory, or conducting training programs. Because several of the specialized agencies are already involved in these or similarly specialized activities, however, a new ocean agency may be limited to coordinating activities.

The Secretary-General has been requested by the General Assembly to formulate proposals for an international ocean resources program with the advice of a group of experts of his choice and "to cooperate" with certain specialized agencies whose activities are supposed to be coordinated by ECOSOC's Administrative Committee on Coordination. As a practical matter the UN is a long way from being effective in the harmonization or coordination of either national or international ocean programs. How to achieve better coordination is really the immediate question. In all probability a stronger mechanism than now exists will be needed to achieve effective exploration and exploitation of ocean resources. ACC is only advisory. The Secretary-General and the General Assembly will need to have greater influence over the specialized agencies and probably more effective communication with other non-UN organizations such as the Organization for Economic Cooperation and Development (OECD) and various intergovernmental fisheries organizations. As in the case of national administration, the special interests of particular established agencies tend to preclude the possibility of any one of them taking a sufficiently comprehensive view of a new problem and may militate against their accepting coordination.

The functions sketched in brief outline above would enable an international marine science agency to perform much as international organizations have performed since the establishment of the European river commissions more than 100 years ago. An international agency performing traditional roles need not foreclose the development of world or regional authorities—general purpose or special purpose—that might take title to, and "govern," ocean resources in the long pull. A more conservative, short-run arrangement would recognize that, for the present, decision centers for resource allocation and management are in national capitals. It would recognize that in market economies industrial and food-processing firms could be encouraged by national authorities to develop the oceans in a way that might be unlikely for the time being with exclusive international jurisdiction. It would recognize that industry and food production in planned economies depend even more on the authority and power of the national state. Finally, such an arrangement would recognize that more can be done by international organization in the here-and-now than *is* being done to meet human needs.

International organization is presently too weak as a governmental or administrative mechanism to manage the sea directly. Despite the fact that ocean space beyond national jurisdiction is uninhabited and unclaimed it is hard to conceive how international organization can be stronger in the water than it has been on the land. Even if this point is conceded, premature control of more than half the globe by an international body, exercising ownership and holding title, is as likely to create controversy as it is to avoid it. It is as likely to be economically inefficient as efficient. International ownership might also dampen incentives for ocean research and discovery. There is no short-run prospect of establishing the world political authority necessary for the political decisions (policy choices) that would in anything like equal terms benefit rich and poor nations or coastal and noncoastal nations. Few governments as yet have any real interest in a financially independent or even financially strengthened UN, however much they may wish increased aid flows and better terms of trade.

Several national governments, however, do have the requisite financial and industrial capabilities for ocean exploitation. The present system of international law and economic exchange has shown a potential for cooperative exploitation of the earth's resources. The first obvious task for international organization, therefore, is to develop ground rules for ocean exploitation and to improve national capabilities through international harmonization to the point of global coordination.

Science and Technology:

The Implications for International Institutions

EUGENE B. SKOLNIKOFF

I. INTRODUCTION

IT is clear that advances in science and technology, particularly technology, have wrought major changes in society. The effects of these advances have been felt directly through the development of major new artifacts such as the automobile, the telephone, and nuclear weapons. Major social effects, often of greater importance, have also resulted from the second-order consequences of this new technology: urbanization, mass culture, pollution, industrialization, etc.

International affairs have been affected by this process of social change induced by development and application of technology. The postwar development of bipolarity, the expansion of capabilities to communicate across and within borders, the emergence of new concerns such as space and atomic energy for international politics, the basic change in the physical meaning of military power, the alteration of the significance of geography in conflict, and other changes all stem in large part from technology.

At the same time I think it can be argued that technology-related changes in international affairs have not been as fundamental in practice as is sometimes assumed. The subject matter of international affairs has greatly expanded; the parameters of traditional issues have been altered; distinctions between domestic and international affairs have been blurred; and the interdependence of national economies has become steadily more marked. Yet, the underlying assumptions which govern international relations, particularly

EUGENE B. SKOLNIKOFF is professor of political science at the Massachusetts Institute of Technology, Cambridge, Massachusetts. The material for much of this article is drawn from *The International Imperatives of Technology* (Berkeley: Institute of International Studies, University of California, forthcoming). His research was supported in part by the Carnegie Endowment for International Peace, the National Science Foundation, and the Center for Space Research at M.I.T.

From Volume 25, No. 4 (1971), pp. 759–75.

the predominant view of the nation-state as the organizational unit of the international system, have not been seriously modified.'

For example, the United Nations as it is presently functioning is a deterrent both to integration of independent states and to development of a countervailing international power. Since the fundamental unit of the UN and the source of its power and resources continue to be individual states, the organization has if anything encouraged the proliferation of sovereign states. Atomic weapons, to take another example, might have been expected (indeed, were expected by many) to cause a fundamental change in the international system by drastically altering the meaning of war as a viable policy alternative. Instead, over time they have become an umbrella under which more traditional or conventional warfare flourishes between states. The emergence of bipolarity, which was greatly enhanced by the development and cost of nuclear arsenals, slowly recedes as a dominant fact of international life. The inutility of nuclear weapons encourages the development of multiple smaller power centers based on nation-states.

Against this background one must view with a skeptical eye the possibility of dramatic change flowing from future technological developments and applications. Barring any catastrophic events in military or political areas, and this is a major caveat of course, I believe that over the next decade advances in science and technology are unlikely to cause any but marginal, though important, changes in international affairs. However, looking beyond this decade as we must in the 1970s, it is possible to see continued intensification of some trends whose cumulative impact may be very much more significant. The normative question of whether there *should* be more fundamental change in the 1970s, especially in light of technology-related trends going beyond the next decade, is a more debatable proposition.

This conclusion—that change will be moderate—is in contrast to some of the apocalyptic literature that has appeared recently arguing that we are on the brink of disaster. Such a picture is overdrawn, though it must be noted that we lack adequate information about what is actually happening to our global environment. In any case uncertain and unprovable apocalyptic predictions do not lead to useful analysis or prescriptions for change. Such predictions cannot be completely ruled out, however, for they cannot be proved wrong and may well be more nearly accurate on a longer time horizon. The weight of the evidence does not yet support them, but the possibility of serious physical danger to our global environment cannot be ignored in foreign policy planning.

Using the 1970s as the primary time frame in this discussion, we must inevitably be much more concerned with technology than with science. It is in any case the applications of technology that have the dominant impact on international relations. There are occasional exceptions—for example, the implications of geophysics for an agreement on a comprehensive nuclear test ban —but in general, and certainly on a short time scale, technology is of greatest interest. Technology as discussed here includes not only the actual techniques and artifacts developed but also the side effects which accompany the application of technology. As we look ahead, it is the side effects which grow out of intensive use of technology by burgeoning populations and economically growing states that are likely to pose the most serious issues for international affairs.

II. GENERAL AREAS OF INTERNATIONAL POLITICAL IMPACT

In order to identify future trends it is helpful to start with a brief review of the major effects which technology has had on international relations in the recent past. One such effect is the dramatic growth of the interdependence and interpenetration of societies. The appetite of technological societies for resources which are widely and unevenly scattered throughout the globe contributes to this phenomenon. So, too, do the "revolutions" in communication and transportation that have led to the international movement of people, information, and ideas on an unprecedented scale. The growth of industry, especially high-technology industry, has increased reliance on markets and capital beyond national borders and thus penetration of these borders. The development of global technologies requires multinational cooperation and creates cross-national dependencies.

Another major effect of technology has been to blur the distinction between domestic and foreign affairs. Interdependence is a significant causative factor in this phenomenon as is the ease with which domestic developments can be publicized and related to foreign policies. Further, the expansion of the subject matter of international relations has brought more elements of society and government into direct participation in foreign affairs. This expansion is facilitated to the extent that the primacy of the Department of State among government agencies in foreign policy making has been seriously eroded. Television has had a substantial impact in making foreign policy a subject of intense and immediate debate and thus has made it easier to relate foreign and domestic issues within the country.

Strategic-military affairs are also obviously strongly affected by technology. Changes in the destructiveness, speed of delivery, and cost of weapons systems have altered the conditions of warfare, the meaning and usefulness of military power, and the time scale of the decisionmaking process. As noted earlier these military developments have not wrought fundamental changes in international relations as might have once been expected, but they have, nonetheless, had important effects.

Technology has also had important effects in the creation of new patterns of relationships between countries, particularly between the developed and less developed worlds. The gap between North and South, as measured by ability to accept and apply modern technology, is presently large and is growing larger. Even among developed countries the notion of a "technology gap" implies concern for the growth of a new kind of dependence relationship, a dependence based on effective monopolies in high-technology industrial fields such as computers, electronics, or applied nuclear energy. Technological monopolies can give the country with the advantage great economic, political, and even cultural influence. Dependence resulting from such monopolies may be more subtle and difficult to overcome than past patterns of direct domination through economic or military power have been.

In institutional terms technology has led to the rise of new elites involved in the decisionmaking process and has contributed to the proliferation of international organizations built around new technologies or newly concerned with the application of technology. The advance and use of technology have contributed to marked alteration in foreign policy machinery, notably in the number of actors involved in policymaking, in the subject and character of the issues, in the information that must be processed, in the role of former major actors (such as ambassadors), in the time allowed for decisionmaking, and in the pressures and interests that must be considered.

There are other ways to evaluate the impact of science and technology on the international scene and many additional specifics to enumerate. For purposes of this article, however, the examples above are adequate. A more interesting question is how any of these trends are likely to change in the future and whether new trends of substantial importance will emerge.

Almost certainly the interdependence and interpenetration fostered by technology will continue to be among the results of advancing technology. In fact, interdependence is likely to be intensified by several technology-related developments. One is the likelihood that multinational corporations, many maintaining their position by dominance of high-technology industries, will continue to expand in size and scope. This will result in substantially more economic integration and will force the development of international political cooperation to meet the relatively independent power of multinational firms. It will also likely lead to more extensive international economic, and particularly monetary, cooperation between governments as a means of regulating the firms.

Another cause of intensified interdependence will be the development of global technologies that automatically create dependence relations: communications, weather forecasting and modification, geologic surveillance, direct broadcasting, and others. In the long run the development of low-cost communications may be the most significant cause of interdependence as it would encourage extensive international data transmission and the growth of electronic technologies for the handling and use of large amounts of data. It is difficult to specify in any detail the effects of this technology, but the growth of "data dependency" relations may prove of crucial importance in tying economies and societies together. At the least the expansion of television exchanges dependent on low-cost communications is also likely to increase cross-national interpenetration.

Other trends, such as the further blurring of distinctions between domestic and foreign affairs and the continued widening of the technological gaps between developed and less developed countries, are also likely to be intensified. Notwithstanding a growing popular reaction against technology, one can also expect a continued enhancement of the role of intellectual elites as essential and powerful elements in the governmental decisionmaking process.

Some trends, specifically the impact of scientific or technological developments related to weapons, are likely to remain substantially unchanged in the next decade. More will be said about this later.

Finally, we can look toward some new trends and some trends that, while not new, are so changed in degree as to be different in kind. One of the latter is the requirement that international political machinery assume much greater functional responsibilities (i.e., regulation, control, allocation, and management of technology or its costs and benefits) than it does today. This conclusion receives more detailed discussion in the next section.

Another likely development will be the creation of new patterns of conflict between nation-states, patterns that grow out of conflicts of interest generated by technology. In the future, controversy may arise from unequal use of unevenly distributed natural resources, increasing gaps in technology utilization (or modernization), reaction to imported technology seen as cultural domination and economic imperialism, divergent objectives over issues such as pollution, decisions about the criteria by which global technologies should be designed and utilized, and allocation of resources found in an international environment. The disputes which arise over these issues will generally be between the technologically advanced countries and those countries aspiring to reach comparable levels.

Examples of such conflicts of interest are cropping up frequently even now: disputes in the International Bank for Reconstruction and Development (IBRD) over the weight to be given to the environmental effects of large development projects such as dams; long delays in agreement on the permanent charter for the International Telecommunications Satellite Consortium (IN-TELSAT) because of questions of control of system design and allocation of benefits; and coordinated action by oil-producing countries to improve their bargaining position against the Western oil companies. Such conflicts of interest will almost certainly be more prevalent and more serious in the future.

The next decade is also likely to see the further substantial enhancement of the role of television, and thus of public involvement, in the making of foreign policy. Instant and vivid exposure to worldwide events, provided with increased ease and at reduced cost, may make the role of public opinion a much more decisive element in foreign affairs than it has been in the past. Television may even make the moral values of a society more relevant elements in the policy process.

We will also move farther down the road toward technologically vulnerable societies in which certain kinds of intervention, willful or inadvertent, can cause the collapse of systems affecting many people at once. The power blackout in the Northeast and the urban chaos resulting from strikes by workers who provide critical services are indicative of the sensitivity of society to small-scale disruption. The increasing technological interdependence of modern societies employing ever more complex technologies within growing concentrations of population is likely to exacerbate this situation and heighten its political importance. It must be noted, however, that technology can also reduce vulnerability through redundancy or system independence although substantial expenditures may be required to do so.

Finally, I would single out a growing reaction in technologically advanced societies against technology itself as a new factor of considerable importance in the 1970s. It is difficult to predict the effects of this attitude. Conceivably, it could work to slow technology-related change and thereby to delay some of the trends mentioned here. In time its effects could materially erode the strength underlying the technological capabilities of advanced countries; it could particularly affect the ability of those countries to use technology to meet some of the longer term needs created or exacerbated by technology (e.g., substitution of nuclear power for conventional power sources to meet problems of atmospheric pollution). More likely, this new antitechnology bias will assert itself, for the 1970s at least, as a major unsettling societal force leading to difficulty in asserting leadership, to sharper questioning of values and of the political process, and to a lack of clear national objectives. The effect could be to contribute to the inward-turning already evident in the United States and to the development of a desire to use technology to achieve autarky rather than interdependence. A trend toward autarky is not likely to be successful (though technology itself would make a considerable degree of autarky a feasible goal) because present technological developments and desires to use technology are leading toward greater interdependence. But the tension between the two pressures could produce major internal contradictions and conflict over goals and use of resources.

III. Specific Areas of Impact

Armaments

During the 1970s it is unlikely that there will be developments in science and technology that will seriously affect the power balance between the superpowers. Such developments cannot be completely ruled out, of course, but the more probable course of events is a continuation of the present standoff between the United States and the Union of Soviet Socialist Republics, though with substantial developments in weapons systems and substantial additional expenditure of resources.

The technology-related area with the greatest potential for destabilizing the present balance lies in the development of means to neutralize offensive missile forces, either by antiballistic missiles (ABMs) after they are fired or by a capability to locate and destroy fixed and mobile missile forces. It is hard to imagine at this time the development of an ABM capability that would give assurance of protection against a missile strike sufficient to imply the capability to neutralize another country's missile force. Such a development by one, or even both, superpowers would certainly change the strategic relationship, but it is most unlikely well into the future. The construction of an ABM system using present technology could also be destabilizing, of course, but the net result would almost certainly be reciprocal construction of ABM systems and more intercontinental ballistic missiles (ICBMs). Such construction would simply restabilize the strategic balance at a higher level of expenditure.

A capability to locate and destroy missile forces, particularly undersea forces, is another matter and one which is receiving much attention. Clearly, the capability to destroy undersea forces, currently the most secure component of a deterrent, before they can be fired could have a destabilizing effect on the superpowers' relationship. But, if such a capability emerges as a serious possibility, the probable result would be the development of new countermeasures and additional offensive weapons. It would be more useful, in fact, to consider any new technology for surveillance of undersea forces as a candidate for arms control rather than for armaments.

Development of more exotic weapons (weather control, genetic weapons, etc.) will take place after the 1970s if at all. Surprise is always a possibility, but it is difficult to imagine any category of development in the near future that, at worst, would have more than a minor and transient effect on the basic power relationship between the superpowers.

Other political developments related to strategic armaments are likely. Specifically, the rise of the People's Republic of China (Communist China) and, conceivably, of Western Europe to "superpower status," as measured by strategic weapons systems, are possibilities which must be considered. But the technologies involved are unlikely to be different in kind from what the United States and the Soviet Union now have or are building.

Weapons developments which would affect the power position of other countries in major ways can be ruled out with less certainty. Leaving questions of nuclear proliferation aside (the problem of controlling proliferation is likely to increase along with the increase in nuclear power installations), substantial change in local war weapons is likely. For example, developments pioneered by the United States in Vietnam are likely to be copied by others when costs permit or when the big powers pay the bill. Use of new antiaircraft weapons may for a time change the significance of air power in small wars, but countervailing tactics and weapons will be likely to redress the balance before long.

Thus, the 1970s are not likely to see armaments developments that appreciably alter the current situation. There may well be increased expenditure to pay for new developments. There is likely to be one, and perhaps two, new superpowers. There may also be some developments with transient effects of significance for particular limited situations, but there will be nothing in the armaments themselves that would constitute a quantum change.

Nation-States

One of the major effects of science and technology on states will clearly be the need for increased reference to the international community in a growing number of politically and economically important fields. In effect, this need to place decisions in an international environment will constitute an erosion of traditional concepts of national sovereignty, an erosion already long in process but likely to be much exaggerated in the next decade. The growing realization of this erosion by governments is in the first instance likely to make them more jealous of the prerogatives they retain. International agreement is therefore likely to become more rather than less difficult to achieve, especially over issues with major economic impact.

The increasing interdependence between states for resources, markets, audiences, capital, and information and the continuing coalescence of domestic and foreign affairs are also leading toward a reduction of the significance of governments as independent actors on the international scene. The state will remain the unit of negotiation and the point of political and diplomatic contact, but its effective freedom and independence of action in most areas will be gradually diminished even if there is no outward recognition of the changed situation.

The costs and technological base required to realize the benefits of some technologies will also create pressures for political developments designed to pool technological resources on an international scale. In some cases such sharing may contribute to political integration; in most instances it will more likely result only in increased cooperation—and interdependence—between sovereign states. The rise of competing centers of power in the multinational business corporation, based largely on leadership in sophisticated advanced technology, is also likely to lead governments increasingly to pool resources and to attempt to work together to control international business.

Thus, in several different ways the 1970s will be a period in which national governments' independence of action and ability to control events will become increasingly compromised in technology-related areas, though without any formal, structural alteration of the nation-state. In fact, the existing structural forms are likely to be reinforced as additional actors become involved. No specific type of technology is predominant among the issues that will concern governments; all types of technology, and particularly the side effects of more intensive use of technology, are implicated.

Less Developed Countries

The problems of development cannot appropriately be dealt with here, but two points relevant to technology and its implications are worth making. The first point is that the role of technology in development is still little understood. Much has been said and written about the importance of the transfer of technology from developed to less developed countries and of the necessity for sound scientific and technological infrastructure, but a good theoretical underpinning to guide policy and investment of resources is lacking. Countries want modern technology as a symbol of modernization, and they need new technology like modified seed strains or communications systems to achieve their development objectives. But the scale of resources required, their mix, and the institutions needed to make them effective remain matters of art.

The second point has to do with so-called technology gaps. However great the politicized gap between the United States and Western Europe, it is as nothing compared to the technology gap between North and South. As noted, most commentators believe that this gap is likely to widen rather than narrow.

In time the problems created by disparities between rich and poor countries are likely to become even more serious an international issue, not only in economic terms as at present but also in a new dimension. Technologically advanced countries may preclude the possibility that others can ever achieve comparable income levels. The issue here is whether the appetite of highly industrialized societies for raw materials and the environmental contamination the use of the resources causes will in the long run set a ceiling on the movement of other societies in the same direction. For example, will necessary natural resources for industrialization be depleted? Will there have to be a total global limit on carbon dioxide (CO_2) emission or heat dissipated in the atmosphere, with developed countries already using most of the quota? There can be no definitive answers to these and similar questions today, nor will all dimensions of these problems be fully clear in the 1970s. But it behooves us to begin to understand that situation for its political implications could be profound: at the very least an irresistible demand to share more equitably the wealth of advanced societies, backed up, perhaps, by a threat on the part of raw material–providing countries to withhold the resources advanced societies must have.

International Machinery

The clearest and most certain international impact of advancements in the application and use of technology will be felt by international organizations, including nongovernmental organizations as well as the United Nations, regional organizations, and other intergovernmental bodies. In effect there will be a rapidly growing need to deal with the many functional implications of technology on an international rather than a national basis. New technologies or the side effects of increased application of technology will "force" a degree of international management and control that goes well beyond what is already in evidence. States will find it necessary to seek international agreement and to accept internationally determined constraints on their actions in a variety of fields of growing political and economic significance, and these developments will raise important questions about the capability of current international machinery and governmental practices to meet the new requirements.

A brief look at a few global issues related to technology will illustrate the point. Many different aspects of the environmental issue, for example, are relevant.[1] Atmospheric effects of the activities of an increasingly technological society are suddenly being recognized. These effects, most often pollution caused by industrial effluents, are largely of regional concern at the moment, but there are also global implications that are as yet little understood. Accumulation of CO_2 or particulate matter could in time have profound effects on the heat balance of the planet and thus alter climate in unknown ways; so, too, could exhaust from high-altitude aircraft or continued transfer of land from agricultural to urban use.[2] Similarly, pollution in the rivers and oceans from agricultural use of pesticides and insecticides, from disposal of atomic waste, or from oil spills could seriously interfere with natural processes essential to life and with the ability to claim living resources from the seas.

These and other pollution problems will undoubtedly require international action. At the very least global monitoring will be necessary in order to obtain

[1] More extensive detail is available from, among other sources, Gorden J. D. MacDonald, "The Modification of Planet Earth by Man," *Technology Review*, October–November 1969 (Vol. 72, No. 1), pp. 27–35; T. F. Malone, "Current Developments in the Atmospheric Sciences and Some of Their Implications for Foreign Policy" (Paper presented at the National Academy of Sciences, Washington, June 16–17, 1968); and *Man's Impact on the Global Environment: Assessment and Recommendations for Action*, Report of the Study of Critical Environmental Problems (SCEP) (Cambridge, Mass: M.I.T. Press, 1970).
[2] *Man's Impact on the Global Environment*.

the necessary information for analysis and to warn of impending problems. Regulations will have to be instituted, at first on a regional basis but ultimately on a global basis, to control those "domestic" activities that cause problems across borders or pose dangers more widely. These regulatory and monitoring functions will have to be internationally based to be acceptable and to ensure equity of application and effect. In turn, such regulatory activity will require the development of institutional capabilities to monitor compliance, inspection, enforcement, and settlement of disputes. The UN Conference on the Human Environment scheduled for 1972 in Stockholm will be seized with the issues of developing such international machinery for regulation and control.

Inadvertent modification of the environment is not the only concern. Large-scale experiments such as Project Westford[3] or underground nuclear explosions in the Aleutians will eventually have to come under some kind of international regulation because of the danger they may pose to all countries. The United States may well come to regret its present assumption of unilateral authority with respect to carrying out such large-scale actions. On a longer time scale (but not much longer for preparation is required during the 1970s) new technology for planned weather and climate modification will require international regulation, allocation of costs and benefits, and perhaps management of the technology itself. Much of the required research and development is already being conducted as international experiments by states under the auspices of the World Meteorological Organization (WMO) and the International Council of Scientific Unions (ICSU). Both of these organizations will certainly be involved in the resulting application and control of this technology.

In regard to the oceans it is already clear that not only the resources of the seabed but also the living resources of the sea do and will require internationally based controls and management. The world is far from innocent with regard to international machinery dealing with ocean matters, but the requirements to be placed on that machinery will grow inexorably. Deep drilling technology is rapidly advancing as a direct result of substantial economic incentives, and fishing technology is also, though not as quickly, moving ahead. Both already require means to control access, allocate resources and benefits, apply and monitor regulations, adjudicate disputes, and so forth. The need for expanding the functions performed by international machinery will only be further emphasized each day that passes. The UN Conference on the Law of the Sea scheduled for 1973 will be faced with that range of issues.

We can also expect continuing development in the applications of technology in outer space, particularly in communications (including direct broadcasting, though it can be argued that that will be a much more limited tech-

[3] Project Westford deployed a belt of copper "needles" in the upper atmosphere for radio communication experiments.

nology than is generally assumed), meteorology, resource mapping, agriculture, navigation, and data transmission.[4] Each of these will have important implications for international machinery. For example, the technology emerging for improved weather forecasting will require international management to ensure the equitable distribution of benefits and to reduce dependence on the continued goodwill of any single state. The United States may provide most of the original technology, but, as in the case of communications satellites today, as soon as the technology becomes important to other countries continued domination of the system by the United States becomes politically unacceptable as a permanent arrangement.

The pattern will be the same for other applications of technology in space because of the international nature of the space environment, the potential economic value of some of the information generated, the need to assure equity and impartiality of operation, the need to allocate radio frequencies and orbital slots, and the cost of the technology. We already have, of course, one major new international institution—INTELSAT—in this area.

The depletion of natural resources is becoming once again a subject of growing concern though in fact serious resource limitations are not likely (rightly or wrongly) to become a prominent issue of international affairs until after the 1970s. The issues here are not only the obvious questions of assuring adequate supplies of needed resources but also those of equitable distribution of benefits from resources and of wise management of a necessarily limited supply. The problem is that an increasingly technological society has been, for example, demanding metals at a rate of growth of 6 percent per year. The entire metal production prior to World War II is about equal to the amount which has since been consumed.

Whether or not we have immediate shortages of resources for which there are inadequate substitutes (itself a controversial issue), it is clear that the world is sitting on a finite resource supply that must eventually be rationed and "managed." Moreover, it may well be that our present use of resources is highly inefficient from the perspective of future needs. The uneven distribution of resources over the globe inevitably raises questions of control and equity. At some time international regulation and allocation of natural resources on a major scale will have to begin, and perhaps the process should start within this decade.

The interaction of population growth and the need for food and other resources is another area that will press on the international community notwithstanding the temporary respite of the Green Revolution. Estimates vary but the UN secretary-general's report on world population predicts close to

4 For details consult *Useful Application of Earth-Oriented Satellites* (Washington: National Academy of Sciences and National Research Council, 1969); and *Selected Space Goals and Objectives and Their Relation to National Goals* (Report No. BMI-NLVP-TR-69-2) (Columbus, Ohio: Battelle Memorial Institute [for the National Aeronautics and Space Administration], July 15, 1969).

a 50 percent growth in population by 1985, and the Food and Agriculture Organization (FAO) estimates that to meet population growth (assuming no change in per capita income) food production must increase between 3.2 and 3.8 percent per year against an average of 2.8 percent in 1962.[5] Coupled with some growth in income, the necessary increase in food supplies will be even higher.

There is little point in attempting to spell this situation out in detail here. It is clear that, even if population growth created no other problems, the magnitude of the task of supplying necessary food will be enormous and will increasingly be of concern to the international community. Whether international organizations will or should be charged with greater responsibility for the production and distribution of food supplies is a matter of judgment.

But there are other complications as well. Increased production of food implies substantial increase in the use of fertilizers and pesticides both of which can have major detrimental ecological effects. If DDT were to be prohibited without an equivalent substitute at the same price, the net effect would be to reduce the production and availability of food supplies. No qualifying substitute is yet available. Furthermore, the new seed strains that are the basis of the Green Revolution are highly vulnerable to disease so that sudden catastrophe could strike if much of the world's population were to become dependent on these varieties.

Population growth itself will of course lead to more pressure on natural resources, to increased production of energy, transportation of fuel, and industrialization, and thereby to more deleterious environmental effects. It will thus add to the need for international management, regulation, and allocation of global resources and of national activities that have international environmental and other effects. On a longer time scale population growth itself will eventually be a candidate for international regulation. It should be noted that in these areas the conflicts of interest between the developed and less developed worlds are likely to become a major source of tension.

The major conclusion to be drawn from these brief illustrations, each of which could be elaborated in great detail, is that the locus of decisionmaking in many technology-related areas *must* move (and is moving) from the national to the international sphere. The imperative results from the international nature and effects of forthcoming technology-related developments and from the apparent inevitability of these developments. They are inevitable because of the dispersed decisionmaking characteristic of technology and also because many of them are already in the process of development or applica-

[5] UN Document E/CN.9/231 (*World Population Situation*, Note by the Secretary-General), table 14, p. 117; and Graham Chedd, "Famine or Sanity?" *New Scientist*, October 23, 1969 (Vol. 44, No. 672), pp. 178–182.

tion. Most of these technology-related developments could not be stopped even if it were the political will to do so.

The need for international machinery is not new. The world is accustomed to international management or regulation and even monitoring in many areas—telecommunications, postal service, standardization of weights and measures, health, communications, and others. What will be different in the future is the degree of international interaction that will be required for many more subjects, the extent of the regulation needed, the fact that substantially more of what have been considered purely national matters will have to come under some kind of international jurisdiction with corresponding limitations on national sovereignty, and the related fact that the political and economic importance of subjects requiring international decision will sharply increase.

A major question for the 1970s, therefore, is whether existing international institutions and the attitudes of governments toward them are adequate to enable the institutions to meet the responsibilities they will have to assume during and after this decade. It is critical to remember that even if the major institutional impact will be after 1980, any institution building necessary must start well in advance if there is to be any hope for its success.

IV. POLICY ISSUES

International Institutions

The first and the clearest question to be asked with regard to existing international machinery is whether it is capable of fulfilling the functions it will have to perform by the end of the decade and beyond. We can think of these functions broadly as 1) provision of service, 2) norm creation and allocation, 3) rule observance and settlement of disputes, and 4) operation. There will be substantially increased demands made on all of these functions and the latter three, particularly, will be politically difficult.

In fact, an examination of present machinery shows that all of these functions are performed at least to a limited extent today. A flight of imagination is not necessary to visualize these functions being performed by an international system greatly expanded in scale and importance in the future. Nation-states today do reach agreement on international regulations and controls (telecommunications, air traffic, health, fisheries), and by and large they adhere to those agreements. There are examples of international inspection (fisheries, atomic energy, health) that work reasonably well, and international operation of large-scale technology has begun (communications satellites, atmospheric research programs).

But there is cause for grave concern. The institutional mechanisms that exist, whether the United Nations and its specialized agencies, regional organizations, or other specialized international machinery, are geared to a scale of activity and degree of responsibility far lower than will be necessary. As these issues grow in political and economic salience, there can be little confidence that the existing machinery is adequate to cope with the changed demands. The United Nations system is too often characterized by highly variable competence, jurisdictional conflict, weak and diffuse authority structures, burgeoning bureaucracy, lack of interest, and inadequate coordination machinery, among other problems. This is not to say that nothing works. In fact several of the United Nations agencies perform quite well, and the reasons for their success can be quite instructively analyzed. Effective performance usually correlates with small organizations, technical nature of missions, relatively high influence of knowledgeable member states, high degree of agreement on scope and objectives, relatively greater reliance on national experts than on international bureaucracy, and other such characteristics.

Regional organizations or other non-UN bodies often work more effectively than universal membership organizations by focusing on a limited range of issues or by operating only among a limited group of like-minded countries. Among these as well wide variations in performance and competence are found, and they of course present different kinds of problems and opportunities for a state's foreign policies than those of the universal membership organizations.

Shortcomings of institutional machinery cannot be blamed simply on the institutions. The attitudes of member states are critical and are equally a basic cause of the existing malaise. States relinquish apparent attributes of sovereignty only reluctantly, especially to organizations in which their control is seriously diluted. The participation of many states in international organizations and particularly in the United Nations is too often characterized by little knowledge and much politics. The quality of national missions is often weak. Domestic coordination of policy is often even poorer than that between international bodies.

In short, current international machinery and national attitudes toward that machinery are inadequate for the tasks that will somehow have to be performed by international machinery in the future. The situation is made considerably more serious when we realize that future responsibilities will be of much greater political significance for they will involve allocation of important resources, management of large systems, inspection and control that reaches into domestic activities, and international settlement of disputes that have substantial economic and political impact.

We are dealing here with a major issue of foreign policy that is only beginning to receive the attention it deserves. Realistically, no state is likely to surrender willingly important prerogatives to institutions over which it has little influence and which do not have the competence to carry out their responsibilities. Nor should they. Some states may have few choices, but the United

States has many. It must take the lead in planning for the development of international institutions that are capable of assuming responsibility and of adequately representing the interests of all countries. Is that a realistic prospect?

Here we have a major job of institution building for the 1970s. We have time, but not much. "Revolutionary" changes in the international system are not necessary now; however, if there is inadequate institution building now, revolutionary changes are likely later when global dangers and inequities release irresistible political forces.

It is not a foregone conclusion that the United Nations ought to be reshaped in order to provide the machinery necessary to meet the new functional needs. Perhaps more organizations like INTELSAT are needed; perhaps more regional bodies; perhaps additional bilateral arrangements. Some proliferation of international organizations may be necessary and desirable, especially when existing machinery is weak and inflexible. Distasteful as proliferation may be, it could quite easily be preferable to granting increased responsibility to machinery unable to fulfill that responsibility.

But, without real study and adequate collaboration between technologically advanced countries, the necessary international machinery and governmental attitudes toward that machinery are unlikely to be available in time. Conflicts of interest with technologically backward countries in the design and operation of international machinery may be unavoidable. A major policy question in the future is likely to be whether or not it is realistic for technologically advanced countries to take a paternalistic attitude toward the third world on these issues. In order to achieve workable, reasonably efficient institutions it may be necessary for advanced countries to take the position that technologies or their effects will have to be left under the control of those with the technological knowledge. The political difficulty and cost of that stance may be great, but there may well be no alternative. Somehow, however, it should be possible to avoid paternalism without dooming the international system to representative but essentially unworkable international organizations.

Control of Technology

The question of the control of technology or its direction into "more useful" channels necessarily arises. In particular one can ask whether it is somehow possible to internationalize science and technology to help both to control and to direct technology more wisely. In this century science and technology have been used primarily to achieve national, rather than international, objectives. This national orientation will undoubtedly continue as a major focus of technological development. However, even on the national scene there is a growing attempt to anticipate the side effects of technology and to include those anticipated effects as part of the original decisionmaking for new technology. This movement is in its infancy and has a long way to go before there are appreciable results.

There are also good arguments, however, for attempting to put some portion of the scientific and technological enterprise under international auspices. There have been proposals, for example, for an international science foundation. Such a foundation may be the only way to get adequate research and development on subjects determined by international needs rather than by national objectives. That argument would be particularly relevant to less developed countries (for example, to meet the need for an economical DDT substitute or to develop health systems based on $100 per capita incomes). It would also be relevant to the development of global technologies that can serve to ameliorate the undesirable effects of technology.

Another argument for internationally sponsored research and development is that such programs can help to keep "dangerous" subjects in the international domain. The ultimate appropriation of such technologies for purely national purposes would, therefore, be less likely and the prospects for their international control correspondingly more likely. Genetic technology, with potentially dangerous as well as beneficial applications, is a case in point.

Lastly, internationally sponsored research and development may also be of great importance in developing "international" expertise. This expertise is likely to be essential for the operation of the international machinery which, in turn, is necessary to cope with the effects and regulation of technology. Looking ahead, one can see the importance of developing some international institutions as the arbiters and controllers of technology that are and are seen to be impartial.

V. Conclusion

Barring major surprise or catastrophe, advances in science and technology and their application in the 1970s are likely to cause substantial but not revolutionary changes on the international scene. However, the potential for cumulative, more drastic change in the subsequent decade is very real. In particular, substantial international institution building and changes in national attitudes will be essential during the 1970s and must be understood and set in motion without delay.

INTERNATIONAL INSTITUTIONS AND THE ENVIRONMENTAL CRISIS: A LOOK AHEAD

David A. Kay and Eugene B. Skolnikoff

DAVID A. KAY is associate professor of political science, University of Wisconsin, Madison, and visiting research scholar, Carnegie Endowment for International Peace, New York. EUGENE B. SKOLNIKOFF is professor of political science, Massachusetts Institute of Technology, Cambridge, Mass.

In the industrialized northern hemisphere we are assaulted daily with evidence of the deteriorating quality of the human environment: Rivers are closed to fishing because of dangerous levels of contamination; the safety of important foods is challenged; the foul air that major urban areas have been forced to endure is now spreading like an inkblot into surrounding areas. Lack of early concern about the implications for the environment of the widespread application of modern technology has allowed the problem to grow rapidly into a critical domestic and international issue.

Certainly one indication of the growing international public and political attention being devoted to the environmental issue was the 1968 decision of the United Nations General Assembly to convene a conference on the environment.[1] The speed with which the organization moved to convene this conference was markedly greater than that shown for earlier UN conferences on trade and development or the peaceful uses of outer space.

We do not propose to summarize here the points made by the contributors to this volume. Our effort, rather, will be to identify some of the implications for international politics and international organizations of the process described and analyzed in these articles.

I.

Central to understanding the drive behind the convening of the Stockholm conference as well as assessing the continuing effects of this new concern for environmental problems is the evidence that has

---

[1] General Assembly Resolution 2398 (XXIII), December 3, 1968.

From Volume 26, No. 2 (1972), pp. 469–78.

developed on the imbalances and strains created in the global ecosystem by the widespread application of powerful new technologies. These imbalances and strains have created problems that are in many cases global in nature and that will in all probability require solutions breaching traditional political, sectoral, and disciplinary boundaries.

Many of these imbalances and strains have been identified. Examples are the 10 percent rise in atmospheric carbon dioxide over the last century; the tremendous increase in the amount of waste products which become pollutants, indicated by the fact that in 1968 solid wastes in the United States amounted to 7 million automobiles, 10 million tons of paper, 48 million cans, and 142 million tons of smoke and noxious fumes; the estimated one billion pounds of DDT that have entered the environment and the additional 100 million pounds that are used each year in the face of growing evidence of the toxicity to some forms of animal life of the concentration of such persistent pesticides in the food chain.[2] Although these and other indicators of environmental imbalance have played an important role in pushing environmental concerns to the forefront of major public policy questions, they have, perhaps more importantly, made us aware of how little is known about the workings of the global ecosystem. While written specifically about the state of scientific knowledge concerning man's impact on climate, the judgment of the recently completed *Report of the Study of Man's Impact on Climate* is appropos in describing the general state of knowledge concerning man's relation to the ecosystem:

> During the past two decades there has been significant and encouraging progress by the scientific community in developing the theory, models and measurement techniques that will be necessary for determining man's impact on climate. We are, however, disturbed that there are major and serious gaps in our understanding of the complex systems that determine climate, and that data in many critical areas are incomplete, inconsistent, and even contradictory. . . . It is clear to us that without additional research and monitoring programs the scientific community will not be able to provide the firm answers which society may need if large-scale, and possibly irreversible, inadvertent modification of the climate is to be avoided.[3]

[2] See *Man's Impact on the Global Environment: Assessment and Recommendations for Action* (Report of the Study of Critical Environmental Problems) (Cambridge, Mass: M.I.T. Press, 1970); *Environmental Quality: The Second Annual Report of the Council on Environmental Quality, together with the Message of the President to the Congress* (Washington: Government Printing Office, August 1971); and *Problems of the Human Environment: Report of the Secretary-General* (UN Documented E/4667).

[3] *Inadvertent Climate Modification* (Report of the Study of Man's Impact on Climate) (Cambridge, Mass: M.I.T. Press, 1971).

One of the clear messages that has emerged from the process leading to the Stockholm conference is that, lacking clear knowledge of our ecological system, we constantly hazard man's future in a game whose rules we do not yet fully understand. Yet the same lack of knowledge makes it difficult to design specific policies and measures. This situation has certain important implications for the activities of international organizations. As many of the contributors to this volume have noted, there is a desperate need, on a continuing basis, for information, research, and analysis about the environment. The objectives of this research and analysis function should be: 1) to provide continuous, up-to-date information on what is happening in the global ecosystem; 2) to determine the likely effects of present trends and to establish tolerances; 3) to develop alternatives to, or modifications of, current practices when necessary; and 4) to establish hard data on the costs and benefits of alternative courses of action for political decision.[4]

In a fragmented manner many international organizations already have taken steps toward these objectives. It seems clear that as a result of the Stockholm process additional pressure will be exerted for the development within the United Nations of a recognized and impartial analytical capability for considering the environmental implications of ongoing and contemplated scientific and technological developments as well as for the development of the capability for making recommendations on the necessary public policies required by these developments. Both Richard Gardner and Brian Johnson in their articles have examined the various institutional shapes that this research and analysis function might assume as a result of the Stockholm conference. But what can be said about its implications for the United Nations system regardless of the exact institutional shape that it assumes?

Any movement toward increasing the responsibility of international machinery for collection, research, and analysis in the highly complex area of environmental affairs will increase substantially the requirements for the effective performance of that machinery. At present it cannot be assumed that the international secretariat of the United Nations system has either the quality or influence required for these new tasks although there are "islands" of technical quality and efficiency. Unless the quality of the personnel and the effectiveness of the institutions engaged in these new functions are clearly respected by governments, the scientific community, other international organizations, and the public, there is little hope that this research

[4] Eugene B. Skolnikoff, "The International Functional Implications of Future Technology," *Journal of International Affairs*, 1971 (Vol. 25, No. 2), p. 274.

and analysis function will be able to have a major impact on environmental developments. It is doubtful that such a level of quality can be developed without substantial institutional change, including a direct challenge to many of the hallowed canons of international secretariats, such as the concepts of career civil service and geographic representation. In very few areas of the United Nations system has effective performance been the standard against which bureaucratic form and organization have been tested. New patterns and altered forms of existing organizational patterns will surely be needed if international machinery of recognized quality and influence is to develop in this area.

Development of international machinery for research, analysis, and policy review of scientific and technological developments concerning the changing environment also is likely to have important implications for the relationship between the United Nations and member states. International organizations already perform a wide variety of regulatory functions, some are engaged in allocation of resources, a few even are engaged in the inspection and enforcement of agreed international rules. States have already delegated appreciable portions of their sovereignty to international bodies—more than most realize—(in addition to watching the erosion of their sovereignty in a multitude of other ways through the rapidly growing and largely unavoidable interdependence of national societies). The essentially boundless nature of the "environment" as an issue area is likely to further narrow the scope of unilateral, national decisionmaking and to increase the role and authority of international machinery.

"Environment" as an issue area has no simple bounds. To be concerned with assessing the impact of scientific and technological developments on the environment requires being concerned with the full array of issues affecting civilization, from disposal of waste to population growth, from the methods and amount of food production to the wise use of resources, from the transfer and control of technology to the calculation of the real costs of economic growth. This is thus not a concern with a new problem for societies but with the oldest and most central of all problems—the allocation of values within and between polities. Inevitably, as international institutions develop their concern and capacity for analyzing environmental impact issues, they will find themselves involved in many questions touching on major political, economic, and social problems.

In this connection it should be noted that the process leading up to the Stockholm conference was designed by the secretariat to go beyond the involvement of traditional diplomatic and government participants and to seek to draw into the preparatory process significant domestic and international interest groups.[5] This conscious effort to penetrate national societies was greatly abetted by the very nature of the issue. One can expect that the post-Stockholm concern of international institutions with environmental matters will involve them with closer and more sustained contact with nongovernmental elements of states than ever before. Such penetration of national societies can be a source of strength for international institutions as well as a source of tension with member governments.

International institutions have traditionally suffered, in their attempts to influence governments, from a lack of significant contact with domestic interest groups. In most cases, the International Labor Organization (ILO) and the European Economic Community (EEC) being the major exceptions, member governments have successfully maintained the claim that they should be the channel of contact between international organizations and their societies. If in the environmental area the responsible international organization is able to deal directly with iterest groups, such as the scientific community or environmentalists, the possibility of bringing added leverage on the policies of government could enhance the influence of that international organization.[6] On the other hand, direct contact between an international secretariat and potent domestic interest groups, which results in attempts to influence the policy of a state in critical areas, can also develop into a significant source of stress between member governments and the international secretariat.[7] On matters as complex as environmental issues, in which clearly conflicting values must be balanced, the national decisionmaker is likely to view as unwelcomed the efforts of an additional contender in the policy process. This is particularly likely in relatively closed polities, such as the communist states, and international secretariats may well find their efforts to develop links with environmentally significant domestic interest groups producing strong reactions from these governments. On the other hand, such development of interest-group politics on a cross-national basis could in time have profound effects on international affairs.

[5] See, for example, *Report of the Preparatory Committee for the United Nations Conference on the Human Environment* (UN Document A/CONF.48/PC.9); and *Statement by the Secretary-General of the UN Conference on the Human Environment* (UN Press Release HE/2, February 8, 1971).

[6] On this point see Maurice F. Strong, *Development, Environment and the New Global Imperatives: The Future of International Co-operation* (Plaunt Lectures delivered at Carlton University, Ottawa, Canada, 1971.) (Mimeographed.)

[7] For an example see Leon N. Lindberg, "Integration as a Source of Stress on the European Community System," *International Organization*, Spring 1966 (Vol. 20, No. 2), pp. 233-265.

II.

One of the most persistent problems surrounding efforts in the United Nations over the last four years to engage the organization's interest in environmental issues has been the reluctance of the developing countries. Joao Augusto de Araujo Castro, ambassador of Brazil to the United States, has expressed in this volume his strong fears that concern with the environment is being used in the United Nations to distract the organization's attention from major political issues that the United States and the Union of Soviet Socialist Republics now prefer to handle outside the United Nations and to limit the economic development of the developing countries and excuse the failure to provide them with adequate resources. Ambassador Castro also has forcefully argued here for separating consideration of the environmental problems of the developed and developing world.

The unenthusiastic attitude of the developing countries for greater United Nations involvement with environmental issues was recognized early in the planning for Stockholm. As Maurice Strong has written:

> Although environment has rapidly become a major preoccupation of both publics and governments in the industrialized countries, it is still endowed with no such magic in much of the developing world. Environment is still seen by many as a rich man's problem, a disease they would be prepared to risk if it is a necessary accompaniment to the economic growth which they want and urgently need. They are understandably concerned about how the preoccupation of the industrialized countries with environment will affect their priority task of meeting the basic and immediate needs of their peoples for food, shelter, jobs, education and health care. They have also been concerned that those whose industrial technology has produced the major part of today's pollution should assume the major cost of dealing with the environmental consequences. They want to be more sure before jumping enthusiastically on the environmental bandwagon just how it is likely to affect their own interests and their own priorities.[8]

We do not propose to assess the merits of the position of the developing countries—both Brian Johnson and James Lee have examined the development-environment nexus in their articles—but rather to point to a few of the implications of this view for international action on environmental concerns.

The developing states compose a clear majority of the membership of the United Nations. A position supported by a majority of these developing states will necessarily command attention. The coolness shown by the developing countries toward UN involvement with

[8] Strong, p. 13.

the environment illustrates the point. It is to be counted as a major success of the secretariat of the Stockholm conference that through diligent efforts involving near-continuous lobbying by Strong the developing countries were so thoroughly engaged in the pre-Stockholm process. The 1969-1970 fears of a developing country boycott of Stockholm have not occurred, at least until now, to a large extent because of this vigorous effort to take their concerns into account.

However, the constant effort of the secretariat to keep the developing countries engaged in the process came at a price. First, it did require an immense amount of the time of the secretariat—time that was not, as a result, available for concentration on technical issues or on the real issues confronting industrialized states. Particularly in the year before Stockholm private complaints have increased from the developed states that the conference secretariat has failed to adequately consult them as a result of its concentration on the developing world. Second, the secretariat has encouraged the developing states to believe that concern with development will not reduce the funds available for development but rather will increase them. This increase is to come in the form of a fund that will bear the cost of taking environmental considerations into account in development projects. This fund, if established, would be financed by voluntary contribution from the developed states.

The developing countries' fears that increased United Nations action in the environmental area will adversely affect their interests will continue to be a factor beyond Stockholm. Hopes that a large fund will be established to bear the incremental cost of taking environmental concerns into account in development planning may fail. They may initially fail because the prevailing attitude in the United States Congress toward foreign aid, in any form, is not likely to support a large United States contribution to such a fund. Over the long run such hopes may fail because at least some economic development projects may not be compatible with sound environmental principles, for example, the Aswan Dam.

The very nature of the United Nations political process will mean that the developing countries are able to ensure that their concerns are taken into account. Whatever continuing bodies are set up by Stockholm will emerge as subsidiary organs of the United Nations, a United Nations that not only places a premium on the concept of one state-one vote but one whose broad range of concerns facilitates inter-issue bargaining.[9] One can expect that the developing states will use their tactical advantage in the UN bargaining process to extract

---

[9] For a discussion of inter-issue bargaining in United Nations politics see David A. Kay, "The Impact of African States on the United Nations," *International Organization,* Winter 1969 (Vol. 23, No. 1), pp. 20-47.

the maximum advantage. If this does turn out to be the case and the procedures of the organization make possible the delay or manipulation of the international community's response to crucial issues of survival, a significant incentive will have been created for bypassing UN involvement with environment issues.

III.

We believe that the articles presented in this volume and the overwhelming weight of available scientific evidence are in agreement that the challenge of environmental management is of a long-term character. There are few final solutions to environmental problems, and the objective of international action must be to seek to establish processes and techniques for identifying environmental problems, developing solutions on a continuing basis, and providing a forum for the clash of differing priorities and values. However, the realization of the long-term nature of the challenge and of the substantial existing international action already underway should not minimize the importance of the policies and actions that must be taken now.

Increasingly, new technologies are global in nature, or the side effects of more intensive application of existing technology have international and global repercussions. In time, and not very far ahead, many functions—regulation, allocation, inspection, enforcement, adjudication, and operation—will have to be performed on a wide variety of subjects in an international arena. There is an early need for the establishment of international norms for effluents, for solid waste disposal, for tanker routing, for actions in the event of ship accidents, and for registration of the thousands of new chemical compounds introduced into the biosphere each year.[10] As Ralph d'Arge and Allen Kneese have shown in their article for this volume, the imposition of national environmental standards can have an important impact on international trade. Continued international trade in a free and orderly fashion soon will require agreement on environmental standards. In areas in which the effects of pollution are subtle and complex and control measures require unaccustomed domestic retraints the political problems will be serious. If limitations must be imposed on the total use made of specific technologies each year or on the spread and introduction of new technologies or if limitations are eventually required on the amount of forest or agricultural land that can be destroyed each year, then we will be seriously affecting areas never before subject to any form of international regulation (or in many countries even subject to national regulation). Limitations on research

[10] Skolnikoff, *Journal of International Affairs*, Vol. 25, No. 2, pp. 274-275.

and development itself may even become a serious political issue if a judgment can be made—as was asserted by some opponents of the supersonic transport—that the direction new technology may take would seriously exacerbate environmental problems.

The establishment of norms will require international decisions on the fair allocation of the burdens involved in obeying these norms. We live in a world of inequality, inequality of wealth, of technological processes, of resource distribution, of resource use, and of the impact of various forms of pollution. Who would bear the burden of a ban on certain forms of activity, such as the use of a pesticide: the producers of the pesticide in the form of lost sales or the consumers of the pesticide in the form of lost crops, disease, and higher price substitutes? The determination of the cost and impact of various environmental decisions and the fair allocation of this burden will require international action of a recognized fair and impartial character. Once norms are established and the burden of compliance allocated, monitoring and enforcement will be needed in many cases to ensure compliance and detect avoidance of critical norms.

Scant attention has been paid to the international conflict potential of environmental change. As awareness grows among the public and governments as to environmental alteration and the sources of such alteration, the possibility of conflict between states increases. Acid rain, polluted waters, a disappearance of fish from a traditional fishing area, tainted foodstuffs, and the inadvertent modification of weather are likely to become new sources of international tension in the future. Similarly, the growing conflict of interest between the developed and developing countries has the potential of exacerbating international tensions. International machinery will be urgently needed if these conflicts are not to lead to interstate violence.

While it would be encouraging to be able to conclude this look ahead with confidence that the international community is moving to establish the needed machinery to perform all those functions necessary if we are to manage effectively on a long-term basis the critical relations between man and his environment, such confidence does not appear warranted. The general performance of the United Nations system today, notwithstanding its effectiveness in some areas, leads to considerable skepticism that it provides an adequate base for expansion in responsibility without substantial modification. This is not just a question of the capabilities of international secretariats but more fundamentally a question of the willingness of governments to encourage the needed evolution and expansion of the functions and authority of the United Nations system in directions that constrain their own freedom of action. The experience on the road to Stockholm is not overly encouraging in this regard. At times governments seemed far more interested in debating, perhaps even at the final price of sabotaging the conference, the merits of the attendance of the Peoples' Republic of China (Communist China) or the German Democratic Republic (East Germany).

There is no easy alternative to seeking to use the United Nations system for dealing with global aspects of the environment. It may be necessary to build some new institutions outside the UN, especially in those subjects requiring high technical efficiency, with limited membership and patterns of control and influence quite different from that which prevails in most United Nations bodies. But the UN system offers the best, and only real, opportunity for providing an institutional base with widespread participation. This political goal is critical, not only because of the global nature of the environment but also because of its importance for any future growth of a democratic world order. Indeed, if the United Nations can demonstrate its ability to deal effectively with the range of environmental issues requiring international action, it could make an important contribution to revitalizing the entire United Nations system, particularly in the eyes of the major powers which have shown growing disenchantment with the organization in recent years.

PART IV

REGIONALISM vs GLOBALISM

REGIONAL ORGANIZATION AND THE
UNITED NATIONS

NORMAN J. PADELFORD

One of the marked features of international relations in recent years has been the growth of regional groupings and organizations. Included among the more notable regional arrangements formed since 1944 are the League of Arab States, the Organization for European Economic Cooperation, the Organization of American States, the North Atlantic Treaty Organization, and the European Coal and Steel Community. In addition to these and other existent arrangements are proposals for the creation of a European Defense Community and a European Political Community, the idea of a Pacific Pact resembling NATO, the concept of a Middle East Defense organization, and a possible linkage of Asian States.

The idea of regional organizations has long held a place in thinking on international politics, going back to some of the classic peace plans and the writings of philosophers. Translation of these ideas into actual compacts and permanent organizations has in the main not been effected, however, until the present.

The current emphasis upon regional arrangements may be attributed in part to the emergence of world political and economic conditions rendering frequent consultation and joint action among numbers of states having shared interests desirable or necessary. Such arrangements have also been called into existence in order to provide for mutual defense and reciprocal assistance to meet the increased threats to security arising from the new range and power of weapons in the hands of an aggressor and from the growth of subversive movements aimed at overthrowing established governments. Recourse to regional arrangements may also be ascribed to beliefs that the United Nations under present circumstances cannot wholly suffice to protect or further the interests of states. Consequently, states have turned to regional groupings as a supplement to unilateral national action and the usual diplomatic relations.

Regional arrangements provide groups of nations having common interests and objectives an opportunity to cooperate, to whatever extent

NORMAN J. PADELFORD, Professor of International Relations at the Massachusetts Institute of Technology, is Editor of *Current Readings on International Relations* and a member of the Board of Editors of *International Organization*.
From Volume 8, No. 2 (1954), pp. 203-16.

they believe desirable, on matters of mutual concern. They thus afford a directness of association which cannot be attained through universal institutions. The development of regional groupings and organizations also acknowledges the fact that it is possible to do some things within limited areas and among a restricted circle of states that cannot be done on a global basis. In the following pages we shall explore some of the variations in existent regional arrangements and their relation to the United Nations.

I

Geographers often find it difficult to say precisely what lands, islands and oceanic spaces are to be included within a given region. There are large "regions" such as the so-called American Hemisphere and small ones such as Western Europe or the Caribbean. There are wide discrepancies in the presence and absence of elements contributing to harmony or discord within the various generally acknowledged regions of the globe. Indeed, so variable in size, configuration, population, and numbers of countries included are the various "regions", and so difficult is it in some instances to define with exactness their limits or boundaries, geographers are not altogether sure how even the presumed fact of a "region" may be determined.[1] Notwithstanding these variations and uncertainties, statesmen find no insuperable obstacle on this account to the formation of regional groupings and the conclusion of regional arrangements.

Broadly speaking, a regional arrangement in the sphere of international politics may be described as an association of states, based upon location in a given geographical area, for the safeguarding or promotion of the participants. The terms of this type of association are fixed by a treaty or other agreement.

Ordinarily the idea of a regional association embraces cooperation between more than two states or political entities and is not localized to the extent of dealing solely with one narrowly confined site or question such as the regulation of the Turkish Straits or the Suez Canal. On the other hand, it does not usually extend to associations of states that are proximately global in their situation, as for example the Commonwealth of Nations. The North Atlantic Treaty Organization, with its membership extending from Canada and the United States whose western borders are on the Pacific; to Greece and Turkey on the south-eastern rimland of Europe, and with a concern admittedly reaching as far as Indo-China, comes close to the geographic extreme of what may be regarded as a "regional" arrangement.

[1] See Richard Hartshorne, *The Nature of Geography* (Lancaster, Pa., 1939), chs., 9–10.

Regional arrangements may take a variety of forms ranging from an agreement that certain rules or principles shall apply in the relations among a group of states to the creation of an alliance or the erection of an elaborate organization with permanent institutions or organs. Such arrangements may be established to serve the interests of states within a comparatively restricted area, such as the Middle East, the Caribbean or the Balkans. Or they may be employed to protect and to advance the interests of a group of states stretching over a large oceanic space as in the case of the ANZUS Pact between Australia, New Zealand and the United States, or embracing an entire continental area and its adjacent waters as in the instance of the Rio Pact of Reciprocal Assistance among the American Republics. Regional arrangements may be designed to serve political, economic, cultural, or defense purposes, or some combination of these. Because of the many ways in which regionalism may manifest itself, attempts to formulate the concept in precise legal terms were rejected at the San Francisco Conference in 1945.[2] Nevertheless it is now generally accepted, at least by the free world, and expressly indicated in Chapter VIII of the United Nations Charter, that these arrangements should serve peaceful and not aggressive purposes.

II

The existent regional arrangements may be grouped for convenience under three broad headings: (1) economic and technical arrangements; (2) arrangements for defense purposes; and (3) arrangements providing an organizational framework for the consideration of broad political issues. Hard and fast distinctions cannot, of course, always be drawn between matters that are of an economic, political, or defense character. They are often intermingled in the activities and deliberations of the Organization of American States, NATO, and the League of Arab States, for example. Moreover, as the interests, objectives, and outlooks of states change, so also do the purposes and activities of the organizations and agencies which they create to further their interests. Thus, any categorization is subject to limitations and must be viewed as having a degree of flexibility.

Numerous multipartite arrangements relating to geographically definable areas larger in extent than a small waterway or internationalized zone, such as those relating to the Suez Canal or the international zone of Tangiers, may occur to readers as being properly conceivable as regional

[2] See Leland M. Goodrich and Edvard Hambro, *Charter of the United Nations, Commentary and Documents* (rev. ed., 1949), p. 310–311 for reference to discussions at San Francisco.

arrangements. It is possible that they should be so considered. Generally speaking, however, the idea of regional arrangements envisages some form of undertaking or action by contracting parties or agencies established by them on a somewhat broader geographical plane. But there are no easily minimal or maximal bounds on this matter. Question may also arise as to the status of the Soviet alliance system as a regional arrangement. Notwithstanding the imperialistic character of Moscow control in Central and Eastern Europe and the reduction of the states in this area allied to the USSR, and to one another to the status of satellites, the undertakings and unified action of countries participating in the Soviet alliance system do partake in part at least of the nature of an alignment.

One feature which is particularly notable with respect to contemporary regional arrangements among the nations of the free world is the extent of United States participation in existent organizations or arrangements. Of nineteen present regional arrangements among the free nations, the United States is a member of eight and closely associated with three others. Supplementing the regional arrangements in various ways are a host of bilateral undertakings which the United States has entered into since 1945. The United States has indeed become the switchboard for most of the regional and joint efforts in the free world. The fact that one nation is closely identified with a number of regional arrangements affords a link among them which can be useful in establishing harmonious relationships and averting duplication of effort or conflict of action.

III

The factors which bring a group of states together into a regional association are often complex. Different motives condition the policy decisions of different states. Moreover, an element which may exert a cohesive effect in one situation does not necessarily operate in like manner in other circumstances.

States situated in relative geographical propinquity are sometimes persuaded that because of this fact their interests can be promoted through concerting together. This argument has been adduced at times in connection with the inter-American movement. On the other hand, in different circumstances, states situated near one another in a more or less clearly distinguishable area have found their interests so incompatible that there has been more friction and conflict than regional accord. Relative geographical proximity in itself is a weak force for unity when states have little in common or are divided by political, cultural, or religious differences. Although the countries south of the Himalaya Mountains have a degree of propinquity and are geographically set off from the rest of Asia, the geographical situation so far has not been a sufficiently uniting factor to bring them together as a regional unit.

Common racial, cultural or religious backgrounds and heritage may predispose certain states toward regional associations, particularly when all of them share some interest in an international political issue. The common Arabic and Moslem background of the Arab states of the Near East undoubtedly facilitated the formation of the League of Arab States in 1945, but it may be questioned whether this element alone would have exerted sufficient force to draw these states together had they not been faced with a common concern with respect to Palestine. And there was also the possibility of playing a more influential role in the United Nations and world politics if their voices and actions could be concerted. Cultural, religious and ideological affinities may be quite insufficient, however, to overcome suspicions and fears which have arisen among a group of states as a result of past wars and conflicts.

The most compelling motivation for the development of regional cooperation in recent years has been the search for security. This has been evident in the Americas, in the North Atlantic and European regions, and in the Pacific. In the Americas a sense of "continental solidarity" and interest in "hemispheric defense" assumed significant form only when the imminence of Nazi aggression appeared in the 1930's. At the beginning this may have reflected, at least on the part of some, an escapism from world dangers and was in effect a form of quasi-isolationism. In any event, the Rio Pact of Reciprocal Assistance of 1947 supplanted a more or less sentimental Pan-Americanism only when a common interest in safeguarding the integrity of the American hemisphere had emerged. The Brussels Western Union Pact, NATO, and the ANZUS Pact in the Pacific each had its basic motivation in the crystallization of mutual concern for national and regional security.

Another factor inducing states in recent years to enter into regional arrangements or establish organizations of a regional character has been the growing realization that standards of living can be advanced, economic well-being assured, and prosperous international trade maintained only through cooperative effort in reducing the barriers to trade and affording mutual assistance to one another by way of economic aid and technical assistance. Such considerations have influenced the establishment of the Organization for European Economic Cooperation, the European Payments Union, Benelux, the European Coal and Steel Community, the Caribbean Commission and the Colombo Plan. Interest in furthering international cooperation for the solution of technical problems has been undertaken by the United Nations regional economic commission. Conviction on the part of the government in Washington that Western Europe cannot resolve the economic and political ills which have afflicted it since World War II, save by economic integration, has been a driving force behind much American effort to convince the governments of Europe that they should take further steps toward regional organization and unity.

A desire on the part of a group of states to handle local or regional questions of particular interest to themselves without the interference of outside parties may also be a motivating influence with respect to regionalism. This, for example, may be said to have been a factor behind the early development of the extensive network of treaty arrangements among the American Republics for peaceful settlement of international disputes within the Americas.

Political factors, such as a desire to create a kind of equilibrium of power within an area, may also condition the policy actions of some states with regard to regional undertakings. In forming the Arab League the signatories of the Pact of Cairo in 1945 undoubtedly had in mind the fashioning of a balance of power favorable to themselves as a deterrent to Zionist aspirations in Palestine. And however effective or weak the Arab League may be as a military force, the concerted efforts of its members have become an important factor in the political equation of Middle Eastern affairs. Likewise, some Latin Americans may have hoped that the inter-American movement, and specifically the Organization of American States, might operate so as to strengthen the position of the Latin states in dealing with the United States. Similarly, it has been suggested that one of the principal interests of France and Belgium in the creation of the European Coal and Steel Community has been to check the industrial power of Germany. A comparable motive appeared to be implicit in French Premier Pleven's proposal of a European Defense Community as a means of providing a collective regional system of checks and balances against the danger of German rearmament.

Before any movement for regional organization is likely to acquire much substance and durability, however, some semblance of community interest must develop among the governments concerned. This was strongly emphasized by General Eisenhower when as Commander in Chief of the NATO Forces in Europe he said in conjunction with his plea for progress toward economic and political union in Western Europe: what must be found in order to make progress is "a principle, a basic objective, and then a broad outline on which all can agree." The absence of community-wide agreement on a principle or a basic objective helps to explain why so few regional arrangements have arisen as yet in the Pacific region, in South Asia, or in the Middle East.

IV

Scanning present-day regionalism it is noticeable that there are many undertakings providing for cooperation on economic, technical and mutual defense matters; while there are relatively few establishing permanent organs for dealing with general political issues. The urgent requirements which have arisen with respect to economic assistance and mutual security have no doubt hastened the cooperation of nations in these respects, even as lingering suspicions, rivalries, and nationalistic sentiments have conversely tended to retard moves in the direction of setting up regional political agencies.

Fashioning a stable European community, for example, requires overcoming difficult obstacles, whatever pathway is chosen toward this end. Fears and suspicions rooted in past wars and conquests linger in the minds of people. Nationalist sentiments and the propensity of political leaders to play upon these feelings for the sake of gaining or holding office or of defeating their political opponents readily tie the hands of policy makers and those in a position to influence the conduct of international affairs.

Regional cooperation, in addition to being affected by the forces which impinge upon international relationships generally, is subject to its own politics. Where there are several powers striving for political ascendency within an area, almost any regional arrangement is likely to be accompanied by competition for the support or control of the smaller states and by maneuvering for power and position. The history of Europe has been studded with this to such an extent that it has been impossible in the past to develop any strong or lasting regional political organization within the continent. Although less competition of this nature may be present in free Europe today, it is by no means absent and it is bound to be augmented in the future by the renaissance of Germany as a strong political entity.

Where there is only one great power in a region the situation may be somewhat different although not necessarily so. There may be fears, real or imagined, as there have been in Latin America, that the great power will dominate the weaker states or interfere in their internal or external affairs. Until the United States vigorously pressed its Good Neighbor policy and pledged itself in formal compacts not to intervene in the affairs of others, suspicions of "Yankee imperialism" were rife within the Americas and there was opposition to United States leadership in a strong inter-American system. Even after twenty years of the Good Neighbor policy and assiduous cultivation of the principle of "continental solidarity", suspicions linger and political capital is sought by some political elements playing on the theme of North American dominance within the region. Equalization of "respect" for the sovereignty of all republics has taken place, but differentiations of power remain and have even increased.

Still another type of regional politics is exemplified in Central and Eastern Europe where successive Great Powers, especially Nazi Germany and now the Soviet Union, have endeavored to establish regional hegemony. Although political opposition was driven underground by Nazi methods, it flourished despite ruthless attempts at extermination and rose for freedom as soon as the opportunity presented itself to throw off the Nazi yoke. Soviet domination in the post-war years has combined with pressure politics the subtler methods of "satellization", alliances, the use of the Communist party apparatus, Moscow-appointed "advisors" in multitudes of public offices, and cleverly schemed joint stock company operations which have placed the vital industries, banks, and transportation properties in the region under Soviet reach. To these other methods Moscow has added an intense campaign of "cultural relations" and propaganda to woo the masses into willing submission to its leadership. Outwardly, the Soviet Union has succeeded in aligning most of this region with itself. But Tito's break with the Kremlin in 1948, the repeated purges of Communist officials in the satellite countries, the continual stream of refugees to the West across the Iron Curtain, and the flood of communications to Radio Free Europe, reveal that many people in this region have not accepted Soviet hegemony as a permanent mode of regional arrangement. Furthermore, the revolt in Eastern Germany and Czechoslovakia in June 1953 demonstrated that the politics of resistance is a living reality in this region.

Quite a different brand of intra-regional politics has prevailed within the League of Arab States. In this case there is no Great Power in the coalition and no member state has power to dominate the area, although Egypt is clearly more powerful than the others. Notwithstanding the unifying elements of race and common religion, and a shared interest with respect to minimizing the power of Israel — factors which were sufficient to bring the states together in the first place in the 1945 Pact and to make possible the conclusion of a Mutual Assistance Pact in 1950 — the Arab League has been rent by internal jealousies and rivalries. Egyptians and Saudi Arabians have suspected the leaders of Syria of conspiring with

Iraq and Jordan for the creation of a Greater Syria. Syrians, Lebanese, and Jordanians, on the other hand, have resented Egypt's efforts to make itself the guiding light of the Arab League and have suspected it of harboring expansionist ambitions in the direction of Palestine as well as to the south in the Sudan. In their failure to prevent the creation of Israel or to choke off its existence, elements of internecine bitterness became injected into Arab relationships. And although motions have been made within the Council of the Arab League for some larger measure of organized political unity among these states, divisions among them have led to the rise of strong opposition to such moves lest one or more of their number be enabled to enhance their power to the possible disadvantage of others. These internal stresses, however, do not prevent the Arab states from exercising a significant political influence within the United Nations. And they have not prevented the members of the Arab League from expressing a powerful voice when issues arise affecting their interests, as for instance over the possible formation of a Middle East Defense Command keyed to the Western Powers.

Viewing the politics of regionalism generally, it is safe to say that the only basis upon which regional arrangements can be made to function smoothly and effectively is that of mutual respect for the sovereignty and independence of all members coupled with a continual search for common values and agreed principles of cooperative action.

V

The principal region groupings active at the time the United Nations Charter was drafted were the American Republics and the League of Arab States. Representatives of both these groups took a prominent part at San Francisco in formulating the Charter provisions with reference to regional arrangements.

The provisions of Chapter VIII of the Charter dealing with "Regional Arrangements" are generally well-known and have been commented upon authoritatively.[3] They permit, by the indirection of saying that nothing in the Charter shall "preclude", the existence of regional arrangements or agencies which are "consistent with the Purposes and Principles of the United Nations". The Charter as a whole contains no definition of what kind of arrangements are covered by this term and the conferees at San Francisco resisted all efforts to introduce a rigid juridical definition of the term. It may be presumed that any regional grouping which exists

[3] See Goodrich and Hambro, *op.cit.*, ch. viii.

to further the maintenance of international peace and security, to facilitate the peaceful settlement of international disputes, to develop friendly relations among states, and to promote international cooperation on economic, social, cultural or humanitarian problems in the broad sense, is not excluded by the Charter.

The provisions of the Charter bearing upon regionalism are not limited to Chapter VIII alone. Article 23, in providing for "equitable geographical distribution" of the elected non-permanent members of the Security Council, has encouraged regional blocs such as the Latin American Republics, the Arab States, the Soviet Union and its Eastern European satellites, and the Western European states, to insist on recurrent bloc representation and to lobby actively for it year after year. The idea of listing regions entitled to such representation was rejected at San Francisco, but practice has led to the regular election to the Council of one or two Latin American states, a Western European state, a state from Central or Eastern Europe (often but not always a Soviet satellite), an Arab or Middle Eastern state, and a Commonwealth member. Continual representation for the Indian Ocean region has been requested but it has not always been accorded, nor can it be with the present limited number of non-permanent seats to be filled. No comparable provision is written into the Charter with respect to elections to other United Nations organs. The political influence of the several regional groups is such, however, that the principle of "equitable geographical distribution" is in fact operative in General Assembly elections of members of the Economic and Social Council, the Trusteeship Council, and many of the committees and offices of the Assembly.

From the point of view of serving the main objectives of the United Nations, Articles 33 and 52–54 lie close to the heart of the Charter. Article 33, by laying a responsibility upon parties to a dispute to seek settlement by pacific means, expressly mentions "resort to regional agencies or arrangements" among the various means which the parties should exhaust or which the Council may call upon the parties to employ. So far as is known to the writer, the Security Council has in no instance thus far called upon disputing parties to seek settlement through a regional instrumentality. But this authority is available for use in time of need and it is conceivable that should another situation such as the War of the Gran Chaco or the Leticia dispute arise among two or more of the American Republics the Security Council might under certain circumstances call upon them to utilize the arrangements of the inter-American system referred to in the Bogotá Charter or elsewhere. The organs of the American Republics have, of course, dealt with international disputes within the Americas on their own initiative.

Article 52, paragraph 2, fortifies the principle of Article 33 through its stipulation that the members of regional arrangements shall make every effort to achieve pacific settlement "of local disputes through such regional arrangements or by such regional agencies before referring them to the Security Council". And the following paragraph of Article 52 complements the provision of Article 33 by stating that the Security Council shall "encourage" the development of such settlement methods "either on the initiative of the states concerned or by reference from the Security Council".

In pursuance of the aim of maintaining international peace and security, the Charter provides in Article 53 for "enforcement action" through the medium of regional agencies, "where appropriate", with respect to threats to the peace, breaches of peace or acts of aggression. But it does so only on the express condition that such procedure shall be utilized by the Security Council and under its authority. Except for the sole case of measures against an enemy state of World War II, "no enforcement action shall be taken under regional arrangements or by regional agencies without the authorization of the Security Council". And it is added that the Security Council must be kept "fully informed" of such activities undertaken or contemplated by a regional group. These provisions are designed to insure that the Security Council shall have full control of enforcement activity wherever it may be undertaken in order to safeguard the general interests in peace and security.

No instance has arisen thus far in which the Security Council has utilized a regional arrangemment for enforcement action. At the time of the fighting in Palestine quite the opposite occurred. The Security Council then called upon all parties engaged in hostilities — both the Arab states and the Zionists — to cease firing, and the Council at no time asked the League of Arab States, which was of course an interested party, to undertake any enforcement measures. In most other cases involving threats to the peace which have come before the United Nations, there has either been no regional organization to which the Security Council might appropriately turn, or the Council has been so impeded by use of the veto that no substantive decision could have been taken by it even if a regional organization were suitably available for assistance. There is indeed no assurance in the Charter that a regional group as such may be authorized to take measures which its members believe necessary for their collective security. This could lead to an invidious situation.

Although the Charter is specific in saying that no regional arrangement may take "enforcement action" without authority of the Security Council, it appears logical to assume that under existing practice and in the light of the Uniting for Peace Resolutions passed in 1950, the General Assembly may call upon disputing states to settle a dispute through the use of a regional agency or arrangement if the Security Council is blocked by the veto. And the inference can be drawn from the sentiment expressed by the overwhelming majority of the United Nations membership in adopting the Uniting for Peace Resolutions, that if action becomes impossible when a threat to the peace or act of aggression occurs because of the casting of a veto in the Security Council, the General Assembly should be able — along with other steps which it may then take — to authorize the members of arrangements or agencies to undertake "action" at its request. Article 51 leaves no doubt, of course, that "nothing in the Charter" shall impair the inherent right of individual or collective self-defense if an armed attack occurs against a Member of the United Nations, until the Security Council has taken the measures necessary to maintain international peace and security. Should action be taken by a regional group it may be presumed that the regional agency would be responsible for keeping the General Assembly informed just as it would be required to notify the Security Council if authorization were given by that organ.[4]

Although Article 51 does not mention regional arrangements or agencies as such, it is self-evident that the members of a regional security pact are as entitled to act together in individual or collective self-defense as are any other states. Speaking at the close of the Committee deliberations at San Francisco which debated and formulated Article 51, the Chairman of the Conference Committee — who was a delegate of an American Republic — formally stated that the right of collective self-defense there provided may "be carried out in accord with regional pacts so long as they are not opposed to the purposes and principles of the Organization as expressed in the Charter. If a group of countries with regional ties," he remarked, "declare their solidarity for the mutual defense as in the case of the American States, they will undertake such defense jointly if and when one of them is attacked. And the right of self-defense," he added, "is not limited to the country which is the direct victim of aggression, but extends to those countries which have established solidarity through regional arrangements with the country directly attacked."

The Rio Treaty of Reciprocal Assistance, the Brussels Pact of Western

---

[4] In passing, it may be noted that Article 47, paragraph 4, incorporates a proviso that the Security Council's Military Staff Committee, with the authorization of the Council "and after consultation with appropriate regional agencies, may establish regional subcommittees." No such subcommittees have been created to date, nor does it seem likely that they will be so long as the Cold War continues to paralyze the Military Staff Committee. There is no impediment to the General Assembly Collective Measures Committee, authorized by the Uniting for Peace Resolutions, establishing a more or less comparable subcommittee if it sees fit to do so, but this does not appear to have become necessary or desirable as yet.

Union and the North Atlantic Treaty expressly refer to the authorization of Article 51. Thus, this Article of the Charter does afford regional groups a substantial ground upon which to plan and to undertake measures of self-defense regardless of whether the Security Council may or may not call upon them to undertake "enforcement action."

The United Nations and some of the technical international organizations and specialized agencies have recognized the utility of dealing with certain problems on a regional basis. With this in view Economic Commissions for Europe, Asia and the Far East, and Latin America have been established, and a number of committees and offices following regional lines have been created by the World Health Organization, the Food and Agriculture Organization and the International Civil Aviation Organization. Unspectacular as are many of the activities being carried on along these lines they nevertheless help to create those "conditions of stability and well-being" which the Charter holds "necessary for peaceful and friendly relations among nations".[5]

VI

Apprehension has sometimes been expressed that the growth of regionalism may result in a weakening of the United Nations or be productive of further conflict. It is of course possible that a regional group may oppose a proposed course of action or a decision of the United Nations. One of the notable features of United Nations' procedure has been the caucussing and bloc voting of members of regional groups.[6] In the Palestine case the Arab states opposed the majority in the United Nations on the question of partition although they subsequently accepted United Nations mediation for a truce in the fighting which occurred in 1948. The Soviet Bloc has refused to allow any United Nations investigation commission to function inside the Iron Curtain since 1948.

The full potentialities and limitations of regional arrangements have yet to be determined. There are political, administrative, and other problems associated with the functioning of regional organizations on which further data is needed. Nevertheless, United Nations' experience on the

[5] See C. Hart Schaff, "The United Nations Commission for Asia and the Far East," *International Organization*, Nov., 1953; W. W. Rostow, "The Economic Commission for Europe," *ibid.*, May, 1949. See also factual summaries of ECOSOC, the U. N. regional economic commissions, and the various regional organizations appearing regularly in this journal.

[6] See M. Margaret Ball, "Bloc Voting in the General Assembly," *International Organization*, Feb., 1951; G. M. Carter, "The Commonwealth in the United Nations," *ibid.*, May, 1950; W. R. Crocker, "Voting in the International Institutions," *Australian Outlook*, Sept., 1951; Raymond Dennett, "Politics in the Security Council," *International Organization*, Aug., 1949; E. S. Furniss, "The United States, the Inter-American System and the United Nations," *Political Science Quarterly*, Sept., 1950; H. N. Howard, "The Arab-Asian States in the United Nations," *The Middle East Journal*, Summer, 1953.

whole has substantiated the view of the late Senator Vandenberg when toward the close of the San Francisco Conference he said: "We have found a sound and practical formula for putting regional organizations into effective gear with the global institution. . . . In my view we have infinitely strengthened the world organization by thus enlisting, with its overall supervision, the dynamic resources of these regional affinities. We do not thus substract from global unity of the world's peace and security; on the contrary, we weld these regional king-links into the global chain."

INTERNATIONAL INTEGRATION

The European and the Universal Process

ERNST B. HAAS

I. European and Universal Integration

The established nation-state is in full retreat in Europe while it is advancing voraciously in Africa and Asia. Integration among discrete political units is a historical fact in Europe, but disintegration seems to be the dominant *motif* elsewhere. Cannot the example of successful integration in Europe be imitated? Could not the techniques of international and supranational cooperation developed in Luxembourg, Paris, and Brussels be put to use in Accra, Bangkok, and Cairo, as well as on the East River in New York? Or, in a different perspective, will not the progress of unity in Europe inevitably have its integrating repercussions in other regions and at the level of the United Nations even without efforts at conscious imitation?

Such a development would be most satisfying. Presumably it would contribute to world peace by creating ever-expanding islands of practical cooperation, eventually spilling over into the controversy-laden fields which threaten us directly with thermonuclear destruction. The functionalist theory of international peace might be put to work by a generalization of the European mode of post-1945 international cooperation. Further, those who hope to contribute to the peaceful solution of conflict could take much solace from such a development, for the post-1945 European mode of resolving conflicts among states has demonstrated that "there often comes a moment when there is a simultaneous revolution of interests on both sides and unity precipitates itself," to quote Mary Follett.[1]

Before abandoning ourselves to such pleasant speculation, however, we would do well to state systematically what we have learned about the causes of European integration and then to investigate where else these causes might be operative. This effort calls for some definitions.

We are interested in tracing progress toward a terminal condition called *political community.* Successful nation-states constitute such communities and subsequent amalgamations of several such states may also form communities. A variety of constitutional and structural factors are compatible with this notion; political community exists when there is likelihood of internal peaceful change in a setting of contending groups with mutually antagonistic claims. The process of attaining this condition among nation-states we call *integration,* the process whereby political actors in several distinct national settings are persuaded to shift

ERNST B. HAAS is Associate Professor of Political Science at the University of California in Berkeley. The author gratefully acknowledges the support of the Rockefeller Foundation and of the Institute of International Studies of the University of California in the preparation of this article.

From Volume 15, No. 3 (1961), pp. 366-92.

[1] As cited in Metcalf and Urwick, eds., *Dynamic Administration,* New York, Harper & Brothers, 1940, p. 40.

their loyalties, expectations, and political activities toward a new and larger center, whose institutions possess or demand jurisdiction over the pre-existing national states. It should be noted that the objective economic, social, and communications "factors" often identified with "integration," in my scheme, are conditions typical of an ongoing political community. At best they may serve as indicators to help us assess the progress of integration.

This focus precludes attention to what may be called the "immanent myth" of European unity which owes its inspiration to cultural-historical antecedents considered equally relevant to the contemporary process of integration. It appears to me that European unity under the Roman, Frankish, and medieval Roman-German imperial realms has no more analytical importance than the unity of all Islam in the eighth century, the domains of the Ming Empire in the fifteenth or the Guptas in the fifth. The mere fact that specific regions were unified politically and culturally at one time seems not to prevent them from subsequently dividing into warring nations denying in their conduct the cultural unity the historian wishes to impute to them: they do not then constitute any kind of political community. If this is so we cannot use some previous historical experience which involved the notion of community as an argument for assuming the natural and inevitable re-emergence of this happy state of affairs. It may indeed emerge, but in response to the factors we shall discuss. Naturally, in the political advocacy of integration by some specific movement, the "memory" of a historical community may play its part in the construction of a myth; but this does not make the past an active causative agent. On the other hand, a series of traumatic events vividly remembered by a generation subjected to inte-

gration may launch and then spur the process. The role of two world wars of unprecedented destructiveness and the threat of the victory of a revolutionary totalitarian movement at the end of the second of these wars were undoubtedly primary among the specific stimuli which, in western Europe, made people receptive to the historical-cultural arguments of the mythmakers. This combination of circumstances does not easily permit repetition elsewhere.

Conflict resolution is a particularly interesting indicator for judging progress along the path of integration. A close study of negotiating processes in international relations suggests the prevalence of three types of compromise, each indicative of a certain measure of integration.

(1) The least demanding we may call accommodation on the basis of the minimum common denominator. Equal bargaining partners gradually reduce their antagonistic demands by exchanging concessions of roughly equal value. Gains and losses are easily identified, but the impact of the transaction never goes beyond what the *least* cooperative bargaining partner wishes to concede. This mode of compromise is typical of classic diplomatic negotiations.

(2) Accommodation by "splitting the difference" carries us a little farther along the path of integration. As before, demands are reduced and concessions of roughly equal value exchanged among autonomous bargaining units. But in this mode of compromise the mediatory services of a secretary-general or *ad hoc* international expert study group may be admitted by the parties. Conflict is resolved, not on the basis of the will of the least cooperative, but somewhere between the final bargaining positions. This type of negotiation is prevalent in international economic organizations and in other deal-

ings permitting financial identification of gains or losses, such as the formulation of a scale of assessments for Members of the United Nations.

(3) Finally, accommodation on the basis of deliberately or inadvertently upgrading the common interests of the parties takes us closest to the peaceful change procedures typical of a political community with its full legislative and judicial jurisdictions, lacking in international relations. To confuse matters further, this mode of conflict resolution is often identified as "integration," as by Mary Follett, who wrote that it, unlike mere compromise, signified "that a solution has been found in which both desires have found a place, that neither side has had to sacrifice anything."[2] If this is so it must mean that the parties succeeded in redefining their conflict so as to work out a solution at a higher level, which almost invariably implies the expansion of the mandate or task of an international or national governmental agency. In terms of results, this mode of accommodation maximizes what I have elsewhere called the "spill-over" effect of international decisions: policies made pursuant to an initial task and grant of power can be made real only if the task itself is expanded, as reflected in the compromises among the states interested in the task. In terms of method, the upgrading of the parties' common interests relies heavily on the services of an institutionalized mediator, whether a single person or a board of experts, with an autonomous range of powers. It thus combines intergovernmental negotiation with the participation of independent experts and spokesmen for interest groups, parliaments, and political parties. It is this combination of interests and institutions which we shall identify as "supranational."

The initial creation of such an agency, of course, demands a creative compromise among the states parties to the effort, based on the realization that certain common interests cannot be attained in any other way. This in turn presupposes that identical and converging policy aims, rather than antagonistic ones, predominated at the moment when the supranational organization was set up.

Each of these modes of accommodation, in addition to specifying a type of outcome relating to intensities of integration, also is typified by appropriate institutional mechanisms. There exists, moreover, a fourth prominent procedural device—parliamentary diplomacy—which is capable of producing any of the three outcomes. Parliamentary diplomacy, as Dean Rusk defined it, implies the existence of a continuing organization with a broad frame of reference, public debate, rules of procedure governing the debate, and the statement of conclusions in a formal resolution arrived at by some kind of majority vote.[3] When bodies like the UN or the Council of Europe define a conflict situation by filtering discussion through this machinery they may also be setting the limits within which eventual settlement comes about, though parliamentary diplomacy rarely defines the actual terms of the settlement. Instead it mobilizes political mediatory forces—the uncommitted states, parties, groups, or persons—whose voice in the settlement process is given volume by the reluctance of the parties to the dispute to annoy the mediating forces. Since the institutional context in which parliamentary diplomacy can be practiced maximizes the representation of a variety of interests emanating from the same nation, it opens up areas of maneuver which are foreclosed in negotiations exclusively conducted by

[2] *Ibid.*, p. 32.
[3] Dean Rusk, "Parliamentary Diplomacy—Debate vs. Negotiation," *World Affairs Interpreter*, Summer 1955 (Vol. 26, No. 2), p. 121–122.

carefully instructed single agents of foreign ministries. To that extent it facilitates a greater amount of integration even though it does not necessarily produce outcomes which upgrade common interests.

Where can these modes of accommodation be identified in the history and institutions of European integration?

II. The Lesson of European Integration

Clearly all these modes of accommodation are part of the European pattern of international adjustment. While they do not provide the only indicators of degrees of integration, they appear to be particularly strategic ones in that they focus on decision-making, thereby acting as a summary of, and an abstraction upon, other factors which could also be used as indicators. Broadly speaking, international institutions maximizing decision-making by means of the second and third modes yield the greatest amount of progress toward the goal of political community.

Parliamentary diplomacy is the chief contribution to European unity which can be credited to the various parliamentary assemblies. They have not meaningfully controlled their various executives nor have they legislated in any real sense, though they have attempted and partially exercised powers in both these fields. But they have acted as a spur to the formation of new voluntary elite groups across national boundaries—the European political groups—and the interplay among these has produced a type of diplomatic problem-solving which takes its inspiration from parliamentary resolutions and is able to upgrade common interests. As examples we may cite the work of the Council of Europe in relation to the Saar, in refugee relief and resettlement, and in the relaxation of frontier formalities. We may add the work of the Nordic Council in the

negotiation of the now superseded Nordic Common Market Agreement. But let it be admitted at the same time that the total contribution of parliamentary diplomacy is not very great. It found no institutional outlet at all in the Organization for European Economic Cooperation (OEEC); yet that organization's contribution to integration was substantial even though it operated primarily on the level of accommodation by "splitting the difference."

The most successful institutions in Europe are the "Commmunities" of the Six, constitutional hybrids which once caused nightmares to the public lawyer. They facilitate the resolution of conflict by virtue of all three modes, but the upgrading of common interests is their true contribution to the art of political integration. All fundamental decisions are made by the Councils of Ministers. But they are decisions based on continuous compromise, constantly informed by generally respected expert bodies with constitutional powers of their own and in constant contact with supranational voluntary associations and interest groups. The character of decision-making stimulates interest groups to make themselves heard; it spurs political parties in Strasbourg and Luxembourg to work out common positions; it creates an enormous pressure on high national civil servants to get to know and establish rapport with their opposite numbers; and it sharpens the sensitivities of the legal profession to European norms and political processes in preparation for the inevitable flood of litigation before the Court of Justice. In short, many of the decisions are integrative in their immediate economic consequences *as well as* in the new expectations and political processes which they imply. It is this indirect result which is maximized by the mixture of institutions which usually achieves accommodation at a higher level

SUMMARY OF INTEGRATION EXPERIENCE OF EUROPEAN ORGANIZATIONS

Organization	Institutions	Mode of Accommodation and Functions		Ideological-Social Environment
OEEC-EPU Age: 12 years	inter-governmental; weak secretariat; strong autonomous expert bodies	upgrading common interests:	remove trade barriers;	mixed ideologically, economically, social structure
		splitting difference:	divide US aid; emergency distribution of goods;	
		minimum common denominator:	planning for long-range economic growth	
Council of Europe Age: 12 years	inter-parliamentary; weak secretariat; rudimentary judicial institution	minimum common denominator:	European integration in general;	mixed ideologically, economically, social structure, though united on democracy
		minimum common denominator plus parliamentary diplomacy:	European legislation;	
		splitting difference and parliamentary diplomacy:	solution of specific short-range problems	
NATO Age: 13 years	inter-parliamentary; strong secretariat; strong autonomous expert bodies	minimum common denominator:	integrated defense policy;	mixed ideologically, economically, social structure, and in military power
		splitting difference:	coordinated foreign policy; joint defense economics;	
		upgrading common interests:	planning for new weapons and strategy	

Nordic Council Age: 8 years	inter-governmental; inter-parliamentary	parliamentary diplomacy plus minimum common denominator:	economic integration; legal standardization; social security harmonization	homogeneous ideologically, but mixed in social structure and economic development
Benelux Age: 17 years	inter-governmental; inter-parliamentary	minimum common denominator:	economic integration	homogeneous on all counts, except role of agriculture
EEC ECSC Euratom Age: 9 and 4 years	supranational	upgrading common interests: splitting difference: minimum common denominator:	economic integration in long run; solution of short-run economic problems; labor mobility; nuclear planning	homogeneous on all counts (except in southern Italy)
Western European Union Age: 6 years	inter-governmental; inter-parliamentary; weak secretariat; strong autonomous expert bodies	parliamentary diplomacy plus minimum common denominator: upgrading common interests:	foreign policy coordination; arms control	homogeneous on all counts except separate UK ideological position and special German military position
EFTA Age: 3 years	inter-governmental; weak secretariat	splitting difference:	remove trade barriers	mixed on all counts

of agreement as compared to the initial bargaining positions of the parties. Earlier decisions, including the ones constituting the Communities, spill over into new functional contexts, involve more and more people, call for more and more inter-bureaucratic contact and consultation, thereby creating their own logic in favor of later decisions, meeting, in a pro-community direction, the new problems which grow out of the earlier compromises.

Intergovernmental institutions of the classic variety, even when assisted by respected international civil servants and advisory boards, have not been able to match this performance. The North Atlantic Treaty Organization (NATO) and OEEC, for reasons to be explored, have continued to make their contribution to integration by means of compromises based on techniques found also in the United Nations. They have transcended these only in relation to certain tasks hinging around the direct implications of the welfare state.

This brings us face to face with the key question of which organizational *functions,* or tasks, have contributed most to the process of integration in Europe. The superficial answer clearly points to the field of economics; but by no means all organizations with an economic competence have performed equally well and few of them solve their problems on the basis of upgrading common interests. Parliamentary diplomacy has apparently been of importance in advancing economic integration only in the Nordic Council; OEEC functioned on the basis of "splitting the difference" or compromising on the level of the minimum common denominator in all areas except those relating to currency convertibility and the removal of quotas (in which common interests were indeed upgraded). The European Free Trade Association (EFTA) has not taken

strides comparable to those of the European Economic Community (EEC) and the European Coal and Steel Community (ECSC).

Not merely economic tasks, therefore, but the degree of functional specificity of the economic task is causally related to the intensity of integration. The more specific the task, the more likely important progress toward political community. It is not enough to be concerned with the reduction of trade barriers or the forecasting of industrial productivity. Specificity of task is essential, with respect to such assignments as creating a common market for narrowly defined products, unifying railway rates, removing restrictive practices in certain branches of industry, removing import quotas by fixed percentage points during fixed periods, and the like. Functional specificity, however, may be so trivial as to remain outside the stream of human expectations and actions vital for integration. This would seem to be the case with the standardization of railway rolling stock, for example, or the installation of uniform road signs. The task, in short, must be both specific and economically important in the sense of containing the potential for spilling over from one vital area of welfare policy into others.

Non-economic tasks have shown themselves much more barren. The cultural activities of the Council of Europe lack a focus on intensely experienced human wants. Its emergency aid measures have been short-range and its contributions to the solution of political tensions non-repetitive. The "European review" function is much too vague to yield observable results. The standardization efforts of the Nordic Council lack the stimulus of controversy and debate: they are so deeply rooted in the Scandinavian setting that one suspects integration of proceeding even without the Council. Continuous contact among civil servants and ministers is capable of contributing to integration in narrowly defined areas even without the participation of parliamentarians. The only functionally specific assignment of the Western European Union (WEU) is the supervision of the arms aspects of the Paris and London Agreements (1954). This function is being carried out in a supranational manner, but the reason is in the non-controversial and non-recurrent aspect of German rearmament, at least at the intergovernmental level. The other activities of WEU are unlikely to be remembered by history.

What about the field of European conventions? Surely these are specific in content and many of them relate to economics and welfare policy. The fact remains, however, that their very content reflects merely the minimum common denominator among the existing practices and policies of the member states, and that the Council had to resort to the device of "partial agreements" to get beyond this level. Conventions which depart from this denominator tend not to be ratified by the country whose standards are below the norms fixed in Strasbourg.[4] Integration, therefore, is advanced by the European conventions only to the extent that their content calls for a new—a supranational—political process which can generate new expectations and policies. This, probably, is the case only with reference to the field of human rights, a very significant field indeed. Moreover, there recently evolved in the Council the practice, among the members of the Committee of Ministers, of reporting annually on the willingness and speed of ratifying conventions. While this practice falls short of supranationality it nevertheless exposes the reporting country to the possibility of criticism and pressure.

Military and defense questions have not displayed a close affinity to integration unless the issue involves the related question of saving and allocating resources for welfare measures. NATO's experience in the financing of infrastructure programs, weapons research, integration of air warning systems, and the switch to centrally-controlled nuclear deterrents indicates that the upgrading of common interests does take place—not without obstacles and delays—when the economic burdens of defense for small countries are considered incompatible with their welfare commitments. But the other activities of the Atlantic Alliance make plain that more primitive modes of accommodation continue to flourish and that integration is more pronounced on paper than in the command post, the procurement center, and the council chamber.

This survey of the functional lessons of European integration leads to the inevitable conclusion that functional contexts are autonomous. Integrative forces which flow from one kind of activity do not necessarily infect other activities, even if carried out by the same organization. OEEC could not repeat in the field of tariff bargaining the results it obtained on questions of convertibility. NATO cannot transfer its success in planning strategy for new weapons systems to the standardization of the enlistment period; and ECSC has shown itself more adept in negotiating cumulative compromises on the creation of a common market than on short-run solutions for the coal crisis. Decisions made by identical officials, in organizations with a stable membership, in a non-revolutionary socio-ideological setting with similar institutional characteristics nevertheless vary sharply, in terms of their integrative impact, depending on the functional con-

---

[4] The conventions dealing with the equivalence of university degrees and the movement of persons are exceptions to this generalization. Both of them involved some measure of upgrading common interests.

text. If this is true even in the European setting, how much more true is it likely to be in the United Nations. But the converse proposition is equally important: the autonomy of functional contexts means that disintegration in one range of relations among certain states does not necessarily imply parallel disintegration in other relations among the same states. Thus the breakdown of the Free Trade Area (EFTA) negotiations did not entail a retreat from monetary convertibility; NATO's work on unifying air raid warning systems was not interrupted by the split between the Six of EEC and the Seven of EFTA.

The attempt to compare the European experience with efforts elsewhere compels attention to the environment in which the process of integration is taking place, what some scholars call the "background" factors. This investigation will show that while "Europe"—in the largest sense of the nineteen countries west of the Iron Curtain—possesses no completely common factors at all, significant islands of almost identical environmental factors exist among certain of them.

Social structure provides one set of factors. With the exception of Greece, Turkey, Portugal, parts of Spain, and southern Italy, the western European social scene is dominated by pluralism. Articulate voluntary groups, led by bureaucratized but accessible elites, compete with each other more or less rationally for political power and social status. The population is mobilized and participates in this process through affiliation with mass organizations. In the countries mentioned, however, effective and functionally diffuse social relations prevail.

Economic and industrial development furnishes a second set of factors. With the exception of the same countries plus Ireland, we are dealing with a very high level of economic development—including that of the countries in which the dominant products are agricultural—from the point of view of productivity, investment, and consumption. Significantly correlated with industrialization we find the usual high degree of urbanization and ever-growing demands for government services and durable consumer goods. We also find increasing demands on limited natural resources and greater dependence on foreign (or regional) trade. But note some partial exceptions: Norway's industrial weakness compared to that of Sweden, Belgium's agricultural inefficiency compared to that of the Netherlands.

Ideological patterns provide the final set of factors. Since policies of integration are, in the first instance, advanced or blocked by the activities of political parties and their ministers, parties may be used as an index of ideological homogeneity. A given cluster of countries is ideologically "homogeneous" if the divisions among the parties are, very roughly, the same among all the countries in the cluster, when the principles professed and the concrete socioeconomic interests represented by the parties are roughly analogous on both sides of a frontier. Given this definition, the Scandinavian countries emerge as ideologically homogeneous among themselves (with the partial exception of Iceland) but quite dissimilar from the rest of Europe. The Benelux countries, West Germany, Switzerland, and Austria seem homogeneous and seem to have considerable affinity for Italy and France. But a disturbing element is introduced here by the large anti-parliamentary minorities in France and Italy. Portugal, Greece, Spain, and Turkey lack the typical European socioeconomic structure and therefore the appropriate party systems; they do not fit into any neat ideological package. The British and Irish parties show some affinity for their continental colleagues, especially the socialists, but the patterns of interest aggregation and political style differ sufficiently to prevent the positing of a homogeneous pattern. We therefore have two large ideological clusters: 1) Scandinavia, and 2) the Six (plus Switzerland and Austria), as well as a number of single national systems whose characteristics seem *sui generis.*

Let us relate these environmental patterns to the integration process. Integration proceeds most rapidly and drastically when it responds to socio-economic demands emanating from an industrial-urban environment, when it is an adaptation to cries for increasing welfare benefits and security born by the growth of a new type of society. In the words of two European scholars:

> For decades industrialism has been revising the workways and consuming habits of people everywhere. It has enabled cities to grow and the urban way of life to spread. Urbanism is the great outreaching dynamic, breaking down isolation and encroaching upon tradition. Modern industrial urbanism is innately inimical to any isolation. It demands access and stimulates mobility. As earlier it resisted being confined to city walls, now it resists being confined to limited political areas. This resistance to confinement is greater than the resistance against the encroachments. In the measure that industrial urbanism has gained in this contest against the rooted barriers —in that measure integration is needed. The effort toward European integration reflects this need of industrial urbanism for wider organization.[5]

I reject the teleological aspects of this statement. In terms of a social process

based on rational human perceptions and motives, no mere concept "calls for" or "needs" anything: a discrete set of group motives, converging with motives of cognate groups from across the border, results in a certain pattern of policy; the aims and the policy reflect demands born from the environment, and the later policies may well change the environment in a wholly unintended fashion. Only in this sense, then, does industrial urbanism favor integration. Because the modern "industrial-political" actor fears that his way of life cannot be safeguarded without structural adaptation, he turns to integration; but by the same token, political actors who are neither industrial, nor urban, nor modern in their outlook usually do not favor this kind of adaptation, for they seek refuge instead in national exclusiveness.

Thus, countries dominated by a non-pluralistic social structure are poor candidates for participation in the integration process. Even if their governments do partake at the official level, the consequences of their participation are unlikely to be felt elsewhere in the social structure. Hence the impact of European integration, in all its aspects, has been minimal in Portugal, Turkey, and Greece. Finally, sufficient ideological homogeneity for value-sharing among important national elite groups is essential for rapid integration. The implications for Europe are obvious as reflected in the differential rates of progress toward political community which have been made within Scandinavia, within the Six, and within Benelux compared to the all-European level represented by OEEC, NATO, and the Council of Europe.

In addition to these environmental considerations, which relate to the internal

⁵ Jan J. Schokking and Nels Anderson, "Observations on the European Integration Process," *Journal of* *Conflict Resolution,* December 1960 (Vol. 4, No. 4), p. 409.

characteristics of the region undergoing integration, there are often external environmental factors of importance. Fear of a common enemy is an absolutely necessary precondition for integration in military organizations: without the Soviet Union there would have been no NATO. But the common enemy may be a more subtle manifestation, such as fear of external groupings of culturally and economically suspect forces: such considerations were not irrelevant to the "third force" argument which entered the integration process among the Six and is apparent in the convergence of interests which resulted in the Organization for Economic Cooperation and Development (OECD). While external environments produce motives favoring integration, they are never sufficient in themselves to explain the rate and intensity of the process.

Institutions, functions, and environments provide useful categories for arranging the human data among which our various modes of accommodation made themselves felt; but they do not exhaust the list of crucial given factors of which we are all aware and without which the process of integration simply cannot be discussed. Variations in national policy, for instance, are fundamental to the life of international organizations, especially in agencies which do not possess the institutional power to influence significantly the policy aims of their member states. However, this truism should not be rendered in the all too common form which asserts that differences in *power* among members determine organizational behavior and the speed and direction of organizational response. Variations in national policy provide a power determinant, not in absolute terms, but only with respect to the functional strength of particular states in relation to the specific task of the organization. The military and economic power of the United States in NATO, for instance, is a meaningful ingredient in the life of that organization only when it is brought to bear on infrastructure or procurement negotiations. The fact remains, nonetheless, that changes in the policy needs experienced by member states, reflecting as they do the pressures of the home and of the international environments, create definite phases in the life of international organizations.

Therefore, lessons about integrative processes associated with one phase do not generally carry over into the next because the specific policy context—often short-range—determines what is desired by governments and tolerated by them in terms of integrative accommodations. This, in turn, forces us to the conclusion that types of accommodation, and the associated procedural norms of an organization, developed in one phase of its life do not necessarily carry over into the next. There is no dependable, cumulative process of precedent formation leading to ever more community-oriented organizational behavior, unless the task assigned to the institutions is inherently expansive, thus capable of overcoming the built-in autonomy of functional contexts and of surviving changes in the policy aims of member states.

The importance of this lesson must be illustrated from the experience of one of the more successful European organizations, OEEC, with multilateral accommodation in liberalizing trade and payments —the aspect of OEEC which contributed most to integration in Europe.[e] The typical OEEC procedure included confrontation, collection of detailed information, mediation in closed sessions, and the work-

[e] My discussion of OEEC benefited greatly from the advice and criticism of William Diebold, Jr., and Robert Triffin.

ing out of specific solutions to crises by autonomous bodies of national experts. The procedures were perfected during the period (1948–51) when the chief task of OEEC was the distribution of United States aid, assistance which was conditional on trade and payments liberalization. During the next phase (1952–56) the procedure continued and was remarkably successful in further removing obstacles to intra-regional commerce, despite the cessation of United States aid. Why? Largely because the major national policies continued to be oriented toward liberalization, and the recurrent French and British payments crises could therefore not successfully challenge the multilateral decision-making process; continuing French and British demands for a relaxation of the OEEC Code resulted in successive compromises along the principle of "splitting the difference," but involving the upgrading of common interests in the system of review and accountability which accompanied the relaxation. Since 1956, all this has changed. Further economic integration has become enmeshed in the political issue of the Six against the Seven, with the result that the procedures which had apparently been institutionalized successfully in an earlier phase of OEEC's life have stagnated with disuse. Fundamental changes in national policies provide the crucial explanatory variable.

This process went on in a setting of intergovernmentalism. More than in the supranational setting, an environment of intergovernmentalism permits great freedom to states strongly endowed in a specific functional context. Let us use monetary cooperation as an example. The history of OEEC suggests—as that of ECSC and EEC does not—that certain types of states can use their special bargaining power more readily to get their way. Thus, economically weak countries

whose trade is not crucial to the system are readily exempted from the governing norms and play little part in decision-making; but economically strong countries, in terms of total foreign trade *and* credit capacity, possess a *de facto* veto power. Structural creditors whose role in regional trade is secondary occasionally assert a veto power and delay decisions, but their influence is never dominant. Structural or occasional debtors (France and the United Kingdom) with a very important stake in regional trade are able to exercise a constant blackmail power and to succeed in obtaining exemptions from regional rules, since they are immune to the threat of retaliation and responsive only to the techniques of discreet mediation and confrontation.

The lesson of European integration can be summarized as follows:

1. *Institutionally,* supranational bodies most readily lend themselves to accommodation on the basis of upgrading common interests. This is equally true of intergovernmental bodies which permit certain of their expert commissions the role usually associated with the Communities of the Six, such as the OEEC Steering Board for Trade, the Council of Europe's Commissioner for Refugees, and WEU's Armaments Control Agency. These institutions are least susceptible to the alternation of phases and most likely to develop cumulative decision-making precedents.

2. *Functionally,* specific economic tasks resolving policy differences emerging from previous imperfect compromises on welfare questions, but involving large mass interests, are most intimately related to rapid integration. Conflicts may be resolved by all the usual methods, but upgrading com-

mon interests predominates. The tendency toward autonomy of tasks can be overcome only by building into the institutions specific assignments which maximize the spill-over process.

3. *Environmentally*, integration fares best in situations controlled by social groupings representing the rational interests of urban-industrial society, groups seeking to maximize their economic benefits and dividing along regionally homogeneous ideological-political lines. Changing national policy inhibits integration unless compensated by strong central institutions maximizing the spill-over process.

Obviously, integration may take place and has taken place among nations which have few of these characteristics and through international organizations which depart little from the classic intergovernmental pattern. But the pace and intensity of such integration is pallid in such a context as compared to the situation in which all optimal conditions are met. Hence it should come as no surprise that the Communities of the Six represent the most, and the Council of Europe the least, successful organizations in a European spectrum in which all organizations make some contribution to some aspect of the integration process.

III. The Lessons Applied to Other Regions

Before proceeding to a projection of these conclusions at the global level of the United Nations, it might be instructive to see to what extent they can be used to explain progress toward political community in other areas of the world. I have selected three such areas, the European members of the Soviet bloc, the Arab

world, and the western hemisphere. Each of these possesses more unifying environmental characteristics in certain aspects than does western Europe. The Arab and Latin American worlds are, respectively, relatively homogeneous with reference to language and religion. They share, less uniformly, it is true, economic underdevelopment and dependence on monoculture. They also share certain ideological commitments, at least if we do not probe too deeply below the surface of ringing affirmations and generous platitudes. The Soviet bloc owes its unity less to any of these considerations than to the organizational and ideological ties among the ruling elites—and these may be undergoing disintegration now!

Whatever assurance may be warranted in our discussion of European integration is not readily transferable to other regional contexts. The generalizations offered for the Arab world and for Latin America do not merit firm theoretical assertion. While recent work on the Soviet bloc enables us to speak with considerable confidence, no similar work has yet been done on integration in the other regions.[1] The generalizations here advanced are therefore far more tentative and should be regarded as strong theoretical possibilities derived from firmer propositions culled from the European context and projected on the basis of information available at the moment.

Soviet Bloc. There are no supranational organizations in the bloc now, nor were the relations which dominated during the Stalin era of a supranational type. On the contrary, the organizations which prevail are intergovernmental and the party meetings which take place seem almost like diplomatic conferences. The law of alternating phases seems to apply, as exem-

[1] See, above all, Zbigniew K. Brzezinski, *The Soviet Bloc*, Cambridge, Mass., Harvard University Press, 1960; and George Modelski, *The Communist International System*, Princeton, Center of International Studies, December 1, 1960, and the literature cited there.

plified by the lack of cumulative decision-making and precedent formation. Organizational tasks expand most readily when they are specific; the most continuous type of integrative activity is in the area of joint economic planning with highly detailed objectives. Environmentally speaking, this activity goes on in a setting dominated by a resolution to industrialize, with growing urbanization and a deepening socio-economic division of labor in each communist country, even though totalitarianism precludes the flowering of a pluralist society.

The truly revealing lesson of the Soviet bloc, however, emerges from the organizational context. Actually, integration was *least* successful when the Communist Party of the Soviet Union possessed an organizational monopoly over the process. The Stalin period witnessed a minimum of military cooperation, no joint economic planning, no exchange of information apart from the slavish imitation in eastern Europe of Soviet examples, and no successful value-sharing among fellow communists. Integration was a one-way process in which the aims of the European satellites were simply subordinated to those of the Soviet Union. The brittleness of the structure stood exposed in the fall of 1956. Now, with the occasional flowering of "revisionism," there is little central direction, but, paradoxically, a good deal of practical integration. The dismantlement of the central apparatus of coercion and manipulation yields to a process of voluntary integration based on a calculation of economic advantage, accompanied by the proper dosages of ideological compromise negotiated among equals. The modes of accommodation are as varied as elsewhere, with the upgrading of common interests by no means always victorious. However, the more varied the centers of power in the bloc become, with the implied insta-

bility of alignments and unpredictability of compromise patterns, the more likely the emergence of some habits of continuous intra-bloc adjustment by techniques not unlike those of western Europe.

Hence, the essential lessons of the western European integration process seem to hold in the communist setting, with the pragmatic value-sharing of allied communist parties taking the place of interaction among kindred democratic parties. However, the continuation of this process clearly depends on the observation by the satellite rulers of the limits to voluntarism imposed by the Soviets. Imre Nagy demonstrates the non-observance of these limits, while Wladislaw Gomulka exemplifies the principle of limited dissent within a framework of fundamental loyalty to bloc objectives. Unlike other regional systems, voluntary integration in the Soviet bloc depends on the patience of *one* national elite.

Arab States. Institutions in the Arab world contain no trace of supranationality. The Arab League as well as the African organs in which certain Arab states participate are intergovernmental conferences, with either weak secretariats or none at all. While their deliberations are eloquently clothed in the phraseology of Arab Brotherhood and often refer to the lofty aims of the Arab Nation, they result in accommodations based on the minimum common denominator, if they achieve accommodation at all. But this is a symptom of the lack of integration rather than a cause.

Much the same is true of the conclusions which can be drawn from a functional analysis. In principle, Arab institutions have tasks which cover collective security and peaceful settlement of disputes among the members, security against external aggression, economic integration, regional investment, legal harmonization, cultural cooperation, coordination of transport and communication—the list of activities is identical with the European prototype. The only functions successfully carried out, however, are of a purely negative character. While the autonomy of functional contexts is fully intact in the Arab world, none of the tasks show a tendency toward spilling over into new areas of common concern, and many show evidence of periodic atrophy. Nothing of consequence has occurred toward economic and legal integration, though some common transport policy measures have been elaborated. The most striking successes were the defense of the Middle East against Western and Israeli policy. Arab unity has been sustained in keeping up the economic-diplomatic boycott of Israel and in making common policy against Western countries suspected of neo-imperialist designs.

Security and peaceful settlement among members of the Arab League has been less consistently achieved. When the total international environment made it seem that the consequences of inter-Arab strife (as in the Lebanese-Jordan crisis of 1958) would be destructive for all concerned, the phrases of Arab Brotherhood enshrined in League proceedings were translated into reality. But the same machinery proved quite useless in settling the differences between Egypt on the one hand and Jordan and Iraq on the other in connection with the liquidation of the Palestine conflict. Nor did it help to smooth the quarrels between Nasser, Kassim, and Bourguiba. Whenever the Arab League served essentially as a front for Egyptian national policy its activities were doomed to failure; whenever the convergence of interests permitted a different internal alignment successful mediation took place. In no instance did the League acquire the role of an integrating mechanism standing above the separate policies of its members. Suc-

cess in highly specific security undertakings, lack of success in other pursuits, the prevalence of the minimum common denominator: these are merely more symptoms, not causes, of lack of integration and progress toward an Arab political community.

The explanation, then, may be found in the environment with its deceptive façade of unity. With the exception of the pan-Arab Socialist Renaissance Party (Ba'ath) there are few ideological links of unity among Arab political groups. Each modernizing elite in power, whether an intellectuals' independence movement or the army, acts and thinks only in the context of its state; each traditional-feudal oligarchical elite is intent on preserving its position and rejects cooperation with hostile Arab groups across the border. They "integrate" in meeting jointly experienced threats from outside the region; they cannot meaningfully work together on normally integrative tasks because they experience no common needs. Even in the area of economic development it is the maximization of national resources which motivates elites, not a pooling of resources. In fact, Iraqi nationalist suspicion that Egypt had its eye on Iraq oil may have been a factor in the split among such similarly motivated leaders as Kassim and Nasser. On the other hand, it is possible that a jointly experienced desire in pooling the major Middle Eastern resource—oil—so as to exert greater control over prices and marketing conditions may eventually result in a sufficiently specific convergence of aims to permit the evolution of a vital regional task administered by supranational techniques. This has not yet occurred, but the example of Europe would suggest this as the most likely area of intense integration.

If Europe is to serve as our model, too few of the preconditions for integration exist in the Arab world to make an imitation of the integration process a likelihood in the near future. If neither the economic nor the social environment bears any resemblance to that of the West, the ideologies which prevail are unlikely to conform to that pattern. Forcible integration—conquest—remains the major possibility, but this would hardly be an application of the European modes of accommodation.

The Americas. Though there are no supranational institutions in the western hemisphere, the fact remains that the prevailing intergovernmental organizations contain bodies which, on occasion, perform as if they were supranational. This is true of the Inter-American Peace Committee and of occasional subcommittees of the Organization of American States (OAS) Council. It is also possible that certain bodies of the projected Central American and Latin American common market organizations will develop such modes of behavior. However, ways of accommodation thus far have never gone beyond the minimum common denominator. They have had distinct integrative consequences because the techniques of consultation have created precedents, subsequently applied in similar situations. Still, it may well be that the determining role of historical phases applies here too, preventing the precedents from becoming cumulative.

Precision can here be gained from functional analysis. Within OAS a growing complexity of economic, social, and cultural organs has resulted only in cumulative inaction: the clashing expectations and demands of the United States and of the underdeveloped Latin American countries have thus far check-mated one another. There has been no expansion of the organizational task, leave alone a spill-over. But the same is not true of the mainte-

nance of security and the peaceful solution of disputes among members of OAS.

A mixture of quiet mediation, admonition, and the threat of economic and military sanctions has sufficed to stop almost a dozen western hemisphere wars since 1945. Why? Essentially because no major ideological issues were at stake. The wars in question involved the mercenary ragamuffins of one oligarchy arrayed against those of another in very minor military skirmishes. It is in these situations that the mediatory prowess of OAS proved itself; here it achieved the institutionalization of precedent. But when this context changes a new picture emerges. Wars involving the issue of outside intervention —whether collective or unilateral—in a civil conflict in which democratic-revolutionary forces are arrayed against a traditional oligarchy (Guatemala, Dominican Republic, Costa Rica, Cuba) cannot be readily settled by OAS conciliation. Costa Rica was saved and the Trujillo regime faced with collective denunciation and sanctions because there was a huge majority in favor of the democratic forces in question. But the Guatemalan and Cuban cases show that OAS intervention is considered hostile to modernization and thus cannot easily receive organizational approval. Is it not likely that the very success of OAS in collective security is possible only as long as the issue of interfering with modernization is not involved? If so, we are now living in a new phase in which past precedents will *not* shape future policy, which may imply a decay in the hitherto successful security function of OAS.

The current preparation by OAS of a convention on human rights and of a document concerning the limits of multilateral intervention on behalf of democracy may prove that common interests, for the first time, can be upgraded in this field.

It would imply institutional growth, new tasks, a spill-over, and a definite advance toward political community. While this has not yet happened, it could suggest that economics need not be the chief carrier of the integration process. In fact, this begs one of the most puzzling of questions: can only industrialized nations integrate or can the very fact of underdevelopment be a spur to regional unity? When one super-developed power confronts twenty disunited nations eager for aid, the answer is no. But would this be true if OAS possessed the power to distribute aid on the scale of OEEC under the Marshall Plan? There are two Latin American common market organizations now projected, each using as its *raison d'être* the need for development and the creation of large markets as a spur to industrialization.[8] The tasks imposed by their respective treaties are less precise and more permissive than the Treaty of Rome, and they lack the power to hold out and withdraw economic rewards to their members. The picture for integration seems unpromising, but again it may be too soon to judge, especially since defense against the export prowess and possible protectionism of a united Europe is another factor making for unity in Latin America. Regional unity in Europe may yet father regional unity in Latin America even though the process obeys different impulses.

If this reasoning is correct, the fact of underdevelopment and the prevalence of monoculture may turn out to be environmental factors favorable to integration, though they were hostile to it in Europe. At the same time, social and economic underdevelopment creates major regional

ideological affinities, especially among radical socialist-nationalist reformist parties of the *Aprista* type. But regimes and parties have a habit of changing rapidly in this area. Even if they remain in power for longer periods, the preoccupation with purely national development has thus far carried the day. The intensification of the national-revolutionary process may still have the same disintegrative consequences here as in the Middle East.

Returning to our initial propositions, then, let us reiterate that intensity of integration is positively correlated with industrialization and economic diversification. These conditions, in turn, imply an interest in social legislation at the national level; when a regional integration process is launched, the need for an intra-regional harmonization of social legislation is frequently expressed. That being the case, the degree of existing uniformity of such legislation, prepared often under the auspices of the International Labor Organization (ILO) and subject to its continuing review, provides a useful indicator for judging the existence of commonly experienced needs and interests. Table 1 makes clear that the indicator of international social legislation confirms our earlier reasoning concerning the impact of industrialism on integration. The ILO conventions involved, of course, were drafted on the basis of global considerations; even so the interest shown by regional organizations grouping underdeveloped countries is minimal. Table 2 offers similar computations for the conventions concluded under the auspices of the Council of Europe, showing their coverage for the important regional organizations within Europe and for certain countries rela-

[8] For descriptions of the Latin American Free Trade Area and the Central American Free Trade Area conventions see *Europa-Archiv*, April 1960 (Vol. 15, No. 7–8), *External Affairs*, April 1960, and *Monthly Review* of the Federal Reserve Bank of New York, September 1960. The scheme is defended by Galo Plaza, "For a Regional Market in Latin America," *Foreign Affairs*, July 1959 (Vol. 37, No. 2). Both conventions have been completed and are awaiting ratification. It should not be overlooked that the driving force behind the negotiations was the UN Economic Commission for Latin America.

TABLE 1

Regional Coverage of ILO Conventions, August 1960

Category of Convention	OAS	EEC	EFTA	NATO	Arab League	All ILO Members
Occupational Hazards (13, 62)	24	67	29	33	19	28
Freedom of Association (11, 87, 98)	48	89	76	75	37	55
Anti-Discrimination (100, 111)	29	33	43	33	25	27
Social Security (2, 3, 12, 17, 18, 19, 24, 25, 35, 36, 37, 38, 39, 40, 42, 44, 48, 102, 103)	21	51	37	33	13	22
Hours and Vacations (1, 4, 14, 20, 30, 41, 47, 52, 67, 89, 101, 106)	24	31	24	22	14	24
Administration of Labor Legislation (26, 34, 63, 81, 94, 95, 99)	29	57	49	41	14	30
Minimum Age and Protection of the Young (5, 6, 10, 33, 59, 60, 77, 78, 79, 90)	25	55	23	29	5	25

"Coverage" is the ratio of actual ratifications to possible ratifications for all the members of a given regional organization, expressed in percent.

Source: International Labour Organization, *International Labour Conventions, Chart of Ratifications.* The computations are the author's responsibility.

tively aloof from the work of integration. Again, the figures support the proposition that environmentally similar countries, with a common basis in pluralism and industrialism, tend to express the joint interests which flow from this environment in harmonizing national legislation. While the over-all coverage of ILO conventions is about 33 percent, that of the European conventions is 59 percent.

IV. The Lesson Applied to the United Nations

If the attempt to apply categories of analysis developed in the European context to other regions must be treated with caution, the same is true to an even greater extent when we shift our focus to the United Nations. Far from being a finished theory of integration at the global level, the generalizations here advanced consti-

TABLE 2

Coverage of Council of Europe Conventions
(as of March 20, 1959)

Type of Convention	Coverage in %							
	Total	EEC	EFTA	Nordic Council	United Kingdom	Greece	Turkey	Ireland
Political Integration (nos. 1, 2, 3, 5, 6, 7, 8, 9, 23)	66	61	81	85	67	50	25	50
Economic Integration (nos. 4, 10, 11, 12, 13, 14, 15, 21, 25)	56	75	60	53	75	11	0	75
Cultural Integration and International Understanding (nos. 18, 19, 20, 27)	62	63	70	56	100	25	50	75
General Convenience (nos. 16, 17, 22, 24, 26)	50	53	64	60	60	20	40	60
TOTAL	59	63	69	64	76	27	29	65

415

"Coverage" is the ratio of actual to possible ratifications of each convention in each category. Possible ratifications were so computed as to exclude countries to which specific conventions are not applicable because of their subject matter.

Source: *European Yearbook*, Vol. VI, for the information on ratifications. The computations are the author's responsibility.

tute merely an attempt to subject a variety of international phenomena to the rigor of a unified set of concepts in an effort to narrow the field of analysis to a few central propositions. Hence I continue to apply the ordering concepts of environment, function, and institution, even though they may lead to less satisfactory results.

To impute environmental homogeneity to the United Nations Member States would be futile. Any superficial examination on the basis of the indicators we used in the case of Europe will demonstrate the absence of pervasive traits common to all Members. More than half of the Member States are non-industrial and underdeveloped; two-thirds, perhaps, lack a rational-pluralistic social structure and continue to exhibit various degrees of traditionalism; totalitarian, democratic, and oligarchical regimes are represented in about equal numbers. Most important, perhaps, the ideals of Member States run the gamut from the advocacy of revolutionary change to the staunch defense of some status quo. The UN environment, in short, is volatile and dynamic: it changes with every admission of a new Member, with every revolution, almost with every election. The western European environment, in contrast, is the epitome of stability.

This, obviously, implies a marked systemic dependence on historical phases. The UN during the period of deceptive inter-allied unity was one kind of system; it functioned very differently during the subsequent period of United States–NATO supremacy, to give way to still another mode of action when neutralism came into its own with the mass admission of new Members in 1955. The advent of the African states and the eventual obsolescence of the whole colonial issue is certain to create a new environment again. Environmental instability is much greater than in any regional example here investi-

gated, and the performance of the UN system is proportionately uneven.

In fact, the environment was singled out for initial attention here because it imposes on the UN an entirely different species of organizational life as contrasted with regional systems. Regional integration responds to certain *common* environmental features, no matter how elusive or temporary; it is based on certain common needs experienced by all participants, often in defense against some outside force. Nothing of the kind is true in the UN. The United Nations system represents the cohabitation of enemies, the institutionalized attack-and-retreat of hostile forces seeking to get the better of each other by peaceful means, but without any intention of deliberately emphasizing what they may share in common. Integrative consequences flowing from this game are wholly unintended, though none the less real when they do occur. Consequently, it is idle to expect stable agreement on the primacy of certain tasks in the UN; the volatile environment is responsible for a shifting perception of necessary and common tasks, thus interfering with the functional specificity desirable for integration.

It would be a mistake to conclude from this picture that the institutions of the UN may be dismissed as irretrievably impotent. The UN institutional structure is so complex and the diversity of tasks so considerable that they extend from pure intergovernmental diplomacy to certain cautious approaches to supranationality. Further, the variety of organs is so great and the conditions under which they function so diffuse that all modes of accommodation can and do flourish under the proper circumstances. Institutionally, then, the system is exceedingly flexible and has shown the most startling constitutional adaptations, often to the chagrin of international lawyers.

But it remains true just the same that the dominant mode of accommodation has been compromise on the basis of the minimum common denominator, though "splitting the difference" is not unknown in the activities of certain specialized agencies. The upgrading of common interests has occasionally been attempted, as indicated in a variety of colonial, economic development, and military proposals, beginning with the Baruch Plan. Yet, the record points to the lesson that *successful* UN action or solution of crises has *always* been based on the minimum common denominator, success being judged by the degree of implementation given to UN resolutions. Resolutions, by contrast, which emerge through the process of parliamentary diplomacy and represent the view of a majority sharply contested by the defeated minority never achieve full implementation. Bona fide compromise may resolve individual crises (as in Korea, Indochina, Lebanon, and aspects of the Palestine war), but unless the process yields to more community-oriented modes of accommodation, these remain *ad hoc* settlements of no integrative significance.

Now it is true that the efforts of the Secretary-General, acting in the name of the UN, to deal with certain crises contain a dose of supranationalism and seek to upgrade common interests. By committing the UN to a given course of action (as in the Congo) and subsequently requesting ever larger authority from the Security Council or the General Assembly to enable him to carry out tasks assumed earlier, the Secretary-General causes the accretion of new powers and responsibilities to the UN as a whole. In the European context such efforts often resulted in a permanent growth of community-oriented procedures; in the UN this has not occurred. Member States, in deference to changing policy at home and shifting

alignments abroad, will acquiesce in such courses of action in New York and then proceed to sabotage them in the field: UN authority has not increased in the Congo context, not because of Mr. Hammarskjöld's mistakes, but because certain crucial Member States blocked the execution of his mandate. Much the same is true of the UN operation in Suez. The claim for supranational powers and the desire to upgrade common interests in peaceful change and relative stability—both of which do grow out of crises dealt with by the UN—run afoul the persistence of Member States to use the techniques only for the advancement of their own local policy aims, as exemplified by the conduct of Ghana, Guinea, Egypt, and Belgium in the Congo crisis.

The prevalence of environmental phases in an institutionally weak system results in a paucity of cumulative decisions creating integrative precedents. While this was also true in certain European organizations and in the western hemisphere, it is much more striking at the global level. The first Charter provisions with respect to collective security and enforcement were changed by the Uniting for Peace Resolution, a change which had fallen into quiet disuse by 1955. Powers given to the Secretary-General vary—but do not necessarily grow—from crisis to crisis. Issues which appeared settled reappear a few years later, including major constitutional questions.

But despite all this, one major procedural advance in the direction of political community has shown a tenacious persistence: the role of a *stable* majority in the General Assembly, through the medium of parliamentary diplomacy, to set the limits and define the direction of certain crucial tasks. In the realm of security and enforcement, this has resulted in the enshrinement of the conciliation process, as executed through the agency of un-committed nations. But a much more sta-ble majority has imposed its stamp on other organizational tasks, which confirms at the global level that functional specific-ity bears the major responsibility for inte-gration, and that functional contexts tend toward autonomy in New York as in Strasbourg. Chief among these tasks is the expanding work of the UN in eco-nomic development and technical assist-ance, followed by the significant accretions of authority in situations involving the peaceful transfer from colonial status to independence. The stable core of the ma-jority responsible for pushing these tasks forward is made up of the bulk of Latin American, Asian, and African nations, joined in certain decolonization ventures by the Soviet bloc.

Environmental heterogeneity and insti-tutional weakness need not prevent global integration around certain tasks which command general interest; but it is the political component of the environment which defines the nature of convergence of national aims. Integration in the UN system has occurred, not in the context of purely non-controversial and technical activities which are of equal interest to all Member States, even though of no trans-cendent importance to any of them, but in areas of convergence due to the major political conflicts of our era. The Cold War, the anticolonial struggle, and the revolution of rising expectations are re-sponsible for the national policy aims which, by converging at the UN, have resulted in new and larger tasks. Further-more, the dependence of the major powers and their allies in their ideological conflict on the support of nations more interested in anticolonialism and economic develop-ment neatly merges these separate strains into one mélange, infusing the Cold War with the colonial issue, and economic de-velopment with the East-West ideological struggle. Thus, the universal military-ideological environment based on conflict begets certain areas of common interest in which organizational tasks have ex-panded.

In the realm of collective security this has resulted in the erosion of a task and in the decadence of institutions of a quasi-supranational character. But in the func-tional realm of economics the picture is otherwise. Originally, the UN task was the elaboration of universal economic pol-icy tending toward a common world trade and payments system, coordinated counter-cyclical policies, and continuous consulta-tion on all issues relating to economic sta-bility, including commodity trade. This task was not successfully carried out in the UN, in the International Monetary Fund, or in the Food and Agriculture Organization. Universal economic policy foundered on the ideologically mixed en-vironment which produced irreconcilable demands.

But more specific economic aims re-sulted in a spectacular expansion of an-other task: international investment and related activities of technical assistance. The history of expanded International Bank for Reconstruction and Development responsibilities and operations, the creation of three new UN investment agencies since 1955, and the integration of invest-ment with highly focused and centrally controlled technical aid, through the UN Special Fund, speaks for itself. Further, each decision to expand the UN task was taken on the basis of majority pressure mobilized by parliamentary diplomacy and followed by detailed compromises among the major contributing powers, in-volving both an upgrading of common interests and a splitting of the difference. Routinized administrative control by in-ternational civil servants may follow eventually, thus submitting national develop-ment programs to an integrating process. The upgrading of common interests would then continue to be manifest in the flow of decisions made by such agencies as the Special Fund. While this has not yet hap-pened, it should at least be noted that the controls exercised by the Special Fund are much more rigorous than is the super-vision of the Technical Assistance Board.

Anti-colonialism suggests a parallel les-son. The irreconcilable demands implicit in the environment prevented the firm but general colonial policy from develop-ing which is suggested by the UN Char-ter. General discussions on colonialism included ample invective but no concrete solutions. Peaceful change, as a regular integrative process in UN organs, was not in evidence with reference to colonial dis-putes. But the very Cold War pressures which resulted in progressive compromises among the major powers in the economic development field also brought pressure on the West to yield to the anti-colonial demands mobilized through parliamen-tary diplomacy. The result was a recurrent pattern of enhanced UN responsibility with respect to assuring a peaceful transi-tion to independence in the case of specific territories facing specific problems, through the processes of the trusteeship system. Somewhat more generally, this constella-tion of forces brought about an institution-alized increase in the procedural powers of the UN to hear and deal with com-plaints. If "peaceful change" means the gradual yielding of one type of policy in the face of the onslaught of another, mini-mizing violence, and relying on parlia-mentary diplomatic pressure allied with Cold War overtones, the demise of coloni-alism under UN auspices provides a strik-ing example of task expansion. In contrast to the collective security function, the ex-istence of a stable UN majority on the colonial issue has brought about cumula-tive precedents on procedure that may sur-vive the historical phases which buffet the universal system.

Let us complete this functional survey with a word about universal human rights. I suspect strongly that here the dominance of phases reasserts itself and that the inte-grative role of this function, which exists at the regional level, will have no global counterpart. The prominence of universal human rights in UN discussion is due al-most solely to the desire of Member States to score propaganda points off one an-other: initially the West used the issue to embarrass the Soviet Union; now the Afro-Asian, Latin American, and Soviet blocs are tactically united in using the issue to embarrass the West on the colonial and overseas investment issues. The im-minent end of colonial rule will destroy this tactical alliance and create a new UN phase. Then, it is highly doubtful that either the Soviet Union or the under-developed countries with totalitarian ten-dencies will be eager to create a system of universal private rights or a scheme of international accountability. In the Euro-pean context the protection of individual rights could have integrative results just because the pre-existing environment was already homogeneous, a point much less strikingly applicable in the western hemi-sphere. But no integrative consequences can emerge at the UN level if many of the Member States are motivated purely by short-run interests which will not survive the current phase.

This analysis suggests further functional areas in which integrative UN activities could well be undertaken. True, neither colonialism nor human rights is likely to provide opportunities for converging inter-ests in a few years. But economic devel-opment will continue to offer a field of action to such aims as long as the current world tripolarity prevails; in fact, that very condition suggests additional common interests. The peaceful uses of outer space, pooled space research, and UN control over extra-terrestrial bodies are obvious candidates. Less obvious but clearly within our framework of analysis is the field of regulated arms reduction and the increasingly international peaceful use of nuclear energy. These activities involve converging interests among conflicting states; they have a very high spill-over potential and require supranational administrative bodies for adequate control. In short, they evoke the upgrading of common interests in the execution of highly specific programs.

But let us guard against the fallacy that *any* non-political program yields greater integrative results than would a concerted political effort to call into life a world political community. Our European survey makes clear that politically-infused economic tasks, flowing from an industrial environment with a pluralistic society, yield the greatest amount of integration. Other regional experiences do not clearly support this conclusion, but the UN experience conforms, at least, to the economic component in the proposition. Yet the economic work of the UN is obviously less integrative than that of Europe for the institutional and environmental reasons stated. The art of manipulating integration consists in isolating functional areas which produce converging interests among moderately hostile states, and in capitalizing upon those "non-political" aims which very soon spill over into the realm of politics when specific programs are envisaged by strong international institutions. The urban-industrial-pluralistic environment is optimal for this purpose, but not unique.

V. Integration as a Discontinuous Process

Five major conclusions can be drawn from this discussion. Processes which yield optimal progress toward the end of political community at the European level simply cannot be reproduced in other contexts because the necessary preconditions exist to a much lesser degree. Therefore, European integration will proceed at a much more rapid pace than universal integration. Further, other regions with strongly varying environmental factors are unlikely to imitate successfully the European example.

However, it is by no means clear that slightly different functional pursuits, responding to a different set of converging interests, may not also yield integration. The Soviet and Latin American examples suggest that this may be the case. But it is also true that if regional integration continues to go forward in these areas, it will obey impulses peculiar to them and thus fail to demonstrate any universal "law of integration" deduced from the European example.

Integration at the universal level obeys still different impulses. It flows from much more intense conflict than the regional process, in deference to the heterogeneity of the environment in which it unrolls. Consequently, the areas of common interest are more difficult to isolate and the proper specific functions harder to define. In view of the prevalence of phases it then becomes very hazardous to forecast any even and consistent pattern of integration.

The UN effort suffers from the built-in defect that the very economic development and technical aid activities which at the moment constitute its integrative task may create the kind of national environment in which *less* integration will take place a

TABLE 3

Cohesion of Regional Caucus Groups in the United Nations General Assembly, 1945–1958

Caucus	Cohesion of Member States								
	Before Creation of Caucus %			After Creation of Caucus %			During the Whole Period %**		
	Identical	Solidarity	Divided	Identical	Solidarity	Divided	Identical	Solidarity	Divided
African*	—	—	—	46.7	33.3	20.0			
Western European	65.0	23.8	11.2	82.4	11.0	6.6			
Asian-African	11.4	36.4	53.9	34.4	42.2	23.4			
Benelux							77.5	17.0	5.5
Scandinavian							68.3	23.9	7.8
Commonwealth							13.0	27.7	59.3
Arab							63.4	27.2	9.4
Latin American							28.8	33.2	38.0
Soviet							96.0	3.9	0.1

Source: Thomas Hovet, Jr., *Bloc Politics in the United Nations*, Center for International Studies, Massachusetts Institute of Technology, 1958, pp. 64–65, 86, 98, 111, 121–122, 131, 155, 172, 187.

Hovet's study is based on the counting of an "adjusted gross" number of roll-call votes. For the meaning of this device, see Hovet, pp. 239 ff. For an "identical" vote the frequency of members voting the same way, not considering abstentions, is counted; for a "solidarity" vote, the frequency of members of a caucusing group abstaining rather than voting against their colleagues is determined; a "divided" vote covers the situations of direct opposition among members of a group.

*The African caucus had functioned for only two sessions at the time these computations were made, thus precluding firm conclusions. Prior to the formation of the caucus there were not enough African Member States to create a meaningful statistical pattern.

**The caucusing groups listed for "the whole period" were formed before or at the time of the first meeting of the General Assembly.

TABLE 4

Cohesion of Members of Regional Pacts in the United Nations General Assembly, 1945–1958

PACT	Before Conclusion of Pact		After Conclusion of Pact	
	Identical Votes %	Divided Votes %	Identical Votes %	Divided Votes %
ANZUS	75.8	13.8	78.2	5.4
Central Treaty Organization	39.2	26.2	55.0	15.0
Council of Europe	51.0	21.0	43.0	30.0
NATO	47.4	21.1	55.4	21.3
Organization of Central American States	48.3	24.2	67.5	29.8
Southeast Asia Treaty Organization	37.0	34.8	75.0	10.0
Western European Union	—*	—*	75.0	3.6

Source: Thomas Hovet, Jr., *Bloc Politics in the United Nations,* Center for International Studies, Massachusetts Institute of Technology, 1958, pp. 196–203.

This computation is based on certain roll-call votes considered as relating to "significant resolutions" on a variety of issues before the United Nations. A panel of outstanding participants in the debates determined which of the votes during each session merited the label "significant." It is Hovet's conclusion that in all instances votes dealing with matters of collective measures and the peaceful settlement of disputes commanded the greatest cohesion among the members of each regional pact.

*Since Italy did not participate in UN debates prior to 1955, no meaningful figure for the pre-pact period can be given.

generation from now. To the extent that the UN effort strengthens national economies and administrative structures it actually may *reduce* the final integrative component. Functionally specific economic tasks found to provide progress toward a political community in Europe may thus have the opposite final effect at the world level. Whether, in some future UN phase, space and nuclear tasks would produce more integration remains an open question.

The element of discontinuity among the various processes is increased by the continued autonomy of the universal and regional decision-making contexts. As Tables 3 and 4 make clear, there is no overwhelming evidence that the members of a cohesive regional system remain united in the UN, nor is there evidence that normally weak and heterogeneous regional systems may not perform cohesively in New York. In short, the contexts remain separate and distinct in the minds of policy-makers, a feature hardly conducive to the elaboration of a unified and global integration process.

A final element of discontinuity must be frankly exposed. Regional integration, because it proceeds more rapidly and responds to a greater number of optimal factors, may eventually slow down universal integration altogether. The regional process may create a relatively small number of integrated political communities, facing each other in the UN system. In fact, the expanded UN task looking toward pooled economic development and regional agencies in Africa, Southeast Asia and elsewhere, may actually contribute to this trend. In that case, the growth of fewer and larger political communities will contribute to regional, but not to universal, peace. The universal system will remain what it now is: the arena for minimizing conflict and maximizing common interests in deference to the minimum common denominator.

PART V

INTERNATIONAL ORGANIZATION: NEW PERSPECTIVES

Transnational Relations and World Politics:

A Conclusion

Joseph S. Nye, Jr., and Robert O. Keohane

World politics is changing, but our conceptual paradigms have not kept pace. The classic state-centric paradigm assumes that states are the only significant actors in world politics and that they act as units. Diverse domestic interests have effects on international politics only through governmental foreign policy channels. Intersocietal interactions are relegated to a category of secondary importance—the "environment" of interstate politics. As Karl Kaiser has pointed out, the reality of international politics has never totally corresponded to this model. Nevertheless, the model was approximated in the eighteenth century when foreign policy decisions were taken by small groups of persons acting within an environment that was less obtrusive and complex than the present one.[1]

Simplification of reality is essential for understanding. A skeptical scholar or diplomat might admit that the state-centric model misses much of the complexity of transnational relations described in this volume, but he might argue that such a simplification is justified because 1) in direct confrontation with transnational actors governments prevail, 2) transnational relations have always existed, and 3) transnational relations do not significantly affect the "high politics" of security, status, or war. We believe that these objections are to a large degree mistaken and that a broader world politics paradigm is necessary if scholars and statesmen are to understand such current problems as the unequal distribution of power and values in the world, the new setting of

[1] Karl Kaiser, "Transnationale Politik: Zu einer Theorie der multinationalen Politik," *Politische Vierteljahresschrift*, 1969 (Special Issue No. 1), pp. 80–109. An English translation of this important essay will appear in *International Organization*, Autumn 1971 (Vol. 25, No. 4), forthcoming.

From Volume 25, No. 3 (1971), pp. 721–48.

United States foreign policy, statesmen's feelings of "loss of control," and the new types and tasks of international organization.

I. Why Change Paradigms?

Before elaborating our world politics paradigm and discussing these problems we set forth our reasons for rejecting the major arguments for the adequacy of the state-centric approach.

"Governments Win Direct Confrontations"

When transnational relations are discussed, those who wish to preserve the limited state-centric view are likely to stress the point that, in direct confrontations with transnational actors, governments generally prevail. Robert Gilpin argues this point in his essay in part I. It is certainly true that national governments are often able to win such confrontations since they have much greater resources of force and popular legitimacy. The Ford Foundation can be expelled from a foreign country or disciplined by the United States Congress. A local Catholic hierarchy can be cut off from Rome. The assets of a multinational business enterprise may be nationalized, and its efforts to impose retaliatory sanctions may come to no avail. IBM and Ford Motor Company may be prevented from investing in the Union of Soviet Socialist Republics. Invading revolutionary guerrillas—or guerrillas operating from a base in an independent state—may be decimated by military force. At a nonorganizational level individuals whose attitudes become too cosmopolitan because of transnational contacts may be deprived of political effectiveness at home.

However, the question "who wins confrontations?" is insufficient. It focuses only on the extreme cases of direct confrontation between a government and a nongovernmental actor. Winning may be costly, even for governments. Transnational relations may help to increase these costs and thus increase the constraints on state autonomy. Expelling a foundation cuts off resources that may be vital to certain important groups. As Ivan Vallier points out, the Roman Catholic church today is better able than ever before to transfer resources across borders. Even where access is restricted, it remains a significant political factor. Nationalization of the local assets of a multinational business enterprise may prove costly in terms of capital, technology, or markets foregone. Restrictions on American business involvement in Eastern Europe may mean that such dealings are handled through European subsidiaries and thus are more easily isolated from the American political process. It may also mean that the market is left to European rivals.[2]

[2] There are currently several hundred joint ventures of private Western and Communist business enterprises in Eastern Europe. "Europe Economic Survey," *New York Times,* January 16, 1970, pp. 49–73; see also Marshall I. Goldman, "The East Reaches for Markets," *Foreign Affairs,* July 1969 (Vol. 47, No. 4), pp. 721–734.

Because of the rise in the costs to national governments of "winning" in direct confrontations with transnational actors there are more incentives for bargaining. More relevant than "who wins" direct confrontations are the new kinds of bargains, coalitions, and alliances being formed between transnational actors and between these actors and segments of governments and international organizations. The essays in this volume provide a wide variety of examples: coalitions between the Roman Catholic church and nation-states; new ecumenical alliances between religious groups; coalitions between locally owned companies and governments to gain protection against foreign companies; coalitions between vertically integrated corporations and trade unions to ensure continuity of supplies; coalitions between government and unions to influence or even help overthrow foreign governments; coalitions between scientists to strengthen their position in lobbying for resources at home; coalitions between trade unions to coordinate pressure on multinational business enterprises; coalitions between foreign intellectuals and United States foundations to protect social scientists against their governments; coalitions between revolutionary groups to strengthen their legitimacy in their struggles against governments.

There is considerable variety among the actors involved, the resources available to them, and the outcomes of their coalitions. For example, boycotts of companies and individuals in the entertainment world by Arab governments are coordinated through regional intergovernmental organizations. In one instance (that involving the Norwich Union Fire Insurance Society in the United Kingdom) a boycott proved effective in changing the leadership of a British corporation. In other cases the costs of boycott were too high, and governments did not enforce the agreed-upon sanctions.[3]

Robert L. Thornton's essay on air transport, to take a different type of activity, illustrates a variety of coalitions and outcomes that are suggested by figure 2 in the introduction. In the 1966 air corridors controversy a transnational actor, the International Air Line Pilots Association, lobbied successfully to prevent an intergovernmental organization, the International Civil Aviation Organization (ICAO), from endorsing the position advocated by the United States government. In general the nongovernmental International Air Transport Association (IATA), run by an oligarchy of airlines, is far stronger than the intergovernmental ICAO in which each state has one vote and minor governments can create obstructions. In some cases airlines have aligned with governments for protection against other airlines or governments. As Thornton describes it, Pan American World Airways and Trans World Airlines tacitly approved of an Alitalia position in the IATA that thwarted the United States government position on charter airline fares. United States airlines

[3] Robert W. MacDonald, *The League of Arab States: A Study in the Dynamics of Regional Organization* (Princeton, N.J.: Princeton University Press, 1965), pp. 118–123.

could not have resisted the United States government as well on their own. In its rivalry with Pan American over South Pacific air routes Continental Air Lines is allegedly attempting to enlist the support of an intergovernmental organization—the United Nations Trusteeship Council—to strengthen its position. The complexity of these coalitions in the political struggle to allocate important resources in the field of air transport is not caught by the state-centric paradigm. Nor, we might add, do national governments always prevail.

A sophisticated analysis of contemporary international politics cannot ignore this variety of bargaining situations or the differences in outcomes among issue areas. The state-centric view often fails to forecast outcomes correctly, and state-centric theories are not very good at explaining such outcomes even when the forecasts are correct.

"Transnational Relations Have Always Existed"

Raymond Aron was among the first to introduce the concept of "transnational society" into international relations theory. He used the term to describe commercial interchanges, migration of persons, common beliefs, ceremonials, and organizations that cross frontiers. However, he arrived at the skeptical judgment that transnational society as he defined it was relatively unimportant for understanding basic interactions in world politics. In his words: "Before 1914 economic exchanges throughout Europe enjoyed a freedom that the gold standard and monetary convertibility safeguarded even better than legislation. Labor parties were grouped into an International. The Greek tradition of the Olympic Games had been revived . . . religious, moral and even political beliefs were fundamentally analogous on either side of the frontiers. . . . This example, like the similar one of Hellenic society in the fifth century, illustrates the relative autonomy of the interstate order—in peace and in war—in relation to the context of transnational society."[4]

Aron is certainly correct when he points to the existence of transnational relations before 1914, as the essay by James A. Field, Jr., abundantly indicates. More generally, as Oran Young has observed, "over the bulk of recorded history man has organized himself for political purpose on bases other than those now subsumed under the concepts 'state' and 'nation-state.' "[5]

Our contention, however, is neither that transnational relations are new nor that they supersede interstate politics but that they affect interstate politics by altering the choices open to statesmen and the costs that must be borne for

[4] Raymond Aron, *Peace and War: A Theory of International Relations*, trans. Richard Howard and Annette Baker Fox (Garden City, N.Y: Doubleday & Co., 1966), p. 105.
[5] Oran R. Young, "The Actors in World Politics," in *The Analysis of International Politics*, ed. James N. Rosenau, B. Vincent Davis, and Maurice A. East (Glencoe, Ill: Free Press, forthcoming); see also Adda B. Bozeman, *Politics and Culture in International History* (Princeton, N.J: Princeton University Press, 1960).

adopting various courses of action. In short, transnational relations provide different sets of incentives, or payoffs, for states. These altered payoffs were not sufficient to ensure peace in 1914 despite the hopes of men like Norman Angell, who argued in 1910 that "the wealth, prosperity, and well-being of a nation depend in no way upon its political power."[6] Nevertheless, World War I by no means refutes the contention that transnational relations influence interstate politics; it merely warns us against the incautious assumption that transnational relations render war impossible between states linked by extensive transnational ties.

In any case, the analogy between 1914 and 1971 should not be taken too seriously when discussing transnational relations any more than it should be regarded as the key to understanding great-power politics. Transnational relations today take different forms than in 1914, and in our view the contemporary forms have greater political significance than the pre-1914 versions. On the one hand, mutual sensitivity of societies has increased; on the other hand, the growth of transnational social and economic organizations has created powerful and dynamic transnational actors capable of adapting to change and of consciously attempting to shape the world to their interests.

SENSITIVITY OF SOCIETIES. The importance of transnational relations depends less on the sheer quantity of such relations than on their political salience and the resulting sensitivity of societies to one another. There are two major reasons for this increased sensitivity. First, improved technology has removed many of the imperfections of communications that once helped separate societies. Second, as we indicate in the introduction and as Edward L. Morse suggests in his essay, a given volume of transnational activity may, paradoxically, have greater effects on interdependence when governments are ambitiously attempting to control their economies than in situations of relative laissez faire.[7] Thus, Gilpin's assertion that "the role of the nation-state in economic as well as in political life is increasing" in no way contradicts our assertion that transnational relations are becoming more important. On the contrary, it reinforces our point. In the liberal nineteenth-century world transnational society remained somewhat separate from interstate politics, but today the result of ambitious governmental policies is that transnational relations affect intergovernmental relations and have themselves become politicized. New subjects enter the realm of international relations. As the May 1971 international monetary crisis made clear, governments must often be concerned

---

[6] Norman Angell, *The Great Illusion: A Study of the Relation of Military Power in Nations to Their Economic and Social Advantage* (3rd rev. and enl. ed.; New York: G. P. Putnam's Sons, 1911), p. 34.

[7] Richard N. Cooper, *The Economics of Interdependence: Economic Policy in the Atlantic Community* (Atlantic Policy Series) (New York: McGraw-Hill Book Co. [for the Council on Foreign Relations], 1968); see also Andrew Shonfield, *Modern Capitalism: The Changing Balance of Public and Private Power* (Oxford Paperbacks on International Affairs) (London: Oxford University Press, 1969), chapter 2.

with the internal economic policies of other governments.[8] This is sometimes referred to as the "domesticization" of international politics. It might better be called the "internationalization" of domestic politics. An important result is that subunits of governments are provided greater opportunities for transnational contacts and coalitions.

By facilitating the flow of ideas modern communications have also increased intersocietal sensitivity. Certainly there have been indirect "contagions" of ideas in earlier periods such as the European revolutions of 1848 or Latin American university reforms in 1917. Field refers to St. Petersburg, Smyrna, Nagasaki, and Canton as "windows on the West" for the transmission of culture in an earlier time. Today, however, television has created a "window on the West" in the living rooms of the elites of the third world. Widely separated elites, whether functionally similar social groups, students, military officers, or racial minorities, become more rapidly aware of each other's activities.[9] Seymour Martin Lipset has noted that "student culture is a highly communicable one, the mood and mode of it translate readily from one center to another, one country to another."[10] Indeed, although many of the leaders of the student disturbances that shook Europe in the late 1960s were aware of each other's activities, they first came into direct contact when British television producers brought them together after the events.[11]

Not all the political effects of transnational communications are so dramatic. The incremental growth, spread, and change of knowledge, doctrines, and attitudes alter the context within which governments operate and change the payoffs available to them. While these ideas and attitudes are often transmitted by transnational organizations, they are also transmitted by individuals through personal travel and communication—subject to the qualifications mentioned in Donald P. Warwick's essay.

TRANSNATIONAL ORGANIZATIONS. Not all types of transnational organizations have increased in importance. Those with explicitly political goals seem to have declined in importance. The close links between Communist parties and the international brigades of the 1930s find only the palest of reflections in the Havana-based Tricontinental or the expeditions of radical American stu-

---

[8] For example, "when the Nixon Administration, with at least one eye on the 1972 election, switched signals and called for easing the money supply and lowering interest rates to stimulate business and employment, the outflow of Eurodollars from the United States was set in motion, and the stage was set for monetary trouble abroad." New York Times, May 10, 1971, p. 52.

[9] "Hating the Pigs," The Economist, August 15, 1970 (Vol. 236, No. 6625), pp. 17–18, gives an example of the similarity of phrasing of demands by racial minorities in the United Kingdom and the United States. For a discussion of transnational communications affecting patterns of military coups or insurrections see Samuel P. Huntington, ed., Changing Patterns of Military Politics (International Yearbook of Political Behavior Research, Vol. 3) (Glencoe, Ill: Free Press, 1962), pp. 44–47.

[10] Seymour Martin Lipset, "The Possible Political Effects of Student Activism," Social Science Information, April 1969 (Vol. 8, No. 2), p. 12.

[11] Anthony Sampson, The New Europeans: A Guide to the Workings, Institutions and Character of Contemporary Western Europe (London: Hodder and Stoughton, 1968), p. 419.

dents to cut sugar cane in Cuba. As J. Bowyer Bell points out, current revolutionary guerrilla groups have a transnational myth to sustain morale and legitimacy rather than a transnational organization to coordinate operations. Robert W. Cox shows that a similar trend away from political organization has occurred in labor movements. The international confederations that aggregated labor interests at a very general level and engaged primarily in transnational political struggles have been replaced in prominence by the international trade secretariats which aggregate more specific economic interests and organize to coordinate operations against multinational business enterprises. The greater reliance of the Roman Catholic church in recent years on moral and humanitarian influence, rather than on political alliances with governments, is consistent with this trend away from explicit political activity by transnational organizations.

In contrast to political organizations, however, transnational organizations whose principal goals are social and economic have increased in importance. These organizations, of course, may have very significant political consequences. By far the most important of these organizations is the multinational business enterprise. Multinational enterprises existed at the beginning of this century but on a smaller scale and with much less important effects.[12] Modern communications technology has greatly increased the feasibility of imposing a central strategy on widely scattered subsidiaries and consequently has increased the challenge that enterprises present to state sovereignty. Unlike those of the Hudson's Bay Company, the activities of today's multinational business enterprises often do not coincide with the decision domains of particular states. Their effects on world trade and production can be judged by the fact that the production of overseas subsidiaries of the ten leading capital-exporting states was nearly twice the volume of trade between those countries.[13] Raymond Vernon indicates that overseas subsidiaries may account for approximately 15 percent of world production. Finally, multinational business enterprises have had strong effects on other transnational actors. Trade unions, banks, and public relations firms have all been lured into increased transnational activity by following the lead of the multinational business enterprise.[14]

Arnold Wolfers pointed out over a decade ago that the ability of international nongovernmental organizations "to operate as international or transnational actors may be traced to the fact that men identify themselves and their interests with corporate bodies other than the nation-state."[15] Transna-

[12] See Mira Wilkins, *The Emergence of Multinational Enterprise: American Business Abroad from the Colonial Era to 1914* (Cambridge, Mass: Harvard University Press, 1970).

[13] Robert L. Heilbroner, "The Multinational Corporation and the Nation-State," *New York Review of Books*, February 11, 1971 (Vol. 16, No. 2), pp. 20–25.

[14] See the essays by Lawrence Krause and Robert W. Cox in this volume; see also Herbert Schiller, "The Multinational Corporation as International Communicator" (Paper delivered at the Sixty-sixth Annual Convention of the American Political Science Association, Los Angeles, September 1970).

[15] Arnold Wolfers, *Discord and Collaboration: Essays on International Politics* (Baltimore, Md: Johns Hopkins Press, 1962).

tional actors therefore flourish where dual loyalties are regarded as acceptable. In totalitarian societies, and in areas in which one version or another of integral nationalism has taken hold, dual loyalties are regarded as treasonous and transnational forces as potentially corrupting and dangerous. It is hard to imagine a good Soviet citizen avowing loyalty to General Motors Corporation or a contemporary Chilean nationalist identifying himself with Anaconda Company or Kennecott Copper Corporation.

In the modernized Western world and its ancillary areas the acceptability of multiple loyalties is taken for granted. Yet, this toleration seems to be extended more readily when the transnational actor is explicitly economic in purpose than when it is explicitly political. Thus, it seems less incompatible to be loyal to both IBM and France, to FIAT and the United States, or to the Roman Catholic church and Belgium than it does for a loyal citizen of the United Kingdom to pledge allegiance to transnational communism or for Americans to identify with Israel. In the West, therefore, nationalism probably hinders overt political organization across boundaries more than it hinders transnational economic activity. Dual loyalties may be more feasible when the foci of loyalty seem to operate in different areas with different goals.[16] When the competition is directly political, the individual is often forced to choose.

These are mere speculations about the reasons for the mixed trends in transnational organizations, reflecting the rise of economic actors in modernized areas of the world and the decline of transnational political organizations. Whatever the reasons for the trends, however, the increased scale of social and economic organizations and their increased effects on the political sensitivity of societies to each other constitute an important new aspect of world politics.

"Transnational Relations Do Not Affect High Politics"

Distinctions between high and low politics are of diminishing value in current world politics. Stanley Hoffmann has described this situation with a useful metaphor: "The competition between states takes place on several chessboards in addition to the traditional military and diplomatic ones: for instance, the chessboards of world trade, of world finance, of aid and technical assistance, of space research and exploration, of military technology, and the chessboard of what has been called 'informal penetration.' These chessboards do not entail the resort to force."[17] Hoffmann observes that each "chessboard"

---

[16] According to Harold Guetzkow "multiple loyalties are quite admissible *provided* the different objects are furnishing compatible solutions to different needs." *Multiple Loyalties: Theoretical Approach to a Problem in International Organization* (Publication No. 4) (Princeton, N.J.: Center for Research on World Political Institutions, Woodrow Wilson School of Public and International Affairs, Princeton University, 1955), p. 39.

[17] Stanley Hoffmann, "International Organization and the International System," *International Organization*, Summer 1970 (Vol. 24, No. 3), p. 401.

has rules of its own but is linked as well to others by "complicated and subtle relations." High and low politics become difficult to distinguish. Thus, during the international monetary crisis of May 1971 it became clear that an implicit bargain had been struck between American and West German statesmen and central bankers by which the willingness of West German authorities to hold United States dollars was a condition for a large United States army in Europe.

This volume has shown that on a number of Hoffmann's "chessboards," or issue areas, transnational relations are extremely important. As sensitivity to other societies increases, new subjects are brought into the realm of world politics. Issue areas that were formerly quite distinct from political calculation have become politically relevant, particularly insofar as governments have attempted to extend their control over domestic economic activity without sacrificing the benefits of transnational intercourse. Since these issue areas are often of great significance to governments, they cannot be merely dismissed as "low politics," allegedly subordinate to a "high politics" of status, security, or war. Butter comes before guns in New Zealand's diplomacy.

In these issue areas, furthermore, force may be neither appropriate nor effective. Insofar as force is devalued for a particular area of interaction, transnational interactions and the activities of transnational relations are likely to be important—even for France, the United Kingdom, and the United States.

We find ourselves in a world that reminds us more of the extensive and curious chessboard in Lewis Carroll's *Through the Looking Glass* than of more conventional versions of that ancient game. The players are not always what they seem, and the terrain of the chessboards may suddenly change from garden to shop to castle. Thus, in contemporary world politics not all players on important chessboards are states, and the varying terrains of the chessboards constrain state behavior. Some are more suited to the use of force, others almost totally unsuited to it. Different chessboards favor different states. For example, relations between Norway and the United States are quite different on shipping questions than on questions involving strategic arms. When international oil prices are negotiated, Iran is more important than it is on world trade issues in general. High and low politics have become tightly intertwined.

II. The World Politics Paradigm

Although we use the word "paradigm" somewhat loosely, we wish to make it clear that we seek to challenge basic assumptions that underlie the analysis of international relations, not merely to compile a list of transnational interactions and organizations. Nor are our concerns merely academic. "Practical men, who believe themselves to be quite exempt from any intellectual influences," are usually, as John Maynard Keynes once pointed out, unconscious captives of paradigms created by "some academic scribbler of a few years back."[18]

In the introduction we define world politics as political interactions between any "significant actors" whose characteristics include autonomy, the control of substantial resources relevant to a given issue area, and participation in political relationships across state lines. Since we define politics in terms of the conscious employment of resources, "both material and symbolic, including the threat or exercise of punishment, to induce other actors to behave differently than they would otherwise behave," it is clear that we are positing a conception of world politics in which the central phenomenon is bargaining between a variety of autonomous or semiautonomous actors.

The difference between our world politics paradigm and the state-centric paradigm can be clarified most easily by focusing on the nature of the actors. The world politics paradigm attempts to transcend the "level-of-analysis problem" both by broadening the conception of actors to include transnational actors and by conceptually breaking down the "hard shell" of the nation-state.[19]

This can be illustrated by a diagram that compares the range of actors included within our world politics paradigm with that included in the state-centric model. Figure 1 displays the characteristics of actors in world politics

	Position		
	Governmental	Intergovernmental	Nongovernmental
Maximal central control	**A** States as units	**C** International organizations as units	**E** Transnational organizations as units
Minimal central control	**B** Governmental subunits	**D** Subunits of international organizations	**F** Subunits of transnational organizations; also certain individuals

A + C = Actors in the state-centric paradigm
B + D = Actors in transgovernmental interactions
E + F = Actors in transnational interactions

FIGURE 1. ACTORS IN WORLD POLITICS

[18] John Maynard Keynes, *The General Theory of Employment Interest and Money* (London: Macmillan & Co., 1957), p. 383.
[19] See J. David Singer, "The Level-of-Analysis Problem in International Relations," *World Politics*, October 1961 (Vol. 14, No. 1), pp. 77–92.

on two dimensions: 1) the degree to which they are governmental or non-governmental in position and 2) the extent to which they consist of coherent and centrally controlled organizations rather than subunits of governments or of transnational organizations.

The first dimension distinguishes actors according to formal position—governmental, intergovernmental, or nongovernmental. It therefore corresponds to the "inverted U" diagram in figures 1 and 2 of the introduction which illustrates our concept of transnational interactions. As a first approximation we found this easily verifiable distinction a useful way to identify certain aspects of world politics that are missed by the state-centric view.

As we also indicate in the introduction, however, there is another dimension of world politics that the classic state-centric paradigm with its assumption of states as unitary actors fails to take into account. This second dimension, centralization of control, involves the realization that subunits of governments may also have distinct foreign policies which are not all filtered through the top leadership and which do not fit into a unitary actor model. Thus, scholars have recently developed a "bureaucratic politics approach" to foreign policy analysis, explaining decisions of governments in these terms.[20]

Bureaucratic politics is not limited to governments but can be applied to nongovernmental actors as well. Multinational business enterprises are frequently unable to act as unitary actors, and we have seen that the Roman Catholic church, the Ford Foundation, guerrilla movements, and organizations of scientists are hardly monolithic.[21] Furthermore, just as American military officers may negotiate with their Spanish counterparts and Congressman Wilbur Mills with Japanese textile companies, so may local divisions of a multinational business enterprise or of the Roman Catholic church strike bargains and form coalitions with national governments or subunits thereof.[22]

The combination of these two dimensions in figure 1 portrays a complex model of world politics in which the state-centric paradigm focuses on only two of the six cells. Another way of illustrating this point is shown by figure 2. The state-centric paradigm covers only four of the 36 possible types of politically important interactions across state boundaries that are identified by the

---

[20] See, especially, Graham T. Allison, *Essence of Decision: Explaining the Cuban Missile Crisis* (Boston: Little, Brown and Co., 1971); or, by the same author, "Conceptual Models and the Cuban Missile Crisis," *American Political Science Review*, September 1969 (Vol. 63, No. 3), pp. 689–718; and also Richard E. Neustadt, *Alliance Politics* (New York: Columbia University Press, 1970).

[21] In his essay, "The Multinational Corporation: Measuring the Consequences," Robert B. Stobaugh argues against images of the multinational business enterprise "as one economic entity controlled by one 'economic man' in headquarters rather than of what the enterprise really is: an organization of numerous staff groups and subsidiaries, some of which are large and powerful in their own rights and among which considerable negotiation takes place." *Columbia Journal of World Business*, January–February 1971 (Vol. 6, No. 1), p. 62.

[22] For details about the Spanish case see Robert O. Keohane, "The Big Influence of Small Allies," *Foreign Policy*, Spring 1971 (Vol. 1, No. 2), pp. 161–182; on the politics of textile quota legislation see the *New York Times*, March 16, 1971, p. 51.

world politics paradigm. This gives us an idea of the richness of possible transnational coalitions that determine outcomes in world politics and that are now largely relegated to the subsidiary and largely undifferentiated category of "environment."

Actor	A States as units	B Governmental subunits	C International organizations as units	D Subunits of international organizations	E Transnational organizations as units	F Subunits of transnational organizations; also certain individuals
A States as units	IS	TG	IS	TG	TN	TN
B Governmental subunits	TG	TG	TG	TG	TN	TN
C International organizations as units	IS	TG	IS	TG	TN	TN
D Subunits of international organizations	TG	TG	TG	TG	TN	TN
E Transnational organizations as units	TN	TN	TN	TN	TN	TN
F Subunits of transnational organizations; also certain individuals	TN	TN	TN	TN	TN	TN

IS = Interstate interactions
TG = Transgovernmental interactions
TN = Transnational interactions
TG + TN = Transnational relations
TG + TN + IS = World politics interactions

FIGURE 2. BILATERAL INTERACTIONS IN WORLD POLITICS

Adding the second dimension, centralization of control, allows us to specify a paradigm of world politics that brings together traditional international politics, the bureaucratic politics approach to foreign policy analysis, and transnational actors as defined in the introduction. Yet, it also poses certain conceptual problems. As defined in the introduction, transnational interactions could be easily identified by the involvement of nongovernmental actors. Thus, definition on the basis of formal position—governmental or non-governmental—led to a clear delineation between transnational and inter-state interactions. This narrowed the issues and omitted problems of central control, but it did achieve an initially useful simplification and clarification. Unlike that of formal position, however, the concept of centralization of control is a continuum—there can be more or less central control, and lines that are drawn will necessarily be somewhat arbitrary. How, then, do we distinguish various types of behavior along this dimension?

Our first step is to introduce a new type of interaction in addition to "transnational interactions" and "interstate interactions" as defined in the introduction. Transnational interactions necessarily involve nongovernmental actors, whereas interstate interactions take place exclusively between states acting as units. Transgovernmental interactions, however, are defined as interactions between governmental subunits across state boundaries. The broad term transnational relations includes both trans*national* and trans*governmental* interactions—all of world politics that is not taken into account by the state-centric paradigm.

As we have defined world politics, any unit of action that attempts to exercise influence across state boundaries and possesses significant resources in a given issue area is an actor in world politics. Thus, this concept of transnational relations calls attention to the activities of subunits of governments or intergovernmental organizations as well as to the behavior of individuals and nongovernmental organizations. Yet, we still need to specify when an actor is behaving "as a unit" and when its subunits possess significant autonomy.

On an abstract level we distinguish transgovernmental from interstate interactions by the extent to which actors are behaving in conformity to roles specified or reasonably implied by the formal foreign policy structure of the state. The problem of discovering deviations from formally prescribed roles is difficult and sometimes impossible because of the ambiguous specification of role at high levels of authority. Nonetheless, such deviation was found among European agricultural ministers in the example cited in the introduction. At lower levels of authority the transgovernmental behavior of those in formal governmental positions is much easier to identify, for example, the coalition of United States and Canadian weather bureaus to overcome a Department of State decision on control of international meteorological research.[23] The difficulties of delineation in this murky area of control are admittedly great, but it would hardly be sensible to promulgate a supposedly "new" paradigm for world politics without including reference to transgovernmental politics.

[23] The example is from the essay by Edward Miles in this volume. Our inclusion of this second dimension is due in large part to his arguments.

To explain this more complex world the study of world politics must proceed by the analysis of particular issue areas and the relations between them. It must take into account the differences in the way the game of world politics is played on Hoffmann's different chessboards or, to escape from bipolar imagery, poker tables. Who are the players? What are their resources? What are the rules? How do the players, resources, and rules differ from game to game? Most important, how are the different games related to each other? Are winnings and resources transferable, and, if they are, at what discount?

A Plan for Research

We are suggesting an approach to the study of world politics through analysis of different types of issue areas (which we define loosely, following Cox, as unorganized or partially organized systems of interaction) and of the relationships between them. The elaboration of this paradigm suggests three foci for research: 1) analysis of issue areas, 2) research on transnational and transgovernmental actors, and 3) studies designed to illuminate relationships between issue areas.

First, we would want to know the types of interaction and interdependence that characterize each issue area. We would further want to know what role transnational actors play within the issue area and how they interact with each other and with components of governments. We would want to know to what extent governments (or some governments) act as centralized units or are characterized by transgovernmental coalitions. We would want to know how these differences have varied over time and how they vary in relation to such factors as salience to the public, technological change, and the number and symmetry of the actors. The essays in part III of this volume suggest a few preliminary answers.

The essays in part II exemplify the second research focus. By studying the internal organization of transnational actors we can shed light on the roles they play. For example, not all trade unions are lured into transnational activity nor are the effects of all multinational business enterprises similar. Both are affected by the nature of their internal structure. Cox points out that unions organized at the plant level are more likely to fight the corporation transnationally and to develop an ideology of internationalism. Unions more strongly organized at the national level are more likely to ally with the government and evidence strong feelings of nationalism. Louis T. Wells, Jr., shows that multinational manufacturing enterprises are more likely to weaken a government's control of economic matters if the firm is organized on a product basis. It would be interesting to know, for example, how the adverse effects alleged by Peter B. Evans vary according to differences in the internal organization of the transnational actor.

Similarly, further research should be focused on the process of formulation of "private foreign policies." The Roman Catholic church has very explicit procedures. The Ford Foundation, as described by Peter D. Bell, seems deliberately to shun such questions. Yet, they are unavoidable. At what point, for example, does a transnational organization withdraw from a country? Does a foundation behave more like a church or more like a bank? How are private foreign policy decisions made?[24]

The third major research focus would explore the linkages between issue areas. Here the essay by Gilpin is very suggestive. Gilpin argues for the primacy of the security issue area and suggests that in the postwar period there were explicit bargains, between the United States and the Federal Republic of Germany (West Germany) and between the United States and Japan, by which security resources were exchanged for trade and financial benefits. He argues further that changing conditions may undo these bargains and adversely affect transnational activity. One problem with Gilpin's argument, however, is that any situation of reciprocal advantage can, often incorrectly, be interpreted as a result of bargaining; one might then infer that if one set of benefits is altered, the other will likewise change. But in the absence of clear historical evidence about the perceptions and actions of decisionmakers the inference that a conscious bargain was made and maintained over a period of time is not necessarily valid. There is a danger here of interpreting the past too much in terms of the present: United States decisionmakers in the 1950s were much less concerned about America's international financial position than they are in 1971. Thus, even if bargains were struck between the United States and West Germany and the United States and Japan, it is not clear that these bargains involved an interplay of issue areas. They can also be interpreted solely in terms of mutual security: the exchange of bases or assured access to a forward position in return for protection. Since then economic elements have become more important. Finally, even if Japan in particular is now receiving economic advantages that cannot continue because political conditions have changed, it does not necessarily follow that the contradiction will be resolved in the direction of restrictions on transnational interactions. It might also be resolved within the economic issue area by increasingly opening the Japanese economy to American business—that is, by an extension of transnational relations. Yet, regardless of the validity of Gilpin's conclusions, his approach raises crucial questions that are ignored when analysts fragment

[24] Transnational actors, like governments, may be unable to make decisions due to bureaucratic politics. Charles P. Kindleberger cites a major oil company that was unable to reconcile the opposing views of its subunits in regard to oil imports into the United States and thus had no position in this seemingly vital issue. See his essay, "European Integration and the International Corporation," in *World Business: Promise and Problems*, ed. Courtney C. Brown (Studies of the Modern Corporation) (New York: Macmillan Co., 1970), p. 105; see also, by Kindleberger, *Power and Money: The Economics of International Politics and the Politics of International Economics* (New York: Basic Books, Publishers, 1970), p. 13.

reality into "strategic" and "economic" sectors and deal only with one or the other.

Thus, our third research focus, and Gilpin's essay, point to crucial questions of world politics. What bargains are struck across issue areas? How fungible are resources in a given issue area—how easily transferable are they to another poker table? Does dominance in the security area provide a state with leverage in another area in which it may be weak? To what extent are all issue areas politicized, and to what extent can some of them be insulated from political competition? Answers to such questions would shed light on the elusive concept of "power" in world politics. If the poker games are not closely interconnected and resources are only fungible at a discount, how useful is a concept such as power, resting as it does on the analogy with money in an economic system?

In summary, we believe that the essays in this volume support our contention that the state-centric paradigm provides an inadequate basis for the study of changing world politics. Transnational actors sometimes prevail over governments. These "losses" by governments can often be attributed to the rising costs of unilateral governmental action in the face of transnational relations. For a state-centric theory this is represented as "environment." But it is theoretically inadequate to use the exogenous variables of the environment to account for outcomes in the interaction of various actors in world politics. State-centric theories are not very good at explaining such outcomes because they do not describe the complex patterns of coalitions between different types of actors described in the essays. We hope that our "world politics paradigm" will help to redirect attention toward the substance of international politics, in which the major theoretical as well as practical questions can be found, and away from the relatively unenlightening application of subtle reasoning or sophisticated methodology to problems that have been narrowly defined by a limited theoretical outlook or the wrong units of analysis. Perhaps for a while we have had enough computer-assisted voting analyses of the United Nations General Assembly except for the routine descriptive purpose of keeping up with recent trends. We may even have a sufficiency of macrohistorical studies of "bipolarity" and "multipolarity" that focus entirely on the strategic level of interaction. The "world politics paradigm" does not provide scholars with an instant revelation, but it does provide them with at least one path toward relevance.

III. ASYMMETRY AND THE ALLOCATION OF VALUES

Broadening the scope of international politics beyond the state-centric view provides a clearer understanding of and base for further thought about one of the most important structural problems of current world politics—the extremely asymmetric relations between states. We have been struck by the lack of serious theorizing about this aspect of international relations. This is attributable at least in part to the prevalence of the state-centric view. The myth of state sovereignty and the emphasis on security issues make the world seem less imbalanced than it is. The popularity currently enjoyed by a variety of theories of imperialism is one result of this vacuum. In the introduction we explain our reasons for believing that the word "imperialism" obscures more than it enlightens. Nonetheless, the problem of asymmetric relations that underlies theories of imperialism is both real and important.

Transnational activity is very unequally distributed. Sensitivity to its impact varies greatly. Multinational business enterprises, foundations, organizations of scientists, international trade union secretariats—all have their origins in advanced Western countries. Kjell Skjelsbaek's data on the distribution of international nongovernmental organizations shows that in 1966, 53.5 percent of all national representations came from Eastern Europe and .5 percent from Communist Asia. Moreover, 88.7 percent of the headquarters of all international organizations were located in the developed Northwest. Data on transnational activity by individuals has shown a similar pattern of distribution— greater participation by individuals from developed Western states.[25]

Several factors account for this uneven distribution. Among the most important seem to be: 1) modernization, 2) decreased costs of transportation and communication, and 3) pluralistic ideology. Skjelsbaek argues that the specialization that accompanies modernity creates an increasing number of discrete interests with a capacity to organize first nationally and later transnationally. The increased economic specialization of advanced countries leads them to become each other's best trading partners. The simple pattern of industrial countries trading manufactures for raw materials from poor countries has been greatly modified. Trade between developed market economy countries accounts for approximately one-half of world trade, while the share of less developed countries (and of raw materials) has been declining.[26]

Several essays in this volume discuss the effects of decreased transportation and communications costs. Advances in communications technology have played a major role in facilitating the development of a central strategy for multinational business enterprises. Lawrence Krause argues that rapid communications have greatly increased the sensitivity of money markets to each other, a point reinforced by the influx of almost $2 billion to West Germany in a few days during May 1971. While these developments in communications technology also affect less developed countries, they generally touch only a small elite and penetrate these societies less deeply.

[25] Robert Cooley Angell, *Peace on the March: Transnational Participation* (New Perspectives in Political Science, No. 19) (New York: Van Nostrand Reinhold Co., 1969).
[26] Michael Zammat Cutajar and Alison Franks, *The Less Developed Countries in World Trade: A Reference Handbook* (London: Overseas Development Institute, 1967); see also Shonfield.

New Perspectives

Not only does the economic and social structure of the developed market economy countries make them the locus of transnational activity, their prevailing pluralistic ideology provides much more legitimacy for such activities than is available in Communist countries or in many less developed states. Moreover, as Cox illustrates, transnational actors tend to develop ideologies of transnationalism to add to their legitimacy, thus reinforcing their positions in areas of strength. It is now stylish for corporations to be "multinational."

If transnationalism has become the ideology of some of the rich, nationalism remains the ideology of many of the poor. In many of the new states transnational processes are (or seem to be) remnants of colonial rule. Politics often revolves around nationalists' efforts to diminish transnational ties. Transnational actors originating in rich countries are vulnerable to charges of illegitimacy. In many less developed countries insecure political elites turn to nationalist ideologies in an effort to integrate or distract populations which are undergoing social mobilization at rates too fast for their institutions to handle. In these circumstances it is not surprising to find resentment of transnational actors that seem to threaten an already shaky sense of sovereign control. The ability to tolerate a public "defeat" by a transnational actor is smaller in Bolivia than in Belgium.

We are not arguing that transnational actors always weaken governmental control in less developed countries. On the contrary, the superior performance of multinational business enterprises in paying taxes and increasing exports or the activities of Planned Parenthood or the Ford Foundation in the field of birth control may actually increase governmental capacities. Nor are we arguing that all elites in less developed countries resist transnational relations. Indeed, governmental elites are often happy to have their countries gain the resources of capital, technology, and markets that multinational business enterprises can provide. Local trade union elites are often happy to gain the organizational resources provided by international unions. Local university elites are frequently pleased to gain the material and moral support of the Ford Foundation which diminishes their vulnerability to control by their governments. The local Catholic clergy is often willing to have the support of additional resources from Rome.

The trouble lies in the gap between elites and masses in less developed countries. The increased mutual sensitivity of societies that is created by transnational relations touches only a tiny proportion of the population. As elites are absorbed into a transnational network, the gap between elites and masses is increased and intolerable political tensions may be created. Transnational trade union activity may create a grossly overrewarded "labor aristocracy" at the expense of the welfare of peasants. One effect of multinational business enterprises or American foundations may be the reinforcement of a local salary structure geared to the world economy rather than to local social conditions. This in turn would mean a grossly inequitable class structure. Experimentation with altered incentives is curtailed by the threat of brain drain since mobile individuals can escape the country. The creation of a single global economy is rational, perhaps, to achieve optimal allocation of global resources, but it is also a severe limitation on national autonomy. The transnationally mobile are rewarded at the expense of the nationally immobile.

As Cox observes in his essay, "Historically, the geographically based power of the state has been the only power capable of counterbalancing unequal forces in the interest of welfare. . . . A Canadian-type solution [of openness to transnational forces] may be feasible where most of the population participates in the transnational society. It is, however, likely to raise considerable tensions in countries in which there is a substantial population marginal to or outside the transnational society and in which there are great disparities in incomes and life-styles which may be further exaggerated by a continuation of transnational relations."[27]

IV. United States Foreign Policy

The issues raised by transnational relations are relevant to all countries, or at least to all modernized Western countries. Yet, as we indicate in the introduction, transnational phenomena raise specific and unique problems for the United States. From a transnational perspective the United States is by far the preponderant society in the world.

United States preponderance in transnational activities has its origins in American patterns of social organization and the American "style" as well as in the size and modernity of its economy. As Field points out, Americans in the nineteenth century were active transnationalists, even when the United States was by no means predominant in the world. Now, the size of the United States means that its largest social units, including some corporations, foundations, and universities, often have annual budgets greater than those of the governments of the countries in which they operate. Furthermore, as a result of this modernity American economic techniques are often more advanced than those of countries on which United States–based transnational actors descend. Thus, by virtue not only of size but also of technological leadership, the United States is somewhat less vulnerable to the effects of transnational relations than are other societies.[28]

This situation raises important issues for United States foreign policy. First, it means that the term "neo-isolationism" is highly misleading when we think

[27] Cox, in this volume, p. 584.

[28] See Kenneth N. Waltz, "The Myth of National Interdependence," *The International Corporation: A Symposium,* ed. Charles P. Kindleberger (Cambridge, Mass.: M.I.T. Press, 1970), pp. 205–223; and Raymond P. Vernon, "International Investment and International Trade in the Product Cycle," *Quarterly Journal of Economics,* May 1966 (Vol. 80, No. 2), pp. 190–207.

in transnational rather than state-centric terms. Although United States government foreign policy may be turning inward, the same is not necessarily true of the private foreign policies of its transnational actors. Thus, an analogy to the 1930s is inappropriate. Second, it means that the preponderant size of the United States is one of the major problems of contemporary world politics. From a state-centric perspective the United States seems highly constrained by the structure of world politics, although analysts have often overstressed the constraints and underemphasized United States freedom of action.[29] Yet, from the perspective of transnational relations the United States often seems to have too much freedom of action—whether in exporting inflation to Europe or unwittingly undertaking the "Coca-Colonization" of the world. It would be difficult to argue that the United States is too constrained in transnational relations.

United States policy toward the third world looks particularly different when viewed in transnational perspective than it does when conceived in terms of the state-centric model. Future problems in United States relations with less developed countries will increasingly revolve around the activities of United States–based transnational actors rather than around the cold-war and anticolonial issues of the past. In many cases it may be extremely difficult to avoid the collision course that Vernon foresees. The interests of United States–based transnational actors are often incompatible with the interests of governments that desire to maintain or extend national political control. Only if the American government is able to disengage itself somewhat from the interests of United States–based business enterprises, and only if American statesmen are willing to make short-term sacrifices of interest, will it be possible for the United States to play a creative role in these conflicts.

If Evans were correct about the limitations placed on national autonomy and economic development by the activities of multinational corporations, a complete disengagement of the United States from the third world might be beneficial. In our view, however, such a complete disengagement would probably not produce autonomous national development in most poor countries but would involve high costs both for these countries and to some extent for the United States. We believe, therefore, that United States foreign policy should attempt to assist poor countries to control, choose between, and profit from transnational actors. In some situations complete disengagement may be necessary; in others, a more active policy may have greater benefits for both parties. Insofar as possible, as we indicate in section VI of this essay, cooperation in helping less developed countries control transnational incursions should be sought from other developed states through intergovernmental organizations.

[29] For a dissenting view see Kenneth N. Waltz, "International Structure, National Force, and the Balance of World Power," *Journal of International Affairs*, 1967 (Vol. 21, No. 2), pp. 215–231.

Yet, if the United States has been predominant in transnational relations, it does not dominate all the issues in which it is interested, nor can it hope to remain as immune from the effects of transnational changes in the future as it has in the years since World War II. Vernon points out that cultural patterns and antitrust legislation produce a more arm's-length relationship between government and business in the United States than is true of other developed countries, and American business leaders have recently begun to complain about this aspect of free enterprise.[30] Vernon also argues that American labor has been one of the few clear losers in welfare terms (at least in the short run) as a result of the shift of production abroad. Edward Miles shows that the United States is less predominant in the ocean issue area than in outer space. Thornton notes that the United States does not always win in the IATA. Krause points out that although the United States is less vulnerable than other countries to loss of control in the monetary field, it is still vulnerable to some extent, and it no longer has the power unilaterally to make policy in this field as it once did.

If we look toward the future, it is apparent that American dominance will be further diminished. This is not likely to be welcomed by the United States government for, as Vallier argues, a country which perceives benefits from its current position in transnational networks will be likely to attempt to preserve the system—a new and subtle form, some might argue, of imperialism. Yet, European countries and Japan are generating more transnational actors of their own, often with more direct governmental support than is provided in the United States.[31] Some people argue that the United States will have to cope with these challenges—by increasing governmental support for United States-based multinational business, as some industrialists desire, by erecting higher tariff barriers, or by other measures. Since neither statism nor protectionism is likely to be attractive to most American leaders, one can expect attempts to find other solutions, perhaps by negotiating changes in the policies of "Japan, Incorporated" or Common Market countries. In any event the outcome will be only partially determined by American policies, and the efforts of other governments will be equally important in shaping the future.

The growth of transnational relations also raises a number of important questions about the management of United States foreign policy. World politics has become more complex. One response to this has been an increase in the machinery of formal intergovernmental diplomacy. In 1914 the United

---

[30] For example, William H. Moore, chairman of the board of Bankers Trust Company, was recently quoted to have said that "the government and the private sector, for the good of the United States, are going to have to join hands in many projects." *New York Times,* July 13, 1971, pp. 43, 45. When business magazines discuss Japan's export activities, the same theme—the need for more active cooperation between business and government in the United States—is often stressed.

[31] Stephen Hymer and Robert Rowthorn, "Multinational Corporations and International Oligopoly: The Non-American Challenge," in Kindleberger; see also Louis Kraar, "How the Japanese Mount That Export Blitz," *Fortune,* September 1970 (Vol. 82, No. 3), pp. 126–131, 170. 172.

States was represented in only ten foreign capitals. In 1970 it was represented by 117 embassies, nine missions to international organizations, 67 consulates-general, 56 consulates, four special offices, and nine consular agencies. At the same time, however, the increased sensitivity of societies and the internationalization of domestic politics have led to a situation in which every Cabinet department and fifteen of 31 principal agencies outside the Cabinet have responsibilities requiring actions beyond national borders. In some embassies Department of State personnel account for as little as 20 percent of the total. In London in the early 1960s, 44 distinct federal bureaucracies were represented in the United States embassy, although in Moscow (where transnational relations were very limited) the embassy reflected more traditional forms of diplomacy.[32]

Increased contact between subunits of different governments both through bilateral diplomacy and representation in multilateral organizations enhances the likelihood of transgovernmental coalitions and makes central control of foreign policy more difficult. The situation is even further complicated by private foreign policies that interact with public ones. On issues involving ocean resources, for example, it is easy to imagine a coalition between international oil companies, some elements in the Pentagon, certain bureaucratic units of the Department of the Interior, and some segments of other governments facing an opposing coalition between international scientific organizations, the Department of State, other elements of the Department of the Interior and the Department of Defense, and certain foreign governmental units. Such situations raise serious questions not just about the democratic control of foreign policy but about *any* control of foreign policy.

V. Loss of Control

The increased complexity described in our world politics paradigm helps us understand the seeming paradox that statesmen in a country as preponderant in world politics as the United States often complain about a "loss of control" over their international political environment. People in government often claim that they spend most of their time just trying to find out what is happening, and some have been heard to question whether a coherent foreign policy is possible in a period of rapid, disorienting change. As we argue in the introduction, however, to speak of a "loss of control" is somewhat misleading. States have never been in full control of their external relations,

---

[32] Henry M. Wriston, *Diplomacy in a Democracy* (New York: Harper & Brothers, 1956), p. 26; Ellis Briggs, "American Diplomacy—The Pelican in the Wilderness," *Foreign Service Journal*, March 1971 (Vol. 48, No. 3), pp. 38–40; see also John Franklin Campbell, *The Foreign Affairs Fudge Factory* (New York: Basic Books, Publishers, 1971). For these citations and statistics we are indebted to a seminar paper prepared at Harvard University for Joseph Nye by G. Robert Dickerman of the United States Information Agency (USIA).

quite apart from the impact of transnational relations. In 1914, for example, the structure of the interstate balance of power severely constrained statesmen. Today the complexity of bureaucracy in modern welfare states and the weakness of institutions in many less developed countries also contribute to the statesman's sense of loss of control. Finally, the impact of transnational relations creates a "control gap" between the aspirations for control over an expanded range of matters and the capability to achieve it. The problem is not a loss of legal sovereignty but a loss of political and economic autonomy. Most states retain control over their policy instruments and are able to pursue their objectives. They are just less able to achieve them.[33]

It seems clear from these essays that this loss of control is not uniform for all types of state objectives. Governments sometimes act as loosely related coalitions of bureaucracies, but they also have central executive and legislative organs which try to integrate these coalitions into a coherent whole. When these central political organs are successful, the unitary model of state behavior becomes a fair approximation of reality, and we would expect to find a lesser role for transgovernmental interactions or for transnational relations in general. It seems that central governmental control tends to be stronger in matters of security than in issues of economic welfare; the "myth" of national security remains an important resource of executive control, and chief executives are likely to spend a large proportion of their time on security issues. But, as Graham T. Allison has shown, even in this area bureaucracies compete to interpret the myth.[34] It is in the nature of bureaucracies to resist policy integration that sacrifices the interest of their special domains for the sake of some allegedly more general interest. Thus, a lack of definition of what constitutes "security" may lead to bureaucratic fragmentation even in this area.

As Evans points out, some governments may be as concerned about loss of control over cultural autonomy and national identity as they are about difficulties in assuring their security against armed attack. Some countries, such as Burma, have been able to isolate themselves from transnational networks, but at considerable economic cost; other countries have attempted more selectively to limit the impact or freedom of action of transnational organizations and transnational communication. For less developed states these policies are politically attractive but difficult to carry out effectively. Controlling transnational communication may become more difficult when direct satellite-to-home broadcasting becomes feasible, and, as multinational copper and oil firms develop greater resources in politically stable areas, the rewards of nationalization may decline.[35]

[33] We are indebted for this point to Richard Cooper, "Economic Interdependence in the 1970's," *World Politics,* forthcoming.

[34] Allison, *Essence of Decision;* or Allison, *American Political Science Review,* Vol. 63, No. 3.

[35] For an interesting discussion of the perils as well as benefits of nationalization see Theodore H. Moran, "The Multinational Corporation versus the Economic Nationalist: Independence and Domination in Raw Materials," *Foreign Policy,* December 1971, forthcoming.

The sense of loss of control is probably most acute, at least among developed countries, in regard to welfare objectives. In part this reflects the expansion of the tasks of government in response to popular pressure. As governments seek to extend control over their own societies, they become increasingly dependent on transnational forces impinging on them from outside their boundaries. Aspirations for increased domestic control broaden the range of relevant issues at the transnational level, thus complicating the problem of controlling the external environment. Complexity and frustration in foreign affairs are among the consequences of the modern capitalist welfare state.

While the range of relevant issues at the transnational level has been greatly broadened by the introduction of the welfare state, technology has increased the mobility of factors and the sensitivity of markets, and societies, to one another. Advances in transportation and communications technology are destroying the fragmentation of markets that is a necessary condition for autonomous national policies. Morse, Krause, Evans, Vernon, and others provide numerous examples of loss of control in the welfare area, largely as a result of technological and organizational change.

Faced with this situation, governments that are unwilling to take a passive position have three major policy options: 1) They can attempt to restore fragmentation of markets through unilateral defensive policies, although this may invite retaliation and eventually prove harmful to the welfare of their citizens; 2) they can follow aggressive policies of extraterritorial extension of national laws to cover mobile factors, but this may also breed resentment and costly retaliation; 3) they can adopt cooperative policies involving joint coordination of policy through international institutions.[36]

For most states cooperative policies have obvious advantages: Conflict can be reduced by joint action and policies coordinated for optimal results. Yet, as Kaiser points out in his essay, this may lead to another kind of loss of control in which legislatures and other democratically responsible bodies continue to lose influence to bureaucrats and technocrats. Once again the close linkage between domestic and international politics becomes clear, and the dangers as well as the opportunities of such interconnections become more readily apparent.

Cooperative policies of response to transnational relations may strengthen ties of interdependence or help create new international organizations, but they do not necessarily do either. States may decide, for example, to amend the rules of an existing institution like the International Monetary Fund (IMF) to create greater exchange rate flexibility, hoping to weaken the mutual sensitivity through the balance-of-payments mechanism and to restore a certain degree of "fragmentation." The net effect may be a reduction of friction

---

[36] Cooper, *World Politics*, forthcoming. In addition, Cooper suggests an exploitative or parasitic policy option, for example, tax havens and flags of convenience, open to a few small countries.

by restricting interdependence. This would be a joint defensive policy rather than a unilateral one. More frequently, however, cooperative action is likely to create new international institutions to cope with increasing interdependence. This brings us to our final concern—the new tasks that transnational relations create for international organizations.

VI. TRANSNATIONAL RELATIONS AND INTERNATIONAL ORGANIZATIONS

Increases in the importance of transnational relations usually reflect the twin dynamic forces of advancing technology and organizational sophistication. Large organizations such as multinational business enterprises profit from new technology and help generate even greater technological advances; their successes stimulate competitors and other threatened organizations into transnational action as a means of protecting their interests. Yet, transnational relations and the advances that promote them often impose significant external costs on interest groups or governments that cannot be controlled without joint international action. By and large, however, governments and secretariats of intergovernmental organizations have been slow to respond to this challenge.

Recent developments in ocean technology and the law of the sea illustrate this point. As Miles observes, in less than a decade the supposed natural limits to national jurisdiction assumed by the 1958 United Nations Conference on the Law of the Sea were rapidly pushed outward by corporations engaged in undersea exploration. The United Nations General Assembly has been able to agree that the seabed should be the common heritage of mankind but unable to agree on where that heritage begins. The exploitation and development of modern technology by transnational organizations have therefore created difficult political problems that may exceed the capacities of intergovernmental organizations to find universally acceptable solutions.

Transnational organizations are also partially responsible for problems of pollution and wastage of natural resources which will be the subject of the United Nations Conference on the Human Environment in 1972. More dramatically, transnational guerrilla groups have accentuated problems of air safety by spectacular hijackings of airplanes. In quieter ways, networks of scientists have collaborated in pressing for intergovernmental cooperation in science policies, and United States–based foundations have taken the lead in sensitive areas such as birth control. The most significant transnational challenge to international organizations arises, of course, from multinational business enterprises. Vernon suggests a number of ways to reduce friction that will depend on coordination of national economic policies through international institutions, and Cox mentions that the International Labor Organization (ILO) is beginning to take account of the importance of multinational business. Paul Goldberg and Charles Kindleberger have elsewhere suggested the possibility of a "GATT" to monitor multinational business enterprises.[37]

A larger question, however, that transnational relations pose for international organizations is the problem of asymmetry. Science and technology, as used by transnational organizations, are having ambivalent effects on world economic interdependence in the 1970s—linking rich countries and reducing their involvements with poor countries. Thus, the North-South cleavage may be widened rather than bridged by the increasing importance of transnational relations.

Such asymmetries are bound to lead to resentments, particularly on the part of countries that strive to develop an indigenous modern identity. These problems are particularly acute for those countries in which only a small part of the population benefits from transnational relations. Resentments of the transnational interactions that impinge on local culture and of the narrow elites that benefit from these processes may lead to internal strife and increasing self-isolation by poor countries. One might conclude from the essay by Evans that such a period of isolation and separation would be beneficial. Only in this way, one might argue, will the third world achieve new societies with economic and cultural autonomy.

Isolation would, however, have costs as well as benefits. These costs would include not only the loss of the potential benefits of capital and technology but also the greater danger that developed countries would turn increasingly inward as well. Producers in rich countries would develop "safe" resources, for example, shale oil and nuclear energy, and synthetic substitutes at higher costs. Then, following the classic pattern of producers prevailing over consumers in questions of economic nationalism, tariffs and protective quotas would be erected around the West European and American markets.[38] Once in place these barriers would be hard to dismantle. Such a situation is not likely to be healthy for the objectives which the United Nations was established to achieve.

To the extent that the United Nations becomes simply an arena for harangues over intergovernmental aid and an administrator of technical assistance, financial support received from rich countries will recede to a level sustained only by a humanitarian constituency. Perhaps with generational change this constituency will grow. A more imaginative strategy would be for the UN to develop capacities that would assist less developed countries to deal with transnational relations and thus enable them to avoid being caught on the laissez faire or statist-isolationist horns of the dilemma we have sketched.

[37] Paul M. Goldberg and Charles P. Kindleberger, "Toward a GATT for Investment: A Proposal for Supervision of the International Corporation," *Law and Policy in International Business,* Summer 1970 (Vol. 2, No. 2), pp. 295–325.

[38] See Harry G. Johnson, ed., *Economic Nationalism in Old and New States* (Comparative Study of New Nations Series) (Chicago: University of Chicago Press, 1967).

Obviously, the UN cannot play this role alone, but its secretariat could provide leadership in the establishment of impartial monitoring of transnational relations, creation of tribunals to mediate disputes, and creation of a divestment fund to ease disengagement.

Kindleberger has argued that harmonization of rules for the multinational business enterprise is necessary if the institution is going to be effective in promoting world welfare. He has suggested a conference on the multinational corporation under the auspices of the UN and the creation of "an international agency which would collect information on direct investment on a systematic basis, overall and case by case, and would have power to prohibit an investment that substantially reduced competition in a given commodity, even if both governments consented. . . . "[39] In addition, "there should be an international Ombudsman, staffed by experts from the smaller countries, to which companies could appeal if they were being unduly squeezed by overlapping sovereignty of two countries. . . . it would be desirable if they bound themselves in advance to adhere to its decision."[40]

The idea that the United Nations should develop a capacity to monitor, mediate, and establish norms for transnational economic activities is an excellent one. The idea of employing the tired old institution of conference diplomacy is a mistake. Given the political schisms of today's world the classic model of the diplomatic conference with a closely associated secretariat is bound to drive the developed countries to create "shadow" institutions where "business can be done." The suggestion that the United Nations Conference on Trade and Development (UNCTAD) develop a capacity to oversee the actions of multinational corporations is unlikely to be accepted even by men of goodwill in Washington. Similarly, many aspects of inspection and monitoring of governmental behavior have become too difficult politically for the United Nations Secretariat to handle by itself. The task of monitoring the problems created by transnational economic activities in the 1970s would best be handled by institutions only indirectly related to the General Assembly. The role of the assembly (and the reason for at least some linkage) is to discuss, criticize, and publicize decisions reached in smaller and less overtly political bodies.[41]

Transnational relations present opportunities as well as problems for international organizations. The hard shell of national sovereignty appears less daunting from a transnational perspective. International organizations provide

[39] Charles P. Kindleberger, *American Business Abroad: Six Lectures on Direct Investment* (New Haven, Conn: Yale University Press, 1969), p. 207.

[40] Ibid.

[41] One of the useful tasks undertaken by UNCTAD has been to study and publicize the activities of the liner conferences—important transnational actors in ocean shipping. See J. S. Nye, "UNCTAD," in *The Anatomy of Influence: Decision-Making in International Organizations,* ed. Robert W. Cox and Harold K. Jacobson (New Haven, Conn: Yale University Press, forthcoming).

meetings and myths that help foster and legitimate transnational personal contacts and transgovernmental coalitions. Transnational and transgovernmental actors can be seen as potential allies for the secretariats of international organizations. Greater efforts might be made to involve the representatives of national and international private associations directly.[42] More institutional imagination will be needed in the future if governments and international organizations are to cope with the problems posed by transnational relations and to avoid the classic international organization syndrome of designing institutions to fight the last battle rather than to prevent the next one.

VII. A FINAL WORD

This volume does not attempt to prove that states are obsolete. We do not contend that transnational relations will necessarily bring world peace or even reduce the likelihood of certain types of conflict. Transnational relations are dependent on the political relations between states as well as vice versa, and world peace in the future will surely depend not only on the forms taken by transnational activities but also on the creativity shown by leaders of states, international organizations, and transnational organizations themselves.

Although transnational relations are not entirely new, they are an important part of world politics, and their importance has been increasing in the years since World War II. The essays in this volume show why we believe that the simplifications of the state-centric approach divert the attention of scholars and statesmen away from many important current problems and distort the analyses of others. We have suggested a "world politics paradigm" that includes transnational, transgovernmental, and interstate interactions in the hope of stimulating new types of theory, research, and approaches to policy. We think that these essays, written within a common framework and in response to our specific questions, illustrate the potential utility of our approach. The authors pose many difficult problems, but they also attempt to provide some suggestions, if not solutions.

We plead guilty, however, to raising far more questions than we or our authors answer. These questions are amenable to research from a normative as well as an empirical point of view. We hope that they will stimulate new types of scholarly research projects and graduate theses. But the questions are not simply "academic." We also hope that they will stimulate new policy perspectives on the part of statesmen in governments and international organizations. If these new perspectives contribute to greater understanding of world politics, which may indirectly contribute to peace and justice, then this imperfect volume will have succeeded.

[42] Cox and Jacobson found surprisingly few efforts to foster such coalitions.

INDEX

Index

Political Science Books from Wisconsin

615. WORLD ECO-CRISIS: International Organizations in Response. Edited by David A. Kay and Eugene B. Skolnikoff. This is the first full-length book to analyze the impact of the world environmental crisis for international organizations. It seeks to define the nature of the crisis, the role of international organizations in meeting it, and the prospects for co-operation among nations in this area. (Reproduces the contents of the Spring 1972 issue of *International Organization.*)
332 pages   1972   cloth $14.00; paper $4.25

605. MAN IN THE LIVING ENVIRONMENT: A report on Global Ecological Problems. Sponsored by The Institute of Ecology (TIE). This report, the work of fifty top-ranking scientists, was prepared to transmit the ecologist's view of global ecological problems to the 1972 UN Conference on Human Environment. Discussed are problems of human ecology, element cycles, ecosystems for human benefit, land management, and management of aquatic resources. An important document in global ecological studies.
312 pages, figs.   1972   cloth $14.00; paper $3.25

621. POLITICS AND PLANNERS: Economic Development in Central America. By Gary W. Wynia. In this original work, the author explains the frequent failures of a new generation of economic planners in five Central American nations. Closely evaluated are the roles of both regional organization and foreign aid in helping — or hindering — national development programs. Wynia's book is the first to explore fully this basic conflict between political self-interest and successful economic planning.
240 pages, figs., map   1972   cloth $17.00

594. THE RUSSIAN REVOLUTION IN SWITZERLAND, 1914-1917. By Alfred Erich Senn. Switzerland, during these critical war years, attracted many Russian political emigrés, including Lenin, who were united there in order to form a new social order in Russia. This is the first integrated study of the various currents within the Russian exile, treating both the movements of the revolutionaries and their ideology. Lenin's wartime activities dominate this carefully documented account.
266 pages   1971   cloth $17.50

561. THE POLITICAL ECONOMY OF MODERN SPAIN: Policy-Making in an Authoritarian System. By Charles W. Anderson. ". . . a splendid study of the functioning of political pluralism in the Franco Regime . . . Historians of contemporary Spain will find new data and deep insight . . . this fuller understanding of the Franco regime will in turn enrich the study of comparative government." — *American Political Science Review.* " . . . his conclusions are convincing . . ." — *The Journal of Politics.*
298 pages, figs.   1970   cloth $17.50; paper $5.00

543. FINANCING POLITICS: Recent Wisconsin Elections. By David Adamany. "Professor Adamany has provided us with a well informed, analytically sound and lucidly written study of campaign finance in Wisconsin. Hopefully, the book will stimulate comparable studies in other states and add to the growing body of research on comparative state politics." — *Midwest Journal of Political Science.* " . . . of great value to political scientists . . ." — *The Book Exchange.*
318 pages   1969   cloth $17.50